From Above
and Below

From Above
and Below

The Mormon Embrace of Revolution
1840–1940

Craig Livingston

GREG KOFFORD BOOKS
SALT LAKE CITY, 2013

Greg Kofford Books
P.O. Box 1362
Draper, UT 84020
www.gregkofford.com

2017   16   15   14   13   5   4   3   2   1

Library of Congress Cataloging-in-Publication Data

Livingston, Craig (Craig Zapata), author.
  From above and below : the Mormon embrace of revolution, 1840-1940 / Craig Livingston.
       pages cm
  Includes bibliographical references and index.
  ISBN 978-1-58958-621-5
  1. Church of Jesus Christ of Latter-day Saints--History. 2. Revolutions--History. 3. Millennialism--History. I. Title.
  BX8611.L65 2013
  261.7088'2893--dc23
                          2013015228

CONTENTS

Acknowledgments, ix

Introduction, xi

1   Secular and Religious Revolutionary Concepts, 1

2   Mormon Observers of the 1848 European Revolutions, 35

3   Mormon Revolutionary Symbolism, 71

4   A Mormon Critique of Industrialization, 1860–1920, 109

5   France And Russia in "The Throes Of Revolution," 1870–71 and 1905, 137

6   Mormon Observers Respond to Colonialism, 159

7   The Mexican Revolution and the Idea of an Indian Nation, 1910–17, 191

8   Post-Revolutionary Mexico, 1920–30, 221

9   The Bolshevik Revolution of 1917, 261

10   The Golden Age of Revolution in South America, 1925–31, 293

11   Fade-Out and Conclusion, 323

Coda, 343

Biographical Sketches, 347

Sources, 373

Index, 417

Dedicated to my youngest daughter, Romney Ellen Livingston,
The Woodlands 2nd Ward Beehive Secretary who likes *Les Misérables*.

Acknowledgments

I am indebted to Christopher Smith at Claremont Graduate University for his assistance in getting this manuscript through the last hundred yards toward publication. Additionally, I thank the LDS Church History Library; the University of Utah's J. Willard Marriott Library, especially Walter Jones in Special Collections; and the Utah State Historical Society. The Harold B. Lee Library at BYU also provided first-rate assistance.

I owe gratitude to the professors who taught me. At BYU Michael Quinn introduced me to primary sources. David Montgomery taught me how to organize research. Richard Immerman at Temple University chaired my dissertation committee. I am grateful for his insights and the encouragement he gave that kept me going.

The library at Lone Star College–Montgomery worked endlessly to maintain the flow of interlibrary loan requests. Thank you Janice Peyton and Suzie Solomon.

Where would we be without colleagues of high esteem? Acquaintances of Lavina Fielding Anderson know why I would thank her. At Lone Star College–Montgomery Ron Heckelman in the English Department works tirelessly to encourage community college professors to aim high in academia. I thank Mark Stelter, Professor of Criminal Justice, for his integrity, courage, intellect, and most importantly, his friendship.

Students of Lone Star College–Montgomery and I live history every day as jointly experienced revelation. For that I am grateful. My students are in my heart forever.

Throughout this project my loving family stood by me. Jennifer, my wife, and three children, Nathan, Dakota, and Romney—I love you. My parents, Jack and Adele, both living, thank you for bringing me to the gates of history.

As in all book acknowledgments, what follows accounts to me.

C.L.
The Woodlands, Texas, April 2013

INTRODUCTION

Mapping Parallel Revolutions

Revolution threatens the conservative view of social and political development. According to conservative ideology change must occur under controlled conditions. The uncontrollable results of revolution can wreck social relations and undermine respect for the rule of law. Among modern-day Latter-day Saints, fidelity to government and rejection of radical change are articles of faith. In *Mormonism in Transition, 1890–1930*, historian Thomas Alexander interprets Mormonism as a movement beyond the reach of revolutionary allure: "There had seldom been much sympathy among church leaders for secular visions of cooperation, whether Marxian or utopian."[1] Articles published in old Mormon periodicals advocated the old communalism, but Church leaders discouraged members from joining labor unions or the Utah Socialist Party. The Mormon hierarchy discouraged leftist solutions partly because the salvationist creed of worker solidarity and the political goals of socialism might rival the Church's spiritual leadership. Unions and organized labor might also compromise the returns Church leaders expected from their investments in capitalist enterprises.[2]

However, as I mined pre-World War II Mormon sources, I found a century-long script that sustained a more revolutionary view of historical development. I do not propose that Mormon thought interlocked with leftist theory or that Mormon leaders indoctrinated their followers

---

1. Thomas G. Alexander, *Mormonism in Transition: A History of the Latter-day Saints, 1890–1930*, 184.

2. John S. McCormick, "Hornets in the Hive: Socialists in Early Twentieth-Century Utah," 225–40. In 1912, 10 percent of Utah voted for Eugene Debs, the Socialist candidate for president, which compares to 6 percent for the nation. See Alan Kent Powell, "Elections in the State of Utah," 159. John McCormick (Salt Lake City Community College) kindly shared with the author his research notes cataloging Church leaders' injunctions against socialism.

with radical discourse and expected revolutionary action from them. The conditions that made Vladimir Lenin and Pancho Villa revolutionaries differed completely from the environment that produced Orson Pratt and Anthony W. Ivins. Most Church leaders remained silent about revolutions between 1840 and 1940, and others adamantly opposed such action and ideas. Furthermore, the Mormon response to revolution varied according to the Church's feelings of security as the dominant culture of America approached and then enveloped the Mormon West. I do, nonetheless, detect revolutionary sympathies in Mormon circles. In commenting on revolution, prominent Mormon leaders engaged in a religious exercise. Revolution conformed to their schema of progress toward the millennium. Mormon observers used the revolutions of other peoples to demonstrate a Mormon view of justice and millennial hope. While not always condoning revolutionary objectives, Mormon leaders conditionally accepted violent methods.

Early Mormons believed that Christ's return represented the millennial "revolution from above" that would catapult them to global leadership. But as the Mormons were driven west, the European revolutions of 1848 opened another narrative: revolt "from below" would overthrow the privileged classes and dignify the masses. Revolution would weaken traditional loyalties and destroy the religious, political, and social monopolies that inhibited missionary work. To express their millennialism Mormon leaders integrated the language and symbols pioneered by secular revolutionaries.

Revolution sustained a Mormon view of history. God was omniscient. He projected his power in the medium of time through human agency. World events became a source of canon. If revolution was possible, ran the logic, then it was God's will to pursue it. Revolution often endowed Mormon scriptural interpretations with up-to-date meaning.

Acceptance of revolution incarnated Mormon millennial theology as a discourse of human progress. Mankind would return to God's presence. The path back would be lighted by lost truths restored through the Church's prophets. Corruption would be eliminated. Finally, humanity, God, and Earth would reunite in paradisiacal glory. The dialectical movement of history would produce global conditions previously imagined by French revolutionaries during the 1790s: the elimination of kings and traditional institutions to clear the way for universal property, brotherhood, and the enshrinement of truths that enabled citizenship in a sanctified republic. Mormons, like revolutionary utopians, condoned the use of force to shape society into what it could become.

After 1890 Mormon assimilation to normative American values accelerated, but the Mormon script resisted total Americanization. Anti-capitalist and anti-imperialist undercurrents continued to inform Mormon views of the external world. The Mexican Revolution and political coups in South America in 1930–31 let Latter-day Saint leaders explore the global implications of their original message for fifty years beyond the abandonment of polygamy and the demise of the political kingdom of God.

The international political and economic crises of the 1930s collapsed Mormon faith in progress toward a rational world illuminated with spiritual understanding. Radicalism lost relevance in a bureaucratic church. That Mormon observers ratified post-revolutionary governments in Mexico and the Soviet Union suggests that they remained uneasy with assimilation and continued to hold out for millennial times.

Others have hinted at this book's thesis. In 1978 Douglas Tobler, a German specialist at Brigham Young University and later president of the Poland Warsaw Mission, suggested that philosophically, Marxists and Mormons were polarities that repelled each other but pursued the same goal. Tobler noticed that communism appealed to younger people. It was not communism's focus on class struggle or scientific analysis of history that attracted, but rather its promise to restore the human race to wholeness. Tobler reiterated the mantra of the sixties: after "the revolution" upended corporate-military domination of the planet, new socialist states would unite people previously fragmented by industrialization. People sectioned off by specialization would become interconnected, and the spiritually alienated would be "reunited into integral selves capable of true art and thought."[3] A British Mormon speaking at an international conference hosted at Brigham Young University in 1976 announced the antecedent of his own beliefs: "If it had not been for Marx, I should not yet be in this Church, if at all."[4] Ironically, the

---

3. Douglas F. Tobler, "Mormonism and the Secular Philosophies: Competing Creeds in the Twentieth Century," 336.

4. Arthur Henry King, quoted in ibid., 356. King (b. 1910) was a prominent British Mormon leader, philanthropist, and university professor. For elements of attraction and aversion to communism, see also the impressions of future Soviet Union Mission President Thomas Franklin Rogers in his account titled "Images and Imaginings: An American in Moscow, 1958."

first converts in Mexico and France—Louis A. Bertrand and Plotino Rhodankanaty—were radicals. Evidently they saw something in Mormonism not discernible today.[5]

A long time ago Mormon missionaries courted Freemasons and French republicans. Church writers tried to understand Russian social democrats. They analyzed Louis Blanc, Karl Marx, Emiliano Zapata, and Peruvian student revolutionaries. Seldom did Mormon observers cast aspersions, even in disagreement; the names and goals associated with revolution were often mentioned in reverent terms. Mormon leaders usually rejected the details of socialistic programs, but understood socialist leaders as sincere people in quest of justice and fair play.

Today Mormons rely on correlated instructional materials and conservative counsel from Church authorities to negotiate worldly terrain. But before World War II, Mormons positioned their movement in the context of history. Mormon observers of revolution linked contemporary events to what they felt the Church taught about its divine mission, producing pro-revolutionary rhetoric in their writings and speeches. Latter-day Saint leaders accepted that the "greatest and most essential truths have [come] from non-ecclesiastical 'revelations,'" writes T. Eugene Shoemaker. God, in partnership with humanity, working through the physical and social sciences, supported a "spiritual and ultimately political revolution led by living prophets." History bound mankind to a single destiny. Mormonism and science were united by "common ends," embraced "all truth," and recognized only "one source."[6] A gesture at the funeral of Brigham Young suggests an antinomianism that implies more than moral resistance to the political order. In 1877 Young laid in state with a flag of the political "kingdom of God" inside his redwood coffin. In similar fashion the caretakers of communism displayed a Communard banner with Lenin's corpse.[7] The revolutionary faith always gloried in emblematic simplicity.

---

5. A Hungarian convert, Paul Petrovitis, fought in the revolutions of 1848 and sailed to California with Samuel Brannan. See Will Bagley, ed., *A Scoundrel's Tale: The Samuel Brannan Papers*, 334–36.

6. T. Eugene Shoemaker, "The Office of Prophet: An Intellectual Look," 34.

7. James Billington, *Fire in the Minds of Men: The Origins of the Revolutionary Faith*, 346; D. Michael Quinn, "The Flag of the Kingdom of God," 111.

Revolutionary Reminders of the Mormon Past

The followers of Joseph Smith, charged with revolutionizing the world, ended up as the champions of corporate values, nationalism, and social conservatism. Historian Paul Edwards suggests that Mormons have "not allowed the revolutionary nature of the movement from which we have sprung to make us revolutionaries." Church-sponsored images of Joseph Smith and his times, Edwards charges, have been "primarily traditional, unimaginative, and lacking in any effort to find or create an epistemological methodology revolutionary enough to deal with the paradox of our movement."[8] But scholars have already begun to reshape Mormon historical memory in a more radical direction. Research strategies used by historians since the 1950s have yielded a rich body of literature on Mormon Americana. Topics studied under the rubric of the "New Mormon History" include millennialism, communalism, institutional development, polygamy, and the Rocky Mountain theocracy.[9]

This is the first study to test Mormon eschatological and sociopolitical concepts against world revolutions. Grant Underwood downplays the view of early Mormonism as a radical, counter-cultural movement. In *The Millenarian World of Early Mormonism*, he writes that pre-1846 Mormonism

> deviated little from the morals and mores of nineteenth-century evangelicalism, at that time the prevailing religious ethos in America. Upon close examination, the attitudes and behavior of early Mormons seem more mainstream and the alleged radicalism of their marital, economic, and political relations more superficial than has often been assumed.[10]

---

8. Paul M. Edwards, "The Irony of Mormon History," 24. See also Paul M. Edwards, "Being Mormon: An RLDS Response," 108; and the quotation from Sterling M. McMurrin in Robert Gottlieb and Peter Wiley, *America's Saints: The Rise of Mormon Power*, 14.

9. For overviews of the New Mormon History, see Newell G. Bringhurst and Lavina Fielding Anderson, eds., *Excavating the Mormon Past: The New Historiography of the Last Half Century*; James B. Allen, "Since 1950: Creators and Creations of Mormon History"; D. Michael Quinn, ed., *The New Mormon History: Revisionist Essays on the Past*; Davis Bitton and Leonard J. Arrington, *Mormons and Their Historians*. For a catalog of LDS historical and sociological works, see James B. Allen, Ronald W. Walker, and David J. Whittaker, *Studies in Mormon History, 1830–1997: An Indexed Bibliography*.

10. Grant Underwood, *The Millenarian World of Early Mormonism*, 9–10.

Underwood further denies overt Mormon political intentions. Angry Mormon rhetoric was directed at politicians believed to have violated the principles of constitutional government. Otherwise Mormons assumed Christ himself would destroy the wicked in his own time and inaugurate the thousand years of peace. Thus freed from social and political concerns, the Saints showed more interest "in the bursting open of graves than in the breaking down of institutions."[11] Underwood's work carries the study of Mormon millennialism to the beginning of the westward migration, but bypasses the political and social content in Mormon millennial discourse excited by the revolutions of 1848.[12]

Some historians insist that Mormonism was part of the American mainstream all along, and that Mormonism never intended a separate political, social, and economic body. Kenneth Winn argues that Smith's establishment of a vertical priesthood clashed with the communitarian republicanism and popular control that converts had inherited from New England. Internal dissent in Ohio and Missouri happened when those who considered themselves republicans "with a difference" objected to Smith's centralization of Mormon economic activity.[13] Those who supported Smith's successor, Brigham Young, migrated west. Once the pioneers mastered the environment in Utah, the argument goes, authoritarianism dissipated. With the rigorous planning of initial settlement no longer needed, the democratic and capitalist character of the Mormon people reemerged.[14]

"Kingdom school" scholars, on the other hand, argue that the Church leadership established a theocracy, organized the Council of Fifty to promote the political kingdom of God, and intended it to survive

---

11. Ibid., 110.

12. Underwood carefully classifies Mormon doctrine as "millenarian" rather than "millennial," but I have opted in the present study for the more familiar term.

13. Kenneth H. Winn, *Exiles in a Land of Liberty: Mormons in America, 1830–1846*, 114–18, 127–28. Robert E. Shalhope identifies several versions of early American republicanism in "Republicanism and Early American Historiography." The Mormon rendition of republicanism favored the "traditional ideas of a moral economy rather than capitalistic enterprise" (ibid., 341).

14. Klaus J. Hansen, "The Metamorphosis of the Kingdom of God: Toward a Reinterpretation of Mormon History," 237–38. See Hansen's note 67 for other works that minimize Mormon theocratic intentions.

through the millennium. The "political implications of the Kingdom of God," writes one historian, "were clearly understood by the leadership of the Church, if not so clearly so by the rank and file."[15] The present study focuses on how Latter-day Saint observers responded to other people's revolutions and how both Mormon eschatology and contemporary secular thought informed that response. The two complement each other. The political ramifications of Mormonism's own universal vision led easily to fascination with the script of upheaval. If the people of the world rose against royalist, capitalist, and imperialist oppression, they could destroy the social and political forms that prevented the nations of the earth from receiving from on high the revelations of a new world order.

Definitions

So far I have used the term "Mormon leaders" to identify the men and women looking out into a world of revolution. From this point forward I will call them "Mormon observers." They are the ones who showed their interest in revolution by publishing in Church periodicals, keeping diaries, and making speeches. Many of these observers were in fact not only leaders, but also "general authorities": members of the upper echelons of the worldwide Church hierarchy. Importantly, however, the Church's ruling councils did not constitute a monolithic group. Until 1976 general authorities resided in three quorums: the First Presidency (three men), the Quorum of the Twelve Apostles (twelve men), and the Presidency of the Council of the Seventy (seven men). The Presiding Bishopric (three men) had jurisdiction over temporal affairs. Additionally, a presiding patriarch dispensed prophetic blessings outlining an applicant's lineage, life mission, and the rewards of gospel obedience. Another institution—the Council of Fifty—met sporadically until 1884. Several general authorities were members of this shadowy organization that Smith commissioned to promote the political kingdom of God. In addition to the different theological and political emphases of the various councils, general authorities also had their own individual differences that were much sharper than they are today.

A second set of observers was even more prolific. They were editors, writers, missionaries, mission presidents, educators, colonists, and leaders, both public officials and local Church officers. Stake presidents

---

15. Keith J. Melville, "Brigham Young's Ideal Society: The Kingdom of God," 5.

preside over a geographic administrative unit roughly analogous to a Catholic diocese. Mission presidents have the same authority as a stake president but preside over proselytizing missions, often in areas where there are not enough members to form stakes. This second set of observers between 1871 and 1914 provided insights into Church attitudes toward revolutions at a time when the general authorities were preoccupied with problems arising over polygamy, politics, missionary work, and the Church's public image in the United States.

As to leftist terminology, Martin Buber, Frank and Fritzie Manuel, and Luce Racine suggest that the chief difference among believers in utopia concerned the means by which mankind would attain it. Utopians, whether writing fantasy novels, establishing peaceful communes, or rising up against rulers, were motivated by hope for a future state of justice and well-being. In secular terms this future state is referred to as utopia. In religious terms it is the "millennium." Each may arrive by either a violent or non-violent path, through either revolutionary or evolutionary action. Two concepts bound the millennial and utopian together. First, a condition of future harmony was possible on earth. Secular and religious utopians fostered environments—laboratories—in which they could test new social mores and economic practices in anticipation of this future harmony. Second, historical development, prophecy, or scientific advances made the future harmony inevitable. Progress was governed by laws. Whether historical, scientific, or providential, these laws could be discovered and applied and predictable outcomes would result.[16] In this book, variations of "utopia," "millennium," and "kingdom of God" are all used to describe the same condition.

Events Mormon observers *perceived* as revolutionary receive attention in this study regardless of how scholars have classified them. This definition admits a spectrum of "revolutions" not always categorized as such. For example, Mormon observers greeted Japan as a liberating power in Asia by 1905, and an apostle interpreted the regime changes in South America during the 1930s as evidence of progress toward the millennium.

---

16. Frank E. Manuel and Fritzie P. Manuel, *Utopian Thought in the Western World*; Martin Buber, *Paths in Utopia*, 7–9; Luc Racine, "Paradise, the Golden Age, the Millennium and Utopia: A Note on the Differentiation of Forms of the Ideal Society"; Lawrence Foster, *Religion and Sexuality: The Shakers, the Mormons, and the Oneida Community*, 3–20; and Catherine Wessinger, "Millennialism with and without the Mayhem."

Sources

In addition to unpublished sources, this study draws heavily from Church periodicals. One of the most important was the *Latter-Day Saints' Millennial Star*, first printed at British Mission headquarters in Liverpool in 1840. This periodical is a gold mine of information about Church history and doctrine, especially during the nineteenth century. Beginning in 1852, the *Millennial Star* appeared weekly. The *Millennial Star* was under the direction of the Quorum of the Twelve.[17] Nearly a century after its first issue a Church official wrote, "The *Star* has felt the pulse of the Church and its people, and has reflected, in truth, what it felt."[18] At seventeen thousand subscriptions in 1849, *Millennial Star's* circulation exceeded that of the *Manchester Mercury*.[19] It ran until 1970.

After the 1845 demise of the *Times and Seasons* in Nauvoo, the *Millennial Star* and the *Frontier Guardian* were the only Church publications in print. The first issue of the *Deseret News* appeared in Salt Lake City in 1850. The *Deseret News* was Church controlled except for 1892–99, and even during that seven-year interlude its editors were strong Mormons. The paper had a worldwide correspondent corps in the form of Mormon missionaries.[20] Along with the *Millennial Star*, the

---

17. James B. Allen, Ronald K. Esplin, and David J. Whittaker, *Men with a Mission: The Quorum of the Twelve Apostles in the British Isles, 1837–1841*, 252; Allen, Walker, and Whittaker, *Studies in Mormon History*, 208; Stanley A. Peterson, "Millennial Star."

18. Richard L. Evans, *Century of "Mormonism" in Great Britain*, 149.

19. "Samples of Mormon Blasphemy and Impudence," *Latter-day Saints' Millennial Star* 11 (February 1, 1849): 45; Hubert Howe Bancroft, *History of Utah, 1540–1886*, Appendix 19. Circulation hit twenty-two thousand in 1852 when the *Star* went from bi–monthly to weekly publication. See Evans, *Century of "Mormonism" in Great Britain*, 144.

20. For the relationship between the *Deseret News* and the LDS Church, see Monte Burr McLaws, *Spokesman for the Kingdom: Early Mormon Journalism and the Deseret News, 1830–1898*, 107, 170; Barbara Lee Cloud, *The Business of Newspapers on the Western Frontier*, xv, 111, 155; and Earl E. Hawkes, "Newspapers, Stern Mormon View," 72. The Cannon family, members of which were in the hierarchy, owned the paper during the privatization phase. It remained the voice of the Church during this time. See Wendell J. Ashton, *Voice in the West: Biography of Pioneer Newspaper*, 207–8.

Deseret News was the "chief organ" of the Church and "championed the cause of Zion in all lands and climes." In 1867 the semi-weekly *News* was supplemented by a new daily edition, titled the *Deseret Evening News*. The daily reverted to the name *Deseret News* in 1920, and the semi-weekly was discontinued shortly thereafter.[21]

For youth the Church published the *Juvenile Instructor*. Apostle George Q. Cannon commenced printing in 1866. To appeal to its target audience, the magazine was richly illustrated. Some of its articles before 1890 are more sophisticated than one would ordinarily expect from a juvenile magazine. In 1929 it became simply the *Instructor*. Publication ceased with the 1970 consolidation of Church periodicals.[22]

The *Contributor* was the Church's main American magazine. Published in Utah, it ran monthly for seventeen volumes between 1879 and 1896. Editor Junius F. Wells selected high quality paper and printed stories related to Church history and world events.[23] The *Contributor* was eventually replaced by the *Improvement Era*. The first issue appeared in November 1897, and the last was in 1970. The *Era* was the organ for the Church's priesthood quorums, Young Men's Mutual Improvement Association, and schools. It was illustrated and tackled a variety of topics.[24] Before the *Era* became the organ for the Church's Young Women's Mutual Association, women had their own publication, the *Young Woman's Journal*. Running from 1897 to 1929 and totaling twenty-six thousand pages, the women's magazine featured many insightful articles.[25]

These various sources sound notes of radical Mormon belief. Individually the notes are discordant. Together, they form a chorus. Often soft but occasionally rising to a crescendo, the theme heard throughout is a steady revolutionary chant.

---

21. Andrew Jenson, *Encyclopedic History of the Church of Jesus Christ of Latter-day Saints*, s.v. "Deseret News." An 1862 poem celebrating the *Deseret News* chimed, "But now the mind's electric fire / Beams forth where'er we be; / The pen and press has gained a name— / Will soon the world set free." See John Lyon, *Songs of a Pioneer*, 23.

22. Jenson, *Encyclopedic History of the Church*, s.v. "Juvenile Instructor."

23. Ibid., s.v. "The Contributor."

24. Ibid., s.v. "Improvement Era."

25. Ibid., s.v. "Young Woman's Journal."

Synopsis

The present book follows major revolutions in the order they occurred, showing how consistently Mormon observers tuned in on these events and studied them as a religious exercise. Interspersed among the major revolutions were smaller anti-colonial revolts, such as uprisings in Ireland and India. Their inclusion in one chapter shows how sensitive Mormon observers were to even slight revolutionary vibrations. Mormon observers were also attuned to worker resistance to industrialism. This background theme also gets spotlighted in a single chapter.

This study begins, in Chapter 1, with the apparent contradiction between the Mormon Church's present conservatism and its earlier rhetoric praising the French Revolution. Unlike modern Mormons, early leaders shared secular utopians' expectations of universal, revolutionary sociopolitical change. This chapter explores the secular revolutionaries' views of time and conflict and compares them to Mormon concepts of how the millennium would come—human co-agency with God—and produce "theo-democracy."

Chapter 2 describes how Mormon observers cheered the rise of the barricades during the revolutions of 1848. The enthusiasm that animated the Young America movement was evident in Mormon commentary on the mid-century European upheavals. Expectations peaked as observers believed the revolutions were the opening act of the millennial era. In their exuberance, Mormon attitudes slid to the left of American opinion. The revolutions addressed the needs of workers and augured a Jewish return to Palestine. Observer disappointment was great when the conservative coalition struck back.

Chapter 3 looks at early Mormon revolutionary symbolism and metaphor. Revolutionaries seeking legitimacy discarded traditional symbols. As they redesigned the future reign of reason, unity, and egalitarianism, they used new emblems—geometric shapes—to simplify the vision and chart the method of getting there. Mormons, both in their roles as religious revolutionaries and as students of revolutions elsewhere, were attracted to these symbols and ways of thinking.

Chapter 4 studies an array of statements by Mormon observers critiquing the status quo. Revolution as a means to an end seemed to offer a solution to the social problems caused by unregulated capitalism in industrialized nations. In 1879 future Presiding Bishop Charles W.

Nibley was radicalized by Henry George's single tax theory in a way that George, who actually intended his theory as an alternative to revolution rather than an argument for it, would neither have recognized nor approved. Another Mormon critic of industrialism was Alice Louise Reynolds, a BYU English professor and future member of the Relief Society's general board. She used the writings of Paris Commune supporter John Ruskin to champion Mormon communalism.

Chapter 5 analyzes Mormon observers' responses to two major revolutions. Heady expectations accompanied the Franco-Prussian War and the Paris Commune (1870–71). The extreme violence of the Commune's destruction by the French army induced a sobering reassessment of class conflict but did not wreck observer fascination with radical action. Similarly, the Russian Revolution of 1905 was viewed initially as a progressive event. Subsequent events tempered Mormon observers' enthusiasm, but they never denied the right of the Russian people to overthrow the czar.

Mormon observers also believed that anti-colonial revolts and the rise of Japan might rejuvenate democracy. Chapter 6 shows how Lenin's theory of monopoly capitalism found expression in Mormon periodicals. According to Lenin, revolution in the underdeveloped nations might trigger crises that would disrupt the industrial nations. Waging their own struggle against federal incorporation, Mormon writers looked for opportunities and inspiration in revolutions against colonial empires.

Chapter 7 moves the scene to Mexico. Anthony W. Ivins and Rey L. Pratt were thrilled by the exploits of Emiliano Zapata and Pancho Villa during the Mexican Revolution of 1910–17. The idea of an Indian nation opened the minds of principal Mormon leaders charged with interpreting events in Mexico to the themes of social justice and revolutionary progress, which they eloquently advocated in sermons and articles.

Mormon observers also followed the efforts of Mexican officials during the 1920s to institutionalize the Revolution, the topic of Chapter 8. Ivins defended the Mexican government's nationalization of the Catholic Church, squaring off in public debate against a Catholic official in Salt Lake City. Pratt, the Mexican Mission president, was cognizant of the land issue in Mexico. As a subtle independent leftist, he suspected that Mexican President Plutarco Calles was more interested in power than land reform.

By 1919 hope for global reform rested on the League of Nations. In Chapter 9 we see how the United States Senate's rejection of the League of Nations disappointed some Mormon leaders. In Russia, communist-inspired social and economic reforms earned praise from Mormon observers.

Chapter 10 follows Mormon enthusiasm for revolution into South America. In 1925 Apostle Melvin J. Ballard opened a mission in Buenos Aires. His assessments and those of his companion, Rey L. Pratt, advocated sociopolitical revolution as crucial to the progress of South American Indians. Economic stress beginning in 1930 sent a wave of political disturbances throughout Central and South America. Although these disturbances are now understood as little more than coup d'états, Ballard's enthusiasm for them nonetheless demonstrates the tenacity with which Mormon leaders clung to revolutionary idealism.

The conclusion shows Mormon observers in the 1930s still clinging to some revolutionary beliefs. In their search for social progress and eagerness to affix it to the Soviet Union and Latin America, Latter-day Saint leaders shared a yearning with intellectuals who traveled abroad. Mormon observers extrapolated their longing for utopia into foreign lands. Social experimentation, even if secular, was preferable to complete amnesia of the original millennial script of the Restoration Church. But the old guard was dying, and the revelations of Soviet repression during the late 1930s made revolution less and less the ordained way to change the world.

Social experimentation, imperialism, and revolution marked the world between 1840 and 1940. The Mormon hierarchy linked its teachings to the synergy of global change. The free space emerging from the wreck of social, political, and religious monopolies portended increased missionary work. Toward this end influential Church leaders demonstrated patient resolve. In their view history, progress, and change occurred in unfolding sequence. They shared the faith of pre-Marxist dreamers—the very apostles of the early Christian church who believed that brotherhood and utopia were possible. Revolution would clear the path toward their attainment.

CHAPTER 1

SECULAR AND RELIGIOUS REVOLUTIONARY CONCEPTS

Martyrs of Revolution

On May 10, 1796, the French Directory executed Francois Babeuf, the chief conspirator in a revolutionary cell known as the Society of Equals. A left-wing remnant of the First Republic, the Equals had attempted to seize the government. Their objective was to achieve the egalitarian state envisioned in the *Rights of Man* and later, in the program of Robespierre. Babeuf was reconciled to his fate. In prison he wrote a touching letter to his family. Before going to the guillotine he told listeners that he looked forward to "a perfectly virtuous sleep." When the blade dropped, communism had its first martyr.[1]

Nearly fifty years later in Illinois, Joseph Smith, founder of the Mormon Church, met his end in similar style. In June 1844 he ordered the destruction of the printing press of a dissident newspaper, the *Nauvoo Expositor*. The *Expositor* had criticized Smith for concentrating too much power. He was mayor of Nauvoo, the biggest city in the state; as prophet he had the loyalty of fifteen thousand Illinois Mormons; as lieutenant general he commanded the four-thousand-man Nauvoo Legion.[2] Charged with violating freedom of speech, Smith remanded himself to Governor Thomas L. Ford under the promise of a fair trial. Like Babeuf, Smith was serene in the face of possible death. "I am going like a lamb to the slaughter," he said, "but I am calm as a summer's morning." Incarcerated in an upstairs room of the jailhouse in Carthage, Illinois, Smith wrote a letter expressing love for his first wife

---

1. James Billington, *Fire in the Minds of Men: The Origins of the Revolutionary Faith*, 77; and Jacob L. Talmon, *The Origins of Totalitarian Democracy*, 196–200.

2. For the Legion's strength see Hubert Howe Bancroft, *History of Utah, 1540–1886*, 146.

and family. On June 27, vigilantes stormed the jail. A hail of bullets killed Smith and his brother Hyrum, the Church's presiding patriarch. As with the Babuevists, "The blood of the martyrs" became "the seed of the Church."[3]

The similarities between the Mormon and communist martyr-doms are rooted in their kindred utopian faiths: too radical to be tol-erated by society, and too powerful to be defeated by death. Despite the New England origins of Mormonism, the followers of Joseph Smith never afforded the attention to John Winthrop's "City on a Hill" that they rendered the barricades of France.

Today the Church of Jesus Christ of Latter-day Saints embraces conservative and corporate values, but its embrace of revolution prior to World War II often rested on leftist precepts. Mormons believed that human action could call into existence the paradise forecast by proph-ets. Social harmony and divine rule were impending earthly realities. Man and God might create this utopia before the millennium without the heaven-sent destruction of the present world. Whether religious or secular, dreamers owed their universalism to a common primeval faith, a faith that ultimately aimed for nothing less than change on a cosmic scale.

The French Revolution

Mormon literature and speeches before 1940 abound with admira-tion for the grandfather of all revolutions, the French upheaval of 1789. Junius F. Wells, editor of the Church's *Juvenile Instructor*, wrote in 1883 that the world rebelled against superstition. Jean Jacques Rousseau, he posited, liberated the downtrodden and assured the triumph of reason.

---

3. For Smith's last days see Richard S. Van Wagoner and Stephen C. Walker, *A Book of Mormons*, 294; "The Murder," *Times and Seasons* 5 (July 15, 1844): 584–86; Joseph Smith Jr. et al., *History of the Church of Jesus Christ of Latter-day Saints*, 6:555; Bancroft, *History of Utah*, 76. For the phrase about Smith's blood being the "seed of the Church," see George F. Reynolds, *The Story of the Book of Mormon*, 112; Seymour Young, February 1, 1892, in Brian H. Stuy, comp. and ed., *Collected Discourses Delivered by President Wilford Woodruff, His Two Counselors, the Twelve Apostles, and Others*, 2:361; Hyrum M. Smith, October 9, 1910, *Report of the Semi-annual Conference of the Church of Jesus Christ of Latter-day Saints*, 68 (hereafter cited as *Conference Report*); and George F. Richards, October 8, 1933, *Conference Report*, 114.

"Institutions may crumble and governments fall," Wells concluded, "but it is only that they may renew better youth."[4] Apostle Franklin D. Richards suggested that revolutions were worth the sacrifice: "No great revolution was ever achieved without some fighting . . . But when the war is over, and the new government is instituted, the grand improvement is then felt."[5] Apostle Moses Thatcher said, "A careful review of the history of this world" shows that "the young giant Democracy arose out of the confusion, chaos and tyranny of the ages" to look "hopefully over the fields of God's eternal progress."[6] Thatcher condemned international warfare, but declared that men should be "happy to die" in revolutions. From them "have arisen throughout the past ages all the highest virtues of humanity."[7] In 1893-94 the Church's *Contributor* ran a fictional series about a man and his son struggling through the French upheaval. The final installment concluded: "France . . . now stands as the leading European exponent of the principles of popular liberty . . . The bloody French Revolution has accomplished its object."[8] Another issue of the *Contributor* positively assessed the Napoleonic Code. This outgrowth of the French Revolution had been a gift of "priceless worth" to Europe. The *Contributor* asserted that the Code's rationalism had abolished aristocracy, spread liberalism, and forced the German and Italian states to catch up to the "requirements of the times."[9]

Praise for the French Revolution continued into the twentieth century. A missionary visiting Paris wrote in his diary: "We saw the home and marriage place of Louis 16 & Queen Anonette [which] only hurried up the war of Freedom."[10] During the Mexican upheaval Apostle Anthony W. Ivins declared at the April 1912 General Conference of the Church that the French Revolution benefited the people.[11] Seventies

---

4. Junius F. Wells, "The Eve of Revolution," *Juvenile Instructor* 18 (March 1, 1883): 78–89, 90.

5. Franklin D. Richards, January 18, 1885, *Journal of Discourses*, 26:103–4.

6. Moses Thatcher, July 4, 1891, in Stuy, *Collected Discourses*, 2:241.

7. Ibid., 2:243.

8. Orson F. Whitney, "La Gironde: A Story of the French Revolution," *Contributor* 15 (September 1894): 740.

9. Orson F. Whitney, "Europe and Napoleon," *Contributor* 14 (February 1893): 190–92.

10. Ernest Hungate Burgess, Diary, September 17, 1907, 163.

11. Anthony W. Ivins, April 7, 1912, *Conference Report*, 63.

president and history professor Levi Edgar Young borrowed from H. G. Wells's *Outline of History* to credit the ascent of Western civilization to the French Revolution.[12] In 1926 Apostle Orson F. Whitney admired the "fierce fires of the French Revolution." Equality, he reminded his audience, was a French invention.[13]

Mormon defense of the French Revolution reflected the contemporary state of the historical craft and literary technique. Historians in those days tended toward a Marxist interpretation that cast the French upheaval in terms of class struggle. The "Jacobin synthesis," which dominated discussion of modern French political and social history until the 1960s, also held that radical leaders had to promote the Terror of 1792–94 in order to secure the liberal principles outlined in 1789.[14] When Mormons objected to the French Revolution, their critique centered on the murderous excesses of Robespierre's regime.[15] But even Church observers known for their conservatism admired the revolutionaries' commitment to "republicanism" and liberty, equality, and fraternity.[16] Use of French revolutionary vocabulary to buttress a

---

12. Levi Edgar Young, April 5, 1924, *Conference Report*, 51. Young also praised the heroics of Italian revolutionary Giuseppe Garibaldi in a sermon delivered October 2, 1936, *Conference Report*, 66. H. G. Wells had suggested that the American Constitution was imperfect, the Terror of France was justified, and France was the true educator of republicanism. See *Outline of History: The Whole Story of Man*, 2:740–41, 745–74.

13. Orson F. Whitney, October 4, 1926, *Conference Report*, 93.

14. Jeremy D. Popkin, *A Short History of the French Revolution*, 135–38.

15. "Executions – The Guillotine," *Times and Seasons* 5 (September 2, 1844): 633; T. Y. Standford, "Charlotte Corday," *Contributor* 13 (November 1891): 33; Whitney, "La Gironde: A Story of the French Revolution," 349; James E. Talmage, *Jesus the Christ: A Study of the Messiah and His Mission According to the Holy Scriptures both Ancient and Modern*, 751; and Hyrum M. Smith, April 9, 1905, *Conference Report*, 47.

16. For French revolutionary metaphor in the discourse of other Mormon leaders, see John Taylor's comments in *The Mormon* 1 (October 6, 1855), quoted in Taylor, *The Gospel Kingdom: Selections from the Writings and Discourses of John Taylor*, 312; Taylor's anti-American tirade in a sermon delivered April 9, 1882, *Journal of Discourses*, 23:63–66; Orson F. Whitney, *Life of Heber C. Kimball*, 37; Charles W. Nibley, October 7, 1906, *Conference Report*, 62; B. H. Roberts, *New Witnesses for God*, 1:27, 181–82, 372–73;

religious position is an example of a "literary trope" (a figure of speech that may appear out of its ordinary context). Discourse analysts suggest that the tropic use of secular words by churchmen conveys a message more "radical in scope" than does schematic usage (words used in their ordinary context).[17]

A revolutionary drumbeat in a church known today for its conservatism seems anomalous.[18] Mormons never filibustered, mounted a barricade, or cranked out revolutionary propaganda. Scholars have suggested that Joseph Smith founded Mormonism to counter, not join, the rationalism unleashed by the French Revolution.[19] The Book of Mormon, the movement's new scripture, also fails to establish any rationale for revolutionary opposition to established government.[20] Moreover, Article of Faith 12 promises obedience to "kings, presi-

---

and David O. McKay, April 9, 1939, *Conference Report*, 111.

17. Geoffrey N. Leech, *A Linguistic Guide to English Poetry*, 74. On the phenomenon of opposition groups adopting the discursive structures of groups they oppose, see Alun Munslow, *Discourse and Culture: The Creation of America, 1870–1920*, 1–22. For a guide to rhetorical analysis, see Ann M. Gill and Karen Whedbee, "Rhetoric."

18. Utah's political conservatism is discussed in Clyde A. Milner, Carol A. O'Connor, and Martha A. Sandweiss, eds., *The Oxford History of the American West*, 528; Ronald J. Hrebenar, Melanee Cherry, and Kathanne Greene, "Utah: Church and Corporate Power in the Nation's Most Conservative State," 113; Thomas G. Alexander, *Utah, the Right Place: The Official Centennial History*, 420. Randall Balmer, "Religions" describes the "fierce conservatism of the Mormons." See also Jean Bickmore White, "Utah Voting Patterns in the 20th Century," 148. On social issues see James T. Duke, "Cultural Continuity and Tension: A Test of Stark's Theory of Church Growth," 84–85, 88. On intellectual authoritarianism and conservatism at BYU, see Dale Allen Roberts, "Academic Freedom at Brigham Young University: Free Inquiry in Religious Context."

19. Robert N. Hullinger, *Joseph Smith's Response to Skepticism*, xv, 21, counters that Smith launched a new religion to challenge deism. Richard L. Bushman, *Joseph Smith and the Beginnings of Mormonism*, 6–7, suggests that Smith was influenced by the Enlightenment more than traditional evangelicalism.

20. Richard L. Bushman, "The Book of Mormon and the American Revolution." Early Church leaders most often quoted from the Bible. See Grant Underwood, "Book of Mormon Usage in Early LDS Theology."

dents, [and] rulers." Neither do American attitudes toward revolution help decode the reasons for Mormon praise of the French Revolution. Public opinion has historically reflected the suspicions of John Adams and Thomas Jefferson. Jefferson initially welcomed the popular violence of the French Revolution but by the end of his life had moved closer to Adams's position: No revolution except one modeled after the American precedent could stay within the confines of acceptable change. Americans usually supported revolutions that established republics or liberalized trade, but opinion turned against the ones seeking a socialist path toward economic development.[21]

But revolutionary rhetoric in a church described by some scholars as the most "American" of all religions is not as strange as it sounds.[22] Cases of people switching from one ideology to another are common to historical biography. Georges Clemenceau, the president of France during World War I, was a Communard in 1871 but became a nationalist by 1914. Benito Mussolini, once an admirer of Lenin and the Left, founded fascism, the extreme ideology of the Right.[23] Most ironic of all may be the association of Karl Marx with dreams of the next world. Martin Buber identifies Marx as an "inward utopian." So do Frank and Fritzie Manuel, "though the language of utopia changed at various stages of his life."[24] Marx scorned non-revolutionary utopians for

---

21. Michael H. Hunt, *Ideology and U.S. Foreign Policy*, 92–124; Charles Downer Hazen, *Contemporary American Opinion of the French Revolution*, 1–53, 120–36, 152–62, 266; Eugene N. Curtis, "American Opinion of the French Nineteenth-Century Revolutions," 263. Walter LaFeber argues that American imperialism fomented revolutions but that the United States restored order in ways that advanced market interests. See LaFeber, *The American Search for Opportunity, 1865–1913*, 235–36. An overview of Wilson's policies toward revolutions is found in David Steigerwald, "The Reclamation of Woodrow Wilson?"

22. For interpretations of Mormonism's "American identity," see Harold Bloom, *The American Religion: The Emergence of the Post-Christian Nation*, 96, 111, 263; Ernest Lee Tuveson, *Redeemer Nation: The Idea of America's Millennial Role*, 185; R. Laurence Moore, *Religious Outsiders and the Making of Americans*, 45; David van Biema, "Kingdom Come," 52; Robert Gottlieb and Peter Wiley, *America's Saints: The Rise of Mormon Power*, 13–14.

23. Billington, *Fire in the Minds of Men*, 17–23, 427–33.

24. Martin Buber, *Paths in Utopia*, 13; Frank E. Manuel and Fritzie P.

their belief that science and morality, under the right conditions, would liberate mankind from exploitation; yet he still spoke a language of self-actualization that testifies of his indebtedness to St. Simon and Charles Fourier. "A time may come," the Manuels suggest, "when the sonorous bits of rhetoric strewn throughout the works of Marx will be fused in a unified liturgical chant whose origins are lost in obscurity."[25]

A deeper excursion into the past moves us closer to understanding how revolution found its way into Mormon discourse. In an exploratory article D. Michael Quinn compares two communities: Joseph Smith's Nauvoo and John of Leyden's short-lived Anabaptist kingdom in Münster.[26] "Widely separated in time," Quinn posits, "they had deep structural affinities."[27] Both men anointed apostles, practiced polygamy, declared a theocracy, and anticipated an imminent, violent millennium. Imperial troops crushed the Anabaptists in 1535, and John of Leyden was lynched.

Babeuf, Smith, Anabaptists, and Mormon observers looked forward to the coming of divine law to sanctify a profane earth. The future state of the world was to be one of social perfection. Spontaneous unity, man's natural reflex, was the corollary of a world void of class conflict and international warfare. In the universal application of their beliefs and the fervency of their faith, Mormon observers and revolutionaries shared an eschatology encrypted with similar codes.

Manuel, *Utopian Thought in the Western World*, 713.

25. Manuel and Manuel, *Utopian Thought in the Western World*, 714. See also Sylvia L. Thrupp, ed., *Millennial Dreams in Action: Studies in Revolutionary Religious Movements*, 25.

26. D. Michael Quinn, "Socioreligious Radicalism of the Mormon Church: A Parallel to the Anabaptists." Other works on the Anabaptist connection include David Brion Davis, "The New England Origins of Mormonism," 148–49; Robert J. McCue, "Similarities and Differences in the Anabaptist Restitution and the Mormon Restoration"; William E. Juhnke, "Anabaptism and Mormonism: A Study in Comparative History"; and John L. Brooke, *The Refiner's Fire: The Making of Mormon Cosmology, 1644–1844*, 6. For the Anabaptist revolt see Norman Cohn, *The Pursuit of the Millennium: Revolutionary Millenarians and Mystical Anarchists of the Middle Ages*, 252–80.

27. Quinn, "Socioreligious Radicalism of the Mormon Church," 379.

Revolution, Utopia, and the Millennium

Mormon leaders felt endowed with a mission. In 1920 Church president Heber J. Grant (1918–45) explained what that mission was: to prepare the people of the world "for the inauguration of that blessed day when the millennium shall come and Christ shall reign as the King of Kings, standing at the head of the universal brotherhood of Man."[28]

Apostle Melvin J. Ballard said that "the purpose of the Christ and his Church [is] to make men brothers no matter what their nationality, to bring them into a brotherhood and a fraternity."[29] Doctrine and Covenants 84:100–101 suggested that this fraternal state would come from above and below:

> The Lord hath brought down Zion from above.
> The Lord hath brought up Zion from beneath.
> The earth hath travailed and brought forth her strength;
> And truth is established in her bowels;
>
> And the heavens have smiled upon her;
> And she is clothed with the glory of her God;
> For he stands in the midst of his people.

A denationalized Christ amid a unified international Zion was more than allegory. Mormon doctrine suggested that even the continents would merge during the millennium.[30] In the worldview to which Mormon observers subscribed, revolutions served an evangelical purpose: they toppled monarchies and pried open societies, allowing missionaries to work more effectively. Converts would form the critical mass necessary to build Zion in North America and evangelize the world. Then Christ would return to complete the one-world transformation. Ascendant peo-

---

28. Heber J. Grant, "A Marvelous Work and a Wonder," *Improvement Era* 23 (April 1920): 472–73.

29. M. Russell Ballard, ed., *Melvin J. Ballard: Crusader for Righteousness*, 231.

30. Mormons believed that the single continent Pangaea existed at the time of Adam. See Parley P. Pratt, *A Voice of Warning and Instruction to All People . . .* , 134; Orson Pratt, October 11, 1874, *Journal of Discourses*, 17:188. For other beliefs about millennial conditions, see "The Millennium," reprinted from the *Gospel Reflector* in *Times and Seasons* 3 (February 1, 1842): 673; John Taylor, *The Government of God*, 114–15; Kent P. Jackson, "The Signs of the Times: 'Be Not Troubled'"; Richard D. Draper, "Maturing toward the Millennium."

ples would welcome the descending Christ. Alienation from God would cease and universal justice and happiness would reign. Revolution was the thematic braid that ran through the Mormon historical narrative. News of people rising from below against illiberal governments was the rehearsal for the ultimate revolution from above.

Mormon leaders were also in touch with the revolutionary movements of their time. Far from being ascetics waiting to greet Christ, they engaged the world. They explored, colonized, embarked on foreign missions, and built cities. They provided spiritual guidance for their people and governed in a vast triangular region between Alberta, Canada, southern California and northern Mexico. Mormon leaders were also students of global events. The social misery and political corruption they saw in Europe and Latin America deeply affected them. They sympathized with oppressed peoples. They believed in representative government. Like other men and women of religion, Mormon leaders often linked their commissions to the causes of other peoples struggling for dignity and justice.

The Revolutionary Idea Evolves

Revolution as a sociopolitical event has undergone definitional change. Mid-seventeenth-century Englishman Thomas Hobbes described revolutions as reversible transfers of power, typified by the ascendancy of Parliament in 1649, followed by the dictatorship of Cromwell, the return of Charles II, and the reassertion of Parliamentary control in the Glorious Revolution of 1688. This circular view of revolution was replaced in the late eighteenth century by the linear model of the French Revolution. The world would never be the same; the clock could not be turned back. Writers trying to make sense of the 1790s argued that revolutions destroyed outmoded political and social forms. New institutions built on republicanism, national citizenship, and constitutional government reflected a new faith in change intended to permanently assure social and economic progress.[31]

---

31. The classic Marxist interpretation is Georges Lefebvre, *The Coming of the French Revolution*. For an essay treating subsequent revisions of the classic interpretation since 1939, see William Doyle, *Origins of the French Revolution*, 7–40. An update of the Marxist interpretation is Eric J. Hobsbawm, *Echoes of Marseillaise: Two Centuries Look Back on the French Revolution*.

Karl Marx bestowed on the progressive interpretation of revolution a theoretical rigor it had not previously had. The *Communist Manifesto*, published by the Communist League in 1848, presented history as a series of stages. The class that controlled production shaped the economic order. In this view the French Revolution marked the transfer of power from the landed nobility to the capitalist middle class. In the next revolution, the workers—exploited but gradually becoming conscious of their strength—would rebel against the capitalists and their allies. They would overthrow the state and use its armaments to crush the counter-revolution. Workers would establish socialism and eventually communism.[32] Marxists argued that communism was a historical inevitability. It would cover the earth. The change, violent though it may be, would mean a better life for all.

The French creed *liberty, equality, fraternity* set the tone for proletarian revolutions the world over. Through the ideal of *liberty*, revolutionaries framed new ideas about property rights and individuality. A liberty-centered revolution removed the most important affairs of state from the purview of monarchs if it did not eliminate monarchy altogether. Examples of liberty-centered revolutions include the Glorious Revolution of 1688, the American Revolution of 1776, and the French Revolution of 1830 that dethroned Bourbon King Charles X. Constitutions assured that the forces of talent and production operated in a liberal environment managed by men of property. For its part, the ideal of *fraternity* inspired nineteenth-century nationalism. Nationalists usually realized their goals in a republic or constitutional monarchy. The unification of Italy in 1861 under King Victor Emmanuel II is a good example.

The most radical of the three was the ideal of *equality*, which fertilized the ideas of socialism and communism. During the 1830s the revolutionary camp split: nationalist revolutionaries fought for a new kind of fraternity, and social revolutionaries vied for a new kind of equality. Then, during the 1840s, there was another split within the social revolutionary camp. Socialists such as St. Simon, Robert Owen, Charles Fourier, and Etienne Cabet—and, to a lesser degree, anarchist Joseph-

---

32. Karl Marx, *The Communist Manifesto* (1848), in David McLellan, ed., *Karl Marx: Selected Writings*, 221–47. The fullest discussion of Marx's version of history is Mandell Morton Bober, *Karl Marx's Interpretation of History*. A good primer on Marxist theory is James R. Ozinga, *Communism: The Story of the Idea and Its Implementation*.

Pierre Proudhon—believed that utopia could be conjured without violence. Philosophy and science held the secret of social perfection. It could begin in one place and gradually spread to the rest of the world. Reaching the utopian state depended on personal moral transformation, separation from society, and voluntary redistribution of wealth. The second branch became the revolutionary communists. Class, the product of man's relationship to the mode of production, was the mainspring of history. Concentration of productive machinery under private ownership destroyed the lives of the workers. Karl Marx believed that through the workings of surplus value of commodity production, industrialists stole rewards from workers who did not obtain the full wage value of their labor. The proletarian army of destitute workers and unemployed backups thrown out of jobs due to cost-effective methods of production would develop a consciousness of their historic duty to lead society from capitalism to socialism. In violent revolution, the workers, led by an intelligentsia that understood the theory, would seize the factories and smash the industrialists with their own mass-produced weapons. The ruling class, shorn of its government support, would disappear. With workers controlling politics, production, and military power, oppression would cease. A gentle glide into socialism came next, so the theory went.

By the time of the revolutions of 1848, the nationalist strain dominated revolutionary movements in Germany, Italy, and Hungary. Failure in 1849 changed the nationalist impulse. Giuseppe Mazzini, the Italian activist who inspired a united Italy, had envisioned a federation of European nations joined in mutual friendship. But Mazzini's international romanticism mutated into the rationale for the New Imperialism around 1870. By 1914 it became patriotic nationalism, which in turn devolved into fascism during the 1920s and 1930s.

The most cogent theorist of revolution during his time was Karl Marx. Marx believed that since the productive power of workers exceeded their wages, the working-class "proletarians" must, according to scientific calculations, violently overthrow the capitalist factory owners. Revolutionary workers' councils would abolish private property, smash the bourgeois counter-revolution, and ultimately attain a communist state.

For Marx this was not just an abstract theory; it was a political program. Marx was a founding member of the International Workingmen's Association, formed in London in 1864 to coordinate the efforts of various labor groups and left-wing political factions. However, not everyone in this "First International" shared Marx's revolutionary approach to class struggle. The Marxist faction won, but not before others contested Marx's leadership. Jacobins from France wished to restore a constitutional republic. The followers of Augusti Blanqui adhered to the conspiratorial method. Most serious was the threat from Joseph Proudhon and Michael Bakunin. They were anarchists who urged warfare against the bureaucratic state instead of against capitalism directly. Ultimately, however, the International avowed the intentions of Marx's 1848 *Communist Manifesto*. The Marxist theory adopted by the International dictated that the capitalist ruling class was ripe for destruction to clear the way for the workers' paradise. In the short term the theory failed. The crushing of the Paris Commune in 1871, discussed in Chapter 5, fragmented the International. The amalgam of French activism and German theory, however, migrated from Paris to St. Petersburg. In 1917, after decades of exile, underground activity, and failed uprisings, Vladimir Lenin midwifed communism into political reality.[33]

Mormon observers appreciated the American Revolution and the republic it created. Without the religious freedom guaranteed by the Constitution, they surmised, Joseph Smith would not have been able to restore his truths.[34] Historians have often interpreted Mormonism

---

33. In the 1840s the communist movement split. Anarchists Pierre Proudhon (1809–65) and Mikhail Bakunin (1814–76) wanted to destroy the state. Marx would destroy capitalism and then state oppression would wither away. See James Billington, *Fire in the Minds of Men*, 287–305; and Ozinga, *Communism*, 26, 57. On the 1847 founding of the Communist League, from which came the *Communist Manifesto*, see Francis Wheen, *Karl Marx: A Life*, 98–113; and Ozinga, *Communism*, 33–34, 51.

34. On Mormon appreciation for the United States, see Orson Pratt, *New Jerusalem; or, the Fulfillment of Modern Prophecy*, 17–18; John Taylor, *The Gospel Kingdom*, 312; George A. Smith, *Deseret News*, July 13, 1854; George Q. Cannon, *Gospel Truths: Discourses and Writings of President George Q. Cannon*, 1:308; Orson Pratt, July 8, 1855, *Journal of Discourses*, 3:71–72; and John Taylor, December 17, 1871, *Journal of Discourses*, 14:267. Eugene E. Campbell discusses the schismatic nature of Mormon patriotism versus millennial kingdom building in "Pioneers and Patriotism: Conflicting Loyalties." Richard L. Bushman, in "Virtue and the Constitution," suggests that Mormons believed the Constitution prevented tyranny but did not

as an expression of American exceptionalism—the idea that God reserved a special role for the United States to play in world affairs. Like fellow Americans, Mormons entered World War I believing the nation was fulfilling a providential role as the redeemer nation.[35] While this interpretation captures the American character of Mormonism, it also overlooks a pre-World War II Mormon mindset that was often anything but nostalgic about America.

Religion and the Revolutionary Mind

Faith in revolution is predicated on the same devotion that the churchman renders his religion. "At a deep, subconscious level," writes James Billington, "the revolutionary faith was shaped by the Christian faith it attempted to replace."[36] Religionists and social revolutionaries used the same template. Frank Tannenbaum, a student of the Mexican Revolution, suggested that Marx's labor versus capital equated to the Christian construct of good versus evil. Communist theory had eliminated God and Satan but retained Armageddon. "The theological drama was shifted from heaven to earth," leaving no possible outcome, according to the theory, except "sudden and violent revolution."[37] In

---

offer a solution to political, legal, or economic problems. The Constitution represented God's commitment to free agency, but public, personal virtue was the only reliable safeguard against bad laws.

35. For American expansion as a religious or ideological expression, see Tuveson, *Redeemer Nation*, 187–214; James H. Moorhead, *American Apocalypse: Yankee Protestants and the Civil War, 1860-1869*; Walter A. McDougall, *Promised Land, Crusader State: The American Encounter with the World since 1776*; Gregory S. Butler, "Visions of a Nation Transformed: Modernity and Ideology in Wilson's Political Thought"; Anders Stephanson, *Manifest Destiny: American Expansionism and the Empire of Right*; Hunt, *Ideology and U.S. Foreign Policy*, 19–45.

36. Billington, *Fire in the Minds of Men*, 8. Hillel Schwartz, "Millenarianism: An Overview," 530, recognizes millennialism as the "taproot of religion and revolution."

37. Frank Tannenbaum, "The Prospect of Violent Revolution in the United States," *Scribner's Magazine* 89 (May 1931): 521–22. Vladimir Lenin's *Imperialism, the Highest Stage of Capitalism: A Popular Outline* (1917) replaced the multi-headed antichrist with finance capitalism. The

Michael Walzer's study of Puritan ideology, "Revolution in its origins was only a particular form of this eternal warfare, the continuation, it might be said, of religious activity by military means."[38]

The early "apostles" of the revolutionary faith—theorists, idealists, romantics, utopians, and conspirators—used religious terminology to communicate their epiphanies to the people.[39] In the festivals of the First French Republic, Catholic icons intermingled with the Masonic "level," the symbol of equality.[40] Proto-communist Thomas Goodwin Barmby established a communist "church" and viewed revolutionary struggle in apocalyptic terms.[41] Karl Schapper of the League of the Just (forerunner to the Communist League) addressed fellow members as "Brothers in Christ."[42] And in 1842–43, when Marx was editing the *Rheinische Zeitung* and was still ambivalent about what it meant to be a communist, Wilhelm Weitling was calling himself a "social Luther" and preaching Christian communist revolution.[43] During the 1840s and 1850s, French socialists awakened peasants to a "progressive dem-

---

millennium was the coming classless society. World War I and foreign intervention enabled mobilization of the masses, prompting him to suspect that the end of history, meaning the completion of historical dialecticism, was near. Mary Holdsworth touches on the dichotomous (good-evil) nature of Lenin's work in her essay "Lenin's *Imperialism* in Retrospect," as does Billington, *Fire in the Minds of Men*, 466. Luc Racine discusses the laicization of millennialism in "Paradise, the Golden Age, the Millennium and Utopia: A Note on the Differentiation of Forms of the Ideal Society," 131. For Latter-day Saint awareness of shared secular/religious utopianism/millennialism, see G. Homer Durham, "The Problem of Evil in 1956," *Improvement Era* 59 (January 1956): 2, 62–63.

38. Michael Walzer, *The Revolution of the Saints: A Study in the Origins of Radical Politics*, 110. For reading on how the same Calvinism that motivated the Puritans also influenced the French Revolution, see Dale K. Van Kley, *The Religious Origins of the French Revolution: From Calvin to the Civil Constitution, 1560–1791*.

39. For religious symbolism in social revolutionary discourse, see Billington, *Fire in the Minds of Men*, 19–20, 25, 182–86, 232, 254–58.

40. Lynn Hunt, *Politics, Culture, and Class in the French Revolution*, 60.

41. Billington, *Fire in the Minds of Men*, 254–57.

42. Ibid., 185.

43. Ibid., 185–86, 266, 269.

ocratic ideology [that viewed] the world in terms of Christian moral principles, but [was] committed to institutions of mass democracy."[44] Revolutionaries found that casting Christ as the leader of their movement lent legitimacy to the revolutionary idea.[45] Babeuf presented Christ as a revolutionary prophet. In 1918 Russian poet Alexander Blok depicted a radical Christ leading an armed band of apostles into St. Petersburg.[46] Influential among LDS general authorities was H. G. Wells, a British writer who described Christ as a "great revolutionist" who had leveled an attack against property.[47]

Mormons inherited the rationale for "just revolution" from the Puritans. Puritans expanded John Calvin's teaching on the covenant between man and God. By himself man was worthless. But in covenant with God, man was magnified by God and shared in God's omnipotence. Man became God's indispensible co-agent in building the kingdom of God. Puritans often referred to this co-agency as "Soul liberty." Historian David Hackett Fisher explains that "soul liberty" was "the principle which held that a Christian community should be free to serve God in the World."[48] At the Battle of Concord, William Emerson,

---

44. Edward Berenson, *Populist Religion and Left-Wing Politics in France, 1830–1852*, xx.

45. Robert M. Price, "Numbered among the Transgressors, the 'Zealot Hypothesis' Reconsidered"; John T. Pawlikowski, "Jesus and the Revolutionaries: A Jewish-Christian Approach to the Current Debate"; and Paul L. Lehmann, "The Transfiguration of Jesus and Revolutionary Politics."

46. N. A. Morozov, *The Revelation in Thunder and Storm*, quoted in Billington, *Fire in the Minds of Men*, 76.

47. Wells, *Outline of History*, 2:770. Other General Authorities who referenced Wells include Melvin J. Ballard, October 7, 1917, *Conference Report*, 107; John L. Herrick, April 6, 1918, *Conference Report*, 49; John A. Widtsoe, October 7, 1921, *Conference Report*, 49; Rulon S. Wells, April 5, 1924, *Conference Report*, 63; Richard R. Lyman, April 7, 1928, *Conference Report*, 72; and James H. Moyle, October 8, 1932, *Conference Report*, 61. H. G. Wells interviewed Stalin and believed that Soviet communism and the New Deal were programs with "spiritual appeal" because of the social cohesion they promoted. See Paul Hollander, *Political Pilgrims: Travels of Western Intellectuals to the Soviet Union, China, and Cuba, 1928–1978*, 22, 138.

48. David Hackett Fischer, *Albion's Seed: Four British Folkways in America*, 23, 203; David Hackett Fischer, *Paul Revere's Ride*, 16.

the town's minister, stiffened young militiamen wavering before the approach of British grenadiers. "Stand your ground," Emerson said to Harry Gould, resting his hand on Gould's shoulder. "Your cause is just and God will bless you!"[49]

In the Protestant ministerial tradition, revolution was justified if the government violated natural rights or forced man to choose between God and secular law.[50] The key to ascertaining the right to revolution lies in understanding God's will. The concept of "horizontal revelation" holds that the canon is always open and that God reveals his will through the unfolding of history and invites man to participate with him in his terrestrial undertakings.[51] In this manner the will of God is read in unfolding events. But how does one know when the time is right for revolution, Puritan clergymen asked? John Knox replied: "If a group has the power to attain its aims, this is a sign that it is God's will to pursue them."[52] Revolution often achieved the same legitimacy among Mormon observers.

Time Befriends the Believer

Another key to understanding the Mormon affinity for revolution is the concept of time.[53] Social revolutionaries of the nineteenth centu-

---

49. Fischer, *Paul Revere's Ride*, 205.

50. Therald N. Jensen, "Mormon Theory of Church and State," 106–7, 113, 117. B. H. Roberts said moral and personal accountability before God empowered man with the right of revolution. See his sermon delivered October 5, 1912, *Conference Report*, 33–34.

51. Lorin K. Hansen, "Some Concepts of Divine Revelation," 53; James Barr, "Revelation through History in Old Testament and in Modern Theology"; John Cobb and Truman G. Madsen, "Theodicy," 1474.

52. Richard Harries, "The Criterion of Success for a Just Revolution," 193; John Knox, *The History of the Reformation of Religion in Scotland*, 323; Walzer, *Revolution of the Saints*, 108–9. See also Joel H. Nederhood, "Christians and Revolution"; and M. M. Thomas, "Social Justice and Just Rebellion."

53. On Mormon concepts of time, see John A. Widtsoe, *Joseph Smith as Scientist*, 66–68; Sterling M. McMurrin, *The Theological Foundations of the Mormon Religion*, 40–46; Max Nolan, "Materialism and the Mormon Faith"; Edwin S. Gaustad, "History and Theology: The Mormon Connection"; Kent E. Robson, "Time and Omniscience in Mormon Theology," 17–24.

ry—persecuted and hounded into exile, if they avoided death in street battles—found an ally in time. If revolution failed in a particular place, the devoted revolutionary could rest assured that at some future time, theory would be vindicated. Workers would come out on top. Marx assured everyone that the laws of history foretold the rise of socialism with the same scientific certainty that governs the sunrise every day.

Mormons also learned to place faith in time. Joseph Smith's revelations designated Jackson County, Missouri as Zion—the Western Hemisphere's sacred center. In 1833 Missourians drove Mormon settlers from the state. The Saints, frustrated, had to postpone the building of Zion in that place and rely on God to make them victorious at a later time. Paul Edwards writes that positioning God in time made "progression . . . not a history of a people in a specific place, but of all people throughout time."[54] Individual revolutions became merely events pegged to specific places and times. What really mattered was the overall revolutionary movement of history. Achievements in one place or another were mere markers ticking off the countdown to the millennium. The triumph of providential design through successive change and upheaval on earth made God's omniscience more important than his omnipresence.

A useful way to understand the Mormon conceptualization of history is to distinguish between "profane" and "sacred" time. Profane time is the time recorded on clocks and calendars that mark off world history. The profane calendar will eventually yield to the millennium, and a new era of sacred time will begin. Heavenly beings will walk the earth, new priorities will be imposed, and things like schedules and getting to a job on time will no longer matter. The difference between profane and sacred time is like the difference between the left and right hemispheres of the brain. The former analytically deals with the world as it is; the latter creatively imagines the world as it could be. Historian Jan Shipps has portrayed an early Mormon Church that believed it was the reincarnation of ancient Israel. Modern temple building gave God a place to commune with man as he had communed with the ancient kings and patriarchs. The trek to the Rocky Mountains recapitulated the biblical Exodus from Egypt. In such reenactments of biblical events,

---

54. Paul M. Edwards, "Time in Mormon History," 388–89.

Mormons dramatized their connection to ancient Israel.[55] Revolution in other countries likewise opened passageways to sacred time. Street fighting and parliaments of the people sprouting from soils plowed by revolution enticed Mormon observers to enter vicariously into sacred time and experience the kingdom coming.

Mormon observers tacitly recognized revolution as a catalyst driving history toward its consummation. Robert Flanders suggests that Joseph Smith energized the egalitarianism of the Jacksonian age by promising "that in God's new time the weak and humble would, in covenant with deity, rise and break down the things of the strong and mighty."[56] Smith's followers believed that his "new American history might yet save the world." For similar "expressions of ecumenism," concludes Flanders, "it is perhaps necessary to look to profane history, to Marx's restructure of time, or to the National Socialist nightmare of the Third Reich."[57] Latter-day Saint time paralleled Marx's chronology. The Marxist equivalent of profane time was humanity's story while it was still in flux. Revolution was the last act of the human drama. The equivalent of sacred time was the awaiting reality—worker control of the factories, socialism and perfection—the end of the story.[58] In 1902 B. H. Roberts connected Mormons' concepts of time and horizontal

---

55. Jan Shipps, *Mormonism: The Story of a New Religious Tradition*, 63.

56. Bruce Flanders, "To Transform History: Early Mormon Culture and the Concept of Time and Space," 117. Joseph Smith once claimed he liked French democrat-republicanism, and he endorsed demands for broader franchise in the 1841–42 Dorr Rebellion in Rhode Island. See Klaus J. Hansen, *Quest for Empire: The Political Kingdom of God and the Council of Fifty in Mormon History*, 87; and Smith et al., *History of the Church*, 6:199. Contemporary accounts indicate that Smith's grandfather Asael Smith embraced Thomas Paine's *Age of Reason*. See Bushman, *Joseph Smith and the Beginnings of Mormonism*, 38. Enemies of Joseph Smith claimed that Joseph Sr., his father, viewed the writings of Voltaire as "the best Bible in extant, and Thomas Paine's *Age of Reason* the best commentary." See "Strafford, Orange County, State of Vermont, February 15, 1844, to the Editor of the *Warsaw Message or Warsaw Signel if that has commenced*," in Dan Vogel, ed. and comp., *Early Mormon Documents*, 1:596–97.

57. Flanders, "To Transform History," 117.

58. Karl Marx, Letter to Pavel Annenkov, [December 1846], in McLellan, *Karl Marx: Selected Writings*, 193.

revelation with those of their contemporaries. The "modern liberal doctrine of man and the optimism of the nineteenth century," Roberts said, connected the Church "with all the other great movements that are bringing to pass the revolutions now going on in the earth."[59]

The Millennium

The second coming of Christ and millennium are the Judeo-Christian version of the secular "unfinished" French social revolution of 1792.[60] The restoration of the monarchy in France and the failure of Prussia to establish constitutional government in 1848 inspired hope for a second revolution that would enshrine the final purpose of the 1789 revolution. The goal was a new, egalitarian world. From Thomas Müntzer to Woodrow Wilson's League of Nations, Western thought shows yearnings for political and moral purity.[61]

Belief in a millennium—one thousand years of earthly harmony—drove early Mormonism and thus it is important in understanding the Church's first hundred years. The current Latter-day Saint emphasis on personal morality—love, charity, honesty, patience—did not receive the same degree of attention that the Church's early apostles paid to events they thought were leading to the millennium.[62] Millennial fervor abated after the American Civil War, but periodically resurged when world events appeared to coincide with Mormon eschatological expectations.

---

59. Quoted in Leonard Arrington and Davis Bitton, *The Mormon Experience: A History of the Latter-day Saints*, 257–58. Roberts's views of time and progress were picked up by Ray B. West Jr., *Kingdom of the Saints: The Story of Brigham Young and the Mormons*, 335.

60. Billington, *Fire in the Minds of Men*, 71. On fixation on the "unfinished revolution," see ibid., 70–71, 75–78, 84–88.

61. General studies include Karl Löwith, *Meaning in History: The Theological Implications of the Philosophy of History*; Ernest Lee Tuveson, *Millennium and Utopia: A Study in the Background of the Idea of Progress*; Jacob L. Talmon, *Political Messianism: The Romantic Phase*; Cohn, *Pursuit of the Millennium*; Talmon, *Origins of Totalitarian Democracy*; Conrad Cherry, ed., *God's New Israel: Religious Interpretations of American Destiny*; Walzer, *Revolution of the Saints*; and McDougall, *Promised Land*.

62. Gary Shepard and Gordon Shepard, *A Kingdom Transformed: Themes in the Development of Mormonism*, 73–80.

Scholars divide on whether Mormons were pre- or postmillennialists.[63] Premillennialists tended to believe that the world was deteriorating. At the moment when affairs could not get worse, Christ would return in glory. His apocalyptic second coming would destroy the wicked, raise the righteous dead, and usher in a thousand years of peace. The Marxist theory of violent revolution and Rosa Luxembourg's "universal strike" had roots in premillennial belief.[64] Postmillennialism,

---

63. For an overview on Mormon eschatology, see Massimo Introvigne, "Latter Day Revisited: Contemporary Mormon Millenarianism." For Mormons as premillennialists see Thomas G. Alexander, "Between Revivalism and the Social Gospel: The Latter-day Saint Social Advisory Committee," 20–23; and Grant Underwood, *The Millenarian World of Early Mormonism.* For postmillennial interpretations see Blaine Carmon Hardy, *Solemn Covenant: The Mormon Polygamous Passage,* 102, 124 note 143; Tuveson, *Redeemer Nation,* 175–86; D. Michael Quinn, *The Mormon Hierarchy: Origins of Power,* 178, 403 note 177; Hansen, *Quest for Empire,* 3–23; Keith E. Norman, "How Long O Lord? The Delay of the Parousia in Mormonism," 48–58; David E. Smith, "Millenarian Scholarship in America," 542; Noel A. Carmack, "Of Prophets and Pale Horses: Joseph Smith, Benjamin West, and the American Millenarian Tradition," 174; and Thomas McGowan, "Mormon Millennialism," 167.

Scholars have also suggested that Mormons began as premillennialists then leaned increasingly toward postmillennialism after 1890. See Louis G. Reinwand, "An Interpretive Study of Mormon Millennialism during the Nineteenth Century with Emphasis on Millennial Developments in Utah," 43–48, 153–60; Dan Erickson, *"As a Thief in the Night": The Mormon Quest for Millennial Deliverance,* 179–211; Arrington and Bitton, *The Mormon Experience,* 416; and David Bigler, *Forgotten Kingdom: The Mormon Theocracy in the American West, 1847–1896,* 367–68. Thomas G. Alexander, *Mormonism in Transition: A History of the Latter-day Saints, 1890–1930,* 13, 237–38 argues that as of 1930, Mormons still assumed the gathering to Zion was a prerequisite for Christ's return. Not until the 1960s did the Church shed the image of a people gathering in urgency for the millennium.

64. Rosa Luxembourg and her colleague Karl Liebknecht were the intelligentsia behind the 1919 Spartacist Uprising in Germany. They believed that a mass worker revolt would almost magically trigger a revolutionary apocalypse more widespread and complete than the Bolshevik Revolution in Russia two years earlier. Discharged German soldiers helped police defeat the Spartacists, and Luxembourg and Liebknecht paid for the

by contrast, derived from the Judaic belief in natural social change. Man was God's partner in the transformation of the inner self, which would lead to the reorganization of society. In Christianity this notion found expression in the belief that Christ would come at the *end* of the thousand years of peace: *after* Christianity had triumphed, *after* the return of the Jews to Israel, and *after* an outpouring of divine knowledge. In this interpretation, revolutions prepared the way for mass conversion during the millennium. Postmillennialism made room for the moral and scientific progress that churchmen believed the Bible foretold.[65] Despite the differences, scholars have noticed that believers in the two different end-of-time camps talked and lived their lives in much the same way.[66]

Mormons had characteristics of both kinds of millennialists. Like those who accepted a remote, postmillennial second coming, Mormons planned for long life in the regular world. They laid out cities, dug irrigation canals, and invested in stocks. In several respects, Mormon enthusiasm for the building of their western Zion configured a world in which the millennial state was a long way off. Mormons were not

---

premature revolt with their lives. Buber, *Paths in Utopia*, 10–11.

65. Postmillennialism in the Protestant world gradually weakened during the 1870s and was dealt a deathblow by World War I (1914–1918). Progressive millennialism yielded to its rival, premillennialism, because postmillennialists could never reconcile the modern and mystical halves of their worldview. World War I destroyed the notion that progress was inevitable, and a burgeoning Fundamentalist movement denounced faith in progress as un- (or even anti-) Christian. Evangelicals abandoned the religious aspect of progress in favor of corporatism, scientific efficiency, and middle class prosperity. James H. Moorhead writes that "the erosion of postmillennialism was part of the waning of supernaturalism." See Moorhead, "Between Progress and Apocalypse: A Reassessment of Millennialism in American Religious Thought, 1800–1880," 541. See also Moorhead, "The Erosion of Postmillennialism in American Religious Thought, 1865–1925," 76–77; and George M. Marsden, *Religion and American Culture*, 157–59.

66. Underwood, *The Millennarian World of Early Mormonism*, 7; Ernest Robert Sandeen, *The Roots of Fundamentalism: British and American Millenarianism, 1800–1930*, 183–86; Timothy P. Weber, *Living in the Shadow of the Second Coming: American Premillennialism, 1875–1925*, 65–81; Catherine Wessinger, "Millennialism with and without the Mayhem," 53–54.

progressives because they believed that Bible societies and missionary work would win over all people (though some did), or that the world was getting better (many did not), or that Christ would come *after* one thousand years of peace (few did). Rather, they were progressives because they believed that revolutions carried out by human action would topple governments incompatible with an expanding Zion. This enthusiasm for revolutionary destruction was not necessarily in anticipation of the end of time. Revolution was about moving history from one epoch to another. Mormons call these epochs "dispensations." In 1870 Orson Pratt talked about an elongated millennium as a "wonderful revolution." However, it would not come about "in one day, or in one year." Pratt also said that kingdoms and thrones would fall, but the destruction of the earth would not come until *after* the one thousand years of Christ's rule.[67]

Millennialism also served a social purpose. John F. C. Harrison, W. H. Oliver, and Bryan Wilson have shown that millennialism was also a "vehicle for emergent socialist thinking."[68] Eschatology blended with social protest—deliverance from a tyrannical master, a tightfisted landlord, or menial subsistence living. Mormon leaders wanted people to break free from their predicaments. Latter-day Saint discourse talked about democratic institutions, wage compensation, state control of economic resources, novel social models, and the defeat of counter-revolutionary enemies.

Wilford Woodruff embodied the Mormon mind in his attitude toward profane and sacred time. He sympathized with oppressed peoples. He looked for the destruction of the old order. He actively built the new. One of the most pro-revolutionary apostles of the nineteenth century, Woodruff epitomized the seamless unity of inner- and other-worldly progress:

> Woodruff saw no incongruity in coupling a firm commitment to building the kingdom in preparation for Christ's second coming with a deep respect and desire for material progress. Since he believed in a holistic religion that recognized no discontinuity between heaven and

---

67. Orson Pratt, April 10, 1870, *Journal of Discourses*, 13:125–26.

68. W. H. Oliver, *Prophets and Millennialists: The Uses of Biblical Prophecy in England from the 1790's to the 1840's*, 216; John Fletcher Clews Harrison, *The Second Coming: Popular Millenarianism, 1780–1850*, 8–9; and Bryan R. Wilson, *Magic and the Millennium: A Sociological Study of Religious Movements of Protest among Tribal and Third-World Peoples*, 9–30.

earth, Woodruff expected material wealth, increased temporal education, and technological improvement to build God's kingdom as readily as sermons, spiritual experiences, and ministrations to the Saints.[69]

As the following chapters will show, revolution warrants installment in Woodruff's "holistic religion."

G. Homer Durham, later president of Arizona State University and member of the Presidency of the Seventy, summed up Mormon thought about the unity of man and God. In *Ethics: An International Journal of Social, Political, and Legal Philosophy*, he wrote that man had always existed with God as intelligence and was, therefore, "capable of unending progress." This doctrine "recognizes man's power to co-operate with God in controlling the universe for human good."[70]

Georg Wilhelm Friedrich Hegel

Mormon belief in dispensations fit within a larger context of religious and secular belief that history unfolds in stages. Joachim of Fiore (1145–1202), Henri de St. Simon (1760–1825), Charles Fourier (1772–1837), and Karl Marx (1818–1883) were among those who divided history into three stages. The periodization of history gave revolutionary and millennial enthusiasm a cadence that guided action and inspired faith.[71] The concept of linear history accented by periodic revolutionary change attracted some Mormon observers to the philosophy of Georg Wilhelm Friedrich Hegel (1770–1831). Subsequent philosophical interpretations of Hegel's works described his theory of history in terms of thesis, antithesis, and synthesis. Hegel never specifically used these

---

69. Thomas G. Alexander, *Things in Heaven and Earth: The Life and Times of Wilford Woodruff, a Mormon Prophet*, 152.

70. G. Homer Durham, "The Democratic Crisis and Mormon Thought," *Ethics: An International Journal of Social, Political, and Legal Philosophy* 52 (October 1941): 112.

71. For Fiore's stages of history, see Manuel and Manuel, *Utopian Thought in the Western World*, 56–59; Cohn, *Pursuit of the Millennium*, 108–13. For St. Simon see Talmon, *Political Messianism*, 35–71. For Fourier see Buber, *Paths in Utopia*, 18–20. For Marx see *The Poverty of Philosophy* (1846) in McLellan, *Karl Marx: Selected Writings*, 212.

terms, but the terminology simplifies the arcane thinking that became the basis of one of the most revolutionary modern ideas: the dialectic.[72]

Young Hegelians suggested that the Berlin professor had unwittingly described the motive force behind revolution by presenting the historical development of the state. According to Hegel, the contradiction between the idea of national unification (thesis) and the vestiges of feudalism (antithesis) would eventually be resolved through the creation of a new synthesis. The synthesis, in this case, was the unification of all Germanic peoples into one nation: Germany. Nationalists took Hegel to mean the creation of the liberal state; communists believed this process would produce socialism. But the realization of the state was just the beginning for new explorations. The evolution of a people continues under nationhood and expresses itself in art, religion, and science. Human history was continually evolving from a lower to a higher condition, and it was doing so through the periodic, revolutionary replacement of old antitheses by new syntheses.

Hegel left a mark on pre-1940 Mormonism. In 1920 Levi Edgar Young, a member of the Council of Seventy, referred to a lesson manual used by seventies quorums. The lesson taught the "modern conceptions of god," including "the fundamentals of philosophy and metaphysics" as taught by great thinkers such as Kant and Hegel. These academic forays were relevant to the motto of the quorum: "To become a Seventy means mental activity, intellectual development, and the attainment of spiritual power."[73] An article in the *Latter-day Saints' Millennial Star* suggested that science and revelation would forge the perfect civilization. Agriculture, cities, commerce, and manufacturing enabled the consolidation of the state. Next to develop would be art, literature, and music—the pursuits mentioned by Hegel. Even the Mormon "divine economy" and the "strictly theocratical society . . . must pass an infancy and travel the progressive stages of growth to maturity."[74] The triadic

---

72. Alfred Weber, *History of Philosophy*, 409–10; Billington, *Fire in the Minds of Men*, 228–29, 267; Ozinga, *Communism*, 16; Warren Lerner, *A History of Socialism and Communism in Modern Times: Theorists, Activists, and Humanists*, 24, 32–33. For Marx's attempt to "demystify" Hegel, see *Capital* (1864), in McLellan, *Karl Marx: Selected Writings*, 420.

73. Levi Edgar Young, "Sociological Aspect of 'Mormonism,'" *Improvement Era* 23 (July 1920): 826–27.

74. "The Essayist: Society—Its Stages," *Latter-day Saints' Millennial Star*

formula stuck with Mormon writers. A *Millennial Star* article in 1891 suggested that nations are like organisms. They experience stages of progression, balance, and deterioration. Deterioration leads to a "passing away," much as Marx dreamed of a "withering away" of the state and the formation of a classless society, or as Hegel dreamed of the replacement of feudalism by a Reich of all Germans.[75]

For Mormon thinkers as for Hegel, historical process dictated the emergence of a single social ideal. Religious pluralism, monarchies, liberalism, and democratic government were steps between the ten kingdoms referred to in Nebuchadnezzar's dream and the one true theodemocracy prophesied to replace them (Dan. 2:24–45). The idea of history unfolding as a series of dispensations, or stages of history, doomed the United States to short life expectancy. The American republic, like all other political institutions, would either decay, be absorbed by the theocratic kingdom, or explode prior to the millennium. Brigham Young preached that American independence from Great Britain was a temporary arrangement that granted "sufficient liberty" for religion. But politicians and their moneyed supporters had since twisted the constitution. In time the American republic would disappear.[76] Orson Pratt preached the same conclusion. The nations of Europe would exist "until a kingdom of divine origin shall come down . . . and then comes the mighty crash of republics, kingdoms, thrones, and empires."[77] The historical process would grant no exemption to the United States: "For all its glory and greatness, it was only a steppingstone to a form of government infinitely greater and more perfect—a government founded upon Divine laws, with all its institutions, ordinances, and officers appointed by the God of heaven."[78] Louis Bertrand, a radical Frenchman

---

21 (January 1, 1859): 3–4, hereafter cited as *Millennial Star*.

75. Willard Done, "The Diversity of Nations," *Contributor* 13 (November 1891): 28–30.

76. Brigham Young, *Discourses of Brigham Young*, 359. Young did not deny the right of revolution but hoped that through "faith in law, even human law" God would resolve the "maladministrations [and] the injustices" according to a scheme of "divine jurisprudence." See J. Keith Melville, "The Reflections of Brigham Young on the Nature of Man and the State," 267.

77. Orson Pratt, *Latter-day Kingdom; or the Preparation for the Second Advent*, 117.

78. Orson Pratt, August 14, 1859, *Journal of Discourses*, 7:215.

converted to Mormonism, wrote in a letter to Napoleon III: "The work of George Washington was only a provisional government, in order that [God's] kingdom might be founded on earth." John Taylor, Young's successor in 1877, credited the United States' founders with hammering the "entering wedge" into the "new era." Still, compared to the "light, the power and union that God alone can impart to the human family," the American republic was a mere "preliminary step."[79]

Conflict, growth, decay, and rebirth drove history. Mormons adapted the conception of Puritan divines who had equated days of progress with days of affliction. Contradictions preventing the consummation of Saintly triumph would be abolished over time.[80] In 1840 Wilford Woodruff pondered the "rise, progress, and fall of the empires of the earth, & the revolutions which must transpire before the winding up scene & the coming of Christ."[81] Convulsion and change, Woodruff wished to remind future generations, remained vital links in the "great chain" of history. Revolution was living, horizontal canon pointing to "the fulfillment of the word of God & the preperation [sic] for the coming of the son of Man." There was no foreboding as Woodruff dropped the curtain on revolutionary drama of 1848: "Look for the great Revolutions in the old world [and for] disunion in the States," Woodruff wrote. "But the Lord will govern the helm of the States and Nations for the final good of the world."[82] The *Frontier Guardian* depicted a violent sequence: "Monarchial, aristocratical, and republican governments of their various kinds and grades, have, in their turn, been raised to dignity, and prostrated in the dust."[83]

---

79. Louis A. Bertrand, "Important Appeal to the Emperor of the French," *Millennial Star* 23 (April 6, 1861): 221. For similar statements see John Taylor, April 9, 1879, *Journal of Discourses*, 21:31–32; and Scott G. Kenney, ed., *Wilford Woodruff's Journal: 1833–1898, Typescript*, January 1, 1876, 7:261.

80. James W. Davidson, "Eschatology in New England: 1700–1763," 229.

81. Kenney, *Wilford Woodruff's Journal*, May 11, 1840 and June 18, 1840, 1:447, 468. See also Warren Cowdery, *Latter-day Saints' Messenger and Advocate* 3 (July 1837): 531–32.

82. Kenney, *Wilford Woodruff's Journal*, December 30, 1850, and January 1852, 3:389, 4:89.

83. Joseph Fielding Smith Jr., comp., *Teachings of the Prophet Joseph Smith*, 249; "The Government of God," *Times and Seasons* 3 (July 15, 1842): 856, reprinted in *Frontier Guardian* (June 27, 1849): 1.

Brigham Young welcomed the tension of a world reaching for the future: "Every government of the world," he said, "has the seeds of its own destruction in itself."[84] His universal republicanism—equated with theocratic rule, as was common among Mormon leaders—would supplant the atomized world of competing sovereignties. The *Millennial Star* similarly condoned the violence that would trigger the "dissolution of nationalities." Through revolt the "Almighty" would clear away "the decaying rubbish of earthly governments, which have for ages caused the people to mourn and Satan to hold sway, that the reign of the King of Peace may be ushered in."[85] Revolution, a *Millennial Star* issue stated, occurred not because it was desired but because it was necessary. "The universal kingdom of God cannot be co-existent with the kingdoms of this world." Revolution was a "demolisher of obstacles in the way of the introduction of a peaceful reign." Therefore, "it is no less in harmony with reason to expect the utter extinguishment of all systems antagonistic to that more improved state." Eventually, internal contradictions would "make a crumbling mass of institutions of the proudest and most powerful governments under the sun."[86] Anthony W. Ivins tacitly interwove Hegelian development with horizontal revelation. "God's hand in the affairs of nations," he wrote in 1898, works in "imperceptible" ways that may make it hard to determine what it means for "the existence of [a] nation, [to] tell what it has accomplished [or to] say why it passes away."[87]

In 1930 B. H. Roberts completed his seven-volume *Comprehensive History of the Church*. At the April Conference he outlined the Latter-day Saint position. History had meaning. It had produced the present. Historical dialectic would inaugurate sacred time in Hegelian manner:

> Your history of one hundred years will be your vindication; . . . Not a sect, but the universal religion founded upon . . . the New Dispensation of it, the complement and fulfillment of all that has gone before, and

84. Brigham Young, August 12, 1866, *Journal of Discourses*, 11:262.

85. "The Sword," *Millennial Star* 41 (April 14, 1879): 233. An apocryphal quote attributed to Wilford Woodruff says, "The American nation will be broken in pieces like a potter's vessel and will be cast into hell." See Robert W. and Elizabeth A. Smith, *Scriptural and Secular Prophecies Pertaining to the Last Days*, 18.

86. "Secret Combinations," *Millennial Star* 41 (April 21, 1879): 248, 250.

87. Anthony W. Ivins, "The Hand of God in the Affairs of the Nations," *Improvement Era* 1 (April 1898): 450–51.

prophecy of what shall be hereafter. To make this appear, however, your historic statement, your history must not be merely a recital of events. The events must be coordinated and so linked together that the rationale of successive events shall be made apparent; and how they link in with the world movements which but spell out God's purposes struggling to get expressed.[88]

Roberts's reprise of man's co-agency with God combines with Hegel's theory of "becoming" through history. Revolution from below was part of the unfailing divine purpose to move history toward its climax in the final act: Christ's return from above.

Theo-Democracy and Totalitarian Democracy

Historian Jacob Talmon has referred to the utopia envisioned by the French First Republic as a "totalitarian democracy." The ideology of totalitarian democracy affirmed human potential but denied that man could be trusted until he had been restored to a natural state.[89] Absolute liberty could only be achieved by eliminating pluralism. The conflict between spontaneity and duty would then cease, and with it the need for coercion. Untainted democracy would allow the true citizen to emerge. Social revolutionaries in France thought that they had come close to creating a virtuous state. In 1792 a radical republican coalition cut off the head of King Louis XVI. The Jacobin faction led by Maximilien Robespierre attempted to de-Christianize France and replace God with a "Supreme Being" who would be the father of republican purity. Enemies shot Robespierre on July 27, 1794, then guillotined him. Despite this setback, Jacobin radicals believed the "Thermidorian Reaction" had merely upset the timetable. Thus did revolutionary scripture acquire the motif of the "unfinished revolution," which prefigured a second upheaval of even greater potency.[90]

Mormon leaders mirrored the effort of French radicals to eliminate pluralism and arrest the rising tide of popular democracy in America.[91]

---

88. B. H. Roberts, April 6, 1930, *Conference Report*, 45.

89. Talmon, *Origins of Totalitarian Democracy*, 46, 105–6, 112, 137–38.

90. Talmon, *Political Messianism*, 20–26.

91. For pre-1850 Mormon efforts to establish communal utopia and theocratic government by rejecting pluralism, see Marvin S. Hill, *Quest*

Dubbed "theo-democracy," Mormon government in Utah during the nineteenth century was half reality and half vision. The unity and happiness Mormon leaders expected from theo-democracy never had a chance to develop due to federal intervention. But when the Mormon "Reformation" approached full implementation in the late 1850s, its more fanatical aspects generated so much fear and disillusionment that rank-and-file Mormons gratefully accepted its dissolution.

Apostle George Q. Cannon touched all the major themes of theo-democracy in an 1869 speech. The communist United Order would be "universally established." Moreover, Cannon noted, "Money is the root of all evil. . . . The Order of which I speak will correct these evils because there will be a treasury in the midst of the people." Surplus will "become the common property of the church." Concerning central administration, Cannon said, "President [Young] can control this people . . . for beneficial ends, for the amelioration of the condition of the human family."[92] Mormon theo-democracy admitted democratic decision-making on the fringes, but once Church leadership rendered a decision, all of Mormondom was expected to obey.

Cannon's suggestion that correct principles would produce mass obedience suggests the influence of French totalitarian doctrine. Spirit fulfilled the same purpose for Mormons as reason did for the revolutionaries. Its unifying effect would enable the "prevalence of universal brotherhood and knowledge of God." Those who resisted would be destroyed.[93] In the Mormon theo-democratic concept, surplus wealth would serve the community and polygamy would regenerate the human family. Robert Flanders suggests that Joseph Smith's "radical ecumenism" paralleled the secular vision of his contemporary, Karl Marx.[94]

Totalitarian democracy and Mormon theo-democracy slid down the same discursive tracks. Substitute "the party" for Parley P. Pratt's use of "God," "theory" for "revelation," and "people" for "church," and one of the Twelve's most revolutionary tracts crystallizes in a revolutionary dictatorship:

---

for Refuge: The Mormon Flight from American Pluralism, 178–81; Hill, "Counter-Revolution: The Mormon Reaction to the Coming of American Democracy"; and John E. Hallwas, "Mormon Nauvoo from a Non-Mormon Perspective," 172.

92. George Q. Cannon, April 6, 1869, *Journal of Discourses*, 13:102–3.

93. "The Sword," *Millennial Star* 41 (April 14, 1879): 232–33.

94. Robert Flanders, "Some Reflections on the New Mormon History," 40.

> The legislative, judicial, and executive powers is vested in [God]. He reveals the laws, and he elects, chooses, or appoints the officers. Hence the necessity of constant intercourse by direct revelation between him and his church.
>
> It is true, the people have a voice in the government of the kingdom of God, but it is secondary. The power, the laws, and the officers do not originate with the people but with the Lord; the voice is rather a sanction, strength, and support to that which God chooses.
>
> The fact is, when the order of the kingdom of God is full established, the Twelve are the only general officers of the church, whose jurisdiction is UNIVERSAL.[95]

Like the French revolutionaries, Mormons countenanced force to achieve consensus. Compulsion might be required at first, but eventually force would yield to spontaneous unanimity. Theocratic violence in Missouri, Nauvoo, and territorial Utah never came close to the terrifying liquidations of revolutionary France, but intimidation and example-making were methods occasionally employed by the Great Basin's rulers.[96] As late as 1941, G. Homer Durham held that Mormonism's "new universalism" included the "rarely-to-be-used monopoly of force."[97]

The talismanic word of utopian totalitarianism was the word "universal." Universalism informed a wide range of secular thinkers, not all of them revolutionaries. Charles Fourier believed his communes called phalansteries would join in global confederation. In 1844 Wilhelm Weitling, an early communist, wrote of the "liberation of humanity [that] is not German or French or North American freedom, but the

---

95. Parley P. Pratt, "Proclamation. To the Church of Jesus Christ of Latter-day Saints: Greeting," *Millennial Star* 5 (March 1845): 150, 152.

96. Brigham Young's enforcers crushed the dissident Joseph Morris and his followers in 1862. See LeRoy C. Anderson, *For Christ Will Come Tomorrow: The Saga of Morrisites*; and Bigler, *Forgotten Kingdom*, 208–13. The Mountain Meadows Massacre of 1857 is treated in several books, but good introductory texts are Will Bagley, *Blood of the Prophets: Brigham Young and the Massacre at Mountain Meadows*; and Ronald Walker, Richard E. Turley, and Glen M. Leonard, *Massacre at Mountain Meadows: An American Tragedy*. For a discussion on theocratic violence in Utah, see D. Michael Quinn, *The Mormon Hierarchy: Extensions of Power*, 226–61.

97. G. Homer Durham, "World Crisis and Mormon Thought," *Improvement Era* 44 (August 1941): 509.

real freedom of man." Marx learned from failure in 1848 that revolution must be international. Only a united labor movement could smash the history-stopping "Holy Alliances" of the aristocracy and its counter-revolutionary bourgeois supporters.[98] Reason and liberty were meant for all people. Neither monarchies nor republics were safe as long as the people remained despoiled of their rights. Rarely did Mormon observers view revolutions as isolated events bringing about local improvement. They linked local sociopolitical disturbances to continental, hemispheric, and global transformations.

The Pratt brothers, the principal expositors of universal theocracy, demonstrate the boundless vision of Mormon globalism. In *A Proclamation of the Twelve Apostles of the Church of Jesus Christ of Latter-day Saints to all the Kings of the World* (1845), Apostle Parley P. Pratt warned that the Saints would be given global dominion.[99] In a *Millennial Star* reprint, he reiterated:

> The government of the church and kingdom of God, in this and all other ages, is purely a THEOCRACY; that is, a government under the direct control and superintendence of the Almighty.[100]

Parley's brother and fellow apostle Orson Pratt similarly exhorted obedience to the future central governing priesthood. Nations might develop independently according to their historical circumstances, but universal historical principles pointed toward a future "oneness of nationality—a unity existing over all the earth." As to the future of Europe and the United States, "No kingdom, no form of government of human invention will be permitted to stand . . . there will be one universal kingdom."[101]

The notion of "one universal kingdom" would never come about through unregulated human activity, according to Levi Edgar Young. In a discussion of Mormonism's "dynamic and constructive" philosophy,

---

98. Manuel and Manuel, *Utopian Thought in the Western World*, 3–4; Billington, *Fire in the Minds of Men*, 188–89, 280–81.

99. Parley P. Pratt, *A Proclamation of the Twelve Apostles of the Church of Jesus Christ of Latter-day Saints . . . to the Rulers and Peoples of All Nations*.

100. Pratt, "Proclamation. To the Church of Jesus Christ of Latter-day Saints: Greeting," 150.

101. "Epistle of Orson Pratt," *Millennial Star* 15 (July 30, 1853): 497–500. See also Orson Pratt, July 8, 1855, and March 26, 1876, *Journal of Discourses*, 3:71 and 18:181.

Young synthesized three perspectives discussed above: Hegel's ideal, French totalitarian democracy and universalism, and the Puritan covenant of co-agency that would enable the building of God's kingdom:

> Man is taught not to adjust his ideals to reality, but to take his higher religious idealism and, with clean heart and broad cosmic outlook, solve the problems of the practical life, which in time will result in a greater spirituality individually and socially.[102]

Young went on to assure readers that the search for "real progressivism justifies the naïve and daily practical hope" that people might obtain "universal happiness." Mormonism is

> interested in the rise of men who will [unify] the great truths of ethics, religion, and philosophy . . . that men may emancipate themselves from bondage and ignorance and become free in will and in mind [and aroused] from dogmatic slumber.[103]

Although reform was preferable, Young argued that revolution might be warranted in some cases to unfetter a people and construct a Christian community. Young also believed that social reorganization would release people from mundane, constant work and allow them to explore the higher world of spirit. Mormonism promised to achieve both.

Toward the Kingdom of God

In 1842 John C. Bennett published his *History of the Saints* and toured the country lecturing against Mormonism. Bennett had held high civil, military, and ecclesiastical rank in Nauvoo, giving his allegations believability. Smith, claimed Bennett, was practicing polygamy and had established a theocracy. The Mormon hierarchy was rife with "deism." In ceremonies of the "Order Lodge," candidates were stripped and paraded before members. Initiates swore loyalty to the hierarchy and its "clandestine" purposes, even readiness to "massacre the gentiles" and "overturn the Constitution."[104] The *History of the Saints* was sensational, and Bennett ignored his own misdeeds. Nonetheless, Bennett's

---

102. Young, "Sociological Aspect of 'Mormonism,'" 829.

103. Ibid., 830. Young borrows heavily from James Quayle Dealey, *Sociology: Its Simpler Teachings and Applications*, 249.

104. John C. Bennett, *The History of the Saints; or, an Exposé of Joe Smith and Mormonism*, 275–76.

charges contributed to the gathering of anti-Mormon forces that led to Smith's death.[105]

Joseph Smith's assassination in 1844 did not trigger the second coming of Christ. Contrary to expectations, theocracy and the future seemed to be unfolding in a postmillennial pattern. On April 6, 1845, Brigham Young announced that the millennium had begun. Zion, where "union and true charity dwells . . . is increasing and spreading wider and wider [and will] stretch all over the earth."[106] The next day the Nauvoo Conference sustained Young "as the President of the Quorum of the Twelve Apostles to this Church and nation, and all nations, and also as the President of the whole Church of Latter Day Saints."[107] The following year Young led his people to the Rockies. Space and time would enable the Saints to rebuild. One day they would march back to Missouri and assume leadership of a united world.

Across the Atlantic, the people of Poland, like the Mormons, experienced pangs of loss. For the Poles, however, there was no western outlet. Treaties during the eighteenth century had partitioned Poland among Austria, Prussia, and Russia.[108] In February 1846, after decades of repression, Polish revolutionaries led by Edward Dembowski proclaimed a republic in Cracow. They called it the "Lord's Kingdom." Austria and Russia reacted swiftly. Troops crushed the Cracow republic. Frustrated in their effort to establish a national fraternity, Polish radicals lifted their gaze to an even higher plane: the sociopolitical transformation of the entire world.[109]

The abortive Cracow Uprising was preamble to a general European explosion. As wagon trains rumbled west in 1848, Mormon observers turned to look eastward over their shoulders one more time.

---

105. On the Bennett-Smith affair, see ibid., vii–xxviii. An exemplary work on the Mormon-Mason connection is Michael W. Homer, "'Similarity of Priesthood in Masonry': The Relationship between Freemasonry and Mormonism."

106. Brigham Young, April 6, 1845, in *Times and Seasons* 6 (July 1, 1845): 956.

107. Quinn, *Mormon Hierarchy: Origins of Power*, 178.

108. Billington, *Fire in the Minds of Men*, 149.

109. For the Cracow Republic see ibid., 230–34.

CHAPTER 2

MORMON OBSERVERS OF THE 1848 EUROPEAN REVOLUTIONS

The Ecumenical Banner

In 1847 Mormons yearned for redemption. On Ensign Peak over-looking the Salt Lake Valley flew a banner referred to as the "flag of the kingdom of God."[1] In the revolutionary tradition, writes French historian Mona Ozouf, display of ensigns and liberty poles was a militant act—a symbolic leaving of the old world and "welcoming the birth of the new."[2] Driven into exile by Illinoisans who feared that Joseph Smith's theocracy would impair the individualism they believed essential to a free-voting republican society, Mormons streamed to the Rockies to nurse their own vision of what society could be.[3] In the mountain valleys they waited for the catalyst that would mark the new beginning. It came quickly.

In 1848 Europe exploded in revolution. The shaking of the European order heralded to some high-ranking Mormons that the world was about to undergo major transformation. Apostle Wilford Woodruff, who a year

---

1. D. Michael Quinn, "The Flag of the Kingdom of God"; Ronald W. Walker, "'A Banner is Unfurled': Mormonism's Ensign Peak," 89–109. Samuel Brannan's ship *Brooklyn* flew a white flag of a crowned woman surrounded by twelve red stars in Will Bagley, ed., *Scoundrel's Tale: The Samuel Brannan Papers*, 154–58. Brannan's flag resembled the iconography of the French Revolution in Joan B. Landes, *Visualizing the Nation: Gender, Representation, and Revolution in Eighteenth-Century France*, 51, 150–51, 160–61.

2. Mona Ozouf, *Festivals of the French Revolution*, 254–55. Mormon liberty poles raised during the early years in Utah seemed to have had this meaning in B. H. Roberts, *A Comprehensive History of the Church of Jesus Christ of Latter-day Saints, 1830–1930*, 3:275, 319 note 25, 375, 493 note 37. On the origins of revolutionary flags, see James Billington, *Fire in the Minds of Men: The Origins of the Revolutionary Faith*, 101, 159, 346.

3. John E. Hallwas, "Mormon Nauvoo from a Non-Mormon Perspective."

before was skirmishing with Indians in Wyoming, wrote from Boston, "Our eyes are turned towards . . . the whole European world."[4]

Woodruff was not alone in his transatlantic orientation. Other Mormon observers similarly rhapsodized about the revolutions of 1848, leaving behind a large body of manuscripts, diary accounts, and published works about events far away from the Latter-day Saint kingdom in the Great Basin. Chief among these observers were three apostles, three mission presidents, a Scottish poet, and a half dozen missionaries and members. They were united by a sense that it was their duty to make their observations a matter of Church record.

Mormon observers made the revolutions of 1848 fit their worldview in three respects. First—ironically, given the negative Mormon experience in the United States—the observers believed that the rise of republics legitimated the revolutionary overthrow of monarchs. Second, they believed the representative governments that resulted from the revolutions would promote religious toleration. Mormon membership rolls would swell, and converts who wished to could migrate to the gathering place in Utah. Furthermore, liberalized legal codes would free the Jews. No longer fettered by prejudicial laws, Jews would be allowed to fulfill their prophesied role in Palestine. Third, Mormon observers felt a kinship with the oppressed peoples who were venting their anger in Europe. For Mormon observers, the rulers and ministers of Europe stood proxy for the American politicos who had forced the Saints—vicars of the future world government—to move west. From a socioeconomic perspective, the poor working conditions and low wages that had aggrieved the revolutionaries pricked the Mormon observers' sense of compassion. The factory owners of the emerging industrial order deserved their chastisement.

Mormons with eyes on Europe in 1848 bent their millennial expectations to match the political developments of the revolutions. The observers found themselves torn between two end-of-time variations. One was the premillennial model, in which the Saints awaited the millennium at the edge of the world. The other was the progressive, postmillennial model. To illustrate the second variation, Apostle Orson Pratt, editor of the *Latter-day Saints' Millennial Star*, transmitted

---

4. Wilford Woodruff, Letter to Orson Spencer, August 21, 1848, in *Latter-day Saints' Millennial Star* 10 (October 15, 1848): 317 (hereafter cited as *Millennial Star*).

to Mormon readers Mordecai Manuel "Judge" Noah's article "Building the Temple at Jerusalem." Noah, a prominent New York Jew, believed the revolutions would allow his people to return to Jerusalem and to establish a free and independent government. Noah's article praised the "Reformers, Socialists, Communists, [and] Philosophers" who were challenging the European political and economic status quo. He also lauded Protestant radicals for renewing their confidence in Christ as an "eminent and illustrious reformer, teacher, prophet, [and] brother."[5]

Pratt's editorial effort to connect the *Millennial Star* with Jewish thought and European movements evinces a shared conviction that man, acting as God's agent, might destroy religious, social, and political monopolies. Once these barriers were removed, man himself might provide the genesis of world unification. Pratt, in other words, offered a progressive narrative. Instead of a world deteriorating in dynastic enslavement, spiritual darkness, and physical destitution that could be cleansed only by the apocalypse and the second coming of Christ, he perceived an uplifting revolution from below. Pratt was quite willing to see the opening act of the eschatological drama played out in revolutionary violence.

For Pratt and other Mormon observers of revolutions, victory was coming now, in calendar time, by human hands. The people would reduce privilege and exploitation in the crucible of revolution, then reforge society in a spiritual union of peace. Faith that the revolutionary wave represented the will of God inoculated Mormon hopefuls against the anxiety induced by the violent restructuring of existing social and political forms. The destruction of the monarchical and industrial orders and the rise of republicanism appeared to be preparing the world for redemption. At a stroke in 1848, Noah and his "Reformers" depicted a world getting better, not worse, before the millennium. Pratt and oth-

---

5. Mordecai Manuel Noah, "Building the Temple at Jerusalem," reprinted from the *New York Tribune* in *Millennial Star* 11 (March 1, 1849): 69. Noah (1785–1851) was the US proconsul in Tunisia from 1816 until his recall due to complications caused by his Judaism two years later. In 1823 Noah proposed the settling of Jews on Grand Island, New York. By 1837 Noah hoped to settle Jews of the Eastern Hemisphere in Palestine, and in 1844 he published his Zionist call in *Discourse on the Restoration of the Jew*. Noah's belief in political liberty, his public notoriety and service, and his participation in Jewish community life earned him the title "the first American Jew." See "Judaic Treasures of the Library of Congress: Mordecai Manuel Noah."

er observers picked up this narrative and recast it for a Mormon audience. For a brief time, the priesthood secrets introduced in Nauvoo and Joseph Smith's dark visions of apocalyptic destruction yielded to the rapture of popular revolt. Understandably, the observers' disappointment would be severe when their heady expectations were frustrated.

Course of the Revolutions, 1848–1851

The revolutionary explosion of 1848 had been building since Napoleon's defeat at the Battle of Waterloo. The French Revolution and Napoleonic Wars had ushered in new concepts of national identity. However, court ministers attending the 1815 Congress of Vienna restored Europe to its ruling families, frustrating nationalists who challenged the dynastic formulas foisted on peoples seeking independence. Also, industrialization was growing more exploitative. Twenty-five years of economic change and low agricultural yields in 1845 and 1846 had produced unsettled conditions by 1848. Economic and political distress climaxed in France. On February 24, Parisian magistrates suppressed a workers' political banquet. The people, joined by the National Guards, revolted. King Louis-Phillipe abdicated, and four days later the provisional government proclaimed the Second Republic.[6]

The fall of the French monarchy triggered urban fighting, separatist movements, and political awakenings all over Europe. The revolutions were dominated by nationalists and intellectuals, but they were broadly supported by peasants, radicals, students, and workers. The first phase of the revolutions between February and November 1848 produced assorted constitutional monarchies, national assemblies, and republics in France, Prussia, the Italian states, the Hapsburg Empire, and Poland. Revolution across the Channel also coincided with "Chartist" reformers in Great Britain presenting their grievances to Parliament. Ultimately, however, none of the revolutionaries managed to build lasting new governments. The forces of reaction began to regroup in June 1848, and by the summer of 1849 a counter-revolution was accomplished.

---

6. On the mid-century European revolutions, see Jonathan Sperber, *The European Revolutions, 1848–1851*; R. J. W. Evans and Hartmut Pogge von Strandmannn, eds., *The Revolutions in Europe, 1848–1849: From Reform to Reaction*; Raymond Postgate, *Story of a Year: 1848*; Mike Rapport, *1848: Year of Revolution*.

Still, the revolutions' beginnings were heady. In March 1848 the provisional government of France charged the Luxembourg Commission to reform labor laws. Under the influence of radical democrats—"Red Republicans"—National Workshops headed by Louis Blanc were set up to employ artisans and workers. Political clubs were organized throughout France as the people felt energized by the nation's resurrected revolutionary heritage.

Revolution also hit the Prussian capital of Berlin in early March. Unnerved by the street fighting, Friedrich Wilhelm IV acceded to a constitution. In May, representatives of the German states met in Frankfurt to draft a formula for a greater Germany. The prospect of a unified nation was greeted with such anticipation that Catholics, Protestants, and Jews embraced in the Rhineland city of Mainz. In Cologne, Friedrich Engels exhorted eight thousand people to demand a republic under the red flag.[7]

Centrifugal forces threatened the Hapsburg Empire, which covered vast tracts in central, eastern, and southern Europe. In March 1848 Chancellor Klemens von Metternich, widely regarded as the personification of dynastic rule, fled the Hapsburg capital of Vienna. Two months later in May, the imperial court followed suit. The temporary eclipse of the Hapsburg fortunes whetted nationalist appetites throughout the empire. Slovaks, Serbs, and Romanians asserted their autonomy in mass rallies. Hungary elected a national assembly. Threatened in September by armies still under imperial control, the Hungarians voted for armed resistance. In October, Hungarian generals pushed Austrian armies back up the Danube toward Vienna. From Budapest and Paris came calls for the restitution of Poland. In March 1848 a Polish National Committee was established in Cracow. Throughout Eastern Europe, peasants ignored baronial rights and invaded the forests to hunt, pick berries, and gather wood.

Great Britain escaped generalized fighting, but tensions ran high. In April the Chartists, widely regarded as the most democratic force in Europe, petitioned Parliament for broader voting rights. The police contained the crowds, but the movement's left wing conspired through the summer to continue the struggle. Meanwhile, the potato famine made Ireland a nightmare. Making the suffering more abysmal was the British government's dogmatic devotion to market theory that mili-

---

7. Sperber, *The European Revolutions, 1848–1851*, 116, 157.

tated against direct relief. Half of Ireland's eight million residents either starved or migrated, squeezed out by Anglo landlords. In June 1848 Young Ireland affiliates staged a rebellion. The uprising failed, but agitation continued into 1849.[8]

Revolution also scorched the states of the Italian Peninsula. In February, constitutional monarchies formed in Piedmont-Savoy and Tuscany. Milan and Venice declared independence from the Hapsburg Empire in March. The "kingdom of the Two Sicilies" split. King Ferdinand of the Spanish Bourbon royal house retained control of Naples after an uprising in May, but he was forced to accept a parliament. Insurrectionists on the island of Sicily ceded from Naples completely. Even Rome's Pope Pius IX was driven from the city after he reneged on a promise to accept a constitution for the Papal States. The "Red Shirts" commanded by Giuseppe Garibaldi, along with Giuseppe Mazzini and other Italian nationalists, prepared to defend the Roman republic against papal retaliation.

The counter-revolution began in June 1848. Paris workers felt frustrated when premature elections returned a government that abolished the Luxembourg Commission; they began to dismantle the public works programs and instigated the "June Days" insurrection. The French army routed the insurgents in three days of the bloodiest street fighting witnessed in all the European revolutions.

Hapsburg and Hohenzollern power also revived. In June 1848 Prince Alfred Windischgrätz of the Austrian army suppressed the Slav Congress in Prague. In November, General Joseph Radetzky recaptured Vienna using artillery bombardments and infantry assaults second in intensity only to the counterattack on Paris. Hapsburg troops executed Robert Blum, the Frankfurt Assembly's well-known democrat. The crushing of constitutionalism on the barricades of Vienna wrecked the nationalists' pan-German aspirations. Friedrich Wilhelm IV refused the crown of a united Germany, and Prussian troops scattered the liberal-minded Frankfurt Assembly in June 1849. Vindicating Mormon observers' suspicions of Europe's established religions, the churches became a potent counter-revolutionary weapon. There were radical "red priests," but, as Douglas Rapport writes, "Protestant Prussian Lutheran

---

8. For a contemporary account of the 1848 Irish uprising, see John Mitchel, *Jail Journal; or, Five Years in British Prisons*, in Peter Berresford Ellis, *Eyewitness to Irish History*, 177–82.

pastors played a leading role in conservative 'King and Fatherland' associations." Throughout Europe, religion was "*the* decisive factor in keeping the population loyal to the old order."[9]

One by one the Italian states also succumbed to royalist forces. In the south, King Ferdinand dissolved the Neapolitan parliament in March 1849. Two months later Bourbon troops defeated the Sicilian rebels. Radetzky smashed the Piedmontese at the Battle of Novara on March 23, 1849. Hapsburg regiments occupied Milan by May. Venice surrendered in August after a three-month bombardment. France, concerned that Hapsburg victories in northern Italy would upset the balance of power, landed troops to restore papal authority in Rome. The republicans resisted, but the city fell on July 3. Garibaldi fled to America.

Romania, Poland, and Hungary also failed to withstand the conservative onslaught. Nicholas I of Russia, anxious to shield his feudalistic state against modern ideas, invaded Eastern Europe at Austria's request. Cracow fell in May 1849. By August, Russian and Austrian forces had subjugated Romania and Hungary.

The ironic denouement occurred in France. In the lull that followed the June Days insurrection, revolutionaries waited for another chance, but Napoleon III seized power from the National Assembly on December 2, 1851. Two years later he declared himself Emperor of the French.

The American Response

The overall American response, driven by reform-minded Whigs and "Young America" democrats who advocated the spread of American ideals across North America, welcomed news of sister republics forming in Europe. President James K. Polk recognized the new French government but gave only moral assurances to the others.

By mid-1849 public ardor had cooled.[10] Hungarian nationalist Louis Kossuth was given a euphoric reception when he landed in New

---

9. Rapport, *1848: Year of Revolution*, 267.

10. For the American response see Merle E. Curti, "The Impact of the Revolutions of 1848 on American Thought"; John Gerow Gazley, *American Opinion of German Unification, 1848–1871*; Emiliana P. Noether, "The American Response to the 1848 Revolutions in Rome and Budapest"; Richard C. Rohrs, "American Critics of the French Revolution of 1848," 359–77; Timothy M. Roberts and Daniel W. Howe, "The United States and

York City on December 5, 1851, which briefly rekindled the initial sentiment. However, northern enchantment with the Hungarian struggle did not endure when Kossuth declined to endorse the antislavery crusade in order to avoid sidelining his own cause.[11] American churches detected a delayed fulfillment of the Protestant Reformation in the overthrow of Pius IX, but otherwise showed little interest in the sociopolitical significance of the revolutionary wave.[12] A recent scholar concludes that "American interest in the Revolutions of 1848" was "transitory" and "superficial."[13]

Mormon Sources and Mormon Observers

While in some respects Mormon observers reflected the opinions of mainstream American territorial expansionists, reformers, and church ministers, they nevertheless outdistanced all three.[14] This chapter measures the distance Mormon thought went by focusing on Mormons assigned to posts that enabled them to track the revolutions, record their thoughts, and address them publicly. Working-class diaries and periodicals of the 1840s focused mostly on daily concerns, with only rare forays into political and social commentary. Converts to Mormonism were no exception.[15] Furthermore, some Mormon officials dismissed the revolu-

---

the Revolutions of 1848."

11. Donald S. Spencer, *Louis Kossuth and the Young America: A Study of Sectionalism and Foreign Policy, 1848–1852*, 14–18.

12. Roberts and Howe, "The United States and the Revolutions of 1848," 165–66; Theodore Dwight Bozeman, "Inductive and Deductive Politics: Science and Society in Antebellum Presbyterian Thought."

13. Roberts and Howe, "The United States and the Revolutions of 1848," 173.

14. On Mormon sympathy with Young America, see Robert Bruce Flanders, *Nauvoo: Kingdom on the Mississippi*, 212. Young America newspaperman James Gordon Bennett, editor of the *New York Herald* and Mormon sympathizer, wrote several articles supporting the European revolutions, many of which were reprinted in the *Millennial Star*. See, for example, "Extracts from Mr. Bennett's Letters from Europe," *Millennial Star* 9 (July 1, 1847): 197–98, and "The Foreign Policy of France—the Final Great Struggle," *Millennial Star* 10 (July 15, 1848): 209–11.

15. John F. C. Harrison, "The Popular History of Early Victorian Britain: A Mormon Contribution"; Billington, *Fire in the Minds of Men*, 335.

tions. Apostle Willard Richards regarded them as mere "anarchy" and "commotion," and fellow Apostle John Taylor believed them completely misguided.[16] But for those who saw them as progressive millennialism in action, commentary was euphoric and voluminous.

One such observer was William I. Appleby (1811–70), president of the Eastern States Mission from February 1847 until he went west in May 1849. Although Appleby was never a polygamist, Church leaders trusted him with important callings. Shortly after his arrival in the Salt Lake Valley, he was appointed regent for the University of Deseret (now the University of Utah) and elected to the territorial legislature. From 1856 to 1857 Appleby served another mission, managing John Taylor's weekly newspaper, *The Mormon*, in New York.[17] The dispatches arriving on packet steamers from Europe aroused Appleby: "There probably never was a period in the history of human affairs in which the movements of the Great Powers of the earth were invested with so much grandeur and solemnity as at the present moment," he wrote in April 1848.[18] To commemorate the drama for future generations Appleby began to write a manuscript that he hoped would become the official Church record of the revolutions titled "History of the Signs of the Times Benefiting the Church of the Latter-day Saints." He supplemented this history with a diary. Together, Appleby's commentaries on revolutions total two hundred handwritten pages.[19]

Wilford Woodruff (1807–98), apostle and future Church president, was a self-styled millennial chronicler. His filled his journals with references to the revolutions and reported his observations to the Church recorder. He firmly believed that the revolutions of 1848 reified the spirit of God. The "rapid succession" of universal turmoil consum-

---

16. Willard Richards, Letter to Elder G. D. Watt, May 16, 1848, in *Millennial Star* 11 (January 1, 1849): 8; John Taylor, *The Government of God*, 24–25. See also "John Taylor's Conference Sermon," Journal History of the Church, April 8, 1853, 11.

17. Andrew Jenson, ed., *Latter-day Saint Biographical Encyclopedia: A Compilation of Biographical Sketches of Prominent Men and Women in the Church of Jesus Christ of Latter-day Saints*, 4:330–31; Obituary of William I. Appleby, *Deseret Evening News*, May 20, 1870.

18. William I. Appleby, "History of the Signs of the Times for the Benefit of the Church of the Latter-day Saints," April 8, 1848, 177.

19. William I. Appleby, Autobiography and Journal.

ing "the whole earth [was] rushing like a mighty cataract to finish its work," he summarized. This new movement in history promised social justice and the triumph of the Saints. The Mormon people therefore welcomed the uprisings as "the ownly [sic] ones who understand their fulfillment . . . and have cause to rejoice therein."[20]

Apostle Orson Hyde managed an outfitting station on the Mormon Trail in Kanesville, Iowa, where he edited the *Frontier Guardian*, a trail journal that provided information for pioneers going overland to Utah.[21] Mormons knew Hyde for his 1841 trip dedicating Palestine for missionary work and for the return of the Jews.[22] Hyde selected dispatches for his paper that reflected favorably on the progress of the revolutions, noting in the *Guardian's* prospectus that the purpose of the paper, in part, was to promote "the spirit that is destined to bless the world."[23] Near the end of the European drama, Hyde printed an extract that linked the pioneers to the struggles of Europe. "In doubt, struggle, suffering unspeakable, dies the Old Order that the New may rise from its ashes," the *Guardian* reminded men and women trudging west. "Terrible . . . is the process, but let us believe that the result will be worth the pain."[24] Hyde even used non-Mormon sources. One in particular was poet John C. Lord, a Presbyterian minister from Buffalo, New York. A contributor to Lord's biography noted "Mazzini himself could hardly have hailed with more enthusiasm the revolutions of 1848."[25]

---

20. Scott G. Kenney, ed., *Wilford Woodruff's Journal: 1833–1898*, December 8, 1848, 3:394–95; "Letter from Wilford Woodruff," *Millennial Star* 11 (April 15, 1849): 117–18. Woodruff's most recent biography is Thomas G. Alexander's *Things in Heaven and Earth: The Life and Times of Wilford Woodruff, a Mormon Prophet.*

21. Jean Trumbo, "Orson Hyde's *Frontier Guardian*: A Mormon Editor Chronicles the Westward Movement through Kanesville, Iowa"; Myrtle Stevens Hyde, "Orson Hyde and the *Frontier Guardian.*"

22. See Orson Hyde, *A Voice from Jerusalem, or a Sketch of the Travels and Ministry of Elder Orson Hyde, Missionary of the Church of Jesus Christ of Latter Day Saints, to Germany, Constantinople, and Jerusalem.*

23. Quoted in Hyde, "Orson Hyde and the *Frontier Guardian,*" 62.

24. "The Tragedy of the Nations," reprinted from the *New York Tribune* in *Frontier Guardian*, June 13, 1849: [3]. The *Frontier Guardian* has neither volume nor page numbers.

25. *Memoir of John C. Lord, D.D.: Pastor of the Central Presbyterian*

The British Mission, which in 1848 had jurisdiction over the whole European continent, saw two presidents between 1848 and 1849. Orson Spencer graduated from Union College and the Baptist Theological Seminary before converting to Mormonism in 1841. In January 1847 he assumed leadership of the British Mission. After a failed attempt to establish a mission in Prussia in 1852, Spencer was called to proselytize among the Cherokee Indians but died in St. Louis. His obituary stated that he had forsaken "an enviable position in society, and an extensive circle of influential acquaintances" to cleave to "down-trodden people."[26]

Orson Pratt, one of the original Twelve, succeeded Spencer in August 1848 and remained in Great Britain until January 1851, during which time he wrote some of his most important doctrinal works. A quasi-scientist, Pratt sought to unite scientific knowledge with his perceptions of revealed truth.[27] To express his view of the revolutions of 1848 he chose the words of Judge Noah: "The people, fighting centuries of bondage, were in arms against their sovereigns [in] a struggle indeed for Liberty and Human Rights."[28]

John Lyon, a Scottish poet and journalist who joined the Church in 1844, was well known to Mormons of his day. Devoted to democratic ideals, he had welcomed the 1832 reform bill as the "thunderous storm" that had "brought doon" the "rogues" who allied with prelates to keep

---

Church for Thirty-Eight Years, 103. Lord, born in New Hampshire in 1805, abandoned a promising law career to attend theological seminary in Auburn, New York and become minister of the Buffalo, New York Presbyterian Church in 1833, a post he held until 1873. In 1841 he was awarded a Doctor of Divinity degree by Hamilton College. Although he supported compromise on the slavery issue in the 1850s, he stood for the Union during the Civil War and denounced southern efforts to make slavery the controlling power on the continent. He wrote revolutionary poetry during the revolutions of 1848, some of which appeared in Orson Hyde's *Frontier Guardian*. Lord died in Buffalo, New York in 1877. For this and other biographical information, see *Memoir of John C. Lord*.

26. Jenson, *Latter-day Saint Biographical Encyclopedia*, 1:337–39.

27. D. Michael Quinn, *The Mormon Hierarchy: Origins of Power*, 526; Breck England, *The Life and Thought of Orson Pratt*; David J. Whittaker, "Orson Pratt: Prolific Pamphleteer"; Erich Robert Paul, *Science, Religion, and Mormon Cosmology*, 128–41.

28. Noah, "Building the Temple at Jerusalem," 68.

"poor folks" subjugated.[29] Lyon also adored the Covenanters, dissidents in Scotland who opposed state interference in the spiritual affairs of the Presbyterian Church of Scotland. He believed they were patriots who "sowed the seeds of liberty and equal rights in the minds of their children, which will at no distant day redeem the world from the thralldom of political and religious oppression."[30] The revolutions of 1848 inspired Lyon to continue his writings amid his duties as a presiding elder in the Worcester Conference of the British Mission. In 1853 he published *Harp of Zion*, a collection of songs intended to illustrate the congruity between world events and the "unique, all-encompassing gospel of the Mormon church"—a purpose British Mission authorities endorsed.[31]

Missionaries and Church members in Europe and the United States also registered their views. Many of these, though they held no high Church office, were influential or historically significant figures. British missionary John Jaques wrote articles on the revolutions for the *Star* under the pseudonym Harvey Locksley Birch. Jaques later became a survivor of the Martin handcart disaster and served a second mission as the associate editor of the *Star*.[32] Thomas Dunlop Brown, a British convert, labored to civilize the Indians of southern Utah during the 1850s with the same devotion he showed as a traveling elder in England in 1848.[33] James Henry Flanigan, missionary and diarist who died of smallpox in Birmingham, was eulogized as "an exception among men."[34] Curtis Edwin Bolton, converted to Mormonism in 1842,

---

29. John Lyon, *Songs of a Pioneer*, 118.

30. Ibid., 169. See also John Lyon, *Harp of Zion*, 123.

31. For John Lyon's political and journalistic activity and the background of *Harp of Zion*, see T. Edgar Lyon, *John Lyon: The Life of a Pioneer Poet*, 92–93, 156–62.

32. For the identity of "Birch," see Stella Jaques Bell, *Life History and Writings of John Jaques*, 25–26. Jaques may have written under a pen name to conceal the fact that he was only twenty-one years old when first published in the *Millennial Star*. For information on Jaques's life, see the Biographical Register near the end of the present book.

33. Juanita Brooks, ed., *Journal of the Southern Indian Mission: Diary of Thomas D. Brown.*

34. Davis Bitton, *Guide to Mormon Diaries and Autobiographies*, 12, 109; Lyman Omer Littlefield, *Reminiscences of Latter-day Saints*, 40–41; Richard L. Evans, *A Century of "Mormonism" in Great Britain*, 248.

fought in the Battle of Nauvoo. He opened the French Mission in 1850 and translated the Book of Mormon into the French language. In 1851 he recorded his observations about how Napoleon III extinguished the revolutionary spirit.[35]

Excitement for Republican Government

In 1848 the European Party of Movement (intellectuals, students, workers, and artisans) and its nemesis, the Party of Order (feudal lords and large capitalists), were colliding. British elder Thomas Dunlop Brown speculated that the revolutions would purge the old order and prepare the way for man and God to rework the political world. His letter to the *Star* left little doubt where the Church stood, wherein he wrote that in the "sudden and unlooked for interchange of institutions," governments of "mere human origins must be broken and ploughed as a field."[36]

Mormon observers like Brown assumed that the revolutions of 1848 would produce republican forms of government in Europe, and similar transformations would follow on a global scale. Actually, nationalists in northern Germany and in the Hapsburg domains of central Europe and northern Italy preferred constitutional monarchy. True Republicans—intellectuals, students, veteran radicals, and labor leaders—were a minority in Europe but found almost everywhere. Republican successes during the revolutions of 1848, notably in Rome and France, particularly riveted the attention of Mormon observers.

Republicanism in 1848 was a legacy of the original French Revolution of 1789–93. Democrats and Socialists, the most ardently egalitarian "Republicans," believed that these years had augured humankind's liberation from the *ancien régime*, but that reactionary forces had cut short the process. Republicans stood for parliamentar-

---

35. Curtis Edwin Bolton, Reminiscences and Journals; Bitton, *Guide to Mormon Diaries*, 253; and Cleo H. Evans, comp., *Curtis Edwin Bolton: Pioneer, Missionary: History, Descendants, and Ancestors.*

36. Thomas D. Brown, Letter to Relations and Friends, December 16, 1848, in "A Letter of Warning," *Millennial Star* 11 (February 1, 1849): 34. The terms "Party of Order" and "Party of Movement" are borrowed from Jonathan Sperber, but Marx also referred to them this way. See Marx, "The Class Struggles in France" [1850], in David McLellan, ed., *Karl Marx: Selected Writings*, 294.

ian government but were more entranced by revolutionary action and the achievement of equality. They hated established churches, believing that clerics opposed the triumph of liberty and reason.[37]

Eastern States Mission President William I. Appleby and Apostle Wilford Woodruff were unruffled by the violence. Whether looking "towards *Babylon* or *Zion*," Woodruff believed he was witnessing God's work. For him, five hundred deaths were a small price to pay for the establishment of a French republic.[38] Appleby similarly approved the roughness with which Parisians seized the throne and burned it.[39] The "hurricane of 1848," Appleby wrote, wiped out the Bourbon and Orleanist aberrations and institutionalized the "liberal ideas" of 1789.[40]

Appleby shared his republicanism with Mazzini, the Italian nationalist who envisioned a "Young Europe" federation of nations joined by the spiritual authority of the people:

> Kings and nobles cannot maintain their positions, and before another year passes, we shall probably see no thrones among the Teutonic, perhaps none among the Latin races. The example of France must soon be followed in Germany and Italy and ultimately in Scandinavia and the Peninsula. England, Spain, Austria, Russia, Prussia, Germany . . . with the Slavic tribes, Hungarians . . . will [break] the fetters of despotism and aristocracy and kingly power.[41]

Revolution, explained Appleby, would produce international harmony throughout Europe. In New York, Appleby admired German-Americans who were loading arms on ships bound for German ports and who volunteered to defend republicanism and the Frankfurt Assembly.[42]

---

37. Robert R. Palmer and Joel Colton, *A History of the Modern World*, 466–67.

38. Kenney, *Wilford Woodruff's Journal*, December 28, 1848, 3:394–95; Wilford Woodruff, Letter to Orson Pratt, March 1, 1849, in *Millennial Star* 11 (April 15, 1849): 117. The number killed in the February revolution was twenty. See Palmer and Colton, *History of the Modern World*, 502.

39. Appleby, Autobiography and Journal, April 1848, 228–29; and Appleby, "History of the Signs of the Times," June 1848, 8.

40. Appleby, Autobiography and Journal, April 1848, 229.

41. Appleby, "History of the Signs of the Times," October 20, 1848, 160–61. On the Mazzinian international see Billington, *Fire in the Minds of Men*, 149–52, 162; Emiliana P. Noether, "Mazzini and the Nineteenth Century Revolutionary Movement."

42. Appleby, Autobiography and Journal, April 1848, 227. On filibustering see

Mormon observers were convinced that France was the bellwether of the revolution. Woodruff and Appleby identified France with the spread of republicanism.[43] When Russia assured Austria in May 1849 that it would invade Hungary to suppress the revolution there, Hyde identified the "Red" (democrat-socialist) Republicans in the French Assembly as the Hungarian nationalists' only remaining friends. If Hungary fell, the republics of Poland, Rome, Naples, and northern Italy might follow. Only with French radicals in the lead could the European Party of Movement check the Russian threat.[44]

Orson Spencer praised the establishment of a French republic but added a word of caution. He warned that this was a "critical period in the political affairs of the French nation," for European monarchs would attempt to neutralize French influence as they had done during the revolutionary and Napoleonic wars of 1792–1815.[45] Spencer's analysis was astute. The suppression of the French Left and Napoleon III's restoration of Pius IX to Rome dashed hopes for republicanism throughout Europe. The "Gallic cock who eighteen months ago assumed republican colors," wrote John Jaques, "now loads the Roman eagle with chains for singing the same tune."[46] Orson Hyde, however, believed French ideals were only temporarily submerged. His paper noted that the scheme to restore the Pope in Rome was "extremely distasteful to the French troops," and predicted that the sell-out of republicanism would boomerang on the conservative government.[47]

The progress of the revolutions in the Austrian Empire and Italy attracted nearly as much attention as events in France. The minis-

---

Roberts and Howe, "The United States and the Revolutions of 1848," 166–67.

43. Kenney, *Wilford Woodruff's Journal*, April 23, 1848, 3:345; Wilford Woodruff, Letter to Orson Spencer, April 24, 1848, in *Millennial Star* 10 (June 15, 1848): 186; Appleby, "History of the Signs of the Times," September 18, 1848, 152–53.

44. Orson Hyde, Foreign News, *Frontier Guardian,* May 16, 1849, [3]; and ibid., June 27, 1849, [3]. On Russia's reactionary stance see Palmer and Colton, *History of the Modern World,* 506.

45. "April 1, 1848," *Millennial Star* 10 (April 1, 1848): 103–4. No author is identified but it reads like Spencer.

46. Harvey Locksley Birch [John Jaques], Letter to Orson Pratt, August 16, 1849, *Millennial Star* 11 (October 1, 1849): 298.

47. Hyde, Foreign News, *Frontier Guardian,* July 11, 1849, [3].

ters of the 1815 Congress of Vienna were swept away, Appleby wrote. Sovereigns across Europe had submitted to popular demands and "the people drove Prince Metternich from his lofty eminences."[48] Stubborn defenses of republican strongholds inspired alternately gritty and romantic images of the fighting. When Austrian Generals Josip Jelačic and Prince Alfred Windischgrätz shelled Vienna and overwhelmed the barricades in November 1848, Appleby memorialized the democratic resisters as "men fighting for freedom and rights and endeavoring to break the chains of despotism and oppression."[49] The *Frontier Guardian* featured several heroic mosaics. Around Palermo, Sicily, women of all classes were digging trenches to counter King Ferdinand's siege lines; inside Ingölstadt, Bavaria, the defenders were fighting to the death under the revolutionary black flag.[50]

The Mormon observers tolerated Pius IX as long as the pope seemed sympathetic to republican government. But when the citizens of Rome proclaimed a republic, Appleby declared the old Papal States "a nullity."[51] Woodruff excused Garibaldi and Mazzini for the "beastly power" of violence used to create the Roman republic and believed the fall of the "Papel Crown" fulfilled prophecy from the biblical book of Revelation. News of the "Pope of Rome laid prostrate & he driven from his Kingdom" led Woodruff to predict that even the Romanovs would not likely survive.[52] John Lyon gloated over "Pope-less . . . 'Forty-nine."[53] Pius was reinstated in 1849, but the *Millennial Star* prophesied: "The papal throne is shaken, and the Holy See disgraced. These great and important movements are destined to prepare the way for the kingdom of Heaven to be established on earth."[54]

---

48. Appleby, Autobiography and Journal, March–April 1848, 221, 229.

49. Ibid., November 20, 1848, 167.

50. Hyde, Foreign News, *Frontier Guardian*, June 27, 1849, [3]; ibid., August 22, 1849, [3]. The black flag had dual meaning in 1848. It was the original banner of proletarian revolution dating back to 1830, and it also symbolized mourning for people fighting a losing struggle for nationhood. See Billington, *Fire in the Minds of Men*, 151, 159, 281.

51. Appleby, "History of the Signs of the Times," November 29, 1848, 169.

52. Kenney, *Wilford Woodruff's Journal*, December 31, 1848, and January 9, 1849, 3:395, 404.

53. Lyon, *Harp of Zion*, 91.

54. "The Destroyer Already Rideth upon the Face of the Waters," reprinted

Hungary's fight received special attention from Mormon observers due to the popularity of Louis Kossuth. Hyde published extracts of Kossuth's speech informing the world that "the women shall dig a deep grave," in which they would "bury the name, the honor, the nation of Hungary or our enemies."[55] Hyde also printed the words of George Lunt, a famous American poet, who deified Kossuth as the eastern incarnation of freedom:

> Has shot a newer gleam.
> The paling despot sees it shine,
> The serf beholds the beam. . . .
> Once more the voice of Ages rolls
> Kossuth! and calls for thee![56]

Mormon observers were aware of Russia's potential for reaction. "The Great Bear of the North," Appleby wrote, "is as yet an unexcited spectator of these magical transformations. Yet even Russia will have to engage in the general strife when the voice of oppressed and unappeased Poland rises high." In the Russian invasion of Poland and Hungary, Appleby believed he was witnessing the timeless encounter "between the spirit of human freedom and despotism."[57] William Gilmore Simms, the famous southern writer, wrote an angry poem, which Hyde reprinted in the *Frontier Guardian*: "Hark! a mighty clamor! a thousand nations rise." The Russian army had routed the Hungarians, but another "day of vengeance dawneth" against the forces of reaction.[58] John Jaques

---

from the *Frontier Guardian* in *Millennial Star* 11 (August 15, 1849): 253.

55. "Kossuth," reprinted from the *Boston Transcript* in *Frontier Guardian*, August 8, 1849, [3]. See also Kenney, *Wilford Woodruff's Journal*, September 23, 1849, 3:483.

56. George Lunt, "Kossuth," *Frontier Guardian*, March 6, 1850, [4]. Lunt (1803–85) practiced law in Boston and in 1849 was appointed United States Attorney for Massachusetts by Millard Fillmore. He began editing the *Boston Courier* in 1857. He retired from journalism in 1862 and pursued literature. Edgar Allen Poe admired Lunt's style and "massiveness of thought." See James R. Elkins, "George Lunt."

57. Appleby, Autobiography and Journal, April 1848, 330; Appleby, "History of the Signs of the Times," March 24, 1849, 177.

58. W. G. Simms, "The Desolation of Babylon," *Frontier Guardian*, August 8, 1849, [4], reprinted from W. Gilmore Simms, *Sabbath Lyrics; or, Songs from Scripture: A Christmas Gift of Love*, 27. William Gilmore Simms (1806–70)

faced reality: Russo-Austrian behavior was an inevitable and irresistible consequence of their "professed principles" of anti-republicanism. With gruesome enthusiasm, Woodruff hoped for the fulfillment of Zechariah 14:12—that the lice infestation afflicting the Russian army would make the soldiers' flesh fall from their bones and their eyes from their sockets.[59]

Godly Republicanism and Jewish Emancipation

Mormon expectations received an added impetus from prophecies related to the establishment of a Jewish state. Mormon doctrine taught that Ephraim, one of the Lost Tribes of Israel, would be gathered out of the world and exercise leadership over the millennial order.[60] Emancipation from restrictive laws, Mormon observers held, would prepare a Jewish political cadre for its historic role.

Jewish emancipation had become a major social, political, and economic issue in Europe by 1848. Jews in France and in the Netherlands enjoyed full citizenship status, but laws in the German Confederation and the Austro-Hungarian Empire made them a segregated, disfranchised minority. Liberal and Jewish delegates to the German and Austrian constituent assemblies wanted to incorporate Europe's Jews. Their arguments rested first on the liberal theory that equality was vital to economic prosperity, and second on the recognition that human rights required free-

---

was a writer and poet born in Charleston, South Carolina. He supported the "Young America" movement during the 1840s and 1850s. Simms wrote several novels describing the history and culture of various regions of the antebellum South. He upheld slavery, and during the Civil War he conferred with leading Confederate politicians and made elaborate proposals for Southern defenses. He is considered the "embodiment of Southern letters" and one of the most influential writers shaping American consciousness of the South. See Mary Ann Wimsatt, "William Gilmore Simms."

59. Birch [Jaques], Letter to Orson Pratt, August 16, 1849; and Kenney, *Wilford Woodruff's Journal*, August 25, 1849, 3:478.

60. Mormon concepts of racial elitism versus universalism are discussed in Armand L. Mauss, *All Abraham's Children: Changing Mormon Conceptions of Race and Lineage*; and Arnold H. Green, "Gathering and Election: Israelite Descent and Universalism in Mormon Discourse."

dom from medieval prejudice.[61] Gabriel Riesser, the Jewish vice-president of the Frankfurt National Assembly, linked emancipation to unification: "The messiah . . . has appeared and our fatherland has been given to us. The messiah is freedom, our fatherland is Germany."[62]

Appleby marveled over the rights granted to Jews in the newly established Roman republic.[63] For Wilford Woodruff, ending the Jewish Diaspora through revolution would uplift humankind. Jewish franchise and civil and landholding rights would prepare them for their future role as co-administrators of the kingdom of God.[64] The events of 1848 supplied the context for Orson Spencer's *Letters Exhibiting the Most Prominent Doctrines of the Church of Jesus Christ of Latter-day Saints*. A reconstituted Israel would become a metaphysical force that would unite the righteous of the world.[65]

Orson Pratt expressed his views by reprinting an essay by Mordecai Noah, who praised the "great men" among the Jews, especially in France and Germany, who had been

> busy amid these revolutions. It was not to be that a people of their literary, political, and commercial influence—the bankers of Europe, the merchants of England, the statesmen of France, the philosophers of Germany, the agriculturists of Poland, the poets of Italy, the artists, the mechanics, the soldiers everywhere, could see these mighty events developing themselves on the Continent without participating actively in the progress and results.[66]

The rise of Jews to "highest stations in governments" would lead to their restoration in Palestine. From there, "those laws which Moses had consecrated to liberty and republican forms of government" would be reinstated throughout the world.[67]

---

61. Simon Dubnov, *History of the Jews: From the Congress of Vienna to the Emergence of Hitler*, 255–314.

62. Glenn R. Sharfman, "Jewish Emancipation of 1848."

63. Appleby, Autobiography and Journal, December 2, 1848, 247.

64. Kenney, *Wilford Woodruff's Journal*, December 12, 1849, 3:517.

65. Quoted in Steven Epperson, *Mormons and Jews: Early Mormon Theologies of Israel*, 182.

66. Noah, "Building the Temple at Jerusalem," 83–84.

67. Ibid., 68. The failure of the revolutions to achieve total Jewish emancipation affected Pratt's later teachings. Revolution and emancipation were insufficient. In 1871 he speculated that Israel would not be restored to

The pairing of "Moses" and "republican" would have resonated among dreamers who also mixed Talmudic imagery with nineteenth-century nationalism.[68] Revolution would eventually produce a sort of theocratic republicanism. In the scenario envisioned by Mormon observers, two hemispheric kingdoms—one with a capital in Jerusalem and the other in Missouri (or, temporarily, the Rocky Mountains)—represented polarities destined to unite humanity. The gathering of Ephraim from among the nations and the return of Judah to Palestine would pave the way for millennial order and global brotherhood.[69]

Revolution Promotes Missionary Work

The Mormon millennial tradition stipulated that before the Second Advent the world must receive the chance to hear the gospel and gather to Zion. Mormon observers of the 1848 revolutions conjectured that these social and political upheavals would expedite the process: "Great convulsive shocks must take place before the gospel can be tolerated universally," stated the *Millennial Star*.[70] Orson Spencer editorialized on missionary prospects after the red flag appeared in Paris:

> The Latter-day Saints feel the effects of poverty, but these commotions must precede the introduction of the gospel to many nations. Therefore we will rejoice in those things which make many sorry. . . . The stumbling blocks of despotism, and bigotry, and aristocratic monopoly, that so frequently deter the poor from obeying the gospel,

Jerusalem until missionaries converted Jews to the Latter-day Saint faith. See Epperson, *Mormons and Jews*, 181, 192–93.

68. Billington, *Fire in the Minds of Men*, 325.

69. Compare ibid., 218–20 to Mormon one-worldism in which revolution and Jewish restoration to Palestine figure prominently, as discussed in Gary James Bergera, ed., "'Let Br. Pratt Do as He Will': Orson Pratt's 29 January 1860 Confessional Discourse—Unrevised," 51; Italian Mission President Jabez Woodard, Letter to Willard Richards, September 18, 1852, in Eliza R. Snow, *Biography and Family Record of Lorenzo Snow: One of the Twelve Apostles of the Church of Jesus Christ of Latter-day Saints*, 229.

70. "April 1, 1848," 104. Similar sentiments are found in "The Gospel Witness," *Millennial Star* 10 (June 15, 1848): 179; and "Letter from Wilford Woodruff," 118.

will be moved out of the way, and a highway cast up for the ransomed to walk in.[71]

In July 1848 the *Star* featured a letter by Presbyterian ministers claiming that "now the word of God is not bound" and Europe thirsted for missionaries of the gospel.[72]

In the spring of 1848, English Mormons, most of them working-class converts, anticipated relief from unemployment, low wages, and Anglican harassment.[73] Expectations ran high that the disabling of repressive regimes elsewhere would be permanent and the weakening of high-church influence in Britain would trigger an explosion of conversions. Appleby published a broadside in Philadelphia endorsing armed struggle as the surest method of emancipating the mind. Only when "kings and nobles stand afraid with terror and dismay," he wrote, could the gospel reach "every kindred and tongue."[74] The revolutions were working their historic role as "recent accounts show that republican doctrines are daily spreading among the people; and that the battle for life between democracy and aristocracy has already begun and will soon be decided. Aristocracy must die. . . . Republicanism will go before and prepare the way for [religious] toleration."[75]

The *Millennial Star*'s glee would not have endeared the mission office to the British government. Fear of republican or nationalist revolt fermented throughout England. In April 1848 the British government, wary of the Chartist left wing, enrolled temporary constables and sent army regulars

---

71. Orson Spencer, "April 15, 1848," *Millennial Star* 10 (April 15, 1848): 120.

72. "A Religious Money Mission to France," *Millennial Star* 10 (July 15, 1848): 211.

73. For the social and religious background of early Mormon converts in Great Britain, see James B. Allen, Ronald K. Esplin, and David J. Whittaker, *Men with a Mission: The Quorum of the Twelve Apostles in the British Isles, 1837–1841*, 323–40; Rebecca Bartholomew, *Audacious Women: Early British Mormon Immigrants*, 32–36; Susan L. Fales, "Artisans, Millhands, and Laborers: The Mormons of Leeds and Their Nonconformist Neighbors," 164; Polly Aird, "Why Did the Scots Convert?" 94; and Phillp A. M. Taylor, *Expectations Westward: Mormons and the Emigration of Their British Converts in the Nineteenth Century*.

74. William I. Appleby, *Lines Suggested and Composed on the Present State of the World*.

75. Appleby, "History of the Signs of the Times," October 20, 1848, 160–61.

to Ireland to ferret out Young Ireland insurrectionists.[76] The nearer revolutionary agitation seemed to approach Great Britain, the more intensely the mission office encouraged British Saints to sail to America: the "revolution in France, and the bloody scenes in the south of Europe, have recently been followed with numerous alarming disturbances in England, Scotland, and Ireland. . . . These things should warn the Saints to secure a safe hiding-place in the kingdom of God and land of Zion."[77]

Orson Spencer, the mission president, suggested that the "abstracting" of good people from their countries would hasten the collapse of old political authority, thus contributing to the revolutionary cause.[78] Spencer exploited class antagonism to loosen the loyalty of British converts to their country. In the *Millennial Star* he printed extracts from the *Black Book of British Aristocracy* (1848), a treatise that denounced ruling-class privileges. Revolution was imminent, Spencer concluded. British workers were taxed twice as much as their French counterparts, and that money went to support upper-class frivolities.[79] Spencer borrowed from the French revolutionary trinity (liberty, equality, and fraternity) to communicate the benefits of migration. In Utah, converts would be "organized on the principles of godliness, fraternity, and liberty."[80] Spencer's use of "godliness" in place of "equality" is a linguistic swap referred to as metonymy, or the substituting of one word for another that is closely related to it. Discourse analysts suggest that such metaphoric switches evoke particularly intense meaning.[81] By as-

---

76. Billington, *Fire in the Minds of Men*, 181–82. Contemporary rumors of French agents in Ireland are discussed in Leslie Mitchell, "Britain's Reaction to the Revolutions," 94. The arming of the peasantry and the troop build-up was reported in "Ireland," *Millennial Star* 9 (January 1, 1847): 1, 3–4.

77. "April 1, 1848," *Millenial Star* 10 (April 1, 1848): 103.

78. "The Gospel Witness," 179; "Black Book of British Aristocracy," *Millennial Star* 10 (May 15, 1848): 145; "The Day of God's Power," *Millennial Star* 10 (August 1, 1848): 227.

79. "Black Book of British Aristocracy," 146. The extracts came from Alice Mann, *Mann's Black Book of the British Aristocracy; Or, an Exposure of the More Monstrous Abuses in the State and the Church, with Black Lists of Pensioners Royal, Aristocratic, Legal, Civil, Diplomatic, Hereditary, Military, Clerical, Etc.* (1848).

80. "Black Book of British Aristocracy," 145.

81. Geoffrey N. Leech, *A Linguistic Guide to English Poetry*, 74, 152.

sociating equality with "godliness," Spencer thus identified the fraternity of Zion with the erasure of poverty, property exploitation, and class privilege. Spencer, in other words, marketed the Mormon gathering to Utah as a kindred project to the 1848 revolutions.

Rank-and-file missionaries joined the chorus of their leaders. Historian Robert Flanders notes that missionaries during the 1840s spoke of a "new heaven and a new earth . . . of Christian revolutionaries, of brotherhood and equality, and of emigration to the Kingdom of God."[82] A British Mission report in August 1848 hinted that the upheavals had humbled heads of state, making them receptive to the "perfect system of government" that would accompany "the second coming of our Lord."[83] James Flanigan attributed growing protest against "popery" in the Anglican Church to the people's newfound courage to withstand authority.[84] The ebullient Jaques added,

> These [revolutions] are fast preparing the nations to receive the message from heaven, removing all obstacles to the spread of truth, by the bursting asunder the chains of tyranny—opening the political and moral prison door . . . and displacing the high minded, proud, and intolerant—liberating the fettered and entrammelled mind, and infusing in the spirits of the people a high tone of independence, resolution, self-reliance, and moral courage.[85]

Converts responded to this message. The membership rolls of the British Mission rose more steeply between 1847 and 1851 than in any other four-year period of the nineteenth century. By 1851, LDS mem-

---

82. Flanders, *Nauvoo: Kingdom on the Mississippi*, 62. See also W. H. Oliver, *Prophets and Millennialists: The Uses of Biblical Prophecy in England from the 1790's to the 1840's*, 230, 238; Hyrum L. Andrus, "The Second American Revolution: Era of Preparation," 91; and Marvin S. Hill, "The Shaping of the Mormon Mind in New England and New York."

83. British Mission, Manuscript History and Historical Reports, August 13, 1848.

84. James Henry Flanigan, Diary, November 11, 1850, 4:112. Since the 1820s the Anglican Church had come under increasing attack. Grant Underwood, "The Religious Milieu of English Mormonism," 33. In 1848 an Anglican bishop lost his libel suit in a publicized court case. See Postgate, *Story of a Year: 1848*, 101–6.

85. Birch [Jaques], Letter to Orson Pratt, August 16, 1849.

bership in the British Isles totaled thirty-three thousand, the highest during the century.[86]

Virtually no news could tarnish Mormon hopes even when reactionary forces began regrouping for a counter-stroke. From Stratford-on-Avon in 1849, John Jaques, writing under his own name for the first time, wrote "Truth"—published later as the hymn "Oh Say, What is Truth?" Jaques alluded to the revolutions with images of the "earth's fountains burst" and the people rising up against the "monarch's diadem."[87] Then God's truth would sweep the scepter from the "despot's grasp, / When with winds of stern justice he copes."[88] Orson Pratt, using Judge Noah as mouthpiece, anticipated that the "blow" delivered by the revolutions to the "powerful union of Church and State" promised freedom: "The Allied sovereigns may succeed in overpowering the people and maintaining their thrones and scepters, but great concessions will be made to the wishes of the people to avoid a hurricane of frightful outbreaks. The people are no longer in chains."[89] Already, Austria was believed to have grown more tolerant of Mormonism, and Woodruff predicted that France would soon supply "efficient preachers" to the Church's cause.[90]

The Script of Social Revolution

While the first sight of social revolution frightened most Americans, Mormon observers were emboldened by it. Mormon observers' embrace of class conflict was one of their sharpest deviations from broader American public opinion. They condoned violence in

---

86. Evans, *Century of "Mormonism" in Great Britain*, 244. Richard L. Jensen, "The British Gathering to Zion," 173.

87. Diadem means crown.

88. John Jaques, "Truth," *Millennial Star* 12 (August 1, 1850): 240. European Mission President Franklin D. Richards republished this poem as a hymn in the ninth edition of the Saints' Manchester hymnal. "Oh Say, What is Truth?" was a favorite of David O. McKay and appears on page 272 of the 1985 edition of *Hymns of the Church of Jesus Christ of Latter-day Saints*. See Bell, *Life History and Writings of John Jaques*, 27–28.

89. Noah, "Building the Temple at Jerusalem," 68.

90. Kenney, *Wilford Woodruff's Journal*, December 28, 1848, January 9, 1849, and February 11, 1849, 3:395–96, 404, 417.

pursuit of social amelioration just as they had affirmed its necessity to achieve national fraternity or parliamentarian institutions. The uprisings and foundational "tremblings" of the people, as Woodruff called them, weighed especially on France, where the "social questions are all pregnant with vast Results."[91]

Appleby assumed that God was orchestrating the social revolution in Europe. "When I . . . see the oppression of the poor and man taking the advantage of his fellow man," he wrote in his journal, "I exclaim surely the Lord is at work among the nations and Kingdoms of the Earth to bring about his righteous purpose."[92] His Philadelphia broadside decried laws that favored the rich and chastised rulers and capitalists who robbed the lower classes.[93] Amid his commentary on the bombardment of Vienna, rioting in Prague, and the Polish uprising, Appleby expressed his desire for a social revolution. He admitted in June 1848 that his views were almost "eutopian."[94] Actually, Appleby's writings differed little from those of the barricade-builders, at least one of whom later converted to Mormonism (as described in Chapter 4).

The class conflict that stimulated Appleby also caught the imagination of several British missionaries. The British Mission log records an upper-class "uproar" in response to suspected missionary agitation among workers.[95] John Jaques believed that the "dismemberment of empires, the clashing of social institutions, the overthrow of feudal governmental systems [and] the outbreaks of . . . democratic violence" would raze the "rotten foundations of men's faith" and indifference.[96] Thomas Dunlop Brown hoped for a leveling of society that would rectify everything that had gone wrong in history. Revolutions were destroying the clay-and-iron feet of the statue in Nebuchadnezzar's dream (Dan. 2:24–45). Dethroned kings, violent displacement of the ruling class, and murder of the "capitalists" were prerequisite to the millennium.[97]

---

91. Ibid., April 29, 1848, 3:345; "Signs of the Times and Remarks upon the Year AD 1849," in ibid., December 1849, 3:517.

92. Appleby, Autobiography and Journal, February 4, 1848, 217.

93. Appleby, *Lines Suggested and Composed on the Present State of the World.*

94. Appleby, "History of the Signs of the Times," June 1848, 7.

95. British Mission, Manuscript History and Historical Reports, October 15, 1848.

96. Birch [Jaques], Letter to Orson Pratt, August 16, 1849.

97. Brown, Letter to Relations and Friends, December 16, 1848.

At mission headquarters in Liverpool, Orson Spencer, a supporter of the Chartist petition, championed the "labouring classes" as "indispensable to the prosperity and very existence of any nation." In a general epistle Spencer assailed the socioeconomic order:

> The nations had endured their erroneous creeds so long, that they have fairly and fully proved them palpably false and insupportably prejudicial to the happiness and peace of the human family. They are beginning to make a violent effort to burst asunder their shackles, and resuscitate long extinguished rights. The effort of the industrial classes to overthrow the sway of iron despotism, seems to be almost simultaneous throughout every nation in Europe.[98]

Spencer attributed the formation of a proletarian army to a spiritual transformation:

> The whole political aspect of numerous and powerful governments changed as it were in a day! A large and warlike army of 80,000 soldiers in the capital of France . . . suddenly converted from their allegiance to the sovereign to . . . the people, and [took] sides with the oppressed against the oppressor! This spirit of sympathy for the laboring people, spreading among so many nations with electric speed, is surely ominous that the hand of the Mighty God of Jacob is at work in turning and over-turning, until He . . . shall come and reign on the earth.[99]

Back in the United States, Orson Hyde printed extracts from a radical journal, Karl Marx's *New Rhenish Gazette*.[100] Both the *Gazette* and Hyde's *Frontier Guardian* favored news, commentary, and gritty portrayals of the human spirit in action. For example, Hyde's account of students and "proletaires" resisting Hapsburg forces from behind the Vienna barricades sculpted a frieze of revolutionary heroism.[101] Both editors also liked to print the work of radical poets.[102] Few items printed in the *Guardian* captured the thrill of revolution so well as the

---

98. Spencer, "April 15, 1848," 119.

99. Ibid., 120.

100. Hyde, Foreign News, *Frontier Guardian*, June 17, 1849, [3]. Prussian authorities suppressed Marx's paper May 19, 1849.

101. Ibid., June 27, 1849, [3].

102. Marx tolerated no one who failed to appreciate his views, but he showed uncharacteristic patience toward radical poet Heinrich Heine. See Francis Wheen, *Karl Marx: A Life*, 64–65.

revolutionary poetry of Reverend John C. Lord: "To exile goes the king, the throne is in the street; / And royal floors are echoing the sound of Plebian feet."[103]

Faith in worker activism, however, proved premature. The workers' uprising in Paris in late June 1848 made clear to Mormon observers the limits of social revolution. The insurrection resulted from the decision to discontinue the public works programs established by the Second Republic. Protesters erected barricades all over the city. Proclamations demanded a social and democratic republic, state-sponsored labor associations, and the impeachment or arrest of conservatives in the National Assembly and Luxembourg Commission. The government responded savagely. General Eugene Cavaignac crushed the uprising; about fifteen hundred were killed on each side. As many as three thousand Parisians were executed in the aftermath, and another forty-five hundred were deported.[104]

Mormon observers and contemporaries sympathetic to the workers believed stories that the Parisian workers' revolt had been instigated by conservative agents working to discredit the Democrats.[105] Elder Flanigan opined that the June Days was a counter-revolution "got up by designing demagogues who had been thrown out of office by the dethroning of Louis Phillipe."[106] Appleby blamed both sides for the disaster. The government had mishandled the situation, and Parisian workers had made economic demands that pushed France to the "verge of anarchy." God had sanctioned the trajectory of French politics until June 1848, but Appleby believed that the workers' revolt was a reminder that the divine task of the revolutionist demanded purity of motivation, discipline, and good timing.[107]

---

103. John C. Lord, "Kings and Thrones Are Falling," *Frontier Guardian*, January 9, 1850, [4].

104. Postgate, *Story of a Year: 1848*, 165–93; Sperber, *The European Revolutions, 1848–1851*, 198–203; Helen Castelli, "June Days (22–26 June 1848)."

105. Appleby, Autobiography and Journal, November 9, 1848, 244; Kenney, *Wilford Woodruff's Journal*, December 28, 1848, 3:395; Sperber, *The European Revolutions, 1848–1851*, 201. T. A. B. Corley, *Democratic Despot: A Life of Napoleon III*, 70–73, 75, makes the same suggestion.

106. Flanigan, Diary, July 14, 1848.

107. Appleby, "History of the Signs of the Times," July 13, 1848, 131–32.

Sympathy for French workers was widespread among Mormon observers despite the unflattering reputation of the French in the United States.[108] In his manuscript history Appleby said that he hoped future generations would remember the "courage and intrepidity" of the French people, recognizing in particular the women who ran messages and poured hot oil on the troops from upper story windows.[109] Orson Hyde reprinted a poem by John C. Lord hailing the workers of France as the vanguard of the coming world:

> At the voice of the Nations,
> Like the roaring of a flood . . .
> The word of power is spoken,
> In accents loud and long . . .
>
> The purple robe . . .
> Is crushed beneath the tread,
> Of masses hunger driven,
> Demanding work and bread . . .
>
> With pike and paving stone
> The maddened people arm,
> And Peace and Freedom fly
> The scene of tumult and alarm.
>
> The Seine is running red
> Through the capitol of France,
> Over ramparts of the dead
> The cry is still advanced!
>
> The terror, pain and sorrow
> Till the travail throes are past,
> But then a glorious morrow,
> And the promised rest at last . . .
>
> King or Priest shall never
> Rebuild the broken wall,
> For thought is freed forever
> And Truth is now for all.[110]

---

108. Gazley, *American Opinion of German Unification*, 284–309.
109. Appleby, "History of the Signs of the Times," July 13, 1848, 131.
110. Lord, "Kings and Thrones Are Falling," [4].

William McGhie, a British member, intimated a less passive role for Mormons to play. He wrote a play script, published in the *Millennial Star*, titled "Priestcraft in Danger—A Drama." In one scene Lord Aimswell, a kindly aristocrat without social pretension, questions Dr. Clamour, a Presbyterian minister, about the value of the state church. Lord Aimswell hints at the direction he is going by arguing that religion should never be "a cat's-paw in the hands of power for the enslavement of mankind." A true church, Lord Aimswell posits, should "effect the perfect freedom, both in mind and body" of his countrymen. And instead of religion being a "barricade to hinder the emancipation of mankind, [it] should be used as the only weapon to effect such a glorious object." Lord Aimswell's progressive attitude worries Dr. Clamour. He confides to a colleague that "a strange, restless spirit, aided by the light diffused by Mormon doctrines" must be countered by more "priestcraft."[111] The play captured the essence of the Mormon encounter with the 1848 revolutions. The metaphor of the barricade and the "light" of Mormon teachings suggested revolutionary entrenchment and a sense of sympathy with the revolutionaries of Europe, where the battle between progress and reaction would be decided.

Militancy among British Mormon leaders grew as the continental revolutions spread. The Church press office in Liverpool demanded reform, and President Orson Pratt may have conversed with British radical George Jacob Holyoake.[112] "Something seems to whisper that wisdom will be given to her Majesty's government," wrote Orson Spencer during the Chartist demonstrations in April 1848, "to devise liberal things for the poor, whereby they may stand, at least for a season; and business

---

111. William McGhie, "Priestcraft in Danger—A Drama," pt. 1, *Millennial Star* 11 (April 15, 1849): 124–25. The play was completed under the same title in *Millennial Star* 11 (May 1, 1849): 172–75; and *Millennial Star* 11 (June 1, 1849): 190–92. During the winter of 1861–62, McGhie's drama played in Heber, Utah, for three nights to "large, appreciative audiences." See Edward William Tullidge, *Tullidge's Histories, Containing the History of all the Northern, Eastern, and Western Counties of Utah: also the Counties of Southern Idaho*, 149.

112. England, *Life and Thought of Orson Pratt*, 155. George Jacob Holyoake, *Bygones Worth Remembering* (1905) does not mention Pratt, but Edward W. Tullidge suggests the relationship in his *History of Salt Lake City and Its Founders*, 33, Appendix.

gain a fresh impulse, and the righteous poor be thereby qualified to effect their deliverance."[113] The next month the whisper crescendoed. The Mormon press hectored Prime Minister John Russell and urged a solidarity movement of workers and the lower-middle class to solve the problems stalking British society. The government had lost its moral authority. The people owned the future.[114]

Disgust with the British government's ineffectiveness during the Irish potato famine intensified criticism of Russell's free-market policies.[115] In January 1847 the *Millennial Star* excoriated the slow British response to the agricultural disaster, adding that Britain's "criminal and murderous tyranny" justified revolution.[116] Nineteen months later the Liverpool office of the *Millennial Star* supported a petition that would secure Irish tenure of the land, stop evictions, and abrogate the privileges of English landlords.[117] Appleby predicted that Irish nationalism would eventually win. The day "must surely come" when the "titled nobility" and "corrupt and wicked clergy" would pay for Britain's "sins and oppression," he wrote.[118] Other observers, including Wilford Woodruff, and Franklin D. Richards—Orson Pratt's successor as British Mission President—shared Appleby's sentiments. They encouraged Irish nationalists to "throw off the Brittish yoak" and destroy the land tenure system.[119]

---

113. Spencer, "April 15, 1848," 120.

114. "Alarming Condition of the Country—Progress of Despotism," reprinted from *Howitt's Journal of Literature and Popular Progress* in *Millennial Star* 10 (May 15, 1848): 146–47. *Howitt's Journal*, published in London, was edited by William Howitt (1792–1879), a historian and social commentator, and his wife Mary (1799–1888). Contemporary liberals and radicals had earlier praised his *Popular History of Priestcraft in All Ages and Nations* (1833). At the time of the 1848 revolutions, the Howitts were making a transition from Quakerism to spiritualism. See "An Inventory of the William and Mary Howitt Papers, 1827–1886"; and Sue Young, "William Howitt 1792–1879."

115. R. F. Foster, "Ascendancy and Union," 166–67.

116. "Ireland," *Millennial Star* 9 (January 1, 1847): 1.

117. "Petition of Irish Tenant Farmers," *Millennial Star* 10 (July 1, 1848): 208.

118. Appleby, "History of the Signs of the Times," August 30, 1848, and October 1, 1848, 143–44, 160–61.

119. Kenney, *Wilford Woodruff's Journal*, December 28, 1848, 3:396; Lord, "Kings and Thrones Are Falling," [4]; F. D. Richards, "Ireland," *Millennial*

The Irish land question and the June Days uprising stimulated Mormon thought on human organization. Elder Charles Derry envisioned a millennium reminiscent of early American communal republicanism. Wars would cease. Agriculture would prevail and "no longer will the tyrant sway his sceptre, nor lord his authority over the heritage of God, but the 'meek shall inherit the earth.'"[120] Orson Pratt published *New Jerusalem, and Equality and Oneness of the Saints: A Forecast of Events to Be Established by a Chosen and Dedicated People*. Pratt assumed that all governments would be "uprooted." National distinctions would disappear, and a unified kingdom would replace the old order. Private property, the "foundation of . . . innumerable evils," would yield to the "union of property" to foster the advancement of the Indians, assist the poor, fund immigration, and build the New Jerusalem.[121]

The Bitterness of Reaction

The imperial reaction that followed the "Springtime of the Peoples" in 1848 jarred Latter-day Saint observers. Overwrought expectations rendered Mormon observers' disappointment even more profound. In July 1849 John Jaques reviewed the previous eighteen months. Providence had sanctioned the street battles: the "civil wars, daring *emeutes* [uprisings], and lawless, unconstitutional disturbances" were "not unapproved."[122] The upper classes had been "confounded" and God, in conjunction with the people, had struck "terror to the heart of kings."[123] But Jaques had been stunned by the conservative reaction. The

---

Star 12 (August 15, 1850): 254.

120. Charles Derry, "Restoration of the Earth," *Millennial Star* 13 (October 15, 1851): 312.

121. Orson Pratt, *New Jerusalem, and Equality and Oneness of the Saints; a Forecast of Events to be Established by a Chosen and Dedicated People*, 58–64. This modern reprint combines Orson Pratt's *New Jerusalem; or the Fulfillment of Modern Prophecy* (1849) with his "The Equality and Oneness of the Saints," *Seer* 2 (July 1854): 289–300. The back cover says, "The World's Answer to Communism."

122. Harvey Locksley Birch [John Jaques], "Miscellanea and Letter to President Pratt," *Millennial Star* 11 (July 1, 1849): 198. *Emeute* means violent outbreak or popular uprising.

123. Harvey Locksley Birch [John Jaques], "A Glance at the World,"

disconsolate missionary compiled dispatches for Orson Pratt. From a French journal Jaques concluded that since the high point of the June Days uprising, gloom and political factionalism had pervaded France. The people were afraid and so ravaged by sickness that further resistance would be a mere act of despair.[124]

As Jaques's earlier democratic optimism faded, he emphasized migration to Zion. Uncertainty due to Joseph Smith's death and the evacuation of Nauvoo ended when Brigham Young commanded the Saints to gather to the Rocky Mountains.[125] The 3,591 who boarded ship in 1849–50 were over four times more numerous than the 828 who migrated in 1847–48.[126] Many who left England for Utah were disappointed by the failed Chartist movement.[127]

As to affairs in France, Mormon observers believed that Louis Napoleon III would act as a republican stalwart, but in this he proved disappointing.[128] Elected provisional president in December 1848,

---

Millennial Star 12 (February 1, 1850): 37.

124. Birch [Jaques], "Miscellanea and Letter to President Pratt," 198.

125. Richard E. Bennett, *We'll Find the Place: The Mormon Exodus, 1846–1848*, 49, 312–13.

126. Conway B. Sonne, *Saints on the Seas: A Maritime History of Mormon Migration, 1830–1890*, 148; and Taylor, *Expectations Westward*, 20. The numbers jumped again in 1852 when Scandinavian Mormons entered the migration stream and the Perpetual Emigration Fund began funding Transatlantic crossings. Sonne, *Saints on the Seas*, 31, 35–36.

127. Flanders, *Nauvoo: Kingdom on the Mississippi*, 62–63; Harrison, "The Popular History of Early Victorian Britain: A Mormon Contribution," 8, 12–13; John F. C. Harrison, *The Second Coming: Popular Millenarianism, 1780–1850*, 189–90. Malcolm Thorp, "Popular Mormon Millennialism in Nineteenth-Century Britain," 110–11, emphasizes the excitement over the restoration and "identity reinforcement" as the best way to explain migration to Utah. Allen, Esplin, and Whittaker, *Men with a Mission*, 325 argue that ideological disillusionment was less decisive than sheer economic hardship.

128. Acclaim for Napoleon III is found in "The Coming European Revolution—Kossuth's Next Movements," *Frontier Guardian*, February 6, 1852, [4]; Appleby, "History of the Signs of the Times," December 6, 1848, 170; "Prince Napoleon on European Affairs," *Millennial Star* 28 (July 28, 1866): 478. Billington, *Fire in the Minds of Men*, 325, 340–41, notes that the rise of another Napoleon mesmerized European leftists as the embodiment

Napoleon III's intentions grew more transparent as he surrounded himself with men determined to establish the Second Empire. A missionary in France writing to the British Mission office predicted that Napoleon III would have to protect his corrupt government against dedicated republicans accustomed to sacrifice: "The streets of [Paris] flowed with human gore [and] batteau [boat] loads of dead bodies went down the Seine . . . to obtain the present liberty of the French Republic, and place a President at its head, but a more fearful onslaught is apprehended."[129] Sure enough, after a pro-Napoleon coup led to the arrest of two hundred members of the Assembly on December 2, 1851, the workers of Paris revolted. The Minister of War hurled the army against them.

After the coup Elder Curtis Bolton, then translating the Book of Mormon, walked the bullet-riddled sections of Paris. Inquiries of passersby confirmed for him that France had ceded its revolutionary leadership: "At a signal given the troops leveled and fired . . . The 33d Regiment of infantry seized a mother of children large in the family way. She had several knives in her possession. They stood her out and shot her. French soldiers did that, not [I]ndians."[130] Orson Hyde, too, believed that France had betrayed republicanism. "Affairs in France had reached the crisis so long dreaded," but Hyde could not imagine that "twelve middle-aged Bonepartists" would survive the onslaught of a hundred million aroused Frenchmen.[131]

The *Millennial Star* reprinted the work of Eliza Cook, a non-Mormon Chartist poet who agreed with Bolton and Hyde.[132] Cook believed Napoleon III, Nicholas I, and "Constitution promising Frederick" were

---

of the revolutionary synthesis.

129. "A Sunday in Paris," *Millennial Star* 13 (November 1, 1851): 330–31. This item was probably written by Curtis Bolton or John Pack.

130. Bolton, Journal, December 5, 1851. However, Bolton's old companion, John Taylor, approved Napoleon's action. He believed French radicals were about to install Robespierre as a God and massacre reactionaries. See John Taylor, April 8, 1853, *Journal of Discourses*, 1:228–29.

131. Hyde, Foreign News, *Frontier Guardian*, January 9, 1852, [1].

132. Eliza Cook (1819–89) was a well-known writer in Chartist circles. She published the periodical *Eliza Cook's Journal* from 1849 to 1854. Cook was popular among Britain's working class and was widely published in anthologies. See *Encyclopaedia Britannica*, 7:71; Gerald Le Grys Norgate, "Cook, Eliza" and "Biography of Eliza Cook."

enemies of progress.[133] She was less sanguine than Hyde, however, about the possibility of eventual democratic triumph. The 1846 percussion rifle exemplified for Cook the new weapons that the ruling class could turn against the population. Quoting from a British colonial administrator, she detailed the effectiveness of rifled ordnance:

> Garibaldi's officers in scarlet were regularly shot down without seeing or hearing from which quarter the shot came. . . . [O]n the Boulevards of Paris, one of these new balls entered the forehead of a Socialist Representative the moment he appeared on the barricade with his red flag; in short, disguise it as one may, 500 men so armed are more than a match for any 3,000 men armed with the present British musket.[134]

Democracy, Cook concluded, was the loser.

Orson Spencer perhaps fell the furthest from the heady days of 1848. In 1853 he submitted a report informing Brigham Young that prospects for democracy in Europe were dim, let alone a mission in the German states. The revolutions had initially "humbled" the Hohenzollern dynasty, but the "spirit of tyranny . . . has returned to the breast of the King of Prussia." He, in partnership with the Holy Quadrangle Alliance, was enforcing the "absolutism . . . present on the whole continent of Europe." Only death promised relief from the people's "hell on earth."[135]

The *Millennial Star* covered the retreat to Utah. Refusing to concede that the ruling class had stomped out the embers of 1848, the voice of Mormonism asserted that "Revolution will succeed revolution. . . . The injured and oppressed will not hesitate to stain their path to liberty

---

133. Eliza Cook, "March of Civilization—Backwards!" reprinted from *Eliza Cook's Journal* in *Millennial Star* 14 (May 22, 1852): 204.

134. Ibid., 205. Brigham Young drew similar conclusions about the impact of weapon technology in a sermon delivered August 26, 1860, *Journal of Discourses*, 8:157. Cook's "Sir Charles Gray" was more likely Sir George Grey (1812–98), explorer and governor of New Zealand and Cape Colony and advocate of social reform. See James Rutherford, *Sir George Grey, K.C.B., 1812–1898: A Study in Colonial Government*. On rifled musket development between 1846 and 1851, see W. H. B. Smith, *Small Arms of the World: A Basic Manual of Small Arms*, 32–33.

135. Orson Spencer, *The Prussian Mission of the Church of Jesus Christ of Latter-day Saints: Report of Elder Orson Spencer, A.B. to President Brigham Young*, 5, 14–16.

with the blood of their oppressors and [lay] the foundation for their universal deliverance."[136]

Two Futures

In the pattern of revolution and reaction between 1848 and 1851, Mormon observers opposed every value associated with the status quo. They ridiculed kings, cheered republicanism, and predicted the end of capitalism. They shared social revolutionaries' hope for the universal destruction of the old order and the birth of the fully equal citizen. Along with the social levelers, Mormon observers also featured nationalist romantics in their pictorials of the disturbances sweeping across Europe.

But the revolutions of 1848 fizzled. Appleby's manuscript remained unpublished in Church archives as the failure of the revolutions sapped the desire to canonize 1848 as a momentous year in God's history. As usual, optimists pressed the reset button and recalibrated the millennium's unfolding. The year 1848 was not forgotten considering that over the next seventy years Mormon critics of political economy would refer to that year's revolutionary aspirations to legitimate certain leftist ideas.[137]

In the meantime, another utopia was emerging. In the spring of 1851, a Mormon delegation visited the Great Exhibition held in London. The display of engines, exotic imports, and mass-produced consumer goods demonstrated that middle-class achievement could be sustained only by mollifying the popular forces that had attacked the European dynastic and economic structure.[138] The diaries of Mormon visitors to

---

136. "The Russo-Turkish War and Its Responsibilities," *Millennial Star* 16 (June 10, 1854): 358–60.

137. J. E. S. Russell, "The Poor," *Millennial Star* 27 (January 21, 1865): 38, suggested that British Mormons were disillusioned Chartists. See also Charles W. Nibley, "Competition," *Millennial Star* 40 (November 25, 1878): 741; Joseph M. Tanner, "The Nineteenth Century," *Improvement Era* 4 (January 1901): 162–63; Joseph A. Vance, "Growth and Development of Socialism," *Millennial Star* 71 (March 25, 1909): 178; B. H. Roberts, *The Life of John Taylor: Third President of the Church of Jesus Christ of Latter-day Saints*, 234.

138. Peter H. Hoffenberg, *Empire on Display: English, Indian, and Australian Exhibitions from the Crystal Palace to the Great War*; Eric J. Hobsbawm, *The Age of Capital, 1848–1875*, 5, 24–26, 32–33, 289. Several

the Crystal Palace recorded their awe at this evidence of material progress. Mormon sightseers, accustomed to "thinking big regarding their religion and its plan to cover the entire earth, were highly impressed by the immense building and the numerous exhibits demonstrating power and speed."[139]

Throughout the remainder of the nineteenth century and into the twentieth, introspective churchmen and women continued to study world events. As they endeavored to place their religion in historical context, they confronted two futures as different from each other as the neatly arranged galleries of the Crystal Palace and the ramshackle barricades of 1848. The rewards of evolutionary capitalism and assimilation stood gleaming on the one hand. On the other lingered the revolutionary epiphany of a terrestrial kingdom of socioeconomic justice. Mormon interest in revolution persisted, but it now competed with an alternative progressive vision that would gradually supplant it in the Mormon mind.

Chartists, socialists, and continental revolutionaries were co-opted by the magnificence of the 1851 Great Exhibition. See Hoffenberg, *Empire on Display*, 127–28; Billington, *Fire in the Minds of Men*, 240, 336.

139. T. Edgar Lyon, "In Praise of Babylon: Church Leadership at the 1851 Great Exhibition in London," 14, 54.

CHAPTER 3

MORMON REVOLUTIONARY SYMBOLISM

Borrowings

Revolutionaries understood the value of symbols. In their minds "the ideal," writes James Billington, "was not the balanced complexity of the new American federation, but the occult simplicity of its great seal: an all-seeing eye atop a pyramid over the words *Novus Ordo Seclorum*." Revolutionaries preferred "primal, natural truths . . . idealizing above all the semi-mythic Pythagoras as the model intellect-turned-revolutionary and the Pythagorean belief in prime numbers, geometric forms, and the higher harmonies of music."[1] In nature and mathematics they found "truth amidst the crumbling authority of tradition."[2] Willard Mullins writes that the belief that history was moving toward a specific end inspired men to formulate laws of social development and to craft political agendas to enforce them. A "coherent system of symbols" reinforced these programs of "collective action."[3]

The New Mormon History has stressed the exchange of ideas between the Church and its host environment. As one researcher has written, Mormon leaders, "sensitive to the movements and conditions of their times," borrowed emblems and invented meanings to separate the Church from orthodox Christianity.[4] Historians have connected Joseph Smith's Nauvoo innovations to Kabbalah and Freemasonry, but in the extended field of symbolism the Mormon mind of the 1840s and 1850s also intersected with iconography, language, and organizational

---

1. James Billington, *Fire in the Minds of Men: The Origins of the Revolutionary Faith*, 6.

2. Ibid., 101.

3. Willard A. Mullins, "On the Concept of Ideology in Political Science."

4. Leonard J. Arrington and Davis Bitton, *The Mormon Experience: A History of the Latter-day Saints*, xiv.

structures familiar to revolutionaries.[5] Indeed, whether Mormonism is viewed as a movement content to live separately in the American West or as a militant theocracy with universal ambitions, we would expect to see the Latter-day Saints use symbols to convey their intentions. In this endeavor Mormons often borrowed revolutionary symbolism, hoping to derive power and inspire hope for the creation of a better world.

Masonry and Illuminism as Revolutionary Organizational

The emergence of Freemasonry has been linked to the beginnings of revolutionary ideology and organization. Masonry is a complex lineage of fraternal associations that make extensive use of symbolism and ceremony. Founded in England in the late sixteenth or early seventeenth century, Masonry came to America during the 1730s. Masonry focuses on creating a moral universe embodying concepts of justice and equality. Inside their lodges Masons ritualistically practiced equality and brotherhood. They dedicated themselves to social improvement, science, and moral philosophy. Masonic architecture represented the proper form of society; the mason's tools symbolized the methods and the principles by which social perfection would be achieved.[6] Masonry's birth in the age of kings and empires, then, attracted suspicions from royalists and the Catholic Church that Masons had radical intentions—suspicions that were not entirely unfounded.

Masonry's practices influenced radical secret societies ranging from the Italian Carbonari to the communistic groups formed by

---

5. On the connection between the ascetic Jewish tradition and Mormonism, see John L. Brooke, *Refiner's Fire: The Making of Mormon Cosmology, 1644–1844*; Lance S. Owens, "Joseph Smith and Kabbalah: The Occult Connection"; and D. Michael Quinn, *Early Mormonism and the Magic World View*. Harold Bloom believes Smith was a religious "genius" who reivented major themes of Kabbalah through a "creative misreading of the Bible." See Bloom, *The American Religion: The Emergence of the Post-Christian Nation*, 84.

6. Billington, *Fire in the Minds of Men*, 92. The role of architecture in utopian thought and social modeling is discussed in Frank E. Manuel and Fritzie P. Manuel, *Utopian Thought in the Western World*, 153–80. Mormon Apostle James E. Talmage believed that "Moses received divine instructions in architecture." See *The Articles of Faith: A Series of Lectures on the Principal Doctrines of the Church of Jesus Christ of Latter-day Saints*, 4.

Filippo Buonarroti.[7] Buonarroti (1761–1837) was particularly important because in many ways he birthed the modern revolutionary tradition. He became the first full-time revolutionist—the first, according to James Billington, "having total dedication to the creation by force of a new secular order." In 1828 he published *The History of the Babeuf Conspiracy*, which Karl Marx and Friedrich Engels planned to publish in German. The importance Buonarroti placed on disciplined leadership and organization went far beyond the goals of Masonry, but Buonarroti's five-year membership with a Masonic lodge in Geneva, Italy, influenced his thinking.[8] Masonic teachings also sustained Mexican liberals in the civil wars of the 1850s and in the struggle against French intrusion from 1861 to 1866. In 1915 Masonry proved a rallying point for Mexican intellectuals opposed to Woodrow Wilson's tacit recognition of Victoriano Huerta's short-lived regime during the Mexican Revolution.[9]

Contemporaries exaggerated the leadership role Masons played in the French and American Revolutions. True, half the generals of the Continental Army were Masons, and Louis XVI's Mason cousin Philippe Égalité voted to guillotine the French king. In reality, though, a Mason could be either royalist or revolutionary. Nevertheless, the belief persisted that Masonic lodges were think tanks of revolution. A historian of Masonry suggests how this attribution electrified the lodges: "If masonic lodges were places where revolutions were planned, that was where ardent young revolutionaries wished to be."[10]

Masonry figured more directly in Russia. In 1825 a group of army officers wanted to continue the reforms of the deceased Czar Alexander I. Some of them even wanted to free the serfs. They planed to use Masonic Lodge Asrea, named after the Goddess of Justice, to model a constitutional

---

7. Billington, *Fire in the Minds of Men*, 92–93; Bernard Fäy, *Revolution and Freemasonry, 1680–1800*; Steven C. Bullock, *Revolutionary Brotherhood: Freemasonry and the Transformation of the American Social Order, 1730–1840*, 225–27, 242, 291; Jonathan Sperber, *The European Revolutions, 1848–1851*, 54; and Lynn Hunt, *Politics, Culture, and Class in the French Revolution*, 198–201.

8. Billington, *Fire in the Minds of Men*, 87, 92, 269.

9. Jaksíc Iván, "Masonic Orders." Antonio Lara Reyes discusses the appeal of both Mormonism and Masonry in Mexico in his article, "Mormonism, Americanism, and Mexico."

10. Jasper Ridley, *The Freemasons: A History of the World's Most Powerful Secret Society*, 137.

empire. The coup failed and five officers were hung, but the Decembrists, as they were called, had started the modern Russian revolutionary tradition.[11]

Several early Mormon leaders, including Joseph Smith's brother Hyrum, were already Masons when the Church was organized in 1830.[12] There is also evidence that Masonic bonding informed the activities of the Danites, a secretive Mormon paramilitary organization founded in Missouri in 1838 that became the enforcement arm of the Church.[13] A former Danite remembered the unit as a "divine brotherly union," a phrase that echoed Masonic fraternalism.[14] The Danites served the dual function of policing the internal utopian standards of the Mormon community and protecting that community from external, reactionary forces.[15] The Danite organization was short-lived, but Mormons remained fascinated with Masonry's esoteric utopianism. Formal Mormon ties to Masonry were completed in 1842 when prominent Mormons received permission to establish a Masonic lodge in the city of Nauvoo. Nauvoo and the surrounding area soon boasted six such lodges, encompassing 1,550 members.[16] The Mormon lodges were known for their seriousness and their esoteric inclinations.[17] John Brooke notes that Mormonism's

---

11. Robert R. Palmer and Joel Colton, *A History of the Modern World*, 484; and Billington, *Fire in the Minds of Men*, 141.

12. For works on Mormons and Masonry, see Brooke, *Refiner's Fire*; Mervin B. Hogan, *Mormonism and Freemasonry: The Illinois Episode*; David John Buerger, *The Mysteries of Godliness: A History of Mormon Temple Worship*, 49–58; Michael W. Homer, "'Similarity of Priesthood in Masonry:' The Relationship between Freemasonry and Mormonism"; D. Michael Quinn, *The Mormon Hierarchy: Origins of Power*, 113–15, 129–31; Reed C. Durham, "Is There No Help for the Widow's Son?"; Joseph Smith Jr. et al., *History of the Church of Jesus Christ of Latter-day Saints*, 4:550–53, 570, 589, 594; 5:1–2, 446; 6:287.

13. Quinn, *Mormon Hierarchy: Origins of Power*, 102–3, 469–78.

14. Brooke, *Refiner's Fire*, 233.

15. See Stephen C. LeSueur, *The 1838 Mormon War in Missouri*.

16. Hogan, *Mormonism and Freemasonry: The Illinois Episode*, 290. One historian places the total Mormon membership in Freemasonry at seven hundred in 1844. At the time of the Mormon founding of Nauvoo in 1839 there were only 100–150 Masons in the state of Illinois and 2,072 in the United States. See Quinn, *Mormon Hierarchy: Origins of Power*, 130; and Buerger, *Mysteries of Godliness*, 58.

17. Hogan, *Mormonism and Freemasonry: The Illinois Episode*, 308.

encounter with Masonry "brought a sharper absolutist strain" to the Mormon tradition than the magical folk practices and evangelical populism that informed it at its founding.[18] Mormon initiates, who included almost the entire leadership of the Church, viewed Smith's temple ritual as perfected Masonry.[19] Further elaboration was achieved when Mormon lodges incorporated elements of the French "Rite de Perfection."[20] Despite subsequent antagonism between Mormons and Masons, scholars insist that the two embraced kindred philosophies.[21]

Freemasonry gave Mormon leaders insights into universal trans-formation. "Humanity never really had but one religion," Freemasonry taught. Through the "vast expansion of individual life," man would grow to understand his obligations in the social state God had intended.[22] The Master Mason, committed to turning thought into action, favored socioeconomic justice and national independence movements.[23] With this attitude in mind, Masons urged revolution to overthrow feudal-ism and empires and to free men's minds from religious superstition.[24] When Smith introduced his own temple endowment ceremony on May 4, 1842, less than two months after his own advance to Master Mason, nine candidates for the new endowment engaged in "fervent prayer concerning the problems of the day."[25] Initiated to beliefs about perfection and divine governance, Mormon Masons were bound in a

18. Brooke, *Refiner's Fire*, 233.

19. Buerger, *Mysteries of Godliness*, 56–58. Smith's gradual and secretive introduction of the temple ceremony and polygamy has a parallel in Bonneville's theory of incremental knowledge, which he justified "not out of cruelty, but in order to secure little by little, universally, the innumerable steps that must be taken on our ladder." See Billington, *Fire in the Minds of Men*, 40.

20. Homer, "'Similarity of Priesthood in Masonry,'" 108–9.

21. Hogan, *Mormonism and Freemasonry: The Illinois Episode*, 323; Allen E. Roberts, *Freemasonry in American History*, 243–44. The use of "brother" as a salutation is common among both Mormons and Masons. See Billington, *Fire in the Minds of Men*, 92.

22. Albert Pike, *Morals and Dogma of the Ancient and Accepted Scottish Rite of Freemasonry*, 102, 197–98.

23. Ibid., 90, 92–95, 180.

24. Ibid., 69, 73–74, 94.

25. James B. Allen, *Trials of Discipleship: The Story of William Clayton, a Mormon*, 127.

special understanding of what Nicholas Bonneville had preached to the Paris Confederation of the Friends of Truth in 1793: a consciousness of themselves as the controlling unit of an international movement.[26]

Lodges and temples were designed to teach truths that guided humans back to heaven. Furniture arrangements, costumes, props, and symbols impressed upon the mind the perfectibility of humanity and society.[27] James Anderson, one of the most quoted Masonic scholars in Joseph Smith's day, linked architecture to social improvement: "Adam, our first Parent, created after the image of God, the *great Architect of the Universe*, must have had the Liberal Science, particularly *geometry*, written on his heart."[28] Orson Pratt and Brigham Young similarly said that the "Great Architect of the Universe" had supplied all human needs. Only "unrighteous monopolies" prevented material enjoyment by all.[29] Mormons adopted Masonic architectural symbolism in their temples. Preference for the Gothic style, writes Laurel Andrew, unified space and time, providing "tangible expressions" of the future political kingdom of God in this world.[30]

Along with Masonry came allegations that Mormon leaders had taken to Illuminism, the occult spark of the revolutionary idea. The Order of the Illuminati, founded in 1776 by Bavarian professor Adam Weishaupt, was a secret order with global ambitions. Its adherents honored Christ as the master Illuminist and were dedicated to rationalism, anti-clericalism, and mastering the art of controlling the consciousness. Christopher McIntosh writes that Illuminism intended to develop a "style of ritual and hierarchy." Its core philosophy preached the overthrow of despots, Jesuits, and all other institutions blocking the worldwide enjoyment of enlightened thought.[31] The intellectuals that

---

26. Brooke, *Refiner's Fire*, 10, 235–36; Billington, *Fire in the Minds of Men*, 40–41.

27. Dolores Hayden, *Seven American Utopias: The Architecture of Communitarian Socialism, 1790-1975*, 39–40, 130–41; and J. Finlay Finlayson, *The Symbols and Legends of Freemasonry*.

28. James Anderson, *The Constitution of Free-Masons*, 7–8, quoted in Quinn, *Early Mormonism and the Magic World View*, 178.

29. Orson Pratt, "The Power of Nature," *Seer* 2 (March 1854): 227; Brigham Young, September 28, 1862, *Journal of Discourses*, 10:3.

30. Laurel B. Andrew, *The Early Temples of the Mormons: The Architecture of the Millennial Kingdom in the American West*, 27, 121–22, 141.

31. Christopher McIntosh, *The Rose Cross and the Age of Reason: Eighteenth-Century Rosicrucianism in Central Europe and its Relationship*

comprised Illuminati cells infiltrated Masonic lodges. The order obtained a membership between two and three thousand before German authorities eradicated it.[32] If Masonry provided the vocabulary for revolution, Illuminism "provided its basic structural model."[33] Antagonists charged that the Illuminati had engineered the French Revolution, won over the New England clergy, and elected Thomas Jefferson as president. Worse still, Illuminists intended to destroy the American republic. The charges were mere myth, but fear of domestic Illuminism continued in the United States until the mid-nineteenth century.[34] It was against this backdrop that John C. Bennett, one of Smith's closest Nauvoo confidants until 1842, claimed after his defection from the Church that Smith had told him to establish the Order of the Illuminati.[35] Illinois Governor Thomas Ford (1842–46) thought he saw a similarity between the loyalty oaths of the Illuminati and those administered to Smith's shadow government formed in March 1844—the Council of Fifty.[36]

Illuminism's impression on Masonic Mormons may well have influenced the genesis of the Council of Fifty (revolutionary France had a Council of Five Hundred) and its stylistic preference for arcane

---

to the Enlightenment, 105.

32. Scholars dispute the degree to which the Illuminati infiltrated Freemasonry. See Billington, *Fire in the Minds of Men*, 94, 594 note 222; McIntosh, *Rose Cross*, 103; Henry Wilson Coil, *Coil's Masonic Encyclopedia*, 545; Arthur Edward Waite, *A New Encyclopaedia of Freemasonry and of Cognate Instituted Mysteries: Their Rites, Literature, and History*, 1:66.

33. Billington, *Fire in the Minds of Men*, 93.

34. For Democrat-Republican and Federalist charge and counter charge, see Vernon Stauffer, *New England and the Bavarian Illuminati*, 345–60; Richard Buel, *Securing the Revolution: Ideology in American Politics, 1789–1815*, 167; Alan V. Briceland, "The Philadelphia Aurora, the New England Illuminati, and the Election of 1800," 3–36.

35. Klaus Hansen, *Quest for Empire: The Political Kingdom of God and the Council of Fifty in Mormon History*, 55.

36. Ibid., 98–99. There is also a parallel between Smith's organizational ideas and Carbonari rituals. The Carbonari believed in an unfinished revolution (to be completed by Christ's second coming), nature over tradition (divine-human connection is natural; denominations are traditional), hierarchal organization, and secret handshakes. See Billington, *Fire in the Minds of Men*, 132.

revolutionary concepts in pursuit of global preeminence.[37] Robert Flanders says that the Nauvoo innovations inaugurated a "new, more sacred American Revolution, from which it was difficult to turn back." At the center of the unfinished revolution was the "mystical" leadership of Joseph Smith.[38] Smith charged the Council with planning a move westward and with campaigning for his presidential run in 1844. But the "kingdom school" of Mormon historiography goes further: the Council was a government-in-waiting ready to seize power on the eve of the millennium. Public outcry against growing Mormon influence in Illinois was partly an expression of concern that the Council of Fifty would install Joseph Smith in the White House with the same alacrity with which the Illuminati had allegedly toppled the French monarchy in 1789.[39] Smith was so sure of his future role as a global ruler that he commissioned ambassadors to foreign courts.[40] To escape the fetters of state

37. Owens, "Joseph Smith and Kabbalah," 170–73; and Klaus Hansen, "The Metamorphosis of the Kingdom of God: Toward a Reinterpretation of Mormon History," 223.

38. Robert B. Flanders, "Dream and Nightmare: Nauvoo Revisited," 80. Marvin S. Hill and D. Michael Quinn date theocratic intentions to the Missouri and Kirtland, Ohio era of the 1830s. See Hill, *Quest for Refuge: The Mormon Flight from American Pluralism*, 55; and Quinn, *Mormon Hierarchy: Origins of Power*, 80–103.

39. The pioneering "kingdom school" study is Hansen, *Quest for Empire*. See also James R. Clark, "The Kingdom of God, the Council of Fifty and the State of Deseret"; Hill, *Quest for Refuge*, xvi; Keith J. Melville, "Brigham Young's Ideal Society: The Kingdom of God"; Andrew Ehat, "'It Seems Like Heaven Began on Earth': Joseph Smith and the Constitution of the Kingdom of God"; Robert Bruce Flanders, "The Kingdom of God in Illinois: Politics in Utopia"; Quinn, *The Mormon Hierarchy: Origins of Power*, 79–141; and D. Michael Quinn, *The Mormon Hierarchy: Extensions of Power*, 262–313. For additional sources on the topic, see Newell G. Bringhurst and Lavina Fielding Anderson, eds., *Excavating Mormon Pasts: The New Historiography of the Last Half Century*, 124.

40. Elder George J. Adams, for example, was the ambassador to Russia. See Matthew S. Moore, "'Joseph's Measures': The Continuation of Esoterica by Schismatic Members of the Council of Fifty," 82, 99. For a list of members of the Council of Fifty and the missions of each member, see D. Michael Quinn, "The Council of Fifty and Its Members, 1844–1945," 163–197.

oversight and to establish a world administrative headquarters, Smith petitioned the federal government for the separation of Nauvoo as an autonomous region within the Union.[41] To ensure secrecy, Mormon leaders adopted pseudonyms like early underground revolutionaries.[42]

Smith's death on June 27, 1844, squelched theocratic intentions along the Mississippi River. But in Utah the "Great Council," one of several names by which diarists referred to the Council of Fifty, persevered in the "unfinished revolution" and continued to nurture aspirations of a global kingdom. At a Fourth of July celebration in Salt Lake City, a reading of a poem by Eliza R. Snow told how Joseph Smith and Brigham Young had renewed the revolution that Americans had allowed to lapse.[43] In 1862 Apostle George Q. Cannon told a group of departing missionaries that the Church was "to become a political power, known and recognized by the powers of the earth," and that missionaries were "its accredited agents . . . at the courts of foreign nations."[44] Brigham Young looked forward to the day when the Council would "give laws to the nations of the earth. . . . Joseph Smith organized this government before, in Nauvoo, and he said if we did our duty, we should prevail over all our enemies."[45]

Geometry and Numbers

While Cannon and Young anticipated earthly rule, British explorer Sir Richard Burton noticed a similarity between Salt Lake's theocratic culture and the techniques of French radicals. In *The City of the Saints*, Burton surmised that the Mormons had adopted doctrines of

41. Hansen, *Quest for Empire*, 80.

42. For secret names and military titles, see Doctrine and Covenants 78, 82, 92, 96, and 104 in editions prior to 1981; Quinn, *Mormon Hierarchy: Origins of Power*, 83, 87, 198; Hill, *Quest for Refuge*, 53; David J. Whittaker, "Substituted Names in the Published Revelations of Joseph Smith"; Kent W. Huff, "The United Order of Joseph Smith's Times," 148–49. For early revolutionaries see Billington, *Fire in the Minds of Men*, 95, 114–15; and Jacob L. Talmon, *The Origins of Totalitarian Democracy*, 186.

43. "Revolutionary Song," Journal History of the Church, July 4, 1854, 4.

44. "Minutes of a General Council Held in Farm Street Chapel, Birmingham, Commencing Jan. 1, 1862," *Latter-day Saints' Millennial Star* 24 (February 15, 1862): 103 (hereafter cited as *Millennial Star*).

45. Journal History, January 19, 1863.

the Illuminati and Pythagorean perfectionism.[46] However strange as it may seem, prime numbers and geometric shapes, especially the triangle, circle, and pentagram, were patterns of revolutionary thought. Historian James Billington suggests that the typical French revolutionary intellectual of the 1790s was a "modern Pythagoras" whose social ideal was the ancient Greek city of Philadelphia. The Circle of Philadelphians, the first revolutionary group to arise after the suppression of the Babeuf revolt in 1797, adopted Greek thought to distill a new breed of revolutionaries committed to the brotherly ideals common to Masonry and Illuminism.[47] The use of geometry and numbers as tools to reconstruct society was common to both these secular revolutionaries and the would-be designers of Mormon theocracy. The evidence is insufficient to demonstrate direct influence of revolutionary geometry on Mormonism, but Mormons and revolutionaries do seem at least to have been common partakers of an esoteric tradition, which looked to numerology and geometry for patterns for utopian social organization.

Secular radicals of the 1790s envisioned truth condensed to the symbolic perfection of the circle. Members of Bonneville's "Social Circle" in the Palais-Royal of Paris believed that men could become like Gods (a belief also held by Mormons) by widening the circle of brotherhood. The center, Paris, was the New Jerusalem over which the sun would radiate light throughout the world. From this center the circumference of perfected society would expand until the Philadelphian vision—brotherly love—was everywhere. Similarily, Buonarroti, the link between Babeuf and Marx, borrowed from the concentric rings of Illuminist ritual to identify levels of revolutionary dedication. The outer ring consisted of liberals. In the next ring were "staunch democrats." A clandestine group committed to absolute egalitarianism occupied the center.[48]

The circle modeled social perfection; the triangle was the organizational form that would build it. The triangle offered the theorists of revolution simplicity. A triangle uses the fewest possible straight lines to enclose a space and was one of the most widely used icons arising from

---

46. Richard Francis Burton, *The City of the Saints and across the Rocky Mountains to California*, 410, 443; and Arnold H. Green and Lawrence P. Goldrup, "Joseph Smith, an American Muhammad? An Essay on the Perils of Historical Analogy," 55.

47. Billington, *Fire in the Minds of Men*, 100.

48. Ibid., 44, 98–99, 101, 103.

the French Revolution. Triangles, pyramids, or representations of "three" were found in the tricolor, the trinity of liberty, equality, and fraternity, and on official seals and stamps.[49] When Buonarroti created his own ceremony in 1808–9, he arranged his room in a way that used triangles to model the universe. At the first point, the altar, the master introduced candidates to the other points of the triangle. The second point represented the ocean, the element of water and life. The third point represented the volcano, the element of earth and revolution. Additional arrangements depicted the circumference of the earth, symbolic of eternal perfection, and the North Star, the guide for its attainment.[50]

Pythagorean numerology came early to Mormonism. Joseph Smith and other early converts dabbled in Pythagorean formulations through their involvement in the treasure-seeking folk magic found among Puritan descendants in New England and New York.[51] William Morgan, whose suspected 1826 murder in New York after he threatened to reveal lodge secrets launched the anti-Masonic party, described Pythagoras as "our ancient friend and brother."[52] In 1854 Apostle Wilford Woodruff recorded that he was trying to apply the character improvement lessons in a study of the *Golden Verses of Pythagoras* by Antoine Fabre d'Olivet, an esoteric writer of the French revolutionary era who considered earthly perfection to reside in the harmonies of music.[53] Brigham

---

49. Hunt, *Politics, Culture, and Class in the French Revolution*, 1–119.

50. Billington, *Fire in the Minds of Men*, 106.

51. Quinn, *Early Mormonism and the Magic World View*; Owens, "Joseph Smith and Kabbalah," 173–78; and James B. Allen, "But Dick Tracy Landed on the Moon," 19.

52. William Morgan, *Illustrations of Masonry, by One of the Fraternity Who Has Devoted Thirty Years to the Subject*, 71. For Masonic interpretations of Pythagorean geometry as symbols of unity and reason, see Pike, *Morals and Dogma*, 11, 487, 861.

53. Scott G. Kenney, ed., *Wilford Woodruff's Journal: 1833–1898, Typescript*, February 4, 1854, 4:247. Compare to Billington, *Fire in the Minds of Men*, 116, and Antoine Fabre d'Olivet, *The Golden Verses of Pythagoras Explained and Translated into French and Preceded by a Discourse upon the Essence and Form of Poetry among the Principal Peoples of the Earth*. Antoine Fabre d'Olivet (1767–1825) was a French playwright better known for his esoteric writings and influence on his century's occultists. See John Renwick, "Fabre d'Olivet, Antoine."

Young and other leading Mormons drew from Pythagoras. According to one scholar, they believed that they were borrowing from a "universal body of truth."[54]

Church leaders adapted Egyptian and French pictography to model the universal reign of justice and the growth of the political kingdom of God. A sacred center was as important to Mormons as it had been to French revolutionaries. Perfection would begin in Zion, the center stake—initially Jackson County, Missouri, and later in the Salt Lake Valley. At the center stood the temple and around it the stakes of Zion would spread. In an article titled "Centralization of Government," the *Latter-day Saints' Millennial Star* recognized that both Peter the Great and Napoleon had "grasped the idea of the formation of a great supervisory power over the nations," the center of which would be Paris or Constantinople. But these were "unscrupulous men." Only men of godly intelligence and pure motives could establish the true "great centre."[55]

The Church as metropole around which the world would orient itself appeared early in Mormon belief. Benjamin Winchester wrote that Joseph Smith designated Kirtland, Ohio "to be the great center of the world. Kings and Queens were to come there from foreign lands to pay homage to the Saints."[56] Parley P. Pratt explained that when Israel gathered from among the nations, a new world center would be established. Along its circumference former empires and nations would be reduced to absolute equality and equidistance from the moral middle. An 1845 *Proclamation of the Twelve Apostles of the Church of Jesus Christ of Latter-day Saints* asserted that Israel would become a unified nation and all others would heed its voice:

> In short . . . The courts of Rome, London, Constantinople, Petersburgh, and all others, will then have to yield the point and do homage, and pay tribute to the one great center, and to one

---

54. Allen D. Roberts, "Where Are the All-seeing Eyes? The Origin, Use and Decline of Early Mormon Symbolism," 39. Other Mormon references to Pythagoras are discussed in Hugh Nibley, "The Meaning of the Kirtland Egyptian Papers," 384; B. H. Roberts, *New Witnesses for God*, 1:446–47; William E. Dibble, "The Book of Abraham and the Pythagorean Astronomy."

55. "Centralization of Government," *Millennial Star* 41 (April 28, 1879): 265.

56. Benjamin Winchester, "Primitive Mormonism," quoted in Hill, *Quest for Refuge*, 55.

mighty Sovereign, or THRONES WILL BE CAST DOWN, AND KINGDOMS WILL CEASE TO BE.[57]

In 1854 Jedediah M. Grant, the bishop of Salt Lake City, claimed that Mormons were inside the "Circle of Truth." They would build Zion and "establish the reign of peace on earth."[58] The *Millennial Star* said it explicitly in 1879:

> Zion is necessarily organized on the principle of a grand, pervading central power. This is observable in all the works of nature, even in the government of the myriad of worlds that bespangle the starry heavens. When Zion is built up in her glory, her center will be in the divinely designated spot, in Jackson County, Missouri, U. S. A. Around this, like so many planets around a central sun . . . her benign influence will radiate to the end of the earth.[59]

The attraction of the circle and triangle as utopian symbols in Mormonism also came as an import through Louis Bertrand, a French convert who became president of the French Mission. Bertrand's 1861 letter to Napoleon III mentions America as the "angular stone of the New World" that would unite the human race.[60] In his memoir

---

57. Parley P. Pratt, *A Proclamation of the Twelve Apostles of the Church of Jesus Christ of Latter-day Saints. To All the Kings of the World; to the President of the United States of America; to the Governors of the Several States; and to the Rulers and Peoples of All Nations*. A version of this work was also printed in the *Millennial Star* 5 (March 1845): 149–53. French and Mormon forecasts of the emergence of a new center of world government were undoubtedly influenced by biblical prophecies such as Isaiah 2:2–4, Daniel 7:9–14, and Ezekiel 5:5 as well as by sacred geometry. Ezekiel even refers to Jerusalem as the "center."

58. Jedediah Grant, February 19, 1854, *Journal of Discourses*, 2:15–16. Other references to the circle as the symbol of "truth," "power," or "perfection" are found in Amasa Lyman, October 11, 1857, *Journal of Discourses*, 5:308; Orson Pratt, August 8, 1880, *Journal of Discourses*, 21:235; Roberts, *New Witnesses for God*, 165–66, 473; Margaret Toscano and Paul Toscano, *Strangers in Paradox: Explorations in Mormon Theology*, 287–88; and Roberts, "Where Are the All-seeing Eyes," 43.

59. "Centralization of Government," 265–66.

60. Louis A. Bertrand, "Important Appeal to the Emperor of the French," *Millennial Star* 23 (April 6, 1861): 221.

Bertrand admitted to the influence of Hoëne Wronski, a "geometrician" who preached global "Messianism." His mentors, Hegel and St. Simon, inspired Bertrand's depiction of Africa, Asia, and South America moving by stages toward industrial harmony and "geometric" perfection. "For me," recalled Bertrand, geometry and universalism were "the torch of mankind."[61]

The triangle provided a popular form of revolutionary recruitment and organization. Each man knew two others in his group plus one from each of the triangles above and below his own. The triangular organization form was popular among revolutionary cells such as the League of Outlaws, Irish Ribbonists, and Bolsheviks. In simple geometric modeling revolutionaries believed they had discovered the sublime perfection that triggered revolutionary action.[62] The pentagram, the symbol of universal love used by the Illuminati, was adopted later by other revolutionary cells.[63] The number five also became the organizing principle of the Council of Fifty.[64] Relatedly, an unpublished monograph found in the LDS Church History Library studies Pythagorean calculation in the structure of the Church's ruling councils. When the ruling councils are diagrammed in a certain way, interlocking circles form the moons, suns, and the five- and six-pointed stars sculpted in nineteenth-century Mormon temple architecture. The study also notes subliminal triadic formulations. From three-man bishoprics up to the Church's three-man First Presidency, two counselors answer to a third person until the whole structure is complete.[65]

------

61. Louis A. Bertrand, *Memoirs of a Mormon*, 2; Billington, *Fire in the Minds of Men*, 218–21, 224–25. Josef Hoëné de Wronski (1778–1853) was an eccentric mathematician who attempted to solve the problem of longitudinal navigation. His esoteric works attract few followers today but some of his published mathematical theories were ahead of their time. See John J. O'Connor and Edmund F. Robertson, "Josef-Maria Hoëné de Wronski."

62. On the triangle as a ceremonial pattern and organizing principle for revolutionary cells, see Billington, *Fire in the Minds of Men*, 105–110, 181.

63. Ibid., 98–99, 110–11, 120, 136.

64. Quinn, "The Council of Fifty and Its Members," 167–69; and Kenneth M. Sundberg, "The Morning Star, A Study of the Symbolism and Design Inherent in the Holy Priesthood as Administered in the Church of Jesus Christ of Latter-day Saints," 34–45.

65. Sundberg, "The Morning Star," 18–20.

In addition to three and five, special significance was attached to the number seven. In *Early Mormonism and the Magic World View*, renowned historian D. Michael Quinn suggests that Smith's understanding of numerology produced the seven presidents who preside over the Latter-day Saint Seventy, the Church's third highest presiding quorum.[66] Mormon observers, numerologists, and early revolutionaries identified the number seven with a range of associations. A *Times and Seasons* piece equated the power of seven with the extinguishment of noble titles and the leveling of society brought about by the French Revolution.[67] Wilford Woodruff claimed a vision in which he saw "seven lions, as of burning brass." They glowed in representation of the combined dispensations that "will appear in the heavens before the coming of the Son of Man."[68] In 1892 James E. Talmage surmised that seven was part of an ancient formula. In his book *Articles of Faith*, he mentioned the Biblical "seven men of honest report" and proceeded to discuss the importance of structural perfection and symmetry in Church organization, which "comprises no superfluities." Talmage believed each quorum of the Church required an exact number of members for "the power to act in the name of God, which power commands both respect on earth and in heaven."[69] Levi Edgar Young expounded on the number seven as late as 1951. In the Bible "the number seems to have been regarded as the symbol of completeness or perfection" and "connected intimately with everything relating to God." To "seven it," Young related among other examples, was how Hebrew elders ratified an oath. Then Young turned to Honoré de Balzac's 1832 novel *Louis Lambert*. The plot, an exploration of mysticism and Illuminism, contains a passage about seven cited by Young: "Seven is the Formula of Heaven. . . . We see the beauty and the sacredness of the word 'seven.' We understand the meaning of the kingdom of God because we

---

66. Quinn, *Early Mormonism and the Magic World View*, 60. Captured Morrisite scepters inscribed with the numbers five and seven identified the owners' status as rulers of a future world order. See Kenney, *Wilford Woodruff's Journal*, June 16, 1862, 6:56.

67. "Millerism," *Times and Seasons* 4, no. 11 (April 15, 1843): 171.

68. Wilford Woodruff, March 3, 1889, in Brian H. Stuy, ed. and comp., *Collected Discourses Delivered by President Wilford Woodruff, His Two Counselors, the Twelve Apostles, and Others*, 1:217.

69. Talmage, *Articles of Faith*, 207, 209–16.

possess its power."[70] Mormon observers were not alone in treating the number seven with reverence. Seven also found expression among early revolutionaries in Italy: Carbonari grand masters initiated meetings with seven ceremonial ax strokes to a tree trunk.[71]

Revolutionary organizers also admired Sparta. Illuminist interest in classical antiquities led them to Sparta, and Jacob Talmon writes that Robespierre, St. Just, and their followers upheld Sparta as the ideal of liberty. They believed that this militarized Greek society molded young men to obey the laws of virtue, to love reason, and to live equally. Superstition and contradiction were eliminated from Sparta, negating the need for politics. Liberty, in this narrative, was freedom from corruption and myth.[72] Revolutionary admiration for Sparta implied rejection of Christian passivity. The revolutionary favored the militant disciplinarian and loathed the moneychanger.

Mormon observers, in similitude with revolutionary organizers, also praised Spartan political, social, and cultural mores. Characteristics singled out for admiration included the "republic" of Sparta's "constitutional ferocity" and "solidarity."[73] Church member Mosiah Hancock re-

70. Levi Edgar Young, April 6, 1951, *Report of the Semi-annual Conference of the Church of Jesus Christ of Latter-day Saints*, 29 (hereafter cited as *Conference Report*). Other references to seven in Mormon, Masonic, and numerological sources include Obert C. Tanner, Lewis M. Rogers, and Sterling M. McMurrin, *Toward Understanding the New Testament*, 379; Toscano and Toscano, *Strangers in Paradox*, 290; Francis Barrett, *The Magus, or Celestial Intelligencer; Being a Complete System of Occult Philosophy*, 117; Morgan, *Illustrations of Masonry*, 40–41; James Hastings, ed., *Encyclopaedia of Religion and Ethics*, s.v. "Numbers"; and Morton Scott Enslin, *Christian Beginnings*, 21, 358.

71. Billington, *Fire in the Minds of Men*, 133.

72. McIntosh, *Rose Cross*, 105; Talmon, *Origins of Totalitarian Democracy*, 142–44; Manuel and Manuel, *Utopian Thought in the Western World*, 573. Proto-communist Joseph-Alexander-Victor Hupay looked to Russia in search of "a Spartan people, the true nursery of a better race of men than ours." Quoted in Billington, *Fire in the Minds of Men*, 80.

73. Letter to Oliver Cowdery, in *Latter-day Saints' Messenger and Advocate* 1 (June 1835): 140 (hereafter cited as *Messenger and Advocate*); "Ancient History—No. 7: The Republic of Sparta," *Messenger and Advocate* 3 (August 1837): 552–53; "Ancient History. No. 8: The Republic of Athens,"

called that the Mormon community was defended against Missourian persecutors in 1838 by "a few staunch men in the Church known as the Spartan group, [men] full of virtue."[74] Similarly, in 1846 the rearguard covering the Mormon crossing of the Mississippi at Nauvoo was referred to as the "Spartan band."[75]

It is difficult to know for sure whether Smith and other Mormon leaders consciously thought of Spartanism, Masonry, or Illuminism as providing the method and rationale for a premillennial seizure of power. Neither can we certify that Mormons knowingly borrowed Pythagorean geometry to model the future. Similarly, Lynn Hunt has studied the influence of Masonry on the French Revolution but cannot ascertain whether uses of Masonic symbols in revolutionary iconography were conscious acts.[76] To corroborate the organizational and numerological connections, the researcher must look for other signs of revolution in Mormon discourse. These additional symbols and metaphors warned of upheavals that would transform a profane world into a celestial orb.

Symbols and Icons

One of the most famous icons of the French Revolution, the liberty cap—or *bonnet rouge*—was present in Mormon iconography. Liberty caps were copies of Phrygian caps, headgear given to freed slaves in the Roman Empire. Artists of the French Revolution exalted Marianne, the Goddess of Reason, and usually adorned her in the gray or red wool cap associated with French republicanism.[77]

Messenger and Advocate 3 (September 1837): 566. Other admirations of Spartan society include Charles H. Hart, October 5, 1913, *Conference Report*, 42; Charles H. Hart, October 5, 1930, *Conference Report*, 116; Marvin O. Ashton, October 7, 1939, *Conference Report*, 63; Blaine Carmon Hardy, *Solemn Covenant: The Mormon Polygamous Passage*, 95; and Hugh Nibley, *Approaching Zion*, 489–90.

74. Mosiah Lyman Hancock, *Autobiography of Mosiah Lyman Hancock*, 15.

75. Journal History, September 11, 1846, 2; ibid., September 12, 1846, 8; ibid., September 15, 1846, 6; Hubert Howe Bancroft, *History of Utah, 1540–1886*, 238; James B. Allen and Glen M. Leonard, *Story of the Latter-day Saints*, 222.

76. Hunt, *Politics, Culture, and Class in the French Revolution*, 113 note 58.

77. John Paxton, *Companion to the French Revolution*, 35; Simon Schama,

The Phrygian cap appeared on the seal of the Quorum of the Twelve Apostles in 1845. The cap is circumscribed by nine stars (significant in Royal Arch Masonry). An acronym circling the seal stands for "Private Seal of the Twelve Apostles in the Last Dispensation All Over the World."[78] One scholar has identified the Phrygian cap on the seal of the Twelve as representative of "human sovereignty."[79] Members of the Quorum of the Twelve commissioned to devise the seal borrowed the image from Jacob Boehme's *Theosophical Works*.[80] The same emblem was pressed into Mormon coins minted in the Utah Territory in 1849 and 1850.

The apostolic Phrygian cap surmounts an all-seeing eye, a symbol associated with Masonry and one of the most enduring icons in Mormon culture.[81] Sometimes referred to as the "eye of Providence" or the "Egyptian eye," the all-seeing eye was part of the Great Seal of the United States, first proposed to a committee of the Continental Congress during the American Revolution. The eye also watched over Festivals of Federation in revolutionary France.[82] Original drawings of the Nauvoo Temple indicate that all-seeing eyes appeared at the top of its semi-circular windows.[83] In Utah Brigham Young ordered that the all-seeing eye be displayed on documents and properties owned by the Church.[84] The eye also adorned stationery and banknotes.[85] When the Salt Lake Temple was completed in 1893, the eye was prominently dis-

Citizens: A Chronicle of the French Revolution, 603–4; Hunt, *Politics, Culture, and Class in the French Revolution*, 59, 75, 86, 112–13, 118.

78. Dean C. Jessee, ed., "The John Taylor Nauvoo Journal, January 1845–September 1845," 34, 105; Quinn, *Mormon Hierarchy: Origins of Power*, 649; Owens, "Joseph Smith and Kabbalah," 149.

79. Hastings, *Encyclopaedia of Religion and Ethics*, s.v. "Crown."

80. Owens, "Joseph Smith and Kabbalah," 147; Brooke, *Refiner's Fire*, 273.

81. Roberts, "Where Are the All-Seeing Eyes?" 36–38, 40–44.

82. Edward W. Richardson, *Standards and Colors of the American Revolution*, 11–12; Hunt, *Politics, Culture, and Class in the French Revolution*, 60.

83. Matthew B. Brown and Paul Thomas Smith, *Symbols in Stone: Symbolism on the Early Temples of the Restoration*, 106–7.

84. Journal History, November 18, 1868. An all-seeing eye still stares at worshipers in the Tabernacle designed by Miles Romney in St. George, Utah.

85. For its use in the Nauvoo and Salt Lake temples, see Andrew, *Early Temples of the Mormons*, 90, 111, 115, 117. A sketch of the Nauvoo Masonic Hall depicts an all-seeing eye in the pediment. See Hayden, *Seven American Utopias*, 134.

played.[86] For European radicals the all-seeing eye symbolized vigilance; its gaze protected revolutionary regimes from counter-revolutionary action. This connection to the revolutionary tradition is reflected in the way Church leaders referred to the all-seeing eye for years after Smith's death. For Mormons it represented the divine gaze that searched the hearts of men and uncovered malefactors.[87]

Another elixir found in revolutionary symbolism is fire and light. "The heart of the revolutionary faith, like any faith, is fire," writes Billington. Flame figured prominently in the rituals of the Illuminati, the Freemasons, and the Philadelphians who opposed Napoleon. The Italian Carbonari who yearned to unite Italy drew inspiration from burning charcoal. Several revolutionary cabals also appreciated the lights of the firmament—sun, moon, and North Star—which also adorn several Mormon temples.[88] When detractors laughed at French Philadelphians for attempting to use a matchstick as a lever to overturn the monarchy, their leader replied, "With a match one has no need of a lever; one does not lift up the world, one burns it." Fire represented the conviction that rationalism would burn away the old world and light the path to the new. For the revolutionary, observes Billington, "there was also the more pointed millennial assumption that on the new day that was dawning, the sun would never set."[89] Festivals in revolutionary France celebrated Paris as the home of the sun.[90]

---

86. Brown and Smith, *Symbols in Stone*, 140.

87. See examples in Orson Hyde, October 6, 1854, *Journal of Discourses*, 2:84; John Taylor, November 16, 1873, *Journal of Discourses*, 16:301; Rulon S. Wells, April 7, 1929, *Conference Report*, 104; Charles A. Callis, October 6, 1939, *Conference Report*, 27; Joseph F. Merrill, April 7, 1945, *Conference Report*, 115; Smith et al., *History of the Church*, 3:lxxiv; Hugh Nibley, "How Firm a Foundation! What Makes It So," 34; and Quinn, *Early Mormonism and the Magic World View*, 61. Owens says the all-seeing eye was an Egyptian symbol that represented divine truth and reason and the "uncreated intelligence" of God. See "Joseph Smith and Kabbalah," 145.

88. Billington, *Fire in the Minds of Men*, 133.

89. Ibid., 6.

90. On the belief in solar (universal) revolution, see ibid., 6, 48, 77, 95, 103; Talmon, *Origins of Totalitarian Democracy*, 213. Tommaso Campanella's utopian novel *City of the Sun* (1602) drew from the sun's imagery and the story of "solarian" citizens who had mastered the secrets of communal

The Latter-day Saints spoke of light and fire in the same revolutionary context. Zion replaced Paris in Mormon geography, but the sun still illuminated the path leading to man's divine potential. The sun represented the highest degree of glory in the Mormon heaven—a reminder, as French radicals had insisted, of what man could become. In 1857, as two thousand federal troops marched toward Utah to enforce federal authority rumored to have been flouted by Mormon leaders, Apostle Lorenzo Snow assured Salt Lake City denizens that their enemy would "melt away as before the morning sun." The radiance of Zion would then "spread and increase until she holds dominion over all the nations of the earth."[91] Orson Pratt once conjectured that the candlepower of the "Great Capital City" of Zion would negate the need for gas lighting.[92]

In 1845 Parley P. Pratt set the future ablaze. Recalling that Joseph Smith said he would "lay a foundation that will revolutionize the whole world," Pratt rejoined: "[Joseph Smith] kindled a fire—We [apostles] will fan the flame."[93] Pratt's rhetoric matched the imagery used by Russian

organization and world government. See Manuel and Manuel, *Utopian Thought in the Western World*, 271–79. For a Masonic interpretation of light as the cause of life and representative of a single unifying deity, see Pike, *Morals and Dogma*, 13.

91. Lorenzo Snow, October 7, 1857, *Journal of Discourses*, 5:326.

92. Orson Pratt, March 10, 1872, *Journal of Discourses*, 14:355. For supporting references to Zion as source of light, perfection, expansion, or truth, see Pratt, "American Exiles' Memorial to Congress" (1838), in David J. Whittaker, ed., *The Essential Orson Pratt*, 142; Kenney, *Wilford Woodruff's Journal*, October 5, 1851, and December 16, 1855, 4:69, 366; Brigham Young, "A Word to the Churches Abroad," *Times and Seasons* 5 (January 1, 1845): 762; Smith et al., *History of the Church*, 7:347; Orson Hyde, April 6, 1853, *Journal of Discourses*, 2:48; Amasa Lyman, December 2, 1855, *Journal of Discourses*, 3:149; Franklin D. Richards, January 11, 1857, *Journal of Discourses*, 4:162; Wilford Woodruff, January 1, 1871, *Journal of Discourses*, 14:4; Moses Thatcher, August 28, 1885, *Journal of Discourses*, 26:307; George Teasdale, October 4, 1897, *Conference Report*, 11–12; J. G. McQuarrie, April 4, 1904, *Conference Report*, 41; German E. Ellsworth, April 4, 1908, *Conference Report*, 43; and Winslow Farr Smith, October 7, 1921, *Conference Report*, 55.

93. Smith et al., *History of the Church*, 6:365. See also Daniel 2:34, 45 in the KJV. For interpretations of Smith's militancy, see Quinn, *Mormon*

revolutionaries. The Decembrists of 1817–25, one faction of which plotted to murder the family of the czar, rallied to the motto "From the spark comes the flame."[94] Several revolutionary journals, including the forerunner of Lenin's *Pravda*, were entitled *Iskra* (The Spark).[95] At the 1849 Fourth of July celebration in Utah Territory, Mormon orators stoked the imagination of the settlers. Elder Phineas Richards, a Danite and member of the Council of Fifty, served notice that the people of the Territory had inherited the "holy fire" of revolutionary ardor.[96] Jane Mason, a Mormon working class woman, wrote a poem that was published in the *Millennial Star* and later in the *Frontier Guardian*. She spoke of a "meteor blaze" that would turn "darkness into day"; then "sons of the mental light" would turn the earth into Paradise.[97]

Mormon Print, Proclamations, and Fiction

"The smell of printer's ink," Billington writes, "is the incense of modern revolutionary organization."[98] Social revolutionaries, following the lead of Irish Chartist George Harney, chose variations of *Star*, *Polar Star*, or *North/Northern Star* as the titles of their organs during the 1840s.[99] One example is Mormonism's British periodical, the *Latter-day*

Hierarchy: Origins of Power, 137; Hill, *Quest for Refuge*, 76–86, 130–31, 136–37, 140–41; Parley P. Pratt, "Proclamation to the Church of Jesus Christ of Latter-day Saints: Greeting," *Millennial Star* 5 (March 1845): 151.

94. Billington, *Fire in the Minds of Men*, 6.

95. Ibid., 322–23. A communist newspaper in America supporting the Republican side in the Spanish Civil War was similarly named *The Spark*. See Allen Guttmann, *The Wound in the Heart: America and the Spanish Civil War*, 158.

96. Eliza R. Snow, comp., *Biography and Family Record of Lorenzo Snow: One of the Twelve Apostles of the Church of Jesus Christ of Latter-day Saints*, 101–2.

97. Jane Mason, "Truth," *Millennial Star* 9 (August 1, 1849): 239; and *Frontier Guardian*, March 20, 1850, [4]. Compare to Orson Pratt's declaration that Zion will "illuminate the nations and the dark corners of the earth" in "Celestial Marriage," *The Seer* 1 (December 1853): 187.

98. Billington, *Fire in the Minds of Men*, 44.

99. Ibid., 106, 188, 321, 332, 374. The Nauvoo-based *Times and Seasons* and Britain-based *Millennial Star* printed extracts from Harney's Chartist paper, *The Northern Star* (founded 1838 in Leeds, England by Feargus

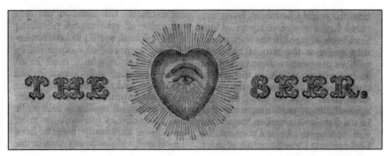

The masthead of Orson Pratt's 1853–54 Washington, DC periodical *The Seer*. Image provided by and used with permission of the Church History Department of the Church of Jesus Christ of Latter-day Saints.

Saints' Millennial Star, first printed in 1840. The first Mormon paper published in France in 1850, *L'Etoile du Deseret* (The Star of Deseret), invoked the North Star, and associated in Mormon symbolism with guidance toward perfection.[100]

Still more striking is the Illuminist iconography employed in Orson Pratt's *The Seer*, an apologetic periodical published 1853–54 in Washington, DC The heart-shaped all-seeing eye radiating light on the paper's masthead looks very similar to a Rosicrucian image depicting a radiant lantern atop a similar all-seeing eye. Arching over the lantern in the Rosicrucian iteration was the word "Illuminor," from which the Illuminati had derived their name.[101] Revolutionary iconography also decorated the masthead of another Mormon paper, *The Mormon*. Printed

---

O'Connor). Harney became a friend of Marx and Engels, who wrote articles for the *Northern Star*. See John Simkin, "The Northern Star."

100. "Appendix 3: Church Periodicals," 1661–63. Mormon speakers often associated the polar star with divine guidance. See Charles H. Hart, April 5, 1921, *Conference Report*, 138; Harold B. Lee, October 1, 1955, *Conference Report*, 55; Harold B. Lee, October 3, 1964, *Conference Report*, 86; Buerger, *Mysteries of Godliness*, 145–46; Brown and Smith, *Symbols in Stone*, 156; Roberts, "Where Are the All-Seeing Eyes?" 42. The German, Scandinavian, and Dutch versions of the *Millennial Star* were also translated *North[ern] Star*.

101. Billington, *Fire in the Minds of Men*, 95; Owens, "Joseph Smith and Kabbalah," 148; Frances A. Yates, *The Rosicrucian Enlightenment*, 210.

An illustration from Daniel Cramer's 1617 Rosicrucian text *Societas Jesus et Rosae Crucis Vera*, as published in Adam McLean, *The Rosicrucian Emblems of Daniel Cramer: The True Society of Jesus and the Rosy Cross*, 29. Used with permission of the author.

by Apostle John Taylor in New York, *The Mormon* featured two crossed ensigns of star-and-stripe design that resembled the kingdom flags discussed later in this chapter. Phrygian caps dangled at the ends of both flagstaves. The masthead also juxtaposed favorite slogans of the French revolutionaries, such as "virtue" and "liberty," with the religious invocation of "faith." "Intelligence" also stands out—the epistemological cousin of "reason." Other symbols used in the masthead included the all-seeing eye, bursting light, stars, and a beehive.[102] The beehive warrants comment. Though Illuminists referred to themselves as "the Perfectibilists," they had also considered calling themselves "the Bees," one of the most widely recognized symbols in Utah and in Mormonism.[103]

---

102. See picture and description in B. H. Roberts, *The Life of John Taylor: Third President of the Church of Jesus Christ of Latter-day Saints*, 246–47. *The Mormon* was headquartered on Nassau and Ann Streets between the offices of *The Herald* and Horace Greeley's *Tribune*.

103. See Billington, *Fire in the Minds of Men*, 94.

In revolutionary circles political and social commentary were supplemented by fiction. While poetry and opera have usually been identified as the preferred expression of national revolutionaries, utopian novels were equally significant. Fictional prose allowed speculative forays into the future state of man, inspiring social revolutionaries in their aspirations to universal harmony.[104] Thomas More's mythical *Utopia* (1516) told of property equality that would abolish scenes of starving people living near the bulging granaries of the rich.[105] In the eighteenth century, Enlightenment philosophers began to question the medieval belief in an inevitable decay from primordial glory. Instead, heaven would come to the profane world and stay. French utopian Louis Sebastien Mercier's novel *L'An 2440* (1768) was among the first to voice hope for a "perfect state of man that might endure as a consequence of inevitable progress" on earth.[106]

The Book of Mormon, according to historian Clyde Forsberg, contains reformist and radical thinking dating to the 1820s and before. Joseph Smith's founding book has "the moral edification of the common people in mind" and shows traces of the revolutionary Anabaptists of the eighteenth century.[107] Between 1850 and 1880 Church leaders took a dim view of novels, but Mormon observers sometimes communicated in fiction to explain the future in a manner parallel to the earliest ideologues of the revolutionary idea.[108]

In 1844 Parley P. Pratt finished a fictional work titled *Angel of the Prairies*. Pratt's story tells of a young man's dream in which self-serving

---

104. For the place of the novel in the formation of utopian and revolutionary thought, see Billington, *Fire in the Minds of Men*, 587 note 81; Sidney Lens, *Radicalism in America*, 151.

105. Manuel and Manuel, *Utopian Thought in the Western World*, 125.

106. Ibid., 415, 458–60.

107. Clyde R. Forsberg, Jr., "Retelling the Greatest Story Ever Told: Popular Literature as Scripture in Antebellum America." Mark D. Thomas discusses the Mormon canon as sophisticated fiction in *Digging in Cumorah: Reclaiming Book of Mormon Narratives*. Viola Sachs ably summarizes the book's retelling of American cosmology in "The Holy Scriptures and the Scripture of the New Cosmogony."

108. After 1880, fiction was regularly featured in Church periodicals. See Matthew Durrant and Neal E. Lambert, "From Foe to Friend: The Mormon Embrace of Fiction."

men seized power in the United States through the electoral process. Disgusted by the corruption of the venal government, the "millennial empire" moved west, restored the purity of the original republic, defeated an invasion force sent against it, and established a world government—all within "one short century."[109] Historians have read *Angel of the Prairies* as a story rooted both in American Manifest Destiny and the early Mormon millennial tradition, but it also brims with revolutionary implications.[110] A "more perfect liberty and freedom" made possible by a second revolution is juxtaposed to degraded Jacksonian individualism. Corruption and individualism had destroyed the first republic, only to be replaced by a more sublime liberty reminiscent of extreme French democracy. Pratt's expectation that liberty would be lost and then permanently restored resembles the idea of the unfinished revolution that sustained French republicans after the Thermidorian reaction of 1794. Having survived the overthrow of Robespierre, radicals consecrated their lives to egalitarian principles. Members of Babeuf's "Society of Equals" saw themselves as Mormon leaders did—as the intelligentsia of the revolution that would "put back the destinies of Liberty in the hands of truth which is eternal, rather in the hands of men who pass."[111]

Noticeably absent in Pratt's fictional narrative is any mention of a role for supernatural power in creating the new order. The "temple of liberty" mentioned in *Angel of the Prairies* was "enlarged" by men acting as God's agents *before* the Second Coming.[112] The "temple of liberty" bears a striking resemblance to the "triumph of reason" celebrated during the French Revolution. During that celebration, young women costumed as the Goddess of Reason sat atop indoor mountains raised in cathedrals. Their purpose was to educate the masses about the new

109. Parley P. Pratt, *Angel of the Prairies; a Dream of the Future*, 19–20.

110. Kenneth H. Winn, *Exiles in a Land of Liberty: Mormons in America, 1830–1846*, 187–93; Ernest Lee Tuveson, *Redeemer Nation: The Idea of America's Millennial Role*, 181–83.

111. Talmon, *Origins of Totalitarian Democracy*, 134; Billington, *Fire in the Minds of Men*, 9.

112. Freemasonry praised the republican ideal but did not exempt republics from revolution should they engage in territorial or commercial aggrandizement or fail to maintain civil virtue. See Pike, *Morals and Dogma*, 69, 73–74.

deity.[113] There are also hints of socialist methods in Pratt's fiction. The novella ends with the dreamer returning to reality when a landlord awakens him. The implicit contrast with the dreamer's utopia suggests that forms of rent had been destroyed in the dream.

Pratt wrote another futuristic piece the following year that underscored the same point: a second, more comprehensive American revolution was near. This time the setting was well into the millennial era, after the merging of the continents. The Saints had built the 145th "City of Joseph," and the people were celebrating the "Feast of the Lord to Joseph and Hyrum Smith." While the people celebrated in the fashion of revolutionary Paris, a time capsule dating to the "old Government of the United States" was opened. In it the people found a coin embossed with the Statue of Liberty, which they interpreted as representing the tyranny of the "old world."[114]

Red and Black, Festivals, Earthquakes, Volcanoes, and Wind

Mormon literature of the nineteenth century is redolent with red—the color most closely associated with revolution. Originally, government troops displayed the red flag to warn that order would be imposed by force. Rioters responded by mockingly brandishing it first. The red flag of revolution appeared for the first time in Paris in 1832 in conjunction with the funeral of popular general Maximilien Lamarque (the setting for *Les Misérables*). By 1848 the red flag, having been "steeped in the blood of the workers," as Karl Marx proclaimed, replaced the black flag as the workers' banner. At an international gathering in 1850, George Julian Harney became the first to disclaim his own national colors in favor of the red flag. Social revolutionaries chose red because it was found in the revolutionary tricolor of virtually every nation. It reflected simplicity and universal transformation.[115]

---

113. Hunt, *Politics, Culture, and Class in the French Revolution*, 63–64.

114. Parley P. Pratt, "One Hundred Years Hence, 1845," *Nauvoo Neighbor*, September 10, 1845, in Peter L. Crawley, ed. and comp., *The Essential Parley P. Pratt*, 143. On the significance of the festival in revolutionary France, see Billington, *Fire in the Minds of Men*, 205; Hunt, *Politics, Culture, and Class in the French Revolution*, 27–28, 60–65, 110–11.

115. Billington, *Fire in the Minds of Men*, 159–60, 281; Diana Lang, "Chinese

In the Mormon context, red emblems and imagery suggested revolutionary intent or militant redemption. Zion's camp, a Mormon force of two hundred men who marched to Missouri in 1834 to take back land lost in 1833, carried a white flag edged with red and emblazoned with an eagle. However, as the group penetrated further into the western part of the state and local hostility rose to a boil, it was deemed prudent to write the word "peace" on the ensign.[116] In 1839 Apostle Parley P. Pratt and other Mormons held prisoner in Columbia, Missouri displayed a white flag colored with a red eagle. Some Mormon writers have linked the eagle with the concept of militant Zion. The fact that the prisoners hung the flag from their cell window on the Fourth of July added to the defiant tone of the display.[117] When Apostle Heber C. Kimball arrived in Penwortham, England in 1840, a red flag was run up a pole at the train station to announce his arrival.[118] On January 8, 1846, shortly before Mormon wagon trains crossed the Mississippi River, John Taylor made a ghostly reference to revolutionary iconography. He related that he had seen seven men crossing the prairie toward Carthage, Illinois, where a mob had martyred the Smith brothers. The corps carried a large red flag while four horses pulled an artillery piece. The flag and cannon symbolized violent revolution; the draft horses may have represented the four horsemen of the apocalypse.[119] The red flag was reported again in September 1846: anti-Mormon agitators claimed that the Mormon Spartan Guard flew a red flag from the tower of the Nauvoo Temple.[120]

Reds"; and Johann Wolfgang von Goethe, *Goethe's Color Theory*, 314–15.

116. Levi Ward Hancock, *Autobiography of Levi Ward Hancock, 1803–36*, 55.

117. Smith et al., *History of the Church*, 3:399.

118. James B. Allen, Ronald K. Esplin, and David J. Whittaker, *Men with a Mission: The Quorum of the Twelve Apostles in the British Isles, 1837–1841*, 1.

119. Juanita Brooks, ed., *On the Mormon Frontier: The Diary of Hosea Stout, 1844–1861*, 1:103. Apostle Lyman Wight wore a red scarf during the 1838 Mormon War in Missouri. See LeSueur, *The 1838 Mormon War in Missouri*, 86.

120. Wandle Mace, *Autobiography of Wandle Mace*, 204. Joseph Smith intended to defend Nauvoo under a "standard of the nations." See Smith et al., *History of the Church*, 6:528. Red imagery is splashed throughout apostolic writings before 1840 as well. See, for example, Orson Hyde, "A Prophetic Warning," *Messenger and Advocate* 2 (July 1836): 344; Kenney, *Wilford Woodruff's Journal*, January 25, 1837, 1:123. In Hebraic usage,

Astronomical sightings of red emblems were also common among Mormons in the British Isles when economic depression struck in 1841–42. Four months after Kimball's red flag arrival in Penwortham, the *Millennial Star* reported that a "perfectly blood red flag was seen flying in the elements" over England, and that it changed to a cross and then to a sword. Following the apparitions was a "beautiful light which shot away toward the western hemisphere." For those too poor to pay for the transatlantic passage, there was another hope. References to "red rain" in the "Signs of the Times" section of the *Millennial Star* and the Nauvoo *Times and Seasons* suggested deliverance in the form of a heaven-sent revolution against the ruling class.[121]

The annihilation of oppressors by supernatural cosmic powers was a common theme among revolutionary millennialists. Norman Cohn and George Shepperson, in their study of colonized peoples and medieval millennialism, contend that social and political disruptions triggered anxiety about the stability of the cosmos. In this sense, believers in flying saucers share an astral fascination with millennialists among the ancient Hebrews and medieval Europeans as well as with Taiping rebels and Amazon Indian tribes who believed that gods or aliens would restore equilibrium to a world upset by foreigners and modernization.[122] Mormons, suspicious of Jacksonian political pluralism and

---

red represented bloodshed, war, and guilt. See Hastings, *Encyclopaedia of Religion and Ethics*, s.v. "Symbolism."

121. "Signs in the Heavens," *Millennial Star* 1 (December 1840): 215; Smith et al., *History of the Church*, 4:252. Other astral references to red during the 1841–44 period include "Earthquakes, and Fall of Red Rain," *Millennial Star* 3 (July 1842): 43–44; "Event of the Times," *Millennial Star* 4 (April 1844): 207; "Remarkable Phenomenon," *Times and Seasons* 2 (September 15, 1841): 549; "Another 'Shower of Flesh and Blood in Our Own Neighborhood,'" *Times and Seasons* 3 (November 1, 1841): 587; "A Shower of Flesh and Blood," *Times and Seasons* 5 (January 1, 1844): 388–90.

122. On the cosmic factor in sign-seeking and revolutionary millennialism, see essays by Norman Cohn and George Shepperson in Sylvia L. Thrupp, ed., *Millennial Dreams in Action: Studies in Revolutionary Religious Movements*, 41, 45. On social change during the early republican and Jacksonian period, see Melvyn Stokes and Stephen Conway, eds., *The Market Revolution in America: Social, Political, and Religious Expressions, 1800–1880*; and Hastings, *Encyclopaedia of Religion and Ethics*, "Sun,

commercialism, fixed their gazes on the cosmos in search of signs. They panted for evidence that the perfect time of the millennium and the perfect place of utopia would be upon them soon.

The year 1848 inspired more cosmic sightings in red. William I. Appleby wrote that "crimson and blood" were seen in the sky over New York. He also linked red imagery to Christ: "Behold the heavenly prince, clad in his garments, his vesture dyed in blood, emblem of vengeance, for the day of his redeemed has come, and . . . to this event the nations are hastening with the rapidity of time."[123] Against the backdrop of the Neapolitan and Swiss revolutions and the Irish potato famine, Appleby thought that "The Lord is making an inquisition for blood, and will bring down the high and exalted where Royalty, Judges, and Rulers now sit."[124]

Red as a theme of revolution and vengeance continued into 1849. Orson Hyde's *Frontier Guardian* assured readers that God stood behind the democratic violence rippling across Europe. The people's misery and thirst for national identity had "ripened into revolutions," "carrying away thrones and royalty on its crimsoned flood."[125] A poem in the *Frontier Guardian* told the story of class conflict in color. The "Purple Robe" of royalty had been crushed, and Germany had risen like "a cyclops—dark his brow with hatred, red his eye with wrath."[126] In the 1849 prospectus of the *Guardian*, Hyde predicted that Christ would return with his robe sprinkled red with the blood of the faithful, exact revenge on behalf of those who had died in the revolutions, and complete the destruction of the nations seen in Nebuchadnezzar's dream.[127]

Moon, Stars." Also, "Atmospheric Phenomenon," *Times and Seasons* 3 (April 15, 1842): 758 explained how "portentous visions" in the sky reveal things to come.

123. William I. Appleby, "History of the Signs of the Times for the Benefit of the Church of the Latter-day Saints," October 1 and November 20, 1841, 159, 167. For Christ's red robe as a symbol of vengeance, see Doctrine and Covenants 133:48 and Brown and Smith, *Symbols in Stone*, 29–30.

124. William I. Appleby, Autobiography and Journal, February 4, 1848, 217.

125. "The Destroyer Already Rideth upon the Face of the Waters," reprinted from the *Frontier Guardian* in *Millennial Star* 11 (August 15, 1849): 253.

126. John C. Lord, "Kings and Thrones are Falling," *Frontier Guardian*, January 9, 1850, [4].

127. Orson Hyde, "Prospectus," *Frontier Guardian*, February 7, 1849, [4].

In the years following the revolutions of 1848, Mormon leaders orchestrated celebrations loaded with revolutionary content. At the 1849 Fourth of July celebration in the Salt Lake Valley, keynote speaker Phineas Richards (Council of Fifty member and former Danite) laced his address with blood and revolution. He portrayed the martyred Smith brothers as revolutionary heroes and said that Brigham Young had "unsheathed his sword" to rescue republicanism from corruption. Mormon militia marched past the reviewing stand carrying staves with the top halves painted red. Waving amidst the ranks of other marchers was a flag bearing the slogan "Liberty or Death."[128] A similar event occurred at the Church's London Conference in 1851 and became commonplace at conferences in the British Isles. The 1851 festival included a band, marching women, and twelve branch presidents carrying staves followed by twelve more staff-carrying "fathers in Israel."[129] These celebrations matched the atmosphere of the French Festivals of Federation. In Salt Lake City, London, and Paris, the "pageant masters of the new regimes" used symbols and choreography to instruct the masses and reinforce their own sociopolitical authority.[130]

In addition to color symbolism and festive gatherings, Mormon observers associated their expectations with earthquakes and volcanoes. Used as religious metaphor, seismic events signaled historical shifts, divine anger over man's injustice, or impending eschatological doom. As usual, the French Revolution invigorated the discussion. Clerical opinion divided as some British and American Protestants feared the irreligious rationalism unleashed by the Jacobins, while others, including radical millennialists, predicted that the fall of the French monarchy portended the destruction of papal dominion.[131] On both sides, ministers and Bible

---

128. Snow, *Biography and Family Record of Lorenzo Snow*, 97.

129. See the program of the British Mission's London Conference on June 2, 1851, at the Masonic Hall on Queen Street, described in Peter L. Crawley, *A Descriptive Bibliography of the Mormon Church*, 2:579.

130. Hunt, *Politics, Culture, and Class in the French Revolution*, 60–61.

131. For American and British clerical assessments of the French Revolution, see Charles H. Lippy, "'Waiting for the End:' The Social Context of American Apocalyptic Religion," 43; Gary B. Nash, "The American Clergy and the French Revolution." For the French Revolution's negative impact on Joseph Smith's New England and New York environment, see Robert N. Hullinger, *Joseph Smith's Response to Skepticism*, 21. American

societies since the French Revolution equated the earthquake mentioned in Revelation 11:13 with political and social upheaval.

Social and national revolutionaries borrowed this seismic symbolism from religionists. During the 1790s, St. Just and Sylvain Maréchal were among the first to use the revolution-as-volcano comparison.[132] Later, in the wake of the 1830 revolution, French revolutionaries alluded to lava to convey the leveling idea of class warfare, and Victor Hugo described the revolution of 1832 celebrated in *Les Misérables* as a volcanic force.[133] Karl Marx, after the abortive worker's revolt of the Paris June Days insurrection, linked the earthquake metaphor to urban revolution.[134] Garibaldi's Red Shirts carried a black flag emblazoned with a volcano. The flag's black color mourned unredeemed Italy, parts of which were ruled by Austrian Hapsburgs and Spanish Bourbons; the volcano belched the explosion that would overthrow foreign dominion.[135] When John Taylor warned of "volcanic fires," he was following an

------

minister Ethan Smith preached against French deism in *Key to Revelation* (1833), 130–48, quoted in Leroy Edwin Froom, *The Prophetic Faith of Our Fathers: The Historical Development of Prophetic Interpretation*, 4:190–93.

Thomas Goodwin, John Philipot, and Robert Flemming predicted a revolution in France before it happened. See Froom, *Prophetic Faith*, 2:642–49. Joseph Priestley linked British and American interpretations of the French Revolution as a universal event destined to eliminate the power of the Catholic Church and inaugurate new forms of government more congenial to evangelizing. See *The State of Europe Compared with Ancient Prophecies* (1794), 25–27, quoted in Froom, *Prophetic Faith*, 2:642–49. John Livingston sermonized that the "last struggle" against the papacy "may be violent." All nations that supported the French monarchy would "suffer the wrath of God." See *Glory of the Redeemer* (1799), 8–29, quoted in Froom, *Prophetic Faith*, 4:71. For popular millennial fervor heightened by the French Revolution, see John F. C. Harrison, *The Second Coming: Popular Millenarianism, 1780–1850*, 67, 75–78.

132. Billington, *Fire in the Minds of Men*, 70.

133. Ibid., 147, 156; and Victor Hugo, *Les Misérables*, 548, 707.

134. Karl Marx, "The Class Struggles in France," [1850], in David McLellan, ed., *Karl Marx: Selected Writings*, 290.

135. Billington, *Fire in the Minds of Men*, 151. The volcano-revolution metaphor was also used by Mazzini. See ibid., 147.

established literary template. According to Taylor, the masses needed "but a spark to set them a flame" in revolution.[136]

References to earthquakes in Mormon literature during the 1840s and 1850s similarly signified political revolution.[137] In 1843 the *Times and Seasons* explained: "Earthquake, when used symbolically, signifies a revolution of a kingdom." Specifically, the statement in Revelation 11:13 that there "was a great earthquake, and a tenth part of the city fell" referred to the occupation of Rome and the ejection of the pope by medieval Germanic tribes.[138] In 1844 the *Times and Seasons* related earthquakes to the structure of the circle. In answer to the question of whether the Church could fail, the paper declared,

> No! Times and seasons may change, revolution may succeed revolution, thrones may be cast down, and empires be dissolved, earthquakes may rend the earth from centre to circumference, the mountains may be hurled out of their places, and the mighty ocean be moved from its bed; but amidst the crash of worlds and the crack of matter, truth, eternal truth, must remain unchanged.[139]

Apostle Lorenzo Snow used earthquakes in the political sense in 1850 when he wrote: "With regard to Romanism, let no one imagine that our difficulties are decreased because the Pope has quarreled with the king of Piedmont. The influence of papal domination does not crumble away before the earthquakes of political controversy."[140] John Taylor employed the earthquake metaphor the same way. "Earthquakes tremble and thrones roll down, and empires are destroyed," he wrote. Taylor affirmed the

---

136. John Taylor, April 9, 1882, *Journal of Discourses*, 23:63.

137. Janne M. Sjödahl, *An Introduction to the Study of the Book of Mormon*, 458. Apostle Bruce R. McConkie, the celebrated Mormon doctrinaire, while not directly interpreting earthquakes as political revolutions, suggested that they were "testimony of the Lord's power . . . to the people on earth." See Bruce R. McConkie, *Mormon Doctrine*, 212. Joseph Fielding Smith Jr. linked political revolution and earthquakes in *The Way to Perfection: Short Discourses on Gospel Themes*, 282–83.

138. "Millerism," *Times and Seasons* 4 (April 15, 1843): 171.

139. "The City of Nauvoo," *Times and Seasons* 5 (December 15, 1844): 744.

140. Lorenzo Snow, Letter to [Willard?] Richards, December 2, 1850, in Lorenzo Snow, *The Italian Mission*, 19.

Mormon view of history, warning that after the prophesying of the elders "will come the testimony of earthquakes, wars, [and] blood."[141]

Fixation on geological dynamics represented the hopes of peoples and the aspirations of nations. In 1848 Appleby led off his discussion of the revolutions with a reference to the "combustions of nature," especially earthquakes.[142] Missionaries in Paris expressed their pleasure at having gained a foothold for the kingdom of God in "the volcanic soil" of France.[143] Hyde, sure that social and political discontent would again reach a flash point, printed selections from other papers that lined up with post-1848 Mormon commentary. "The bloody scenes of 1848 . . . are about to be re-enacted," Hyde editorialized in the *Frontier Guardian* two months after Napoleon III's coup. "The volcanic fire, once kindled in France . . . when and where it will be quenched?" The coming upheaval, Hyde wrote, will be "the great struggle of the people for independence."[144] Louis Bertrand, a socialist republican turned Mormon, compared revolutionary fervor to Mount Vesuvius.[145] In 1859 Orson Pratt discussed the "revolutionary elements" of Europe as "fomenting, igniting, and belching forth [the] hot lava of destruction."[146] In Mormonism's materialistic theology, God's spirit trembled through the earth the same way he moved men's minds toward truth.

Mormon references to earthquakes, volcanoes, and other forces of nature paralleled Masonic and Illuminist usage. Italian students, excited by the 1789 revolution in France, borrowed from Illuminist phraseology when they compared the force in Europe to "the energy of the winds, which are bursting forth violently against oppression."[147] Masons taught that the forces of nature had their "parallelism in the moral word, in individuals, and nations. . . . The earthquakes that rend nations asunder, overturn thrones, and engulf monarchies and repub-

---

141. John Taylor, "John Taylor Letter, Hamburg, Germany, to W. Phillips, Wales, 1851 November 24."

142. Appleby, Autobiography and Journal, February 4, 1848, 217.

143. "A Sunday in Paris," *Millennial Star* 13 (November 1, 1851): 331.

144. "The Coming European Revolutions—Kossuth's Next Movements," *Frontier Guardian*, February 6, 1852, [4]; "The Tragedy of the Nations," reprinted from the *New York Tribune* in *Frontier Guardian*, June 13, 1849, [3].

145. Bertrand, *Memoirs of a Mormon*, 161.

146. Orson Pratt, August 13, 1859, *Journal of Discourses*, 7:213.

147. Billington, *Fire in the Minds of Men*, 98.

lics, have been long prepared for, like volcanic eruptions."[148] Mormons equated seismic and meteorological activity with the spirit of God acting in a revolutionary way. The *Evening and Morning Star* stated at the time of the abortive revolution in France in 1832 that a "wind that blows before a storm is sent forth to purify the world."[149] Orson Pratt referred to Book of Mormon prophecy in 1877 when he told a General Conference audience that not only would governments of Europe and western Asia be overthrown, but judgments "swift and terrible" would also hit the republics of the Western Hemisphere "like a fierce wind when they expect it not."[150] Brigham Young declared that Mormonism, "born in poverty, cradled in storms and reared in hurricanes, won't faint in earthquakes."[151]

Wilford Woodruff was also inclined to use the metaphor of wind as a revolutionary expression of the Church's destiny. "Three elements seem to have been chosen to go forth on a mission to visit the nations," he said: "fire, water, and wind." On another occasion he compared God's work to "wind sweeping across the nations." The Church was like an army, Woodruff assured Tabernacle attendees, and "no weapon formed against it would stop it."[152]

In summary, Mormon observers used tectonic and meteorological metaphors as a way to synchronize natural history, worldly revolutions, and sacred time.[153] Editors of the *Millennial Star*, for example, grouped earthquake and volcano reports together with sociopolitical and foreign news. Heavy concentrations of such reports were published in 1841–42, 1848–52, and 1853. They correspond with the second Chartist movement, the revolutions of 1848, and the year Napoleon III was crowned and the Crimean War began.

---

148. Pike, *Morals and Dogma of Freemasonry*, 90.

149. "Signs of the Times," *Evening and Morning Star* 1 (October 1832): 38.

150. Orson Pratt, February 25, 1877, *Journal of Discourses*, 18:339.

151. Journal History, July 4, 1854, 7.

152. Wilford Woodruff, October 23, 1881, *Journal of Discourses*, 22:345; and Wilford Woodruff, June 12 and 13, 1892, in Stuy, *Collected Discourses*, 3:83.

153. Ernest Robert Sandeen, *Roots of Fundamentalism: British and American Millenarianism, 1800–1930*, 22, 52.

The Flag of the Kingdom of God

On July 26, 1846, just two days after the vanguard pioneer company arrived in the Great Basin, Brigham Young and seven companions hiked to the top of Ensign Peak, overlooking the Salt Lake Valley. At the summit they unfurled the flag of the millennial kingdom of God. A later version of this standard featured blue and white horizontal stripes with twelve stars arranged in a circle in the upper-left canton. At the center of the circle was a single star. Another rendition had a plain white field and, in the canton, three stars in a triangle pattern surrounded by a circle of stars.[154] The circled stars resembling the American flag adopted in 1777 may have been derived from the Masonic symbolism of a "new constellation" in the firmament.[155] The canton with stars arranged in a triangle, reminiscent of Buonarroti's master grade sign of three triangularly arranged dots surrounded by a circle, probably represents the First Presidency.[156]

There are other variants of the flag of the Mormon millennial kingdom. Wilford Woodruff's diary contains a drawing of a pennant containing rectangular and triangular forms beneath a star, moon, and sun.[157] Most interesting is a flag purported to have been the "kingdom flag" of the Mormons brought by Samuel Brannan to California aboard the *Brooklyn*. The flag shows a robed woman crowned and surrounded by twelve stars. She could be Maiden Columbia, but she also bears a rough likeness to women depicted in French revolutionary illustrations representing republican government.[158]

---

154. For discussion of the "Flag of the Kingdom of God," see Ronald W. Walker, "'A Banner is Unfurled': Mormonism's Ensign Peak." Descriptions of Mormon ensigns paraded publicly may be found in Snow, *Biography and Family Record of Lorenzo Snow*, July 4, 1849, 97; Journal History, July 4, 1854, 1; and B. H. Roberts, *Comprehensive History of the Church of Jesus Christ of Latter-day Saints, 1830–1930*, 3:270–76. On revolutionary flags see Billington, *Fire in the Minds of Men*, 101, 159, 346. For a picture of the flags, see D. Michael Quinn, "The Flag of the Kingdom of God."

155. Billington, *Fire in the Minds of Men*, 562 note 59.

156. For Buonarroti's master sign and ritualistic layouts, discussed earlier in this chapter, see ibid., 106.

157. Kenney, *Wilford Woodruff's Journal*, May 29, 1847, 2:188.

158. Will Bagley, ed., *Scoundrel's Tale: The Samuel Brannan Papers*, 155–56; and Joan B. Landes, *Visualizing the Nation: Gender, Representation, and*

Whatever the "flag of the kingdom of God" looked like, it endured as a symbol of Mormon intentions. The flag represented the unification of the nations while simultaneously reinforcing Mormons' sense of separation from the United States. To stress both points Mormon officials ran the flag up liberty poles over a hundred feet high in full view of federal officials.[159] The blue color on the more popular versions of the flags also conveyed special meaning. In Hebraic symbolism blue stood for revelation.[160] The Mormon elite viewed the blue sky as a cosmic opening through which they might access the mysteries of the earth's millennial governance. From the skies, divine knowledge shone upon the earth.[161] Several early Mormon hymns signified universal salvation by the image of a flag. One penned by Parley P. Pratt proclaimed, "Come ye sons of doubt and wonder, / Indian, Moslem, Greek, or Jew; / All your shackles burst asunder— / Freedom's banner waves for you."[162]

From Models of Revolution to the Mountains of Utah

Masonic councils, ritualistic bonding, and simple geometric shapes had modeled the future state of the world and outlined the

---

Revolution in Eighteenth-Century France, 150, 161.

159. Roberts, *Comprehensive History of the Church*, 3:319, 274, 375, 493.

160. Hastings, *Encyclopaedia of Religion and Ethics*, s.v. "Symbolism"; Brown and Smith, *Symbols in Stone*, 140. At the July 4, 1849, celebration in Salt Lake City, twenty-four women in white with blue shoulder sashes marched past the reviewing stand. At a June 2, 1851, London Mission Conference celebration it was twenty-four young men. See Snow, *Biography and Family Record of Lorenzo Snow*, 97; and Crawley, *Descriptive Bibliography*, 2:579.

161. On the political importance of open-air events held in Paris, see Billington, *Fire in the Minds of Men*, 48–59; Hunt, *Politics and Culture in the French Revolution*, 60–61, 96–98, 110–11. Cloud stones on the center tower of the east façade of the Salt Lake Temple symbolize either providential knowledge or the Coming of Christ. See Andrew, *Early Temples of the Mormons*, 112, 116.

162. "Lo! The Gentile Chain Is Broken," in *Sacred Hymns and Spiritual Songs for the Church of Jesus Christ of Latter-day Saints*, 103. The same lyrics are found in "High on the Mountain Top," hymn no. 5 in *Hymns of the Church of Jesus Christ of Latter-day Saints*.

method to attain it. The presence in Mormonism of bloody skies, red flags, Phrygian caps, seismic events, and utopian fiction suggests fertilization from revolutionary thought. Mormon observers of the 1840s, alienated from national culture, welcomed predictions and movements that promised the destruction of the sociopolitical order preparatory to the redemption of Zion. Universal brotherhood was coming, but before the consummation God would see the world tinged with red.

Although revolutionary organization began in esoteric circles, secrecy gradually gave way to openness. As in 1792 when French radicalism arose from the underground cafés of the Palais-Royal to the open festivals of the Champ de Mars, the Mormon movement shifted venues as well. The secret meetings of Nauvoo were left behind for the open skies and mountaintops of the West.

CHAPTER 4

A MORMON CRITIQUE OF INDUSTRIALIZATION, 1860–1920

Resistance to the Mainstream

From the Civil War to 1889, the attention of the Mormon hierarchy was consumed by the struggle to live polygamy, sponsor migration to Utah, expand the Mormon settlement zone, and sustain an insular economy and a shadow government. But goals eventually shifted. In 1890 the Manifesto began a process that phased out the practice of polygamy. Utah statehood in 1896 transformed the Mormon kingdom into the Mormon Church. These changes produced rhetoric more deferential to capitalism and conventional American politics. In 1901 the editors of the *Improvement Era* deleted references to the overthrow of capitalists and aristocrats in a reprint of Parley P. Pratt's 1841 *Letter to Queen Victoria*.[1] Church leaders castigated labor unions and discouraged members from registering with the American Socialist Party.[2] Meanwhile, several Church leaders were prominent capitalists themselves. The Church's shift toward normative American culture led to administrative reform, rewriting of history, and changes in doctrinal

---

1. Parley P. Pratt, "Letter to the Queen of England: Touching the Signs of the Times and the Political Destiny of the World," *Times and Seasons* 3 (November 15, 1841): 593–96, reprinted in *Improvement Era* 4 (October 1901): 883–94.

2. For example, the moral of the story in "The Strike," *Contributor* 15 (October 1894): 744–58, was that strikers were cowardly whelps. The Church's Liverpool office urged workers to wait until "revealed religion was accepted by all" in "The Labor Problems of the Day," *Latter-day Saints' Millennial Star* 56 (May 7, 1894): 296–98 (hereafter cited as *Millennial Star*). "The Strike Craze," reprinted from the *Juvenile Instructor* in *Deseret News*, June 15, 1903, posited that strikers were extremists "devoid of the spirit of reason and common justice."

works. Statements appeared that denied that Joseph Smith, Brigham Young, and John Taylor had ever intended to establish an earthly theocratic kingdom. In 1907 the First Presidency declared that "overthrow of earthly governments" violated timeless Church principles: our "loyalty to the United States [has] outlived the memory of all the wrongs inflicted upon our fathers and ourselves."[3] In 1924 a new edition of *Articles of Faith* by Apostle James E. Talmage dropped references to equality.[4] The charismatic leadership of the pioneer Church appeared to be giving way to the bureaucratic style of a mature institution. Prophets turned into managers, universalists into nationalists, and separatists into assimilationists, or so it seemed.[5]

But Mormonism's revolutionary dream did not die. The task of conveying the dream devolved upon younger Mormon leaders yearning for the justice anticipated under a divinely inspired government of global span. The Mormon observers of this generation bridged the gap between the expectations of 1848 and the Mexican Revolution of 1910. They studied the writings of revolutionaries like Karl Marx, and also considered non-revolutionary utopian options like those of Charles Fourier, Edward Bellamy, and Henry George. The disturbing effects of industrialization offered Mormon observers scenarios that tested the validity of their revolutionary theories. The slow burn of worker discontent alerted them to coming conflict. Far from viewing the clash with trepidation, Mormon observers viewed worker empowerment and even social revolution as contingencies laden with millennial possibility.

---

3. "An Address to the World," March 26, 1907, in James R. Clark, comp., *Messages of the First Presidency of the Church of Jesus Christ of Latter-Day Saints, 1883–1964*, 4:150–54. For other examples of rewriting and de-emphasis, see Klaus Hansen, *Quest for Empire: The Political Kingdom of God and the Council of Fifty in Mormon History*, 185; Thomas G. Alexander, *Mormonism in Transition: A History of the Latter-day Saints, 1890–1930*, 182, 247–48.

4. Compare the 1899 edition of James E. Talmage's *The Articles of Faith: A Series of Lectures on the Principal Doctrines of the Church of Jesus Christ of Latter-day Saints*, 454 with page 409 of the 1924 edition of the same work.

5. On the Church's shift from social justice to pro-management advocacy, see Alexander, *Mormonism in Transition*, 186–89; and Davis Bitton, "Anti-Intellectualism in Mormon History," 125.

Preamble to Full-blown Industrialism

During the outburst of 1848, Mormon observers established a tradition of giving voice to social and political discontent. Mormon solutions to socioeconomic problems often edged closer to radicals like Augusti Blanqui, Karl Marx, and John Goodwin Barmby than they did to reformers like Robert Owen or Charles Fourier. Revolution—not reform—would end injustice. Awareness of class conflict came early to the Mormon mind. In 1832, a year after the first labor strike in America, the *Evening and Morning Star* reported that members of the upper classes held "Cholera Dances" that mocked the poor. But while the sick died by the thousands and the courtiers danced, "mobs were preparing to slay their tens of thousands." Revolution broke out in France that year. In England the 1832 Reform Bill was before Parliament. The *Star* summarized English sentiment with the phrase, "Reform or Revolution!"[6]

Class consciousness ripened among Mormon leaders as the Church turned its attention to Europe. From 1840 to 1841 nine members of the Quorum of the Twelve Apostles served missions in the British Isles.[7] In the words of one historian, the 1840s was "a decade of crisis, even in terms of classical economics."[8] Wilford Woodruff wrote that "the poor are in great bondage like the children of Israel"; in Ireland there was "much crying for bread."[9] John Taylor was likewise annoyed. When he

---

6. Foreign News, *Evening and Morning Star* 1 (July 1832): 14.

7. Malcolm R. Thorp, "The Setting for the Restoration in Britain: Political, Social, and Economic Conditions," 45; James B. Allen, Ronald K. Esplin, and David J. Whittaker, *Men with a Mission: The Quorum of the Twelve Apostles in the British Isles, 1837–1841*, 107–8; James B. Allen and Malcolm R. Thorp, "The Mission of the Twelve to England, 1840–41: Mormon Apostles and the Working Classes," 512–13. An economic slump in the potteries thirty miles south of Manchester, a major center of Mormon proselytizing, was reported in *Millennial Star* 3 (November 1842): 127–28. For the general European condition setting the stage for this chapter, see William L. Langer, *Political and Social Upheaval, 1832–1852*, 181–98.

8. Christopher Harvie, "The Rule of Law, 1789–1851," 450. An 1848 railroad boom employing a quarter of a million workers defused revolutionary ambitions in all but the most dedicated agitators. Ibid., 455.

9. Scott G. Kenney, ed., *Wilford Woodruff's Journal, 1833–1889, Typescript*, January 14, 1840, 1:405; Thomas G. Alexander, *Things in Heaven and*

saw a Mormon woman leave her husband and children to go to work, he lamented the "breaking up [of] those social endearments that united the family."[10] The apostles in England saw retribution from God as boiling up from the people as well as coming like lightning from above. Woodruff employed a literary metonym to warn capitalists how deliverance would occur: the workers, embodied in "Judah & Ephraim," would be the agents of their own emancipation and would "rise again & fulfill the word of God on thee!"[11]

Orson Spencer, president of the British Mission, ran an editorial in the *Latter-day Saints' Millennial Star* that critiqued the effects of uneven economic growth. "The rod of the Oppressor," he wrote, "has caused wailing and sorrow among the honest poor for a long time. The hire of the labourer has been kept back by fraud." High grain prices, a centralized currency, and railway speculation would benefit the rich at the expense of the poor. In this description of the maldistribution of wealth, Spencer treated readers to the "portentous signs of want, rebellion, and revolution."[12]

In 1840 the *Millennial Star* published an extract from the *Manchester Advertiser* that attacked the "lords and ladies" for living luxuriously while skyrocketing potato prices forced desperate Irishmen to plunder grain ships. The *Advertiser*'s analysis showed that Irish workers, "blank idle" one-fourth of the year, could not sustain a living. In the face of famine and exploitation, the paper's Dublin correspondent asked, "Dare we contemplate the end?"[13]

Earth: The Life and Times of Wilford Woodruff, a Mormon Prophet, 77, 89. For Woodruff's Irish observation see "The Year 1840" in Kenney, *Wilford Woodruff's Journal*, January 1, 1841, 2:4.

10. Allen, Esplin, and Whittaker, *Men with a Mission*, 108.

11. Kenney, *Wilford Woodruff's Journal*, June 8, 1840, 1:469. Woodruff's mention of Ephraim and Judah refers to Mormons' belief that they are blood descendents of the House of Israel. See Armand L. Mauss, "In Search of Ephraim: Traditional Mormon Conceptions of Lineage and Race," 143–49. For schemes and tropes in literary analysis, see Geoffrey N. Leech, *Linguistic Guide to English Poetry*, 152–53.

12. Editorial, *Millennial Star* 9 (November 1, 1847): 330–31.

13. "Distress of the People of Ireland," reprinted from *The Manchester Advertiser* in *Millennial Star* 1 (August 1840): 99–100. The article was also reprinted in *Times and Seasons* 2 (December 1, 1840): 231–32; and *Times and Seasons* 6 (April 1, 1845): 862–63. The second *Times and Seasons*

Mormon observers zeroed in on Irish discontent as one of several indicators pointing toward European upheaval. The Church's *Millennial Star* picked up stories demanding repeal of the 1800 Union Act (which joined Ireland to Great Britain) from *The Nation*, the militant "Young Ireland" journal of William Smith O'Brien. The *Millennial Star* also aired the views of Daniel and John O'Connell. The O'Connells were "Old Ireland" reformers advocating an independent Dublin parliament and Catholic access to senior legal positions but otherwise retaining ties to the British Crown. Both the Young and Old Ireland groups countenanced violence. Both wanted an Irish republic.[14]

During the 1840s Mormon observers also attacked the status quo in England. In a letter to Joseph Smith, missionary Alfred Cordon reviewed the labor problem. The wage system either drove men to work fifteen hours a day or denied them employment for long stretches. Gone were the old social bonds between master and laborer. Instead there were the "groans, and tears and wretchedness of the thousands." Great Britain, Cordon concluded, was "on the eve of a mighty revolution."[15]

In a tract published in 1841, Apostle Parley P. Pratt warned Queen Victoria of a revolutionary wave "more important in its consequences, than any which man has yet witnessed upon the earth: a revolution in which all the inhabitants of the earth are vitally interested, both reli-

---

printing attributed the extract to the *Northern Star*, a periodical owned by Chartist and Irish nationalist Feargus O'Connor. After 1844 the paper was edited by Julian Harney, who printed contributions by Karl Marx and Friedrich Engels. Harney would later print the first English translation of the *Communist Manifesto* in his paper *The Red Republican*. See John Simkin, "George Julian Harney." Terrible peasant conditions of the 1840s are described in Michael Donheny's *The Felon's Track* (1848), quoted in Peter Berresford Ellis, *Eyewitness to Irish History*, 170.

14. "Ireland," *Millennial Star* 9 (January 1, 1847): 2–3; R. F. Foster, "Ascendancy and Union," 157–59; Richard Davis, "Young Ireland." On the popularity of the O'Connells in Ireland, see "Liberation of O'Connell," *New York Herald*, October 3, 1844, in Ellis, *Eyewitnesses to Irish History*, 168–69. An Anglo-Irish treaty dissolved the 1800 Union Act and gave Ireland independence in 1922. Northern Ireland, however, opted out of the Irish Free State and remains part of the United Kingdom today.

15. Alfred Cordon, Letter to Joseph Smith, February 17, 1842, in Joseph Smith Jr. et al., *History of the Church of Jesus Christ of Latter-day Saints*, 4:515–16.

giously and politically." The timbre of Pratt's open letter mirrored the Ranter admonitions meted out to the Cromwellian Parliament in the 1650s.[16] Pratt exhorted the queen, nobility, gentry, and clergy to "dispense with their pride and extravagance" and to hear the "cries of the poor." He offered an escape route: the rulers of England could become agents of relief if they satisfied human need over the interests of capital. If not, Pratt warned, they would be "overthrown . . . and perish from the earth."[17]

Bombastic proclamations like Pratt's were a revolutionary staple. Michael Walzer suggests that the "rhetoric of opposition and struggle . . . played an important part in the development of the idea of revolution." Calvinist theologians living during Queen Mary's persecution of English Protestants (1553–58) had incorporated the imagery of medieval warfare to oppose Catholic absolutism, as there was no method short of war to effect political change before the advent of democracy.[18] Pratt's missives likewise suggested war. His belief in revolution outran his faith in reform. Sweeping predictions of impending destruction were written to kindle a small revolution that would mystically flare into a universal conflagration due to the very novelty of the idea. On another level, Pratt's *Letter to the Queen of England* did not intend to show power or threaten a general social leveling. His letter and open letters like it were texts meant to discredit the present, light up the future, and legitimate the torchbearers. Such manifestos, according to James Billington, were less about inspiring immediate action than seeking the sanction of moral opinion.[19]

The social tension missionaries encountered as they fanned out in Great Britain and the eastern United States sharpened their sensitivity

---

16. Abiezer Coppe, *A Fiery Flying Roll: A Word from the Lord to All the Great Ones of the Earth, Whom This May Concerne: Being the Last Warning Piece at the Dreadfull Day of Judgement* (1649), quoted in Norman Cohn, *The Pursuit of the Millennium: Revolutionary Millenarians and Mystical Anarchists of the Middle Ages*, 322–24.

17. Pratt, "Letter to the Queen of England."

18. Michael Walzer, *The Revolution of the Saints: A Study in the Origins of Radical Politics*, 110–11.

19. On the role the press played in establishing revolutionary legitimacy, see James Billington, *Fire in the Minds of Men: The Origins of the Revolutionary Faith*, 44–45, 306–23.

to social conflict. Elder George J. Adams preached the imminent down-fall of the political order.[20] Copying from Pratt's *Letter to the Queen of England*, Adams warned US President John Tyler that disregard for the plight of the lower classes would result in the destruction of the American republic.[21]

In 1845 a round of anti-rent violence flared in New York. Tenant farmers in the Hudson River and Mohawk River Valleys rebelled against lease hold customs dating back to the colonial era. One historian points out that as pre-Revolutionary War patterns of social deference yielded to expanding concepts of free labor and social mobility, "militant farm-ers placed the land question at the center of political debate."[22] William I. Appleby, president of the Eastern States Mission, sided with the ten-ants. Recalling an 1845 incident, he wrote that the people had risen "en masse" against their landlord, shot deputy sheriff Osman Steele who had come to exact rent payments, and "proclaimed themselves the victors." Whether popular violence was appropriate in America, Appleby wrote, "We will leave for others . . . to determine, but it stopped the Rent."[23] The following year an amendment to the state constitution banned lease holds in excess of twelve years.

---

20. Steven Epperson, *Mormons and Jews: Early Mormon Theologies of Israel*, 147–48.

21. George J. Adams, *A Letter to His Excellency John Tyler, President of the United States, Touching the Signs of the Times, and the Political Destiny of the World*, 14–15. Other works by Adams which suggest revolution include the lecture summarized in *Times and Seasons* 3 (July 1, 1842): 835–36; and *A Few Plain Facts, Shewing the Folly, Wickedness, and Imposition of the Rev. Timothy R. Matthews; Also a Short Sketch of the Rise, Faith and Doctrine of the Church of Jesus Christ of Latter-day Saints*, 14–16.

22. Reeve Huston, "Land and Freedom: The New York Anti-Rent Wars and the Construction of Free Labor in the North," 38. For similar interpretations see David Maldwyn Ellis, *Landlords and Farmers in the Hudson-Mohawk Region, 1790–1850*, 312; and Charles W. McCurdy, *The Anti-Rent Era in New York Law and Politics, 1839–1865*.

23. William I. Appleby, "History of the Signs of the Times," August 30, 1848, 143–44. Appleby based his assessment on recollections. Steele was shot August 7, 1845. Appleby erroneously dated the event in 1846. On the shooting of Steele, see Ellis, *Landlords and Farmers*, 265–66.

Mormon Sympathy with Socialist Goals

Labor disturbances in the United States after 1870 served to make socialism and other economic alternatives more politically viable. Marxism and socialism came to America from Europe following collapse of the First International Workingmen's Association (1864–73).[24] The Depression of 1873 and the Great Railroad Strike of 1877 further stimulated socialist activity. The Socialist Labor Party (1877) gravitated toward "revolutionary" socialism, while the American Socialist Party (1901) championed "reform" or "ballot-box" socialism. The "golden age" of American socialism climaxed in 1912, when socialist presidential candidate Eugene Debs attracted 6 percent of the vote, one socialist congressman was elected, and twelve hundred socialists won seats on city councils.[25]

Mormons observers of these developments used print to expose the excesses of capitalism and to remind old Mormon constituents why their church had appealed to working-class converts and middle-class religious dissenters in the first place. The observers' tactics resembled the oppositional strategies of reformers of the late nineteenth and early twentieth centuries who waged, as one historian put it, a "conflict over norms and values where utopian and radical discourse could find a hearing."[26] In 1869 the *Millennial Star* published a paper by Elihu

---

24. The Social Democratic Party (SPD) of Germany, founded by Ferdinand Lasalle, was repressed by Bismarck. It was revived under the leadership of Karl Kautsky in 1890. Kautsky abandoned the socialist position of worker victory through enfranchisement alone. A Marxist, Kautsky reasoned that the workers would have to push the liberals into the modern era. By reinstating the thesis of class revolution the SPD invoked the millennial mystique that made the party attractive to intellectuals and to disadvantaged workers. See Albert S. Lindemann, *A History of European Socialism*, 133–78; Eric J. Hobsbawm, *The Age of Empire, 1875–1914*, 116–18.

25. Paul Buhle, "Socialist Labor Party," 711–16; and Paul Buhle, "Socialist Party," 716–19. For the "golden age" in the early twentieth century when being a leftist was poetic and bohemian rather than Marxist and bloody, see John Patrick Diggins, *Rise and Fall of the American Left*, 56–84; James Weinstein, *Ambiguous Legacy: The Left in American Politics*; and Richard W. Judd, *Socialist Cities: Municipal Politics and the Grass Roots of American Socialism*.

26. Francis Robert Shor, *Utopianism and Radicalism in a Reforming*

Burritt, former US consul in Birmingham and widely-known advocate for world peace.[27] Burritt explained the plight of British workers in terms of class exploitation. The demands of the military budget forced a ploughman to work six months to pay for an eleven-pound artillery shell, while military recruitment took the most physically fit men. No country, cried the *Star*, should allow so much "honest, patient labour" to be "swallowed up in the wolfish maw of war!"[28]

Another *Star* article reprinted from the *Morning Advertiser* suggested that conditions were ripe for revolution. Families living on insufficient wages were as desperate as the urban *sans culottes* (radical workers who wore trousers instead of the silk knee britches of the middle class) of the French Revolution.[29] Privilege and worker exploitation lay exposed. An article reprinted from *The Civilian* finished the story: "If the practical good sense of the mass of the people does not actively protest against this state of things, nothing but a social revolution or a violent convulsion will clear away the vices of civilization."[30]

The *Millennial Star's* editors idealized working class life during the coming millennium. The profit motive and "labor-saving machinery" that produced "semi starvation among the masses" would disappear. Instead, production would be "governed by the demands of consumption." Workers, freed from exploitation, would have "more time to devote to the cultivation of the higher powers of their natures." In this article, a form of socialism was divinely appointed. Through "well di-

America, 1888–1918, xvi. For the impact of Bellamy and other utopian novelists, consult Frank E. Manuel and Fritzie P. Manuel, *Utopian Thought in the Western World*, 759–61.

27. For the life of Elihu Burritt (1810–1879), see Charles Northend, ed., *Elihu Burritt: A Memorial Volume Containing a Sketch of His Life and Labors, with Selections from His Writings and Lectures, and Extracts from His Private Journals in Europe and America.*

28. Elihu Burritt, "Labour and War," *Millennial Star* 31 (October 27, 1869): 710.

29. "The Awful Destitution," reprinted from the *Morning Advertiser* in *Millennial Star* 31 (November 17, 1869): 760.

30. "Social Rottenness," *Millennial Star* 33 (June 6, 1871): 355–56. *The Civilian* was the organ of the Civil Service and was printed in London under that name from 1869 to 1925. From 1926 to 1928 it was called *The New Civilian*.

rected study and divine inspiration, the knowledge of God will cover the earth as the waters do the channels of the great deep."[31]

Mormon observers condemned capitalism when the wealth it generated became the object of living. Scandinavian Mission President Edward H. Anderson defined wealth in 1890 as surplus "accumulated by a person over and above what is necessary to properly provide for his every welfare, including bodily and mental requirements." Anderson attacked the "palatial residences," clubhouses, and restaurants of the rich. The protagonists of justice in his view were the "proletarians." "Humble people," who Anderson equated with Jesus and courageous men of action, would save civilization. Anderson also displayed awareness of Marx's theory of the surplus value of labor: capitalists, he argued, were withholding the full reward of a day's labor.[32] B. H. Roberts expressed similar views. According to Roberts, selfishness, the basis of American industrial enterprise, bred two classes: the proud and the envious. Class struggle followed.[33] Just before his death in 1894, John Morgan, one of the seven presidents of the Seventy, faulted both labor and capital for the violence during the ongoing economic depression. Morgan suggested, however, that "those who are possessed of the wealth" bore primary responsibility; it was they who were in a position to "employ a little conciliation [to] endeavor to make the condition of the human family better and more bearable." In Social Gospel style, Morgan called the rich to repentance.[34]

---

31. "Centralization of Government," *Millennial Star* 41 (April 28, 1879): 265.

32. Edward H. Anderson, "Effect of Wealth on Morals," pt. 1, *Contributor* 11 (September 1890): 423–25; "Effect of Wealth on Morals," pt. 2, *Contributor* 11 (October 1890): 464–66. See also "Poverty and Economy as Applied to Young Men," *Millennial Star* 43 (May 16, 1881): 317. Marx's *Capital* was not published in English until 1886, but his theory of the surplus value of labor was known as early as 1863. See Francis Wheen, *Karl Marx: A Life*, 302–3, 413 note 302.

33. B. H. Roberts, *New Witnesses for God*, 1:396–97.

34. John Morgan, April 15, 1894, in Brian H. Stuy, ed. and comp., *Collected Discourses Delivered by President Wilford Woodruff, His Two Counselors, the Twelve Apostles, and Others*, 4:97. For general study of the Social Gospel movement, see Donald K. Gorrell, *The Age of Social Responsibility: The Social Gospel in the Progressive Era, 1900–1920*. On Social Gospel influence on Mormonism, see Scott G. Kenney, "Personal and Social Morality in a

The highest-ranking Mormon observer to overtly sympathize with socialism was Apostle Moses Thatcher. In *A History of Utah Radicalism*, John R. Sillito and John S. McCormack show that by 1900 Utah newspapers identified Thatcher as a socialist. Typical of "gas and water" socialists of the day, Thatcher urged municipal control of utilities to eliminate price gouging by private sector companies. At Brigham Young College in Logan, Thatcher spoke openly in favor of socialism and showed that labor and capital were in constant tension. In a short time, Thatcher preached, private property would be abolished. As Thatcher aged, his enthusiasm for socialism faded. But in his younger years, he was schooled in Mormonism's revolutionary tradition at a time when the fire still burned hot.[35]

The *Millennial Star* credited German socialism with stopping subsidies to churches in the German states,[36] but the potential unintended consequences of socialist promises were worrisome to Mormon observers. Especially dangerous was the possibility that party mystique would mesmerize the masses, leading to secular displacement of spirituality and worship of the material world. Hence the Church was always keenly aware of the challenge posed by secular socialism and sought ways to counteract it.[37] The *Millennial Star* reprinted an editorial from the *New York Forum* in 1890 stating that the programs of the Paris Commune, nihilism, anarchism, and Social Democracy could become the religion of the people. Industrialists had exaggerated the people's affinity for communist doctrine, but given the "ostentation of wealth," the people might still organize under the red flag. Should that happen and revolution follow, the governing classes would be forced to "convert [wealth] into military

---

Religious Context: Reinhold Niebuhr and the Mormon Experience," 20; Armand L. Mauss, "Assimilation and Ambivalence: The Mormon Reaction to Americanization," 36; and Thomas G. Alexander, "Between Revivalism and the Social Gospel: The Latter-day Saint Social Advisory Committee, 1916–1922," 19–39. Richard T. Ely, a Social Gospel advocate and well-known economist, praised the Mormon spirit of cooperation in "Economic Aspects of Mormonism," *Harper's Monthly Magazine* 106 (April 1903): 668.

35. John S. McCormick and John R. Sillito, *A History of Utah Radicalism: Startling, Socialistic, and Decidedly Revolutionary*, 61–62.

36. "Socialists in Germany," *Millennial Star* 53 (August 24, 1891): 542–43; "Social Democracy and Religion," *Millennial Star* 65 (November 5, 1903): 712.

37. McCormick and Sillito, *History of Utah Radicalism*, 384–86.

power" to maintain order.[38] Another *Star* editorial worried that socialism promised too much, and that social democracy would become a "world party" and replace religion.[39] Joseph M. Tanner, president of what later became Utah State University, agreed with many of the aims of ballot-box socialism. He was offended, however, when European socialists failed to send condolences to the Portuguese royal family following the assassination of King Carlos and the crown prince in 1908. He worried that socialism could lose its discipline and devolve into anarchism.[40] Nonetheless, as late as 1920 Tanner believed that "among millions of the human family there is an awakening of a new consciousness . . . which has given rise to the demands of labor and which is gradually molding the conduct of the rulers of the world.[41]

In summary, Mormon observers sympathized with socialist grievances and were willing to follow along with at least the theoretical rationale for revolution. At the same time, they saw socialism as a competing revolutionary faith. Socialism was acceptable as long as it maintained discipline as an antidote to random violence. Most importantly, revolt from below could not be allowed to swallow faith in the final consummation from above.

Mormon Communalism in the Revolutionary Context

During the 1830s Mormons were one of many groups endeavoring to establish common property communities.[42] Joseph Smith established collectivist communities in Ohio and Missouri, but they failed.[43] In sub-

---

38. "Signs of a Revolution," *Millennial Star* 52 (September 22, 1890): 605–6.

39. "Social Democracy and Religion," 712. Six years later the *Star* continued to respect socialists as "sincere and honest men," but was suspicious of the anti-religious element. See E. A. Cooke, "Altruism vs Socialism," *Millennial Star* 71 (December 23, 1909): 804–7.

40. Joseph M. Tanner, "The Portuguese Tragedy," *Improvement Era* 11 (March 1908): 400.

41. Joseph M. Tanner, "A New Consciousness," *Improvement Era* 23 (October 1920): 1077–78.

42. Francis Robert Shor, *Utopianism and Radicalism*, 99–116.

43. See Doctrine and Covenants 42, 51, 56, 70, 72, 78, 82, 85, 90, 101, and 105 for revelations directing the establishment of communal property ownership and surplus management.

sequent years Mormon leaders tried to revive the idea. In 1849 Orson Pratt published a tract championing the "union of property." Property would be allotted equally; profits would belong to the Church and would be used for capital improvements and missionary work.[44] In 1862 French Mission President Louis A. Bertrand published *Mémoires d'un Mormon* (*Memoirs of a Mormon*). Bertrand, former editor of a radical Parisian journal, was one of the first Mormon converts in France. A barricade leader in 1848, Bertrand admitted his attraction to "the ranks of militant democracy."[45] The economic ideas of Pratt and Bertrand mirrored programs set forth by French democratic-socialists.[46] Bertrand's book is particularly instructive because it shows Mormon thought creatively fusing with some of the most revolutionary concepts of the latter half of the nineteenth century.

Bertrand came to believe that the French Revolution had been "huge negation." It was as powerful as Mount Vesuvius, but being "sterile," "skeptical," and utterly rational, it was devoid of the knowledge that would "lead the world toward divine unity."[47] The structure and revelations of Mormonism would rescue the act of revolution from mere negation. Revolution had delivered people from the false power of kings and greedy bourgeois, but the excesses of the French experience had to be avoided.

Bertrand wanted to wipe out the "terrible law of social inequality." The plan he advanced resembled ideas described in Victor Hugo's 1862 novel *Les Misérables*. Bertrand, who knew Hugo and moved in French Democratic-Socialist circles even after his conversion to Mormonism, proposed a plan to achieve the harmony envisioned by like-minded French and Mormon contemporaries. The key was the "universalising" of property as opposed to the mere extinguishment of individual title.[48] Private property would be consolidated to form "national property,"

---

44. See Chapter 2 of the present book.

45. Bertrand was likely the man identified as "A. Bertrand" who fought on the Paris barricades during the June Days insurrection. See Gary Ray Chard, "A History of the French Mission of the Church of Jesus Christ of Latter-day Saints, 1850–1960," 17–18; and Christopher H. Johnson, *Utopian Communism in France: Cabet and the Icarians, 1839–1851*, 267.

46. Jacob L. Talmon, *Political Messianism: The Romantic Phase*, 458.

47. Louis A. Bertrand, *Memoirs of a Mormon*, 160–61.

48. Victor Hugo, *Les Misérables*, 706–9.

then redistributed according to need as a non-transferable stewardship. There would be no individual profits, no lawyers, and few bankers. Hard money, Bertrand suggested, would freely circulate. The law of tithing would temporarily be a "mitigated consecration" that allowed Mormons to enjoy 90 percent of their income. One day the "school" session would end. The socialism that started in Utah would go on to demonstrate the obsolescence of capitalism, preparing the way for its "universal" application.[49]

In 1873 the *Millennial Star* presented a review of American socialism based on contemporary sources interspersed with laudatory commentary. "Unless the masses" in the United States adopted some scientific "means of salvation," concluded the *Star*, "their doom is sealed." The *Star* suggested that Marxism offered a sequence of attainment but that socialism achieved through violence would weaken incentives to produce. The answer lay instead in the "old socialism." The Owenite and Fourierist period from 1820–50 had been a period when "a noble and beautiful faith" had filled the minds of young Americans. Their enthusiasm portended a new start for humanity. Just as the architects of the French Revolution symbolically recalibrated the calendar of 1792 to herald the beginning of a new human history, the social innovators of the 1840s likewise had anticipated "year one of universal human perfection."[50] The yearnings of the old socialists had survived. The people, prevented by politicians, generals, and technocrats from attaining true freedom, might still reorganize society. In "Apostolic communism" the "refined and cultivated but unwealthy class" would be free from the "avaricious few." The success of the Oneida community (minus its practice of free love) and of the earlier Owenite and Fourierist communities provided data "valuable to all future cooperators."[51] Common property, however, was not enough. The community must also be bound by a common religious faith.[52]

---

49. Bertrand, *Memoirs of a Mormon*, 162–69.

50. "Socialism in America," *Millennial Star* 35 (July 15, 1873): 433. This article was based on Samuel Leavitt's 1873 pamphlet, "Township Coöperation: The Legitimate Fruit of the Protectionist Theory; Also, The History of American Socialism: Two Lectures before the New York Liberal Club by S. R. Wells."

51. "Socialism in America," 434–35.

52. Ibid., 436; and Frank E. Manuel, *Prophets of Paris*, 154. Colonel

Amid an 1874 downturn in the Utah mining industry, Brigham Young, nearing the end of his life, attempted to resuscitate Joseph Smith's communitarian dream. The "United Order of Enoch," as the movement was called, incorporated many of the findings presented by Pratt and Bertrand. Three models emerged. The most radical one, the "Gospel Plan," abolished private property and imposed close living arrangements reminiscent of John Humphrey Noyes's Oneida Community and the *Phalanxes* of Charles Fourier. Within two years, two hundred communities had been organized. Optimism abounded, but the movement was virtually shut down by the early 1880s. Several factors explain the failure: competition from non-United Order towns, lack of capital, half-hearted leadership participation, poor planning in the big city Orders, and freedom to leave the Orders.[53]

The Mormon communal movement offers insights. Mormons modified revolutionary and socialist thought to create their own itera-

---

Thomas L. Kane (1822–1833), long-time friend of the Mormons and secretary in the US legation in Paris, had studied St. Simon and Fourier. See George Q. Cannon, February 23, 1890, in Stuy, *Collected Discourses*, 2:12; and Leonard J. Arrington and Davis Bitton, *Saints without Halos: The Human Side of Mormon History*, 31. Kane forms a link between the doctrines of St. Simon and Mormon insistence on the religious component of social organization. Kane never joined the Church but his service as the recruiter of the Mormon Battalion (1846) and advisor to Brigham Young made him a trusted representative of Mormon interests in Washington, DC. Under Kane's influence, George Q. Cannon showed regard for the St. Simonians. See Cannon, February 23, 1890 and March 11, 1894, in Stuy, *Collected Discourses*, 2:12 and 4:23. Kane's service in Mormon interests is discussed in Leonard J. Arrington, "In Honorable Remembrance: Thomas L. Kane's Services to the Mormons"; and Albert L. Zobell, Jr., "Thomas L. Kane, Ambassador to the Mormons."

53. For nineteenth-century Mormon economic experimentation, see Donald E. Pitzer, ed., *America's Communal Utopias*; L. Dwight Israelsen, "An Economic Analysis of the United Order"; L. Dwight Israelsen, "Mormons, the Constitution, and the Host Economy"; Leonard J. Arrington, *Great Basin Kingdom: An Economic History of the Latter-day Saints, 1830–1900*; Leonard J. Arrington, Feramorz Y. Fox, and Dean L. May, *Building the City of God: Community and Cooperation among the Mormons*, 135–301; Dean L. May, "Brigham Young and the Bishops: The United Order in the City."

tion. The Mormon cooperatives were supposed to unite science and religion to create a social order that would spread across the world. Elements of the St. Simonian doctrine are evident. In 1870 Young urged the Saints to view science and revealed religion as the same thing. Organizations built on the scientific organizational principles of pure religion can resist "anarchy and confusion."[54] George Q. Cannon likewise criticized concentrated wealth, class distinctions, poverty, and the lack of political freedom—all of which he blamed on the "incorrect organization of society."[55]

Like Bertrand, Orson Pratt sought peaceful revolution through religious reform. Pratt emphasized his lifelong conviction that straightlaced individualism would disappear and a determined effort by the Saints would revive the utopia of Joseph Smith. "How much of a revolution would it accomplish in Salt Lake City," he asked a congregation, "if this order of things should be brought about?" If the people dedicated themselves to their historic mission, they could "work a greater revolution . . . than has ever been witnessed amongst them since they had an existence as a Church."[56]

Property, Factories, and Observer Philosophies of Change

The shortcomings and collapse of the United Order movement sensitized Mormon observers to social demolition and reconstruction. Some of it followed a reformist course. Among alternatives capturing Mormon attention were the theories of Henry George. In *Progress and Poverty* (1879) and *Social Problems* (1883), George attacked the "land monopoly." He proposed a 100 percent capital gains tax on the appreciated value of land. As the sole source of government revenue, such a tax would suppress rent increases. More money and productive capital would remain in the hands of the people instead of going to pay land speculators, thus closing the gap between rich and poor. George's redistribution plan was not a socialist proposal, but it inspired socialists, unionists, and progressives to pursue their own versions of socioeconomic reorientation.[57]

---

54. Brigham Young, November 13, 1870, *Journal of Discourses*, 13:306–7.

55. George Q. Cannon, April 6, 1869, *Journal of Discourses*, 13:97–99.

56. Orson Pratt, March 9, 1873, *Journal of Discourses*, 15:357.

57. Lindemann, *History of European Socialism*, 144; Jacob Oser, *Henry George*, 32–50.

With all arable land in Utah claimed, George's ideas captured the attention of Mormon leaders. First Counselor George Q. Cannon told the Saints in 1878 to be grateful they live in a region where men cannot "monopolize large bodies of land to the exclusion of their poorer neighbors."[58] Apostle John Henry Smith recorded in his journal that Henry George himself gave Smith a copy of George's *Social Problems* while on a visit to New York.[59] The most obvious George advocate, however, was Charles W. Nibley, future presiding bishop of the Mormon Church and future second counselor in the First Presidency.

Nibley's writings represent a larger body of Mormon literature that took on a more radical tone. In 1878 Nibley was a missionary in England, and he did not like what he saw. International rivalry had depressed wages as nations tried to undersell competitors. Everything, Nibley suggested, was such a "polluted mass that our senses sicken at the sight. This arch-enemy to the welfare of society—competition—has here been most actively, desperately and cunningly at work." He suggested that Louis Blanc, a socialist in the French provisional government of 1848, had it right: "'If society is badly made make it over again;' . . . In this matter, as in many others, the Latter-day Saints take the lead of the age. They are the revolutionists of the latter days. Where error exists, the truth, when introduced, creates a revolution; but truth will prevail."[60] Karl Marx's encouragement to the Communist League compares to Nibley's radical call: "For us the issue cannot be the alteration of private property but only its annihilation . . . not the improvement of existing society but the foundation of a new one."[61] Nibley refrained from referring to class struggle, but the terms "revolution" and "will

---

58. George Q. Cannon, July 7, 1878, *Journal of Discourses*, 20:35. Cannon also mentioned the attractiveness of Edward Bellamy's 1890 utopian novel *Looking Backward, 2000–1887*. See Cannon, February 23, 1890, in Stuy, *Collected Discourses*, 2:12. Bellamy's novel envisioned strong national government to eliminate inequality.

59. Jean Bickmore White, ed., *Church, State, and Politics: The Diaries of John Henry Smith*, 132.

60. Charles W. Nibley, "Competition," *Millennial Star* 40 (November 25, 1878): 741.

61. "Address to the Communist League" (March 1850), in David McLellan, ed., *Karl Marx: Selected Writings*, 280.

prevail" seem close enough to Marx's theory to establish young Nibley as a proponent of revolutionary determinism.

Nibley continued to plead labor's case in a series of lectures delivered in the Logan Temple in 1886. Bending Adam Smith to his purposes, Nibley ruled that "wealth is the result of labor." He then tinctured Henry George with Karl Marx. In juxtaposing the wealth of Leland Stanford against the poverty of Chicago, he noted that capitalists "rob" the laborer and consign him to subsistence living. Left untouched, fat profits and thin wages would drive history toward revolution. "Where such a state of society exists," Nibley said, "something is radically wrong and needs changing, or it will change itself in a manner not pleasing to behold, nor very healthy to the capitalist."[62]

Nibley disdained insistence on property rights and distrusted the ability of reformers to work effectively within the system. Constitutional property rights were a travesty, and laws upholding private land ownership were construed to favor the rich. They would have to be abolished. "From this fundamental injustice," Nibley thought, "flow all the injustices which distort and endanger modern development, which condemns the producer of wealth to poverty and pampers the nonproducer in luxury."[63] Nibley echoed another leftist theme when he bemoaned the detachment of man from society, leaving him an unprotected individual. Whereas slaves of the antebellum South might have enjoyed the care of a benevolent owner, Nibley thought modern capitalists escaped accountability for their workers' welfare.[64] On this point Nibley was downright iconoclastic. He denounced the nation's founding documents and the Emancipation Proclamation. Unless the consolidation of property in the hands of a few was arrested and society reformed, modern "slavery . . . must grow and deepen," resolving itself in social revolution.[65]

The antidote to individualism, Nibley believed, was a return to the Church-guided plan of common landholding and profit regulation.[66] Nibley calculated that under Church-sponsored communalism, only

62. Charles W. Nibley, "Logan Temple Lectures: Political Economy," *Contributor* 7 (January 1886): 135, 139.

63. Ibid., 137.

64. Ibid., 139.

65. Ibid., 140.

66. Ibid., 141–42.

six four-hour days would be required from workers each week. This formula was even more optimistic than the expectations of Ira Steward, the crusader of the "8-hour millennium."[67] "Such a state of society," Nibley promised, with time allowed for education, recreation, worship, and brotherhood, "would be a millennium" indeed.[68]

From the loftiness of a man-made utopia, Nibley brought his listeners back to earth. The "soulless corporations" have produced a "fool's prosperity," he said. The rich were reaping the rewards of labor's surplus value. The Robber Barons had made themselves the targets of "the poor [who] are ready, nay anxious," to murder them.[69] Rhetoricians, he argued, deceived the people every Fourth of July with "sovereignty of man" talk, but Nibley believed he saw through the façade. Classless brotherhood was possible only when surplus wealth came under a single controlling body audited by the people or responsible to God.[70]

Joseph M. Tanner added political philosophy to Nibley's critique. History, he explained, unfolds in a series of conflicts. The interplay between historical determinism and the freewill of individuals lays the basis for change:

> The great social reforms that have moved the nations of the earth, have had their forces husbanded in the beginning by all kinds of opposition, as if whatever the works of God had given birth to must

---

67. Steward believed that wages earned during an eight-hour shift would result in spending during leisure time, thus boosting industry and ensuring prosperity. See Sean Dennis Cashman, *America in the Gilded Age: From the Death of Lincoln to the Rise of Theodore Roosevelt*, 146.

68. Charles W. Nibley, "Logan Temple Lectures: Political Economy—Work and Wages," *Contributor* 7 (August 1886): 429. John Wells, Nibley's future second counselor in the Presiding Bishopric (1918–25) was influenced by Nibley's thinking. He urged members to keep capital in Utah and to build the spirit of economic cooperation within themselves to prepare for a Church-led communal plan. See John Wells, "Thoughts on the United Order"; John Wells, October 7, 1921, *Report of the Semiannual Conference of the Church of Jesus Christ of Latter-day Saints*, 51–53 (hereafter cited as *Conference Report*); and John Wells, "Cooperation and Mutual Helpfulness," *Improvement Era* 25 (February 1922): 295–96.

69. Nibley, "Logan Temple Lectures: Political Economy—Work and Wages," 425.

70. Ibid., 428.

come forth in pain. Social progress, then, seems to be one of destiny, while the relative position of man in weaving the fabric of civilization is evidently one of option.[71]

Tanner viewed conflict as essential to political and social advancement. His philosophy read like Hegel's *Philosophy of the Right*. States are constantly recast as they move through time until they arrive at some form of national existence. Otherwise they wither or suffer annexation.[72] Tanner echoed Hegel's supposition that the institutions, religion, and values of a society reflect its character at a given point in time:

> The principles and history of political institutions warrants the conclusion that no nation ever enjoyed a government, absolute or liberal that was not in exact accordance with the wants, necessities and virtues of the people who made it, and for whom it was made.[73]

Tanner was suggesting that people progress by their own way in their own time. What worked for one country might not work for another. This lack of an absolute until the final consolidation of a people's historical development is what permits revolution. Tanner asserted the sovereignty and changeability of the people. His depiction of nations as evolving organisms allowed the most up-and-coming segment of society to determine historical direction. The process of history, therefore, superseded constitutional boundaries. Revolutions were justifiable acts, at least until the state outgrew its subordination to human subjectivity and became an ideal object in finished form.

Tanner admired bourgeois intellectuals. This new class, he argued, had been able to "revolutionize the social fabric in one generation." Beginning with the 1830 revolution in France, middle-class intellectuals had built political structures that in "their form, dimensions, and finish" represented propertied interests. Triumphant, the bourgeois nonetheless created another set of problems. Tanner suggested that when wealth and power became the "end rather than the means, the

---

71. Joseph M. Tanner, "Political Institutions," pt. 4, *Contributor* 5 (March 1884): 207.

72. For a discussion of Hegel on the "idea" and the "absolute" as the relationship between man's perfected state and historical process, see Alfred Weber, *History of Philosophy*, 423–35.

73. Tanner, "Political Institutions," pt. 1, *Contributor* 5 (October 1883): 13.

distinctions created by it are unfavorable." Enlightened labor leaders, a new intelligentsia, might affect the next leap forward.[74]

Themes of conflict and historical progress also informed the writings of Alice Louise Reynolds. Reynolds was as much a radical as any Mormonism would produce. A BYU English professor and later a member of the General Board of the Relief Society, Reynolds added her voice to the chorus of the American "Lyrical Left," a left that could be enjoyed in terms of thought and culture without having to reconcile with the "Old Left" of 1917 and Bolshevik dread.[75] Reynolds demanded the vote for women and sympathized with the "New Women" of Greenwich Village who advocated individual female fulfillment, including sexual pleasure. Politically, Reynolds bore a likeness to Jane Addams. Reynolds doubted, however, whether the refurbished republic for which Addams hoped could achieve the justice the Left demanded.[76]

Reynolds began writing in the wake of the 1893 Depression and the Pullman Railroad strike. The crisis "provoked an intense social and political reaction against the regime of free market liberalism" that governed national life.[77] By 1898, Reynolds's faith in reform had collapsed. The government and the "rich monopolist" had subverted the millennium. Reynolds eschewed the middle-class progressives who used politics and journalism to restore themselves as the nation's moral leaders but curbed ideas from the Left. From *Message of Jesus to Men of Wealth*, an 1891 tract by Christian socialist George D. Herron, Reynolds quoted, "The blood of Abel cries out through toiling millions."[78] The expecta-

---

74. Ibid., pt. 3, *Contributor* 5 (December 1883): 90.

75. Diggins, *Rise and Fall of the American Left*, 98.

76. For Jane Addams, see Victoria Brown, "Advocate for Democracy: Jane Addams and the Pullman Strike."

77. David Montgomery, "Epilogue: The Pullman Boycott and the Making of Modern America."

78. Alice Louise Reynolds, "God's Social Order," pt. 1, *Young Woman's Journal* 9 (May 1898): 202. Reynolds was quoting from George D. Herron, *The Message of Jesus to Men of Wealth*, 9; and George D. Herron, *The Christian Society*, 102. Herron (1862–1925) launched his leadership of the Social Gospel movement with *Message of Jesus*. Divorce hurt his reputation and he moved to Italy. After a life in academia he worked in the State Department of President Woodrow Wilson as a "secret negotiator." See "Guide to the George D. Herron Papers."

tions of the poor could not be postponed any longer. "Another social system" was "demanded by humanity." Reynolds drew from British communist reformer John Ruskin to deride constitutional law as the basis for mollifying Abel's righteously vengeful millions: "No arrogant reply as to the historical and legal rights of private and corporate property will silence these voices."[79]

In articles appearing in the *Young Woman's Journal*, Reynolds reviewed the history of socialism, beginning with Thomas More's *Utopia*. She memorialized James Oglethorpe, Robert Owen, Charles Fourier, Henry George, and Edward Bellamy as pioneers of social reform. Only the lack of unifying religious principles had prevented their social experiments from flowering. The United Order of Enoch would restore the religious component that St. Simon had belatedly recognized as vital to offset the materialism of an industrial order. In the binary of material output tempered by faith, participants would find "primitive Christianity" and brotherhood. There was no need to wait for an apocalyptic descent of divine power to impose universal justice. Reynolds described the Biblical city of Enoch the same way she referred to the secular societies: they were "temporal" forms of social organization achievable by mortal men and women.[80]

Reynolds proposed the United Order as the spiritual and organizing principle for the state. She rejected the literal leveling she found in other utopian schemes in favor of endowments disbursed to individuals and families from a central storehouse. Disbursements proportionate to productive capacity while accounting for particular need would boost output without sucking the humanity out of people with "machine-like regularity." Reynolds believed her views were more optimistic than those of other modernists. The "wretched pessimism" and naked self-interest of Herbert Spencer and Arthur Schopenhauer, she thought, would embarrass even primitive patriarchs like Abraham and Moses.[81]

---

79. Reynolds, "God's Social Order," pt. 1, 202. John Ruskin (1819–1900) was a writer, social thinker, and artist, and is remembered as a "Victorian sage." He described himself as a "Communist of the old school—reddest also of the red" in "Charitas" (July 1, 1871), published in John D. Rosenberg, ed., *The Genius of John Ruskin: Selections from His Writings*, 374.

80. Reynolds, "God's Social Order," pt. 1, 200.

81. Ibid., pt. 2, *Young Woman's Journal* 9 (June 1898): 257–58. Schopenhauer (1788–1860) was the German philosopher of pessimism

Reynolds called for a commonwealth of communes harmonized by the state. In Hegelian fashion the nation would become "the expression of the highest common thought of the people, the work of the people's faith."[82] The submission of capitalists to the people's will was essential. The institutions of a new state under righteous directorship would eliminate the "anarchy" and "nihilism" of free enterprise.[83]

Virginia Snow Stephen is worth noting because of who she was. In *A History of Utah Radicalism*, John R. Sillito and John S. McCormick describe Stephen's involvement in the Mormon Church as "minimal," but she was the daughter of former Church President Lorenzo Snow and Mary E. Houtz, one of his polygamous wives. Stephen taught at the University of Utah's art laboratory starting in 1907. Shortly thereafter, under the influence of Unitarian minister William Thurston Brown, Stephen made a lifelong commitment to socialism. Stephen was fired from the University of Utah in 1916, after which she sought to organize domestic servants under the banner of the Industrial Workers of the World—a labor union despised for its Marxist rhetoric. America's foremost anarchist, Emma Goldman, described Stephen as a "very courageous and able woman."[84]

Another Mormon advocate of socialism was Joseph A. Vance, a teacher respected by renowned Mormon educator Karl G. Maeser. In March 1909 some Presbyterians invited Vance, a missionary in the Birmingham Conference at the time, to address the topic of socialism before a Presbyterian guild in Wombourne, England. Why Presbyterians chose a Mormon missionary to educate them on socialism is unclear. The *Millennial Star* said Vance relied on contemporary sources but also added "thoughts and illustrations of his own."[85] Vance proceeded to

---

who inspired Friedrich Nietzche. His *The World as Will and Representation* suggests the primacy of will over spirit and intellect. Spencer (1820–1903) was one of the pioneers of "social Darwinism," arguing in *The Principles of Ethics* that morality and intelligence endow certain populations with greater powers of survival and adaptation.

82. Reynolds, "God's Social Order," pt. 2, 259.

83. Ibid., 260.

84. Quoted in McCormick and Sillito, *History of Utah Radicalism*, 126.

85. Joseph A. Vance, "Growth and Development of Socialism," *Millennial Star* 71 (March 25, 1909): 177. The *Star* reported that Utah socialists invited Vance to make the same presentation in Utah.

review socialist thinkers: Utopians Robert Owen and Charles Fourier, Nibley's hero Louis Blanc, Marx's early rival Joseph-Pierre Proudhon, and Ferdinand Lasalle, the leader of German ballot-box socialism, repressed by Bismarck. Vance also considered the writings of Karl Marx and Friedrich Engels, the founders of revolutionary socialism. The challenge for socialists, Vance stated, was how to convert private property—land and capital—to collective property. Socialist leaders were tutoring the working class for its "great mission" to win political power in order to redistribute wealth.[86] Fulfillment of their goals would have global impact. "The evils [socialism] seeks to remedy are vast and real," Vance said, "and are found under the most illiberal and most highly-developed constitutional governments."[87] Vance described Blanc as an "eloquent enthusiast of the highest character." Lasalle was a "social innovator" who "looked with compassion upon the depressed and disabled working classes under the iron law of wages." Lasalle's answer to labor indignity was "productive associations." This plan would raise working class living standards by grafting workers into factory decision-making (what some might call syndicalism). Marx and Engels were cogent theorists in Vance's estimation. Their work on labor's surplus value in *Das Kapital* exposed "the secret of modern economic movement." The impact of the 1864 First International Workingmen's Association, Vance believed, would be "great, far-reaching and enduring."[88]

In his conclusion Vance urged serious consideration of socialist proposals, rededication to the defunct Mormon communal effort, and faith in the ongoing American Progressive Movement. Trusts and monopolies warranted the "most serious consideration" from President Roosevelt and the electorate. Once the government dissolved business combinations, Vance argued, "the private appropriation of the instruments of labor must cease."[89]

B. H. Roberts was another Mormon leader who argued, in his book *New Witnesses for God* (1911), that Mormon communalism was still relevant. The "communists"—St. Simon, Fourier, Cabet, and Owen—having failed to prevent the development of a "deadly conflict" between labor and capital, had left the world to corporations. "Distrust and jeal-

---

86. Ibid., 180.
87. Ibid., 181.
88. Ibid., 178–80.
89. Ibid., 181.

ousy" were rampant. Despite the free market's "manifest absurdities in the waste of energy, the unfairness in the distribution of the products of industry, still mankind has, so far, preferred to endure its known evils and incongruities rather than to trust their fortunes to the proposed systems of the socialists and communists."[90]

Neither the state nor capitalism was the solution. Roberts advocated a return to Joseph Smith's Law of Consecration, but with the stipulation that change had to first come from within the individual. "It is vain," Roberts said, "for men to seek to build up communities in which selfishness shall be abolished, and love and goodwill abound." First, men needed to acquire the "same qualities that are to be characteristic of the community; for communities can be no better than the individuals that compose them." Once an individual signed up, he would make a full consecration to the Church. The "stewardship" of property, capital, or commodities would represent an inviolate pact. Surplus would accrue to the Church, and withdrawal from the system would entail forfeiture of rights of recovery.[91] The people, relieved of burden and exploitation, would be free to reach upward. Roberts concluded, "It is a system which contemplates the humiliation of the rich and the exaltation of the poor."[92] Roberts thus anticipated that reactionaries would reject the "temporal salvation of mankind revealed through Joseph Smith" just as they had denied the viability "of socialists and communists so far as the industrial phase of their plans is concerned."[93]

The influence of Marx is evident in Roberts's theory of economic development. Roberts's system would retain the incentives of ambition and "fear or want" during the developmental phase of his agro-industrial communes, meaning that participants would be compensated based on their labor input. Eventually, efficient production would allow humanity to make the transition from the realm of "necessity" to the realm of "freedom." Labor would still be required, but Church directorates would disburse from the central repositories according to wants, no longer according to work performed. The two-step move beyond capitalism that Roberts proposed—from conventional rewards for

90. Roberts, *New Witnesses for God*, 1:396.
91. Ibid., 1:397–400.
92. Ibid., 1:401.
93. Ibid., 1:403.

work to automatic endowment—paralleled Marx's Phase I and Phase II communism.

Taut Expectations

In 1912, a year after Roberts published *New Witnesses for God*, the *Improvement Era* suggested that the US government had not properly dealt with inequalities.[94] American utopians of the period hoped to reconstruct society through "reasoned choice."[95] Mormon observers shared this hope but were also open to violent revolutionary change. From the vantage point of Mormon critics, capitalism and the corporatist governments that supported it must inevitably reform or be destroyed.

The lives of two men illustrate the influence of leftist thinking on Mormon thought. First is Charles W. Nibley, who experienced the full range of ideological orientations. Whereas in 1878 he virtually preached the overthrow of capitalism as a young missionary, by 1909 he had become a political ally of Apostle Reed Smoot, a conservative Republican who held a Senate seat from 1902 to 1932 and built an impressive business portfolio.[96] Nibley represented a new strain in criticism of socialism by LDS leaders. Mormon assimilation into American culture necessitated embrace of capitalism and stepped-up attacks on socialism. McCormick and Sillito write: "Previously, [the Church] had been critical, first of utopian Socialism, and then of other forms of Socialism, from the perspective of its own utopian Socialism. Now it was critical as an incipient capitalist."[97]

The young Nibley's demand for a restructuring of society was echoed by Henry Lawrence. Lawrence was a confidant of Brigham Young who had urged the Church to end its isolation from the mainstream of American society. A stalwart member who once defended polygamy, Lawrence left the institutional Church to become a leader in the Utah populist movement. In 1911 he won election on a Socialist ticket

---

94. Elmer G. Peterson, "Equality of Opportunity," *Improvement Era* 15 (October 1912): 1093–97.

95. Shor, *Utopianism and Radicalism*, xiv.

96. Milton R. Merrill, *Reed Smoot: Apostle in Politics*, 25, 99 note 28; D. Michael Quinn, *The Mormon Hierarchy: Extensions of Power*, 212, 337, 676–78.

97. McCormick and Sillito, *History of Utah Radicalism*, 389.

to the Salt Lake City Commission.[98] Like most socialists, Lawrence believed that capitalism was a stage of history destined to disappear when the workers gained control of the machinery of production. Lawrence's biographers suggest that for him, "the world was essentially divided into two groups, the party of progress and the party of order, and it was clear where he stood."[99]

Nibley and Lawrence ended up in different places, but they imbibed the same Mormon inheritance. They believed that distributive justice could be achieved within history by men acting to reduce upper-class privilege and uplift the lower classes. The delay of utopia kept expectations taut. The radicalism of Mormon observers was proving persistent but the attraction of democratic capitalism was increasing. Two revolutionary upheavals in industrialized nations, one in France and the other in Russia, would test continued observer comfort with violent change.

98. David Griffiths, "Far Western Populism: The Case of Utah, 1893–1900," 398, 403, 404; John S. McCormick and John R. Sillito, "Henry W. Lawrence: A Life in Dissent."
99. McCormick and Sillito, "Henry W. Lawrence," 238.

CHAPTER 5

FRANCE AND RUSSIA IN "THE THROES OF REVOLUTION," 1870–71 AND 1905

Introduction

Despite changes following the pioneer era that laid the foundation of modern Mormon identity, the belief lingered that the Saints would someday literally rule the earth. Apostle Anthony W. Ivins recorded in his journal in 1898 that Church leaders still expected to return to Jackson County, Missouri, the place designated by Joseph Smith as Zion—the Second Jerusalem. But unless the Church became financially solvent, purchase of the land was out of the question. In solemn assembly in the Salt Lake Temple, Joseph F. Smith said the Lord would send "Cyclones, Whirlwinds and devouring fire and the way will be prepared for the fulfilment of His purposes." He reminded the apostles that the elders might have to return to Missouri "as Ancient Israel wint into the Promised Land, by the shedding of blood." The time was rapidly approaching—ten to twenty years ahead, "maybe sooner."[1] With this commentary, Smith hit upon a revolutionary article of faith. If the divine director required it, the true believer in utopia understood that its realization might require violence and death.[2]

Mormon study of the bloody 1871 uprising of the Paris Commune, the 1905 Russian Revolution, and various colonial revolts managed to remain grounded in sympathetic critique. "The Latter-day Saints," said Apostle George Q. Cannon in 1900, "take great interest in that which transpires in our own nation and in foreign nations. . . . The wars, the commotions, the revolutions among the inhabitants of the earth, and also

---

1. Anthony W. Ivins, *Autobiography and Diary Excerpts of Anthony W. Ivins*, July 2, 1898.

2. Frank E. Manuel and Fritzie P. Manuel, *Utopian Thought in the Western World*, 716.

the elemental disturbances that occur, are noticed by us because in our minds they have a bearing on the great future that lies before the earth."[3] Latter-day Saint literature and speeches refracted the era's revolutionary events. In the continued belief that the workings of history were manifestations of divine revelation, Mormon observers showed a sympathy toward revolution best understood as an exercise of faith. Postmillennialism, the idea that Christianity would triumph and the world would merge into the thousand year's peace through regular historical processes, dominated Protestant theology between 1870 and 1920; but Mormon observers extended further and with greater hope the notion that revolutionary violence might advance the sacred narrative of human history.

The Franco-Prussian War (1870) and the Paris Commune (1871)

Despite domestic distractions such as the 1857–58 Utah War, Mormons remained strongly interested in Europe. In 1860 Garibaldi's Red Shirts seized the Two Kingdoms of Sicily and handed them to King Victor Emmanuel II in the name of the people of Italy. In 1870 Napoleon III withdrew French troops from Rome. Italian soldiers occupied the city, completing the unification of Italy. Next came German unification.

The hundred years of peace among European nations between Napoleon's defeat at Waterloo in 1815 and the onset of World War I were marred only by the very short wars of German unification, culminating in the Franco-Prussian War of 1870. That conflict began when German Chancellor Otto von Bismarck manipulated France's Louis Napoleon III into declaring war on Prussia to shore up his sagging popularity at home. In a war that lasted just six weeks, the German Confederation led by Prussia trounced France. The French army surrendered at Sedan and Napoleon III abdicated. The Prussians swept forward and besieged Paris. In the meantime, Bismarck completed the unification of Germany in the Versailles Palace Hall of Mirrors.[4] Radicals in Paris, humiliated by the terms of ca-

---

3. George Q. Cannon, April 6, 1900, *Report of the Semi-annual Conference of the Church of Jesus Christ of Latter-day Saints*, 11 (hereafter cited as *Conference Report*).

4. For the Franco-Prussian War, see Lawrence Dinkelspiel Steefel, *Bismarck, the Hohenzollern Candidacy, and the Origins of the Franco-German War of 1870*; and Michael Howard, *The Franco-Prussian War: The*

pitulation and the subsequent parade of German troops under the Arc de Triomphe, formed the Paris Commune in March 1871. The holocaust that followed in May remains the biggest urban insurrection in history.

American opinion sided with German unification. Napoleon's attempt to install Maximilian I in Mexico during the American Civil War had weakened American goodwill toward the French emperor.[5] Additionally, few Americans could understand how a cultured nation such as France could tolerate a ruler who had wasted money in the renovation of Paris, over-centralized the government, and sapped free enterprise.[6]

The Mormon press shared their countrymen's dislike of Napoleon III's France. The gambit to restore a French presence in North America via Mexico doomed the regime in Mormon eyes, as the Book of Mormon stated that kings would not be tolerated in the Americas.[7] In 1864, owing to poor convert returns, Mission President Louis Bertrand closed the French Mission on the grounds that police surveillance and revived Catholic influence made missionary work in France impossible. Before he departed Paris, Bertrand wrote to Napoleon predicting the destruction of his regime.[8] During the Franco-Prussian War, Apostle

---

German Invasion of France, 1870–1871.

5. John Gerow Gazley, *American Opinion of German Unification, 1848–1871*, 264–309.

6. Ibid., 406–7, 418–19. A minority supported France after Adolphe Thiers proclaimed the Third Republic following the surrender at Sedan. Americans criticized the shelling and occupation of Paris in January 1871. Nonetheless, the pro-German consensus held. See ibid., 382–98.

7. George C. Ferguson, "Book of Mormon and Napoleon III," *Latter-day Saints' Millennial Star* 42 (October 4, 1880): 636–39 (hereafter cited as *Millennial Star*). See also Anthon Hendrik Lund, Diary, August 16, 1914. Book of Mormon injunctions against monarchies in the Americas include 2 Nephi 1:7 and Mosiah 29:17–31.

8. For Bertrand's correspondence with Napoleon III, see Louis A. Bertrand, "Important Appeal to the Emperor of the French," *Millennial Star* 23 (April 6, 1861): 220–21; Louis A. Bertrand, Letter to George Amasa Smith, March 6, 1865, in Paris Branch, France Mission, Manuscript History and Historical Reports. Harassment and dismal proselytizing returns of the French Mission are recorded under the entry for June 30, 1864, in the same collection; and in Gary Ray Chard, "A History of the French Mission of the Church of Jesus Christ of Latter-day Saints, 1850–1960," 41–42. The law of 1850

George Q. Cannon, editor of the Church's *Juvenile Instructor*, published vignettes that pitted French pride against Teutonic ruthlessness. The French people, arrogant but brave and resourceful during the siege of Paris, paid the price for Bonapartist ambition.[9]

In February 1871 British Prime Minister Benjamin Disraeli warned that Bismarck's victory threatened the European balance of power. However, the German threat to British security failed to engender sympathy in the office of the *Latter-day Saints' Millennial Star*.[10] The *Star* featured a futuristic account of England's overthrow as "retold" in 1925 by an old man. The narrator described how interest rates had soared; coal mining, industry, and trade had declined; the leisure class had grown; paupers had become "a caste in the state;" and how uprisings in India and Ireland had tied up the army. These developments had weakened Great Britain, which succumbed to German conquest in 1875.[11] The message was that the disorder caused by the rise of German power would embolden exploited classes and oppressed nations, culminating in revolution.

To Mormon observers, it appeared that the established orders of England, Europe, and even the whole world were under siege. The support Mormon observers showed for Irish nationalism and worker

---

allowed Catholic influence in education at the primary and secondary levels, reflecting the adage that "fear of the Jacobins outweigh[ed] fear of the Jesuits." See William L. Langer, *Political and Social Upheaval, 1832–1852*, 454–55.

9. "Before the War," *Juvenile Instructor* 6 (April 15, 1871): 61; "French Declaration of War," *Juvenile Instructor* 6 (April 29, 1871): 65–66; "The Declaration of War at Berlin," *Juvenile Instructor* 6 (May 13, 1871): 73; "Expelled from Paris," *Juvenile Instructor* 6 (June 10, 1871): 89; "The City of Strasbourg," *Juvenile Instructor* 6 (June 10, 1871): 93–94; "Flight of French from Paris," *Juvenile Instructor* 6 (June 24, 1871): 101; "A Strike in the Factories of France," *Juvenile Instructor* 6 (July 8, 1871): 109; "Cutting Down the Bois de Boulogne," *Juvenile Instructor* 6 (July 22, 1871): 117–18.

10. Gordon A. Craig, *Germany: 1866–1945*, 103; "Nearly a European Conflagration," reprinted from *Daily News* in *Millennial Star* 33 (April 11, 1871): 229–30.

11. "The Impending Ruin of England," *Millennial Star* 34 (October 1, 1871): 626–27. A Ribbonist uprising in Ireland in 1869–70 raised concern in England as British officers complained that Fenianism (Irish republicanism) was infiltrating security forces. See Virginia Crossman, "The Army and Law and Order in the Nineteenth Century," 361, 366, 367.

grievances exemplified the moral and historical force that revolution continued to exert upon the Mormon consciousness. Three days before the French surrender at Sedan on September 2, 1870, an editorial in the *Deseret Evening News* eagerly weighed in:

> The political and social condition of the masses . . . was never more unsatisfactory. Wars and Revolution are threatened. . . . It is like a volcano, whose pent up fires are ready to burst forth at any moment. . . . The monarchs and magnates of almost every land, with all the immense machinery at their command, find it impossible to govern and control the people, who, smarting under the wrongs and tyranny of ages, are ready to rise in their might to wrest from their rulers their misused power, and to institute systems of government under which "life, liberty, and the pursuit of happiness" will be guaranteed to all.[12]

The editorial tied the "varied movements" to God's will: an "all-wise Providence was at work "for the accomplishment of its purposes and the promulgation of the gospel of the kingdom."[13]

January 1871 brought more incredible news. Victor Emmanuel II of Italy had seized the Vatican. Wilhelm I received the crown of a united Germany. The French Empire had fallen and Adolphe Thiers was elected president of the Third Republic. From his editor's desk George Q. Cannon read the changing barometer and wrote that a propitious moment for the Church had arrived:

> The throes of revolution which Europe is undergoing are signs of that freedom that shall soon dawn on that continent. Then the Elders of this Church will go through Germany, France, Italy and Spain, and through every land in Europe; for the "sick man" [Ottoman Empire] will yet open his doors . . . and Russia will unfold her gates. [The missionaries] will go forth . . . proclaiming unto them that God has established a government which will be the means of restoring to the earth the blessings for which mankind have sighed, panted and labored for ages in vain.[14]

Eight days after the proclamation of the Paris Commune on March 18, Orson Pratt spoke in Salt Lake City. "One great revolution," he said,

---

12. "Revolutionary Tendencies of the Age," *Deseret Evening News*, August 30, 1870.

13. Ibid.

14. George A. Cannon, January 8, 1871, *Journal of Discourses*, 14:28.

would cast down kingdoms and thrones. While Pratt did not directly identify Germany, France, or the Commune, he had ongoing European events in mind: "Empire will war with empire, kingdom with kingdom, and city with city."[15] The unfolding civil strife, in Pratt's estimation, was a foretaste of things to come.

Paris withstood the besieging German army until January 28, 1871. The new government, led by Adolphe Thiers, signed the Treaty of Frankfurt and proclaimed the Third Republic. Then formed the Paris Commune. The Communards—a gaggle of artisans and destitute workers, anarchist Proudhonists, conspiratorial Blanquists, some Marxist representatives of the First International, and old-fashioned Jacobin radicals—rejected the treaty. The Commune protested the loss of Alsace-Lorraine to Germany, the lack of municipal elections in Paris, and the election of a monarchist majority to the National Assembly in February. Gabriel-Constant Martin, a Communard leader, captured the stubborn mood when he declared that the Commune would never surrender.[16]

Monarchists and the wealthy fled the city. Meanwhile, the Communards enacted social reforms. Poor people entered the half-abandoned neighborhoods of Paris's wealthy western side, but there was little time for much else. The Thiers government regrouped at Versailles and persuaded Bismarck to release French troops for the purpose of squashing the Commune. During the week of May 21–28, 1871, the French Army destroyed the Commune in horrific street fighting. Fires consumed sections of Paris, mostly set by republican troops or started by gunfire.[17] Twenty thousand insurrectionists were killed or executed. Thirty-eight thousand were arrested and seventy-five hundred deported

---

15. Orson Pratt, March 26, 1871, *Journal of Discourses*, 14:65–66.

16. Stewart Edwards, *The Paris Commune 1871*, 338. Karl Marx had hoped the Communards would rally behind the Third Republic in exchange for worker gains. He lionized the Commune's defiance and explained its failure only after its destruction. See Francis Wheen, *Karl Marx: A Life*, 324; Karl Marx, "The Civil War in France" (1871), in David McClellan, ed., *Karl Marx: Selected Writings*, 539–57. For a Marxist interpretation of the Commune, see Alexander Trachtenberg, "The Lessons of the Paris Commune."

17. John M. Merriman, "Contested Freedoms in the French Revolutions, 1830–1871," 206.

to New Caledonia. The European Party of Order had once again served notice of its intent to hold the barrier against social change.[18]

The sympathy that the Paris Commune engenders today among social activists masks the fear that the insurrection originally generated. Even those sympathetic to the Commune were appalled by the death toll of its fanatical resistance.[19] Few Americans understood the Commune or its fundamental aims. Influenced by newspaper reports, Americans viewed the Communards as enemies of civilization fighting against a republican government during a time of sensitive national transition.[20]

Mormon observers and press editors accepted the first round of accounts of the Commune's irrationality. The Commune did not represent a new society modeled on the purity of the people. Instead it degenerated into a mass riot in the midst of which atrocities were committed by both Communards and government troops. This episode momentarily doused Mormon observers' enthusiasm for revolution. The *Deseret Evening News* denounced the Communards as "the worst element to be found in France," an element that had led the "most ignorant portion of her population under the specious watchwords: reason, liberty, equality, and fraternity." Fortunately for civilized man, the reign of the "desperados" was short.[21] The editor of the *Millennial Star* warned that the "whole civilized world is seething and bubbling with [social, political, and religious] revolution." The horrific fighting in Paris could be repeated in America, a nation "still an experiment" whose "sorest trials are yet to come."[22]

---

18. For the Paris Commune see Alistair Horne, *The Fall of Paris: The Siege and the Commune, 1870–71*; Robert Tombs, *The War against Paris, 1871*; Merriman, "Contested Freedoms in the French Revolutions," 202–8.

19. Royden Harrison, ed., *The English Defence of the Commune, 1871*, 23.

20. George L. Cherry, "American Metropolitan Press Reaction to the Paris Commune of 1871." Other works treating American contempt of the Commune include M. J. Heale, *American Anticommunism: Combating the Enemy Within, 1830–1970*, 23–24; and Michael H. Hunt, *Ideology and U.S. Foreign Policy*, 105.

21. Editorial, *Deseret Evening News*, May 26, 1871.

22. "The Coming Conflict," *Millennial Star* 33 (May 16, 1871): 307. Another article linked women's suffrage and Victoria C. Woodhull's "free love" movement to the Paris Commune. See "A Growing Evil," *Millennial Star* 33 (June 20, 1871): 385–86. Ironically, Utah in 1870 had become one

Eliza R. Snow, president of the LDS Church's female Relief Society, inscribed her support of Adolphe Thiers in a poem entitled "Farewell to Paris." Snow denounced the Communards as "suicidal bands" fomenting "internal strife" and "fraternal hate."[23] Her quickness to judge, however, is understandable. After all, Thiers did head a republican government that had regained power thanks to the Prussian victory over Napoleon III's empire, much as George Q. Cannon had hoped would happen. But Snow, like other observers, was not fully aware of the Commune's grievances. Snow saw the Communards as simply reactionaries animated by a mob mentality.

Subsequent news of the reprisals softened the anti-Communard bias. As early as April 1871, the *Millennial Star* worried that the Thiers government planned to force all nations to respect Papal territory and the stabilizing role of the Catholic religion in the moral and philosophical foundation of Europe.[24] Similarly, the *Deseret News* presented evidence of a royalist revival, Catholic resurgence, and "White Terror" (ruling class revenge).[25] Editor George Q. Cannon matched these reports with word that the Commune had seized clerical property, an act Mormon readers would likely have approved, given Catholic harassment of Mormon missionaries.

The fiery end of the Commune also elicited religious similes. Russian novelist Fyodor Dostoevsky compared the inferno in the Tuileries palace (destroyed by the Communard rebels) to the flames of the Last Judgment. Lenin described the Commune's final days as "the struggle for heaven."[26] The *Millennial Star* likened the siege of Paris and the destruction of the Commune to the Roman siege and Jewish defense of Jerusalem in 70 AD: "Many gallant feats were performed on both sides: the Romans [German troops] evincing military skill combined with strength, the Jews [Parisian defenders], reckless impetuosity and unbridled fury." In the liquidation of the Commune, "Shame led on

---

of the first US territories to grant women the right to vote.

23. Eliza R. Snow, "Farewell to Paris," *Woman's Exponent* 1 (February 15, 1873): 138.

24. "Bad Prospects for Peace," *Millennial Star* 33 (April 4, 1871): 215.

25. Foreign News, *Deseret Evening News*, June 1, 1871; Editorial, *Deseret Evening News*, June 9, 1871; Editorial, *Deseret Evening News*, June 21, 1871.

26. James Billington, *Fire in the Minds of Men: The Origins of the Revolutionary Faith*, 357.

the one party"—French soldiers atoning for their defeat in the Franco-Prussian War, and "necessity"—Communards fighting for their lives spurred on the other. In this metaphor, drama blurred ideological distinctions. The Thiers government had failed to behave like a magnanimous winner. Labeling Third Republic officials as "cowardly absentees from Paris," first for partnering with the conquering Germans during the siege, then for killing and mistreating prisoners after the Commune street fighting, the *Star* reported that the "clemency of Titus is without its modern analogue, and we may look in vain among the letters from Versailles for a hint of any such merciful consideration" as shown by the Roman emperor to the ancient rebel Jews.[27] France, in the brutality of repression, had lost its "religious faith and public spirit."[28]

Some Latter-day Saints outside the mainstream of the Church agreed with the fundamental aims of the Paris Commune. In 1871 two prominent Mormons, E. L. T. Harrison and William S. Godbe, established the Liberal Institute in Salt Lake City. Free-Thinkers, spiritualists, non-Mormons, and anyone else who chafed against Mormon rule found solace in the pages of the Institute's organ, the *Salt Lake Daily Tribune*. The Communards, the paper declared, embodied the American republican spirit. In class conflict the *Tribune* anticipated the moral and physical victory of the workers:

> Educated labor will yet triumph; and when these matters are fully understood it will be found that the power of wealth is on the wane. It has ruled the world from its infancy up through all the ages of ignorance which have marked the past, but its day of humiliation is coming, and the uprising of the people is at hand.[29]

---

27. "Paris and Jerusalem," reprinted from *Liverpool Journal* in *Millennial Star* 33 (June 13, 1871): 372.

28. Ibid., 374.

29. "The Commune," *Weekly Salt Lake Tribune and Utah Mining Gazette*, July 20, 1871. Godbe and Harrison were eventually excommunicated from the Church but retained the admiration of Apostles Heber J. Grant and Charles Penrose. See Ronald W. Walker, "When Spirits Did Abound: Nineteenth-Century Utah's Encounter with Free-Thought Radicalism," 319, 324. The convictions of the Godbeites were also shared by Henry Lawrence. See John S. McCormick and John R. Sillito, "Henry W. Lawrence: A Life in Dissent," 230.

Class warfare waged in Paris encouraged research into the European sociopolitical system. American Protestant ministers rejected the atheism of the Communards but sought to understand them by analyzing the roots of European social unrest.[30] Mormon observers shared the same concerns. Less than a month after Thiers regained control of Paris, Cannon, relying on "one of the ablest and accurate statisticians in Europe," led off a June 1871 issue of the *Deseret Evening News* with an examination of the late Napoleonic regime's fiscal policies. Cannon concluded that high taxes, public debt, and arms expenditures had contributed to the revolutionary outburst of 1871. Also, the same factors that triggered the formation of the Commune might have repercussions in Great Britain: "A nation may stagger under such a burden of expense for a long period, as England has done," concluded the editorial, "but it cannot last always. Her people, the working classes, upon whom the weight of [taxation] rests, will not quietly endure it much longer. Already they manifest a restiveness which . . . may break out in riots and revolution."[31]

Mormon observers had mixed feelings about the immediate implications of the uprising and the destruction of the Commune. British Mission President Horace Sunderlin Eldredge, on tour in Germany in spring 1871, was impressed by the "warm greeting" the cheering crowds gave a Bavarian regiment as it paraded through town on its return from France.[32] A year later, a missionary visiting an exhibition in Paris was awed by the Commune's fortifications.[33] In 1872 Apostles George A. Smith and Lorenzo Snow met Adolphe Thiers and congratulated him on his triumph. But after viewing the old embattled districts in Paris, Snow was circumspect. He confided to a correspondent that the "political prospects of France are shrouded in fearful mystery—at any moment the most terrible scenes may burst upon the country."[34] On the

---

30. Philip M. Katz, "'Lessons from Paris:' The American Clergy Responds to the Paris Commune."

31. George Q. Cannon, Editorial, *Deseret Evening News*, June 23, 1871.

32. Horace Sunderlin Eldredge, Letter to Brigham Young, January 21, 1871; and Horace Sunderlin Eldredge, Diary, March 22, 1871.

33. Samuel Stephen Jones, Diary, March 27, 1872, 2:154.

34. Lorenzo Snow, Letter III, December 15, 1872, in Eliza R. Snow, comp., *Biography and Family Record of Lorenzo Snow: One of the Twelve Apostles of the Church of Jesus Christ of Latter-day Saints*, 510.

other hand, eighteen months after the destruction of the Commune, Orson Pratt still pictured a beneficial revolution from below. He looked for "great change and revolution among the inhabitants of our globe." Mankind would "rise by degrees into that high position that God intends for his children." Pratt proceeded to describe a postmillennial state. The earthly kingdom of God would advance until "there will be no more death, no more sorrow nor crying, for all things will become new." Christ would not necessarily reign on earth, but he would have "a connection" with it. Distance would "make no difference."[35] Later in the decade, the memory of France's 1789 revolutionary heritage prompted speculation that France might again liberate peoples from oppression. During the Russo-Turkish War of 1877–78, the *Millennial Star* suggested that another Bonaparte might seize power and launch a "democratic revolution" that would confine Russia north of the Danube and retake Alsace and Lorraine from Germany.[36]

In the United States, the memory of the Commune was negatively recalled following the scare of the Pennsylvania railroad strikes in 1877. Labor historian Eugene Leach has documented how the idea of the mob was used to discredit worker dissent.[37] Further worrying the Mormon

35. Orson Pratt, November 24, 1872, *Journal of Discourses*, 15:239.

36. "Speculation: Coming Results of the Russo Turkish War," *Millennial Star* 39 (June 18, 1877): 391. Protestant ministers were ambivalent toward the role of the Bonapartes, referred to in this article as the "Napoleonic Antichrist." The revival of Ultramontanism (universal papal authority) after 1815 turned attention to Louis-Napoleon III as an agent of anticlericalism as his uncle had been. In a popular millennialist version, antichrist Bonaparte (Napoleon, Louis-Napoleon, or Jerome) would destroy the papacy, and in turn be destroyed by Christ's coming. Some ministers denied that Napoleon was the antichrist. After all, the Napoleonic Code repressed the Jesuits and curbed Catholic influence in much of Europe. See Leroy Edwin Froom, *The Prophetic Faith of Our Fathers: The Historical Development of Prophetic Interpretation*, 2:759–60; 4:148, 150–51.

37. Eugene E. Leach, "Chaining the Tiger: The Mob Stigma and the Working Class, 1863–1894," 187–215. See also David Brion Davis, ed., *The Fear of Conspiracy: Images of Un-American Subversion from the Revolution to the Present*, 150, 162. The fear of Communist International influence in the 1877 strike is discussed in Robert V. Bruce, *1877: Year of Violence*, 226–60. Strike-breaking detective Allan Pinkerton published his belief in

mind was the 1879 Reynolds case in which the Supreme Court ruled polygamy legally indefensible. "Secret Combinations," Mormons believed, had been formed against Zion itself.[38] Anarchists, unions, Marxists and, for that matter, the Republican Party, were cabals determined to seize power and deprive the people of God's law and individual liberty.[39] Mormons sometimes expressed their discontent through revolutionary talk. George Q. Cannon, Utah's representative in Washington DC between 1872 and 1882, himself a target of the anti-polygamy campaign, took up the refrain: Corruption would build until the United States "convulsed with revolution."[40]

But if Mormon observers succumbed briefly to fear of mobocracy and conspiracy, they nevertheless got back to the positive effects of revolution. Before long they resumed the championing of popular revolutions and industrial democracy in foreign countries. Their social critiques grew more sophisticated, and some of those critiques admiringly recalled Paris of 1871. Alice Louise Reynolds, endeavoring to illustrate that likenesses of the United Order of Enoch had surfaced from time to time in

---

working-class conspiracy in *Strikers, Communists, Tramps and Detectives*, 67, 77–79.

38. George Q. Cannon, "Editorial Thoughts," *The Juvenile Instructor* 13 (July 1, 1878): 150; George Q. Cannon, July 7, 1878, *Journal of Discourses*, 20:34–35; "Signs of the Times," *Millennial Star* 40 (September 30, 1878): 615; "Secret Combinations," *Millennial Star* 41 (April 21, 1879): 248–50; "Terrorism in Russia," *Millennial Star* 41 (June 16, 1879): 371–72; John Taylor, April 9, 1882, *Journal of Discourses*, 23:62–63; George Q. Cannon, "Topics of the Times," *Juvenile Instructor* 18 (May 1, 1883): 133–34. The Church's near disincorporation averted by the Manifesto likewise provoked cries of "secret combination" from the increasingly conservative *Millennial Star* toward the 1892 Pittsburgh Homestead strike in "Combinations That Bring Trouble," *Millennial Star* 54 (August 8, 1892): 504–6.

39. On Mormon opposition to the courts and the Republican Party on the issue of polygamy and theocracy in Utah, see Sarah Barringer Gordon, *The Mormon Question: Polygamy and Constitutional Conflict in Nineteenth Century America*, 147–49; Edwin Brown Firmage and Richard Collin Mangrum, *Zion in the Courts: A Legal History of the Church of Jesus Christ of Latter-day Saints, 1830–1900*, 151–59; Blaine Carmon Hardy, "Self-Blame and the Manifesto," 44–45.

40. Cannon, January 8, 1871, *Journal of Discourses*, 14:28.

"profane history," suggested that one such moment was the rise of the Commune. Writing for the *Young Woman's Journal* in 1898, she referred to the Commune as a reasonable proletarian response to laissez-faire capitalism. Workers, "remembering with no degree of satisfaction the republican government of the past . . . clamored that the nation's wealth be equally distributed and that a united industrial commonwealth be organized." Their intent was pure; absent only were the "doctrines of primitive Christianity."[41] Three years later the Church's *Improvement Era* listed the "general outbreak of revolution throughout Europe" during 1870–71 as one of the "natural miracles" of the nineteenth century.[42]

Some Mormon observers believed the Franco-Prussian War and the Paris Commune episode had incrementally advanced the Kingdom of God. Apostle Franklin D. Richards thought in retrospect that the Franco-Prussian War had made Germany receptive to missionary activity. Bismarck's subsequent religious toleration and crackdown on the Catholic Church encouraged LDS Church representatives to reconnoiter Germany. In 1875 Apostle Joseph F. Smith and European Mission leaders reopened the German Mission.[43] B. H. Roberts applied the same thinking to France. In *The Life of John Taylor*, Roberts reminded readers that Napoleon III had snuffed out the gains the French people had made in 1848, installing "despotism as absolute as any kingdom of the middle ages." Roberts referred to German arms and the Commune when he wrote that Napoleon III himself was "violently overthrown" by "another revolution" years later. In Roberts' view the fall of the Second Empire and birth of the Third Republic fulfilled prophecy. The kingdom of God grows like an oak, "fixing its mighty roots deeper in the earth and increasing in strength."[44]

In 1905, the year of the first Russian Revolution, the *Deseret Evening News* ran a story on Louise Michel, the Communard "Red Virgin." Known for her kindness to animals and commitment to the

---

41. Alice Louise Reynolds, "God's Social Order," pt. 1, *Young Woman's Journal* 9 (May 1898): 201.

42. "The Nineteenth Century," *Improvement Era* 4 (January 1901): 162–63.

43. Heber J. Grant, *Diary Excerpts of Heber J. Grant, 1887–1899*, October 7, 1898; Zachary R. Jones, "'War and Confusion in Babylon': Mormon Reaction to German Unification, 1864–1880," 25–26.

44. B. H. Roberts, *The Life of John Taylor: Third President of the Church of Jesus Christ of Latter-day Saints*, 233–34.

ideas of revolutionary theorist Wilhelm Weitling, Michel was an old friend of the Chartists and Christian communists who had challenged Marx's secular vision of a proletariat stripped of religious sentiment.[45] The *Deseret Evening News* story portrayed Michel as a revolutionary hero. She had "fought like a demon" during the Paris insurrection and in the wake of the street battles had risked her life as a "veritable angel of mercy" to the wounded.[46]

Michel's defiance of the military court that tried her for insurrection evoked the old Mormon rejection of earthly authority. Just as Mormons had taken their utopian dreams west, Europe's revolutionary leadership migrated east from France to Russia.[47] Revolution there and in the colonized regions of the globe kept Mormon hope alive for the restoration of Pangaea.

The 1905 Russian Revolution

Mormon observers had not been particularly hard on the Russian czars during the latter-half of the nineteenth century. After all, the popular Alexander II had abolished serfdom and pardoned dissidents, and Nicholas II had convened a disarmament conference in The Hague. The Mormon press was particularly appreciative of imperial edicts decreeing religious toleration.[48] Russian intellectuals reciprocated this admi-

---

45. Billington, *Fire in the Minds of Men*, 188, 266.

46. "Red Virgin is Dead," *Deseret Evening News*, January 16, 1905.

47. Billington, *Fire in the Minds of Men*, 346, 349.

48. "Ecclesiastical Reform in Russia," *Millennial Star* 31 (July 17, 1869): 471–72; "Coronation of the Czar," *Millennial Star* 58 (June 4, 1896): 365–66; "Evils of War," *Millennial Star* 62 (March 1, 1900): 137. Mormon elders visited Russia during the 1880s, and Mormon Apostle Francis M. Lyman dedicated Russia for missionary work in 1903. Outside a family of converts from St. Petersburg, no members lived in Russia until the 1990s. For Lyman's mission see A. J. Höglund, "Introduction of the Gospel in Russia," *Millennial Star* 57 (June 27, 1895): 413–15; Joseph J. Cannon, "President Lyman's Travels and Ministry," *Improvement Era* 6 (November 7, 1903): 12–23; Thomas G. Alexander, *Mormonism in Transition: A History of the Latter-day Saints, 1890–1930*, 228. For administrative coverage of the Russian mission before 1917, see Gary L. Browning, *Russia and the Restored Gospel*, 3–12.

ration, praising the Mormon proclivity for organization and settlement despite perceived latent militancy.[49]

But the assumption that revolution or an outside power would overwhelm Russia outweighed Mormon admiration of the Romanov dynasty. Many Mormon observers were convinced that Russia was ruled by barbaric expansionists when Nicholas I invaded Hungary and Poland in 1849 to crush revolutionary governments. In 1871 Russian anti-Mormon literature began to appear.[50] When *narodniki* terrorists stepped up their attacks on imperial authorities in the late 1870s, ultimately killing Alexander II in 1881, Mormon writers tacitly legitimated the bomb throwing by blaming czarist incompetence.[51] Mormon observers also abhorred czarist pogroms targeting Russia's Jews.[52] The *Millennial Star* charted the czar's narrowing options: unable to "turn to the right or left," he could maintain his imperial status only by force. The future was bleak. The conservative dynasty manifested the "shaking of thrones and the agitation of empires," the "premonitory symptoms of a fatal political malady."[53]

---

49. Leland Fetzer, "Russian Writers Look at Mormon Manners, 1857–72," 77–79.

50. Ibid., 81–82.

51. "Napoleon's Prophecy," *Millennial Star* 40 (March 4, 1878): 135; "New Picture of the Czar," *Millennial Star* 41 (September 29, 1879): 611–12; "Impending Doom of Russia," 41 (April 28, 1879): 268–69; and "Condition of Russia," 41 (May 26, 1879): 326–27.

52. Church articles explained anti-Semitic violence sociologically. Causes discussed included social stress among the peasantry caused by over-taxation, dependence on "capitalistic traders," increased Jewish landholding and merchant activity, racism, provincial-level ploys to divert popular attention from economic hardship, and fear among Russians that the Zionist movement was angling for land grants in western Russia. See "Russians and Jews," *Contributor* 3 (August 1882): 343–44. Sympathy for Jews and criticism of Russia's anti-Semitic policies are found in "Text of the Memorial to the Czar," *Millennial Star* 53 (January 19, 1891): 35–36; George Q. Cannon, "Religious Intolerance in Russia," *Millennial Star* 58 (September 10, 1894): 589–91; Joseph M. Tanner, "Topics of Moment," *Improvement Era* 9 (January 1906): 244–45; and Edward H. Anderson, "Russian Affairs," *Improvement Era* 9 (October 1906): 991.

53. "Attempt on the Czar's Life," *Millennial Star* 41 (December 8, 1879): 778.

The malaise reached full fever in 1904. Economic hardship and political opposition brewed revolutionary conditions in Russia. State- and foreign-owned industry was concentrated in large factories, making it easier for workers to organize. Peasants were still saddled with taxes, while the government exported the wheat. Between 1898 and 1905 the Constitutional Democrats, Social Revolutionaries, and Social Democrats demanded that the czar agree to more popular control of the government. Vyacheslav von Plehve, the interior minister, anxious to divert attention from domestic problems, organized pogroms and waged a war against Japan over rights in Manchuria and Korea. Plehve was subsequently assassinated. On January 2, 1905, the Russian garrison at Port Arthur surrendered to a besieging Japanese army. In May the Japanese navy annihilated the Russian fleet at the Battle of Tushima Strait.

Living costs in St. Petersburg soared. Hunger spread. Czarist police, hoping to mollify worker agitation fomented by the Social Democrats, allowed a priest, Father Gapon, to take the grievances of the workers to the czar. Gapon led a peaceful march to the Winter Palace and there, on January 22, soldiers opened fire. In the "Bloody Sunday" massacre, czarist troops killed over 130 and wounded twice as many.

News that Nicholas II had fired on the people started a revolution. Peasants, egged on by Social Revolutionaries, destroyed manor houses. Constitutionalists demanded representative government. Marxist Social Democrats in St. Petersburg organized workers into *soviet* councils and coordinated strikes. The czar's tepid concessions in March were ignored and the revolt spread to the army and navy. Nicholas II and his advisors, hoping to appeal to the constitutionalists and split the revolutionary movement, issued the October Manifesto promising constitutional government and an elected assembly called the Duma. Against the backdrop of the stunning Japanese victory at Tushima, the October Manifesto bought time. Unchecked, the revolution might have produced a socialist republic. President Theodore Roosevelt kept the czarist government solvent by brokering the Portsmouth Treaty that ended the Russo-Japanese War.[54] In the meantime, Russian troops returning from the Far East drove the revolutionaries underground. The

---

54. Arthur W. Thompson and Robert A. Hart, *The Uncertain Crusade: America and the Russian Revolution of 1905*, 52–68; and Eugene P. Trani, *The Treaty of Portsmouth: An Adventure in American Diplomacy*, 50, 157.

Duma convened but had no voice in foreign policy, government appointments, or the budget.[55]

Americans condemned the Bloody Sunday massacre. Public opinion viewed the Constitutional Democrats that dominated the Duma as the catalyst of an incipient Russian republic. American encouragement of the revolution continued until the summer of 1905, when socialists agitated for still more representation. American support for repression by returning Russian troops indicates that few Americans viewed a socialist victory with pleasure.[56]

Some articles in Mormon periodicals initially urged caution. Joseph M. Tanner, for instance, expressed worry over a "civil conflict in the labor world . . . more appalling than the world has ever seen." He hoped for moderation but discerned that the "universalists" who stood for peace and justice in the world were outnumbered by "the contentious."[57] Later, however, he changed his tune and forgave the actions of some of the more radical revolutionary groups. Edward H. Anderson, assistant Church historian and assistant editor of the *Improvement Era*, warned that Social Democrats and Social Revolutionaries might steer Russia down a dangerous path. Given the radical alternative, the safest bet was the more moderate Duma. Anderson also reported favorably on Count Serge Witte, who was visiting the United States to garner support for Romanov concessions already given.[58] Anderson too, however, felt torn between moderation and sympathy for the revolution. What Mormon observers ultimately wanted from the revolution was justice and progress in any form.

Despite this initial hesitancy, the writings of Mormon observers generally outdistanced mainstream American opinion and welcomed the calamity that befell the Russian government. Japan's victory augured change in the global balance of power. The drama of peasants and workers challenging four hundred years of Romanov rule compelled Mormon observers to give the left wing of the revolution its due. Student riots and the meeting of the provincial *Zemstovs* all reinforced

---

55. Thompson and Hart, *Uncertain Crusade*, 68–91.

56. Ibid., 29–31, 75–76.

57. Joseph M. Tanner, "A Tottering Empire," *Improvement Era* 9 (February 1906): 320, 323.

58. Edward H. Anderson, "Affairs in Russia," *Improvement Era* 9 (September 1906): 911.

the claim in a *Millennial Star* article that "reforms would not be prayed for but demanded as of right." Further evidence of the *Star's* acceptance of immediate radicalization appears in the line that said Russia's assassinated interior minister was a "butcher" who deserved to be "removed from the face of the earth" by the Social Revolutionary who shot him.[59] Editorials condemning the czar appeared after Bloody Sunday in the *Deseret Evening News*. One compared conditions in Russia to those that launched the French Revolution of 1789. Others applauded the assassination of czarist officials, lionized the people's fight against imperial troops and "class privilege," and warned that that Russian diplomats were lying to conceal the severity of anti-democratic repression.[60]

As in 1848, one of the main functions of the 1905 revolution in the Mormon view was Jewish emancipation. Revolution might free Israelites of the "Lost Tribes"—notably Ephraim (northern Europeans) and others languishing unnoticed under Russian rule—as well as Judah, the "visible" Jews of the world.[61] One element of Mormon thinking at this time was that Israel's restoration would be determined by "the *territorial* terms of the covenant, not in its conversion to, or identity with, the Church."[62] In this view, the mere physical gathering of the Jews presaged the millennium. Mormons scanned Europe for laws that emancipated the Jews or movements that might lead to Jewish nationhood.[63] By the

---

59. "The Awakening of Russia," *Millennial Star* 66 (December 8, 1904): 782–84.

60. "History Repeating Itself?" *Deseret Evening News*, January 27, 1905; "Anarchy in Russia," *Deseret Evening News*, November 5, 1906; and "Autocracy Breeds Anarchy," *Deseret Evening News*, July 31, 1907.

61. On Israelites in the "north countries," see Ether 15:11 in the Book of Mormon; Anthony W. Ivins, "Church and State—British-Israel Movement," *Improvement Era* 30 (December 1926): 97–98; and Arnold Green, "Gathering and Election: Israelite Descent and Universalism in Mormon Discourse," 195–228.

62. Steven Epperson, *Mormons and Jews: Early Mormon Theologies of Israel*, 30.

63. "The Jewish Question," *Millennial Star* 41 (August 4, 1879): 491; Joseph M. Tanner, "The Zionist Movement," *Improvement Era* 3 (November 1899): 1–8; "Concerning the Jews," *Millennial Star* 62 (June 21, 1900): 386–87; "Rabbi Discusses Possibilities of Colony of Jewish Farmers in Utah," *Salt Lake Telegram*, March 15, 1912; B. H. Roberts, April 4, 1902, *Conference Report*, 15. See also Epperson, *Mormons and Jews*, 212.

1890s, civil rights conferred on Jews throughout Europe had enabled Jewish leaders to convene a Zionist Congress and to begin laying plans for the establishment of a national Jewish homeland.

Only Russia continued to harass its Jewish subjects. Mormon editorials and articles set forth revolution as part of a divine plan that would enable God to fulfill his covenant with the Jews. Overthrow of the czar and the strengthening of the more liberal Duma would terminate the pogroms and free the empire's Jewish population to dispose of property and migrate to Palestine. Jewish concentration in the Holy Land would restore the continuity of sacred history, galvanizing an all-out missionary effort and eventually the unification of the world.[64]

By the beginning of 1906, the revolution had succeeded as far as Mormon observers were concerned. The aforementioned Edward H. Anderson hailed the seating of the first Duma in May 1906. St. Petersburg, he wrote, was "dressed bride-like, awaiting the coming of the Lord":

> The most exclusive court in Europe lowered its bars for the first time to admit to the Emperor's presence plebian men who came, not by virtue of his invitation, but by the solemn mandate from the people struggling for the day-dawn of freedom.

Change had come. Not from a benevolent ruler, but from the people who had stolen their own "onward march of civilization."[65]

Mormon observers recognized this new front of socialism as a standard around which "plebian men" had rallied diverse groups in Russia. The *Deseret News* identified socialist leaders among the factory workers as "the most active in bringing about the change." They had "facilitated the propaganda and strengthened the liberal cause until it grew beyond the power of the police" to repress it. Furthermore, worker organization had stimulated peasant solidarity.[66] Anderson credited the coalition of Social Revolutionaries, liberals in the Duma, and mutinous sailors of the Sveaborg and Kronstadt garrisons with having led "one of the great-

---

64. "The Jews Awakening," *Deseret Evening News*, December 18, 1905; Tanner, "Topics of Moment," 245; and Joseph M. Tanner, "The Struggle in Russia," *Deseret Evening News*, March 26, 1907.

65. Edward H. Anderson, "Auspicious Day for Russia," *Improvement Era* 9 (June 1906): 659.

66. "Russia Free," *Deseret Evening News*, October 31, 1905.

est struggles for liberty in modern times."[67] Joseph M. Tanner suspected that "the example of the industrial classes in Russia . . . will give courage and aggressiveness to the industrial masses" all over the world.[68] Recent scholarship confirms that middle-class leaders had indeed given the factory workers and sailors of St. Petersburg a sense of empowerment and had made peasants a force that could not be ignored.[69]

During the latter half of 1906, Mormon observers assessed the results of the revolution with guarded optimism and wondered whether Russians could turn their revolution into an act of human betterment. Mormon writers tuned in to the worker factory councils (*soviets*), the rural radicalism of the Social Revolutionaries, and the political factions vying to promote their agendas in the Duma.[70] They also recognized the challenge von Witte and Pëter Stolypin faced as they attempted to reform without surrendering the essence of autocracy.[71] Anderson suggested amnesty as the antidote to the continuation of agitation and violence.[72] Some observers harbored biases common to many Americans of the day and doubted the capacity of Slavic peoples for self-government.[73] Joseph A. Vance gave high marks to German and British socialists but warned that Russian, Spanish, Italian, and French socialism were "menacing."[74] Tanner suspended judgment. The "revolution must

---

67. Anderson, "Affairs in Russia," 912.

68. Tanner, "Topics of the Moment," 242.

69. Gerald Surh, *1905 in St. Petersburg: Labor, Society, and Revolution,* 5–8; Laura Engelstein, "Revolution and the Theater of Public Life in Russia," 316, 343–54.

70. Anderson, "Russian Affairs," 990–91; Tanner, "A Tottering Empire," 320–23; Joseph M. Tanner, "The New Russian Duma and the Conditions Leading Up to It," *Improvement Era* 10 (April 1907): 457–62; Edward H. Anderson, "Political Progress in Russia," *Improvement Era* 11 (June 1908): 645–46.

71. Peter Stoltypin (1863–1911) administered limited rural reforms while ruthlessly using secret police. Prime Minister Count Sergi Yulevich von Witte (1849–1915) promoted the Trans-Siberian Railway and helped reform the Duma.

72. Anderson, "Auspicious Day for Russia," 660.

73. Hunt, *Ideology and U.S. Foreign Policy,* 78–79, 111–12.

74. Joseph A. Vance, "Growth and Development of Socialism," *Millennial Star* 71 (March 25, 1909): 181. Similar sentiment found in "Anarchy, Not Revolution," *Deseret Evening News,* November 3, 1905. A 1931 editorial said

prove largely successful," he thought, but he gave Slavs a middle rating for constitutional aptitude.[75] Russian ministers, Tanner opined, would have to walk a middle path. On one side they would be under pressure from conservatives to hold the line. On the other side, worker and peasant revolutionaries whose image of Nicholas II as a benevolent father had been destroyed represented incipient violence. The czar had to reform, redistribute power, and recognize the industrial *soviets* to prevent further dissolution.[76]

Faith in Revolution Untarnished

The overall Mormon attitude toward revolution edged slightly to the left between 1870 and 1905. Mormon observers of this period affirmed the people's right to resort to arms to change the form of their government and gain a greater share of the rewards of economic activity. As long as revolutions were justified, supported by the masses, led by men of integrity, and/or fulfilled God's purposes in ushering in the millennium, Mormon observers could endorse them.

The Mormon response to the revolutions of 1871 and 1905 followed a three-stage pattern. News of revolutionary outbreaks was initially received with enthusiasm. The early stages of upheaval seemed to portend the beginning of the long-awaited new age. Gabriel Kolko terms this initial, uninformed response to revolution "mechanistic optimism"—the habit of construing events to fit a preconfigured schema.[77] The second stage was marked by criticism. Excessive casualties, the damage done to Paris in 1871, and the possibility of a radical take-over of the Russian Revolution of 1905 from a moderate coalition forced Mormon writers to analyze the composition of the revolutionary move-

---

revolts in Teutonic or Nordic regions occurred on principle. These were the revolutions anticipated "with trepidation." Latin revolts, by contrast, occurred out of "personal enmity." Therefore a revolt against Mussolini would be meaningless; a revolution in Germany "would probably change the future of the history of the world." See "Revolution," *Deseret News*, April 11, 1931.

75. Tanner, "Topics of Moment," 242.

76. Ibid., 243.

77. Gabriel Kolko, "The Decline of American Radicalism in the Twentieth Century," 198.

ments and correlate the ideologies of these combinations with possible outcomes. In the third phase, concern or disillusionment led to revision. Revolutions could go astray, the observers saw, but the observers most unwilling to let go always reinstated revolution in the providential process. Explaining away unfulfilled expectations allowed the observers to continue to nurture faith in the inevitability of a universal millennial kingdom achievable through human action.

CHAPTER 6

MORMON OBSERVERS RESPOND TO COLONIALISM

From Colonial Revolt, Hope

The New Imperialism—a new wave of European colonial acquisition and exploitation—rolled over the globe between 1870 and 1930. The era tested Mormon observers' belief in humanity's usefulness in working with God to achieve an earthly system of justice and brotherhood. Mormon observers watched Irish, Chinese, Cuban, Filipino, Mexican, Boer, and Indian nationalists rise against colonialism. "A nation is internationally free," wrote an editor of the *Latter-day Saints' Millennial Star* in 1881, when it is not "abridged of its just rights and privileges by other nations." Arguing that progress toward "higher civilization" requires self-restraint, the editor reasoned that nations that indulged in exploitation and expansionistic warfare risked revolution in their colonies and at home.[1] Mormon observers heard the rumblings. In them they anticipated a possible world movement.

The New Imperialism

The New Imperialism was a moral and economic crusade to spread Western culture throughout the world. Protestant missionar-

---

1. "True Liberty – What is It?" *Latter-day Saints' Millennial Star* 43 (August 8, 1881): 498 (hereafter cited as *Millennial Star*). Mormon admiration for freedom-fighting peoples went back to Germanic tribes resisting Roman imperialism and to Mexico's fight against Spain. In 1898 Mormon colonist Joel H. Martineau wrote that the War of Independence ending in 1821 had freed Mexico from "oppression far worse than that which the American colonies abjured in 1776." See "Mexican Independence," *Deseret Weekly*, October 1, 1898, 493–94; and "In the German Woods," *Contributor* 8 (November 1886): 29–33.

ies returning to the United States and Europe from the "field" brought back stories of benighted peoples waiting for the arrival of civilization. There were also economic motives. Europe had become dependent on foreign imports—both raw materials and exotic goods. Russian theorist Vladimir Lenin argued that imperialism resulted from competition between monopolistic firms to amass as much capital and gain control of as many markets as possible. The advantages afforded by imperial preference within one's own colonial system triggered intense rivalry among the European powers and Japan. Battle fleets, coaling stations, and control of canals and waterways were needed to protect lines of supply and communication that connected the Great Powers to their far-flung colonies. Mormon observers toured European capitals and felt the rising tension. Joseph M. Tanner wrote that Constantinople crawled with foreign intrigue. In light of the "mysterious movements among the European nations, if . . . war comes . . . it will be hard to say what nations shall not be involved."[2]

Beginning in 1877, Conservative British Prime Minister Benjamin Disraeli launched a series of military expeditions in Africa, Asia, and the Mediterranean. The economic motives driving Disraeli's imperialism stirred negative sentiments in the Church's Liverpool office. A *Millennial Star* article loathed the "repulsive" and "appalling" struggles for economic supremacy between the European powers.[3] But why had capitalist abuses not yet brought revolution? In *Imperialism, the Highest Stage of Capitalism* (1916), Vladimir Lenin attempted to show that industrialized nations had bought off their own working classes. The imperial powers had exported capital to underdeveloped regions and converted a portion of the profits into higher wages.[4] Revenue and raw materials extracted from annexed territories enabled governments and firms to keep workers in metropolitan centers employed and supportive of colonial expansion. The *Millennial Star* anticipated Lenin's theory in 1879:

---

2. Joseph M. Tanner, Letter to Francis M. Lyman, March 1, 1886, 4, in Francis M. Lyman, Scrapbook.

3. "The Coming Crash," *Millennial Star* 41 (February 17, 1879): 104.

4. Vladmir I. Lenin, *Imperialism, the Highest Stage of Capitalism: A Popular Outline*, 146–54. For an interpretation of Lenin's work as apocryphal writing, see James Billington, *Fire in the Minds of Men: The Origins of the Revolutionary Faith*, 466.

If men would be statesmen for the world instead of narrowing themselves down to a national focus, they would see clearly that if one, two or more nations should be successful in monopolizing the trade to any extent, they could only do so at the expense of other countries. This makes it perfectly clear that instead of this apparent success removing the evil [of unemployment and poverty], it only shifts it to or intensifies it in some other portions of the globe.[5]

But the attempt to bribe workers would not succeed. *Millennial Star* editors believed that the international scramble for more colonies only aggravated the lingering labor problem. "So long as calamity is removed from their own doors," the *Star* admitted, people do not care. But the paper's editors believed that economic difficulties were coming. Imperialism was only a "desperate expedient," a temporary stopgap. The only sure solution to the labor problem was divine government, under which production would be tailored to meet "the demands of consumption" rather than to maximize power and profit for a wealthy few.[6]

The 1880s saw the worst working-class agitation in England since the Chartist movement of the 1840s. Great Britain had led the free trade movement, but now competing nations—even former British colonies such as Canada—raised tariffs. Making matters worse, these nations began to penetrate British markets with manufactured goods, driving down prices but putting British laborers out of work. The British labor movement was strategically divided. The London Workingmen's Association, made up of skilled mechanics, demanded protective tariffs. The Marxist Social Democrat Federation (SDF) wanted to take its chances with continued free trade. Because Britain had intentionally begun to import duty-free foodstuffs with the repeal of the Corn Laws in 1846, Social Democrats feared the re-imposition of the "tax on the people's food." Unemployment stalked London in 1886. The upper class obsessed over the incipient social conflict simmering in the metropolitan slums.[7]

James Walter Paxman, a missionary in the British Mission, sensed a clash was coming. In a January 21, 1886, diary entry, Paxman revealed his anguish at seeing working-class sufferers line the route down which

---

5. "Centralization of Government," *Millennial Star* 41 (April 28, 1879): 264–65.

6. Ibid.

7. Discussion on the interplay between empire, free trade, and protectionism is found in Robert R. Palmer and Joel Colton, *A History of the Modern World*, 596–600, 648–49.

Queen Victoria's entourage traveled. "In their faces could be seen traces of hard labor . . . while between them rode the wealth and nobility of Gt. Britain with all the honors & pomp and dignity imaginable." Paxman predicted the "near approach of revolution in which the poor will rise against the rich and plunder their fine houses."[8] He was right. "The depression of trade is intense and in consequence of this & the laborers starving the unemployed held a demonstration," Paxman noted. He was becoming witness to "Black Monday." Fifteen thousand SDF and Workingmen's Association followers massed in Trafalgar Square. The two organizations voiced their competing views without incident, but die-hards and a rogue element then marched to Hyde Park. A red flag went up and the rhetoric got hot. Paxman recorded that angry leaders who had come to do violence against the wealthy then ignited the "spirit of revolution." The police were unable to quell the ensuing riot. Five thousand men rampaged down Pall Mall, Picadilly, and Oxford Street, vandalizing clubs, shops, and houses. Paxman toured the damage and concluded,

> Surely the poor have arisen against the rich in fulfillment of prophesy, to accomplish the purposes of the Lord; and who can wonder at it when such phenomonens as the above are usual.[9]

Desirous to see justice for humanity, the *Millennial Star* refused to sanctify empire. An article dismissed garrison chapel prayers asking for God's protection for British troops in Afghanistan and Zululand as "hollow" and "empty." The Latter-day Saint task of spreading the gospel militated against asking for divine help for nations to aggrandize themselves. The European powers, said the *Star*, were "full of confusion and perplexity" inflicted by their own colonial machinations.[10]

At first, the United States was immune to the New Imperialism. During the 1890s, however, the nation began to display the symptoms of industrialization that had caused the outward projection of European power. During the "Long Depression" from 1875 to 1894, American cap-

---

8. James Walter Paxman, Diary, January 21, 1886, 2:41.

9. Ibid., February 8, 1886, 2:49. For descriptions of the "Trafalgar Square Riots," see Victor Bailey, "The Metropolitan Police, the Home Office, and the Threat of Outcast London," 95–104; and Robert F. Haggard, *The Persistence of Victorian Liberalism: The Politics of Social Reform in Britain, 1870–1900*, 32.

10. "Lip Worship," *Millennial Star* 41 (April 28, 1879): 267.

italists made good on bad times. They hired more workers and ran their plants at full bore. Raw materials and wages were cheap and immigrants plentiful. By 1897 American steel production outstripped Germany, France, and Britain. Looking for new markets in the Caribbean, Central America, and Asia, President William McKinley and his successors alternately fomented or crushed revolutions to serve the expanding scope of American corporations. At the same time, colonized peoples challenged the rule of Europe, Japan, and the United States.[11]

Joseph M. Tanner treated the US stake in colonialism in two seminal articles. In "Territorial Expansion," published in 1899, Tanner expressed his belief that British and American expansion had a civilizing effect on peoples lucky enough to come under their control. However, the real motive was commercialism, and the stakes were high. To better protect the American mission abroad, Tanner anticipated later reforms in the diplomatic corps calculated to recruit and retain high-caliber personnel.[12] Tanner also warned that whatever the new foreign policy entailed, "it is doubtful whether any constitutional barriers can be erected that will thwart the determined purpose of the people."[13] In 1907 Tanner published an article titled "A New Imperialism." The "watchword of the hour," he wrote, "is commercial expansion." Tanner reminded readers that the United States would be driven to defend commerce in order to keep up even with smaller powers like King Leopold and his Belgian Congo Free State.[14] Tanner considered colonies burdensome, but necessary to avoid eclipse by more ruthless imperialists. As long as Britain and the United States granted their colonies a degree of home rule, he hoped, empire building could at least be a benevolent mission.

----

11. Walter LaFeber, *The American Search for Opportunity, 1865–1913*, 21–82; Eric J. Hobsbawm discusses imperialism and anti-colonial revolts in *The Age of Empire, 1875–1914*, 276–301, especially 279.

12. In 1905, for example, President Theodore Roosevelt imposed a system that required Foreign Service candidates to pass exams before appointment. See "A Short History of the Department of State: Rise to World Power, 1867–1913."

13. Joseph M. Tanner, "Territorial Expansion," *Improvement Era* 2 (April 1899): 432–33.

14. Joseph M. Tanner, "A New Imperialism," *Improvement Era* 10 (January 1907): 222.

Ireland

Britain's oldest colony, Ireland, continued to attract Mormon attention. Missionary work in Belfast and Dublin had not enjoyed the same success as efforts in the rest of the British Isles. Nevertheless, Church leaders believed that social conditions, religious superstition, and famine had rendered the Irish a receptive people to the Mormon message. Famine and migration had cut the island's population in half during the 1840s. During the 1850s Mormon missionaries converted hundreds of Irishmen who had migrated to Manchester and Liverpool, and several Church leaders of the time had been born in Ireland. Rowdy mobs made public preaching difficult, but English landlords and the Catholic clergy were viewed as the real obstacles, threatening to evict tenants or excommunicate those who listened to Mormon elders.[15] By the time the Irish mission reopened under new leadership in 1885, Mormon observers had long been affirming that missionary success would be served by reform or revolution, and vice versa.[16]

In 1868 the heat generated over the Irish land reform bill then before Parliament stirred the pro-Irish tendencies of the *Millennial Star*. British authorities had broken up a Fenian (Irish republican) uprising in 1867, but the event had forced Parliament to discuss land reform and in 1869 pass an act disestablishing the Anglican Church in Ireland and distributing some of the proceeds for education and poverty relief. The *Millennial Star* thought that landlords and Anglican bishops, addicted to the $60 million in Irish revenue, would resist the "entering wedge of revolutionary change," but that revolutionaries would never be satisfied until an independent republic was established.[17] In 1881 the British

---

15. Brent A. Barlow, "The Irish Experience."

16. Irish revolutionaries were condemned, however, in the "secret combination" scare of 1879 in "The Revolutionary Movement in Ireland—A Sign of the Times," *Millennial Star* 41 (December 1, 1879): 762–73.

17. "The Irish Church Establishment," reprinted from the *Deseret Evening News* in *Millennial Star* 30 (June 6, 1868): 358–60. Land and independence issues were as intertwined during the 1870s as they had been in the 1840s. See J. C. Beckett, *The Making of Modern Ireland, 1603–1923*, 369–75. Rebels of the 1867 insurrection were the last to be publicly executed in England. Fenian bombings continued against English targets until the Irish Republic was established in 1924. For contemporary accounts and commentary on

government passed a more comprehensive act that reduced landlord prerogative to raise rents and evict tenants. In Ulster the act was well received, but the Irish Republican Brotherhood in the south and west exhorted the people to violence in protest of an act that did nothing to alleviate the hardship of peasants already in arrears. A government crackdown in 1882 further fanned Irish demand for home rule, a movement led by Charles Stewart Parnell.[18]

Robert S. Spence, a feature writer for the *Contributor*, traveled through Ireland. In 1883 he rejected disorganized violence as the way to eliminate Ireland's "social evil." Nonetheless, the situation demanded that an "ax be laid to the root." Spence suspected that the social consciousness of the people was sufficiently developed to remove the landlords through a minor revolution. New laws would incorporate national lands and eliminate proprietors. Rents paid to officers of the state would give "equal freedom" to all men.[19] If the Fenians and people of Ireland were wrong, Spence argued, then the Church must "reverse [its] theology and accord to Deity other attributes than those of love and justice."[20]

Spence placed the Irish movement in global context. The Irish question "is infinitely more important than any mere local question could be; it is nothing less than the question of transcendent importance which is everywhere beginning to agitate, and if not settled must soon convulse the civilized world."[21] Spence, quoting nearly verbatim from Henry George's *Irish Land Question*, wanted *Contributor* readers to contemplate the inevitability of social revolution. George asked whether, even if the people achieved "political equality,"

> the masses of mankind are to remain mere hewers of wood and drawers of water for the benefit of a fortunate few, whether, having escaped feudalism modern society is to pass into an industrial organization more grinding and oppressive, more heartless and hopeless, than feudalism, whether amid the abundance their labor creates, the produc-

---

the failed 1867 insurrection and disestablishment, see Peter Berresford Ellis, *Eyewitness to Irish History*, 183–88.

18. Beckett, *Making of Modern Ireland*, 389–94; David Reed, *Ireland: The Key to the British Revolution*, 29–30.

19. Robert S. Spence, "Ireland and the Irish," pt. 2, *Contributor* 5 (November 1883): 66–67; ibid., pt. 3, *Contributor* 5 (December 1883): 99–100.

20. Spence, "Ireland and the Irish," pt. 3, 101.

21. Ibid., 100.

ers of wealth are to be content in good times with the barest of livings and in bad times to suffer and starve?[22]

Spence's answer resembled that of Marxist theory: inevitably, the people would organize and rise. The distortions caused by capitalism, imperialism, and autocracy must necessarily be counteracted by revolutionary movements.

> Logical reasoning will manifest to us the same spirit in its various guises—the Communism of France, the Socialism of Germany, the Nihilism of Russia—and the Fenianism of Ireland—it is the bitter war of capital and labor inaugurated under different auspices and continued under circumstances best suited to its growth and proportions.[23]

While distancing himself from illiberal socialists, Spence believed land belonged to its users. He upheld the universal cry "of all tillers of the soil," whether in Ireland, England, or America." The Irish land agitation was not merely a local problem; it was a precursor to global revolution.[24]

Boer War

Dissatisfaction with British imperialism soured Mormon assessments of British military action in South Africa. In 1899 Dutch-German settlers took up armed resistance to British policies in the Boer colonies of the Orange Free State and the Transvaal. Conflicting land claims and Britain's policy of incorporating Boers as British subjects without immediate voting rights led to war. The British won, but only after bringing in heavy reinforcements, concentrating Boer civilians in squalid camps, and waging a costly and bloody counter-insurgency. In the Treaty of Vereeniging (1902), Britain annexed the Boer republics as the basis of the future Union of South Africa. In return, London granted the Boers war indemnities and assurances of representative government. During the war, prominent Democrats and Boer propagandists in the United States tried to raise money to help the rebels, but

---

22. Ibid. Quoted from Henry George, *The Irish Land Question: What It Involves, and How Alone It Can Be Settled. An Appeal to the Land Leagues,* 13.

23. Spence, "Ireland and the Irish," pt. 3, 100. For background on Hawaii as the focus of European, Canadian, and American expansion, see LaFeber, *American Search for Opportunity,* 91–95.

24. Spence, "Ireland and the Irish," pt. 3, 101.

embezzlement and non-recognition from the McKinley and Roosevelt administrations killed the effort.[25]

The tone of the *Millennial Star* remained fairly anti-imperialist throughout the war. One editorial equated Boer settlement of South Africa to Mormon enterprise in the American West.[26] As the two sides careened toward a fight in 1896, a *Star* article fervently hoped for a peaceful settlement.[27] In a 1900 issue of the *Star*, the "Signs of the Times" column linked the Boer cause to revolutionary heritage. The article reported that the Paris Exhibition that year had featured a South African pavilion, and that a Russian prince, Leon Galitzine, had placed a silver crown in front of the bust of Boer President Kruger. Inscribed on it was, "To the representative of a little people, homage, and admiration.—*La Liberté*."[28]

Stronger anti-imperialist content came from the *Young Woman's Journal*. Author Vera Edgeworth was representative. The Boers deserved the land, she wrote, because they had defeated the "treacherous natives" (Zulus and others). Until prospectors discovered gold and diamonds, the Boers had lived happily. Then "thousands of strangers known as *uitlanders* (outlanders)" invaded the Transvaal.[29] Edgeworth rued the loss of the Boers' independent life. The "treasure squandered" and the "lives that must be sacrificed," all so that "Great Britain's possessions may be extended," angered her. Edgeworth reminded readers that the Boers had put a price of $25,000 on the head of the British arch-imperialist Cecil Rhodes during an earlier dispute.[30]

---

25. Richard B. Mulanax, *The Boer War in American Politics and Diplomacy*, 162–68.

26. "Mormons and Gentiles," *Millennial Star* 52 (March 10, 1890): 148.

27. "England's Difficulties," *Millennial Star* 58 (January 9, 1896): 25.

28. "Signs of the Times!" *Millennial Star* 62 (October 18, 1900): 660–61. Leon Galitzine was probably Prince Lev Sergeevich Golitsyn (1845–1916). He hailed from a noble family and pioneered modern industrial winemaking. He became winemaker to Czar Alexander III in 1891. Golitsyn was interested in law, archeology, and politics. See "Prince L. S. Golitsyn: The Founder of Russian Industrial Winemaking"; and Ernest Mehew, ed., *Selected Letters of Robert Louis Stevenson*, 82 note 1.

29. Vera Edgeworth, "Most Important to Us," *Young Woman's Journal* 10 (December 1899): 571.

30. Ibid., 572.

The Boers had the upper hand until March 1900. Then British forces captured Bloemfontein, the capital of the Orange Free State, and launched a campaign against Pretoria, capital of the Transvaal (South African Republic). Joseph M. Tanner dominated Mormon discussion of the conflict. He submitted six articles, published serially in the *Improvement Era*, followed by many pieces in a column called "Some Leading Events in the Current Story of the World." Tanner's stories read like government intelligence reports. Together they covered the political, military, and social ramifications of the Boer War. Always careful in making predictions, Tanner suggested that Britain would subdue the Boers in the "unfortunate conflict.[31] After the British victory against the Boer field army and the taking of Bloemfontein in 1900, Tanner predicted a protracted guerrilla war. He delved into tactics, noting that the mobility of Boer commandoes offset the eight-to-one numerical advantage enjoyed by British forces. Tanner praised both sides. The British soldier is the "same plucky, fearless fighter as in bygone days," Tanner wrote. If any discredit fell on British arms it was generalship. Generals Frederick Roberts and Horatio Kitchner had sterling reputations, but they had never before encountered a foe like the Boers.[32] Tanner, highly attuned to military skill, gave Piet Joubert, the Boer supreme general, high marks. Joubert died during the war, but Tanner's obituary showed the depth of his research in a biographical sketch of Joubert's life. *Improvement Era* readers learned that Joubert descended from a Protestant line and was "more liberal than Kruger." Tanner recounted how British officers and Queen Victoria sent letters of condolence to Joubert's widow and to the Kruger government, illustrating that even amid the cruelty of the war there was chivalry.[33] But there would be

---

31. Joseph M. Tanner, "The South African War," pt. 1, *Improvement Era* 3 (December 1899): 142.

32. Ibid., pt. 6, *Improvement Era* 3 (May 1900): 534–36.

33. Ibid., 537. Compare Tanner's insight to Joubert's modern biographer, Johannes Meintjes, *The Commandant-General: The Life and Times of Petrus Jacobus Joubert of the South African Republic, 1831–1900*, 1, 199. Tanner's assertion that Joubert was the liberal one probably comes from the belief of many of Kruger's friends that Kruger belonged to the seventeenth century. Joubert also believed Kruger was too hard on Uitlanders. Joubert was more willing than Kruger to negotiate with the British—even with Cecil Rhodes, the most hated man among the Boer Republics. See Meintjes, *The*

no winners in this war. Crushing Boer resistance, Tanner concluded, would isolate Britain in Europe and saddle its government with the "extremely undesirable burden" of a second Ireland problem.[34]

The *Deseret News* gave a blow-by-blow account of the war. Tales of British General Hector MacDonald, the beloved commander of the Highland Brigade at the Battle of Magersfontein, appeared alongside stories about Boer general Pierter A. Cronje. At the Battle of Paardeberg, Cronje withstood a terrible shelling on the Modder River and lost four thousand men as prisoners. The road was open for the British advance on Bloemfontein, but the *Deseret News* admired Cronje's skill and lauded his "magnificent courage" in directing delaying actions.[35]

Despite Utah's strong British heritage, editorial opinion there favored the Boer cause.[36] The fight of hardy settlers struggling against the tide of colonial incorporation reminded Mormons of their own battle against the federal government. Mormons invited Boer prisoners and refugees to settle in the western United States: "Industry, frugality and patriotism are qualities much appreciated in this country and in these they have proved themselves great, both in peace and war."[37] Paul Kruger received special attention. Edgeworth noted that despite his illiteracy, imperious "Uncle Paul" knew the Bible and commanded enormous respect among his people.[38] A BYU student reviewed Kruger's visit to the United States in 1900. Comparing the Boer uprising to Holland's resis-

---

Commandant-General, 42, 108, 137.

34. Joseph M. Tanner, "War in the Transvaal," *Improvement Era* 4 (January 1901): 210.

35. "Major General Hector MacDonald," *Deseret Evening News*, February 21, 1900; and "Cronje's Courage is Magnificent," *Deseret Evening News*, February 24, 1900.

36. "Boers and the British," *Deseret Evening News*, January 19, 1900, "Boer and British," *Deseret Evening News*, February 1, 1900; Sympathy for Boers," *Deseret Evening News*, February 14, 1902; Loyalty of the Boers," *Deseret Evening News*, June 16, 1902; and "In Behalf of Boers," *Deseret Evening News*, October 1, 1902.

37. "Boers in America," Journal History of the Church, July 22, 1902, 7–8. There were also proposals to settle Boers in Chihuahua, the location of the Mormon colonies. See "Boers for Mexico," *Deseret Evening News*, June 15, 1903.

38. Edgeworth, "Most Important to Us," 572.

tance to England in the seventeenth century, the student concluded that Britain would win, but Kruger had achieved a place in the pantheon of liberty-loving heroes.[39]

Spanish-American War and Philippine Insurrection

Americans rallied behind Cuban independence when an anti-Spanish revolt broke out on the island in 1895.[40] Many called for intervention on the rebels' behalf, appealing to humanitarian concerns and the belief that the Anglo-Saxon race had an obligation to spread civilization.[41] American opinion grew more bellicose when Senator Redfield Proctor detailed Spanish atrocities recorded during a fact-finding mission to Cuba. In February 1898 the USS *Maine* mysteriously exploded while making a port call in Havana. The following April, Congress declared war on Spain.[42] Like the rest of the country, the Mormon hierarchy endorsed the war. According to historian D. Michael Quinn, the Church's previous "selective pacifism" was discarded as the hierarchy sought to soften anti-Mormon animosity by aligning with American public opinion. Mormon support for the Spanish-American War of 1898 was another adjustment to the reality of existence as part of the

---

39. Malcolm Little, "An Opinion of Paul Kruger," *Improvement Era* 3 (August 1900): 731.

40. Robert L. Beisner, *From the Old Diplomacy to the New, 1865–1900*, 116; Michelle Bray Davis and Rollin W. Quimby, "Senator Proctor's Cuban Speech: Speculations on a Cause of the Spanish-American War," 131–41; John Hope Franklin and Alfred A. Moss Jr., *From Slavery to Freedom: A History of African Americans*, 298; David F. Trask, *The War with Spain in 1898*, 11. Howard H. Quint shows that the Socialist Party opposed American annexationist and expansionist policy, but that several socialists succumbed to the excitement of a patriotic empire. See Howard H. Quint, "American Socialists and the Spanish-American War," 132–54. G. Wayne King argues that business opposition to the war delayed US entry. See G. Wayne King, "Conservative Attitudes in the United States toward Cuba."

41. King, "Conservative Attitudes in the United States toward Cuba," 95–96.

42. A naval board of inquiry later concluded that an explosion in the coal bunker, not Spanish saboteurs, caused the destruction of the ship. See Hyman G. Rickover, *How the Battleship Maine Was Destroyed*, 104.

American nation now that the Church had abandoned its separatist, theocratic ambitions.[43]

Mormon support for the first phase of the Cuban uprising contained themes of revolutionary idealism. The *Contributor* endorsed guerrilla tactics and the burning of Spanish-owned sugar plantations.[44] In 1897 Congressman William H. King, a Utah Mormon, visited Cuba and praised the "valor and patriotism" of the revolutionaries. King believed that Spanish misrule justified US intervention on moral grounds.[45] When seventeen thousand US troops intervened in 1898 to finish what Cuban revolutionaries had started, the Mormon press followed the exploits of General William Shafter's V Corps and kept readers up to date on negotiations.[46] The Mormon press presented the war in Cuba as a crusade, and race was no barrier. In April, the 24th Infantry Regiment, an all-black outfit stationed at Camp Douglas, Utah, trained to join the V Corps in Tampa. The send-off review of the 24th suggested that Black emancipation in the Civil War legitimated the Cuban revolution:

> Cuba is to be invaded that Cubans may be free; and the invasion is to be made by troops who were themselves made free . . . by a war that caused a deluge of blood. Those troops will do for another race

---

43. D. Michael Quinn, "The Mormon Church and the Spanish-American War: An End to Selective Pacifism."

44. "The Cuban Revolution," *Contributor* 17 (March 1896): 267.

45. William H. King, "Through War-Stricken Cuba," *Improvement Era* 1 (March 1898): 354–66. Other Utah Mormon articles supporting intervention in Cuba include "Origin of the Cuban Rebellion," *Millennial Star* 60 (March 24, 1898): 190–91; George Q. Cannon, "The War with Spain," reprinted from the *Juvenile Instructor* in *Millennial Star* 60 (June 9, 1898): 366–68; "The Spanish-American War," *Millennial Star* 60 (September 15, 1898): 586; "The Cause is Just," *Deseret Weekly*, April 30, 1898; "The Case of Spain," *Improvement Era* 1 (April 1898): 451–53; and "The War with Spain," *Improvement Era* 1 (May 1898): 519–24.

46. "Progress of the War between Spain the United States of America," pt. 1, *Improvement Era* 1 (June 1898): 584–85; ibid., pt. 3 *Improvement Era* 1 (August 1898): 750–51; "Minor Incidents of the War," *Improvement Era* 1 (August 1898): 770–71; and Susa Young Gates, "The War and the Women," *Young Woman's Journal* 9 (June 1898): 284–85.

what was done for theirs, and the mighty coincidence will mark another epoch in the tremendous evolution of human liberty.[47]

A *Millennial Star* piece reprinted the congratulations the captain of the battleship *Texas* gave his crew after the destruction of the Spanish fleet at Santiago de Cuba. President William McKinley and all the admirals and commodores of the US Navy were "religious men," carrying out God's will "to benefit mankind by their works."[48]

Mormon articles supported the war in Cuba but drew the line at the United States' annexation of the Philippines following the revolution of the islands against Spanish rule. In the United States, opponents of Philippine annexation were known as anti-imperialists. Moralistic anti-imperialists felt it was wrong for the United States to impose its will on other peoples. Further, "no standard of justice or morality would sustain the transformation of a war that had begun as a crusade to liberate Cuba from Spanish tyranny into a campaign of imperialist conquest."[49] Mormon commentators tended to be "political fundamentalists," meaning they believed that American intervention must further democratic ideals or else be canceled.[50]

At first, arguments for Filipino independence did not impress Mormon observers as much as the rationale of Cuban revolutionaries. The *Improvement Era* described Filipino revolutionary leader Emilio Aguinaldo as an "insolent dictator" trying to establish rule over a people unfit for republican government.[51] Attitudes changed, however, as ideological dissonance arose and the problems inherent in imperial

---

47. "Departure of the Troops," *Deseret Weekly*, April 30, 1898. See also "Progress of the War between Spain and the United States of America," pt. 4, *Improvement Era* 1 (September 1898): 841.

48. "Acknowledging the Hand of God," reprinted from the *Juvenile Instructor* in *Millennial Star* 61 (February 9, 1899): 86–87. The army received recognition in "Honor to the Philippine Heroes," *Millennial Star* 61 (September 7, 1899): 575.

49. Robert L. Beisner, *Twelve against Empire: The Anti-Imperialists, 1898–1900*, 219.

50. Ibid., 220.

51. "Progress of the War between Spain and the United States of America," pt. 7, *Improvement Era* 2 (December 1898): 129; Thomas Hull, "Events of the Month," *Improvement Era* 3 (December 1899): 157–58; Edward H. Anderson, "Election in the Philippines," *Improvement Era* 10 (August 1907): 844.

administration became evident. Major Richard W. Young of the Utah Artillery Volunteers became the correspondent in the Philippines for the *Improvement Era*. American retention of the islands, he wired in April 1899, had caused Filipino leaders to revolt in the name of independence.[52] The editor of the *Improvement Era* wished that Admiral George Dewey, who destroyed the Spanish fleet in the Battle of Manila Bay, had just sailed away "without so much as looking back." For the "Philippine Republic," when established, there should be "ultimate and absolute independence . . . with no further ties connecting it with the United States of America than those dictated by a grateful remembrance of the part we took in bringing to pass their freedom and independence."[53] Another article took comfort in the belief that US protectorates and annexations were selfless acts compared to the aggrandizement sought by other imperial powers.[54]

The price of imperial policing also caused Joseph M. Tanner to reappraise the price of US occupation of the islands. He lectured Mormon readers on the benefits and risks of empire and "dollar diplomacy." Tanner recognized that annexation of the Philippines would accrue economic benefits to the United States and provide a training ground for American statesmen, much as how the British administration of India had improved the quality of its government personnel. However, the United States needed an exit strategy.[55] Tanner mirrored the feelings of other Americans who wished to extend commerce into the Pacific but felt uneasy about counter-insurgency operations and perpetual colonial rule.[56]

China

Latter-day Saint support for anti-colonial revolutionaries carried over to the 1901 Boxer Rebellion, a revolt by Chinese who were resentful of foreign domination. In 1899, as European powers and Japan

---

52. Richard W. Young, "The Story of a Philippine Crime," *Improvement Era* 2 (May 1899): 482.

53. "The Philippine Problem," *Improvement Era* 2 (March 1899): 381–82.

54. "Secretary Taft in Manila," *Improvement Era* 11 (December 1907): 156.

55. Joseph M. Tanner, "A Trip to Cuba," pt. 5, *Improvement Era* 7 (October 1904): 911; Tanner, "Territorial Expansion," 434; Tanner, "A New Imperialism," 221–24.

56. Richard E. Welch Jr., "Organized religion and the Philippine-American War, 1899–1902."

carved up China into colonial concessions, US Secretary of State John Hay circulated the Open Door Notes. The Notes asked the Great Powers of Europe and Asia to treat China as an open economic sphere and to respect its territorial integrity. This Open Door policy was a statement that the United States did not need its own colonial zone; if the playing field were level and trade advantages eliminated, the United States felt confident it could win the China market on a free trade basis.[57] Unfortunately the policy was too little too late, and in 1900 the proto-nationalist Boxer Rebellion erupted. The "Boxers," as foreigners called them, were members of the Society of Righteous and Harmonious Fists: a revolutionary secret society that sought to purify China of foreign influences. The Boxer armies murdered missionaries and laid siege to the foreign legation in Peking. The movement, suppressed by twenty thousand foreign troops, prompted a second round of Open Door Notes. The Great Powers ostensibly agreed to support China's "territorial and administrative integrity," but demanded a $333 million indemnity.[58] American negotiator William Woodville Rockhill, fearful that the penalty would render China dependent on foreign loans, sought to scale down the indemnity requirements, but he was unsuccessful.[59]

Mormon observers had understood the lure of China's markets, while sympathizing with Chinese sovereignty, since the 1860s.[60] An *Improvement Era* story in 1901 blamed the Boxer Rebellion on European and Japanese provocations. In the *Era's* opinion, Russian savagery against Boxers in Peking, the wanton shelling of fortifications at Taku, and the shooting of Chinese "for sport" had given the Boxers the

---

57. Beisner, *From the Old Diplomacy to the New*, 146. The United States wished to downplay its colonial pretensions after the Spanish-American War and to champion the dignity of China, with whom many Americans felt a "special relationship" existed. The weakness of the Open Door policy was the lack of military or naval muscle to enforce it. See ibid., 151–53.

58. LaFeber, *American Search for Opportunity*, 173–76; Michael H. Hunt, *The Making of a Special Relationship: The United States and China to 1914*, 185–88.

59. Paul A. Varg, "William Woodville Rockhill's Influence on the Boxer Negotiations."

60. "A Great Social Revolution—The Treaty with China," reprinted from the *New York Herald* in *Millennial Star* 30 (August 15, 1868): 524–26. Criticism of French demands for extraterritoriality appear in "War in China," *Millennial Star* 46 (September 1, 1884): 552–53.

right to demand the "heads of certain European generals."[61] Future US President Herbert Hoover, then working in China for an engineering firm, would have agreed with the *Era*. Hoover and his wife, along with other Europeans, were besieged by Boxers in Tientsin. The shelling of the Taku forts, Hoover wrote, was an "act of aggression which marked the downfall of the moderate party in Peking" and handed power to those inciting the Boxers.[62]

Joseph M. Tanner partially validated the anti-commercial and anti-foreigner points of the Boxer cause and endorsed the Chinese right to revolution. "A mighty conflict is on in that vast empire. The forces at work cannot be stayed, but they may be wisely directed."[63] Adjustments were necessary to keep pace with the "radical transformation likely to go on in the near future throughout Asia" due to the rising aspirations of peoples under colonial control.[64] Tanner's solution to the Chinese question followed the reasoning of Rockhill. In 1898 Tanner believed that "apprehension [in] the industrial classes" revealed the high-stakes competition generated in the Chinese market.[65] The key to stability lay in protecting China from predatory empires, especially Russia. Since the United States had no territorial ambitions, it, along with Britain and Japan, should protect China. Continued training and equipping of Chinese forces would enable China to better defend itself against interlopers. Eventually, Western ideas would endow China with republican government.[66] Ultimately, Tanner proved too sanguine about the United States' ability to direct either Chinese nationalism or fellow Great Powers. Western ideas and the Open Door did not create

---

61. "Relief of the Legations in Peking—the Other Side," *Improvement Era* 4 (April 1901): 453.

62. Quoted in Diana Preston, *The Boxer Rebellion: The Dramatic Story of China's War on Foreigners That Shook the World in the Summer of 1900*, 112.

63. Joseph M. Tanner, "The Revolution in China," pt. 3, *Improvement Era* 3 (October 1900): 931.

64. Ibid., pt. 2, *Improvement Era* 3 (September 1900): 856.

65. Joseph M. Tanner, "China and the European Nations," *Improvement Era* 1 (April 1898): 419–24.

66. Joseph M. Tanner, "The Revolution in China," pt. 1, *Improvement Era* 3 (August 1900): 734–40; ibid., pt. 2, 854–67. See also Joseph M. Tanner, "Situation in China," *Improvement Era* 4 (December 1900): 123–35; and "China Advancing," *Improvement Era* 11 (February 1908): 316.

the hoped-for reforms in China.[67] Instead, they started China down the path of revolution.

Mormon observers endorsed the later popular overthrow of the Manchu Dynasty in 1911. The people of China had become "conscious of their strength and asserted it. And no revolution was ever more just. . . . It meant liberty and the granting of human rights to three hundred million human beings."[68] Another editorial voted Sun Yat-sen, the intellectual behind the revolution, as "the greatest man in the political field." He not only led the revolution, but also then stepped aside to allow the election of Yuan Shih-kai. Such self-abnegation represented revolutionary purity at its best: "As long as [Sun's] spirit obtains, the republic will be safe."[69]

Japan

Revolution in China coincided with the modernization of Japan. Since 1865 Japan had been industrializing and expanding its military and naval capabilities under its Meiji rulers. Japan demonstrated its rising power by defeating China and Russia in military conflicts (in 1895 and 1905 respectively).[70] Viewing Japan at first as an inspiring example of modernization along Western lines, Europeans and Americans only later came to view Japan as a competitor.[71]

Mormon observers welcomed Japan's rise to Great Power status. The *Improvement Era* regarded Japan's modernization as a "natural" miracle without parallel in the nineteenth century.[72] Tanner marveled at the "wonderful developments of the Japanese Race."[73] Japanese an-

---

67. Hunt, *Making of a Special Relationship*, 272–312.

68. "Chinese Republic," *Deseret News*, February 5, 1912.

69. "A Truly Great Man," *Deseret News*, February 19, 1912. Other supportive editorials in the *Deseret News* include "Tells Dramatic Story of America's Part in the Chinese Uprising," November 18, 1911; "Silent Rise of New Leader," March 29, 1912; "Republic Due to Sun-Yat Sen," April 11, 1912; and "China North and South," February 14, 1912.

70. Charles E. Neu, *Troubled Encounter: United States and Japan*, 41–42; LaFeber, *American Search for Opportunity*, 203.

71. Akira Iriye, "Japan as Competitor, 1895–1917."

72. Joseph M. Tanner, "The Nineteenth Century," *Improvement Era* 4 (January 1901): 162.

73. Joseph M. Tanner, "The Zionist Movement," *Improvement Era* 3

nexation of Korea would stimulate foreign trade, enlarge Korean opportunities for intellectual growth, abolish the Korean emperor, and extend liberties to the Korean people.[74] Aboard a train in Korea, David O. McKay recorded his impressions of Japan: "a nation of men and women capable of physical endurance, and keenness of intellect and sturdiness of character that puts them at least on an equality with other civilized peoples. . . . By their superior intelligence they will control all Manchuria one day."[75]

Mormon admiration for Japanese culture mirrored the sentiments of Protestant missionaries in Japan.[76] Congressional acts of 1917–24 limited Asian immigration, partly because American missionaries had enjoyed little success in China and Asian immigrants did not easily assimilate.[77] But Japan seemed to hold more proselytizing promise. Horace S. Ensign, an experienced missionary who spoke Japanese, served as the Japanese mission president from 1903 to 1905. The thirteen or so Mormon elders in Japan converted few, but were optimistic that they were proselytizing among the lost tribes of Israel.[78]

(November 1899), 4.

74. Joseph M. Tanner, "The End of Korea," *Improvement Era* 9 (January 1906): 241.

75. David O. McKay, Diary, January 5 and 7, 1921. McKay prayed for stable government for China—which he believed would come through the interposition of a foreign (Japanese) power—in "Dedication of China," *Millennial Star* 83 (March 24, 1921): 187. For other sympathetic treatments of Japan, see "Russia as Gog and Magog," *Millennial Star* 66 (December 29, 1904): 823–24; Frank J. Hewlett, "The New China and Japan," *Improvement Era* 10 (August 1907): 813–19; "Restoration of the Jews," *Relief Society Magazine* 6 (September 1919): 549.

76. Sandra Caruthers Thomson, "Meiji Japan through Missionary Eyes: The American Protestant Experience."

77. Martin E. Marty, *Modern American Religion*, 2:82–83.

78. Armand L. Mauss, "In Search of Ephraim: Traditional Mormon Conceptions of Lineage and Race," 167; and "Restoration of the Jews," 549. For an administrative history of the Japanese mission and admiration for Japanese culture and power, see Spencer J. Palmer, *The Church Encounters Asia*, 54–59; and R. Lanier Britsch, *From the East: The History of the Latter-day Saints in Asia, 1851–1996*, 43–70.

President Ensign defended Japan's expansionist ambitions in the Far East. He quoted from an article that appeared in *Taiyo* (the Sun), "published in the interest of peace and prosperity" and written by Jeshei Hashiguchi, "a man of note and influence." Hashiguchi envisioned a decolonizing and civilizing role for Japan in East Asia:

> Japan's victory [in the Russian war] will inspire her sister nations to uprise against the psychological domination by the Europeans. . . . The Chinese—seemingly incapable of progress—are not wood nor stones, but men. When they awake from their long slumber, they will regain the prestige of their forefathers. The Koreans, the Siamese, the Hindoos, and the Fillipinos, who are at present considered to be ineligible quantities, when combined under the hegemony of the Japanese, will become formidable allies of the latter. Should all these rise and urge Japan to lead them against the European races, Japan cannot but satisfy their desire.[79]

Ensign's enchantment with Japan embodied the tendency in the Mormon mind to see revolutionary movements as forces transcending time and space to acquire teleological purpose. Popular revolutions pointed toward the millennium. United under Japanese rule, the liberated Asiatic races would be an unstoppable force for good. They would surpass Europe, abolish tyranny and political corruption, and bring the world "nearer to a state of perfection for the benefit of all classes of people."[80]

Persia and the Ottoman Empire (Turkey)

Within a few years the editors of the *Improvement Era* reported the spread of the revolutionary spirit from Japan to Persia. The defeat of Russia in 1905 had prompted "a spirit of inquiry as to why the triumph of Japan cannot be repeated elsewhere" among the Persians. Persia established constitutional government in 1906, the first step in the "extinction of the old [imperialist] rule."[81]

---

79. Horace S. Ensign, "The 'Yellow Peril' as Seen in Japan," *Improvement Era* 8 (April 1905): 434.

80. Ibid., 435.

81. "The Awakening," *Improvement Era* 11 (November 1909): 79. In 1907 Russia and Britain scattered the Persian awakening by dividing the country into zones of influence. See David Fromkin, *A Peace to End All Peace: The*

The Ottoman Empire was another area of interest. Turkey itself was not the colony of a European power, but there were modernizers within the government as well as Arabs, Armenians, and Jews in the sultan's domains who wanted greater freedoms. Mormon missionaries had limited success after they began work in Constantinople, Jaffa, and Haifa in 1884. Small branches were established; in 1899 and 1900 the branches in Aleppo and Aintab established factories that produced cloth and Turkish rugs for export to Zion's Cooperative Mercantile Institution in Utah.[82]

Mormon views on Turkey varied. The decline of Ottoman fortunes in the last quarter of the nineteenth century drew the attention of the Church's leading diplomatic intelligencer, Joseph M. Tanner. In 1887 Tanner produced a seven-article series for the *Contributor*.[83] Tanner's series, "The Eastern Question," showed him to be a friend of the Turks. He accused Greeks and Armenians of taking advantage of Moslem strictures against usury by charging high interest rates, which compounded Ottoman financial difficulties.[84] Tanner even took a moderate view of harem culture in Istanbul, a position perhaps calculated to induce sympathy among Church readers whose own struggle to preserve the doctrinal practice of polygamy was reaching its climax.[85] Twelve years later Tanner proposed that Istanbul sell Palestine to the Jews to liquidate its debts to European creditors. Sale of the Holy Land would also satisfy the newly formed Zionist movement.[86]

Fall of the Ottoman Empire and the Creation of the Modern Middle East, 31.

82. Seçil Karal Akgün, "Mormon Missionaries in the Ottoman Empire," 347–57; Edward H. Anderson, "M. I. A. Work in Turkey," *Improvement Era* 9 (October 1906): 992; and Andrew Jenson, *Encyclopedic History of the Church of Jesus Christ of Latter-day Saints*, 888–90.

83. Joseph M. Tanner, "The Eastern Question," published in seven installments: pt. 1 in *Contributor* 8 (February 1887): 129–34; pt. 2 in *Contributor* 8 (March 1887): 171–76; pt. 3 in *Contributor* 8 (April 1887): 209–23; pt. 4 in *Contributor* 8 (May 1887): 259–63; pt. 5 in *Contributor* 8 (June 1887): 291–95; pt. 6 in *Contributor* 8 (July 1887): 341–44; and pt. 7 in *Contributor* 8 (August 1887): 369–73.

84. Ibid., pt. 5, 295.

85. Ibid., pt. 5, 291.

86. Joseph M. Tanner, "Emperor William's Visit to Palestine," *Improvement Era* 2 (January 1899): 207. Tanner foretold Germany's alliance with the Ottomans during World War I.

In 1908 modernizers known as "Young Turks" staged an army coup that imposed the 1876 constitution on Sultan Abdul Hamid. Every ethnic and religious group in the Ottoman Empire rejoiced.[87] The rise of the Young Turks also attracted Mormon optimism. The editors of the *Improvement Era* welcomed the 1876 constitution. If foreign powers did not interfere, one Mormon author thought, the country would be "revolutionized" for the better—a prescient statement considering Sultan Kemal Ataturk's transformation of the empire into a republic after World War I.[88] Turkish Mission President Joseph Booth was disinterested in Ottoman political maneuvering, but he recorded in his diary how happy the Christians were when the Young Turks deposed Sultan Abdul Hamid in 1909.[89]

Such optimism was short-lived. Young Turk reformers failed to halt the disintegration of the empire. Arabs in Palestine, Arabia, and Iraq chafed under Ottoman imperial rule. Zionism was bringing unwanted European attention to the region. The Young Turks had also wanted to ease persecution of Armenians, who had looked for Russian support ever since the Russian-Turkish War (1877–78), but failed to improve relations with this Christian minority. Ill-feeling grew, culminating in the Armenian genocide during World War I.[90] Elder John T. Woodbury had hoped constitutional government would weaken Islamic influence, allowing Mormons with their "true Christianity" to heal the division between Turk and Armenian, but this was not to be the case.[91] Tanner had likewise hoped that modernizers in the Ottoman Empire might unite Christians and Turks, but the Empire's malaise ran too deep. As a result of these complications, the LDS mission closed between 1909–1921. Meanwhile, the crisis of the Ottomans deepened. Bosnia-Herzegovina was lost to the Austrians in 1908. The Ottomans lost more territory in two Balkan wars, 1912–13. The treasury and the people's patriotism were sapped by political discord. The Empire's survival came down to

---

87. Arthur Goldschmidt Jr., *A Concise History of the Middle East*, 186.

88. John T. Woodbury Jr., "Turkey's Revolution," *Improvement Era* 12 (June 1909): 644–45.

89. Joseph Wilford Booth, Diary, April 26, 1909, 10:92.

90. Goldschmidt, *Concise History of the Middle East*, 187.

91. Woodbury, "Turkey's Revolution," 652.

playing Austria against Russia during the First World War (1914–18).[92] Turkey fought on the losing side, forever extinguishing Ottoman rule.

Genocide against the Armenians during the war appalled Mormon observers. A 1916 article in the *Improvement Era* told the story of Miko, the legendary defender of the Armenians. He conducted raids from his mountain stronghold, "athirst for vengeance against those who had subjugated him to a merciless slavery."[93] On a train tour of the country in 1919 to rally support for the League of Nations, President Woodrow Wilson chose the Tabernacle in Salt Lake City to call for an Allied mandate to protect this tortured minority.[94]

Other Mormon observers took up the chorus of Jewish emancipation. Protestant ministers had long preached that the Ottoman Empire had to be destroyed before the Jews could return to Palestine in fulfillment of biblical prophecy.[95] Mormon observers put a unique spin on this theme. One Mormon missionary wrote that the rise of a constitutional government heralded the end of the Ottomans' role as protector of the Jews from "corrupted Christianity." Jew and Turk would merge under sponsorship of the Latter-day Saints, fulfilling God's will and ushering in the universal government that Mormonism allegedly embodied.[96] In 1917 two events occurred that seemed to hasten the culmination of these millennial conditions: Britain promised in the Balfour Declaration to work toward the creation of a Jewish national homeland in Palestine, and British General Edmund Allenby, commander of the Egyptian Expeditionary Force, captured Jerusalem from Ottoman forc-

---

92. Joseph M. Tanner, "Conditions in Turkey," *Improvement Era* 16 (April 1913): 630–31.

93. M. A. Denolan, "Miko," *Improvement Era* 19 (April 1916): 501.

94. Michael Bobelian, *Children of Armenia: A Forgotten Genocide and the Century-long Struggle for Justice*, 45. Mormon opinion mirrored anti-Turkish sentiment in the United States. See ibid., 41–44. An earlier call to help the Armenians appeared in "England's Difficulties," 25.

95. See Presbyterian minister Amazi Armstrong's *Syllabus of Lectures on the Visions of the Restoration of Israel* (1814–15), quoted in LeRoy Froom, *Prophetic Faith of our Fathers: The Historical Development of Prophetic Interpretation*, 4:199–200, 266.

96. Ferdinand F. Hintze, "Testimony Derived from the Balkan War," *Improvement Era* 16 (January 1913): 243–47.

es.[97] Mormon observers attached eschatological significance to these British initiatives. Apostle Melvin J. Ballard, for instance, argued that defeat of the Ottoman armies had liberated Jerusalem from the "power that had ruled over the land and the destinies of that people for ages."[98] Although Palestine was populated mostly by Muslims and even some Orthodox and Catholic Christians, the tiny Jewish population was most pertinent to Mormon observers. David O. McKay understood that strategic considerations mandated the drive on Jerusalem, but he linked Allenby's victory to the Zionist cause and the merging of all nations into one universal history. "Fifty thousand Jews were with General Allenby working for the freedom of the Holy Land," he told a General Conference. Out of the "peril and pain" of this great conflict, God would bring "blessings to humanity of which they scarcely dream."[99]

But Jewish nationalism, McKay also believed, would trigger a war. While visiting Jerusalem in 1921, McKay responded to an Arab denizen who assured him that the Jews would not enter the city without a

---

97. On the Balfour Declaration see Leonard Stein, *The Balfour Declaration*. A description of Allenby's campaign is found in Anthony Livesey, *Great Commanders and Their Battles*, 132–39.

98. Russell M. Ballard, ed., *Melvin J. Ballard: Crusader for Righteousness*, 241.

99. David O. McKay, October 5, 1918, *Report of the Semi-annual Conference of the Church of Jesus Christ of Latter-day Saints*, 47 (hereafter cited as *Conference Report*). McKay's "fifty thousand" is an overstatement, but Jews formed the 39th Battalion of Royal Fusileers in Allenby's army and another group was organized by Vladimir Jabotinsky as the Jewish Legion. See Martin Gilbert, *The First World War: A Complete History*, 371; and Fromkin, *A Peace to End All Peace*, 333, 446–47. Support for Zionism during the war and Mormon coverage of Allenby's campaign and the Balfour Declaration are found in Mary Foster Gibbs, "The Passover and the Lord's Supper," *Relief Society Magazine* 6 (April 1919): 189–210; "The Gathering of the Jews," *Millennial Star* 81 (April 17, 1919): 244–46; Anthony W. Ivins, April 5, 1925, *Conference Report*, 50–51; James H. Moyle, April 8, 1932, *Conference Report*, 27. The Balfour Declaration is mentioned in B. H. Roberts, April 3, 1927, *Conference Report*, 38; Janne M. Sjödahl, *An Introduction to the Study of the Book of Mormon*, 208; Joseph Fielding Smith Jr., *The Restoration of All Things*, 151–52. For a secondary source outlining Mormon responses, see also Arnold H. Green, "A Survey of LDS Proselyting Efforts to the Jewish People," 431.

fight. "The streets . . . undoubtedly will flow with blood," McKay wrote in his diary, "but that will not prevent the Jews possessing their land." McKay pictured "doorways and store steps covered with blood in the great struggle that is impending, of which the spirit of this day is but the rumbling as of a pent-up volcano!" The imagery of the volcano describing a Jewish revolutionary seizure of Jerusalem nonetheless worried McKay. For the time being he was content to postpone the revolution: "I was glad to see the British Tommies around with . . . bayonets fixed, and to see the armored cars pass through the streets—They had a subduing influence upon the rising spirit."[100]

India

The Church did little missionary work in India after 1856, but this did not diminish Mormon interest in the subcontinent. Mormon observers skewered Great Britain for transplanting the conditions of Ireland to India. In 1883 the *Contributor* characterized the governor-general of India as an "absolute despot." Increased home rule and an end to the practice of exempting European nationals from arraignment in colonial courts would be "entirely in accordance with the spirit of our age, which is in favor of enlarged liberties of peoples everywhere."[101] Gradually, Hindu activism flickered to life. In 1905 the Indian National Congress Party, made up mostly of Anglicized Hindu elites, petitioned for increased self-government. The Muslim League wanted much the same. Also in that year, the *swadeshi* movement protested a British plan to partition Bengal. National Congress Party leaders appealed to the masses, telling the people to boycott imports, buy native products, and burn foreign clothing. Radicals denounced the Indian princes for collaboration with foreign capitalists and rulers. But the subcontinent was difficult to mobilize. The British administration passed reforms that enlarged native voices in councils of state, but it otherwise kept its footing.[102]

Joseph M. Tanner tried to awaken "sympathetic interest" in India's disadvantaged position in the British Empire. Drought in 1908 had driven up grain prices. The people were living on the "ragged edge of

100. McKay, Diary, November 2, 1921.

101. "The Indian Empire," *Contributor* 4 (May 1883): 317.

102. For British reforms under the 1909 Indian Council Act, see William Golant, *The Long Afternoon: British India, 1601-1947*, 148–54.

existence." Public relief efforts were overburdened and crime was increasing.[103] Britain, said the editor of the *Improvement Era*, may have the monopoly on artillery, but strikes and boycotts by the people would cripple British manufacturing. The "signs of an upheaval" are "on so huge a scale that it may prove formidable itself."[104]

Despite strong internal divisions of religion, caste, and culture, India lurched toward independence during the 1930s. Mohandas K. Gandhi's program of non-violent resistance loosely united India's masses, the princes, and nationalist and socialist leaders against British rule. Britain tried to appease the protesters by passing the 1935 Government of India Act granting greater self-rule, but retention of a Crown-appointed governor-general and a clause for suspending the constitution in time of crisis satisfied few. The National Congress Party condemned the act as a "new charter of bondage."[105] The Muslim League temporized. As usual, the princes stood with the British government.[106]

The *Improvement Era* cast India as the leader of a worldwide anti-imperialist crusade. Guest author Daljit Singh Sadharia informed readers that Indian independence was coming. The religions of Hinduism and Islam that had "inculcated passivity and reduced the people to impotence and death" had been dispelled. European thought in the fields of politics and science had "disturbed the old mental stagnation of the Indian people and infused a new life in the dry bones of their society."[107] The example of Japan's 1905 victory against Russia had proven to India that Asian peoples could beat a European power. The success of the Young Turks, Sun Yat-sen, and the Persian revolutionaries had "bred a furious hatred for alien authority."[108] Singh credited Gandhi as the supreme animating spirit of this new India. Gandhi had "revolutionized the ways of thinking

---

103. Joseph M. Tanner, "Conditions in India," *Improvement Era* 11 (June 1908): 642.

104. "The Awakening," 79.

105. Golant, *Long Afternoon*, 175.

106. Ibid., 176, 195; William Manchester, *The Last Lion, Winston Spencer Churchill: Visions of Glory, 1874–1932*, 835.

107. Daljit Singh Sadharia, "As a Native East Indian Views the Situation," *Improvement Era* 34 (March 1931): 261.

108. Ibid., 262.

and doing things of the Indian people and united them on a common fraternal basis."[109] The people, once in awe of the British colonial elite, were no longer intimidated. Singh lit the path to the future with words that Mormon observers had long been using: "liberalism, constitutional freedom, nationality, and the French Revolution."[110] The Era's managing editor, Hugh J. Cannon, endorsed Sadharia's message. Cannon expressed his admiration for Gandhi and sympathized with "brothers and sisters" imprisoned by British authorities for their solidarity with him.[111]

G. Homer Durham, a future member of the First Quorum of the Seventy, recognized the inevitability of Indian self-rule. He felt that the Indian National Congress's boycott of British-sponsored elections "breathes the spirit of Sam Adams and revolution."[112] Gandhi's "genius" had been to unite Muslim and Hindu behind an independence movement. Durham also noticed that for Gandhi, political repression was inseparable from socioeconomic subservience. Gandhi's boycott of British textiles and his 1930 "salt march" to the sea had generated a "mass-awakening." Nevertheless, Durham discounted the non-violent approach of Gandhi as "unrealistic" considering Britain's determination to retain control over the subcontinent.[113] On the other hand, Jawaharlal Nehru, Gandhi's compatriot, was "developing for the Congress a left wing philosophy of revolutionary proportions."[114] Nehru's downplay of class struggle in an effort to attract the native elite to the independence movement appeared to contradict some of his more fiery speeches, but Durham felt confident that radicalism would win the day. British rule in India was as good as over. In a matter of time, nationalism—and possibly socialism—would suffuse the Indian masses. Where the three hundred million people go, Durham concluded, "so goes India."[115]

---

109. Ibid., 263.

110. Ibid., 261.

111. Hugh J. Cannon, "Land of Castes and Outcasts," *Improvement Era* 34 (March 1931): 251.

112. G. Homer Durham, "The Indian National Congress and Swaraj: The Question of Political Power in India," *World Affairs Interpreter* 8 (Winter 1938): 355. *Swaraj* means "independence" in Hindi.

113. Ibid., 363.

114. Ibid.

115. Ibid., 366.

One-Worldism

Throughout the era of New Imperialism and its gradual decline after World War I, the goal of a global socioeconomic system threaded its way through Mormon thought. Heber C. Kimball, a counselor to Brigham Young known for his earthiness, rejected national chauvinism: "I am not national or sectional, and God forbid that I should be, for I have that Spirit that delighteth in the welfare and salvation of the human family. . . . I will not bow my head to that national spirit, nor to any spirit that is not of God."[116] "What is wanted," read an 1879 *Millennial Star* article, is a "general directorship for the whole earth. . . . The question of employment and subsistence is no longer a national one—it belongs to humanity."[117] A second *Star* article contemplated violent upheaval in quest of global oneness:

> Before so desirable a consummation as the harmonious blending of the affairs of this creation can be reached, it must necessarily be preceded by a condition diametrically opposite. The introduction of a new system of government, to be universal, with one grand central head, renders the demolition of all systems antagonistic to it a foregone conclusion. This view is not only scriptural but strictly logical.[118]

Peace and "universal brotherhood" would prevail during the millennial era, but the logic of social revolution compelled but one outcome:

> If the existing fragmentary governments and nationalities were willing to submerge into the promised grand theocratic order, which will yet prevail, their destruction would be averted. This acquiescence being beyond the remotest expectation, their doom is certain . . . for the decrees of Jehovah cannot be overturned.[119]

Revolutionary globalism was a European idea to be revived in America. "Peter the Great and Napoleon," the *Star* suggested, "grasped the idea of the formation of a great supervisory power over the nations." Their plans anticipated a "great centre" at Constantinople or Paris but denied the requirement for the "intelligence and purity of God." The Saints not only understood the divine geometry, but also had the divine

---

116. Heber C. Kimball, January 25, 1857, *Journal of Discourses*, 4:278.
117. "Centralization of Government," 264.
118. "The Sword," *Millennial Star* 41 (April 14, 1879): 232.
119. Ibid.

wisdom that "unscrupulous" men ignored. "Zion is necessarily organized on the principle of a grand, pervading central power. This is ob-
servable in all the works of nature.... When Zion is built up in her glory,
her centre will be in the divinely-designated spot, in Jackson County,
Missouri, U. S. A."[120] A grand alliance of the world's nations would re-
volve "around a central sun." Light and power would "cover the whole
American continent, and thence her benign influence will radiate to the
ends of the earth."[121] The transformation from many sovereign nations
to a single universal order, wrote another *Star* contributor, would "not
take years and centuries to settle." Revolutionary suddenness put the
moment of reckoning within normal time, inside the bounds of natural occurrences. The "unity which will prevail" would occur before the
"near approaching millennium."[122]

Alongside the dialectic of one epoch yielding to another by revolution, the Mormon press also epitomized the lingering romantic revolutionary ideal. Europe, enjoying internal peace and prosperity except for
the short wars of German unification in 1866–70, seemed ready for a
federation of nations of the type envisioned by Mazzini in the nineteenth
century. Eric Hobsbawm writes that to contemporaries, internationalism at the turn-of-the-century "seemed readily manageable within the
framework of bourgeois liberalism ... and a liberal world would consist
of nations."[123] The LDS Church press in Great Britain and the United
States reflected these sentiments—a world in which nationalities were
"united according to their affinities instead of held together by the hand
of oppression" in order to achieve "universal peace."[124] The "fraternization of the nations" would ensure the spread of "religion and civilization, the development of science and art, all projects and enterprises for
the uplifting of humanity."[125] Unificationist zeal came to a head at the

---

120. "Centralization of Government," 265.

121. Ibid., 266.

122. "The Harmony of the Gospel," *Millennial Star* 43 (March 21, 1881):
184–85.

123. Eric J. Hobsbawm, *The Age of Capital, 1848–1875*, 97.

124. "The Poor and the Rich," reprinted from the *Deseret News* in
Millennial Star 62 (December 20, 1900): 806.

125. "The Broken Up Nations," *Millennial Star* 62 (December 13, 1900):
790; and Charles W. Penrose, "Socialism, the False and the True," *Millennial
Star* 70 (October 29, 1908): 698.

dawn of the twentieth century. An 1899 *Deseret News* article entitled "The Millennium" noted that the nations of the world lined up behind three empires—Britain, the United States, and Russia. The two Anglo-Saxon powers represented democracy; Russia represented autocracy. All were empire builders, but the Anglo empires had a "preponderance of power" and were the "jealous guardian[s] of the divine oracles." The days of the ancient philosophers' belief in a "spiritual" millennium were over. The time for a "terrestrial" millennium had come.[126]

Church President Lorenzo Snow took up the one-world discourse. In a 1901 speech also widely distributed as a tract, Snow showed that his views had not changed since his 1851 mission to Italy when he praised the liberal reforms in the Kingdom of Savoy.[127] He allotted no role for the United States of Theodore Roosevelt, Josiah Strong, or Alfred Thayer Mahan—a nation consummating its visions of greatness through imperial expansion.[128] In Snow's version of universal history, American exceptionalism faded behind two broader concepts: romantic nationalism and social revolution. The idea of Mazzini's Young Europe stood out: "The aim of nations should be fraternity and mutual greatness." Snow urged the presidents and monarchs of the world to "Disband your armies, take the yoke from the necks of the people, arbitrate your disputes; meet in royal congresses, and plan for union instead of conquest."[129]

Snow preached non-violence, but the discourse of proletarian struggle informed the section of his address that dealt with labor. Aware that industrialism menaced the temporal salvation of workers, Snow called on capitalists and rulers to meet the demands of social justice through legislation and philanthropy. If they would not, then a special millennium awaited the workers. "Ye toiling millions," he promised,

---

126. "The Millennium," reprinted from the *Deseret News* in *Millennial Star* 61 (December 28, 1899): 821–23.

127. Lorenzo Snow, Letter to Brigham Young, November 1, 1850, in Lorenzo Snow, *The Italian Mission*, 11.

128. For American exceptionalism at the turn of the century, see Michael H. Hunt, *Ideology and U.S. Foreign Policy*, 19–45.

129. Lorenzo Snow, "Greeting to the World," *Improvement Era* 4 (February 1901): 302. The talk was printed under the same title in pamphlet form, available from the LDS Church History Library. Similar ideas about the "uplifting of humanity" through technological process and the "fraternization of nations" were also printed in "The Poor and the Rich," 806.

"look up and greet the power from above which shall lift you from bondage! The day of your redemption draweth nigh." Snow counseled against anarchism, a term synonymous with terrorism in turn-of-the-century Utah, but he did not castigate revolution in the broader sense. He refused to equivocate with the rights of people. His rise of "toiling millions" pictured an old Mormon understanding. Snow preferred that democratic liberalism distribute the rewards of industrial output, but the language of his youth remained unchanged. Providential history would side with the people if the brokers of political and economic power failed to preempt divine anger with liberality and goodwill.[130]

Mormon observers placed the Church at the center of the global transformation. Mormonism, to these observers, was a utopian faith fired by the revolutionary method. Charles Nibley believed the Latter-day Saint mission "is one that will make poverty extinct in the world. All that men struggle for in socialism . . . is to be found . . . in Mormonism."[131] The Mormon system of "true socialism" would become "the universal order, promoting universal joy, prosperity and peace."[132] Shortly after the defeat of the League of Nations a member asked, "How long, O Lord" before millionaires and paupers were eliminated and the United Order established on a universal scale?[133] Another looked for the Church to perpetuate "the brotherhood of man" through the establishment of communes. The power of the Mormon example would spread until the world became what the "ancient seers have looked forward to, and poets have written about."[134]

From the Center to the Periphery

Mormon support for revolution was not limited to major centers of power in Europe or to light-skinned peoples. Mormon observers perceived revolutionary movements in Ireland, Asia, Africa, and Latin America as the opening acts of a wider drama of global change, cli-

---

130. Snow, "Greeting to the World," 302.

131. Charles W. Nibley, October 7, 1906, *Conference Report*, 62.

132. Penrose, "Socialism, the False and the True," 699.

133. C. L. Olsen, "How Long, O Lord, How Long?" *Improvement Era* 23 (February 1920): 332–35.

134. Carl Pingree Tanner, "Communism in America," *Improvement Era* 27 (August 1924): 991–92.

maxing ultimately in the one-world government and economic system promised in the millennium. Examples of rising peoples in colonial areas prevented the concept of revolutionary millennialism from going dormant in Mormon literature. In 1912 Levi Edgar Young touched upon every Mormon anti-colonial and globalist theme of the preceding forty years. The monotheistic religions of Christianity, Islam, and Judaism, he said, would eventually "see alike on the big things" and work for the "federation of the world that has so long been the dream of men." Revolution would generate a higher form of life:

> The times are filled with the common man's expression of individuality. There are revolutions today, but these revolutions are going to result in man's freedom and independence; in his rights and privileges of free men. Governments are going to receive all of their powers from the consent of those governed and the brotherhood of mankind is going to come about by the working out of that ideal given by the prophets of ancient times.[135]

The highest expression of the divine-human relationship was action. Truth would come to earth from "God to man, together with man's recognition of his own great divine strength and light."

As Young spoke, revolutionaries in Mexico were ready to act. Smoldering discontent was about to flare into full-scale war, threatening the peace and prosperity of Mormon colonies. With material interests at stake but also with a doctrine teaching the special destiny of Indians, the beliefs of Mormon observers about revolution would be put to the ultimate test.

---

135. "Professor L. E. Young Speaks at Synagogue," *Deseret News*, February 17, 1912.

CHAPTER 7

THE MEXICAN REVOLUTION AND THE IDEA OF AN INDIAN NATION, 1910–17

Reprise of 1848

Mormon Apostle James E. Talmage published *Jesus the Christ* in 1915. Postulating as to what Pontius Pilate was thinking as the accused Galilean stood before him, Talmage concluded that it "was clear to the Roman governor that this wonderful Man, with His exalted views of a kingdom not of this world, and an empire of truth in which He was to reign, was no political insurrectionist."[1] Sixty-two years later Church President Spencer W. Kimball, speaking in Bogota, Colombia, echoed Talmage: Christ was not a revolutionary. The Messiah acknowledged the existence of class strife, Kimball admitted, but "his was a way of teaching equalities the slow, free-agency way rather than by revolutionary force."[2] These pronouncements by Talmage and Kimball surprise no one familiar with the LDS Church's conservative reputation. Less well known is the degree to which the shapers of Mormon policy in Mexico during the upheaval of 1910–17 would have disagreed with them.

Revolution undergirded a Mormon view of history. An omniscient God projected his power in the medium of time through the agency of man in accordance with laws and stages of historical development. World events became a source of canon. From Puritan and Presbyterian theology Mormon leaders inherited a theory of "just revolution." If the overthrow of unrighteous authority was possible, ran the logic, then it was God's will to pursue it.[3]

---

1. James E. Talmage, *Jesus the Christ: A Study of the Messiah and His Mission According to the Holy Scriptures both Ancient and Modern*, 634.

2. Spencer W. Kimball, March 6, 1977, in Edward L. Kimball, ed., *The Teachings of Spencer W. Kimball*, 409–10.

3. Michael Walzer, *The Revolution of the Saints: A Study in the Origins*

Mormons' millennial fervor and anger against their enemies joined with profane philosophy and Calvinist justification to produce rhetoric that paralleled the discourse of secular revolutionaries. Both Mormon and secular radicals waited for conditions to ripen that would midwife their epiphanies into worldwide reality. Whereas Michael Bakunin and Karl Marx believed the working class would shake the earth from below, Mormons looked for fire from above. Universally transformative events in each scenario would obliterate all contradictions. In the secular versions, societies would either divide into anarchist communes or be recast in the socialist state. The millennial alternative would install the Saints as rulers in a thousand-year kingdom. A revolution in Mexico in 1910 reprised for Mormon observers the excitement of 1848.

Mormon Point Men in Mexico

Two Mormon officials dominated discussion of the Mexican Revolution in high-level LDS leadership circles: Apostle Anthony W. Ivins (1852–1934) and Mexican Mission President Rey L. Pratt (1878–1931). Both spoke Spanish, and between the two men, they had lived in Mexico for a total of forty-three years. Ivins was one of the most respected general authorities the Church has ever known. His death marked the only time in the history of the *Deseret News* that the paper was distributed gratis.[4] In 1895 the Church's First Presidency appointed him to preside over the Mormon colonies in Chihuahua and Sonora. Ivins moved to Salt Lake City in 1907 when he was called to the Quorum of the Twelve Apostles.

Ivins was active in politics and business. In a state generally dominated by Republican Senator Reed Smoot's "Federal Bunch," he was one of a few key figures around whom the Utah Democratic Party rallied. By profession Ivins was a rancher, though his interests intersected with college trusteeship, mining, banking, and other enterprises.[5] The New

---

of Radical Politics, 108–9; and Kevin Phillips, *The Cousins' Wars: Religion, Politics, Civil Warfare, and the Triumph of Anglo-America*, 179.

4. Wendell J. Ashton, *Voice in the West: Biography of a Pioneer Newspaper*, 311.

5. For biographical information on Ivins, see "Anthony W. Ivins," Anthony W. Ivins Papers, box 1, fd. 2; D. Michael Quinn, *The Mormon Hierarchy: Extensions of Power*, 662–63; Richard S. Van Wagoner and Steven C. Walker, *A Book of Mormons*, 131–34; Thomas Cottam Romney, *The Mormon Colonies*

West type, Ivins was tough, intellectual, and practical.[6] Noble Warrum, a member of the Mexican Claims Commission during the 1920s, described him this way: "There is no man more dedicated to justice—he is [the] triple combination of the Spartan, the Stoic, and the Christian."[7] In the Mexican context Ivins endorsed the centralization of political authority, a liberal statist view echoed in the works of Ernest Gruening, editor of the *Nation* and later a senator from Alaska.[8]

Rey L. Pratt was the grandson of murdered Apostle Parley P. Pratt. Church work and a (monogamous) thirteen-child family kept Pratt busy. In 1907 he succeeded Ammon M. Tenney as president of the Mexican proselytizing mission—a post separate from Mormon colonial administration but loosely supervised by the North Mexico stake president at Colonia Juárez under the broader direction of the Twelve. Pratt headed the Mexican Mission until his death. In 1925 he became a general authority, moving into a position on the First Council of the Seventy left vacant by the death of Seymour Bicknell Young.

Unlike Ivins, Pratt listed himself as a Republican. The party's organ in Salt Lake City, the *Salt Lake Herald-Republican*, often consulted him on Mexican affairs. Church officials, recognizing his talents as editor, commentator, and translator of the Spanish language, appointed Pratt to head the Zion's Printing and Publishing Company, a Church press in Independence, Missouri.

Pratt was a people person. Slightly swarthy looks and fluent Spanish allowed him to travel incognito throughout Mexico and gather information in regions penetrated by few Americans. Admiration for Mexican

---

in Mexico; Nelle Spilsbury Hatch and B. Carmon Hardy, *Stalwarts South of the Border*; Bryant S. Hinckley, "President Anthony W. Ivins," *Improvement Era* 35 (November 1931): 5–8, 39; Herman Hoffman Birney, *Zealots in Zion*, 215–18, 293–310; Kristen Smart Rogers, "'Another Good Man': Anthony W. Ivins and the Defeat of Reed Smoot."

6. In 1958 Ivins was inducted into the Cowboy Hall of Fame. See "Hall of Great Westerners."

7. Noble Warrum, Letter to W. W. Armstrong, September 17, 1926, Ivins Papers, box 11, fd. 5.

8. John A. Britton charts American intellectual attitudes toward Mexico in Britton, *Revolution and Ideology: Images of the Mexican Revolution in the United States*, 17. For Gruening's statism see ibid., 72–73. Gruening's most important work was *Mexico and Its Heritage*.

Indian communalism put Pratt in an intellectual camp staked out by his contemporary Frank Tannenbaum, the widely-known Mexicanist scholar representative of the old "independent left."[9] Rhetorical skill and genuine concern for the welfare of others magnified the influence Pratt exerted in Church and public circles. Mexican members adored him.[10]

Mormon Economic Elitism in Mexico, 1886–1910

By the time Francisco Madero launched his revolution in 1910, nearly forty-five hundred Anglo-American Mormons lived in eight colonies in Chihuahua and Sonora—between 6 and 25 percent of all Americans living in Mexico.[11] The colonies had prospered, but the way in which Mormon settlers, land companies, and mercantile co-operatives had obtained their wealth had strained relations with their

---

9. Britton, *Revolution and Ideology*, 17, 122–23, 161–63. Tannenbaum's most important work on ejidal development was *Peace by Revolution: Mexico after 1910*.

10. For biographical information on Pratt, see Quinn, *Mormon Hierarchy: Extensions of Power*, 679; Dale F. Beecher, "Rey L. Pratt and the Mexican Mission," 294–95; Mary Pratt Parrish, "Look to the Rock from Which Ye Are Hewn," 54–112; Elizabeth Hernandez, *Mormonism Comes of Age in Mexico*, 17–18; "A New Member of the Council of Seventy," *Improvement Era* 28 (June 1925): 762–63; and Melvin J. Ballard, "President Rey L. Pratt," *Improvement Era* 34 (June 1931): 451.

11. Helen Delpar concludes from Mexican national census data that about twenty-one thousand Americans resided there. See Helen Delpar, *The Enormous Vogue of Things Mexican: Cultural Relations between the United States and Mexico, 1920–1935*, 1. President William H. Taft put the number of Americans living in Mexico at between forty and fifty thousand. Historian Ronald Atkin estimates there were seventy-five thousand. John Mason Hart accepts US Ambassador Henry Lane Wilson's similar estimate of seventy thousand. See Ronald Atkin, *Revolution! Mexico, 1910–1920*, 20; John Mason Hart, *Revolutionary Mexico: The Coming and Process of the Mexican Revolution*, 281; *Papers Relating to the Foreign Relations of the United States, with the Annual Message of the President Transmitted to Congress December 3, 1912*, xiv; and Henry F. Pringle, *The Life and Times of William Howard Taft*, 2:701. If the lower figure of forty thousand is accepted, then forty-five hundred Anglo-Mormon colonists accounted for just over 11 percent of Americans in Mexico.

Mexican neighbors. Mormon immigrants benefited from land laws enacted in 1856, 1883, and 1905. Under each of these laws, big landowners expropriated the lands of Indian communities and free peasants with the blessing of Mexican President Porfirio Díaz and the oligarchs who guided his regime. Additionally, the Mexican government leased or sold other large sections of the national domain to foreigners. Changes in land tenure hit Mexican merchants hard. Native middle-class businessmen sold their businesses as their old customers—the independent peasants and ranchers—disappeared. Into the void moved Mormon agents, backed by capital from Salt Lake City, who bought the alienated tracts and Mexican-owned businesses. Mormons soon controlled water access and major commercial, agricultural, and industrial enterprises in Chihuahua and Sonora.[12] By 1910 Mexican lands under Mormon title totaled more than a half-million acres.[13] Ivins wrote in 1912 that Mexican investments returned good dividends to Mormon leaders. He estimated the colonies' worth at $1 million.[14]

---

12. On Mormon commercial success see Journal History of the Church, June 18, 1890, 7–8; and ibid., April 5, 1903, 3. See also Blaine Carmon Hardy, "The Northern Colonies in Northern Mexico: A History, 1885–1912," 115–17; Friedrich Katz, ed., *The Life and Times of Pancho Villa*, 90–91; Jane-Dale Lloyd, *El proceso de modernización capitalista en el noroeste de Chihuahua, 1880–1910*, 87, 90, 123–24, 141; Mark Wasserman, *Capitalists, Caciques, and Revolution: The Native Elite and Foreign Enterprise in Chihuahua, Mexico, 1854–1911*, 98, 112; F. LaMond Tullis, *Mormons in Mexico: The Dynamics of Faith and Culture*, 57–60; Clarence F. Turley and Anna Tenney Turley, comps., *History of the Mormon Colonies in Mexico: The Juarez Stake, 1885–1980*, 296; and testimony by Joseph Lillywhite titled "The Story of the Theft of the Land of the Colony Morelos (Mormon) in the State of Sonora, Mexico," in *Investigation of Mexican Affairs: Preliminary Report and Hearings . . . to Investigate the Matter of Outrages on Citizens of the United States in Mexico*, 2:3254.

13. I added up the total acreage of land in Mormon hands and arrived at a conservative total of 509,600 acres. See Craig Livingston, "From Above and Below: The Mormon Embrace of Revolution, 1840–1940," 290, 329 note 48. Jane-Dale Lloyd puts the 1907 Chihuahua holdings alone at 445,000 acres; see Lloyd, *El proceso de modernización*, 89–90. For land companies and their activities, see Hardy, "Mormon Colonies in Northern Mexico," 150–58.

14. Anthony W. Ivins, Diary, 1912, 272; and "Believed at Church Offices

The growing Mormon presence in northwestern Mexico worried Mexican officials. In 1905 the political authority of the Galeana District, Chihuahua, observed, "Mormons are constantly broadening property and purchasing land tracts to the point that it has become alarming. Soon, all those who had shown them hospitality will themselves become tributaries."[15] Nonetheless, state authorities counted on Mormon support. Resentment grew as Mormon militia consistently mustered in defense of the status quo.[16] Emilio Kosterlitzky, the German-born commander of the Sonora constabulary known as the *rurales*, offered to kill any Mexican whom Mormon settlers found bothersome.[17] "Thus the Mormon position was ambiguous," writes F. Lamond Tullis. "Ideological commitment to Mexican spiritual liberation" clashed with

---

that Mexican Colonists Leaving," clipping from the *Deseret Evening News* in Journal History, January 30, 1917, 3.

15. Lloyd, *El proceso de modernización*, 90. For other local sentiments see Tullis, *Mormons in Mexico*, 89.

16. "'Mormon' Settlers in Mexico Aid the Government," clipping from the *Deseret Evening News* in Journal History, January 19, 1892, 6. In 1893 Celso Anaya and Simon Amaya, inspired by the Tomóchic rebellion the previous year in Chihuahua, called for the overthrow of Díaz. Government troops crushed the uprising. Survivors rallied in the United States, then recrossed the border and occupied Palomas, north of the Mormon colony zone. Mormons turned out with government troops to contain this proto-insurrection. See Orson P. Brown, Autobiography, 21–23; "Mexican Rebels and 'Mormon' Colonists," *Latter-day Saints' Millennial Star* 56 (January 8, 1894): 21–23 (hereafter cited as *Millennial Star*); Romney, *Mormon Colonies in Mexico*, 310–14; Turley and Turley, *History of the Mormon Colonies in Mexico*, 82. On the Anaya and Amaya revolt, see Katz, *Life and Times of Pancho Villa*, 26. The 1892 Tomóchic rebellion was fanned by government expropriations and village attraction to a religious mystic. Loss of land and elite posturing for power triggered other uprisings during the same decade. See Katz, *Life and Times of Pancho Villa*, 21–26; Hart, *Revolutionary Mexico*, 360–61; and Paul J. Vanderwood, *The Power of God against the Guns of Government: Religious Upheaval in Mexico at the Turn of the Nineteenth Century*.

17. Hatch and Hardy, *Stalwarts South of the Border*, 313. For a biography of Kosterlitzky and his relations with Mormon settlers, see Cornelius C. Smith Jr., *Emilio Kosterlitzky: Eagle of Sonora and the Southwest Border*.

"political support of an oppressive and economically ambitious regime based on foreign capital and foreign technicians."[18]

Dazzled by the positivism of the *científucos*—the "scientific ones" who managed Mexico's economy—Ivins overlooked the revolutionary conditions brewing in Mexico.[19] He imbibed the axioms of legalism and gradual reformism. Personal wealth and access to Church credit made him the archetypal post-Manifesto Mormon merging into the mainstream of corporatist America. In a 1901 article Ivins praised Díaz. "Life, property, and personal liberty," he concluded, were "as secure in Mexico as in any country in the world." The absence of sustained opposition had proven the dictator's ability to make "Mexican sentiment the incarnation of his own master mind."[20]

During the Second Yaqui War (1899–1909), Ivins revealed how far he was willing to go in support of Mexico's oligarchs. The Yaqui had assimilated Spanish ways but had resisted taxation and mineral extraction on their lands. Ivins admired them but bemoaned that they were not playing their part in Díaz's "master mind." The slaughter and deportations, as sad as they were, taught a lesson: history and nature had combined to ensure Mexico its due progress under the mandate of Díaz.[21]

---

18. Tullis, *Mormons in Mexico*, 89.

19. The *científucos* were guided by positivist ideas. Positivism was a philosophy of science pioneered by French philosopher Auguste Comte. The *científucos* extended invitations to foreigners to invest in Mexico in order to foster development. Ordered economic growth under European tutelage, they believed, would bring stability to Mexico. However, their policies also empowered elites to suppress the lower classes and to convert them and their lands into adjuncts of the new economic order. On positivist philosophy see Marilyn S. Smith, *Living Issues in Philosophy: An Introductory Textbook*, 482–83.

20. Anthony W. Ivins, "Porfirio Diaz," *Improvement Era* 4 (April 1901): 437.

21. Anthony W. Ivins, "The Yaquis and the Yaqui War," *Improvement Era* 4 (March 1901): 333–36. Ivins's views were typical. See Arturo Warman, "The Political Project of Zapatismo," 321–22. Juxtaposed to Ivins's imperialistic view was an article from the Mormon press sympathetic to Mexican miners in the wake of the Cananea, Sonora strike of 1906. See "Race Troubles in Sonora, Mexico," *Juvenile Instructor* 41 (July 15, 1906): 435–36.

The Madero Revolution

The leader of the Mexican Revolution was Francisco Madero. An upper-class politician with a strong belief in democracy, Madero opposed the attempt by dictator Porfirio Díaz to seek a sixth term as Mexico's president. Madero spoke out against Díaz's subversion of the constitution, repression of workers, seizure of village lands, and terrible treatment of Yaqui Indians. The crowds cheered Madero everywhere he went. Díaz ordered him arrested, but Madero escaped to the United States. From exile in Texas, Madero announced the Plan of Potosi. Unless Díaz resigned, Madero called for revolution. Despite evidence of Madero's appeal, Ivins declared for Díaz at the outset of the revolution. The Mormon colonists were well-armed with .30-30 Winchesters and plenty of ammunition, the apostle said, and they "will fight for the government against the insurrectos."[22] Church leaders considered arming the colonies, but rejected the move as adventurist. Determined Mormon colonists, with permission from the United States government, smuggled weapons in anyway.[23]

On March 6, 1911, Madero crossed the border and attacked Casas Grandes, Chihuahua with 130 men. The attack failed, but as news spread that "The Apostle of Democracy" was back in Mexico, so did revolt against Díaz. Despite their initial support for the existing Mexican government, Mormon observers took note of the revolutionary surge. The Church periodical *Improvement Era* called the situation in Mexico a "social revolution" of the landless masses against the *hacendados*, or feudal landlords. The peasants were in a mood to embrace anyone who offered hope of progress and liberty.[24] The article anticipated the potential for open civil war. Peasant yearning for land, the *Era* worried, might threaten the less radical agenda of the revolution's middle- and upper-

---

22. "Colonists Are Armed," clipping from the *Deseret Evening News* in Journal History, November 28, 1907, 7.

23. Livingston, "From Above and Below," 299–300; Blaine Carmon Hardy and Melody Seymour, "The Importation of Arms and the 1912 Mormon 'Exodus' from Mexico." The colonists bought the guns from the Payne-Shelton Company of El Paso. For gun-running in El Paso and along the border, see Charles H. Harris III and Louis R. Sadler, *The Secret War in El Paso: Mexican Revolutionary Intrigue, 1906–1920*.

24. "The Revolution in Mexico," *Improvement Era* 14 (March 1911): 452–54.

class leadership. The Anti-Reelectionists supporting Madero were "wealthy and intelligent" men previously absent from among Mexico's power brokers.[25] At root, their grievances were constitutional. However, Madero himself, educated in France, was "strongly imbued with the extreme democracy that characterizes French socialism."[26]

A key ally to Madero was General Pascual Orozco, the "soul of the revolutionary movement in Chihuahua."[27] Orozco, a native-born Chihuahuan, figured prominently in the Mormon exodus from Mexico the following year. On May 10, 1911, Orozco and Francisco "Pancho" Villa, another Chihuahuan, captured Ciudád Juárez.[28] Fifteen days later Porfirio Díaz resigned. The new governor of Chihuahua, Abraham Gonzalez, vowed to dismember the huge landed estates called *haciendas*. The announcement tantalized Mormon landholders. The implementation of revolutionary policies might break *hacendado* control over vast territories that had heretofore blocked a Mormon takeover of northwest Chihuahua.[29] In November 1911 a colony resident named Ammon M. Tenney informed Ivins that the

---

25. The Anti-Reelectionist party, headed by Madero associate Abraham Gonzalez, opposed the unconstitutional extension of Díaz's presidency and demanded fair elections, constitutional reform, independence of the judiciary, and freedom of the press.

26. "The Revolution in Mexico," 455. Some suggest that Madero's dalliance with spiritualism outweighed his interest in political philosophy during his 1901–2 stay in France. Others conclude that Madero was impressed by French equality and Anglo democracy. Compare Enrique Krauze, *Mexico: Biography of Power. A History of Modern Mexico, 1810–1996*, 246–47 to Stanley R. Ross, *Francisco I. Madero: Apostle of Mexican Democracy*, 7–8, 10, 224–25.

27. "The Revolution in Mexico," 455.

28. Friedrich Katz argues that Chihuahua's role in the revolution of 1910 was similar to Boston in 1776, Paris in 1789, and Petrograd in 1917. See Katz, *Life and Times of Pancho Villa*, 57.

29. Mormon expansion was at an end unless surrounding landowners offered to sell at reasonable prices. See Anthony W. Ivins, Letter to James G. Bleak, February 19, 1898, in Stanley S. Ivins, ed., "Letter from Mexico: Impressions of a Mormon," 179; and Harold W. Taylor, comp., *Memories of Militants and Mormon Colonists in Mexico*, 122. On the policies of Gonzalez, see Katz, *Life and Times of Pancho Villa*, 127–30; and William H. Beezley, *Insurgent Governor: Abraham Gonzales and the Mexican Revolution in Chihuahua*, 4, 97–99, 103–11.

revolutionary government of Chihuahua had abrogated certain municipal taxes on livestock, land, and farm products. His predictions for the future under Madero were reassuring: "Anticipated changes in the laws of this country under the present administration is certain to give a great impetus to agriculture in this country, and . . . we are already beginning to feel the benefits of the change in government."[30]

Ivins agreed. He now linked personal profit and increased Church revenues to Madero's assumption of power. In fact, Ivins advocated the revival of Indian settlement on Church lands in the colonies. The communitarian aspects of Mormonism would replace the *ejido* (Indian communal lands) as the organizing principle but would absorb its spirit. Idle lands would become productive, community cooperation would increase tithing to Salt Lake City, and the downtrodden Lamanites could rise to yeoman respectability.[31]

Ivins's comments reveal his understanding and sympathy for an important dimension of the Mexican Revolution—the spiritual rescue of the Indian. Revolutionary Indianism struck a familiar chord. Mormon doctrine taught that as heirs of the Abrahamic covenant, Indians were to work in partnership with the Latter-day Saints to establish God's kingdom on earth. The apparent inability of the Indians of the United States to play their ordained role, however, had confounded their self-appointed Mormon benefactors. Revolution in Mexico offered a new venue. Perhaps the descendants of the Aztecs and Mayans would succeed in their divine role where US Indians had apparently failed.[32]

---

30. Ammon Tenney, Letter to Anthony W. Ivins, November 10, 1911, Ivins Papers, box 11, fd. 1. Tenney was noted for his friendly relations with Indians. See Winn Whiting Smiley, "Ammon M. Tenney: Mormon Missionary to the Indians."

31. Anthony W. Ivins, Letter to Hyrum S. Harris, August 4, 1911, Ivins Papers, box 10, fd. 2. Previous efforts to promote Indian and *mestizo* settlement had failed. See "Meeting of the First Presidency in Salt Lake City Temple," Journal History, January 20, 1909, 4; Tullis, *Mormons in Mexico*, 60–65, 83; Agrícol Lozano Herrera, *Historia Del Mormonismo en Mexicó*, 41–42; Thomas W. Murphy, "From Racist Stereotype to Ethnic Identity: Instrumental Uses of Mormon Racial Doctrine," 463–64.

32. On Mormon disappointment with North American Indians, see David J. Whittaker, "Mormons and Native Americans: A Historical and Bibliographical Interpretation," 38.

The Madero revolution and Mormon hope for the peaceful south-ward extension of Zion faced a new challenge beginning March 2, 1912. Madero's most successful general, Orozco, initiated a new uprising in the belief that Madero's revolutionary government had reneged on promises of reform.[33] A month later Ivins addressed the Mormon faith-ful at the Church's semi-annual General Conference. Ivins's remarks showed cautious tolerance for the revolutionary process. Revolution and civil war, he reminded the audience, had produced the liberties en-joyed by France, England, Germany, and the United States. Struggle—not consensus—marked the modern world, though Ivins lamented that violence should be necessary in the supposed age of reason and logic. Ivins upheld the example set in 1789: "The French revolution with all its horrors, its injustice, and the barbarous things which characterized it, nevertheless, made for the betterment of the French people."[34]

Ivins sanctified the supremacy of law, but a close reading quali-fies this devotion. Ivins referred to universal rights: freedom of wor-ship, representative government, and physical security. He disdained laws that preserved special privilege. The antagonists in his sermon were Catholics, high-church Protestants, royalists, and monopolists—the same groups defeated by low churchmen and emergent social and

---

33. Historians disagree about what motivated the leaders of the anti-Maderista revolt. The origins of the Orozco revolt are located in the antecedent revolt of Emilio Vázquez Gómez, the brother of Francisco Vázquez Gómez, the provisional vice-president. Emilio turned against Madero because of Madero's order in June 1911 to demobilize the revolutionary forces before land and labor reforms were completed, and also because of the replacement of radical F. Vázquez Gómez with moderate José Pino Suárez in the 1910 election. Orozco supported Emilio Vázquez Gómez, but the Ciudád Juárez garrison viewed Orozco as its true leader. Sympathetic historians argue that Orozco sincerely sought reforms similar to Zapata's Plan de Ayala. See Michael C. Meyer, *Mexican Rebel: Pascual Orozco and the Mexican Revolution, 1910–1915,* 7, 17; and Hart, *Revolutionary Mexico,* 255. Others conclude that Orozco aligned himself with oligarchic factions that would advance his rise to power. See Katz, *Life and Times of Pancho Villa,* 143; and Krauze, *Mexico: A Biography of Power,* 265.

34. Anthony W. Ivins, April 7, 1912, *Report of the Semi-annual Conference of the Church of Jesus Christ of Latter-day Saints,* 63 (hereafter cited as *Conference Report*).

economic groups in each of the civil wars and revolutions that swept Britain and America from the 1640s to the 1860s.[35] Ivins did not predict how the Mexican Revolution would resolve itself at this time, but he suggested that elite Creoles (Spaniards born in Mexico) had provoked a social uprising: "Whenever a government or an administration shall assume to pervert the law, shall entrench itself with power, and disregard the cries of the masses it cannot expect but that confusion will result."[36]

Ivins accepted temporary dislocation and uncertainty in Mexico and praised President William Howard Taft's commitment to non-intervention.[37] Anti-foreigner agitation among Orozco's Red Flaggers posed a real threat to the colonies, Ivins said, but it would take a hundred thousand troops to "pacify" the country. Furthermore, the Mexican government would naturally tax the prosperous Mormon settlements to defray reconstruction costs incurred by war and occupation.[38]

At this point, Ivins's attitude toward Mexico's revolution was driven by economic considerations as much as ideological ones. He was permissive, but ultimately conservative. Although he understood the appeal of socialism, anarchism, and armed struggle, he rejected their prescriptions for utopia. He acknowledged that industrialism and imperialism had agitated labor and caused destructive international competition, but he could not endorse a violent corrective. He embraced the idea of a "universal brotherhood," but denied its attainment except through the teachings of Christ.[39] Ivins's economic stake in the stability of Mexico led him to articulate an evolutionary rather than revolutionary model of social reform. Soon all that would change.

Expulsion and Recalibration, 1912–13

In July 1912 the halcyon era of the Mormon colonies ended. General Victoriano Huerta, commissioned by Madero, smashed

---

35. Phillips, *Cousins' Wars*, 163.

36. Ivins, April 7, 1912, *Conference Report*, 62.

37. P. Edward Haley, *Revolution and Intervention: The Diplomacy of Taft and Wilson with Mexico, 1910–1917*, 31–32.

38. Ivins, April 7, 1912, *Conference Report*, 61; Anthony W. Ivins, Letter to O. M. Strafford, May 11, 1912, Ivins Papers, box 11, fd. 2; and Anthony W. Ivins, "Mexico," *Young Woman's Journal* 24 (May 1913): 260–61.

39. Ivins, April 7, 1912, *Conference Report*, 65.

Orozco's army at the Battle of Bachimba on July 3. The remnants diffused throughout the Mormon settlements of the Galeana district of northwestern Chihuahua.[40] After the Battle of Bachimba, the anti-American elements within Orozco's army could no longer be contained. Inez Salazar, an Orozco lieutenant, confiscated Mormon settlers' provisions, horses, and livery items. An attempt by Salt Lake authorities to mollify Orozco with a tribute of $5,000 in gold failed.[41] Finally, Salazar ordered the settlers to disarm. In exchange for the token surrender of some old guns, Salazar let the Mormons retreat unmolested north of the border. Beginning July 28, 1912, over four thousand fled by train or wagon. Few ever returned. The property losses and emotional trauma resulting from this expulsion scarred the Mormon psyche for decades to come. A disconsolate Ivins admitted to a friend that the revolution had completely wiped out his financial interests.[42]

As the revolution dragged on, however, economic questions concerned Ivins less. He recommended that the expatriate settlers accept their losses, as by "cheerfully" doing so they would protect lives and establish a better claim for protection and good faith in the future. The high-profile murder of William S. Benton, an English *hacendado*, drew no sympathy from Ivins. He condemned the Englishman for his stand on property rights: "[Benton] should have known better. It is another case of the bull trying to butt the locomotive off the track. I trust that we may learn wisdom from such experiences."[43]

In February 1913 General Victoriano Huerta killed Madero and seized the government. The Constitutionalists—Pancho Villa, Emiliano Zapata, and Venustiano Carranza—marched on Mexico City. Though

---

40. Alan Knight, *The Mexican Revolution*, 1:327–29.

41. Anthon Hendrik Lund, Diary, July 23, 1912.

42. Anthony W. Ivins, Letter to George S. Spencer, December 13, 1912, Ivins Papers, box 11, fd. 3.

43. Ivins, Diary, February 21, 1914. Benton was a ruthless Chihuahua landowner. In 1910, backed by twenty armed guards and a contingent of the Chihuahuan *rurales*, he annexed ejidal lands belonging to the village of Santa Maria de las Cuevas. See Wasserman, *Capitalists, Caciques, and Revolution*, 111–12. For accounts of the Benton affair, see Katz, *Life and Times of Pancho Villa*, 326–30; Atkin, *Revolution! Mexico, 1910–1920*, 170–71; and Knight, *Mexican Revolution*, 2:109–10.

their hatred of Huerta united them, each would claim the mantle of the revolution in his own way.

Mormon leaders never accepted Huerta's coup. But because a return to the *Porfiriato* was unthinkable, a new paradigm replaced the old emphasis on privilege and order. Key Mormon leaders experienced what Michael Walzer has called the "ideology of transition." Heightened awareness of human needs arises "whenever traditional controls give way and hierarchical status and corporate privileges are called into question."[44] By expelling the Mormon settlers, Orozco's *Colorados* had mentally liberated Ivins and Pratt. Freed from concerns about the colonists' physical safety, their minds soared to the more rarefied air of scriptural fulfillment and nation-building.

In March 1913 Pratt publicly joined the discussion on Mexico's ongoing revolution. In an article for the *Improvement Era*, he detailed the same horrors that John Kenneth Turner had exposed in *Barbarous Mexico* (1910). Pratt confirmed stories of twenty-five thousand Indians enslaved on *haciendas* as large as fifteen million acres, unfair labor contracts, laborers paid low wages and charged 500-percent markups in company stores, debt peonage, and the dreaded threat of military conscription or worse—deportation to plantations in the Yucatan. Pratt identified the disturbances in Mexico as a social upheaval: "The present revolution . . . has as its basic cause the age-old desire for freedom, the desire of the oppressed to throw off the yoke of the oppressor."[45]

Like Ivins, Pratt opposed US intervention. He deemed the United States a potentially counter-revolutionary force that would reinstate the *científucos* who catered to foreign capitalists. In 1913 Pratt was living in Mexico City, where he acquired intimate knowledge of events leading to Madero's overthrow. US Ambassador Henry Lane Wilson was singled out for Pratt's unvarnished contempt. Pratt averred, quite correctly, that the ambassador had conspired to depose Madero.[46]

Many of Pratt's observations from this period were recorded in a chronicle he kept between February and August 1913. The manuscript reveals a man even more class-conscious than his public writings and

---

44. Walzer, *Revolution of the Saints*, 312.

45. Rey L. Pratt, "The Gospel to the Lamanites," *Improvement Era* 16 (April 1913): 582–85.

46. Rey L. Pratt, "Account of What Happened in Mexico City between February 9 and 18, 1913," 26–27, 48, Rey L. Pratt Papers Papers, box 3, fd. 2.

speeches suggest. Pratt indicted the rich, the Catholic Church, and the army for being in league against the poor. With historical dialecticism on his mind, he understood the motive force of class struggle in a way that might have pleased Mao Zedong: "When the poor native comes to a point to sufficiently know his own interests . . . then will come the redemption of the native of the land. The time is ripe for that class that had been held down to rise and be on top."[47]

Pratt's sense of inevitable triumph rivaled the optimism of Karl Liebknecht. "We are used to being thrown from the heights to the depths," Liebknecht said after Germany's failed Spartacist Uprising, "But . . . our program will live on; it will rule over the world of redeemed humanity."[48] The death of Madero had stalled national progress, Pratt likewise conceded, but he urged continuation of the class struggle: "Whether it comes now or whether the people again submit to long years of slavery and serfdom at the hands of the rich . . . there must and will come a time when the native people of this land will rise up and throw off the yoke of slavery and raise above the condition that now holds them down."[49]

Pratt grouped Indians, workers, and liberty-minded *mestizos* (the middle class of mixed Indian and European ancestry) into a single revolutionary unit. The bourgeoisie of Mexico City who spoke well of Madero were the "best people" of their class. After a visit to Madero's grave, Pratt venerated the displays of working-class solidarity in his special journal. Of the Indians Pratt wrote, "Years of preaching . . . among them has taught me that the best people in the nation are those that are

---

47. Ibid., 27. This private side of Pratt is represented in his influence on Margarito Bautista, an organizer of the Third Convention movement in 1936 that established an independent Mormon Church in Mexico for a period of nine years. Bautista's *La evolución de México sus verdaderos progenitores y su origen: el destino de América y Europa* reflects a class-consciousness fostered and encouraged by Pratt. Another Third Conventionist, Isaías Juárez, was a founder of the national farmworker's union (*Confederación Nacional Campesina*). See Livingston, "From Above and Below," 463. On the Third Convention see F. Lamond Tullis, "A Shepherd to Mexico's Saints: Arwell L. Pierce and the Third Convention"; Tullis, *Mormons in Mexico*, 137–68.

48. Quoted in Helmut Trotnow, *Karl Liebknecht (1871–1919): A Political Biography*, 203.

49. Pratt, "Account of What Happened in Mexico City," 11.

now suffering the most." He cheered the exploits of the Morelos-based Zapatistas. As long as they and Carranza's coalition refused to acknowledge Huerta, Pratt said, the revolution lived.[50]

A Messianic Revolution?

During 1914 Pratt and Ivins became increasingly supportive of radical measures. On February 3 President Woodrow Wilson lifted the arms embargo after deciding that Huerta had to go. As US arms poured into Veracruz, Pratt's optimism for revolutionary change rose. At the Latter-day Saint University in Salt Lake City, Pratt lectured students on the "social uprising" in Mexico. It must continue unabated, he said. Pratt castigated "the aristocratic, estate-holding tyrants, the rich and well born, the politicians of the country." This class that abused Mexico and enslaved the Indians had to be "removed." Once the people had overthrown elite rule, Pratt theorized, teachers, ministers, and Indian leaders would "rejuvenate Mexico" and restore the sophistication it had achieved before the Spanish conquest.[51]

Pratt glowed as Pancho Villa slugged his way toward Mexico City. After Villa's Division of the North mauled Huerta's forces at the Battle of Zacatecas on June 23, 1914, Pratt wrote,

> "Who can doubt that out of the present struggle will grow a great and better Mexico with an absolute liberty, based on human rights, for *all* her people? And after all, will not the way be prepared for the teaching of the true Gospel unto the people of that land, the Gospel that is to bring about their redemption and make them a people favored of the Lord?"[52]

Pratt was positing a spiritual dialectic for Mexico. The degraded condition of the Indians was symptomatic of their ancient loss of faith in the one true god. But glory would follow the fall. This narrative—the Lamanite people are favored of the Lord, dwindle in unbelief, are con-

---

50. Ibid., 9–11, 35, 36. Pratt also expressed these opinions in verse. See his poem "The 'Cuartelazo'" in Rey L. Pratt, *Just Thinking*, 40–46.

51. "Revolution Marks Social Uprising Is Pratt's Statement," clipping from the *Salt Lake Herald-Republican* in Journal History, February 11, 1914, 4.

52. Rey L. Pratt, "Book of Mormon Prophecies and the Mexican Situation," *Young Woman's Journal* 25 (September 1914): 539.

quered, and then await salvation from the gentiles—was Pratt's way of explaining how Mexico went from an empire of 30 million to an impoverished population of 15 million ruled by a dictator. With nine-tenths of the Indian population wiped out, Pratt announced, the time had come to reverse the process. The revolution, therefore, was a dialectical step toward the cultural return of the Indian.[53]

Other Church officers followed Pratt's lead. In a speech to the Associated Collegians of Brigham Young University, Charles McClellan, formerly a counselor in the Juárez stake presidency, registered his preference for gradual change. But given that Madero was "butchered" when he tried it, McClellan felt that the Mexican people must be pardoned for relying on the "power that a 30-30 rifle gives them." Then McClellan came to the point: "[I]t is not a question of this man or that man in Mexico. It is a question of principles, of human rights; and you and I, under the same circumstances, would take up arms. Our fathers did for even less provocation in the days of Bunker Hill, and we honor them for it." In Mexico, McClellan argued, class revolt would weaken the old order. Once the revolution was accomplished, Mexico must develop a "national spirit" and receive training in constitutional government to overcome *científuco* and *hacendado* influence, class division, and the ethnic differences that would hinder further development.[54]

Ivins began to reconstruct his image of Mexico after the shock of expulsion and financial loss subsided. Previously he had related to Mexico based on the model of Arielism. Frederick Pike describes Arielism as an alliance of elites in the Western Hemisphere who would increase their personal wealth by banding together to limit "barbarous" democratic influences.[55] But the heat of revolution had melted the old

---

53. Ibid., 539–40. Pratt reviewed the population devastation suffered by other Latin American countries to underscore his point. For the unfolding of Mormon racial doctrines toward Mexico's inhabitants, see Murphy, "From Racist Stereotype to Ethnic Identity," 458–61. For a discussion of Mormon views of Indian identity, see Thomas W. Murphy, "Other Mormon Histories: Lamanite Subjectivity in Mexico."

54. Charles E. McClellan, "A Bird's-Eye View of Mexico's Troubles," *Improvement Era* 17 (March 1914): 441–44. McClellan later studied at Stanford and Columbia and became a professor at Utah State University. See Hatch and Spilsbury, *Stalwarts South of the Border*, 422–25.

55. Fredrick B. Pike, *The United States and Latin America: Myths and*

Porfirio-Mormon "alliance-for-progress." Ivins ultimately repudiated the Arielian model and began to seek communion with the masses.

The advance of the northern and southern revolutionary armies toward Mexico City invigorated Ivins's mind with prospects of scriptural fulfillment. Just days before Villa and Zapata culminated the revolution with a dramatic entry into the city on December 5, 1914, Ivins met with the Twelve Apostles and the First Presidency of the Church in the Salt Lake Temple. He reviewed the situation in Mexico and referred to a verse in 3 Nephi in the Book of Mormon. The Mexican people, Ivins declared, "having been trodden down by the gentiles, will become like a lion among a flock of sheep, so plainly set forth by the Savior himself."[56] The trope of peasants and workers as lions united in a providential fight to eradicate their overlords' marks another step in Ivins's reinvention of himself. At a chapel dedication in San Diego, he concluded that liberty would be established in Mexico, but only after the conflict that pitted "servants against pitiless masters" had been won.[57]

The apostle had come to celebrate the violence that was purging Mexico. Both he and Pratt now dismissed the Mormon colonists' expulsion from Mexico as a sidebar in a much bigger event. The fighting that spread across the country was but the antithesis to Spanish imperialism and Creole exploitation. Missionary work, redemption of the Lamanites, and the possibilities of an Indian nation embossed the revolution with the imprimatur of divine approval. The upheaval had assumed scriptural and social proportions that exceeded the legalisms of American property holding in Mexico.

Stereotypes of Civilization and Nature, 194, 218–20.

56. "Minutes of Meeting of the First Presidency," Journal History, November 25, 1914. Cf. 3 Ne. 20:16, 21:12. Ivins was not the first to suggest that an uprising in Mexico would fulfill prophecy. Elder George C. Ferguson said the failure of Napoleon III to install French rule over Mexico validated Book of Mormon scripture. See George C. Ferguson, "Book of Mormon and Napoleon III," *Millennial Star* 42 (October 4, 1880): 636–39.

57. Anthony W. Ivins, May 21, 1916, in "Conditions in Northern Mexico," *Improvement Era* 19 (July 1916): 843. See also Anthony W. Ivins, March 30, 1916, quoted in "War with Mexico Is On, Says Ivins," clipping from the *Salt Lake Tribune* in Journal History, March 31, 1916, 2.

Carranza and the Constitutionalists

Inevitably, revolution became civil war. Huerta resigned July 15, 1914. At the Aguascalientes Convention the following October, the Constitutionalist alliance fell apart. The Carranzistas wanted to defuse revolutionary radicalism and realign Mexican politics along upper-class lines. To enlist urban and rural support, Carranza offered the return of illegally seized ejidal lands and the recognition of labor unions.[58] The Zapatistas, angered by Carranza's elitism and distrustful of his sincerity, insisted on the more sweeping agrarian reforms called for in the Plan de Ayala. Carranza and Villa were divided by personal rivalry and social class, but on a deeper level their incompatibility is explained by the historic division over the nature of Mexican federalism. Carranza would centralize the government in Mexico City; Villa personified the regionalist view that political power should remain in the states.[59] Villa's supporters dominated the Aguascalientes Convention, which therefore chose Eulalio Gutiérrez, a general with agrarian proclivities, to succeed Carranza as president. Carranza refused to accept the Convention's choice, evacuated Mexico City, and formed a second government in Veracruz. On November 19, 1914, General Álvaro Obregón, acting under Carranza's order, declared war on the "Conventionists," Villa and Zapata.

---

58. City workers believed that Carranza's formation of "Red Battalions" to fight the Conventionists and his endorsement of the *Casa del Obrero* indicated his acceptance of syndicalism, a concept that championed unions as the organizing dynamic of society. But to the workers' dismay, Carranza defined his Constitutionalist party in terms of his upper-class background and nationalist sentiment; the worker alliance was a temporary expedient. See Hart, *Revolutionary Mexico*, 306–7, 318–19; Knight, *Mexican Revolution*, 2:433.

59. On Zapata versus Carranza see Krauze, *Mexico: A Biography of Power*, 291; Hart, *Revolutionary Mexico*, 267–69. Katz, *Life and Times of Pancho Villa*, 388–96, reviews the hagiography of the Villa-Carranza split. He concludes that the long-standing dispute in Mexican politics that centered on "centralization versus regionalism is probably the least controversial" explanation for the onset of civil war between the former Constitutionalist allies (ibid., 391). Hart insists that the civil war pitted agrarians and laborers (Villa and Zapata) against the foreigners and *hacendados* (Carranza). See Hart, *Revolutionary Mexico*, 276–77, 327.

US President Woodrow Wilson took the view that Carranza personified the intent of the Madero revolution. The US policy response was pinned on the belief that if Carranza could be induced to concentrate on the land reform issues that attracted the people to Villa and Zapata, the threat to foreign interests in Mexico would diminish.[60] Subsequently, Carranza assured Wilson that he would muzzle revolutionary nationalism in exchange for US recognition. He received it October 19, 1915.[61]

A month later Plutarco Calles, an Obregónist general, annihilated Villa's Division of the North at Agua Prieta. Villa, maddened by US recognition of Carranza, raided Columbus, New Mexico, on March 9, 1916. He hoped that American columns streaming across the border in pursuit would galvanize Chihuahuans against Carranza.[62] In the scenario of renewed desert warfare, the Mormon colonies were again strategically located. Juárez and Dublán served the logistical needs of both US General John J. Pershing's Punitive Expedition and Villa's Mexican Division of the North.[63]

---

60. Lloyd C. Gardner, *Safe for Democracy: The Anglo-American Response to Revolution, 1913–1923*, 61–65.

61. Thomas F. O'Brien, *The Revolutionary Mission: American Enterprise in Latin America, 1900–1945*, 263; and Lloyd C. Gardner, "Woodrow Wilson and the Mexican Revolution," 28.

62. Clarence C. Clendenen, *Blood on the Border: The United States Army and the Mexican Irregulars*, 199–200; and Katz, *Life and Times of Pancho Villa*, 566.

63. Villa, who hoped the United States would not believe he had ordered the Columbus raid, was trying to avoid a two-front war, one against Pershing's expeditionary force and the other against General Francisco Murguía advancing from the south. Accusations of another attack on a property center with ties to the United States (like a Mormon colony) would be ruinous to Villa's policy of gaining the "good will" of his neighbors while he liberated his people from the "slavery and evil condition that had been brought on by the tyrants of his country." See Report to General John J. Pershing, December 16, 1916, quoted in Katz, *Life and Times of Pancho Villa*, 604. On the strategic location of Colonia Dublán, see Clendenen, *Blood on the Border*, 220. Villa refitted his army in Casas Grandes, Dublán, and Juárez in September–October 1915 preparatory to his attack on Agua Prieta. A colorful description of Villa's Division of the North is found in

Despite the unraveling of the Constitutionalist alliance and the violence of Villa's cross-border attack, Ivins and Pratt remained committed to the idea of revolution, though with some differences between the two men. After the Columbus raid, Ivins chose to support institutionalization of revolutionary gains in the Constitutionalist government at Veracruz. On this point he had come into harmony with Wilson's commitment to Carranza. The statism that later became a hallmark of Ivins's defense of the Mexican government's 1926 nationalization of church properties began to take shape. Ivins told a citizens' military preparedness group that the revolution should continue until equal rights for all Mexicans was assured. But since no faction had gained a clear advantage, leaving Mexico mired in unproductive violence, Ivins revised his earlier disinclination to invade. The "turbulent elements" in the armies of Zapata and Villa, he reasoned, had to be quelled long enough for constitutional reforms to proceed. The risk of provoking Mexico was worth taking if the presence of US forces allowed Carranza to consolidate his government under republican principles.[64]

Invasion, however, did not imply general war. In Dublán, General Pershing invited Ivins to address his troops. Standing on a makeshift platform, Ivins reflected on the army's mission. The objective of the Punitive Expedition, he told them, was not to demonstrate imperial power, menace Mexico, destroy Villa, or redeem American honor. To the contrary, the army was to contain Villa in order to assist a sister republic.[65] Before the October 1916 Conference, Ivins was similarly sober in his injunction against aggression. Referring to former Indiana Governor Frank Hanly, a Republican running for the Prohibition Party who said he would attack Mexico if elected president, Ivins said, "it may seem a simple thing" to have a war with America's weaker neighbor.

Grace Zenor Pratt, "Glimpses of Villa's Army," *Improvement Era* 19 (March 1916): 395–401. Several Mormons were pressed into service as teamsters on the Division of the North's fateful march over the Sonoran mountains. See Raymond J. Reed, "The Mormons in Chihuahua: Their Relations with Villa and the Pershing Punitive Expedition, 1910–1917," 73.

64. See "War with Mexico Is On, Says Ivins." For Ivins's reluctant support of Carranza, see also Anthony W. Ivins, "On Villa's Trail in Mexico," pt. 1, *Improvement Era* 19 (September 1916): 1015–16.

65. Mary Foster Gibbs, "General John J. Pershing," *Relief Society Magazine* 6 (January 1919): 22–23.

But like Austria found out against Serbia, the demand for reparations in Mexico could likewise result in a "condition of degeneracy" on both sides "that a generation never can eradicate."[66]

Ivins was ready to believe that the damage done to the old ruling class in Mexico had been sufficient to begin the process of rebuilding, but he remained emotionally tied to Villa. The dashing image he harbored of Villa's 1913 raid on Casas Grandes at a time when Villa was an aspiring revolutionary commander had never worn away.[67] A series of articles authored by Ivins, titled "On Villa's Trail," reads like a heroic western adventure.[68] Ideology is subordinated to drama as narrow Villista getaways to mountain hideouts thrill the reader as much as US Cavalry marksmanship and riding skill. Ivins's description of Villa's plan for the cross-border New Mexico raid is highly complimentary: "The details of the enterprise were carefully worked out, and executed with boldness and dispatch, which illustrate the intelligence and natural genius of this uneducated leader of men."[69] In these narratives Villa executes Americans without condemnation. According to biographer Friedrich Katz, Villa increasingly condoned rape and murder after 1915, when he began a "moral decline."[70] American and Mexican ad-

---

66. Anthony W. Ivins, October 8, 1916, *Conference Report*, 66. That the United States should exercise caution to avoid full-scale war was also suggested in "The United States and Mexico: Shall We Have War or Peace with Mexico Our Neighbor?" *Improvement Era* 19 (May 1916): 584–90.

67. Anthony W. Ivins, Letter to Joseph C. Bentley, June 28, 1913, Ivins Papers, box 9, fd. 3. On Villa's first raid as a Maderista, see Katz, *Life and Times of Pancho Villa*, 204–13.

68. Ivins, "On Villa's Trail in Mexico," published in five installments: pt. 1 in *Improvement Era* 19 (September 1916): 1014–19; pt. 2 in *Improvement Era* 19 (October 1916): 1095–97; pt. 3 in *Improvement Era* 20 (February 1917): 355–59; pt. 4 in *Improvement Era* 20 (March 1917): 397–400; and pt. 5 in *Improvement Era* 20 (April 1917): 500–504.

69. Ivins, "On Villa's Trail in Mexico," pt. 1, 1018. Bishop Joseph Bentley of Juárez, a friend of Ivins, touted Villa as "the greatest fighter of them all." See Joseph C. Bentley, "Some Mexican Revolutionists," *Juvenile Instructor* 55 (October 1920): 488.

70. Katz, *Life and Times of Pancho Villa*, 623–25.

herents lost faith in Villista methods and purposes, but Ivins continued to nurture the image of Villa as a romantic bandit.[71]

Ivins shared his attraction to Villa with other well-known Americans. Army Chief-of-Staff Hugh Scott found common ground with Villa within the "cowboy code of honor."[72] Theodore Roosevelt expressed a general appreciation for Latin cowboy-aristocrats who, like himself, possessed "to a very high degree, the stern, manly qualities that are invaluable to a nation."[73] Ivins, himself the consummate frontiersman, saw in Villa a self-made rebel. As late as December 1918 he defended the old renegade, saying that Villa's visits to the Mormon colonies and his brief but spectacular occupations of Chihuahua City were his way of embarrassing the Mexican government.[74] Still, as John Reed had concluded, Villa could not "fuse creatively with the masses," and Ivins deferred to Carranza.[75]

Carranza, in the meantime, tightened his grip. In the south a Carranzista offensive slowly pushed back Zapata's forces and strangled his revolution.[76] Carranzista General Pablo Gonzalez executed people indiscriminately and laid waste to Morelos. Then, suddenly, fortunes changed. The Zapatista high command shifted its headquarters to Tochimilco, at the foot of the Popo volcano, and launched raids against

---

71. Ivins's reference to Villa as a bandit with honor is similar to the definition of "Bandit" in Edward S. Farrow, *Farrow's Military Encyclopedia: A Dictionary of Military Knowledge*, 1:135–36.

72. Katz, *Life and Times of Pancho Villa*, 319.

73. Quoted in Pike, *United States and Latin America*, 203–4. For a pre-revolution Mormon reflection on the benefits of Spanish and middle-class rule in South America, see "Chili [sic]," *Juvenile Instructor* 27 (May 1, 1892): 265–71.

74. Journal History, December 26, 1918, 6. Bishop Arwell Pierce in El Paso stated that Villa's forced loans and horse and grain expropriations had cost the settlements $7,210. Yet Pierce remained sympathetic to Villa, adding that the Villistas did it because it was their only source of income. The raiders had also been "cordial to the women." See Journal History, March 30, 1919, 1.

75. Pike, *United States and Latin America*, 218–19. Villa's revolutionary elitism is discussed in Jim Tuck, *Pancho Villa and John Reed: Two Faces of Romantic Revolution*, 214–15.

76. John Womack Jr., *Zapata and the Mexican Revolution*, 247.

Mexico City. The Zapatista counter-offensive was so potent that General Gonzalez withdrew from Morelos in November 1916.[77] Evidence suggests that while Mexican Mormons tried to remain neutral, many, especially in the Indian villages, sided with the Zapatistas. Some Mormons paid the price of deportation, arrest, conscription, despoliation, and execution by the Carranzistas. Pratt personally intervened in several cases.[78] The Zapatista execution of two other Mormons for alleged Carranzista collaboration so upset Pratt that he permitted a family member to participate in a government firing squad in retaliation.[79]

Against the backdrop of these events, Pratt spoke at the LDS Church's October 1916 General Conference. The revolution must continue, he averred. The people thirsted for land and political representation. Madero would have realized these dreams, but counter-revolutionaries Orozco and Huerta, "bought off by the millions of the privileged and wealthy classes," had temporarily squashed Mexican aspirations.[80] Unlike Ivins, Pratt peremptorily rejected Mexico's new president: "General Carranza is . . . an aristocrat—one of the privileged classes of Mexico, and he is a man who cannot inspire in the Mexican people any confidence."[81]

Pratt voiced the resolve of peasant soldiers in the south. He never publicly identified sufferers and fighters during this period; they remained a collective abstraction. Still, Pratt personified the revolution with a sensitivity derived from his intimate relationship with Mexico. On the slope of a Puebla volcano, ragged Zapatistas had told Pratt that "We . . . shall inherit something besides the misery that we have had to live in, and we never again will lay down our arms until there is estab-

---

77. Ibid., 302; and Knight, *Mexican Revolution*, 2:368–69.

78. "Mormon Mexicans are Persecuted," clipping from the *Salt Lake Telegram* in Journal History, April 5, 1918, 11; Tullis, *Mormons in Mexico*, 96–103; Parrish, "Look to the Rock," 78–79; Beecher, "Rey L. Pratt and the Mexican Mission," 299–300; and Mark L. Grover, "Execution in Mexico: The Deaths of Rafael Monroy and Vincente Morales."

79. Rey L. Pratt, Diary, May 19, 1917.

80. Rey L. Pratt, October 8, 1916, *Conference Report*, 146.

81. Ibid., 147. The general conclusion among scholars is that Carranza's outlook, despite his nationalist goals, remained tied to the upper-class, was friendly to foreigners, and offered the Catholic Church salutary indifference. See Hart, *Revolutionary Mexico*, 333.

lished for the humble class of Mexico liberty."[82] Pratt drew from a mystical, religious faith in revolution. Like the half-secular, half-religious utopian epiphanies that had fired the minds of men during the nineteenth century, Pratt's discourse was at once religious and revolutionary—"a language in the making: a road sign pointing to the future."[83]

As Pratt concluded his discourse, he collapsed the distance between Mormon colonists and Mexican revolutionaries. "[The revolutionaries] may have committed against us depredations," he admitted, "and if it were only a political issue, if it were only a national issue, if we were only Americans, we might have resentment toward them, but we have received the word of the Lord that they are our brethren." Pratt posited for Mexicans and Mormons a sacred kinship and a shared utopian destiny. He prayed that the light of a new age would shine, and that "when the clouds of war rolled by . . . the servants of the Lord will be permitted to come again and carry the gospel to their brethren and to their sisters who are yet in darkness."

The "They are our brothers" speech employed the discursive technique of enthymeme. An enthymeme is the unstated portion of an argument. The speaker relies on the audience to fill in the gaps based on shared historical experience or commonly held mental references. In the enthymematic shadow, the speaker reveals his philosophy of history, politics, or religion.[84] For Pratt, the revolution was testing Mormon doctrine against his own allowance of raw social forces at work in Mexico.

From an enthymematic standpoint Pratt achieved reconciliation. The Mormon audience could decode a message confirming that the Mexican Revolution was an extension of their own sacred history. The Mexican people were not alien malefactors or barbaric rebels. They were brothers and co-agents in redeeming mankind. The reclamation of the Indians reminded the Saints of their commission to proselytize the remnants of Israel before the Second Coming. Mexico's suffering masses conjured the Missouri and Illinois persecutions; the armies of Villa and Zapata were figments of the 1834 march of Zion's Camp to win back Jackson County, a symbolic rehearsal of the hoped-for future Mormon return to Missouri. Revolutionary Mexico, emerging into a brighter fu-

---

82. Pratt, October 8, 1916, *Conference Report*, 147.

83. James Billington, *Fire in the Minds of Men: The Origins of the Revolutionary Faith*, 7.

84. Teun A. van Dijk, ed., *Discourse as Structure and Process*, 171–72.

ture, prefigured the literal advent of Zion—the New Jerusalem, Christ's future terrestrial capital.

Pratt's oratory animated his audience. Conservative Church President Joseph F. Smith followed Pratt to the pulpit and rejoined: "I do not want war; but the Lord has said it shall be poured out upon all nations. I would rather the oppressors should be killed than to allow the oppressors to kill the innocent."[85]

The topic of Pratt's discourse came at the request of conservative Apostle and US Senator Reed Smoot. Smoot's object was to counter the support Ivins had displayed for Wilson's Mexico policy and the League of Nations.[86] Pratt accepted the invitation but could not be co-opted to Smoot's political purposes. He had scorned the *Salt Lake Herald-Republican*'s endorsement of the Huerta regime as a means of stabilizing the country. But neither did Pratt support Wilson. He believed that US recognition of Carranza had betrayed the Mexican people. Had Pratt known of Wilson's private views prior to October 1915, he would have discovered that he was in agreement with Wilson's earlier initiatives, which had called for a "provisional government essentially revolutionary in character" that "should institute reforms by decree before the calling of a constitutional convention."[87] The disappointment Pratt nevertheless felt toward the US policy shift in favor of Carranza suggests his agreement with the *Herald-Republican*, though for a very different reason, that Wilson had failed as the "president of humanity."[88]

The passion with which Pratt opposed Carranza outdistanced the revolutionary ardor of Kenneth Turner, one of Pratt's closest ideological companions. Turner defined "liberty" like Pratt did: "a concrete, tangible

---

85. Joseph F. Smith, October 8, 1916, *Conference Report*, 154. At the April 1916 General Conference, Pratt gave a sermon similar to his October "They are our brothers" address. George Albert Smith, apostle and president of the Church from 1945 to 1950, came next to the pulpit and voiced his desire to overthrow "the oppressors" in Mexico. See George Albert Smith, April 9, 1916, *Conference Report*, 123–24.

86. Kristen Smart Rogers, "'Another Good Man': Anthony W. Ivins and the Defeat of Reed Smoot," 61.

87. Woodrow Wilson, Letter to Robert Lansing, August 11, 1915, quoted in Gardner, "Woodrow Wilson and the Mexican Revolution," 28.

88. "Concerning Two Pictures," clipping from the *Salt Lake Herald-Republican* in Journal History, October 10, 1916, 2.

thing that means ... not only the broader liberties of the mind but the more
pressing needs of the body."[89] But Turner thought Villa was a "scoundrel"
being manipulated by reactionaries to force a US intervention.[90] Pratt, on
the other hand, extolled Villa. A poem composed by Pratt in 1916 disdained
the alliance between the United States and the Constitutionalist enemies of
Villa. Seventeen American deaths resulting from the Columbus raid had
been the price for allowing Carranza to transport troops across US territory
to reinforce the garrison of Agua Prieta:

"Villa's Raid"[91]

1

So darker grew [Villa's visage]
  And hatred filled his heart,
Against that foreign country
  For their ignoble part
In aiding thus for money,
  Against both nations' laws,
His foe, and brought disaster
  To freedom's struggling cause ...

2

He watched his ragged comrades,
  Their blood-stained feet so sore;
He watched them march in silence,
  Then in his wrath he swore:
"By those who died in battle
  By those who march with me,
I'll take revenge on that proud
  land, Their blood the price must be ..."

3

With lives full many a thousand
  And treasure yet untold,

---

89. John Kenneth Turner, "Mexico's 'Bandit Armies,'" *Collier's* 51 (April
5, 1913): 11, 21, quoted in Britton, *Revolution and Ideology*, 38.
90. Ibid., 39.
91. Pratt, *Just Thinking*, 69–73.

> The gringo army had to pay
>   To this marauder bold.
> Nor did they ever take him back,
>   As they at first had said,
> That they would bring him back alive,
>   If not, bring him back dead . . .

>   4
> But after months of fruitless toil
>   Back home again marched they;
> Left Villa and his dauntless men
>   The victors in the fray;
> His vow made good that pay they should
>   Their act of perfidy
> For helping for a price of gold
>   The foes of liberty.

Pratt's sympathies are clear. Continued violence was preferable to premature consolidation—a position Pratt continued to embrace after the nation he admired most, the United States, endorsed Carranza. "Liberty," as Pratt envisioned it, could only be realized through the decrees of an Indian state. Legitimacy rested on the inclusion of other still-fighting revolutionary constituencies. Pratt's independent leftist view would not allow him to ignore the contradictions he saw between the social origins of Carranzistas and the condition of the people. Neither would he admit defeat as the power of the Carranzista state slowly began to reshape Mexican life.

An Indian Nation Born in Revolution

With the promulgation of the 1917 constitution, the decline of Villa, and the subsequent assassination of Zapata, revolutionary activity in Mexico subsided. Ivins toured the Mormon colonies in November 1917. He surveyed the devastated stores, the idle mills, the uncultivated fields, and the Mormon town of Díaz—destroyed because it was named after the ousted dictator. While these scenes troubled Ivins as much as they did other American observers, he put the destruction into perspective: "Barbarous Mexico has proven herself childlike, humane, and merciful, when compared with the [world war] across the sea."[92] In Ivins's opinion, Mexico had at least forged a new nation through armed struggle. Conflict in Europe was tearing the continent apart. The futility of World War I contrasted sharply with the noble purposes for which Mexicans had fought.

To the ends of their lives, Pratt and Ivins kept faith with the Mexican Revolution. In their speeches, articles, and letters, they fought to reconcile the tension between the spiritual and the secular worlds—between individual salvation and social activism. They engaged in battles of discourse to promote their views on the utility and meaning of revolution. As they did, they often found themselves groping for self-discovery. When they struck the core, both found that they stood for the idea of an Indian nation born in revolution.

Two LDS leaders had articulated a "liberation theology" at a time when Utah was undergoing the transition from a communitarian theocracy to a Wall Street dependency.[93] Pratt and Ivins sublimated the "American" in themselves and spoke a revolutionary language. They made Mormonism fit in Mexico by drawing from a radical past that promoted a social vision no longer advisable in America. During the revolution the people of Mexico had struggled to redefine their place in the Mexican state. Pratt and Ivins intellectually aided and abetted that revolution, believing that the reduction of Catholic influence and realization of socioeconomic justice would promote the rise of an Indian nation—an eventuality that they believed scripture and revelation supported. Twenty more years of revolutionary nation-making in Mexico would test that vision.

---

92. Anthony W. Ivins, "Mexico after the War," *Improvement Era* 21 (June 1918): 715–19.

93. Thomas G. Alexander divides Utah's economic history into four time periods: (1) theocratic kingdom, 1846–1890; (2) colony of Wall Street, 1870–1933; (3) colony of Washington DC, 1933–1980; (4) commonwealth economy (Utah-based entrepreneurship), 1980–present. See Thomas G. Alexander, *Utah, the Right Place: The Official Centennial History*, 408–12.

CHAPTER 8

POST-REVOLUTIONARY MEXICO, 1920–30

Extension of Revolutionary Action

The post-revolutionary consolidation of power in Mexico between 1920 and 1930 riveted the attention of Mormon observers. From President Álvaro Obregón came land reform. In 1926 Plutarco Calles began to enforce the anticlerical clauses of the Mexican Constitution. "It is necessary that we enter into a new phase of the Revolution," he said, "which I shall call the psychological revolutionary period; we must enter into and take possession of the minds of children . . . because they do belong . . . to the Revolution."[1] These measures plunged Mexico into eight years of civil war. Undaunted, Mormon observers recognized and accepted Calles's point: the revolution was not yet complete.

The touchstones of the revolution—liberation, nationhood, and justice—tested the Church's commitment to progress. It was important to leading spokesmen such as Anthony W. Ivins and Rey L. Pratt that the Mormon message conform to the new state of Mexican affairs. To them and others of a like mind, revolutions were not random acts of violence in a degenerate world. Revolutions were historical necessities that met with divine approval. Latter-day Saint observers were in touch with the *zeitgeist* of their age. They lived in a world shaped by the productive power of science, capitalism, and the corporatist state, yet it was the ideological transformations in Mexico that compelled them to either agonize or thrill over the results.[2] Mormon observers spoke a language of social progress.

---

1. John Lloyd Mecham, *Church and State in Latin America: A History of Politico-Ecclesiastical Relations*, 406.
2. For national developments see Emily S. Rosenberg, *Spreading the*

Triumph was certain, but the path toward the great transition was strewn with obstacles. God had left it to man to dream about the millennium, to struggle for it, and to sacrifice for it. Mormon idealism, transplanted to Mexico, found the pull of the revolutionary thinking that informed its origins hard to escape.

The New Mexico

Between 1920 and 1934 the Sonoran dynasty of Obregón and Calles began to consolidate the revolutionary gains of the preceding decade. The formation of the National Revolutionary Party (*Partido Nacional Revolucionario*, or PNR) in 1929 became the vehicle for change.[3] PNR, destined to govern Mexico until 2000, used its authority to confer favors on constituencies deemed helpful to the regime. As a state-sponsored party, PNR proved corrupt and authoritarian, but it also made important social advances.[4] Education minister José Vasconcelos broadened

---

American Dream: American Economic and Cultural Expansion, 1890–1945; Warren I. Cohen, *Empire Without Tears: America's foreign Relations, 1921-1933*, 1–99; and Joan Hoff Wilson, *Herbert Hoover: Forgotten Progressive*, 152. Apostle John A. Widtsoe said, "The history of man's progress is knowledge that science may contribute to religious thought and faith." See Paul R. Green, comp., *Science and Your Faith in God: A Selected Compilation of Writings and Talks by Prominent Latter-day Saints Scientists on the Subjects of Science and Religion*, 206.

3. PNR is known today as the Institutional Revolutionary Party (*Partido Revolucionario Institucional*, or PRI).

4. Alan Knight argues that the state was one of several players in a broad social revolution. See Alan Knight, "Mexico, c. 1930–1946," 1–8. Donald Hodges and Ross Gandy, in their book *Mexico 1910–1982: Reform or Revolution?* suggest the Mexican Revolution conferred economic control upon an indigenous bourgeois, while political power was diffused among various social groupings. Ramón Eduardo Ruiz argues in *Triumphs and Tragedy: A History of the Mexican People* that revolution empowered new elites but left Mexico exposed to foreigners and did little for peasants, Indians, and workers. Ruiz in fact goes so far as to suggest that Mexico today is returning to the Porfiriato. John Womack agrees in *Rebellion in Chiapas: An Historical Reader*, 9. Mary Kay Vaughan treats negative and positive views of the revolution in "Cultural Approaches to Peasant Politics in the Mexican Revolution."

public education under Article Three of the 1917 Constitution. The goal was to rescue Mexico from foreign domination and to cultivate a distinct "Mexicanidad." Government artists cultivated Mexican cultural values and portrayed Indians and *mestizos* as the prototypical revolutionaries in their art.[5] Obregón's labor policy empowered the Regional Confederation of Mexican Workers (*Confederación Regional Obrera Mexicana*, or CROM).[6] Agrarian reforms redistributed over 921 hectares (2,276 acres) of land, five times more than Carranza had during his tenure as president.[7] The 1923 Bucareli agreement confirmed the right of American oil companies to drill in areas tapped before 1917, but in return, Obregón received recognition from the United States.[8]

Historians disagree as to whether the Mexican Revolution was truly "revolutionary" or simply continued the economic policies of the Porfiriato under the guise of a new party. Alan Knight suggests that Mexico had created the largest inclusive political entity in Latin America. Though not the liberal democracy Madero had envisioned, neither was it a closed autocratic system. Obregón and Calles presided as bosses over a "form of mass politics—restless, sometimes radical, often violent and corrupt."[9] In 1938 President Lázaro Cárdenas revoked the Bucareli agreement and nationalized Mexico's oil reserves. Knight argues that the Cárdenas "surprise," bold as it was, evidenced more government control, not necessarily national redemption or radicalism.[10] One historian splits the period between 1910 and 1940 into two revo-

---

5. Richard Haggerty, "Historical Setting," 42–43; Carleton Beals, *Mexican Maze*, 191; Charles Nash Myers, *Education and National Development in Mexico*, 42–44; and Frank Tannenbaum, *Peace by Revolution: Mexico after 1910*, 303.

6. Mexican labor militancy is discussed in Thomas F. O'Brien, *The Revolutionary Mission: American Enterprise in Latin America, 1900–1945*, 252–53, 261.

7. Enrique Krauze, *Mexico: Biography of Power*, 395.

8. O'Brien, *Revolutionary Mission*, 265; Ludwell Denny's 1928 book *We Fight for Oil* discussed Great Power rivalry over Mexican oil. For a summary of "tagged land," subterranean rights, the Bucareli Agreement, and the generally favorable outcome for the United States up to 1928, see J. Reuben Clark Jr., "The Oil Settlement with Mexico," *Foreign Affairs* 6 (July 1928): 600–614.

9. Knight, "Mexico, c. 1930–1946," 3.

10. Ibid., 7.

lutions. The first one, a radical transformation of society and politics that sought to destroy the old order, had failed. The second, a reduction of foreign influence and broadening of productive power within the framework of government institutions, succeeded.[11]

Despite the ambiguity of the revolution's results, something profound had nonetheless occurred. While it is true that only 9 percent of the total value of land redistributed in 1930 went to *ejidos* (local agricultural communes), the mentality of rural Mexicans had been transformed. Formerly docile peasants and workers had awakened to the power of collective action and organized themselves during the 1920s into a formidable political force. They and their leaders compelled government officials to carry through with land redistribution plans. Unions demanded recognition.[12] It was in light of these heightened expectations that Mormon observers would judge post-revolutionary Mexico.

The new Mexico sought to define itself through the creation of a new national culture. Raw materials for the construction of this new identity were sought in the nation's most ancient folkways. The government sponsored archeological digs to recover the nation's prehistory. CROM co-opted Aztec warrior images to represent the labor movement. Spanish conquistadors furnished artists with villains, and balladwriters praised revolutionaries as heroes. In song and art the secular mixed with the religious, creating a national blend that succeeded in developing a Mexican mass popular culture.[13] During the 1920s, indigenist thought emphasized the supremacy of *mestizaje* (Spanish and Indian admixture), an integrationist trend that promoted national consolidation. The art of Diego Garcia and others celebrated *mestizaje* as

---

11. Stuart F. Voss, "Nationalizing the Revolution: Culmination and Circumstance," 273–74. Mexican historian Octavio Paz interprets the revolution much the same way Ivins did in 1926. What started as a social revolution became a middle-class reform movement more dedicated to modernization. The hope was that material and educational progress would socially uplift the country. See Paz's interview with Jerry Johnston, "Mexican Author Forged Conscience of His Country," *Deseret News*, October 25, 1989, C1.

12. Paul J. Vanderwood, "Explaining the Mexican Revolution."

13. Alan Knight, "Revolutionary Project, Recalcitrant People: Mexico, 1910–1940," 248–50.

a new "cosmic race."[14] Vasconcelos articulated the idea that the mixing of races—achieved in Mexico and applicable to the rest of the world—would lead to a "new human type." His 1925 book envisaged a new age of creativity, joy, imagination, and love.[15]

The communal and spiritual values of Mexican peasants made them particularly attractive to American observers as "romanticized primitives" with whom the new leaders of Mexico could form a partnership for a more equitable future. American reviewers of the Mexican national scene installed Indian leaders, radical peasants, and *agraristas*—supporters of land reform—in their catalogs of revolutionary heroes.[16] Carleton Beals, the best-known Latin Americanist in the United States, proposed the full incorporation of the *ejido* as the basic building block of the Mexican state.[17] Frank Tannenbaum similarly urged a continued revolutionary shift from the traditional power centers of Mexico to the Indian *ejidos* and the rural *mestizo* villages.[18] Cultural exchange between the two countries accelerated during the 1920s. Ambassador Dwight Morrow, in partnership with his wife, funded Mexican art and facilitated the cross-border trade. The display of Mexican works at New York's Metropolitan Museum of Art in 1930 showed Americans that "Mexico was not a backward country full of bandits, as so many had previously imagined; instead it was revealed now as a nation of culture."[19]

---

14. Alan Knight, "Racism, Revolution, and *Indigenismo*: Mexico, 1910–1940," 92.

15. José Vasconcelos, *The Cosmic Race/La raza cósmica: A Bilingual Edition*. See also Colin M. MacLachlan and Jaime E. Rodríguez O., *The Forging of the Cosmic Race: A Reinterpretation of Colonial Mexico*, 3, 334–37.

16. For Indianism in Mexico see John A. Britton, *Revolution and Ideology: Images of the Mexican Revolution in the United States*, 57–66, 215; Fredrick B. Pike, *The United States and Latin America: Myths and Stereotypes of Civilization and Nature*, 219–20; Fredrick B. Pike, *FDR's Good Neighbor Policy: Sixty Years of Generally Gentle Chaos*, 93–94; Helen Delpar, *The Enormous Vogue of Things Mexican: Cultural Relations between the United States and Mexico, 1920–1935*, 9–10, 91–124.

17. Beals, *Mexican Maze*, 203–4.

18. Tannenbaum, *Peace by Revolution*, 125, 127; and Britton, *Revolution and Ideology*, 121.

19. On art see Delpar, *Enormous Vogue of Things Mexican*, 62–64, 143–46.

American leftists and liberals saw Mexico as a land of regeneration. The revolution, they believed, had broken the grip of positivism that had destroyed Mexico's idyllic Indian communities. All agreed that the revolution had been a precursor to the return of a lost utopia. More problematic was the question of whether the post-revolutionary state should centrally guide this reconstruction or confer power on regional constituencies.

Mormons in Mexico after 1917

Mormon excitement about the new possibilities for Mexico's future coincided with the attitudes of American romantics, leftists, and liberals. The Mexican people, sanctified by their revolution, were struggling to forge a modern state. State orchestration of corporate, popular, religious, and military institutions, Mormon leaders believed, would generate a favorable social climate for Latter-day Saint proselytizing.

The Latter-day Saints continued their presence in Mexico after the 1910–17 revolution. As the number of missionaries increased, however, the colonies declined or were altogether abandoned. In 1921 the larger Chihuahua colonies contained only a tenth of the 1912 population, and the smaller colonies were never rebuilt.[20] In Sonora local hostility induced Mormon landholders to divest completely for $100,000.[21] The

---

20. An October 1921 report from the US consulate in Chihuahua showed that of the 657 people living in Colonia Juárez, García, and Dublán, 450 were Mormons. See US Consulate, Letter to US State Department, March 10, 1920. The post-revolution histories of the Chihuahua colonies are chronicled in Lucile Pratt, "A Keyhole View of Mexican Agrarian Policy as Shown by Mormon Land Problems"; Elizabeth H. Mills, "The Mormon Colonies in Chihuahua after the 1912 Exodus"; Clarence F. Turley and Anna Tenney Turley, comps., *History of the Mormon Colonies in Mexico: The Juarez Stake, 1885–1980*; and LaVon Brown Whetten, *Colonia Juarez: Commemorating 125 Years of the Mormon Colonies in Mexico*. A post-Exodus wrap-up for the Sonora colonies is found in Thomas H. Naylor and Barney T. Burns, "Colonia Morelos: A Short History of a Mormon Colony in Sonora, Mexico"; and Naylor, "Colonia Morelos and the Mexican Revolution: Consul Dye Inspects an Evacuated Mormon Colony, 1912."

21. On Sonoran difficulties see Journal History of the Church, January 25, 1918, 3; and ibid., January 29, 1918, 3. See also "Word Received Here That Two Colonists Have Been Murdered," *Deseret News*, November 7,

abating Mormon enterprise in Mexico altered local patterns of land tenure. From Colonia Juárez, Anthony W. Ivins received reports that the distribution of vacant land to local Mexican peasants had improved their condition.[22]

The failure of the colonies was offset by the flourishing of the Mexican Mission under the leadership of Rey L. Pratt. In the context of revolutionary nationalism, Mexican Mormons were eager for Spanish translations of all major Mormon doctrinal works. Pratt worked hard to oblige them, translating many of the tracts and books himself. The second and third Spanish editions of the Book of Mormon were completed under his direction in 1919 and 1929.[23] Of the older tracts, the most significant reprint was Parley P. Pratt's A Voice of Warning (1837). Written by Rey's grandfather, this tract contained millennial overtones and preached the redemption of the Indians.[24] Membership and branches (congregations) multiplied. By 1930, there were 3,882 Mexican members and twenty branches, half of them south of the Rio Grande. Fifty-six North Americans were serving missions in Mexico.[25]

1921; and *Investigation of Mexican Affairs: Report and Hearing Pursuant to Senate Resolution 106, 66th Congress, 2nd Session, Document 285*, 2:3254. For the settlement amount see "'Mormon' Lands in Mexico Are Bought by Government," *Deseret News*, June 11, 1921.

22. Joseph Bentley, Letters to Anthony W. Ivins, dated June 6, July 29, and August 5, 1913, February 13 and March 16, 1914, and January 17, 1917, Anthony W. Ivins Papers, box 9, fd. 3; and "Colonists at Morelos May Lose Property," *Deseret News*, August 24, 1917. Widespread landholding by peasants in the Galeana District was reported in Joel Hills Martineau, "Colony Conditions Told by Correspondent," *Deseret News*, November 28, 1925.

23. "Passing Events," *Improvement Era* 22 (October 1919): 1098; Andrew Jenson, *Encyclopedic History of the Church of Jesus Christ of Latter-day Saints*, s.v. "The Mexican Mission." The 1919 Spanish edition of the Book of Mormon, a joint project by Ivins and Pratt, was printed in Independence, Missouri in a run of ten thousand copies. The first full Spanish translation had been made by James Z. Stewart and Meliton G. Trejo in 1886. See Hugh G. Stocks, "Book of Mormon Translations," 213.

24. Mary Pratt Parrish, "Hew to the Rock from Which Ye are Hewn," 27.

25. Totals for the Mexican Mission do not count the Juárez Stake (the colonies) or Anglo wards (congregations) in cities like El Paso. Stakes and wards represent a higher degree of organizational development than do

In addition to transforming the ethnic makeup of Mexican Mormonism, the revolution triggered a terminological shift in Mormon discourse, giving a new meaning to the land of Mexico. Beginning with Obregón's assumption of power, Mormon observers began referring to the "Republic of Mexico" and the "New Lamanites." A survey of Rey L. Pratt's writings and speeches before 1921 shows no use of the formal title "Republic of Mexico." After 1921 Pratt publicly used this title eight times alongside the normal references to "Mexico." The term "old Mexico" disappeared from Pratt's public addresses altogether. Anthony W. Ivins, who referred to the "Republic" only twice before 1902 and not at all between 1910 and 1920, used the formal title six times after 1921. Other Mormon leaders who made references to Mexico showed the same change in diction. Mormon observers consigned "old Mexico" to memory. New usage described the post-revolutionary state.[26]

Germane to the future of the Church in Latin America was the return of the Indian to Mormon thinking and the new habit of making the Mexican Revolution testify to the truthfulness of Mormonism.[27] No

---

mission districts and branches. Rey L. Pratt reported twenty branches in a sermon delivered October 7, 1927, *Report of the Semi-annual Conference of the Church of Jesus Christ of Latter-day Saints*, 29 (hereafter cited as *Conference Report*); and again in "Rey L. Pratt Here on Visit from Mexico," *Deseret News*, February 18, 1931. Andrew Jenson listed only six Mexican branches, but his list was incomplete and did not include the Ozumba Branch. See Jenson, *Encyclopedic History of the Church*, s.v. "The Mexican Mission."

26. I examined speeches and articles written by Church general authorities in the *Improvement Era*, *Journal of Discourses*, *Conference Report*, and diaries of Pratt and Ivins for 1880–1934. I looked for instances of the term "Republic of Mexico" or "southern Republic" versus "Mexico" or "Old Mexico."

27. Since the break-up of the church-state partnership in the running of Indian missions in the mid-1890s, Protestant and Mormon interest in the Indian had been declining. In 1911 B. H. Roberts could only muster that "God had not forgotten" the Lamanites. Andrew Jenson admitted that "the North American Indians have so far disappointed us. . . . For compared with some of the missions among white people in our own country, and in foreign lands, the fruits or results have not been satisfactory." See R. Pierce Beaver, *Church, State, and the American Indians: Two and a Half Centuries of Partnership in Missions between Protestant Churches and Government*,

longer was Mexico merely a safe haven for polygamists or an opportune place to invest. It had become the future. In his October 1921 General Conference address, Church historian Andrew Jenson identified Mexico as a "sister republic" and a spiritual ally with a global mission:

> We, therefore, cast a glance . . . down through Central America and South America, where there are millions and millions of Lamanites, direct descendants of Father Lehi. . . . I therefore look for the Mexican mission . . . to flourish by and by, and become one of the best and most important missions of the Church, and I would further suggest that whenever the time comes that these Lamanites in the south shall embrace the Gospel, there shall be a sufficient number of them to fulfill every prediction contained in the Book of Mormon concerning the Lamanites, and justify every expectation that we have had in regard to the help which these remnants of the of the house of Israel shall render in building up Zion in these last days.[28]

The liberation of Mexico's Indians had rescued the Church from stagnation. Mexico would produce an international cadre of missionaries that would "preach the gospel in Russia, in the Balkan peninsula, in Persia, India, and all over the world."[29]

Re-entering sacred time through the gateway of Latin America taxed the rhetorical skills of Mormon observers sympathetic to Mexico. Along with favorable presentations, American images of Mexico during the 1920s remained mired in stereotypes of Indian violence and Latin cultural inferiority.[30] In this racially-charged milieu, prejudice tinctured some of the general authorities' attitudes. Presiding Bishop Charles W. Nibley told a General Conference audience that the Mexican people could never have constitutional government because "they are not as intelligent as are the people of this nation."[31] Prejudice forced those with progressive views toward Mexico to contend obliquely with their own colleagues.

207–8; David J. Whittaker, "Mormons and Native Americans: A Historical and Bibliographical Interpretation," 38; B. H. Roberts, *New Witnesses for God*, 1:21–23; Andrew Jenson, October 9, 1921, *Conference Report*, 119; Andrew Jenson, October 8, 1922, *Conference Report*, 131.

28. Jenson, October 9, 1921, *Conference Report*, 120.

29. Jenson, October 8, 1922, *Conference Report*, 132.

30. Delpar, *Enormous Vogue of Things Mexican*, 16.

31. Charles W. Nibley, April 4, 1925, *Conference Report*, 24.

Mexican Mission President Rey L. Pratt attempted to foster understanding between the Hispanic and Anglo-American worlds. He accepted the "unknowability" of ultimate political solutions and urged tolerance in matters "twixt nations and men."[32] Pratt combated biases wherever he found them. In the realm of Mexican-American relations, he excoriated Americans as "deceivers" and "truce-breakers." "I am constantly kept in hot water," he told a Church conference in April 1922. "I came up here . . . from the interior of Mexico, and I find here, in the newspapers and among the people, things that are slanderous to the Mexican people [in] the southern republic." The situation, said Pratt, forced him to "act in the [role] of a pacifier in both countries." Blame lay with "that class" of "agitators" in the United States who had whipped up ill feelings toward Mexico's revolution.[33]

Rather than violent revolutionaries, Pratt portrayed the *ejido* Indians as gentle and noble by nature. He spoke of their "chivalry" and sense of "honor and justice." In Indian villages, he said, missionaries of the Church—male and female alike—were safer than anywhere else in the world.[34] Modernism, he believed, had contaminated a primitive and Christ-like culture.[35] Pratt's Mexican poetry collection, published in 1928, contains elements of Indian romanticism alongside criticism of government bureaucrats.[36]

---

32. Rey L. Pratt, untitled manuscript, March 2, 1922, Rey L. Pratt Papers, box 2, fd. 20.

33. Rey L. Pratt, April 9, 1922, *Conference Report*, 121–22. Negative imagery of Mexico in the United States between 1920 and 1935 is discussed in Delpar, *Enormous Vogue of Things Mexican*, 167–91.

34. Pratt, October 7, 1927, *Conference Report*, 30. Other Mormon observers believed that the revolution had released the latent spirituality of the people of Mexico. One of Pratt's missionaries alluded to the spiritual "gifts" of Native Americans in Philip Foremaster, "Chastened, but Not Forgotten," *Improvement Era* 26 (September 1923): 995–97. Levi Edgar Young suggested that "Indians are naturally believers in the Great Spirit." See Levi Edgar Young, April 5, 1924, *Conference Report*, 52. Pratt's successor in the mission presidency, Antoine R. Ivins, believed that Porfirio Díaz had "owed his sterling quality" to his Indian ancestry. See Antoine R. Ivins, "The Mexican Mission," *Improvement Era* 36 (July 1933): 540.

35. Pike, *United States and Latin America*, 219–20.

36. Rey L. Pratt, *Just Thinking*.

Apostle Ivins's references to Mexico in the early 1920s were a mix of romantic remembrances, forgiveness, and future certitude. To ease the pain of colonists who had lost property in Mexico during the revolution, Ivins reportedly cancelled $60,000 in loans.[37] Carranza's demise did not elicit comment from Ivins, but he publicly supported Obregón. An avid watcher of the Mexican political scene and frequent visitor to Mexico on inspection tours, Ivins called for "peaceful settlement" of the 1923 oil dispute. US invasion, he argued, would cost millions of dollars and thousands of lives. After all, the stability achieved since 1918 had created opportunities conducive to mining and agricultural investment. With a touch of nostalgia, Ivins added that Villa was busy "attending to his ranch."[38] Soon, however, Ivins would have to come out of the bullpen to defend the post-revolutionary Mexican state against foreign capitalists and domestic religious *insurrectos*.

The Church-State Controversy in Mexico and Civil Religion

Since Huerta's coup in 1913, Mexican revolutionaries had perceived the Catholic Church as an enemy of the state. On July 31, 1926, the government of President Plutarco Calles began enforcement of Articles 3, 27, and 130 of the 1917 Quérataro constitution. Article 3 secularized education. Article 27 nationalized ecclesiastical property. Article 130 required clerics to register with the federal government, a measure that enabled the government to limit the number of licensed priests. Calles also invoked these articles to prohibit public religious celebrations, disfranchise the clergy, and outlaw the wearing of priestly attire except inside church. The "Calles Laws" shocked the Catholic bishops. Archbishop Moray del Rio, under orders from Rome, suspended Catholic services in the hope of triggering mass protest. By the middle of August, two hundred Roman Catholic priests had been expelled and eighty-three convents and monasteries closed. The government suspended the operation of more than a hundred parochial schools.

---

37. Anthony W. Ivins, "A Sermon on Sacrifice," *Latter-day Saints' Millennial Star* 96 (November 8, 1934): 708 (hereafter cited as *Millennial Star*).

38. Journal History, December 3, 1919, 3, 5; "Passing Events," *Improvement Era* 24 (February 1921): 369; and "Mexico Subject of Talk at Luncheon," *Deseret News*, May 18, 1921.

Others modified their curriculum to satisfy government censors. On August 1, 1926, fighting erupted between Roman Catholics obedient to the Pope and Mexican nationalist Catholics known as *Cismáticos* (schismatics).[39] Government forces, supported by radical workers and *agraristas*, attempted to quell the unrest. In the countryside dissident Catholic armies began to form.[40]

In the United States, Protestant churches stood by President Calles in the hope that repression of the Catholic Church would open Mexico to more effective evangelization.[41] Hubert Herring of the Education Society of the Congregational Church concluded that Mexico was experiencing a "spiritual rebirth."[42] North American ministers and missionaries complied with the Mexican order to leave the country. Mission President Rey L. Pratt, writing from Buenos Aires, concluded that the LDS Church would "just have to make the best of [the situation]."[43] Predictably, American Catholics campaigned for interven-

---

39. David C. Bailey, *¡Viva Cristo Rey! The Cristero Rebellion and the Church-State Conflict in Mexico*, 53. A Mormon missionary and Mexican member were nearly killed when people in Tenango del Aire mistook them for *Cismáticos* (Mexican nationalist Catholics) who had renounced their allegiance to the Pope. See Weston N. Nordgren, "A Missionary Mobbing," *Improvement Era* 31 (May 1928): 594–98; Leland A. Mortensen, Letter to American Consulate in Mexico D.F., [1925], in Mary Pratt Parrish, "Look to the Rock from Which Ye Are Hewn," 71–72; and "Missionaries Dragged from Friends' Home," *Deseret News*, March 30, 1925.

40. General works on the church-state controversy in Mexico include Bailey, *¡Viva Cristo Rey!*; Robert E. Quirk, *The Mexican Revolution and the Catholic Church, 1910–1929*; and Jean A. Meyer, *The Cristero Rebellion: The Mexican People between Church and State, 1926–1929*.

41. For the North American religious reaction to the church-state controversy, see Mollie C. Davis, "American Religious and Religiose Reaction to Mexico's Church-State Conflict, 1926–1927: Background to the Morrow Mission"; and G. Baez Camargo and Kenneth G. Grubb, *Religion in the Republic of Mexico*.

42. Davis, "American Religious and Religiose Reaction," 86.

43. Rey L. Pratt, Letter to Mary Pratt, April 20, 1926, Pratt Papers, box 2, fd. 10. Seventy Spanish-speaking missionaries worked north and south of the Rio Grande River. Female missionaries were withdrawn as tension rose between Roman Catholics and Mexican nationalist Catholics. See Rey L. Pratt, Letter to Mary Pratt, April 7, 1926, Pratt Papers, box 2, fd.

tion. American bishops did not explicitly urge armed insurrection, but they praised the firmness of Mexican bishops loyal to the papacy and pledged their support "to the end."[44]

Commentary on Mexico's church-state controversy provided an outlet for many American anxieties of the era.[45] Exaggerated fears of Mexican communism and oil nationalization topped the list.[46] William Randolph Hearst, invested in Mexican oil, used his newspaper the *New York World* to urge a US invasion. Hearst ostensibly did this to prevent the nationalization of the Mexican Church, but really to position military forces should Mexican nationalists seek control of coastal oil deposits. Oil companies owned by Protestants likewise urged intervention.[47] President Calvin Coolidge, however, committed his administration to neutrality. Calles received an "official frown" from Ambassador James Sheffield, but nothing else. In the meantime, violence spread in Mexico.

Implicit in the modern church-state relationship is the hope that secular institutions can ease tensions among competing religious groups. Individual churches subordinate some of their particularistic

---

10; Anthony W. Ivins, Letter to LDS Mission Headquarters, El Paso, Texas in Journal History, July 25, 1926, 5; and "Church Submits to Law Against Alien Preachers," *Deseret News*, July 26, 1926.

44. Bailey, ¡*Viva Cristo Rey!* 100–101.

45. For the response of the United States government to the church-state controversy, see Bailey, ¡*Viva Cristo Rey!* 14–26; and L. Ethan Ellis, "Dwight Morrow and the Church-State Controversy in Mexico." For a Mormon prediction that communism would find "fertile ground" in Mexico due to the "ignorant" nature of Mexican peasants, see "Mexican Political Changes," *Deseret News*, October 22, 1931.

46. The State Department's inflated worry over the influence of communism in Mexico is discussed in L. Ethan Ellis, *Frank B. Kellogg and American Foreign Relations, 1925–1929*, 38; Robert Freeman Smith, *The United States and Revolutionary Nationalism in Mexico, 1916–1932*, 237; Britton, *Revolution and Ideology*, 79–87; James J. Horn, "U.S. Diplomacy and the 'Specter of Bolshevism' in Mexico (1924–1927)." In 1929 the Comintern ordered its Mexican subsidiaries to overthrow Calles. The attempt failed, and Calles repressed the Mexican Communist Party (PCM). See Karl M. Schmitt, *Communism in Mexico: A Study in Political Frustration*, 15.

47. Davis, "American Religious and Religiose Reaction," 88–90; Bailey, ¡*Viva Cristo Rey!* 101–2.

aims to a broader "civil religion" which exalts democracy, pluralism, and rule of law. Ivins espoused this model, as did contemporaries John Dewey and some Social Gospel ministers.[48]

The papers of Anthony W. Ivins demonstrate his commitment to a secular state.[49] Diversity and pluralism were cardinal features of his political ideal. At one Church conference, Ivins reminded an audience that "The Lord did not give the dominance of the United States to a certain race, that the traditions, language and prejudices of the old world might be established here as they were in all of the great country to the south of us."[50] Each ethnic and religious group had woven its share of the American tapestry:

> To the devoted faith of the Puritan separatists of New England was added the industry and patriotism of the Dutch reformers who had settled at New York, the gallantry and chivalry of the English cavaliers of Virginia, and the light-hearted energy and patriotism of the French at New Orleans. Protestants, Catholics and people without church affiliations united together.[51]

Ivins endorsed the Lockean view of religious toleration.[52] He recognized no limits to plurality, suggesting that "wise men, good men, patriotic men are to be found in all communities, in all political parties, among all creeds."[53] Even the Catholic Church had a role to play in the social betterment of Mexico, provided the prelates submitted to the government.

---

48. Russell E. Richey and Donald G. Jones, "The Civil Religion Debate," 14–18. For civil religion as a method of mending internal division, see Andrew Shanks, *Civil Society, Civil Religion,* 2–3. Ivins's civil religion fit with the Social Gospel teachings of Congregationalist minister Charles Stelzle. Stelzle, a visiting minister at Calvin Coolidge's First Congregational Church in Washington DC, suggested that churches should work to ensure justice and promote democracy and should remain open to all social, political, and economic solutions. To exclude any possible solution in the modern age would be "absurd." See Charles Stelzle, "The Religion of the New Democracy," *Outlook* 143, no. 11 (July 14, 1926): 382.

49. See "The Issue Is Joined" and other papers in the Ivins Papers, box 17, fd. 1. See also Anthony W. Ivins, April 7, 1917, *Conference Report,* 54.

50. Anthony W. Ivins, October 5, 1928, *Conference Report,* 15.

51. Ibid.

52. Alan Ryan, "Liberalism," 369.

53. Ivins, October 5, 1928, *Conference Report,* 16.

A neutral civil religious landscape was essential for state development. Ernst Haas argues that the rationalization of state and social institutions requires tolerance; without it, national unification is difficult. Further, according to Haas's theory of state modernization, Calles had to diminish the influence of the Catholic Church. The Mexican state could modernize under a church-state alliance, but this would be a throwback to the Porfiriato. The neutral civil religion model would create harmony between various groups and supply the kind of transcendent ideology necessary to hold a nation together.[54] The president of the nation was the crucial link. Ivins had remarked on the death of US President Warren Harding that "The president stands at the head of our entire system. He is the embodiment of the divine ideals for which Americans live, and for which real Americans are willing to die."[55] From Madero to Calles, Ivins designated the president of Mexico as the embodiment of revolutionary ideals.

Expanding the Revolution:
The Ivins-Hunt Exchange, 1926

The turmoil in Mexico led to hot debate in Salt Lake City. At a Church conference, Ivins put the controversy in a global perspective:

> The present attitude of the civil government in the Republic of Mexico toward the dominant church in that Republic is of greater importance to the world than we generally understand. It is not a question which involves Mexico alone, but is one which involves all of the churches of the world, and the results which shall be achieved there, whether the civil government of Mexico shall prevail in its present attitude, or whether the church which is opposed to it shall prevail, will have a great influence upon the relationship of the church and state everywhere.[56]

---

54. Ernst B. Haas, *Nationalism, Liberalism, and Progress: The Rise and Decline of Nationalism*, 53 note 24, 54–55.

55. Anthony W. Ivins, "Ft. Douglas Speech," August 10, 1923, Ivins Papers, box 15, fd. 1. Martin E. Marty describes the role of president as priest in "Two Kinds of Two Kinds of Civil Religion," 145–47.

56. Anthony W. Ivins, October 3, 1926, *Conference Report*, 14.

In a speech delivered to the Exchange Club in Hotel Utah on August 5, 1926, Ivins defended Plutarco Calles. The Mexican president was enforcing laws that would empower government-certified clergymen to appoint priests and bishops and to oversee religious functions in Mexico. If the state failed to triumph, asserted Ivins, then the Clerical Party—the political wing of the Catholic Church—would regain its dominance, blocking social and political reforms.[57]

The Exchange Club speech elicited a reaction from Monsignor Duane Garrison Hunt, the nationally renowned rector of Salt Lake City's Cathedral of the Madeleine.[58] Hunt based his argument on constitutional logic and religious rights. He complained about the "Bolshevistic attitude" among Mexican officials and their "determination to crush to the earth all those who stand in their way."[59] He appealed to constitutional law, arguing that the restrictions on the clergy's participation in politics denied them their "inalienable human rights." The Mexican government was undermining other rights as well: free speech, the right to have private schools, the freedom of worship, and the right to own property. In fact, Hunt argued, the Catholic dilemma in Mexico was similar to the challenge faced by Mormons in their confrontation over religious rights during the nineteenth century.[60]

---

57. "Mexico Is Right in Conflict Says President Ivins," *Deseret News*, August 6, 1926.

58. Duane Garrison Hunt (1884–1960) was actually the rector of the Madeleine Cathedral. In 1937 he became the fifth bishop of the Salt Lake Diocese, which had been established in 1891. Hunt's speeches and writings drew national attention. See Bernice M. Mooney, "The Catholic Church in Utah," 78; and Bernice M. Mooney, "Duane Garrison Hunt," 264.

59. Donald L. Herman says the church-state controversy gave communist agents in Mexico a "ready-made issue." They supported the state against the Catholic Church, partly in an attempt to attract the "small but politically powerful middle-class" and partly to show that unity of church and state justified overthrow of the state altogether. See Donald L. Herman, *The Comintern in Mexico*, 32–36.

60. D. G. Hunt, Letter to Anthony W. Ivins, August 7, 1926, Ivins Papers, box 11, fd. 5. This letter was printed the following day in the *Salt Lake Tribune*. For a view similar to Hunt's in the national press, see Reverend John A. Ryan, "The Religious Persecution in Mexico," *Outlook* 143, no. 16 (August 18, 1926): 534–35. Exchanges between Protestants and Catholics

Ivins replied to Hunt in an open letter, in a personal letter, and in a tract titled *The Right Relation of Church and State*, published in 1926. These sources, plus conference talks and other correspondence between 1926 and 1931, reveal continued concessions to revolutionary development and a persistently secular view of the state. In a private letter Ivins informed Hunt that in the coming argument he would not accept the constraints imposed by faith, doctrine, or religious and constitutional custom. "I am trying to live in the light of the present rather than the past," he wrote. "Our lives must be somewhat changed to conform to the day in which our work is to be accomplished. [The gospel's] fundamental truths never change . . . but our methods of applying these doctrines are not to be bound by the traditions of the remote past, but must be brought into harmony with the thought of the present."[61] Ivins located Mexico's conflict at a particular point in historical time. As to Hunt's assertion of communist influence and the more convincing parallel to the LDS Church's battle with the federal government over polygamy, an issue loaded with church-state issues, Ivins ignored both.

In an open letter Ivins claimed authority to speak for Mexico:

> The Greater part of my life I have devoted to work in Mexico. I have been intimately acquainted with her presidents during that time, have had large business transactions with her state departments, have been in the homes of the wealthy and have slept in the hovels of her oppressed and down-trodden peasantry. . . . I have lying on my desk the story of the lives of the Mexican people during the past 400 years as it is told by the Abbe Domenech, by Father Las Casas, by Solis, Bernal, ... Prescott, Bancroft, Von Humboldt, Abbott, and others . . . I also have copies of the current daily press published in the City of Mexico, which come to me every morning."[62]

---

in reference to the Mexican church-state controversy occurred in a few other places throughout the United States. See Delpar, *Enormous Vogue of Things Mexican*, 49.

61. Anthony W. Ivins, Letter to D. G. Hunt, August 14, 1926, Ivins Papers, box 11, fd. 5.

62. Anthony W. Ivins, *Right Relation of Church and State*, 8. The text also appeared in the *Salt Lake Tribune*, August 15, 1926. Abbé Emmanuel Domenech, an administrator of Catholic charities in the French expeditionary force supporting Mexico's Emperor Maximilian (1864–67), criticized the Mexican clergy in *Mexico as It Is; the Truth of Its Climate,*

Both the Mexican War of the Reform (1858–61) and the American Revolution, said Ivins, originated in the same universal aspiration. He praised Benito Juárez, the "Republican" war leader who defeated French-backed Emperor Don Maximilian I and thus extinguished "the last hope of the Clerical party to establish a Catholic empire" in Mexico. Ivins also lauded Miguel Mendez, a Oaxacan liberal who had envisioned a nation based on "secular learning and civic virtues."[63] Ivins identified both men as "pure blooded Indians" whose names "will live in the hearts of the Mexican people as long as those of Washington, Jefferson, and Lincoln live in the hearts of loyal citizens of the United States."[64] Mexico's emergence from colonialism, Ivins wrote, was one of "Patriotism, courage and self-sacrifice, unsurpassed by the patriots of our own country."[65]

Inhabitants, and Government (Fr., 1867). Bartolomé de Las Casas (1474–1566) was a Spanish historian and priest who criticized Spanish exploitation of Indians and fought to abolish slavery. Antonio de Solís y Rivadeneyra (1610–86) wrote *The History of the Conquest of Mexico by the Spaniards* (Sp., 1684), considered to be some of the finest prose of the seventeenth century, though it ignores the destruction of the Aztecs while glorifying Cortez. Bernal Díaz del Castillo (1492–1581) was a Spanish conquistador and chronicler. He was with Hernan Cortez in 1519 during the Aztec campaign. His notes published in *The True History of the Conquest of New Spain* (Sp., 1632) focus on the concerns of the common soldier. William Hickling Prescott (1796–1859) wrote *History of the Reign of Ferdinand and Isabella the Catholic* (1837), *History of the Conquest of Mexico* (1843), and *History of the Conquest of Peru* (1847). Hubert Howe Bancroft wrote *History of Mexico* (1883–1888), *The Native Races of the Pacific States of North America* (1875), and *Life of Porfirio Díaz* (Sp., 1887). John Stevens Cabot Abbott (1805–1877), a minister from Maine, wrote *History of Hernando Cortez* (1855) and *The Romance of Spanish History* (1869). Abraham Lincoln credited Abbott's writing "for about all the historical knowledge I have." Alexander Freiherr von Humboldt (1759–1869) was best known for his explorations of South and Central America and Mexico.

63. Matt Frierdich, "Oaxaca and Its Political Culture of Conflict," 7.

64. Ivins, *Right Relation of Church and State*, 19. Ivins mentioned the role of the Oaxaca Institute of the Arts and Sciences as discussed by John Stevens Cabot Abbott. The Oaxaca Institute taught law and was attacked by the Catholic Church as a revolutionary institution. Ivins praised Oaxaca because it produced Juárez and Mendez before its abolishment.

65. Ivins, *Right Relation of Church and State*, 8. Joel Martineau, a well-

Ivins defended the nationalization of the Catholic Church by deferring to civil religion. The main function of religion, Ivins argued, was to teach the "principles of equality, justice, righteousness and morality . . . upon which national existence can be perpetuated."[66] Quoting the Abbe Emanuel Domenech, Ivins wrote that, "The Mexican is not a Catholic—he is simply a Christian because he has been baptized." The Catholic Church could be one of many religions in Mexico, but it had forfeited its opportunity to claim exclusive spiritual leadership. With few exceptions, the Catholic Church had abetted the enslavement, despoliation, and genocidal massacre of Mexico's Indians and actively undermined their native cultures. Ivins identified Calles's secularization program as the renewal of revolution. Ivins felt that the people of the United States, regardless of religion, must allow the government of Mexico to uproot the power of the Catholic Church. This was a political rather than religious imperative: "millions of people in Mexico who are fighting today for personal liberty will no longer be held in bondage, kept in ignorance . . . and denied those privileges of progression which everyone is entitled to."[67]

In conference with newspaper reporters, Ivins assessed the impact of the church-state conflict on Latter-day Saint activities. The Mormons had submitted to the anti-clerical laws. Business was depressed, but Ivins rated Mexican national confidence high. He also praised Mexican educational efforts, observing that more schools had been built in Chihuahua during the past ten years than in the preceding two hundred.[68] One day, he predicted, Mexico would develop a system similar to the United States. Until then, foreign capitalists and clerics alike would have to wait to see precisely how they would fit into the new order.[69]

---

known Mormon colonist in Mexico, had earlier suggested that the Mexican War of Independence in 1821 freed Mexico from "oppression far worse than that which the American colonies abjured in 1776." See J. H. Martineau, "Mexican Independence," *Deseret Weekly*, October 1, 1898, 493.

66. Ivins, *Right Relation of Church and State*, 11.

67. Anthony W. Ivins, April 8, 1928, *Conference Report*, 119; Ivins, *Right Relation of Church and State*, 9.

68. "L.D.S. in Mexico Accept New Law Churchman Says," *Deseret News*, July 19, 1928; "Conditions in Mexico," Journal History, July 19, 1928, 4.

69. Untitled draft for a *Juvenile Instructor* article, Ivins Papers, box 1, fd. 2. The Church tested its young people with foreign policy questions.

Ivins believed in a Mexico moving toward one critical goal: the creation of a state empowered to restore Indian grandeur and dignity through democratization and land redistribution. As early as 1916, Ivins suggested at a LDS General Conference how far the powers of the state extended: "The state controls the church absolutely, controls your property, controls your lives. It takes your property from you if it wishes, it presses you into service, it declares war or makes peace and you cannot avoid it. . . . After all, the finality is that the state controls us."[70] Since government reshapes society regardless of religion's role, Ivins felt that Mormons and other religious people should embrace government's revisionary power and take an active hand in directing it toward just and beneficial ends. The degree to which Ivins would empower the government to reshape society is revealed in his comments on the state's confiscatory prerogatives. Ivins subordinated contract law to the power of the state: "If I obtain . . . property by unfair means," he essayed, "it may be rightfully taken from me, and restored to its proper owner."[71] Ivins referred at this point to land stripped from the *ejidos* and peasants during the Porfiriato. To achieve justice, land obtained legally but unfairly must revert to the entitled owner, even if that meant retroactive enforcement of laws. The state "may declare war or maintain peace, it may bring peace and good order to society, or tribulation, confusion and final dissolution. It controls your property and mine. . . . Our very

---

Against the backdrop of the church-state controversy in Mexico, the Young Men's Mutual Improvement Association editorial board asked Latter-day Saint teenagers and young adults to evaluate the American occupation of Nicaragua. See "Current Events: A Study for the M. I. A. Senior Classes, 1926-27," *Improvement Era* 30 (March 1927): 476-77.

70. Anthony W. Ivins, April 7, 1916, *Conference Report*, 59.

71. Ivins, *Right Relation of Church and State*, 11-12. Throughout the second half of the nineteenth century, liberals had grown suspicious of the compatibility of democracy with contract law. The new liberalism would use regulation and trade unionism to restrain the excesses of proprietorship, thus preserving economic freedom and freedom from tyranny. See Ryan, "Liberalism," 371-72; John Stuart Mill, *Principles of Political Economy with Some of Their Applications to Social Philosophy*, 766-69; Thomas Hill Green, "Lecture on Liberal Legislation and Freedom of Contract," 366-70; and John Dewey, *Individualism, Old and New*.

life depends upon the proper use of it."[72] To those who bristled at such political theory, Ivins rejoined, "You know that people with these tragedies, . . . struggling for real civilization and religious liberty, are entitled to sympathy, even if in some instances they go to extremes."[73]

The admiration Ivins had cultivated for the French Revolution was coming to full maturation. Robespierre and St. Just believed that the destruction of privilege for the few would guarantee work and happiness to the masses. Ivins embraced some of their ideas about economic control. Property, distributed by state authority, would generate more producers. Since more self-sufficient sellers meant fewer purchasers, prices would fall, assuring equilibrium among farmers, artisans, and workers. Ivins encouraged this unfinished revolution. The government, having established itself as the principal power broker in Mexico, had a historic opportunity to create a unique social system. Prerequisite to democratic rule was the destruction of all obstacles that blocked the people's impulse to think and act in unison.[74]

Ivins further crystallized his liberal statism. Refusing to be baited by Hunt's challenge to view the church-state controversy through the lens of the Mormon experience, Ivins asserted that the 1887 Edmunds-Tucker Act to eliminate Mormon polygamy had been a legitimate use of state power. The US government had acted within its purview when it threatened confiscation of Church property, disfranchised Church members, and imprisoned religious polygamists.[75]

The *Right Relation* tract and the Ivins-Hunt exchange in the *Salt Lake Tribune* generated discussion in Utah. One LDS Church member wrote, "I know of the conditions [in Mexico], and . . . I am proud that a leading Mormon official rises in defense of these poor and mistreated people in that very rich country." Another letter said to Ivins, "I know of no one more capable of speaking the truth . . . than you, and you

72. Ivins, October 5, 1928, *Conference Report*, 16. On this point Ivins departed from Doctrine and Covenants 134:2, which says no government can exist in peace unless it inviolably secures individual property rights and free exercise of conscience.

73. Ivins, *Right Relation of Church and State*, 21. Ivins later admonished members to hold on to the "rod of government," a metaphor drawn from 1 Nephi 8:19–24. See Anthony W. Ivins, April 9, 1933, *Conference Report*, 101.

74. Jacob Talmon, *Origins of Totalitarian Democracy*, 162–64, 189.

75. Ivins, *Right Relation of Church and State*, 12–13, 20–21.

will certainly have [my] support."[76] C. M. Gaxiola, the Mexican consul in Salt Lake City, gratefully acknowledged Ivins's support of the Calles government.[77] Arwell Pierce, the bishop of El Paso Ward and later a key figure in the history of the Church in Mexico, rated Ivins "one hundred percent accurate." He translated *Right Relation* into Spanish for distribution in Mexico.[78]

The most insightful analysis of the 1926 Ivins-Hunt exchange came from a well-known Utahan: Noble Warrum. In July 1924 Secretary of State Charles Evans Hughes had appointed Warrum to the secretariat of the American-Mexican Special Claims Commission charged with arbitrating cases dating from the Mexican Revolution.[79] Warrum wrote to a banker, "The old regime is over. The educated and aristocratic class which recognized the value of alien support and friendship, which understood the oral and mutual obligations of international relationship, has disappeared in one way or another."[80] Warrum prognosticated the future of Mexico. He excused Calles and the new men in power. Execution of the anti-alien ownership and anti-clerical clauses of the constitution would consolidate the government. Capital might be invited back later.[81] Warrum's correspondence shed light on the attitude Ivins had adopted toward the Mexican working class. In a September 17 letter, Warrum intimated that Ivins supported the demands of the Mexican labor movement (CROM):[82]

---

76. J. P. May, Letter to Anthony W. Ivins, August 16, 1926, Ivins Papers, box 5, fd. 13. See also John G. McQuarrie, Letter to Anthony W. Ivins, August 16, 1926, Ivins Papers, box 11, fd. 5.

77. C. M. Gaxiola, Letter to Anthony W. Ivins, August 17, 1926, Ivins Papers, box 11, fd. 5.

78. Arwell L. Pierce, Letter to Anthony W. Ivins, August 20, 1926, Ivins Papers, box 11, fd. 5.

79. "Warrum Given Mexican Post," *Salt Lake Tribune*, July 16, 1924. For the work of the claims commission, see Frank W. Fox, *J. Reuben Clark: The Public Years*, 573; and A. H. Feller, *The Mexican Claims Commissions, 1923–1934: A Study in the Law and Procedure of International Tribunals.*

80. Noble Warrum, Letter to W. W Armstrong, August 27, 1926, 5, Ivins Papers, box 11, fd. 5.

81. Ibid., 5–6.

82. CROM was the leading labor union consortium during the early 1920s. The Confederation of Workers of Mexico (*Confederación de*

President Ivins, who is a close student and keen observer, knows the pitiable mental, social, and physical condition of the Mexican masses; he senses the darkness in which they have groped for centuries without hope or purpose, until rational appreciation of light and truth died within them; he is therefore enabled to view with kindly tolerance the frantic efforts of a frenzied proletariat.[83]

Warrum admitted that he did not share Ivins's capacity to tolerate proletarian "savagery," but acknowledged that "there was no man more dedicated to justice."[84]

Ivins's defense of Mexico was part of a larger effort in two countries. Protestants in the United States and Mexico were united in their support for the Mexican government. Mexican Protestants argued that the Catholic Church, backed by its political prestige and wealth, had no concept of civil religion. Its recalcitrance toward the government was a gambit calculated to perpetuate the privileges of the Holy See.[85] American Protestants agreed with the religious pluralism urged by Ivins but condescended toward Mexico's rising ethnic and lower class-consciousness. Episcopal Bishop Frank W. Creighton predicted that the Indians would look for leadership to the "more ambitious" *mestizos*, who only reluctantly realized that the "national life of Mexico can never develop without the Indian."[86]

Liberal statists—that is, liberals who understood the institutions of the state as the chief guarantors of individual rights and national values—shared Ivins's support of Mexican anti-clericalism.[87] Ernest Gruening, a reporter and historian who later became an Alaska senator, wrote extensively about Mexico. Like Walter Lippmann, John Dewey, Herbert

---

Trabajadores de México, or CTM) superseded CROM in 1934.

83. Noble Warrum, Letter to W. W. Armstrong, September 17, 1926, 1, Ivins Papers, box 11, fd. 5; Ernest Gruening, *Mexico and Its Heritage*, 390. The *Improvement Era* suggested Church support for labor at the outset of the church-state crisis. See "Passing Events," *Improvement Era* 29 (September 1926): 1123. The British-Israel movement, which Ivins vigorously advocated, supported Britain's Labor government in 1924.

84. Warrum, Letter to Armstrong, August 27, 1926, 2.

85. Camargo and Grubb, *Religion in the Republic of Mexico*, 81.

86. Frank W. Creighton, "Aztecs of To-morrow," *Forum* 82, no. 4 (October 1929): 231–34.

87. Britton, *Revolution and Ideology*, 96–99.

Croly, and other liberal statists, Gruening believed in the reforming and guiding power of a socially integrated state. In *Mexico and Its Heritage* (1928), Gruening indicted the Catholic Church. He assailed the practice of flagellation, "clerical commercialism," and misconduct and promotion of superstition by priests in general.[88] He also deplored the clergy's resistance to land reform.[89] If the Catholic Church reformed from within, however, Gruening opined that "the opportunities for service are still immeasurable."[90] Lippmann argued that the "crux of the conflict was whether the Mexican clergy would accept and cooperate with the régime resulting from the social revolution." He concluded that Mexican Church officials, having been tutored during their exile in the United States by liberal Catholic bishops, would abandon their alliance with conservatives and seek an accommodation with the government.[91] As historian Helen Delpar has shown, the American Left's defense of the capacity of the Mexican people to "effect psychological and aesthetic change" through revolutionary measures "defused" the attacks by American business leaders, diplomats, Congressmen, and Catholic religious leaders.[92]

Three weeks after the Ivins-Hunt exchange, John Dewey published related articles in the *New Republic*. The contemporaneous writings of Dewey and Ivins offer instructive points of comparison. Both were liberals who engaged selectively with world politics. Temperamentally, however, the two men operated from different perspectives. Dewey never married and lived cloistered in academia. Ivins had witnessed the firing squad execution of John D. Lee, one of the perpetrators of the Mountain Meadows massacre, had ridden horseback into Mexico wearing pants he made himself. Ivins had performed scores of polygamous marriages in Colonia Juárez, was himself a skilled capitalist, and had once claimed a reward for producing the body of the outlaw Apache Kid. Christian idioms and ethics dot the writings of Dewey, but he had essentially be-

---

88. Gruening, *Mexico and Its Heritage*, 229–74.

89. Ibid., 216–19.

90. Ibid., 284–85, 286. Others who thought the Catholic Church had squandered opportunities to lead a reform movement but thought the possibility remote by 1926 include Beals, *Mexican Maze*, 303–5; Tannenbaum, *Peace by Revolution*, 47, 64–65.

91. Walter Lippman, "Church and State in Mexico: The American Mediation," *Foreign Affairs* 8 (January 1930): 206–7.

92. Delpar, *Enormous Vogue of Things Mexican*, 52–53.

come an atheist halfway through his life.[93] Conversely, Ivins believed that God revealed himself to modern prophets and that world events fit a divine plan. Both men accepted violence, but Ivins countenanced armed revolution to a greater degree than Dewey.[94] Revolution purified; Ivins had no regrets.

Their differences notwithstanding, Dewey and Ivins shared a utopian ideology. The application of "intelligent action," to borrow Dewey's phraseology, was the surest way to social amelioration. For Dewey, the harmonization of science, technology, and government supplanted the metaphysics of religion to serve the "human community," an approach that echoed Ivins's assertion that his own religious philosophy must step in "harmony with the thought of the present."[95] Dewey and Ivins agreed in 1926 that Mexico was a nation still in flux. The uncertainty of the future and the lingering foreign influence emanating from the Catholic Church excused measures that would have been unacceptable in a mature democracy. As Dewey put it, "events in Mexico must not be judged [from the standpoint] of legalities and methods of countries where political and social institutions are stabilized."[96]

Dewey and Ivins also embraced similar views on the topic of civil religion. Each of them recognized the plurality of societies within the state. Each advocated religion and education to help cement the edges together.[97] Mexico had a long way to go, but both men believed that

---

93. Biographies of Dewey include Robert B. Westbrook, *John Dewey and American Democracy*; Douglas E. Lawson and Arthur E. Lean, eds., *John Dewey and the World View*; and Alan Ryan, *John Dewey and the High Tide of American Liberalism*.

94. The concept of revolution drew Dewey's commentary, but he rejected it as an option for men capable of "intelligent action." Ryan, *John Dewey*, 29, 178, 227. See also John Dewey, "Church and State in Mexico," *New Republic* 48 (August 25, 1926): 10. Frank Tannenbaum and Carleton Beals, like Ivins and Dewey, deplored violence, but they too recognized its legitimacy against repressive governments. See Tannenbaum, *Peace by Revolution*, 115–83; Beals, *Mexican Maze*, 9–54.

95. John Dewey, *A Common Faith*, 87.

96. Dewey, "Church and State in Mexico," 10.

97. Dewey suggested that religions had a role to play in social reform. Government and religions could cooperate on a "natural and equal basis" in the search for solutions to social problems. See Dewey, *Common Faith*,

despite the collapse of progressive ideals in Mexico during World War I, the country stood out as a place where the state might still restructure society along liberal and democratic lines.[98] Since 1914, Ivins had not wavered in his belief that revolution was a divinely ordained mode of national development. Religion, government, and capital could work as partners only once the primacy of civil law was established. Ivins trusted that the situation in post-revolutionary Mexico was developing according to divine purposes: "The Lord in his mercy, and undoubtedly by means so natural and common that many will not see his hand in it, will redeem [the Indians]" from their dependent and helpless condition.[99]

Ever the historian, Ivins said that the American "state" established by the revolution of 1776 had struck the hour by which "kingcraft and priestcraft, which for ages had held the struggling masses of the world in thralldom, under perverted control both in civil and religious life, were to be stricken and the people of the world were to be emancipated from the shackles with which they had been bound."[100] Ever since, it had been the right—indeed, the obligation—of other peoples and other governments to do likewise.[101]

Ivins was rebuilding authority in the form of the state and linking it to the Mormon understanding of the world historical process. The supremacy of the state would propel history forward at a faster rate. At the October 1926 General Conference, two months after his exchange with Hunt, Ivins clarified the imperative of civil supremacy over ecclesiastical authority: the "Latter-day Saints are perhaps more directly interested in [the church-state question] than any other people in the world [because] the Republic of Mexico is made up in the great majority of its citizens of people whom the world calls Indians, but to whom the Latter-day Saints refer as Lamanites."[102] To Mormon audi-

---

83. On Dewey and religion see Ryan, *John Dewey*, 32–33, 36–37, 102, 235.

98. Britton, *Revolution and Ideology*, 88–89, 94–96; and Dewey, "Church and State in Mexico," 10.

99. Ivins, October 3, 1926, *Conference Report*, 16.

100. Anthony W. Ivins, October 8, 1933, *Conference Report*, 86.

101. Ibid., 88.

102. Ivins, October 3, 1926, *Conference Report*, 15. This sermon also appeared in Anthony W. Ivins, "Church and State—British-Israel Movement: Significance of the Construction of the Pyramid of Gizeh," *Improvement Era* 30 (December 1926): 93–101.

ences, Lamanites were a people of destiny. If a revolution occurred by them or on their behalf, God must have willed it.

At the same time Ivins acclaimed the anticlerical decrees of the Calles government, he also dabbled in the pseudo-science of pyramidology. Some early twentieth-century thinkers believed that ancient architects had designed the internal chambers of the pyramids in a way that would communicate to modern people the course of human history and the year time would end.[103] To Ivins, four hundred years of Mexican history seemed to be converging like the sides of a pyramid slanting toward the apex. The 1910 revolution and its consolidation in the 1920s fulfilled prophecies in Mormon scripture as they related to Indian destiny.[104] Ivins's belief in dispensational transitions and his interest in pyramidal prophecy revealed the enduring legacy of occult symbolism in Mormonism's revolutionary worldview. An admirer of the French Revolution, Ivins may have seen in the pyramids a variant of the geometric simplicity that attracted his earlier co-religionists.

For Ivins and other pyramidologists, the architecture of the pyramids suggested that history was drawing to a close:

> More than ninety per cent of the events chronicled, according to measurements, have already been fulfilled. The scholars of Great Britain tell us that between the present date and 1936 or 1938, the record so far as it applies to this monument in stone will have been completed. There is nothing which appears after that date. And so they look for the accomplishment of great events during this period.[105]

---

103. See for example John Edgar and Morton Edgar, *The Great Pyramid Passages and Chambers* (1910); and David Davidson and H. Aldersmith, *The Great Pyramid, Its Divine Message: An Original Coordination of Historical Documents and Archaeological Evidences* (1924).

104. For scriptural references to the imperative of missionary work, see Acts 3:20–21 and Doctrine and Covenants 45:28, 133:37. For the role of Indians see 2 Nephi 12:2–4; 3 Nephi 5:23, 20:22, 21:20–25; and Ether 12:2–11.

105. Ivins, October 3, 1926, *Conference Report*, 19. Ivins's suggestion that "great events" were coming in 1936 or 1938 seems influenced by a diagram in Francis M. Darter's *Zion's Redemption: The Return of John the Revelator, the Elias, the Restorer, the Gatherer of All Israel and Forerunner of Christ's Second Coming*, 153. Other Mormon speculation set the date around 1931. See "When Will End 6,000 Years of This World's Human History?" *Liahona: The Elders' Journal* 24 (February 8, 1927): 394–95.

Ivins enjoined the Latter-day Saints to wait, for time was short. The urgency of his appeal was typical of the utopian/messianic impulse. "Christ will prevail," Ivins averred at the October 1926 General Conference. "He will rule over this earth, the right of which he won by the shedding of his blood, and redemption will come to his covenant people. Every word spoken by the prophets inspired of God, as it applies to this land, to this people, and to this great dispensation . . . will be fulfilled."[106]

The *Cristero* Rebellion, 1927–29

The church-state crisis continued until 1929. Representatives of the Catholic Church, lay groups, the Vatican, and the United States negotiated with the Mexican government in an attempt to modify the anti-clerical decrees. Talks stalled when the National League for the Defense of Religious Liberty (*Liga Nacional Defensora de la Libertad Religiosa*, or LNDLR), the most militant of the Catholic political parties, made reconciliation impossible. Catholic bishops did not openly organize armed insurrection, but LNDLR did, with tacit support from the Mexican bishops in exile. In January 1927 LNDLR struck. Severe fighting flared in Mexico's western states as federal troops battled units ranging from guerilla bands to whole brigades of *Cristero* fighters. (*Cristero* comes from the Catholic battle cry, "*Vive Cristo Rey!*" meaning "Long live Christ our King!") The scope and violence of the battles escalated between 1927 and 1929. Federal troops augmented by *agraristas* invaded west central Mexico. Pitched battles and sieges, some of which lasted several days, punctuated prolonged guerilla warfare. Both sides committed atrocities. Rape was commonplace. Prisoners were summarily executed. The war took the lives of forty thousand *Cristeros*; in return the *Cristeros* killed sixty thousand federal soldiers. By the beginning of 1929, the *Cristeros* were winning.[107]

In June, US Ambassador Dwight Morrow and Walter Lippmann of the Council on Foreign Relations brokered a deal between the Mexican government, the Vatican, and the Mexican bishops who saved the Mexican army and ended the standoff. Had it not been for chronic ammunition shortages and US aid to Calles, the Catholic fighters would

106. Anthony W. Ivins, April 5, 1929, *Conference Report*, 16.

107. The best account of military operations of the "First *Cristiada*" (1926–29) is Meyer, *Cristero Rebellion*.

likely have defeated the federal army.[108] The truce was a compromise. Calles promised not to foist unwanted priests on the Mexican Church and to refrain from criminal prosecution of all but the most reactionary clergymen; in exchange the Catholic Church agreed to submit to the reform dictates of the revolution.[109] Not all *Cristeros*, however, stood down. Intermittent fighting continued until Lázaro Cárdenas relaxed some of the tighter restrictions in 1936. The Cárdenas administration raised the number of authorized priests and churches per state, lifted the ban on parochial schools, and allowed the distribution of religious literature. The Church reciprocated by reaffirming its commitment to social reform. From 1936 to the present, the truce between church and state in Mexico has held.[110]

Several scholars have advanced interpretations to explain the Catholic revolt. American historians have usually viewed the *Cristero* Rebellion as a doomed attempt by the Catholic Church to recapture privileges it lost to the reform laws of 1857. The Church belatedly advocated social reform, but because it was unwilling to accept either socialism or liberalism, it had only one other place to go—backward.[111] The Church commanded the devotion of millions of peasants and Indians, but the urban middle and working classes increasingly viewed it as a foreign entity that stood in the way of the beneficial restructuring of Mexican society.[112]

---

108. Ibid., 176–78.

109. Bailey, ¡*Viva Cristo Rey!* 281–83, 311–12; Ellis, "Dwight Morrow and the Church-State Controversy in Mexico," 503–4.

110. On the truce ending the "Second *Cristiada*," see Albert L. Michaels, "The Modification of the Anti-clerical Nationalism of the Mexican Revolution by General Lázaro Cárdenas and Its Relationship to the Church State Détente in Mexico," 35–53; Knight, "Mexico, c. 1930–1946," 17; Bailey, ¡*Viva Cristo Rey!* 297; Robert E. Quirk, "Religion and the Mexican Revolution," 71. Mexico City restored relations with the Vatican in 1992. Constitutional and legislative adjustments made by PNR have enabled Mormons, Catholics, and other denominations to offer religious instruction in private schools, establish religious orders, and obtain property-holding rights. The state, however, reserves the right of intervention. See Roberto J. Blancarte, "Recent Changes in Church-State Relations in Mexico: An Historical Approach"; and *Deseret News 1993–1994 Church Almanac*, June 29, 1993.

111. Quirk, "Religion and the Mexican Revolution," 67.

112. For a historiographic overview see Donald J. Mabry, "Mexican

French historian Jean Meyer challenges this image of a reactionary Catholic Church digging in against the revolutionary reforms by
whipping up the religious zeal of the people. The *Cristero* Rebellion,
Meyer explains, had less to do with religious devotion than with who
had already benefited from the Mexican Revolution and who had yet
to get what they expected. By 1927, the revolutionary state had begun
the final stages of institutionalization. The government would not tolerate any competing party, organization, or church capable of attracting
mass support. This automatically pitted the Catholic Church, despite
its belated interest in social improvement, against the Calles regime.
Secondly, the *Cristeros* fought for some of the same ideals that had inspired the Zapatistas. They perceived that state-disbursed land allot-
ments to individuals threatened communal lands. On this score the
Mexican peasantry was divided. *Agraristas* and lumber workers who
benefited from land redistribution fought alongside federal troops; the
peasants who had not received land more often found themselves following priests and generals of the Catholic National Action Party.[113]
Consequently, land reform—not religion—often determined whether
one became a rebel or supported the government. This division between beneficiaries of reform and those who felt victimized by it was
most severe in the state of Jalisco, the heart of the rebellion. Religion,
of course, also played an important role. Insurgents who fought in the
Catholic armies believed they were fighting for their religion against the
encroachment of secular power. They were traditional, but not necessarily counter-revolutionary.[114]

Except for Pratt, LDS Church leaders in the United States viewed the
Cristero movement as a reactionary counter-revolution led by Catholic
holdouts against public education and constitutional government. In July
1928 Ivins returned from a trip to Mexico. As he re-crossed the border,

---

Anticlerics, Bishops, Cristeros, and the Devout during the 1920s: A
Scholarly Debate."

113. Obregón had redistributed over 921,000 hectares, but far more
land needed to change hands to satisfy aggrieved peasants in villages
despoiled by the Porfiriato. By comparison, President Cardenas distributed
18,000,000 hectares. Only by 1940 had 47 percent of Mexico's cultivated
land been returned to the *ejidos*. See Knight, "Mexico, c. 1930–1946," 20.

114. Meyer, *Cristero Rebellion*, 88–91, 100, 181–90. See also Jrade Ramón,
"Inquiries into the Cristero Insurrection against the Mexican Revolution."

a Catholic angry with government decrees against the Catholic Church shot and killed President-elect Obregón. The following year rebel forces briefly cut communications to the Mormon colonies. Nevertheless, Ivins believed that the government would quickly defeat the *Cristeros*.[115] His optimism, though premature, was not unfounded; Gruening had already declared the insurrection suppressed in July 1927.[116] When moderate Catholic Bishop Pascual Díaz y Barreto was elevated to Archbishop of Mexico, sealing the compromise between the Vatican and the Calles government, B. H. Roberts was putting the finishing touches on his six-volume *Comprehensive History of the Church*. In the section updating Mormon work in Mexico, Roberts pronounced that the "anarchy" loose in Mexico since 1911 had finally ended.[117]

Rey L. Pratt: The Revolution Must Continue

The trouble between the government and Catholic Church began while Rey L. Pratt and Apostle Melvin J. Ballard were in Argentina opening the South American Mission (see Chapter 10). Ballard supported the land redistribution programs and the anti-clerical enforcement undertaken by Obregón and Calles. He believed that the Mexican state would prevail in the battle against "obnoxious" ecclesiastical influence and would continue to provide "true leadership for all the Latin American Republics."[118] When Pratt heard of the Catholic rebellion he wrote: "I am hopeful that the government will be able to put things down."[119] As the Mexican Mission president, Pratt understood that warfare impaired proselytizing efforts. However, the crackdown on re-

---

115. "L.D.S. in Mexico Accept New Law Churchman Says," *Deseret News*, March 19, 1928; and "L.D.S. Heads Fear Attack on Colonists," *Salt Lake Tribune*, March 10, 1929.

116. Gruening, *Mexico and Its Heritage*, 285.

117. B. H. Roberts, *Comprehensive History of the Church of Jesus Christ of Latter-day Saints, 1830–1930*, 6:263.

118. Melvin J. Ballard, "Significance of South American Revolutions," *Improvement Era* 34 (April 1931), 320.

119. Rey L. Pratt, Letter to Mary Pratt, January 13, 1926, Pratt Papers, box 2, fd. 9.

calcitrant clergy, he reasoned in the *Improvement Era*, would "result in greater religious liberty than has been enjoyed in this land."[120]

The government's crude war of pacification in the countryside altered Pratt's focus. In his closing remarks at the October 1927 General Conference he said, "There are underlying reasons why [the *Cristeros*] fight, and I want to tell you that if I were suffering as they have suffered for four hundred years, I would be ashamed if I did not fight." His nine-month experience in South America had reinforced his impression of Indian exploitation. "I pray God will right the wrongs of the oppressed people," he announced, "and that freedom and liberty may come to them. I bespeak for them your sympathy and your love."[121] Pratt's support for the *Cristeros* showed he had recovered from the shock of the executions of Monroy and Morales twelve years earlier. He made no mention of religion or Catholicism specifically. The Virgin of Guadalupe, under which the *Cristeros* fought, had ceased to be a symbol of religious fanaticism. Instead, he understood the conflict in chiefly social and economic terms. In probing the roots of the rebellion, Pratt had anticipated in broad strokes the findings of Jean Meyer.

Pratt adhered to the idea of an extended social revolution. In a small notebook Pratt compiled economic data. The statistical gap between the wealth of Mexico's elites and the poverty of its common people deeply troubled him. Pratt's solution to the problem shows his concord with earlier Mormon observers who had reviled against overconcentrated capital and social injustice.[122] The Mexican Revolution, Pratt contended, had been fought to localize economic and political power in the hands of peasants and *ejidores*. Those still fighting had not received the benefits that were promised in 1917.

American leftists and, to a lesser degree, liberal statists observing the same conditions shared Pratt's apprehensions. Suspicion of Mexico's

120. Rey L. Pratt, "The Mexican Mission," *Improvement Era* 31 (May 1928): 579; Parrish, "Hew to the Rock," 33. See also the letter from a niece of Rey L. Pratt in "LDS Colonist Writes about Mexican Revolt," *Deseret News*, May 3, 1929.

121. Pratt, October 7, 1927, *Conference Report*, 30. Later that month, Carleton Beals criticized the repression of the Yaquis Indians but praised the execution of army officers who had revolted. See Carleton Beals, "The Revolution in Mexico," *New Republic* 52 (October 26, 1927): 253.

122. See for example Rey L. Pratt, Notebook, Pratt Papers, box 1, fd. 8.

centralizing state apparatus and disillusionment about stalled land reforms muffled their earlier enthusiasm for the new Mexico.[123] Gruening wrote that the Catholic Church may have been "medieval," but the corruption of revolutionary government deserved censure as well.[124] Pratt's emphasis on the transformative capabilities of rural villages put him close to Tannenbaum and Beals. Tannenbaum feared Hispanic authoritarianism in the government but held out hope for national education centered on the communal *ejido*.[125] Beals worried about the impact of modernism. Indian leaders "traduced by the trappings of power" would yield to corruption, wastefulness, and moral laxity.[126]

During the Great Depression, Mexico again became an "oasis of revolutionary values." Artists, intellectuals, and Marxists in Mexico and the United States believed that Mexico was a developing utopia even more accessible than the USSR.[127] Indigenous thought of the 1930s shifted. Instead of promoting integration of the Indian, radical *indigenismo* (Indianism) exalted the superiority of Indian race and culture.[128] Pratt pointed to the advantages of *ejido* self-sufficiency. During a 1931 tour with Franklin Harris, the president of Brigham Young University, Pratt reported that Mexico had not experienced the same hardships from economic depression as were then ravaging the United States.[129] The "greater resourcefulness" of the Mexican people, Pratt noted, had "prevented any serious condition of unemployment and avoided any serious want of necessities. . . . The Mexican people always are able to provide for themselves. . . . When a peon is released from work in a mine or anywhere else, he always has a small plot of ground upon which he makes a living for himself and his family."[130] Stuart Chase, an

---

123. Britton, *Revolution and Ideology*, 116–27. Britton argues that independent leftists (such as Pratt and Tannenbaum) were more likely to be pessimistic about prospects for revolutionary principles in Mexico after 1926 than were liberal statists (such as Ivins and Gruening). See ibid., 219.

124. Gruening, *Mexico and Its Heritage*, 284.

125. Tannenbaum, *Peace by Revolution*, 305.

126. Carleton Beals, *The Great Circle: Further Adventures in Free-Lancing*, 308.

127. Pike, *FDR's Good Neighbor Policy*, 64. For general discussion see ibid., 57–79.

128. Knight, "Racism, Revolution, and *Indigenismo*," 81, 92–93.

129. Knight, "Mexico, c. 1930–1946," 8.

130. See "Rey L. Pratt Here on Visit from Mexico."

American journalist-economist, confirmed Pratt's appraisal of Mexican village resiliency in his 1931 book *A Study of Two Americas.*[131]

Still, Pratt affirmed the continuing need of villages for government protection. The state had to preempt the political pretensions of the Catholic hierarchy. He never suspected anything organic in the people's religious customs that dedicated missionary work would not overcome. The Mormon message would dispel the religious superstitions of the people and open their eyes to the promises God made to their ancestors. The influence of the prelates and bishops was a different issue. They were the "power behind the conquest," Pratt said, that "fastened upon the people of Mexico."[132] Opposed to military operations against the people, Pratt urged the government to promote education and to find ways to enforce the religious decrees of the 1917 Constitution without prodding the people into revolt.[133]

J. Reuben Clark, the Surprise Revolutionist

Under the Cárdenas administration, Mexican state consolidation accelerated.[134] Additionally, broader constituencies began to participate in

---

131. Writing at the same time Pratt and Harris visited Mexico, Chase concluded from a visit to Tepoztlán that Mexican craftsmen lived in harmony with seasonal cycles and their own moods. American workers, by contrast, worked according to the factory schedule and the economic cycle. Mexican villages could benefit from mechanized agriculture, sanitation, and electricity, but dependence on cars and American cultural products such as movies should be rejected. Independence from consumer goods would provide the economic and social security lacking in the United States. See Stuart Chase, *Mexico: A Study of Two Americas,* 222–27.

132. Pratt, "The Mexican Mission," 579; Parrish, "Hew to the Rock," 33. Pratt's views of the upper clergy paralleled Gruening, *Mexico and Its Heritage,* 281–83.

133. Quoted in Dale F. Beecher, "Rey L. Pratt and the Mexican Mission," 306 note 44. Neither archivists at the LDS Church History Library nor Beecher himself could locate the December 9, 1929, correspondence he quoted. Nevertheless, the analysis quoted from Pratt is consistent with his views expressed elsewhere.

134. For a narrative of this period, see John W. F. Dulles, *Yesterday in Mexico: A Chronicle of the Revolution, 1919–1936.* For the nationalism

the affairs of state. The revolution had obliterated old forms of deference, and the spread of education imbued the people with a sense of identity and higher expectations.[135] Workers wanted control of their own workplaces and more equitable distribution of rewards earned on foreign capital investment.[136] The cancellation of foreign oil rights and the formation of PEMEX in 1938 capped the high tide of *Cárdenismo* nationalism.[137]

The assertiveness of Mexico's government did not deter Mormon support for the revolution. J. Reuben Clark's initial response to the Mexican Revolution as solicitor general of the State Department had been negative. A proponent of international arbitration, Clark was disappointed by the collapse of negotiations in the spring of 1927, deepening his dislike of postrevolutionary Mexico.[138] He opposed the *ejido* movement and believed Mexicans were incapable of constitutional government.[139] In his subsequent post as US undersecretary of state (1928–30), Clark had rendered legal advice to Ambassador Morrow, assuring him that the *Cristeros* had no legal status and were "common outlaws."[140] But the conservatism and domestic anti-communism for which Clark was later known during his tenure as a counselor in the LDS First Presidency (1933–61) never impaired his belief in revolution as an authentic Mormon expression. Clark's views

---

of the Cárdenas years, see Nathaniel and Sylvia Weyl, *The Reconquest of Mexico: The Years of Lázaro Cárdenas*; and Robert J. Alexander, *The Prophets of the Revolution: Profiles of Latin American Leaders*, 31–52. During the years from 1928 to 1934, known as the *Maximato*, PNR's head Plutarco Calles was the real power behind the throne, wielding influence through Presidents Portas Gil and Ortiz Rubio.

135. Knight, "Revolutionary Project, Recalcitrant People," 255; and Laurence Whitehead, "State Organization in Latin America since 1930," 10 note 8.

136. O'Brien, *Revolutionary Mission*, 252–53.

137. Knight, "Mexico, c. 1930–1946," 44. The anti-American slant of the nationalism eased when Mexico and the United States found themselves as allies against Nazi Germany. See ibid., 64. The president of the Mexican Mission reported improved Mexican feelings toward the United States in "Missionaries Welcome Now, Leader Reports," *Deseret News*, March 28, 1941.

138. Fox, *J. Reuben Clark*, 451–55, 474–75.

139. Ibid., 482; J. Reuben Clark, Letter to Dwight W. Morrow, September 26, 1927, Clarkana Papers of Joshua Reuben Clark Jr., box 128, fd. P8, v. 1.

140. Bailey, ¡*Viva Cristo Rey!* 245.

on the Mexican Revolution shifted after his appointment as ambassador to Mexico in 1930 by President Herbert Hoover. His review of the oil controversy and his service in Mexico increased his sensitivity to revolutionary grievances.[141] On the topic of foreign oil companies claiming exemption from Mexican law (extraterritoriality), Clark's biographer Martin Hickman concludes that Ambassador Clark scorned "those who wished to reap economic advantages in Mexico without bearing the burden which the attainment of those advantages entailed."[142] In the concluding remarks of his farewell speech to the Mexican government in 1933, Clark reconciled with a movement he had once despised. He praised the people's "grope upward for the light of the sun," and expressed his "sympathy with the aspirations and ideals proclaimed in [the Mexican] revolution."[143]

The conservative diplomat of the pre-World War II State Department learned from his own self-tutoring. In a letter to historian L. Ethan Ellis, Clark explained how he, like Ivins and Pratt a generation earlier, had become a sympathizer of the Mexican Revolution:

> I had a definite, strong prejudice against Mexico and the revolutionary regime in control. I thought they were a group of adventurers, dictators, and thoroughly lawless despots. I am afraid this was a reflex of the Department's attitude. When I got to Mexico [in 1927], I began my first independent study of the situation. . . . As I went forward in my work and learned more about the [oil dispute], the law of Mexico, the centuries of inflictions made by the Church and State upon the great Indian (Mexican) population, and got a better understanding of the purposes and activities of the revolutionists (guilty of many excesses, some of them tragically cruel), I found it necessary to reappraise my views and modify my prejudices.
>
> I recall the one day as I reflected, I said to myself, almost orally, "Well, you have thought you were pretty smart in your appraisals of the Mexican Government and its activities in this revolution, which, after all, did away with the curse of peonage, practical slavery, and what would you have done to work out the Mexican problem without the elements that occurred?" After a good deal of thought I concluded that I could not have worked out the revolutionary purpose with less

---

141. Fox, *J. Reuben Clark*, 502.

142. Martin B. Hickman, "The Ambassadorial Years: Some Insights," 410.

143. "Speech at Banquet before Leaving Mexico," February 10, 1933, Clarkana Papers, box 49.

bloodshed, less hardship to the people, less injury to the great landed class, than had the revolutionary leaders.[144]

Clark's newfound patience with the revolution harmonized with the views of Pratt and Ivins. Like those men, Clark's service in Mexico and South America helped him understand the political and cultural barriers that impeded spiritual and material progress there. All three of these observers perceived that spiritual liberation via the Mormon message was by itself insufficient for the people of Latin America. Neither did they believe that capitalism or American models of political organization would suffice to free Latin America from the legacy of the Porfiriato. Mormon observers advocated fundamental changes in the social and political structures of Latin American nations. They risked the undesirable consequences of revolution in exchange for a state that incorporated all constituents of society, especially Indians and workers.

Satisfaction with the Revolution

The Mormon attitude toward post-revolutionary Mexico occupies a place in international history. The efforts of sympathetic American reporters during the 1920s, the popularity of Cárdenas as a protégé of Franklin D. Roosevelt, and the sense of cross-border solidarity during the Depression slowly eroded American assumptions about Mexican ethnic inferiority and political incapacity.[145] American political and cultural ambassadors laid, as Helen Delpar writes, "the basis for permanent linkages between the United States and Mexico that became a routine though valuable part of the relations between the two countries."[146] Mormon observers played an important role in this process.

Looking backward and forward, Pratt, Ivins, and Clark befriended the Mexican Revolution. Pratt shuttled tirelessly between Mexico, Los

---

144. J. Reuben Clark, Letter to L. Ethan Ellis, January 3, 1957, Clarkana Papers, box 256. In a meeting with Church leaders Clark said that he had studied "the history of the people, their oppression—they were downtrodden and had been for 400 years under the heel of despotism," and that he had learned to love that "soft-voiced and generally gentle people." See "J. Reuben Clark to Bishop's Meeting," April 5, 1956, Clarkana Papers, box 151.

145. Britton, *Revolution and Ideology*, 171.

146. Delpar, *Enormous Vogue for Things Mexican*, 208.

Angeles, and Salt Lake City. He urged Latter-day Saints to withhold pejorative judgment of Mexico. Sympathy with Indians and workers made him sensitive to the nuances of local conditions. Land redistribution and decent wages were about human dignity and justice, he believed, but the institutionalization of the revolution would also determine the course of world history. It was a process that required thinking anew: Anglos would have to shed their ideological biases and yield to the leading role of Indian cultural values if they wanted to realize the utopian vision of brotherhood and security that capitalism imperiled. To develop Mexicans' consciousness of their historic role, Pratt embraced Mexican nationalism without letting it fracture the fraternity he wished for all humanity.

Ivins endorsed centralized state power as the surest method to protect Mexico from religious reaction and capitalistic exploitation. He defended the enforcement of anti-clerical laws and accepted his own property losses with grace. In insisting that "this is a church which is progressive," Ivins preached the essence of civil religion.[147] In defense of civil religion in Mexico, Ivins taught Utah Mormons to accept the important yet subordinate role that religion played in the life of their own nation.

State development theory identifies two types of progress, "cognitive progress" and "substantive progress."[148] The cognitive model prevails when people believe they are entitled to expect more. Rey L. Pratt's idealism and defense of Catholic rebels who felt cheated by unrealized land grants made him a champion of cognitive progress. The substantive model differs in that it occurs when there is broad consensus on national goals and policies, such as Franklin D. Roosevelt's New Deal. Ivins held that the state was the ultimate arbiter of national objectives. This judgment made Ivins a spokesman for the substantive model.

The revolution had accomplished as much as could be expected. Class-based privilege had ended, and the "idle rich," as Ivins termed them, had lost exclusive claim to land resources.[149] Indian nations had

---

147. Anthony W. Ivins, "Tabernacle Speech," July 8, 1934, 7, Ivins Papers, box 15, fd. 1.

148. Haas, *Nationalism, Liberalism, and Progress*, 10–11.

149. Anthony W. Ivins, "Fort Douglas Speech," August 10, 1923, 1, Ivins Papers, box 15, fd. 3; and "Meeting of Legislators, Farmers, Flockmasters, and Other Interests," text of a speech delivered February 10, 1933, Ivins

begun to form in Latin America, and the grip of Catholicism had begun to loosen. Now it was time for wise men to develop and modernize the secular states of the Western Hemisphere. Ivins's faith in schools, roads, mines, farms, and the building of cities in Mesoamerica did not differ much from the type of progress advocated by Alexander von Humboldt, Carleton Beals, or the St. Simonians.[150] Mankind, Ivins reiterated, would unite in a "single brotherhood" to build the kingdom.[151] From the southern Zion the example would spread to the rest of the world. It mattered little whether the moment was near or distant. The point was that man had acted according to God's dictates to revolutionize the Western Hemisphere. Ivins preached the man-God-science triad and a special role for the Indians. "What of the future?" he asked a crowd in the Salt Lake City Tabernacle. We must, he said, work to "hasten the day when the promises made by [the Lamanites'] father may be fulfilled."[152] Concerned Mormon observers shared the vision of a modern Zapatista: in Mexico there would be "democracy" and "no more inequality . . . a life worth living, liberation, just like God says."[153] Rifles in the hands of peasants had inaugurated the millennium. A *Book of Mormon* in their hands would consummate it.[154]

Papers, box 15, fd. 1.

150. Víctor Raúl Haya de la Torre in *Thirty Years of Aprismo* (1956) rejected pure communism and welcomed foreign capital to serve national growth based on traditional Indian cooperatives. See also Alexander, *Prophets of the Revolution*, 106. Beals turned increasingly toward statism during the 1930s, suggesting Latin America could integrate more closely with the United States. He praised Ambassador Morrow's policy in Mexico of rural development, education, and diversification and other programs that would benefit Mexicans. Increased purchasing power would prevent a worker turn to Marxism. See Carleton Beals, "Latin-American Social and Political Progress," *New York Times Current History* 32 (August 1930): 932–37.

151. Ivins, October 5, 1930, *Conference Report*, 118.

152. Anthony W. Ivins, "Tabernacle Speech," April 7, 1933, 5–7, Ivins Papers, box 15, fd. 1.

153. Womack, *Rebellion in Chiapas*, 12.

154. Post-1940 Mormon support for the Mexican Revolution includes G. Homer Durham, "Mexico," *Improvement Era* 57 (June 1954): 378, 478; and Marion G. Romney, April 6, 1958, *Conference Report*, 126.

Mormon observers of Mexico sustained a utopian vision. Whether they pinned their hopes on cultural rejuvenation or state power, these Mormon spokesmen for Mexico viewed the nation as a place where justice, political rights, and the universal Church would germinate. They hoped that the example of Mexico would spread to the southern hemisphere. In Peru, social activist Haya de la Torre also imbued Mexico with world-historical meaning.[155] But before the Church pushed into South America, it would have to confront the promise and reality of Russian communism.

---

155. Hodges and Gandy, *Mexico 1910–1982: Reform or Revolution?* 2–3.

CHAPTER 9

THE BOLSHEVIK REVOLUTION OF 1917

Reordering the World

American entry into World War I in April 1917 ensured that President Woodrow Wilson would play a role in the peace settlement. To promote his Fourteen Points for world peace, Wilson needed an American army in France under all-American command. A military victory won by his soldiers and generals would show that America, too, had paid the price in blood. Without this example, says historian Ernest May, Wilson would have been forced to "sacrifice America's prestige and moral influence" in the peace talks. With a show of the flag in the trenches, however, Wilson would be able to get hard-bitten Allied leaders to go along with the last and most cherished of his Fourteen Points: a League of Nations.[1] The League would bind nations to a common standard of conduct. Through joint action, member states could contain nations threatening global stability. European heads-of-state wanted much the same thing, but not before punishing Germany. The appeal of Wilson's message in the United States and Europe reached messianic proportions. Thomas J. Knock suggests that the effusive reception Wilson received when he arrived for the Paris peace talks "transcended mere pageantry. Indeed, [it was] an articulate expression of mass political opinion—and one, significantly, set in motion by the liberal, labor, and socialist movements within the Allied countries."[2]

---

1. Ernest R. May, *The World War and American Isolation, 1914–1917*, 427. For a view that intervention resulted from Wilson's awareness that American economic strength empowered him to create a new world order free from imperialism and revolutionary socialism, see N. Gordon Levin Jr., *Woodrow Wilson and World Politics: America's Response to War and Revolution*, 21–22, 123.

2. Thomas J. Knock, *To End All Wars: Woodrow Wilson and the Quest for*

Mormon observers saw World War I, the 1917 Bolshevik Revolution in Russia, and the pending League of Nations fight as events representing a righteous cause. Amidst the ruins of European military power, men and women inspired by transcendent ideas might design a new world order founded on self-determination and international cooperation. Richard Gamble writes that American ministers went from pacifists to crusading internationalists: missionaries for the creeds of democracy and collective security.[3] For example, Harry F. Ward, author of the Methodist Social Creed, had once chaired the antiwar American Union against Militarism, believing capitalists and imperialists had caused the war. As the war progressed, however, Ward came to accept it as necessary for the reconstruction of the world order. As the Paris Peace talks got underway, he worried that Allied ministers would sabotage solutions to problems that stood in the way of global solidarity and peace. Equating communism with Christianity and capitalism with anti-Christian selfishness, Ward warned that if "democracy does not make a way for economic change without class war, Western civilization is headed for complete and overwhelming disaster."[4] Not all Protestant churchmen agreed; in 1919 the Federal Council of Churches decried Bolshevism as a new absolutism.[5] Several Mormon observers, however, came close to Ward's assessment.

For Mormon observers, intervention in World War I and membership in the League of Nations were essential to human progress. Apostle Charles A. Callis invoked the memory of Joseph Smith to justify the terrible drama on the "bloody battlefields in France:"

> We hold that Joseph Smith was one of the foremost exponents and champions of human liberty. Our soldier boys are fighting for the cause of human liberty. They are battling for a cause which God looks upon and approves."[6]

---

a New World Order, 195. The appeal of Wilson's messianism and language of human liberation is also discussed in Ernest Cassara, "The Development of America's Sense of Mission," 90–91; and Ernest Lee Tuveson, *Redeemer Nation: The Idea of America's Millennial Role*, 211.

3. Richard M. Gamble, *The War for Righteousness: Progressive Christianity, the Great War, and the Rise of the Messianic Nation.*

4. Quoted in ibid., 221.

5. See ibid., 221–24 for Protestant opposition to Ward's views.

6. Charles A. Callis, April 5, 1918, *Conference Report*, 106.

Orson F. Whitney denied that the United States declared war to gain territory or riches; it fought because it was a moral force for good that could not be restrained: "God loves the whole world; he gave his Son to save it; he is using America and her allies as instruments for the spread of the Gospel of Liberty, and in their wake, after they have cleared the way, will follow the missionaries of the Lord Jesus Christ."[7] Janne M. Sjödahl, editor of the *Millennial Star*, spoke of crowns toppled by war and revolution, followed by the immediate unity of humankind:

> Through this war, three empires—all oppressors of men and morally rotten to the core—have been swept away. Militarism lies prostrate in the dust. . . . Nations held in chains for centuries have been set free and are rejoicing in the new day that is dawning over them in glory. On the ruins of the old world the foundation of a new structure has already been laid, upon the portals of which, when completed, the inscription in letters of blazing glory will read: 'The Brotherhood of Man.'[8]

The anticipated post-war peace aroused millennial expectations. A new world harmony would replace the overblown nationalism that had caused the war. Mormon rhetoric swelled with phrases like "higher plane" and "world's spirit" to describe the new internationalist fervor that transcended partisan interests and class warfare. Mexican Mission President Rey L. Pratt predicted that the "great world conflict will eradicate the spirit" that divides people according to "what blood flows in [their] veins."[9] B. H. Roberts looked for the League to suppress nationalism. An "empire of humanity," he suggested, borrowing

---

7. Orson F. Whitney, April 7, 1918, *Conference Report*, 77. Years later, Mormon eschatologist Duane S. Crowther also wrote that revolutions overthrow "those despotic governments that do not allow the Gospel to be preached within their borders." See Duane S. Crowther, *Prophecy—Key to the Future*, 160.

8. Janne M. Sjödahl, "Constitution of the World League," *Latter-day Saints' Millennial Star* 81 (February 27, 1919): 138 (hereafter cited as *Millennial Star*). The three empires to which Sjödahl referred were Germany (House of Hohenzollern), Russia (Romanov), and Austria-Hungary (Hapsburg). He might have added a fourth: the Ottoman Empire.

9. Rey L. Pratt, October 6, 1918, *Report of the Semi-annual Conference of the Church of Jesus Christ of Latter-day Saints*, 81 (hereafter cited as *Conference Report*).

from Wilson, would spiritually redeem civilization. Moral rejuvenation might, therefore, preempt further class revolution.[10] Apostle George F. Richards, the European Mission president, believed that the nations were being united to "receive the King of all and a reign of universal peace." Democracy, revolution, socioeconomic justice, and millennialism merged into a single cause. The details were lost, but the essence suggested one world reordered by saintly men.[11] Communist revolution in Russia would test whether Mormon observers would accept a new partner in the reconstruction of the world.

Mormon Observers Applaud the Czar's Overthrow

By 1917 the Russian war effort was in shambles. On March 15, strikes and riots in St. Petersburg forced Czar Nicholas II to abdicate. American public opinion greeted his fall warmly. Russian liberals, headed by Alexander Kerensky, captivated American attention. Americans hoped a republican government brought to power by a modest revolution would reinvigorate Russia's war effort against Germany. The czar's fall also resolved the disquieting incongruity of an autocratic dynasty in alliance with Great Britain, France, and the United States.[12] Russia's war effort continued to falter during the summer of 1917. A second shock— the Bolshevik Revolution of November 7—forced Wilson to balance the principle of self-determination with strategic realities. There was little to

---

10. D. Craig Mikkelsen, "The Politics of B. H. Roberts," 38. For Roberts's views on the necessity of world government to "uplift and better the conditions of the lowly and underdeveloped," see B. H. Roberts, *The Truth, the Way, the Life: An Elementary Treatise on Theology*, 97.

11. George F. Richards, October 5, 1919, *Conference Report*, 163. Other Mormon leaders similarly linked the League of Nations with the coming millennium. See James E. Talmage, April 6, 1918, *Conference Report*, 159; Janne M. Sjödahl, "Birthday of the League of Nations," *Millennial Star* 81 (February 6, 1919): 90; Joseph A. West, "Present World Conditions and Prophecy," *Improvement Era* 23 (February 1920): 347; Thomas G. Alexander, *Mormonism in Transition: A History of the Latter-day Saints, 1890–1930*, 52.

12. Peter G. Filene, *Americans and the Soviet Experiment, 1917–1933*, 10–17; Leonid I. Strakhovsky, *American Opinion about Russia, 1917–1920*, 3–20; and Meno Lovenstein, *American Opinion of Soviet Russia*, 7–8.

do except help Russia achieve stability, even if under Bolshevik control. Americans could only hope that the fundamentally liberal program of Kerensky's March revolution would survive.[13]

Mormon attitudes paralleled national public opinion in the United States. At first Utah newspapers believed the March revolution would strengthen the Allies' military position and bolster the notion that the Allies were fighting to "make the world safe for democracy." The Russian people had mustered "the courage to strike" against the czar, a *Deseret Evening News* editorial said, despite the horrendous military casualties and economic strain that had rendered the suffering of the Russian people worse than that of the Belgians under German occupation.[14] The "Russian Republic" was better prepared for self-government than France had been in 1789, another writer asserted. The people might be illiterate, but "given the other qualities which tend to make a nation self-governing and free, the lack of book learning need constitute no bar—it is merely a misfortune or neglect that can be easily and speedily remedied."[15] Yet another editorial hoped the March revolution would strengthen the eastern front against Germany by sweeping away the inefficiencies that hampered Russian command, supply, and transportation.[16] The ramifications of the March revolution aggregated into a rationale for American intervention in the war. The democratic movement in Russia would enable the United States to sit at the peace table "no longer estranged from their colleagues by the taint of obscurantism and reaction."[17]

Optimism, however, was tempered by warnings against overconfidence. The *Deseret Evening News* suggested that sheer national exhaustion might make it impossible for Kerensky and the Duma (Russia's elective assembly) to continue the war. "The masses," said the *News*, "sensing for the first time their freedom and power, are by no means certain to stretch

---

13. Filene, *Americans and the Soviet Experiment*, 18–23; and Betty Miller Unterberger, "Woodrow Wilson and the Russian Revolution," 51–54.

14. Editorial, *Deseret Evening News*, March 16, 1917. Throughout the rest of 1917, the *Deseret Evening News*, *Salt Lake Herald-Republican*, and *Salt Lake Tribune* ran editorials and reports expressing sympathy with the Kerensky revolution for democratic, anti-czarist, or strategic reasons.

15. "The Moujiks and Self-Government," *Deseret Evening News*, April 25, 1917.

16. "Cause and Effect of Revolutions," *Deseret Evening News*, March 24, 1917.

17. "Russia Roused, but Running," *Deseret Evening News*, July 26, 1917.

their new-found sinews in the exercise of that which the world calls patriotism."[18] Another editorial accurately described the challenges faced by the new Russian government as "unparalleled in history." Power in the hands of people "unequal to governing themselves" had not, despite the fall of the Romanovs, "brought the millennium."[19] The *News*'s second thoughts on the advisability of revolution in Russia during a critical time of the war muted the normal Mormon sympathy for Irish independence. One editorial urged Irish nationalists to accept dominion status and the permanent attachment of Ulster to the United Kingdom.[20]

Still, the weeklies and monthlies of the Church press largely disregarded such cautious assessments. Mormon reception of the March revolution rang with President Wilson's messianic language.[21] The *Millennial Star* manifested the yearnings of the British people for an end to the war. The misery and anxiety of Britain served to cast the revolution in Russia as a scene in an eschatological play. The world should not fear a "free, democratic Slavonic power." The Russian example, like the fraternal and egalitarian principles of the French Revolution, would sweep across Europe, dooming German militarism. Global disarmament would follow the end of the war, which was now sure to come quickly. Next would follow the millennium.[22] By April the *Millennial Star* touted Russia as a paragon of the "Brotherhood of Man." Janne

---

18. "A Giant Aroused from Torpor," *Deseret Evening News*, March 17, 1917.

19. "The United States of Russia," *Deseret Evening News*, March 19, 1917. Other articles advocating caution include "Treachery That Threatens Russia," *Deseret Evening News*, May 9, 1917; "Russia's Supreme Need—A Man!" *Deseret Evening News*, May 26, 1917; "In the West or the East," *Deseret Evening News*, May 29, 1917; and "Bending to the Conqueror," *Deseret Evening News*, August 4, 1917.

20. "Ireland's Fate in Her Own Hands," *Deseret Evening News*, May 29, 1917.

21. On the religious content of Wilson's efforts to create a "transcendent order of meaning," see Gregory S. Butler, "Visions of a Nation Transformed: Modernity and Ideology in Wilson's Political Thought."

22. Janne M. Sjödahl, "Change of Government in Russia," *Millennial Star* 79 (March 29, 1917): 201–2. Mormon writers did not display the prejudice toward Slavic peoples that American Protestants, Austrians, or Magyars did. Compare Martin E. Marty, *Modern American Religion*, 2:67, to John A. Widstoe, "Opening the Gospel Doors to the Slavs," *Improvement Era* 33 (December 1929): 117–19.

Sjödahl praised the establishment of *soviets*. These workers' councils represented "industrial liberty" and raised expectations of a radiant future.[23] Articles and speeches in Utah also celebrated the change in Russia. The *Improvement Era* focused on the prospects of a more efficient Russian war effort and republican government.[24]

Speeches delivered at the April and October 1917 General Conferences suggest that the Russian revolution and the US declaration of war on April 6 had stamped out any remaining doubts among Mormon observers regarding intervention. With Russia in the hands of men dedicated to representative government, America could unite with the Allies with a clear conscience.[25] Northwest Mission President Melvin J. Ballard said, "Other nations like Russia will take off their shackles and come forth unto their own, to the enjoyment of liberty and freedom and truth, and right. There shall be an emancipation of the people, and they shall look up to America."[26] The war became a crusade to liberate the entire world. Revolution was clearing the way.

Patriotism suffused public opinion in Utah as much as it did elsewhere, but universalism always glimmered on the horizon. Ivins installed the American constitutional experiment in the context of universal history—it, like the Church, was "world-wide and belongs to no race of people."[27] Melvin J. Ballard reminded the audience that the United States and the LDS Church together will "go forward in the

---

23. Janne M. Sjödahl, "Freedom in Russia," *Millennial Star* 79 (April 26, 1917): 265.

24. Joseph M. Tanner, "The Break with Germany—The Czar Dethroned," *Improvement Era* 20 (April 1917): 545; "Russian Revolution," *Improvement Era* 20 (June 1917): 756.

25. For Utah and Mormons during World War I, see Alexander, *Mormonism in Transition*, 46–48; James B. Allen and Glen M. Leonard, *Story of the Latter-day Saints*, 490–92; Ronald W. Walker, "Sheaves Bucklers, and the State: Mormon Leaders Respond to the Dilemmas of War," 279–82; Alan Kent Powell, "Our Cradles Were in Germany: Utah's German American Community and World War I"; and Noble Warrum, *Utah in the World War: The Men behind the Guns and the Men and Women behind the Men behind the Guns.*

26. Melvin J. Ballard, April 8, 1917, *Conference Report*, 122.

27. Anthony W. Ivins, April 7, 1917, *Conference Report*, 53. Congress declared war on Germany the same day.

future fulfilling their mission, and holding up to the nations the ensign of freedom and of truth."[28] At the next conference, B.H. Roberts said the "destructive forces" of war and revolution were "under the control of God." Roberts reiterated Mormon postmillennialism: humanity was God's partner in earthly progress.

> There shall come larger liberty to the inhabitants of the earth; there shall come a more profound security and joy of life, of liberty, and the pursuit of happiness. There shall come a better distribution of the wealth that is created by a combination of the efforts of men, by their daily toil and the supply of the capital that makes possible the labors of men's hands. And so I look forward to better times, to improved conditions, and out of this crucible through which the world is passing and being tried as gold seven times tried in the fire—I anticipate the development of larger opportunities and greater blessings than the world has yet known.[29]

"No nation in the history of this world drew the sword in a more righteous cause and in a more unselfish spirit" than the United States was doing in this war against "the Imperial Government of Germany," Roberts declared. "I am happy to live in this day of the purification of the nations of the earth."[30] German E. Ellsworth, president of the Northern States Mission, said that Mormon soldiers would "return with victory upon their banner and a wreath of laurel woven out of the evergreen of Russia, the roses of England, and the lilies of France."[31]

Apostle Orson F. Whitney extolled the transcendent aims of the war. The American gift to the world was spiritual progressivism, not material abundance. Far from being a bastion of unchanging conservative values, America was a place of constant progress and experimentation with new social and religious institutions. Without "a new mission in history" to fulfill, America would "decay." Whitney vouched for Latter-day Saint participation in the global mission. The membership would eschew the economic benefits of imperialism and reject consumerism in order to focus the redemptive powers of the United

---

28. Ballard, April 8, 1917, *Conference Report*, 123.
29. B. H. Roberts, October 7, 1917, *Conference Report*, 102–3.
30. Ibid., 103.
31. German E. Ellsworth, October 7, 1917, *Conference Report*, 131.

States.[32] Wilson, seen by Mormons and evangelicals as leading an effort to secure permanent world harmony, had stuck a responsive chord. Ron Walker suggests that "If Mormons deviated from wartime sentiment, they 'out-Wilsoned' Wilson by making the religious overtones of his speech explicit."[33]

The idealism attached to the Allied cause shows how far Mormon eschatology had diverged from premillennial dispensationalism, the dominant Protestant Fundamentalist viewpoint. Early in the war, Fundamentalist theologians such as James Gray of the Moody Bible Institute and Methodist minister Arno Gaebelein prophesied that the postwar division of territory would turn Europe into the ten-nation, Roman-like empire mentioned in the Book of Daniel. The Antichrist would rule this new European confederation.[34] Mormon leaders rejected this dismal interpretation of the war's possible outcomes. Despite depressing battlefield communiqués from Europe, they clung to their faith in progress.[35]

Lenin's autumn 1917 victory could not have come at a worse moment for the Allies. True to their promise, the Bolsheviks removed Russia from the war. Under the terms of the Treaty of Brest-Litovsk on March 3, 1918, Russia concluded peace with Germany and affirmed independence for the Baltic States, the Ukraine, and Finland. The implications were sobering. The Russian withdrawal released forty German divisions for service on the Western Front to deliver the knockout blow to France and Britain before the United States could effectively intervene. Americans had been led to believe that the March revolution was evidence that the Russian people wanted to continue the war and establish democracy. But American opinion makers had underestimated the level of crisis in Russia. Former Secretary of War Elihu Root had led a delegation to Russia during the summer of 1917 and returned with the ridiculous report that all the Russian army needed to boost morale

---

32. Orson F. Whitney, October 5, 1918, *Conference Report*, 41–44.

33. Walker, "Sheaves, Bucklers, and the State," 281.

34. Paul Boyer, *When Time Shall Be No More: Prophecy Belief in Modern American Culture*, 101.

35. Robert Erich Paul, *Science, Religion, and Mormon Cosmology*, 153, discusses Mormon imperviousness to disillusionment from World War I. For the forebodings of premillennialists who scorned the idea of progress resulting from the war, see Boyer, *When Time Shall Be No More*, 100–104.

was wholesome activities supplied by the YMCA.[36] Disillusionment ensued when Americans discovered that five million casualties had rendered Russia so desperate that the people would turn to anyone offering peace. Socialists in the Allied countries concurred with public opinion that branded the Bolsheviks in Russia as traitors.[37] Lenin's seizure of power exacerbated the old John Adams suspicion of revolutions, but this reaction was mixed with attempts to understand the Russian dilemma. In the confusion, editorials accused the new Russian leaders of being German agents, enemies of civilization, or dissolute radicals who wished to nationalize everything from land to women.[38]

Editorials in the Church-owned *Deseret Evening News* that reflected the negative themes found in the national press competed with positive reviews of the Bolshevik Revolution.[39] One editorial described the Brest-Litovsk treaty as a "monstrous farce" when weighing Kerensky's patriotism against the "mercenary cowardice and treachery" of Lenin and his radicals. However, opinion makers in Church periodicals and the *Deseret News* showed that while they loathed Bolshevik policy, they also recognized the appeal of socialism's claim to be the antidote to war and imperialism. The "revolution which overthrew imperialism," one writer stressed, "derived its power from Socialism" in both the Kerensky and Leninist phases.[40] Another editorial suggested that Russia had never been a homogenous nation. Held together only by the mystique of the Romanovs, the regime was destined for destruction. The editorial's tolerance of the communist phase of the 1917 revolutions followed the same discursive tracks laid down by previous Mormon observers.

------

36. Strakhovsky, *American Opinion about Russia*, 18.

37. Albert S. Lindemann, *A History of European Socialism*, 207.

38. Michael H. Hunt, *Ideology and U.S. Foreign Policy*, 114–15; Filene, *Americans and the Soviet Experiment*, 39–63; and Strakhovsky, *American Opinion about Russia*, 29–41.

39. "In Their True Colors," *Deseret Evening News*, July 11, 1918; "Man's Home His Castle," *Deseret Evening News*, March 6, 1919; "Which Message Will America Heed," *Deseret Evening News*, March 14, 1919; "Our Responsibility in the League," *Deseret Evening News*, April 21, 1919; "A Hardy Growth and Noxious," *Deseret Evening News*, April 12, 1919; "Bolshevism Losing Ground in Russia," *Deseret News*, September 20, 1920; and "Revolution vs. Progress," *Deseret News*, June 20, 1921.

40. "Russia's Bid for Chaos," *Deseret Evening News*, December 3, 1917.

Revolutions were progressive events. They corrected injustices and destroyed or reshaped outdated institutions.

> There may be many days of red terror before the symptoms of returning reasons shall be manifested, old leaders may go down while others arise and every pillar of the state may seem shaking to its ruins. But even these are conditions not without promise and hope. This is one of the movements that must in the end make for progress and improvement. Revolutions do not go backward, and this one, chaotic though it may appear at present, will prove no exception to the general rule.[41]

Wartime stress on Russian society received treatment in the *Improvement Era*. Two months after an abortive July 1917 uprising of soldiers and sailors in Petrograd (now St. Petersburg), Joseph M. Tanner argued that the injustices and deprivation suffered by the proletariat had become so severe that revolution was the only recourse. Tanner recognized that the Petrograd Soviet of Workers' and Soldiers' Deputies that revolted in July had previously been a "dominating factor" in Kerensky's March revolution against the czar. He reminded readers that those at the head of the "great revolution are themselves aristocrats" and would have to demonstrate that "their hearts, their interests are with the proletariat . . . before they shall eventually gain the confidence of the people."[42] Tanner sympathized with labor, but the prospect of Bolshevik leadership of the international worker's movement concerned him.

For Mormon observers, violence was part of the process that would give birth to the new world. Mormons' reactions to the murder of Nicholas II and his family at Ekaterinburg on July 16, 1918, continued their historic lack of sympathy for the Romanovs. The *Millennial Star* suggested that the czar might have saved himself with timely reforms. The people never forgave him for the 1905 Winter Palace massacre, and the world had not forgotten the pogroms. His fall vindicated the prophecy that "kingdoms would be rent asunder" prior to the Second Coming.[43] Joseph West, a contributor to the *Improvement Era*, asked, "What greater punishment could be meted out to the 'high ones and

---

41. "A Giant, but Loose-Jointed," *Deseret Evening News*, December 10, 1917.

42. Joseph M. Tanner, "What the Russians Suffer," *Improvement Era* 20 (September 1917): 1012–13.

43. Janne M. Sjödahl, "The Late Czar Nicholas," *Millennial Star* 80 (October 10, 1918): 648–50.

the kings of the earth' than that which has overtaken them as a result of the war just passed?"[44] The *Millennial Star* represented the destruction of outmoded governments with the classic metaphor of a universal revolutionary wind:

> We have lived to see the overthrow of Russia, Austria-Hungary, Germany, and the dissolution of numerous governments. In the language of John the revelator, it might be said of the crowns that have dropped during the last few years, that they have fallen "even as a fig tree casteth her untimely figs, when she is shaken in a mighty wind."[45]

The opportunities created by war and revolution permeated the thinking of evangelically-minded progressives in the internationalist movement. Wilson originally wrote an article for universal religious toleration into the League Covenant.[46] Anthony W. Ivins, a Wilson admirer, declared in October 1918 that the world must be made safe for Christianity first, and then democracy would follow.[47] Western States Mission President John Herrick urged the Christian churches to fortify with spiritual strength the young men who were shipping out by the hundreds of thousands for the trenches of France. The need for religion was immediate, and the LDS Church did its part. The Church's soldiers did not use tobacco. They refrained from illicit sex. They did not turn the military camps into alcohol sumps. "Mormonism" represented the truth "more today than ever in the history of the world before." God was using the war to give events "forward movement." In reviewing the situation, Herrick credited wartime events with the "betterment of nations, of communities, [and] of individuals."[48]

Absent from Mormon assessments of the October Revolution during this period were allegations that Bolshevik atheism would block religious impulses in Russia. To the contrary, Mormon observers believed the revolutionaries would prove more tolerant than the old regime. The Communist Party differentiated between the Party's attitude toward

---

44. West, "Present World Conditions and Prophecy," 349.

45. "The Gathering of the Jews," *Millennial Star* 81 (April 17, 1919): 246.

46. The religious clause was dropped in the final draft. See Knock, *To End All Wars*, 224.

47. Anthony W. Ivins, October 5, 1918, *Conference Report*, 52. See also Rey L. Pratt, Diary, October 5, 1918.

48. John L. Herrick, April 6, 1918, *Conference Report*, 49–50.

religion and the religious policies of the state. The Party did subject the Greek Orthodox Church to repressive campaigns between 1917 and 1941, and each wave was also followed by a period of less vigorous activity against other churches. But while the Marxist denial of non-material forces was certainly a motivating factor, the main reason for repression was to consolidate Party control over institutions once loyal to the czar.[49] In the meantime, Mormon observers supposed that the change in government would stimulate Jewish migration to Palestine, deprive the Orthodox Church of its spiritual hegemony, and open the door to missionary work in Russia.[50]

A momentary shift in Mormon attitudes occurred early in 1919. In January the communist-inspired Spartacist Uprising in Germany threatened the centrist socialist government of Friedrich Ebert. The episode drew more condemnation than praise in Utah.[51] However, even editorials that sympathized with the execution of Spartacist leaders Rosa Luxembourg and Karl Liebknecht saw German communism as a force that would smash the "iron and clay feet" of Europe's militaristic

---

49. For sources on religion in Russia during this period, see Max Heyward and William C. Fletcher, eds., *Religion and the Soviet State: A Dilemma of Power*; Robert Conquest, *Religion in the USSR*; and Richard H. Marshall Jr., ed., *Aspects of Religion in the Soviet Union, 1917–1967*.

50. Sjödahl, "Change of Government in Russia," 201; Sjödahl, "Freedom in Russia," 265–66; and "Religious Freedom in Russia," *Millennial Star* 79 (September 6, 1917): 573–74. Several Protestant churchmen viewed the Bolshevik Revolution with similar optimism. See Filene, *Americans and the Soviet Experiment*, 84–86. Dispensationalist premillennialists shared the Mormon belief in the necessity of Israel's restoration to Palestine as a sign of Christ's immanent return. However, the dispensationalists had no faith in Russian progress and forever after branded Russia as the scriptural Gog and Magog. See Boyer, *When Time Shall Be No More*, 102.

51. Anti-Spartacist editorials appeared in "Hun 'Red' Routed," *Salt Lake Tribune*, January 16, 1919; "Must Maintain Law," *Salt Lake Tribune*, January 19, 1919; "Fate Deserved," *Deseret Evening News*, January 18, 1919; "Seed of a World Upas-Tree," *Deseret Evening News*, January 24, 1919; and "Two European Rebellions," *Deseret Evening News*, October 8, 1919. On the Spartacist Uprising see Werner T. Angress, *Stillborn Revolution: The Communist Bid for Power in Germany , 1921–1923*.

empires.[52] Predictably, Utah newspapers were no more sympathetic to reactionary German conservatism than to the Spartacist rebels. In 1920 the *Deseret Evening News* praised Ebert's Weimar government for beating back a right-wing putsch led by Wolfgang Kapp.[53]

The spring of 1919 brought disappointing news. Hints surfaced that the League of Nations was not going to pass muster. On March 2, "reservationists" in the Senate signed the "Round Robin," a circular declaring that no consideration would be given to the League Covenant until the peace treaty with Germany was concluded. Wilson fought the senators. The League, he said, was inseparable from the treaty. When Wilson returned to Paris on March 9, French ministers threatened to undermine the peace by demanding an unspecified amount of reparations and occupation rights in the Rhineland. Meanwhile, the Communist International convened in Moscow with the goal of fomenting communist revolution in other nations, and the Red Army captured Kiev. In the United States, the "Red Scare" began.[54]

Fear of communism in 1919–20 tempered the earlier Mormon affirmations of 1917–18. Apostle George Albert Smith approved the deportation of pacifists and "Reds" like Emma Goldman and Alexander Berkman.[55] Joseph M. Tanner called Bolshevism "the greatest of all world problems." He hoped that Poland, the bulwark of Europe, would block the storm surge.[56] Sjödahl revoked his earlier positive refer-

---

52. "Those Killings in Berlin," *Deseret Evening News*, January 18, 1919; and "Clay and Iron—A Poor Welding," *Deseret News*, September 7, 1921.

53. "The German Revolution," *Deseret Evening News*, March 13, 1920; and "Looks for Revolution in Germany," *Deseret News*, July 19, 1922. For the Kapp Putsch, see Gordon A. Craig *Germany: 1866–1945*, 429–32.

54. Robert K. Murray, *Red Scare: A Study in National Hysteria, 1919–1920*. For Wilson's difficulties in the United States between his two trips to France during the treaty negotiations, see Knock, *To End all Wars*, 227–45.

55. George Albert Smith, Letter to Nettie L. Fulton, February 20, 1920, George A. Smith Family Papers, box 45, fd. 21. Smith opposed "Bolshevism, Socialism, [and] Anarchy," but only because he believed "absolutely in the [US] government." See George Albert Smith, Letter to German E. Ellsworth, March 3, 1919, Smith Family Papers, box 45, fd. 21.

56. Joseph M. Tanner, "Bolshevism," *Improvement Era* 23 (March 1920): 434–37. Poland held and was even able to extend its territory beyond the eastern border recommended by the Allied Supreme Council after World War I.

ence comparing the Russian revolution to the French Revolution. The "earthquake shocks" of the Red Terror had struck Russia; the attempt to inaugurate utopia through mass arrests and atrocities was absurd.[57] Apostle David O. McKay accused the Bolshevik government of splintering families in order to compel loyalty to the worldwide socialist movement.[58] Sjödahl also portrayed Lenin as trying to cash in on the people's religiosity by using theatrics calculated to rival any church claiming to be the earthly kingdom of God. "Strange devices were suspended above the streets [of Moscow] to represent clouds," he wrote. The idea was to represent Bolshevik communism as "Heaven on earth."[59] The danger Mormon observers perceived in Bolshevik trickery was both political and religious.

Pocatello, Idaho Stake President William A. Hyde, a known conservative, agreed with Sjödahl: communism was a religion competing against Mormonism for the heart and soul of the world. In Hyde's writings, like John Taylor's a generation before, the attraction to political messianism was evident. But Hyde's subconscious radicalism lay not in the content of his articles but in the structure of his discourse. Hyde disdained popular government and egalitarian principles. In place of intelligent men who governed through tradition or constitutional devices, the Bolsheviks invoked liberty, equality, and fraternity. Ancient Israel, Hyde argued, had made the same mistake. Into the "theo-democratic" form of government first established by Moses, the Israelites had introduced "elements" of "democracy" to "liberate themselves in measure from Divine authority." Apostasy followed and the Hebrews fell.[60] Hyde, aware of the appeal of communism, borrowed its concepts. Ideologies

---

57. Janne M. Sjödahl, "One of the Signs of the Times," *Millennial Star* 81 (March 20, 1919): 185.

58. McKay admitted his information came from a pre-1917 source. See David O. McKay, June 2, 1919, *Conference Report*, 77.

59. Sjödahl, "One of the Signs of the Times," 185. Similarly, had Babeuf's communist revolt succeeded in 1797, he intended to stage a theatrical display of banners coming from the clouds to celebrate the regenerated republic. See Jacob L. Talmon, *The Origins of Totalitarian Democracy*, 230.

60. William A. Hyde, "Bolshevism in Religion," *Deseret News*, October 15, 1921. For another article suggesting that democratic liberalism had destroyed the unity of Israel, see "Concerning the Jews," *Millennial Star* 62 (June 21, 1900): 386.

often adopt or emulate aspects of rival systems of thought, and Hyde followed this pattern by portraying the migration of nineteenth-century converts to Zion as having "realized the finest dreams of the social democrat." Hyde's resort to the lexicon of Russian communism shows again the influence of secular terminology in Mormon discourse about revolution. Similarly, one historian has shown that leading progressives and socialists of the late nineteenth and early twentieth centuries ironically couched their arguments for labor rights and social improvement within the framework and language of corporatism.[61] Hyde, in co-opting the label of Lenin's original party (the Social Democrats of the 1905 revolution), recapitulated one of the reasons for Mormonism's nineteenth-century appeal in Great Britain.[62]

The fluctuating Mormon response to the Russian revolution was caused in part by the legacy of the French Revolution. Eric J. Hobsbawm suggests that students of global politics viewed revolution not as an event, but as a "process." Russian radicalism had been expected to face the same conservative backlash and moderating pressures as the Jacobins of the French Revolution.[63] The unexpected permanency of the radical Bolshevik government concerned Mormon observers, but the continuity of their attitudes toward revolution remained intact. In emerging revolutionary movements Mormons continued to read providential messages.

The League of Nations as a Revolution in World Affairs

Two types of internationalism vied for Wilson's attention. The first, conservative internationalism, had the advantage of the world's biggest peace organization, the League to Enforce Peace (LEP). The president of the American chapter was former US President William Howard Taft. Chairman of the Senate Foreign Relations Committee Henry Cabot Lodge, Wilson's Republican nemesis, was also a member of the LEP until

---

61. Alun Munslow compares five progressive reformers with the speeches of Andrew Carnegie and finds that they spoke a corporate discourse. See Alun Munslow, *Discourse and Culture: The Creation of America, 1870–1920*.

62. Hyde, "Bolshevism in Religion."

63. Eric J. Hobsbawm, *Echoes of the Marseillaise: Two Centuries Look Back on the French Revolution*, 33–66.

February 1917. Conservative internationalists sought to maintain peace through a stable balance of power. They wanted Wilson to get into the war on the Allied side to punish Germany for disrupting this balance. Those who championed this version of internationalism tended to be Anglophiles, imperialists, and advocates of the gold standard as the only secure basis for currency. They wanted a League of Nations that would impose penalties on the defeated aggressors and prevent the resurgence of their power. Progressive internationalists wanted a League of Nations too, but the similarity to conservatives ended at that point. Progressives stood for disarmament, freedom of the seas, and self-determination for all peoples. Unlike conservatives who blamed Germany, progressives thought that defects in the world system had caused the war—especially imperial and industrial competition. The United States, progressives believed, should use its moral example in addition to legalisms to guide the world to a lasting peace.[64] Wilson's Fourteen Points were clearly a progressive charter, though Wilson did come to believe that German militarism posed a unique threat to global stability.[65]

Several leading members of the Mormon hierarchy were internationalists and embraced Wilson's Fourteen Points, or at least his League of Nations. They saw the League charter as the nucleus of a new divine center around which the people of the world could rally to promote democratic principles. So adamant were they for the League that eleven prominent Latter-day Saint leaders joined the LEP. These included President Heber J. Grant and Apostles Anthony W. Ivins, Richard R. Lyman, John A. Widtsoe, and George Albert Smith. Also appearing on the list is a surprise: Presiding Bishop Charles W. Nibley, an ally of Republican Senator Reed Smoot. Levi Edgar Young of the First Presidency of the Seventy was named as a delegate to the Mountain Congress to promote the League in February 1919. Other well-known Mormons in the LEP include A. C. Rees, future German Mission president; John Q. Cannon, executive editor of the *Deseret News*; and Nephi L. Morris, journalist and former Republican gubernatorial candidate. Also on this list as honorary chairmen are Utah Governor Simon

---

64. Knock, *To End All Wars*, 55–58.

65. A newspaper printed a confidential memo written by Taft in which Taft expressed reservations about the League Wilson proposed. The public revelation strengthened the Senate faction of "Reservationists" opposed to US membership in the League as Wilson wanted it. See ibid., 258.

Bamberger (1917–21) and two former governors, John C. Cutler and William Spry.[66]

The Utah LEP delegation urged a US declaration of war to save the Allied powers, but the views of many of the delegates reflected the economic concerns of the progressives. For them the LEP was a prestigious organization that allowed them to exercise their passion for a united world movement. The content of their speeches and writing reflects the progressive internationalists' desire for decolonization and cultivation of the socioeconomic underpinnings of global peace.[67]

Some Mormon observers opposed the League. Opponents were generally what historians call "strong reservationists." These included David O. McKay, Joseph Fielding Smith, and Reed Smoot. Anti-Leaguer J. Reuben Clark also spoke regularly in Salt Lake City, but he was not a member of the First Presidency until 1933. Clark at the time was serving in the US Attorney General's Office. A loyal Republican with isolationist tendencies, Clark had ironically supported the war to "make the world safe for democracy." He received a major's commission and wholeheartedly prosecuted pacifists.[68] But in 1919 Clark denounced the League in the Tabernacle, charging that Senate ratification would "waste the strength God has given us . . . in petty squabbles over a few rods of miserable European blood-sodden soil." Clark's talk did not go unchallenged; a Mormon group supporting Wilson's League accused

---

66. "Utah Branch League to Enforce Peace," April 1, 1919, Smith Family Papers, box 44, fd. 11; and "Appointment by the Governor as Honorary Delegate for a League of Nations," February 10, 1919, Smith Family Papers, box 44, fd. 11.

67. Mormon leaders who viewed the League within a framework of Anglo-American supremacy and traditional power politics nonetheless accepted the League Covenant. Heber J. Grant felt that the failure to ratify the League imperiled the world with "violent revolution." Junius F. Wells knew the terms of the Versailles treaty were harsh, but hoped it would accomplish its purposes. He and Second Counselor Anthon H. Lund preached that German ambition was "unlimited" and that modern technology had shrunk the oceans, making it imperative that the United States conclude a military alliance with Western Europe to protect the Western Hemisphere. See Anthon H. Lund, April 5, 1918, *Conference Report*, 10–12; Heber J. Grant, October 3, 1919, *Conference Report*, 16, 19; Junius F. Wells, "Comments on the Treaty," *Millennial Star* 81 (May 22, 1919): 328–31.

68. D. Michael Quinn, *Elder Statesman: A Biography of J. Reuben Clark*, 279–80.

Clark of being a traitor.[69] Even Presiding Bishop Charles W. Nibley, a staunch Republican, supported a modified League Covenant.[70] Taken as a whole, Mormon opponents of the League were overwhelmed by supporters. That so many expressed their faith within the framework of Wilsonian internationalism was a testament to the enduring post-millennial belief that man could be God's instrument to transform the world within profane, "calendar" time.

The modern understanding of Wilson's intent with the League of Nations focuses on ideology. Historians N. Gordon Levine, Lloyd Gardner, and David S. Fogelsong have argued that Wilson fashioned policies and used American power to thwart social revolutions.[71] But a more convincing interpretation of Wilson's intentions is proffered by Thomas J. Knock in his book *To End All Wars*. Knock challenges the portrayal of Wilson as a mild reactionary. The president had shunned national aggrandizement and pursued a multilateral world order. Committed to solving the economic problems that were among the causes of World War I, Wilson often found himself cavorting with the more progressive internationalists. Most Mormon observers shared the progressive belief that a new chapter in world affairs was about to begin.

Mormon leaders never equivocated on self-determination and representative government. Before his death in 1918, Joseph F. Smith recognized that all nations contain some "wickedness," but asserted that this does not negate the "inalienable rights of men to organize national governments [and] choose for themselves their own leaders."[72] In Britain, Sjödahl believed the war had put government into the hands of "plain people" and viewed the League Covenant as a world-trans-

---

69. Ibid., 280.

70. Historians have mislabeled Nibley as anti-League, probably because of his association with Smoot. However, Nibley is listed on the "Committee on Information and Speakers" in a Utah chapter LEP document. See "Utah Branch League to Enforce Peace," April 1, 1919, 3, Smith Family Papers, box 44, fd. 11.

71. Levin, *Woodrow Wilson and World Politics*, 7; Lloyd C. Gardner, *Safe for Democracy: The Anglo–American Response to Revolution, 1913–1923*, 162; David S. Foglesong, *America's Secret War against Bolshevism: U.S. Intervention in the Russian Civil War, 1917–1920*, 68–72.

72. Joseph F. Smith, "A Message to the Soldier Boys of 'Mormondom,'" *Improvement Era* 20 (July 1917): 823.

forming, anti-imperialist charter.[73] Apostle James E. Talmage wrote that democracy had been carried to every land "in accordance with Divine intent."[74] Noble Warrum's *Utah in the World War* (1924) recounted the results of the war. Popular government had replaced military despotisms in Germany, Austria, and Russia.[75]

Despite the Treaty of Versailles's punitive excesses, Mormon observers worried about the consequences should the Senate fail to ratify it. Yes, Germany was forced to accept blame for the war and pay the winners for their losses. Germany lost territory to Poland; its colonies in China and the Pacific went to Japan. The German army was reduced to a hundred thousand men and the navy was strictly limited. French troops occupied the Rhineland. But at least the treaty called for a League of Nations, the most important of the Fourteen Points, to correct mistakes in the hoped-for new international order. Follow-on treaties were also determined to punish Germany's allies—Austria, Turkey, Hungary and Bulgaria. Italy was awarded an Austrian province populated by two hundred thousand Austrian citizens; Middle East mandates were carved out of the Ottoman Empire; and the Greeks, with Allied support, invaded Turkey. Continued imperial and anti-democratic habits, Mormon observers believed, were what the world could expect if the US failed in its mission. For progressives like Anthony W. Ivins, it was only this mission—the creation of a "great confederacy of nations"—that had justified American intervention in the war.[76] President Heber J. Grant urged American participation in the League to force Japan to return the Shantung Peninsula to China. Grant believed immediate ratification of Treaty and League "without amendment" was imperative to begin the reconstruction of the world order.[77]

At one point Wilson considered for inclusion in the League Charter a measure that addressed labor conditions and socioeconomic

---

73. Sjödahl, "Birthday of the League of Nations," 5–6.

74. James E. Talmage, "Democracy of American Origin," *Millennial Star* 81 (March 6, 1919): 147.

75. Warrum, *Utah in the World War*, 146. Melvin J. Ballard also discussed the theme of self-determination in a sermon delivered April 6, 1918, *Conference Report*, 64.

76. Anthony W. Ivins, October 8, 1916, *Conference Report*, 67.

77. Heber J. Grant, September 19, 1919, *Conference Report*, 16. Grant repeated the "without amendment" phrase two more times during the speech.

problems.[78] David Starr Jordan, president of Stanford University and regular correspondent with Wilson, spoke in favor of this measure in Salt Lake City. A progressive internationalist, Jordan impressed Apostle Ivins, who filed Jordan's speeches linking issues such as military expenditures to socioeconomic stress.[79]

Mormon observers wanted solutions for economic distortions that had caused the war and triggered revolutions. On October 7, 1917, just prior to the Bolshevik "Red October," B. H. Roberts told a General Conference, "There shall come a better distribution of wealth that is created by a combination of the efforts of men, by their daily toil and the supply of capital that makes possible the labors of men's hands."[80] Joseph M. Tanner accused Austria of violating communal customs in the Balkans in a bid to build an empire that favored the privileged classes. In 1920, while the Red Army was fighting to defeat various anti-Soviet factions in Russia, Tanner presented the workers' cause around the world as a giant engine of reform. "Among millions of the human family," Tanner wrote, "there is an awakening of a new consciousness . . . which has given rise to the demands of labor and which is gradually molding the conduct of the rulers of the world." Tanner rejected violent revolution but adapted some socialist ideas. Workers, for example, were the agents of historical change. Tanner agreed with English and American workers' rejection of Bolshevism, but he also remonstrated in the *Improvement Era* that capitalists often stymied justifiable labor reforms.[81]

Six years later Apostle James E. Talmage might have questioned Tanner's belief that the English worker lacked militancy. In 1926 he was

---

78. Knock, *To End All Wars*, 90–93, 97–98, 260–61.

79. Ivins collected Starr's speeches and writings. The following are examples found in the Anthony W. Ivins Papers: "David Jordan Starr on Building Warships," *Deseret Evening News*, October 14, 1910; "Dr. Jordan on Peace Lookout," *Deseret Evening News*, August 16, 1912; and "Cost of War Mounts Rapidly," *Evening Sun*, March 17, 1918. Starr's connection to Wilson is discussed in Knock, *To End All Wars*, 67–68.

80. Roberts, October 7, 1917, *Conference Report*, 102–3.

81. Joseph M. Tanner, "What the Nations of Europe Are Fighting For," *Improvement Era* 19 (July 1916): 816–19; Joseph M. Tanner, "A New Consciousness," *Improvement Era* 23 (October 1920): 1077–78. On workers as agents of change between the world wars, see Lindemann, *History of European Socialism*, 206–7.

the president of the British Mission. After reminding an audience that Mormons are loyal to their government, Talmage learned that "members who had been present had expressed dissent and manifested feelings that were nothing less than revolutionary."[82]

Overall, leaders in the upper Mormon hierarchy spoke in sympathy with international labor. President Grant warned that unfulfilled expectations among workers would lead to revolution. Should this happen, fault would lie not with the Bolsheviks but with "the conspiracy of speculator and profiteer."[83] When David O. McKay felt he had been overcharged for ferry passage to Naples in Italy, he recorded, "The mercenary commercialists fleece the public! No wonder the people are revolting against the capitalists!"[84] Orson F. Whitney used the context of the war to reprise the universal relevance of the American Revolution. "Justice, freedom, and equality" belonged to the world. "The fetters of tyranny were not stricken for America . . . alone," Whitney reminded a Tabernacle audience. Americans and their allies must "break the chains our brothers wear."[85] George Albert Smith concurred: "The result of this war will be greater liberty for the people generally, better conditions for the working man, and some kind of harmony between capital and labor that will make this world a desirable place in which to live."[86]

Paradoxically, some of these same Mormon leaders adopted a harder line against union activity. Presidents Joseph F. Smith and Heber J. Grant, along with Presiding Bishop Charles W. Nibley, endorsed the "American Plan," a policy that would deny employment to union-affiliated workers. These Mormon leaders tacitly approved of labor crackdowns between 1919 and 1921 but rejected the extremists in the Associated Industries who wished to annihilate unions altogether. Fundamentally, Grant advocated the right to work without compulsion to join a union. But in February 1919 Grant presided over the "Mountain Congress for a League of Nations" held in the Salt Lake City Tabernacle. Printed at the top of the fourth session program was "Labor's Demand for a League

---

82. James E. Talmage, Diary, May 8, 1926.

83. Grant, September 19, 1919, *Conference Report*, 16.

84. David O. McKay, Diary, November 17, 1921.

85. Whitney, April 7, 1918, *Conference Report*, 72, 77.

86. George Albert Smith, Letter to William S. Kline, September 17, 1918, Smith Family Papers, box 44, fd. 10.

of Nations." Nibley was a delegate at this same congress.[87] Eight months later Grant stated to a Church conference, "I am perfectly willing that men shall join labor unions."[88] Perhaps enthusiasm for unionism, labor reform, or outright labor victory over owners was strongest when its prospects were visionary rather than real.

League Defeated—Observers Recalibrate and Take Refuge in Time

At the Versailles peace talks, Wilson encountered opposition from Allied ministers. Unable to formulate a consistent standard for self-determination and other issues, Wilson sacrificed nearly all the Fourteen Points in exchange for Allied endorsement of the League Covenant, which became Article 10 of the Versailles Treaty with Germany. Time, Wilson hoped, would restore the missing pieces. Wilson returned to the United States and hand-delivered the Versailles Treaty to the Senate.

On November 19, 1919, the Senate rejected Wilson's treaty by a 53–38 vote. With it went US membership in the League of Nations. Utah Republican Senator Reed Smoot was among those who voted against the Treaty. But Smoot and other strong reservationists were not the Treaty's only opponents. According to historian Arthur Knock, defections by Democratic senators were as decisive in the League's defeat as reservationist intractability. For the "absolutists," as they were called, Wilson had betrayed internationalism by compromising the Fourteen Points. The absolutists were irreconcilably opposed to a treaty that they believed would perpetuate the old imperial status quo.[89] Smoot's fellow Utah senator, Mormon Democrat William H. King, supported Wilson. King worked hard to persuade reservationists and absolutists to relent in their views, but to no avail.[90]

Most Mormon observers, like Senator King, stood by Wilson to the end. To several general authorities and lower-ranking Church

---

87. "Mountain Congress for a League of Nations," February 21–22, 1919, Smith Family Papers, box 44, fd. 11.

88. Grant, September 19, 1919, *Conference Report*, 13. See also Alexander, *Mormonism in Transition*, 187–89.

89. Knock, *To End All Wars*, 252–57.

90. Leonard Schlup, "William H. King and the Question of League Membership."

leaders, Wilson was a demigod.[91] Support for Wilson was also strong at Church-owned Brigham Young University. Wilson had visited the campus in September 1919 during his famous tour of the country to try to rally popular support for the League of Nations. Students who heard the president's speech urged Utah's senators to vote for the League, as did fifty-two faculty members. Senator Smoot sparked outrage when he replied that he would not vote for the League. The editor of the BYU yearbook, Nels Anderson, publicly said Smoot had the intelligence of a monkey.[92] Fervor among the LDS leadership was so intense that infighting erupted in the Church's highest councils between the majority that supported the League and the minority that opposed it.[93]

Side by side with passion among Mormon observers was doubt. The possibility of vindictive peace treaties, economic depression, and a "Red Scare" in the war's immediate aftermath led to private rumination. Days before the armistice George Albert Smith, an LEP supporter of Wilson, was ready to believe another war would ensue "even more terrible than this."[94] Apostle Smoot confessed a premillennial inclination: nothing but apocalyptic power from heaven could save the world.[95] Junius Wells, the assistant editor of the *Millennial Star*, complained that

---

91. Additional examples of support for Wilson's League include George Albert Smith, Letter to John Barrett, January 1, 1919, Smith Family Papers, box 45, fd. 16; "League Wanted by All the World," *Deseret Evening News*, March 15, 1919; Richard R. Lyman, October 5, 1919, *Conference Report*, 109–11; Richards, October 5, 1919, *Conference Report*, 163–65; Anthony W. Ivins, July 20, 1919, in *Salt Lake Tribune*, August 16, 1919; Janne M. Sjödahl, "The Coming Peace Congress," *Millennial Star* 81 (January 16, 1919): 40–42; and Sjödahl, "Birthday of the League of Nations," 90.

92. Gary James Bergera and Ronald Priddis, *Brigham Young University: A House of Faith*, 175.

93. Mormon leadership response to the League of Nations includes James B. Allen, "Personal Faith and Public Policy: Some Timely Observations on the League of Nations Controversy"; D. Michael Quinn, *The Mormon Hierarchy: Extensions of Power*, 63, 356; Richard E. Bennett, "James E. Talmage and the League of Nations."

94. George Albert Smith, Letter to Nicholas Smith, November 9, 1918, 2, Smith Family Papers, box 45, fd. 3.

95. Thomas G. Alexander, "To Maintain Harmony: Adjusting to External and Internal Stress, 1890–1930," 52–53.

ministers had failed to grasp the spirit of "universal patriotism."[96] In summing up the year 1919, Wells, who criticized ongoing labor strikes as an inappropriate response to the transition from a war footing to a peacetime economy, nevertheless sympathized with the reasons for workingman embitterment:

> The bloody revolution of the Bolshevics in Russia, the continued warfare among the smaller powers of the Near East, the prospect of disastrous economic warfare continuing for generations, have all worked havoc with the illusory notion of a democratic settlement of the world. As a consequence, the proletariat of certain allied countries and America have all but repudiated their respective governments, in their disappointment over the labors of their respective representatives in the Peace Conference, and the apparent impossibility of uniting upon a treaty of peace that should make for prosperity and the general welfare of the world, without imposing unnatural and ungrateful burdens upon the nations.[97]

Ivins tried to sustain himself with pyramidology. The year 1915 had marked the termination of the "Second Dispensation, the destruction of all the present evil institutions, in order to the setting up of the Third Dispensation, the first thousand years of which have been set apart as Christ's Kingdom."[98] But the pyramids proved a false oracle. The United States did not put its signature on the League Covenant—the charter of the new dispensation. Sacred time would not be inaugurated by an American-led League of Nations. No major indicator of God's will had been revealed in history. Instead of a new world order, there was bad news. Chinese warlordism, the invasion of Outer Mongolia by Russian armies, an uprising of Kurds against the British in Iraq, and the Greco-Turkish War were painful reminders of old world chaos.

Devout internationalists among Mormon observers eased their pain by keeping alive the memory of what might have been. When Wilson died in 1924, Ivins eulogized him in the Salt Lake Tabernacle as

---

96. Junius F. Wells, "The Real Covenant of Peace," *Millennial Star* 81 (October 2, 1919): 632.

97. Junius F. Wells, "The Waning Year," *Millennial Star* 81 (December 18, 1919): 809.

98. John Edgar and Morton Edgar, *The Great Pyramid Passages and Chambers*, 1:76. Compare to Anthony W. Ivins, October 3, 1926, *Conference Report*, 19.

"God's instrument."[99] An editorial published in the *Utah Democrat* used the text of a conference talk by Ivins to put the American rejection of the League into a context Mormon Utah might understand:

> Had the nations with one mind and one heart entered the League and made a beginning at overcoming war the condition of the world would be far different today. But it turned out the people of today are but little different from the ancient children of Israel. Moses went high upon the mountain to get the divine law which the finger of God had carved on the tablets of stone for the salvation of men. While he was away the people set up an image of gold and worshipped it.[100]

Like Moses ascending Sinai, three years earlier the most "inspired statesman" in the world had gone to the "pinnacle of human achievement." Wilson's League, like Moses's Law, would have reconciled man's efforts with God's will. The blessing would have been a single, rationally unified world. But "while he was receiving the light and inspiration . . . the people went back to the mire of materialism and the vision was partially blotted out. They could not endure the new revelation." Like a romantic revolutionary, Wilson died on "the scaffold," and his vision had shared his fate. But over the "grave of the patriot who led the way, and over the multitude of sorrow and woes that will come because of the nation's stubbornness, the light shall burst forth anew."[101]

In 1918, as war raged in Europe and revolution convulsed Russia, Talmage had intimated that the "portentous events of the current day" do not signal the "end of time."[102] He made the statement when several Mormon leaders were pushing hard for ratification of the League of Nations. Mormon observers viewed the establishment of a central world tribunal as more than a diplomatic instrument. Much like Wilson's, theirs was a messianic belief in universal redemption from the accumulated mistakes of history. Disappointed by the Senate's non-ratification of the

---

99. Janne M. Sjödahl, "The Passing of President Woodrow Wilson," *Improvement Era* 27 (March 1924): 448–51.

100. "It Might Have Been," *Utah Democrat*, December 9, 1922. Ivins's talk was also published as Anthony W. Ivins, October 8, 1922, *Conference Report*, 84–93.

101. "It Might Have Been." For another rumination revealing disappointment with the war's resolution, see Alice Louise Reynolds, "The Editor Abroad," *Relief Society Magazine* 12 (May 1925): 255.

102. James E. Talmage, April 7, 1918, *Conference Report*, 159.

League, Mormon observers in Utah were again compelled to affirm faith in gradual historical progress above the immediacy of an earthly millennium. Faith in horizontal revelation and acceptance of the time it takes for God to work His will among men served to buoy the hopes of Mormon observers like Talmage after World War I. The *Millennial Star* called the League of Nations a "long step forward on the road to human progress."[103] Apostle Orson F. Whitney spoke of history as "inter-related links . . . of one great chain. How many dispensations there are, I know not," he said, but "whatever their number or [their] names . . . each from the beginning, has prepared the way for its successor."[104]

Latter-day Saint Praise of the Post-revolutionary Soviet Union

Many internationalists who were disappointed after World War I emerged in the 1920s and early 1930s as supporters of the Soviet Union.[105] For churchmen, the degree of religious freedom tolerated in Russia became a benchmark in assessing the new communist government. Soviet attitudes toward religion were erratic. Programs intended to weaken religious commitment included the formation of anti-religious societies such as the League of the Godless. The Soviet government also arrested Orthodox prelates, prohibited the celebration of Christian holidays, and made it illegal to teach religion because religion had been an instrument of the ruling class. At the same time, the Soviet government realized that pushing too hard stiffened popular resistance. Near the end of Joseph Stalin's first Five-Year Plan for the National Economy of the Soviet Union (1932), antireligious propaganda began to subside. In 1936 the new Soviet constitution conceded that "freedom of religious worship and freedom from anti-religious propaganda is recognized for all citizens."[106]

---

103. Sjödahl, "Birthday of the League of Nations," 90.

104. Orson F. Whitney, April 4, 1927, *Conference Report*, 97. For another contemporary example of the view that history was unfolding with teleological purpose, see Edward H. Anderson, "Prophecy and History," *Improvement Era* 27 (October 1924): 1133.

105. Filene, *Americans and the Soviet Experiment*, 187–210.

106. Conquest, *Religion in the USSR*, 25–27. Islamic regions of the USSR did not recover from government repression until after World War II. See

Soviet policies elicited either suspended judgment, acceptance on legal principle, or outright excitement among Mormon observers. In 1929 J. Reuben Clark, future first counselor in the Church's presidency, was an undersecretary in the US State Department. At that date, the US had not yet extended diplomatic recognition to the new Russian regime. Clark told some Soviet representatives that

> I was not frightened of their communism [and] I considered that the Russian people had a perfect right to have any sort of government they wished; that the kind of government which they had [Stalinist] was their business and not mine; that I would regard it as most improper and unfriendly for my government to send propagandists to persuade the Russian people that theirs was a bad form of government, and that ours should be adopted instead thereof.[107]

Clark maintained this perspective the rest of his life. He campaigned vigorously against domestic communism but wished Godspeed to any other country that wanted it.[108]

Mormon observers who had viewed Latin American revolution with favor searched for the most positive signs emanating from fluctuating communist attitudes toward religion. Ivins stressed Jewish emancipation and religious freedom. In 1929 he suggested that the Ottoman collapse and the Russian revolution had enabled more Jews to migrate to Palestine. As for the rest of the Russian people, "the most down-trodden, priest-ridden people in the world who profess to be civilized," they could now worship as they pleased.[109]

Ballard went further in his praise. Communism, he suggested, was the "crucible" in which Russia would find "liberty and freedom."[110] He

---

ibid., 67–76.

107. J. Reuben Clark, Work Diary, January 18, 1929, quoted in Quinn, *Elder Statesman*, 259.

108. Quinn, *Elder Statesman*, 259.

109. Anthony W. Ivins, October 6, 1929, *Conference Report*, 100. After World War II an article stated that Latter-day Saint activities were easier to conduct in Soviet-controlled East Germany than in the western zone. See Arthur Gaeth, "Our Members in the Russian Zone," *Improvement Era* 49 (September 1946): 566, 584.

110. Melvin J. Ballard, April 6, 1925, *Conference Report*, 132.

emphasized that social and political revolution had to precede missionary activity in the Soviet Union:

> I am sure that God is moving in Russia. Much as we are disturbed over the oppression that is waged against religion in that land today it is not a new thing, for that has been the order for ages. But I can see God moving also in preparing the way for other events that are to come. The field that has gone to wild oats needs to be plowed up and harrowed and prepared for a new seed.

Collectivization and industrialization would forge a new environment in Russia, Ballard suggested, that would release the minds of the people for philosophical rumination. Land and machinery under control of the *soviets* would more equitably distribute the rewards of economic activity. The people, provided with the material well-being that allowed time for meditation, could then contemplate the Mormon message when it came:

> It may seem appalling to us but God is using events [in Russia] to break up and destroy an older order of things, and the result will be the accomplishment of God's purposes within a very short period of time, whereas it normally may have taken generations.[111]

Ballard apparently viewed the Five-Year Plan as a dialectical force. Time was the ally of Mormon and Soviet purposes.

Mormon assessments of Russia weathered doubt from Salt Lake City's Protestant clergymen. At a March 24, 1930, meeting in the Tabernacle, several area churchmen denounced the Soviet Union based on reports that the regime was suppressing religious liberty. Reverend Arthur L. Rice countered that news from Russia was "not trustworthy" and that the available information was "not sufficient to warrant a formal protest from the United States." President Heber J. Grant, advised by Ivins (his counselor) and other leading apostles and educators, also suspended judgment: "If the reports are not true, we are not protesting; but if they are true they violate the beliefs of the church."[112]

Churchmen and intellectuals who visited the Soviet Union "put the best possible face on communist repressions of religion and economic experiments in Russia."[113] To the Protestants' optimism Latter-day

111. Russell M. Ballard, ed., *Melvin J. Ballard: Crusader for Righteousness*, 243.

112. B. H. Roberts, *Comprehensive History of the Church of Jesus Christ of Latter-day Saints, 1830–1930*, 6:534.

113. Marty, *Modern American Religion*, 2:282–83.

Saint professors added their own affirmations. In 1929 the American Association for Jewish Colonization invited Brigham Young University President Franklin S. Harris to lead a group of agricultural experts to Birobidzhan, Siberia (the Jewish Autonomous Region) to investigate the possibility of creating an alternative Jewish homeland. Jews were indeed enjoying unprecedented freedom under the Bolsheviks. Anti-Semitism dissipated and the Soviet government promised to end economic and social inequality.[114] The Russian spirit impressed Harris even if socialism seemed to be a trial-and-error enterprise. The people were "sacrificing and struggling that better human [conditions] might be worked out, . . . even though in many cases their methods appeared to be so much in error."[115] Concerning the religious restrictions Harris echoed Ballard. The Soviet Union's trajectory might accelerate an otherwise lengthy historical process. "Russia never had the Reformation," he wrote, "and as a result has to do in a short time what Western Europe required several hundred years to do. Naturally, there are a lot of growing pains coming out of the situation."[116] In the *Improvement Era*, Harris commended Soviet efforts to free workers for more leisure time.[117]

BYU agronomist Thomas L. Martin likewise praised Russia. After touring Russian communes in 1930 Martin wrote that socialism had surpassed the achievements of the czars. The Soviet "experiment" had proliferated religious denominations, curbed military adventurism, and reduced the influence of the Orthodox Church.[118] This approval of Soviet society did not go unnoticed by critics, who accused Harris and Martin of teaching communism at BYU.[119]

---

114. Robert Weinberg, *Stalin's Forgotten Zion. Birobidzhan and the Making of a Soviet Jewish Homeland: An Illustrated History, 1928–1996,* 14–15, 28.

115. Bergera and Priddis, *Brigham Young University,* 16.

116. Ibid.

117. Franklin S. Harris, "A Demonstration of Leisure-Time Activities in Russia," *Improvement Era* 33 (January 1930): 183–85.

118. Bergera and Priddis, *Brigham Young University,* 191–92; Thomas L. Martin, "What of Russia?" *Improvement Era* 34 (May 1931): 381–84, 392.

119. Bergera and Priddis, *Brigham Young University,* 192.

The Will to Believe

Some Mormon observers, before events of the mid-1930s showed how insensible Soviet communism was, believed that post-revolution Russia stood for the denial of imperialism, the raising of living standards, and the destruction of religious monopoly. The "will to believe" in the Soviet system was strong. Despite the starvation caused by communist agricultural collectivization under the first Five-Year Plan, American intellectuals clung to the belief that communism offered an alternative socioeconomic philosophy to the perceived greed of the 1920s. The Great Depression of the 1930s appeared to many progressive thinkers to be the final crisis of capitalism.[120]

Historian Paul Hollander writes that "a significant portion of Western intellectuals" traveled to distant places to find authentic social revolution, the future of mankind being played out in a radical state.[121] Intellectuals visiting post-revolutionary Russia and Mexico generally rejected the economic individualism of the United States. Host governments gave these "political pilgrims" carefully orchestrated tours, which avoided unsavory realities and showed them what they wanted to see. With their objectivity compromised by a combination of selective sampling and a sense of alienation from their own society, these travelers "exchanged their more traditional role of hardbitten social critic to that of the trustful admirer, and . . . their more typical stance of skeptical questioning gave way to zealous affirmation."[122] Dedicated to their cherished values of social improvement and utopian faith, intellectuals traveling to the Soviet Union indulged the façade.[123]

Mormon intellectuals resembled their American counterparts as they tried to rescue themselves from the banality of assimilation. History had produced an ambivalent situation. Latter-day Saint leaders living after 1890 were caught in transitory era between early Mormon

---

120. Paul Hollander, *Political Pilgrims: Travels of Western Intellectuals to the Soviet Union, China, and Cuba*, 74–101.

121. Ibid., ix.

122. Ibid., 102–76, 416. For other works on the positive reviews accorded to Stalinist Russia, see Eugene Lyons, *The Red Decade: The Stalinist Penetration of America*; and Harvey Klehr, *The Heyday of American Communism: The Depression Decade*.

123. Hollander, *Political Pilgrims*, 3–39.

militancy and later Mormon embrace of the mainstream culture that the hierarchy had historically scorned. In extending sympathy to other people's revolutions and, significantly, to the Soviet Union, Mormon leaders projected their own agency. Evidence of other radicals at work showed that history moved in a specific direction and that conditions were being prepared for future Mormon expansion. At this point, Mormonism's progressive millennialism compared to the odyssey of the American Left. "Striving for another world in defiance of reality," writes Diggins, was the "Left's categorical imperative." Mormons, forced to accept reality, experienced the same inner philosophical tension, for they too sought the "impossible victory" while adjusting to the "inevitable defeat."[124]

As the future direction of the Soviet Union remained uncertain, a revolutionary wave swept South America. Perhaps, Mormon observers came to believe, revolution suffused with Latino values would restart the world movement where Europe and Mexico had left off.

---

124. John Patrick Diggins, *The Rise and Fall of the American Left*, 23.

CHAPTER 10

THE GOLDEN AGE OF REVOLUTION IN SOUTH AMERICA, 1925–31

Missionary Work or Socio-religious Radicalism?

The Mormon move into South America coincided with a general American Protestant missionary effort. In 1919 the Protestant Committee on Cooperation devised proselytizing strategies and divided South America into geographical areas assigned to different churches. The Committee, meeting from 1925 to 1929, softened its view of Catholicism, emphasized personal transformation, and focused on converting the upper classes. During the early 1930s the Protestant churches championed a middle path between leftist revolution and fascism, fashioning themselves as the "spearhead of . . . progressive, modernizing, participatory democracy."[1] The Church of Jesus Christ of Latter-day Saints embraced the outlook of its Protestant co-religionists. However, the Mormon outreach was on the lookout for more revolutionary possibilities. The Mormon incursion into South America coincided with Mexican President Plutarco Calles's nationalization of the Catholic Church. Indianism and the demise of the *Porfiriato* had invigorated Mormon observers. And despite the uncertainties of the Mexican political situation, Mormons sailing to South America to open it for missionary work hoped Mexico would serve as an example for the rest of the hemisphere.

The energy that had driven Mormon observers prior to the 1890s still had enough steam to generate a revolutionary vision for Latin America. Animated by the radical faith that inhered in their recapitulation of the Hebraic experience, they had no intention of merely exporting capitalistic and pluralistic American values. Those values were part of the problem

---

1. José Miguez Bonino, "Protestant Churches in Latin America since 1930," 583–88.

to be corrected: the isolated individual seeking his own ends with no understanding of God's plan. This was what Mormonism proposed to heal. From Mormonism's beginning, writes historian Philip Barlow, Joseph Smith intended something bigger than a church, community, or even an empire. He wanted to "mend a fractured reality." Polygamy, priesthood, and family "sealing" would repair humans' alienation from God and each other, "making the world of human (and divine human) systems cohere again."[2] Smith would have resonated with the diagnosis of G. K. Chesterton: "It was not the conception of life outlined in the Declaration of Independence that was wrong; it was the thousand things that have come since to perplex it. . . . America has become the dumping ground of all the most dismal ideals of decaying epochs in Europe from Calvinism to Industrialism."[3] In the Mormon view, the act of revolution would clear the ground of those "dismal ideals," making way for something new. The flame had died in the United States, but revolution in foreign lands might light the path to a more meaningful future.

Mormon observers were displaying some of the symptoms of disillusioned intellectuals. Disappointed by failure to establish a liberal peace at the end of World War I and alienated from the materialism of their own culture, intellectuals often looked to distant or unfamiliar countries engaged in social remodeling because in them the perfect society might be in the making. In the Mormon adaptation, a mission to South America kept utopian hope alive and made Mormon observers feel they still stood at the cutting edge of sacred time. South America was inhabited by Lamanites, a covenant people. The Mexican Revolution had torn down Mexico's old order and opened vistas into the next dispensation of time. Mormons hoped that South America would follow suit. There was a feeling that a new age was beginning that would allow the Church to practice an older Mormonism—the original version never intended to remain just a church. The goal was a literal kingdom of God.

Consecration of South American Revolution

Mormonism, like Protestant and Pentecostal denominations, has grown rapidly in Latin America since the 1950s, but for a long time it

---

2. Philip L. Barlow, "To Mend a Fractured Reality: Joseph Smith's Project," 32.

3. G. K. Chesterton, "The Virtues of Revolution," *Fortnightly Review* 131 (May 2, 1932): 586–87.

was not evident that Mormonism would thrive there.[4] In 1851 Apostle Parley P. Pratt sailed to Chile, possibly hoping that an ongoing revolution there would open the country to Mormon missionaries. Pratt's effort failed because he could not speak the language well enough and because the wrong side prevailed in the civil war: the ruling conservatives defeated the liberal movement whose reforms were necessary for a Mormon planting.[5] Pratt had been optimistic about the mission's potential. Two-thirds of South Americans, he believed, were "descendents of Lehi," people ethnically destined to embrace the Mormon faith.[6] However, after Pratt's departure, South America remained outside Mormon activity for seventy-five years.

The impetus to organize another mission effort came from two sources. In 1923 Andrew Jenson submitted a favorable report to the First Presidency following his tour of Latin America. Also, German converts who migrated to Argentina wrote letters to Salt Lake City beginning in 1924 requesting missionaries to support their branch.[7] On

---

4. On Mormon and Protestant growth in Latin America, see James R. Moss, R. Lanier Britsch, James R. Christianson, and Richard O. Cowan, *The International Church*; David Clark Knowlton, "Mormonism in Latin America: Toward the Twenty-first Century"; and David Martin, *Tongues of Fire: The Explosion of Protestantism in Latin America*. In 1993, 31 percent of the Mormon Church's 8.7 million worldwide members lived in Latin America. See Gustav Niebuhr, "Milestone Highlights LDS Growth in Latin America," *Deseret News*, December 12, 1994, A1. Mark L. Grover predicts Latin America will hold more than 50 percent of all Church members by 2020. See Mark L. Grover, "Maturing of the Oak: The Dynamics of LDS Growth in Latin America," 85–86.

5. For Pratt's efforts in Latin America, see Parley P. Pratt, *Autobiography of Parley Parker Pratt*, 396–402; Peter L. Crawley, ed. and comp., *The Essential Parley P. Pratt*, xx; South American Mission, Manuscript History and Historical Reports, 1:1851–52; Gordon Irving, "Chile"; and David Clark Knowlton, "Parley Pratt and the Problem of Separating Latin and Anglo America," 198–99.

6. Parley P. Pratt, "The Gospel in South America," *Latter-day Saints' Millennial Star* 14 (February 15, 1852): 54–55 (hereafter *Millennial Star*).

7. Events leading to the twentieth-century opening of the South American Mission are treated in Theodore M. Tuttle's vignettes of the various South American missions in "South America, Land of Prophecy and Promise,"

September 3, 1925, Church President Heber J. Grant, in conjunction with the Twelve Apostles, commissioned Apostle Melvin J. Ballard, Rey L. Pratt, and Rulon S. Wells to open the South American Mission.[8]

Melvin J. Ballard, the group's leader, had held numerous positions before his calling to the Quorum of the Twelve in 1919. Since 1898 he had been an industrialist and businessman, the owner of a woolens mill in northern Utah and founder of the Logan Commercial Club. He also served as a local political leader. His first passion, however, was Church work; consequently, he was considered one of the Church's most energetic evangelizers and orators. Ballard presided over the Northwestern States Mission from 1909 to 1919. Taking a special interest in Native Americans, he established a school for reservation Indians. During the 1920s Ballard was the managing editor of the *Improvement Era*, in which capacity he upgraded the magazine's editorial content and boosted circulation to forty-five thousand by 1929. Thousands of young adults knew Ballard as president of the Church's Young Men's Mutual Improvement Association (YMMIA). In 1936 Ballard was named to chair the Church's welfare program, which was a difficult assignment as the Great Depression pounded Utah. Ballard's affinity for Indians led him to take a strong interest in Latin America during his tenure as an apostle. Of the thirty-nine general authority visits to Colonia Juárez between 1919 and 1939, Ballard made fifteen.

Ballard was an insightful leader. His views on politics, science, and society paralleled the New Deal consensus of the 1930s, tinctured with a streak of support for revolutionary development in foreign nations. The influence of his father shaped his attitude toward the working classes.

Improvement Era 66 (May 1963): 352–74. See also Frederick S. Williams and Frederick G. Williams, *From Acorn to Oak Tree: A Personal History of the Establishment and First Quarter Century Development of the South American Missions*, 17–34. Ballard kept a diary, but it was lost sometime after 1966. Excerpts related to the opening of the South American Mission are found in M. Russell Ballard, ed., *Melvin J. Ballard: Crusader for Righteousness*, 75–84. For the tour Andrew Jenson and Thomas Page made through Latin America, see South American Mission, Manuscript History and Historical Reports, 1:1923–24; Journal History of the Church, May 11, 1923, 1–37; and Williams and Williams, *From Acorn to Oak Tree*, 18–20.

8. Health problems forced Wells to return to Salt Lake City on January 14, 1926.

He embraced science as "the greatest ally the Mormon Church has," but qualified that embrace with careful analysis of both its blessings and its spiritual dangers.[9] Contemporaries credited Ballard for understanding "the temporal as well as the spiritual needs of man." His experience and progressive views "fitted him," in the words of the *Improvement Era*, "for leadership in these modern days."[10]

The move into South America resulted partly from the changing dynamics of immigration. Millions of Europeans were heading to South America now that the United States had cut immigration quotas to 3 percent per country. For decades LDS mission efforts had focused heavily on northern Europeans, especially potential migrants to the United States. As the mission program's target audience traveled to a new set of receiving countries, the missionaries followed.[11]

Equally important, however, was a surge of Mormon interest in the conversion of Indians. When Ballard and his colleague Rey L. Pratt discussed the significance of their South American Mission, they emphasized the Indians' identity as the "sons and daughters of father Lehi, who have dwindled in unbelief."[12] "The people that we go to preach to are of the house of Israel," Pratt declared. "They are our brethren and sisters, they are our blood relatives, they have an inheritance upon this land, they are heirs to the Gospel. The Lord has foretold us in words of plainness this day that has now dawned upon us."[13] Pratt scoured indigenous cultures in search of Book of Mormon connections and captivated US audiences with lectures and slide presentations on Aztec and Mayan ruins.[14] Notes found among

---

9. Melvin J. Ballard, April 9, 1930, *Report of the Semi-annual Conference of the Church of Jesus Christ of Latter-day Saints*, 154 (hereafter cited as *Conference Report*).

10. See Biographical Register for sources on Ballard's life.

11. Melvin J. Ballard, October 5, 1925, *Conference Report*, 129–30.

12. Ibid., 130. Also reported in Melvin J. Ballard, "Answering the Call," *Millennial Star* 88 (March 18, 1926): 166. Ballard asked European Mormons to contact him if they had relatives who had migrated to South America.

13. Rey L. Pratt, October 6, 1925, *Conference Report*, 170.

14. "President of Mission Has Picture of Ruins Recently Discovered," *Deseret News*, October 12, 1921; and Rey L. Pratt, October 5, 1924, *Conference Report*, 143–44.

his papers, taken from Diego Muñoz Camargo's *Historia de Tlaxcala* (1892), chronicle Indian legends about three "ends" of the world. The Bible and the Book of Mormon, Pratt believed, record the first two: the great flood in the time of Noah and the destruction that accompanied Christ's visit to the Americas after his resurrection. The third would come "by fire."[15] Light, fire, and revolution were themes that surfaced whenever Mormon observers spoke of South America's march into the future.

A banquet was held for the three newly commissioned South American missionaries on October 28, 1925. Anthony W. Ivins spoke at the event. Comparing their journey to his own nine-month foray on horseback into Mexico fifty years earlier, he said, "this trip will take the brethren into Book of Mormon lands. We shall watch their work with interest."[16] The reading of a poem by Ruth May Fox commemorated the elders' departure. The "men of Israel" (Mormon elders) would "teach the remnant of that land the prophecies to understand." The light of spiritual knowledge would "twinkle forth the glorious news" like a "luminous holy flame." In the glorious future that would begin in South America, God would be the "rising sun," igniting the utopian faith so that "Mankind may reach the perfect day."[17] The opening of South America would activate the Hebraic covenant. Exposure to divine knowledge would awaken peoples of Indian descent to their spiritual heritage and invite them to rebuild the world.

On December 6 the *Voltaire* anchored in the Rio de la Plata, Buenos Aires, Argentina. German Mormons greeted the three missionaries on

15. Rey L. Pratt, notes on Quetzalcoatl, 4–5, Rey L. Pratt Papers, box 2, fd. 18. For essays on revolutionary millennialism absorbed by colonized peoples and adapted to their native legends of cosmic regeneration, see Sylvia L. Thrupp, ed., *Millennial Dreams in Action: Studies in Revolutionary Religious Movements*, 55–165.

16. "Banquet, Program, and Reception," *Improvement Era* 29 (December 1925): 167–68.

17. Quoted in Orson F. Whitney, "For Auld Lang Syne," *Improvement Era* 29 (December 1925): 170–71. The imagery of Fox's poem parallels Ballard's own rhetorical use of the phrase "light of Zion." See Melvin J. Ballard, April 6, 1921, *Conference Report*, 170.

the docks.[18] A week later the first six converts—all Germans—were baptized.[19] The missionaries made numerous observations. Pratt wrote:

> Buenos Aires is a wonderful city . . . much like Mexico City, but much more so. . . . I mean there is evidence of more widely spread . . . wealth. . . . Avenida de Mayo, the principal street, runs from east to west between Plaza Mayo and Plaza Congresso [and] there are many small parks. . . . The people here are fine looking but there does not seem to be nearly as great an Indian mixture as there is in Mexico.

Pratt also commented on the religious situation. When he saw a statue of the Virgin of Carmen featured in a religious parade, he wrote that processions of this size had not been allowed in Mexico "since the time of Juárez."[20]

The Latter-day Saint emissaries quickly arranged meetings with state and national representatives. American Ambassador Peter Augustus Jay was not enthusiastic about Mormons coming to do missionary work in Argentina. Pratt wrote that the ambassador "seems to be something of the same type as Henry Lane Wilson in Mexico."[21] The mayor of Buenos Aires, Carlos M. Noël, received the missionaries more warmly. "We are up against a real issue in trying to start something here," Pratt wrote. "However, we have been given to understand that there is religious freedom."[22] Later contacts with authorities in Callao, Peru were similarly cordial. Privately Pratt confided in his diary that he had been assured of religious liberty in Peru, but the Catholic Church is "the state church and receives subventions."[23] Generally, the missionaries gained permission to preach in most of the places they visited in Argentina and Peru. The opening of Tucumán, Argentina to LDS mis-

---

18. Rey L. Pratt, Diary, December 6, 1925.

19. Pratt, Diary, December 13 and 16, 1925; Rey L. Pratt, Letter to Mary Pratt, December 21, 1925, Pratt Papers, box 2, fd. 9; and "Passing Events," *Improvement Era* 29 (March 1926): 519.

20. Pratt, Diary, December 8, 1925.

21. Rey L. Pratt, Letter to Mary Pratt, December 15, 1925, 6, Pratt Papers, box 2, fd. 9. For Peter Augustus Jay as the US ambassador to Argentina during this period, see David Shavit, *The United States in Latin America: A Historical Dictionary*, 297, 412.

22. Rey L. Pratt, Letters to Mary Pratt, December 8, 9, and 11, 1926, Pratt Papers, box 2, fd. 9; Pratt, Diary, June 3, 1926.

23. Pratt, Diary, August 18, 1926.

sionaries in 1927 was the first time non-Catholic missionaries had been allowed to enter the town.[24]

On Christmas Day in 1925, the missionaries dedicated all of South America for missionary work. They began by singing "The Morning Breaks" and reading promises in the *Book of Mormon* regarding the salvation of the Lamanites. Then, under a tree in a Buenos Aires park, Ballard declared that he as an apostle did "turn the key, unlock, and open the door for the preaching of the Gospel in all these South American nations, and . . . rebuke and command to be stayed every power that would oppose the preaching of the Gospel in these lands."[25] Ballard also said, "we are bearers of these glad tidings to the people of the South American nations, and we also pray that we may see the beginning of the fulfillment of the promises contained in the Book of Mormon to the Indians of this land."[26] Referring to Simon Bolivar (1783–1830), the leader of independence movements in several South American countries, Ballard thanked God for the freedom made possible by the "valiant liberators of these lands." And in the same revolutionary spirit that had ended colonialism in the Western Hemisphere, Ballard prayed that righteousness would obtain "and full liberty for the preaching of the gospel prevail."[27] When Ballard said "Amen," the missionaries gave egress to their emotions. Many Europeans would receive the gospel, they concluded, but "ultimately the great import of the mission would be to the Indians."[28] Ballard's January 1926 dispatch to the *Deseret News* concerning the event portrayed an apostle fired with passion.[29] Recalling the event at a later General Conference, Ballard said he

---

24. South American Mission, Manuscript History and Historical Reports, March 14, 1927, December 6, 1930, and January 8, 1931.

25. "Prayer: Dedicating the Lands of South America to the Preaching of the Gospel," *Improvement Era* 29 (April 1926): 576.

26. Ibid., 575.

27. Ibid., 576.

28. Ibid., 577.

29. "Outlook Promising," *Deseret News*, January 11, 1926. See also excerpts from Melvin J. Ballard, Letter to Heber J. Grant, December 15, 1925, in *Liahona: The Elders' Journal* 23 (January 12, 1926): 312. On July 4, 1926, Vernon Sharp (one of the first four missionaries in Argentina) recorded Ballard's prediction that "The South American Mission will be a power in the Church." See Ballard, *Crusader for Righteousness*, 84.

and the others had felt that "Father Lehi's children" were on the verge of a revolution that would break the "shackles, politically" and hasten the "day of retribution . . . [and] deliverance."[30]

Ballard, Pratt, and the first four missionaries who joined them worked vigorously. They held meetings, translated texts, printed tracts, strengthened the local membership, countered Baptist agitation, and gave film and slide presentations. Ballard alone distributed 11,500 tracts. Pratt wrote a broadside in February 1926 to announce a general meeting at which he and Ballard would preach and then field questions. The meeting promised a seventy-five-frame slide show of ancient American civilizations and an account of God's promise to redeem the Indians. Two hundred people attended.[31]

The Mormon elders immersed themselves in the study of South American history. Pratt recorded that he was "studying Argentine history and found that the early conquistadors were just as cruel to the Indians here as they were in Mexico. . . . The Indians were enslaved and reduced to a remnant."[32] Pratt especially trained his attention on social conditions. In the provincial capital of San Salvador de Jujuy, where the Argentine flag had first been "consecrated" after the Argentine War of Independence a century before, Pratt learned that "90% of the people here are Indian and seem to be fine people. Good place for missionary work."[33] Traveling between Juliaca and Sicuani, Peru, Pratt recorded in his diary that "the land and Indians are in the hands of great land owners. The Indian is in just as great peonage and poverty as they ever have been in Mexico."[34] Nonetheless, Pratt believed that missionary work would yield results, especially in the upper Andes where Spanish and Catholic rule were less pronounced.[35] Ballard, too, took notes related to

---

30. Ballard, April 9, 1930, *Conference Report*, 156.

31. Rey L. Pratt, "Gran Estreno," February 28, 1926, Pratt Papers, box 2, fd. 18; Williams and Williams, *From Acorn to Oak Tree*, 26–27. A day-by-day account of the mission's activities is recorded in South American Mission, Manuscript History and Historical Reports, November 11, 1925–June 14, 1926.

32. Pratt, Diary, January 15, 1926. A synopsis of Ballard's observations is found in his sermon delivered October 3, 1926, *Conference Report*, 38–40.

33. Pratt, Diary, July 28, 1926.

34. Ibid., August 8, 1926.

35. Ibid., July 28 and 31, 1926.

culture, economics, and society. His observations led him to conclude that Indians lived in social conditions that ranged from colonial patterns of landholding to mixed economic activity that presented a "high state of civilization."[36] American mining operations and other forms of investment seemed to have displaced European influence. Ballard also wondered what effect popular Hollywood films would have.[37]

The missionaries left for home in late July of 1926, stopping in Peru and Bolivia along the way to inspect Incan ruins.[38] Ballard rendered a favorable report of the mission at the next General Conference. Despite— or perhaps because of—his sympathy with the South American Indians, Ballard announced that the Spanish conquest was providential. Without this phase in history, violent though it was, there would never have been a common South American tongue. The imposition of Spanish and Portuguese, Ballard believed, would facilitate both missionary work and the future construction of Zion.[39] "We met no opposition, as far as the government is concerned," Ballard concluded, "notwithstanding there is a union of church and state in all the South American republics." What Catholic opposition there was would not last long. Ballard predicted future upheaval. Bolivia and Peru "shall pass through the same changes that are going forward in Mexico."[40]

Ballard then began to shake the Tabernacle with revolutionary rhetoric. "I have wept over [the Indians] . . . as I looked upon these poor, wretched souls," he said. "God is crying repentance to the world in the testimonies of thunder, of lightning and tempests." Ballard declared that people everywhere "shall come out of their serfdom and bondage into the light of freedom in religious, as well as in political matters," and that the "day of retribution and their redemption . . . is not far distant."[41] Ballard spoke the liturgical chant of a millennialist. South American

---

36. "South American Mission," *Liahona: The Elders' Journal* 24 (October 5, 1926): 186.

37. Ibid., 186–87.

38. Pratt, Diary, August 6–7, 10, 12, 1926.

39. Ballard, October 3, 1926, *Conference Report*, 36–37. Andrew Jenson made a similar observation in a sermon delivered October 9, 1921, *Conference Report*, 120.

40. Ballard, October 3, 1926, *Conference Report*, 37. Ballard published a review of South American Indians in the *Children's Friend* (June 1929): 12.

41. Ballard, October 3, 1926, *Conference Report*, 39.

Indians, downtrodden for centuries, would unite to "thresh the nations." His discourse also paralleled the language of social revolutionaries. The responsibility for action, Ballard reminded listeners, "rests upon this Church." He prayed that when the present dispensation had passed and God had redeemed the world, the LDS Church would be found having discharged its obligation as the vanguard of the millennium.[42]

Ballard longed for something beyond middle-class comfort. "Men have seen visions and have dreamed dreams."[43] The establishment of utopian kingdoms in Latin America would rally the people of the world to the Mormon banner. People would stream from the "East and the West, from the North and the South, to learn of our ways and to walk in our paths." Then, Ballard added, they would build a "civilization the like of which the world does not know."[44] Ballard's speech echoed the words of Fyodor Dostoevsky:

> The Golden Age is the most implausible of all dreams. But for it Men have given up their life and strength; for the sake of it prophets have died and been slain; without it people will not live and cannot die.[45]

At a time when utopian contemplation was largely dead, suggests one scholar, Ballard's optimism is noteworthy.[46] It was the same univer-

---

42. Ibid., 40.

43. Ballard, April 9, 1930, *Conference Report*, 154.

44. Ballard, October 3, 1926, *Conference Report*, 40–41. John Dewey used similar words to express his conviction about Russia. In 1928 he said, "Perhaps the most significant thing in Russia . . . is not the effort at economic transformation, but the will to use an economic change as the means of developing a popular cultivation, especially an aesthetic one, such as the world has never known." See John Dewey, *John Dewey's Impressions of Soviet Russia and the Revolutionary World: Mexico—China—Turkey*, 31.

45. Fyodor Dostoevsky, *A Raw Youth*, 462. Dostoevsky (1821–81) became involved with a group of utopian radicals around 1846, but imprisonment (1849–54) and subsequent service in the czarist army turned him against Western liberalism and atheism. In 1861, as editor of the Russian magazine *Vremja*, Dostoevsky featured an anonymous article titled "Mormonism and the United States." I'm grateful to Vladimir Zakharov for bringing this to my attention.

46. Frank E. Manuel and Fritzie P. Manuel, *Utopian Thought in the Western World*, 10.

salism contemplated by Mazzini and Marx, and Ballard admitted the probability of violence to achieve it.

Depression and the South American Predicament, 1930–31

As Mormon observers had anticipated, revolution struck South America in 1930. Revolutions toppled governments in Argentina, Bolivia, Brazil, and Peru. In Argentina, the most politically stable country of all and the one with the largest middle class, a military junta drove President Hipólito Yrigoyen into exile.[47] Yrigoyen's fall has been attributed to several factors. The Argentine export sector had crumpled under the weight of economic depression. Yrigoyen's practice of awarding army commissions to radicals in order to enhance his populist image rankled the officer corps. Divisions within Yrigoyen's party, rumors of his senility, and popular disenchantment with government austerity measures further weakened his grip. On September 6, 1930, with considerable popular backing, General José Félix Uriburu overthrew the government, announcing that he would liberate Argentina from the "old order." This was not a simple military power grab, but rather the vanguard of a popular uprising led by army officers with nationalistic instincts.[48]

In neighboring Bolivia, the overthrow of President Hernando Siles bore features of a social revolution. Bolivia's government had been abusing the Indians and the working classes for decades. From 1874 to 1880, the government, in collaboration with the tin industry, had divested Indians of their land, converting them into *hacienda* peons.[49] Tin exports were a Bolivian economic staple until their peak in 1929, but then global economic depression caused a collapse in prices. As the price of tin fell and Bolivian military expenditures consumed 20 percent of the budget, discontent with Siles grew. The struggle began on June 12, 1930.

---

47. For Argentine political history between 1900 and the revolution of 1930, see David Rock, *Argentina, 1516–1982: From Spanish Colonization to the Falklands War*, 164–213. For the role played by the Argentine military, see ibid., 212; Marvin Goldwert, *Democracy, Militarism, and Nationalism in Argentina, 1930–1966: An Interpretation*, xix, xviii, 4, 23–29, 70; and Mark Falcoff, "Argentina: The Twentieth Century," 155.

48. Goldwert, *Democracy, Militarism, and Nationalism in Argentina*, 28.

49. Erick D. Langer, "Bolivia: Since 1825," 370.

Battles occurred in places ranging from the Argentine frontier to the streets of La Paz, where students fought side-by-side with military cadets against pro-Siles forces. On June 27 Siles abdicated. Revolutionary General Carlos Blanco Galindo, who took over as caretaker president after Siles's ouster, stopped an outright military takeover by calling a general election. After consolidating the revolution, Galindo relied on the capable Daniel Sánchez Bustamante to administer the country until Daniel Salamanca took victory after the election. The provisional government took immediate steps to revise the constitution, reward the revolutionary students, and initiate other reforms.[50]

Ideology played a greater role in the Bolivian revolution than it did in the Argentine revolution. A combination of workers, students, reformist army officers, Indians, and willing political leaders formed the nucleus of Bolivia's revolution. The student and worker contingent, in particular, was animated by Marxist and radical thought; resentment against vestiges of the *latifundia* (plantation) system motivated Indians. The rebel manifesto read, "Our revolution is a *Social Revolution*, which comes to save Bolivia, demanding economic transformation of the nation and the liberation of the force and brains of the producing classes, which is the only basis on which to build true republican and democratic institutions."[51] One scholar has suggested that the "radical movement [in Bolivia] in the late 1920s and early 1930s finally began to assume a decided revolutionary advanced reformist tone more in harmony with leading radical elements elsewhere in the hemisphere."[52]

Revolution in neighboring Brazil was sparked by regional conflict and a collapse of coffee prices. As in other South American countries, young Brazilian army officers viewed themselves as the catalyst for national rejuvenation. This led to the *Tenente* (Lieutenants') Revolt of 1924–27. Led by Luís Carlos Prestes, the "Prestes column" conducted a fifteen thousand-mile march through the interior of Brazil, harrying government forces in protest of the fraud and corruption that had brought Artur Bernardes to the presidency. As one historian put it, the nation-

---

50. The Bolivian revolution is covered in Herbert S. Klein, *Parties and Political Change in Bolivia, 1880–1952*, 97–98, 105–29; and Waltraud Q. Morales, "Daniel Salamanca," 14.

51. Robert Hinojosa, *La revolución de Villazón* (1944), quoted in Klein, *Parties and Political Change in Bolivia*, 110.

52. Klein, *Parties and Political Change in Bolivia*, 122.

alism inherent in the Prestes column was a "military expression of the middle-class against dominance by coffee growers."[53] The rebellion failed and the Prestes column disbanded, but many of its veterans participated a few years later in the successful Brazilian Revolution of 1930.[54]

The 1930 revolution over presidential succession began when a stand-off between the Brazilian states of São Paulo and Minas Gerais made it possible for a swing state, Rio Grande do Sul, to lead a national movement that redressed the defects of the republican constitution.[55] On October 3, 1930, a liberal-military alliance launched the revolution. One historian suggests that Brazilians preferred social reform guided by popular elites to the vagaries of political liberty.[56] Rio Grande do Sul politician Getúlio Dornelles Vargas was installed by the revolutionaries as president.[57] Vargas enacted labor legislation and arranged state

53. Ronald M. Schneider, *"Order and Progress": A Political History of Brazil*, 112. Ilan Rachum draws a different conclusion. Despite the heroic legend surrounding the Brazilian *tenentes*, Rachum argues, the real prerequisite to the 1930 revolution was the emergence of left-oriented nationalism and ideology, the fountainhead of which was Brazilian political philosopher Alberto Torres (1865–1917). See Ilan Rachum, "Nationalism and Revolution in Brazil, 1922–1930: A Study of Intellectual, Military, and Political Protesters and of the Assault on the Old Republic," 1–59, 297–300.

54. On the Prestes column and the vague nationalism it inspired, see Gene D. Pace, "Brazil's 'Long March': Opposition to the Economic Elite of the Old Regime"; Jose Murilo de Carvalho, "Armed Forces and Politics in Brazil, 1930–1945"; Michael L. Conniff, "The Tenentes in Power: A New Perspective on the Brazilian Revolution of 1930"; Peter Flynn, "The Revolutionary Legion and the Brazilian Revolution of 1930"; Ann Quiggins Tiller, "The Igniting Spark—Brazil, 1930"; Jordan M. Young, "Military Aspects of the 1930 Brazilian Revolution"; and Schneider, *"Order and Progress,"* 110–11.

55. Jordan M. Young, *The Brazilian Revolution of 1930 and the Aftermath*, 81–97. The mission's official history detailed how the cities of Minas Gerais, Paraíba, and finally São Paulo joined the Rio Grande do Sul garrison of Porto Alegre to topple Artur Bernardes's hand-picked successor. See South American Mission, Manuscript History and Historical Reports, October 5, 1930.

56. Alceu Amoroso Lima, "Voice of Liberty and Reform, in Brazil," 299–300.

57. For an account of the October 3, 1930, Brazilian Revolution, see Schneider, *"Order and Progress,"* 115–18.

purchase of surplus coffee. His defense of national interests represented a "non-ideological program of fascism" that appealed to left- and right-wing statists alike.[58]

In Peru, revolution took the form of a military-led operation with backing from every socio-economic and ethnic group in the country. In 1924 farm workers, industrial workers, and the small middle-class united in Peru's first mass party, the American Popular Revolutionary Alliance (*Alianza Popular Revolucionaria Americana*, or APRA), under the guidance of socialist intellectual Víctor Raúl Haya de la Torre and Marxist theoretician José Carlos Mariátegui. As APRA's popularity rose, President Augusto B. Leguía (1919–30) tried to repress it. He built a national constabulary that rivaled the army in firepower. During the 1920s he cracked down on students and labor activists. In the election of 1930, Leguía's Civilista Party resorted to fraud to prevent Haya de la Torre from winning the presidency. Economic depression exacerbated popular grievances and stretched the government's resources to the limit. To make matters worse for Leguía, the United States ruled in favor of Colombia in a border dispute. National chaos set the army in motion. Luis Miguel Sánchez Cerro, a young nationalistic colonel with fascist sympathies but backed by a "groundswell of civilian nationalist" sentiment, toppled Leguía and the army's high command. Cerro won the election of 1931 due largely to the credit he received as the one who had actually terminated Leguía's rule.[59]

The United States recognized the new South American governments.[60] Between the stock market crash and the rise of Nazi Germany, the revolutions of 1930 did not cause much consternation. American

---

58. Rollie E. Poppino, "Vargas, Getúlio Dornelles," 262–64; and Eulália Maria Lahmeyer Lobo, "Brazil: Since 1889," 427.

59. For the Peruvian revolutions see Rex A. Hudson, ed., *Peru: A Country Study*, 37–41, 269–70; Vincent Peloso, "Peru: Since Independence," 370; and Daniel M. Masterson, *Militarism and Politics in Latin America: Peru from Sánchez Cerro to Sendero Luminoso*, 32–34. On Cerro's political leaning see Robert J. Alexander, *Prophets of the Revolution: Profiles of Latin American Leaders*, 93.

60. Argentina, Peru, and Bolivia received US recognition on September 18, 1930. The Brazilian government of Getúlio Vargas was recognized on November 8. See *Papers Relating to the Foreign Relations of the United States, 1930*, 1:387–88, 451; 3:756–57.

policy toward Latin America had already undergone significant changes during the 1920s. Washington's inclination to overreact to southern disturbances was weakened by growing Latin American stability, reduced fear of European intervention, and the realization that interventions rarely paid off and hardly ever implanted democracy. President Herbert Hoover exercised the restraint that these trends dictated. He downplayed the right of the United States to intervene in the affairs of Latin American nations, extended recognition to regimes that came to power by unconstitutional methods, and refrained from landing troops in Panama or Cuba in 1931–32. In 1933 he ordered the Marines out of Nicaragua. High US tariffs thwarted greater cooperation, but Hoover's policies laid the groundwork for his successor's "Good Neighbor Policy" toward Latin America.[61]

National periodicals evaluated the revolutions by different criteria. Some sympathized with the deposed presidents, especially Leguía.[62] The Catholic paper *Commonweal* condemned the "nihilism" from which the revolutions stemmed.[63] *Current History* criticized the "personalist" nature of most South American governments but hoped that those remaining would learn from the Bolivian upheaval that statesmanship, negotiation, and good relations with the United States were the proper path to development.[64] The *Saturday Evening Post* featured a liberal capitalist appraisal. The article suggested that Brazil's revolutionary president befriend his country's "business element" to develop

---

61. Wayne S. Smith, "The United States and Latin America: Into a New Era," 279; Donald Marquand Dozer, *Are We Good Neighbors? Three Decades of Inter-American Relations, 1930–1960*; James William Park, *Latin American Underdevelopment: A History of Perspectives in the United States, 1870–1965*, 133–35; and Joan Hoff Wilson, *Herbert Hoover: Forgotten Progressive*, 200–202.

62. "Peru's President Out," *Literary Digest* 106 (September 6, 1930): 8; "Leguia: 'Lincoln' or 'Mussolini' of Latin America?" *Literary Digest* 106 (September 20, 1930): 32, 34; and "A Prolonged Bastile for the 'Roosevelt of Peru,'" *Literary Digest* 110 (August 1, 1931): 32.

63. E. R. Pineda, "Spanish-American Revolutions," *Commonweal* 12 (October 22, 1932): 629–32.

64. Henry Grattan Doyle, "South America," *Current History* 32 (July 1930): 771–74.

Brazil's rubber export potential to the United States.[65] The *Nation* believed that although a well-intentioned middle- and lower-class revolution had ousted Peru's Leguía, rule by Cerro was probably the preamble to military dictatorship.[66]

The majority of American press coverage, however, was optimistic about the social ramifications of the revolutions. An article in *Current History* concluded that "with a wise governmental policy in the hands of young Bolivians, the nation could become before long one of the most prosperous of Latin America."[67] *Living Age* featured an interview with a young Latin American who rejected European culture in favor of cultivating a more authentically American one.[68] *New Republic* urged careful investment in Peru to ensure social progress and not just the enrichment of elites.[69] *Nation* celebrated Peru's "brilliant Marxist writer" José Carlos Mariátegui. He spoke for Latin American youth seeking to "revive the Indian influence in art and thought."[70]

Argentina's revolution attracted the most support in the United States. *World Tomorrow*, a magazine associated with the Social Gospel movement, assessed the historical and future implications of the September 1930 revolution in Buenos Aires. Just as the St. Simonians had seen the "new Argentina" in 1816 as a promised land from which to stage a global positivist revolution, the article likewise hoped the twentieth-century turnover would do the same for liberalism: "The crowd destroyed . . . that for which they had no respect and which they wished to obliterate. Once more Argentina has a remarkable opportunity to take her place among the great nations. . . . Amid all the rejoicing the voice of democracy and law is heard."[71] Other stories in *The Literary Digest*,

---

65. Isaac F. Marcosson, "Brazil and the Future," *Saturday Evening Post* 204 (January 9, 1932): 92, 96.

66. Arnold Roller, "Revolt in Peru," *Nation* 131 (September 17, 1930): 291–94.

67. Diomedes de Pereyra, "The Constitutional Triumph in Bolivia," *Current History* 32 (September 1930): 1149.

68. "South America Changes Heart," *Living Age* 341 (February 1932): 559.

69. Lawrence Dennis, "What Overthrew Leguia," *New Republic* 64 (September 17, 1930): 117–22.

70. Roller, "Revolt in Peru."

71. Anne Guthrie, "A New Argentina," *World Tomorrow* 13 (November 1930): 462–63.

Outlook and Independent, and *New Republic* portrayed the overthrow of Yrigoyen and other dictators as a sign of emergent democracy.[72]

Two articles appeared in *Foreign Affairs.* One commended the Hoover government for de facto recognition of revolutionary regimes. Too often the United States had fallen back on "trading recognition for a consideration," or invoked the "Holy Alliance" façade of withholding recognition until a constitutional reorganization occurred. A second article said, "These recent revolutions in South America are evidence of social progress rather than of retrogression [and] cannot seriously be denied."[73]

Books published in the United States also reviewed Latin America favorably during this era. Philip L. Green, for example, spoke favorably of the French revolutionary influence, the diversity and pride of Indian heritage, the gains made in social legislation, and the desire for democracy reflected in the South American revolutions. He urged his countrymen to display "sympathetic understanding and, above all, an open mind" toward Latin America.[74]

Mormon Observers Revel in Revolutionary Jubilation

The office of the LDS Church's South American Mission, led by Mission President Reinhold Stoof, welcomed the revolutions. The killing of students in Buenos Aires, Argentina justified a "change of government in the country."[75] Stoof sent a *Book of Mormon* to the new Argentine President José F. Uriburu, who acknowledged the gift with

---

72. "Irigoyen Out," *Outlook and Independent* 156 (September 17, 1930): 94; "'Contagious Revolt' in Latin America," *Literary Digest* 106 (September 20, 1930): 10; and "The Argentine Revolution," *New Republic* 64 (September 17, 1930): 112–13.

73. Lawrence Dennis, "Revolution, Recognition, and Intervention," *Foreign Affairs* 9 (January 1931): 205–21; and Clarence H. Haring, "Revolution in South America," *Foreign Affairs* 9 (January 1931): 296.

74. Philip Leonard Green, *Our Latin American Neighbors,* 20–38, 107–8, 157–58, 160–63, 173; and Samuel Guy Inman, *Latin America: Its Place in World Life,* 417–26.

75. South American Mission, Manuscript History and Historical Reports, September 5, 1930.

thanks.[76] The mission office also reported favorably on the revolutionary Liberal Alliance in Brazil. The revolutionaries showed "good discipline and were . . . received with enthusiasm by the population in nearly all the cities."[77] The Mormon press afforded the revolutions similarly favorable reviews.[78]

Other Mormon observers went beyond the immediate requirements of justice for dead students or the chance to welcome a new president. They looked for evidence that the South American revolutions were seismic events endorsed by God. Anthony W. Ivins used affairs in Latin America to reiterate the concept of revelation through history. Speaking at the October 1930 General Conference, he referred to "the parts of Brazil, Argentina, and Peru which were in open rebellion to their governments" as the fulfillment of scriptural prophecy that said that the chosen people of Israel, once downtrodden, would rise again. In the fashion of early revolutionaries who believed revolution a force of nature, Ivins compared revolutionary action to the voice of God: "He would speak to the people of the world by the voice of thunderings, and the voice of lightnings," and then Christ would come in "power and great glory."[79]

The most prolific and enthusiastic proponent of the revolutions was Melvin J. Ballard. Ballard transmitted his assessment to Church members in an October 1931 *Improvement Era* article titled "The Significance of South American Revolutions." The article's first page was illustrated with a sketch of a revolutionary wearing a sombrero, with ammunition belts crisscrossing his chest. Mormons, Ballard wrote, are especially interested in foreign affairs because "Theirs is a world church, and occurrences everywhere have a broader significance to them than to most other people. Therefore . . . the revolutionary disturbances among men [and] the pre-

---

76. Ibid., June 14, 1931.

77. Ibid., September 5, 1930.

78. See "Brazil Revolt," *Deseret News*, October 31, 1931; "Salvador," *Deseret News*, January 28, 1932; and "Cuba's New Revolution," *Deseret News*, September 6, 1933. For the Sergeants' Revolt in Cuba, see Louis A. Perez, "Cuba, c. 1930–59," 430–55. Sergeant Fulgencio Batista (later promoted to colonel) threw his support behind disaffected liberal Carlos Mendieta, and then ruled a string of successive puppet governments until his own overthrow by Fidel Castro in 1959.

79. Anthony W. Ivins, October 5, 1930, *Conference Report*, 118–19.

dicted signs of the times have a special meaning."[80] Ballard's article reviewed the revolutions in Argentina, Bolivia, Brazil, and Peru. Ballard devoted the first part of the article to the political, economic, and social activators of each revolution. The topics of literacy, land, Catholic political influence, and imperialism headed the docket.

First, Ballard said, literacy requirements for voting had served to disfranchise the common people. This was a deliberate strategy by elites to control the political systems of South American countries by effectively barring the lower classes from the political process. As a result, Ballard charged, "there is only one way the majority of the people can express themselves, and that is through a revolution."[81]

Second, Ballard exposed the unfairness of land tenure. He traced the historical pattern, showing how colonial systems of labor and land tenure had concentrated land in the hands of few. The situation was exacerbated after the early nineteenth-century wars of independence, when army officers and soldiers loyal to the new governments were rewarded with chunks of Indian land. Ballard illustrated the results: "Eighty-five per cent of the land is owned by fifteen per cent of the people."[82]

Third, Ballard highlighted church-state relations. The union of church and state in most Latin American countries perpetuated elite rule and made it hard for Ballard and his fellow missionaries to proselytize.[83] Ballard saw South American revolutions as necessary precursors to future severance of the church-state connection. "Liberty," he concluded, "must come before the Gospel message can be very effectively

---

80. Melvin J. Ballard, "Significance of South American Revolutions," *Improvement Era* 34 (April 1931): 318.

81. Ibid., 317. Frank Tannenbaum concluded the same. When societies become divided by class and illiteracy, "No compromise is possible between God and the devil on any issue, [making] the acceptance of a sudden and violent revolution the only way out in theory—and if you grant the premises, in fact." See Frank Tannenbaum, "The Prospect of Violent Revolution in the United States," *Scribner's Magazine* 89 (May 1931): 522.

82. Ballard, "Significance of South American Revolutions," 318. Compare to Susan E. Ramírez, "Haciendas," 162–63.

83. Compare Jeffrey L. Klaiber, "Anticlericalism," 106. Ballard identified Chile as the only South American country with separation of church and state. See Ballard, October 3, 1926, *Conference Report*, 37.

proclaimed among the millions of Indians."[84] In the meantime, Ballard and President Stoof urged missionaries to prepare themselves for the rigors of South American service.[85] Finally, Ballard supported both the nationalistic and socialistic implications of the South American revolutions. He sympathized with South American anger over the high 1930 US tariff, which restricted South American exports to the United States. Concerned about European encroachment in the Western Hemisphere, Ballard also pointed out the humiliating rebuff of Germany following that nation's attempt to intervene in Peruvian internal affairs.[86] Expropriations such as Argentina's nationalization of the oil industry in 1925 left Ballard unfazed. Nor did Ballard ever show any special enmity toward Marxism, which was beginning to gain a little influence in several Latin American countries due to the success of the Russian and Mexican revolutions.[87] Military involvement in the revolutions also posed no problem for Ballard. He wrote of General Carlos Galindo as a "liberator and reformer" and was encouraged by Bolivian army collaboration with the students and the people in the overthrow of Siles.[88] Ballard was in the company of left-of-center writers like Carleton Beals, who admitted that disciplined armies could be useful in safeguarding revolutionary governments from reactionary elements.[89]

---

84. Ballard, "Significance of South American Revolutions," 319.

85. Journal History, February 14, 1931, 3; and Reinhold Stoof, "The South American Mission," *Improvement Era* 31 (October 1928): 1054.

86. Ballard, "Significance of South American Revolutions," 318. For German machinations see "The Bolivian Turn-Over," *Literary Digest* 106 (July 12, 1930): 10; and Pereyra, "Constitutional Triumph in Bolivia," 1144.

87. Hudson, *Peru: A Country Study*, 39–41, 269–70; Rock, *Argentina*, 200–201. On the negligible impact that communism had on South America during this period, see Sheldon B. Liss, *Marxist Thought in Latin America*; Rollie E. Poppino, *International Communism in Latin America: A History of the Movement, 1917–1963*; Klein, *Parties and Political Change in Bolivia*, 97–98; and Harry E. Vanden, *National Marxism in Latin America: José Carlos Mariátegui's Thought and Politics*.

88. Ballard, "Significance of South American Revolutions," 318. Ballard mistakenly gave Galindo's first name as "José."

89. Carleton Beals, *Mexican Maze*, 44. Beals and Samuel Inman identified fascism in Latin America as a greater threat than communism and urged hemispheric solidarity against it. See Carleton Beals, *The Coming Struggle*

At the core of Ballard's beliefs was the inevitable triumph of the Indian people. According to Ballard, the events of 1930–31 portended a new beginning for South American Indians. Around 1650 the Indian population in South America had reached its nadir. At that time only about 5 percent of pre-conquest population had remained. Beginning in the early eighteenth century, however, the Indian population in several Latin American regions had begun to recover. Then, during the middle decades of the nineteenth century, liberal governments, land owners, and armies had renewed their repression of Indians In Argentina, as elsewhere, disease and displacement accounted for a large proportion of Indian decline. By the 1880s, Argentine military operations had subjugated the country's last Indian territories.[90] Bolivian policies were similarly brutal. In 1921 the government of Juan Bautista had ordered the army to crush an Indian revolt in the village of Jesús de Machaca, and in 1923 Bautista had permitted the massacre of mine workers at Uncía. Four years later Hernando Siles had acquiesced in the killing of hundreds of Indians in the Chayanta uprising.[91] Ballard was aware of these repressive measures. His condemnation of them surfaced in his support for revolutionary action as the only way to stop the destruction of Indian culture. Once the Lamanites rectified their historical condition through revolution, Ballard believed, knowledge of Christ's gospel would prepare them for the final task of redeeming Zion with their North American Anglo-Mormon partners. Revolution would satisfy the requirements of both social justice and prophecy.

Ballard's view of the Indians differed from Pratt's in one vital respect. Ballard believed that conversion to Mormonism would alter the Indians' genetic code and make them more white.[92] Ballard also be-

---

for Latin America; and Inman, *Latin America: Its Place in World Life*, 314–23, 346–49.

90. For General Julio A. Roca's campaign in Argentina in 1879–80, see Falcoff, "Argentina: The Twentieth Century," 150; Langer, "Bolivia: Since 1825," 370; Karl H. Schwerin, "The Indian Populations of Latin America," 41.

91. Waltraud Q. Morales, *Bolivia: Land of Struggle*, 52; Langer, "Bolivia: Since 1825," 371–72.

92. Ballard, "Significance of South American Revolutions," 320; Ballard, *Crusader for Righteousness*, 81. For a review of Ballard's racial typing, see Lee Copeland, "From Calcutta to Kaysville: Is Righteousness Color-Coded?" 90. The Book of Mormon teaches that as Indians accept the gospel

lieved this racial transformation would improve the Indians' social status and increase their capacity for self-rule.[93] On the other hand, Ballard showed some signs of influence from Pratt and radical "Indianists" who exalted non-European traits. Indianists, according to historian Alan Knight, believed in the autonomous development and special cultural contribution of the Indians while maintaining their racial identity.[94]

In addition to Indians, Ballard also noticed the prominent role of students in the South American revolutions. Several reporters covering South America emphasized that the young were the driving force in many of the revolutionary social changes. *Current History* praised the "patriotism and ambition" of the students.[95] In *The Nation* Anita Brenner wrote that the youth of Latin America rightfully looked to anti-imperialist role models like Rafael Sandino and Haya de la Torre.[96] Crane Brinton, writing in the 1930s, noted that "weak and decadent societies do not undergo revolutions. . . . Revolutions are, perversely, a sign of strength and youth in societies."[97]

University students had been involved in popular uprisings, anti-clerical movements, and university reform movements throughout Latin America since the 1890s.[98] In 1918 a movement known as *La Reforma*

---

their dark-colored skin will turn whiter (2 Ne. 5:21; Jac. 3:8; 3 Ne. 2:15).

93. The Anglo-Saxon picture of the alternately Negroid, feminine, and childlike Latin American is treated in Michael H. Hunt, *Ideology and U.S. Foreign Policy*, 61–62; and Park, *Latin American Underdevelopment*, 90–91. A Mormon version is found in Philip Foremaster, "Chastened but Not Forgotten," *Improvement Era* 26 (September 1923): 995–97.

94. Alan Knight, "Racism, Revolution, and *Indigenismo*: Mexico, 1910–1940," 81.

95. Pereyra, "Constitutional Triumph in Bolivia," 1149.

96. Anita Brenner, "Student Rebels in Latin America," *Nation* 127 (December 12, 1928): 668–69.

97. Crane Brinton, *The Anatomy of Revolution*, 263; James Billington, *Fire in the Minds of Men: The Origins of the Revolutionary Faith*, 199–200, 275, 389.

98. The first organization with heavy student involvement was the Civic Union of the Youth (*Union Cívica de la Juventud*), which formed the core of the barricade fighters in the abortive 1890 revolution against Argentine President Miguel Ángel Juárez Celman. In 1892 students of the Student Federation in Bolivia had unsuccessfully attempted to divorce the Catholic

(the Reform) began in Argentina, and a similar movement arose in Peru around the same time. Influenced by the Mexican Revolution, Marxism, and the democratic forces unleashed by World War I, students at the universities of Córdoba, Argentina, and San Marcos, Peru demanded more control over the curriculum. As one Argentine student put it, "We rebelled against an administrative system, against a method of teaching, against a concept of authority."[99] In Peru, students formed a major constituency in Haya de la Torre and Mariátegui's APRA. Further developments in student organization occurred in Bolivia. Radical intellectuals in Cochabamba who founded the Federation of Bolivian University Students (*Federación Universitaria Boliviana*) in 1928 called for nationalization of natural resources, agrarian and labor reform, and integration of Indians into Bolivian life. By 1929, they called for outright social revolution. Ironically, both Hernando Siles of Bolivia and Yrigoyen of Argentina endorsed the early efforts of the university activists.[100]

Ballard joined those who magnified the students' role, citing Bolivia as a telling example. The revolutions, Ballard said, "are supported and often brought about by the students, the most intelligent part of the citizenship of those countries."[101] And indeed, historians Waltraud Morales and Samuel Inman have both emphasized the leadership role of Bolivian students in what was more of a "popular street revolt" than a classical military coup. Students stood side-by-side with military cadets in the face of machine-gun fire, and it was the students who "induced the workmen to participate."[102] Ballard hailed the emerging generation as a force that would erase ethnic and class distinctions. "A great body of Indians," he wrote, "marched into the [Bolivian] city of La Paz and offered their thanks to the students who led the revolution."[103] From youthful aspirations progress would ensue. Along with General Galindo and "the people," Ballard assured his readers that the students in Bolivia "and in the other republics" were planning "great political reforms."[104] The student subculture, feared by European conservatives

---

Church from the state. See Rock, *Argentina*, 159–60.

99. Ibid., 200.

100. Robert J. Alexander, "Bolivia: Organizations," 377.

101. Ballard, "Significance of South American Revolutions," 320.

102. Morales, *Bolivia: Land of Struggle*, 53; Inman, *Latin America*, 456–67.

103. Ballard, "Significance of South American Revolutions," 320.

104. Ibid., 318. For the most prominent young leaders voicing opposition

during the nineteenth century, had become in Ballard's mind a catalyst of hemispheric social justice.[105]

For Ballard, temporal and spiritual salvation were intertwined: revolution and the rise of the Indians were part of the second coming of Christ. World War I had not damaged Ballard's millennial hopes. Progress, though tragically interrupted, had continued. Sacred time for Ballard was a synthesis of pre- and postmillennialism. Christ was coming soon, but in contrast to the classical premillennial teaching that the moment of the advent would destroy wickedness and transform the world through divine power, Ballard conceived the advent as the culmination of a constructive, human process. He envisioned Indian emancipation, the overthrow of old regimes, and the triumph of democracy and technological progress. After man had accomplished his part in the divine plan by evangelizing the world and building up Zion, the latter-day promise would be consummated: Christ would return and unify all nations and peoples under a single kingdom of God.

Events convinced Ballard that the moment of millennial fruition was near at hand. Revolution in South America reprised the excitement Mormon observers felt during the 1848 revolutions. There was no trepidation. "I would prefer to be on the earth today, in the year 1930," Ballard said, "rather than any other period the world has ever known."[106] From time to time Ballard referred to natural disasters as "signs" of the approaching eschaton. He did not obsess about them, but the edge of immediacy remained. Ballard admitted that he did not know the exact moment, but thought there was "reason to believe that we are coming to the close of the period of the times of the Gentiles." Then, Ballard added, "dawns a new day."[107] The "gentile" phase of Mormon recruitment in northern Europe had peopled the Rocky Mountains. Now, Ballard concluded, God was opening a new phase in the nations of Latin America.

---

to the coffee oligarchy in Brazil, see Boris Fausto, "Brazil: The Social and Political Structure of the First Republic, 1889–1930," 828.

105. On the role of students in European revolutions, see Billington, *Fire in the Minds of Men*, 136–37, 389–99, 402–3.

106. Ballard, April 9, 1930, *Conference Report*, 153.

107. Ibid., 155. Other examples of Ballard's millennialist views are found in Ballard, April 9, 1922, *Conference Report*, 84; and Ballard, April 8, 1928, *Conference Report*, 116. See also Robert W. Smith and Elizabeth A. Smith, *Scriptural and Secular Prophecies Pertaining to the Last Days*, 83.

Reminiscing on his and Pratt's days in Buenos Aires, Ballard anticipated the day "that the shackles, politically, would be broken, the day of retribution would come, the day of deliverance, and that [the Indians] would come into a full realization of the promises of the Almighty."[108]

Ballard reiterated the Mormon belief in revelation through history and progress through revolution. Fascists and reactionaries might block political reform and resist redistributive justice, but "out of each struggle and conflict will come victory for truth." Ballard combined the divine and secular dimensions of Latin American revolutions. "These numerous revolutions are steps toward [an] end," he wrote. They would promote sociopolitical conditions conducive to missionary work. "The Latter-day Saints do not, therefore, see disaster in these political disturbances, but rather progress, growth, and development."[109]

Ballard was not just offering an interpretation of revolutions; he was issuing a call for Mormons to nourish them. After reviewing the progress made in Mexico, Argentina, and Chile toward the disestablishment of religion, Ballard asked, "Now what shall we do?" The reply was militant:

> Our sacred duty is to stand by the fires that have been kindled, keep them ablaze that they shall never die, that they shall never perish. . . . For this is the age when truth shall be triumphant and victorious, [when] error, darkness, and superstition, whether in the church or in the state, shall perish.[110]

The imagery of light and fire continued the tradition of revolutionary symbolism in Mormon literature. The tendency for revolutionaries to diagram the world in geometric shapes was evident when Ballard drew a circle around the revolutionary movements and placed Mormonism at "the hub and the center."[111] Further, Ballard recapitulated man's partnership with God. From the epicenter the Latter-day Saints would prepare the world for a "glorious" future:

> You Latter-day Saints . . . though you too were cast into the wilderness, driven away, in your isolation God has been with you. He is preparing to bring you out of your isolation, even as he did Joseph, to

---

108. Ballard, April 9, 1930, *Conference Report*, 156.
109. Ballard, "Significance of South American Revolutions," 320.
110. Ballard, April 9, 1930, *Conference Report*, 155.
111. Ibid., 157.

glorify you and to make you the saviors of the whole house of Israel, the light of the world.[112]

Still, human effort was merely preparatory to the final consummation by Christ. Ballard attacked religious collusion in government: "Union of church and state under the leadership of the head of a church, is not a principle that is in harmony with modern democracy."[113] However, the division of secular and ecclesiastical power was temporary. Ballard divided history into two phases. In the first, man fights for political liberty and separation of church and state. That much, revolutions had achieved. In the second phase, Christ returns and church and state "shall be united again." The end of religious and national pluralism inhered in the ideals of medieval millennialists, proponents of social revolution, and nineteenth-century Mormon theo-democrats. But it had "never been given to mortal man" to consummate universal plenipotentiary power, Ballard said. Christ would receive a world renewed by revolution and the Saints, but would govern as "King of kings in matters political while he also presides as Lord of lords in his Church."[114]

An Exercise in Hope

From Latin America Ballard hoped to reconstruct the world. Humanity would be elevated. Obsolete political and social forms would yield to divine rationalism and millennial happiness. Since the 1840s, Mormon observers had narrated this process by subconsciously drawing from the rhetoric of the Left. The vision only slowly constricted until the Cold War closed it off altogether. In the meantime, Ballard believed in Latin America's future. He championed student protest. He stood for the liquidation of the alliance between landowners, the Catholic Church, and foreign imperialists. He wanted a more equitable distribution of wealth through a form of industrial democracy. And finally, he believed Indians would be integrated into civil society and would ultimately play a leading role in revolutionizing the hemisphere prior to the millennium. Ballard's platform followed the outlines of the socialist, indigenist reform program of Peru's Haya de la Torre and Mariátegui.

---

112. Ibid., 155.
113. Ballard, "Significance of South American Revolutions," 320.
114. Ibid., 320; and Ballard, April 9, 1930, *Conference Report*, 157.

Both men rejected Russian-imported communism and incorporated moral and religious overtones into their programs to mobilize workers and peasants.[115] Whether through democratic means or violence, Ballard embraced a similar vision of the future.

Ballard identified the South American revolutions as steps toward national development and separation of church and state, but failed to see that they brought little in the way of social change. Each coup came swiftly, and, except for Bolivia, without much violence, leaving little time for lengthy reflection. Given the timing of his *Improvement Era* article and his speeches, Ballard could not have foreseen that as a result of these revolutionary takeovers, fascism would take hold in several South American countries. Viewed in its historical context, the quality of his analysis compares favorably to contemporary pundits.

Many of the revolutions during this pivotal time in South America were army-led coup d'états. They had broad popular appeal, however, as working classes, middle classes, intellectuals, Indians, and nationalists came together in different combinations to offer their support. Large and diverse segments of the affected nations' populations supported what appeared to be spontaneous democratic movements to replace a decayed order with one that was fresher, younger, more progressive, and more adaptable to the crush of the Great Depression. Each revolutionary movement acted to free its host country from inefficiency, arbitrary government, economic hardship, and political corruption. Although the revolutions rattled the status quo, little was permanently achieved in the way of democracy or benefit for the poor. Neither were Indian nationalists able to fulfill Book of Mormon prophecies. Colonial injustices continued to afflict Lehi's children. Despite revolutionary advances, Indians did not achieve the critical mass necessary to grow Zion in the Americas. Looking back, it can be argued that only Mexico experienced real sociopolitical revolution between 1810 and 1940. The other Latin American revolutions simply replaced one group of ruling elites with another.[116] Ballard had hoped for much more than the displacement of colonial elites by military juntas, populists, and middle-class liberals.

---

115. Robert J. Alexander, *Prophets of the Revolution: Profiles of Latin American Leaders*, 75–108; Jeffrey L. Klaiber, "Religion and Revolution in Peru: 1920–1945."

116. Ilan Rachum, for example, argues that the Brazilian coffee oligarchy supported the revolution only to restore confidence in the coffee market by

No new civilization was realized through the gateway of Latin America. Missionaries briefly proselytized among Indians in the Argentine provinces of Tucumán, Jujuy, and Chaco. In La Paz, Bolivia, missionary Vernon Sharp recorded that the Indian population was relatively emancipated and displayed a happy, progressive view of life. However, disease, illiteracy, lingering colonial conditions, and Catholic opposition defeated Mormon proselytizing efforts elsewhere. The Indian effort was abandoned and the missionaries concentrated on urban areas.[117] Not until the mid-1960s would LDS missionaries return to South American Indians by moving into the Bolivian highlands. By that time, Ballard's vision of a new world civilization based on mass Indian activism had long been dormant.

---

installing a government that would buy the surplus. See Ilan Rachum, "The Brazilian Revolution of 1930: A Revision."

117. The effort to proselytize Indians is chronicled in South American Mission, Manuscript History and Historical Reports, Vol. 2. The "explorations" are listed as follows: Jujuy exploration, March 10, 1927; Tucumán exploration, March 14, 1927; La Paz exploration, April 25, 1927; and Chaco exploration, May 11, 1927. The history contains entries under each of these dates giving a summary of the missionaries' activities, which in each case lasted from a few days to as long as five weeks. A detailed account, usually from the journal of Vernon Sharp, follows each summary. The unresponsiveness of the Indians to missionary efforts is also mentioned in Journal History, June 4, 1932, 3.

CHAPTER 11

FADE-OUT AND CONCLUSION

A Shifting Response

Up to this point a pattern is discernible in the Mormon response to revolution: the further away the revolution and the more anxiety the Church felt, the thicker was the revolutionary rhetoric of Mormon observers. Anxiety came from various sources: hostile governments, bad press coverage of the Church, or the queasy feeling of having surrendered too much for the sake of assimilation into mainstream culture. Conversely, when radicalism hit closer to home and Mormon observers felt more comfortable with assimilation and the secular state, rhetorical support for revolution was more scattered. News of revolutionary outbursts nevertheless aroused their interest at all times. Revolutions indicated that the divine plan was on track and global justice and unity would eventually triumph.

Several factors dampened the Mormon enthrallment with revolutions around 1936. For a hundred years Mormon discourse had hummed with revolutionary rhetoric. The hoped-for South American Indian nations did not arise, but events in Mexico, India, and the Soviet Union continued to enamor Mormon observers into the early 1930s. The onset of the Depression gave some of them further cause to contemplate the prospect of "just revolution." By 1936, however, the breakdown of the international order, the persistence of the Depression, and other factors iced the last vestiges of Mormon radicalism.

Reprise: The Great Depression
and the Sensation of Revolution

The Great Depression (1929–39) struck hard in Utah. Unprepared for the magnitude of the economic hardship and faced in 1932 with a Utah unemployment rate of 36 percent, Church leaders encouraged members to take advantage of government relief programs. In 1936 J.

Reuben Clark, uneasy with New Deal programs, organized the Church Welfare Plan. The intent behind the Church's work-for-food system was to diminish reliance on the direct-aid Federal Emergency Relief Administration and, to a lesser extent, agencies like the Public Works Administration. In actuality, Church welfare only supplemented New Deal efforts. Starvation was prevented, but the rush of applicants strained Church and federal resources.[1] During the 1930s, suggests one scholar, "F.D.R. was more relevant than God."[2] Not surprisingly, 70 percent of Utah voted for Roosevelt in 1936.

The Depression induced Church leaders to grope for explanations. Discontent and hardship prompted Church leaders to stress patience and brotherly love. Richard Rubenstein suggests that millennialism became a device through which devalued, out-of-work people revalued themselves. The unemployed became the "worthy poor" elected by God to help save the world; the wealthy could assure their own salvation by contributing their surplus to the war against poverty.[3] Within the Church, government help and renewed millennial hope served to avert outright despair and civil discord. But nipping at the edges of public fortitude and Roosevelt's New Deal were clerics who countenanced violence to even out the disparities between the classes.[4] Added to these

---

1. For the Depression in Utah, see Thomas G. Alexander, *Utah, the Right Place: The Official Centennial History*, 308–32. On Church leaders' criticism of the New Deal but rank-and-file endorsement of it, see Wayne K. Hinton, "Some Historical Perspective on Mormon Responses to the Great Depression." On the Mormon Church's welfare program, see Garth L. Mangum and Bruce D. Blumell, *The Mormons' War on Poverty: A History of LDS Welfare, 1830–1990*, 136–46; and Betty L. Barton, "Mormon Poor Relief: A Social Welfare Interlude," 81–87. For the role of Church women during the Depression, see David Hall, "Anxiously Engaged: Amy Brown Lyman and Relief Society Charity Work, 1917–45," 84–89. The Church encouraged government relief and work programs in George Stewart, Dilworth Walker, and E. Cecil McGavin, *Priesthood and Church Welfare: A Study Course for the Quorums of the Melchizedek Priesthood for the Year 1939*, 105–10.

2. James L. Clayton, "The Challenge of Secularism," 68.

3. Richard L. Rubenstein, "Religious Modernization and the Millennium," 223–46.

4. Martin E. Marty, *Modern American Religion*, 2:327. In box 273 of the

was another round of pyramid-based predictions.[5] In 1931 Anthony W. Ivins made his last assertion that the measurements and features of the Grand Gallery and the King's Chamber in the Pyramids of Giza foretold the arrival of the final dispensation.[6]

Some lay members started making predictions of their own. In geometric forms and Pythagorean numbers they rediscovered old Mormon beliefs about the revolutionary significance of contemporary events. Francis M. Darter, Heber Bennion, and Robert and Elizabeth Smith were eccentric Church members whose treatises on eschatology sold well. Their works raised hope for the reestablishment of communalism and the elimination of poverty. Social revolution before the return of Christ was presented as a distinct possibility.[7] Darter, a self-proclaimed Mormon eschatologist living in Long Beach, California,

---

Clarkana Papers of Joshua Reuben Clark Jr. are clippings collected by Clark during the 1930s on the subject of ministerial militancy.

5. For example, David Davidson, *The Great Pyramid's Prophecy on the Current Economic Depression* (1931); and Stewart Basil, *History and Significance of the Great Pyramid and the Theories and Traditions Held about It from the Earliest Days to the Present* (1935).

6. Anthony W. Ivins, October 4, 1931, *Report of the Semi-annual Conference of the Church of Jesus Christ of Latter-day Saints*, 87–93 (hereafter cited as *Conference Report*); and D. Michael Quinn, *Early Mormonism and the Magic World View*, 220. The influence of pyramidal and Anglo-Israel works on Ivins is also evident in Anthony W. Ivins, April 6, 1930, *Conference Report*, 15–17; and Anthony W. Ivins, October 5, 1930, *Conference Report*, 118–19. Apostle Charles A. Callis echoed the sense that the fullness of times was approaching in his sermon delivered April 5, 1935, *Conference Report*, 18.

7. The Smiths' works include Robert W. Smith and Elizabeth A. Smith, *Scriptural and Secular Prophecies Pertaining to the Last Days* (1931); Robert W. Smith, *Mystery of the Ages Containing Information Regarding the Great Pyramid of Gizeh in Egypt and the Pyramids and Peoples of Ancient America* (1931); and Robert W. Smith, *Mysteries of the Ages Pertaining to Prehistoric People and Pyramids of Ancient Egypt and America* (1936). BYU professor A. C. Lambert studied pyramidology in his notes entitled, "The Ancient Symbolical Significance of the Triangle and the Circle Related Particularly to the Pyramid as a Symbol." See Samuel W. Taylor, "The Golden Dream and the Nightmare: The Closet Crusade of A. C. Lambert," 56.

published a chart mapping the approach of the millennium. Around 1936, the chart showed, wars and social disturbances would lead to a crisis that required the rescue of the Constitution by the elders of the Church. What role the Constitution was to play from that point was unclear. The final phase of Darter's chart, however, conformed to the earlier Mormon theo-democratic concept. Surmounting the scenery of the pictogram's final phase was the "light that breaks forth" over the "universal brotherhood of man." In the Mormon context, it meant "the temporal or political government" of God.[8]

In 1932 a former bishop in the Salt Lake Valley published a tract entitled *Prosperity without Depression.* "God will not tolerate [the rule] of millionaires," wrote Heber Bennion, "neither will mankind. They will rise in rebellion against it as an intolerable monster." Bennion's revolution was preparatory to the true objective: the revival of the United Order. "The whole world," he wrote, "is ripening for revolution into the millennium." Following the destruction of the rich, the Church would set up "central store houses" and direct the Saints to live "in common."[9] In the Bennion and Darter versions, Christ would return to earth to find the sociopolitical structure of the thousand-year kingdom already established by the Church.

The apocryphal visions of Bennion and Darter were no longer in harmony with the changing tone of the Church's public rhetoric, but they did reflect a wider Mormon anxiety about possible social dissolution in the United States. Adolf Berle, a presidential aide, warned Franklin D. Roosevelt on the eve of his 1932 inaugural, "[W]e may have anything on our hands from recovery to a revolution. The chance is about even either way."[10] In 1934, two thousand labor strikes rippled across the

----

8. Francis M. Darter, *Zion's Redemption: The Return of John the Revelator, the Elias, the Restorer, the Gatherer of All Israel and Forerunner of Christ's Second Coming,* 49. Darter's other works include *The Gathering of Israel from a Scriptural Standpoint* (1915); *Our Bible in Stone: Its Divine Purpose and Present Day Message* (c. 1931); *The Kingdom of God: The U.S.A., British Empire, the House of Judah including the Ten Lost Tribes of Israel* (1941); and "*The Time of the End*" (1928).

9. Extracts of Bennion's pamphlet are printed in Smith and Smith, *Scriptural and Secular Prophecies,* 113, 127.

10. Quoted in David M. Kennedy, *Freedom from Fear: The American People in Depression and War, 1929–1945,* 117.

country. Men were killed in Toledo, San Francisco, Minneapolis, and Woonsocket, Rhode Island. The biggest strike, which included 325,000 textile workers throughout the South, left seven dead and twenty wounded in South Carolina.[11] Communist-organized "unemployment councils" combated urban eviction.[12] Destitute farmers abandoned rural lands and anger spread across the farm belt. From Kansas came a letter to the White House saying people worked like slaves, driven to do the work of two men for the pay of one. "Unless someone can get industry to awaken itself," the letter said, "there will be a revolution in [the] United States, just as surely as the sun comes up in the morning."[13] Apostle Richard R. Lyman acknowledged that the "American right to revolt" had brought progress to humanity, particularly when the Civil War led to the emancipation of the slaves. He argued, however, that denser populations, industrialization, and increased interdependence had rendered the prospect of social upheaval in the modern United States too destructive for its intended purpose.[14]

In 1931 Eastern States Mission President James H. Moyle spoke in the context of rumored mutiny in the Royal Navy, Russian communism, German fascism, and the revolutions in South America. Even in the United States, Moyle said, "it is not an uncommon sight to see armored cars equipped with machine guns to protect the transportation of wealth . . . through the thickly populated streets of the city, and from one bank to another." Moyle proceeded to validate the urban tension:

> Revolution is threatening this very nation because of the unsatisfied demand of the many for social justice, or as we would put it, the lack of brotherly love that the Savior advocated when he said to the wealthy young man, "Give unto the poor that which thou hast."

---

11. On labor strikes see Howard Zinn, *The Twentieth Century: A People's History*, 124–29; Arthur M. Schlesinger Jr., *The Coming of the New Deal, 1933–1935*, 387–88, 390–93; and David M. Kennedy, *Freedom from Fear: The American People in Depression and War, 1929–1945*, 288–302.

12. Zinn, *The Twentieth Century*, 120–21.

13. Eugene S. Simmons, Letter to Franklin D. Roosevelt, March 17, 1937, in Lawrence W. Levine and Cornelia R. Levine, eds., *The People and the President: America's Conversations with FDR*, 176.

14. Richard R. Lyman, October 3, 1930, *Conference Report*, 29–30.

The solution offered by Jesus and Joseph Smith, Moyle believed, was a "Christian socialistic system in which there were no poor and no rich but all things were held in common."[15]

Apostle Melvin J. Ballard suggested that the Great Depression was a social revelation from God to challenge the Church to care for the poor. Asked in 1936 if the Church welfare program meant the reconstitution of the United Order, Ballard replied, "No, . . . [but] the Lord may be giving His people an examination to see how far they have come toward a condition where they might live as one."[16] Still, the magnitude of the Depression overwhelmed Church resources, forcing reliance on New Deal programs. Near the end of the decade, Ballard looked to government rather than Church welfare as the solution to poverty. If the New Deal administration failed to spend "vast sums of money," he suggested, the nation would experience a "revolution."[17]

Fade-out: History, Time, and Revolution Lose Canonical Authority

The revolutionary imprint on Mormon discourse dissipated in the late 1930s. Generational turnover provides a partial explanation. Several key Mormon observers died in 1931, including Orson F. Whitney, Charles W. Nibley, and Rey L. Pratt. Pratt's sudden death on April 14 after a hernia operation shocked the Mexican Mission. His successors relocated the mission headquarters to Los Angeles, and either ignored everything south of the Rio Grande River or proved unable to accept the new ethnic consciousness that the Mexican Revolution had planted and Rey L. Pratt had nurtured. A mission crisis followed. Mexican Mormons, fired by revolutionary nationalism and their sense of destiny as a remnant of Israel, petitioned for Mexican nationals to preside over the mission. Salt Lake City refused. In 1936 a third of Mexico's twenty-four hundred Mormons left the Church. The dissidents formed their own leadership while retaining Latter-day Saint

15. James H. Moyle, October 2, 1931, *Conference Report*, 40–41.

16. Quoted in Harold B. Lee, October 5, 1941, *Conference Report*, 112.

17. *Deseret News*, October 7, 1938, quoted in Hinton, "Some Historical Perspective on Mormon Responses to the Great Depression," 26; Melvin J. Ballard, June 1939, in M. Russell Ballard, ed., *Melvin J. Ballard: Crusader for Righteousness*, 268.

doctrines. Church officials were outraged by this challenge to their authority. They denounced the "Third Convention," as the schismatic movement was called, and excommunicated its members. One of the excommunicated dissidents was Isaías Juárez, a founder of the National Peasant Confederation (*Confederación Nacional Campesina*). In 1945 most Third Conventionists returned to the Latter-day Saint fold thanks to Mission President Arwell Pierce, who promised that the next mission president would be a native Mexican.[18]

When B. H. Roberts died in 1933, a curtain fell on intellectual inquiry in Mormon leadership circles.[19] Ironically, the calling of the enigmatic revolutionary sympathizer J. Reuben Clark to the First Presidency the same year also marked the beginning of a conservative, anti-intellectual trend in the Church. A conservative orthodoxy replaced the century-long vision of revolutionary progress. Mormons' continued assimilation to mainstream American values also dulled their interest in reading the divine messages revealed through the unfolding of history. With the canon of revelation-through-history effectively closed, the new Mormon orthodoxy emphasized past achievements over an unfinished future. Scriptural literalism marginalized efforts to correlate religion with science, philosophy, and social change. Obedience, once harnessed to kingdom-building, became the new discipline of laying aside creativity for the sake of corporate cohesion.[20] Most destructive of all to the old Mormon worldview was a God considered to be absolute

---

18. On the Third Convention see F. LaMond Tullis, "A Shepherd to Mexico's Saints: Arwell L. Pierce and the Third Convention"; F. LaMond Tullis, *Mormons in Mexico: The Dynamics of Faith and Culture*, 137–68; and F. LaMond Tullis and Elizabeth Hernández, *Mormonism Comes of Age: The Third Convention in Mexico*.

19. Sterling M. McMurrin, "Brigham H. Roberts: A Biographical Essay," xxi.

20. Bernard DeVoto claimed that Utah was devoid of intellectualism. He later admitted that he had overstated his point and Utah was just more "provincial" than the rest of the nation. See Bernard DeVoto, "Utah," *American Mercury* 7 (March 1926): 319–21; and Bernard DeVoto, "A Revaluation," *Rocky Mountain Review* 10 (Autumn 1945): 8–10. Other works tracing the decline of Mormon intellectualism to the influence of Clark or the decade of the 1930s include Davis Bitton, "Anti-Intellectualism in Mormon History," 127–28; and Armand Mauss, "Assimilation and Ambivalence: The Mormon Reaction to Americanization," 43, 52–54.

and omnipotent. Man became commensurately ignoble; his importance in pushing providential history forward amounted to less.[21]

To the end of his life, Anthony W. Ivins carried forward his belief in a denationalized, universal Christ. "The daydawn is breaking," he stated in a 1933 General Conference address, "when Christ our Lord shall come, not only to assume dominion over his Church, of which we form a part, but over the world at large."[22] Ivins died on September 23, 1934. The *Deseret News* was distributed for free throughout Utah to announce his death. At his funeral, members of the Mexican branch in Salt Lake City covered his bier with the Mexican flag.[23] Ivins's passing removed another observer whose understanding of Mexican affairs would likely have prevented the Third Convention schism.

The end of the decade took more of Mormonism's international observers. Alice Louise Reynolds, for instance, died in 1938. Those who did not die became uncharacteristically pessimistic. The indomitable David O. McKay expressed the sentiments of many colleagues: "We seem to be slipping backward in the long march of progress."[24] Amidst the onslaught of economic depression, Mormonism lost some of its forward-looking vitality. Church leaders showed less faith in the working out of God's millennial will through the agency of man in historical time. Instead, it appeared that all humanity's efforts throughout history had produced little more than a catalog of accumulated failures.

The Depression and breakdown of the international order further eroded Mormon faith in this worldly harmony. The pillars supporting global liberalism—debt management, disarmament, democracy, the gold exchange system, and US solvency—fell one by one. Japan invaded China in 1931. Germany turned to Adolph Hitler and the Nazi Party. Italy invaded Abyssinia. The German-Soviet Non-Aggression Pact of 1939 stunned American diplomats. Two totalitarian governments

---

21. O. Kendall White Jr., "The Transformation of Mormon Theology." Mormon philosopher E. E. Ericksen noticed some of these tendencies in his 1922 dissertation on Mormonism. See Scott G. Kenney, "E. E. Ericksen: Loyal Heretic," 20.

22. Anthony W. Ivins, October 8, 1933, *Conference Report*, 90.

23. Wendell J. Ashton, *Voice in the West: Biography of a Pioneer Newspaper*, 311; Betty G. Ventura, ed., *The History of the Salt Lake Mexican Branch, 1920–1960*, 189.

24. David O. McKay, October 6, 1940, *Conference Report*, 102.

thought to be ideologically opposed to each other had joined together and secretly decided the fate of Poland. In 1940 Germany, Italy, and Japan formed the Axis Alliance. There was growing fear that totalitarian nations would gobble up other countries at the expense of democracies unprepared for the challenge.

Americans responded to the tension in different ways. Stalin's truce with Hitler disillusioned some intellectuals who had believed that Russian socialism still held out the promise of international rejuvenation. Liberal internationalists refashioned themselves as interventionists in order to preserve the world economic order.[25] Meanwhile, the isolationist impulse also strengthened.[26] While some Mormon observers remained admirers of Russian socialism, others, including J. Reuben Clark and German Mission President Alfred C. Rees, admired Nazi efficiency and defended Nazi policies as harmless to Christianity.[27] In April 1938, shortly after Germany's annexation of Austria and at a time when Hitler was asserting the right of ethnic Germans in Czechoslovakia to unite with the Reich, Clark challenged a general authority who had criticized German expansion: "Has Great Britain ever seen anything lying loose that she did not pick up? France is in no better position. So, brethren, let us be quiet at any rate about this matter."[28]

According to science historian Erich Robert Paul, by the late 1930s the failure of the western democracies to stop totalitarian advances eroded Latter-day Saint faith in the social sciences and international diplomacy.[29] Shortly before his death, Anthony W. Ivins admitted to

---

25. Joan Hoff Wilson, *Herbert Hoover: Forgotten Progressive*, 208; Akira Iriye, *The Globalizing of America, 1913–1945*, 127–29, 139–48, 153–69; Warren I. Cohen, *Empire without Tears: America's Foreign Relations, 1921–1933*, 125–26.

26. Wayne S. Cole, *Charles A. Lindbergh and the Battle against American Intervention in World War II*; Justus D. Doenecke, "Non-Intervention of the Left: The Keep America out of the War Congress, 1938–1941." For a historiographic overview see Doenecke, "U.S. Policy and the European War, 1939–1941."

27. Alfred C. Rees, October 7, 1939, *Conference Report*, 72, 75; D. Michael Quinn, *J. Reuben Clark: The Church Years*, 201–2, 206–7, 225–28; and D. Michael Quinn, *Elder Statesman: A Biography of J. Reuben Clark*, 283–92.

28. Quoted in Quinn, *Elder Statesman*, 286.

29. Erich Robert Paul, *Science, Religion, and Mormon Cosmology*, 163–64.

Brigham Young University students that the only recourse to offset the American failure to join the League was a unilateral strengthening of the national defenses.[30] David O. McKay worried that totalitarianism had struck at "beliefs and teachings which were accepted a decade ago as fundamentals and unassailable."[31] Apostle John A. Widtsoe, noted for being the first Church official awarded a PhD and for his attempt to blend science and religion, warned that in addition to fascism and communism, socialism also menaced democracy.[32] Faith in progress had declined in proportion to economic depression and the impotency of the Western democracies to curb foreign aggression.

The growing unattractiveness of the world also soured Mormon assessments of governments undergoing post-revolutionary reconstruction. The Show Trials orchestrated by Stalin between 1934 and 1938 tested the credulity of sympathetic American intellectuals. Many still excused Stalin's purges, but no Mormon observers were fooled.[33] Against the backdrop of the Show Trials and Stalin's 1936 announcement that socialism had been achieved, Ballard said that Russia had "turned away from all hope of anything beneficial."[34]

In July 1936 the First Presidency appointed J. Reuben Clark to write a statement warning against communism. The joint declaration targeted Mormons who had either joined the Communist Party or who thought communism reflected the principles of the United Order. Clark's objective was to disabuse members of this equation and to warn them about the "popular front" policy of the Seventh World Congress of the Communist International. The "popular front" was an

---

30. Anthony W. Ivins, "BYU Address," 1933, Anthony W. Ivins Papers, box 15, fd. 1.

31. McKay, October 6, 1940, *Conference Report*, 102.

32. John A. Widtsoe, *Evidences and Reconciliations: Aids to Faith in a Modern Day*, 377.

33. For the Show Trials and Purges as Stalin's final consolidation of power, see James R. Ozinga, *Communism: The Story of the Idea and Its Implementation*, 112–13; Ronald Hingley, *Joseph Stalin: Man and Legend*, 237–57; and Nicholas V. Riasanovsky, *A History of Russia*, 503–8. The credulity of American intellectuals who justified Stalin's Purge Trials is discussed in Paul Hollander, *Political Pilgrims: Travels of Western Intellectuals to the Soviet Union, China, and Cuba, 1928–1978*, 160–67.

34. Ballard, June 1939, in Ballard, *Crusader for Righteousness*, 266.

international alliance of liberal and leftist parties to stop the spread of fascism. Because the Communist International functioned during this period as the Kremlin's agency for exporting communist revolution, Clark worried that the popular front would first contain fascism and then serve as a Soviet beachhead to undermine Western democratic governments. Communism wasn't just another political party. It would replace American traditions with "a system of government that is the opposite of our Constitutional government, and it would be necessary to destroy our government before Communism could be set up in the United States."[35] However, Clark limited his points to domestic application. Below we will assess his views about communism for other people.

American anticommunism found expression in negative judgments of Mexico. Travelers to Mexico began to detect the flaws hidden from them by the "techniques of hospitality" Mexican officials had employed.[36] Utah editorials blamed communism for everything disagreeable in Mexico, from socialist education to hostility to foreign capital.[37] Articles and books appeared in the Mormon press pining for the days of Porfirio Díaz.[38] In 1934, nineteen years after the fact, the *Deseret News* reprinted the stories of two Mexican Mormons executed

---

35. J. Reuben Clark, July 3, 1936, in James R. Clark, comp., *Messages of the First Presidency of the Church of Jesus Christ of Latter-day Saints, 1833–1964*, 6:16–18; and D. Michael Quinn, *Mormon Hierarchy: Extensions of Power*, 304–5. For another example of suspicion toward Communist International objectives in the Utah press, see "Red Communists Still Active," *Deseret News*, December 19, 1934. Americans in general responded with aversion to the 1935 Communist International Congress. See Iriye, *Globalizing of America*, 146–47. The United States' radical left responded to the "popular front" directive by aligning itself more closely with Roosevelt. See Sidney Lens, *Radicalism in America*, 315; and James Weinstein, *Ambiguous Legacy: The Left in American Politics*, 57–86.

36. John A. Britton, *Revolution and Ideology: Images of the Mexican Revolution in the United States*, 24.

37. "Mexican Political Changes," *Deseret News*, October 22, 1931; and "Closing Churches in Mexico," *Salt Lake Tribune*, November 27, 1934.

38. Leah Ivins Cardon, "The Land of Manana," *Improvement Era* 37 (April 1934): 212–14, 222–23; and Leslie L. Sudweeks, "When Mormon Enterprise Won the Acclaim of President Diaz," *Improvement Era* 48 (October 1945): 570–71, 609.

by the Zapatistas in 1915.[39] These stories did not instill confidence in the course Mexican politics had taken.

Neither was news from the old Mormon colonies encouraging. Bishop Joseph C. Bentley of Colonia Juárez wrote disconsolately to Ivins in 1933:

> I doubt if we stand as well today with the Mexican people as we have done in the past, and I sometimes wonder if those of us who are here measure up to the standard the Lord expected of us? And if new blood will not have to be brought into the Colonies in order to accomplish the Work of the Lord?[40]

Bentley's appeal was unlikely to find a patron willing to rekindle the cooling embers. Michael Walzer explains in *Revolution of the Saints* that when Puritans became members of the English Parliament, the Puritan colonies in New England and the political radicalism they represented became obsolete. The Protestant work ethic found application in British society, but its original purpose—to build the self-discipline required of a Biblical commonwealth—was no longer relevant.[41] Mormon kingdom-building was likewise transmutable to capitalism and the exercise of democracy.[42] In other words, the work and discipline it takes to build the kingdom of God were exactly the same attributes needed to become productive citizens of a republic. By the 1930s the LDS Church was entering the final stages of assimilation to mainstream America, and the Mormon colonies in Mexico, like the Puritan ones in New England, were becoming obsolete.[43]

---

39. "I Will Make One Last Request," *Deseret News, Church Section,* December 1, 1934.

40. Joseph C. Bentley, Letter to Anthony W. Ivins, September 16, 1933, Ivins Papers, box 9, fd. 3. Little intercourse between Anglo and Mexican nationals was reported forty years later. See "Colonia Juárez Today," Journal History of the Church, June 3, 1972.

41. Michael Walzer, *The Revolution of the Saints: A Study in the Origins of Radical Politics,* 310–20.

42. Mark P. Leone, *Roots of Modern Mormonism,* 162; Thomas G. Alexander, *Mormonism in Transition: A History of the Latter-day Saints, 1890–1930,* 180–89; and Leonard J. Arrington, *Great Basin Kingdom: An Economic History of the Latter-day Saints, 1830–1900,* 380–412.

43. Jan Shipps, *Sojourner in a Promised Land,* 51–97; Alexander, *Mormonism in Transition,* 75, 256–57; and Armand L. Mauss, *The Angel and the Beehive: The Mormon Struggle with Assimilation,* 1–60.

The LDS Church's increasingly visible middle-class ethics and welfare efforts won praise, but they also raised awareness that Joseph Smith's restoration was undergoing a major overhaul. Hugh J. Cannon, editor of the *Improvement Era*, felt the tension. "Every true Latter-day Saint desires to be broad-minded and liberal," he wrote. But he also reminded the Saints that Christ had demanded radicalism: "Woe unto you, when all men shall speak well of you!" How far, Cannon wondered, could the Church's original principles be stretched before "too high a price is paid for the friendship of the world?"[44] During the Mormon Reformation of the late 1850s, Mormon leaders in the Rocky Mountain valleys had been determined to establish an independent kingdom. By the 1930s, Church leaders were behaving as though convention had more relevance for Mormonism than saintly revolution. Mormonism emerged from the transition with a high degree of flexibility. The "combination of traditions," contends historian Thomas Alexander, "allowed church members to support both public and private social action and hold the somewhat contradictory ideals of cooperation and corporate capitalism at the same time."[45]

One scholar writes that the best explanation for the shift from a universal to an Americanized Mormonism is the delay of Christ's second coming, or *parousia*. As it became evident that man's concept of "imminence" differed from God's, the millennium became a distant abstraction.[46] Ivins, the last to anticipate the "accomplishment of great events" as imminently as "1936 or 1938," set up the final expectation.[47] But this time, non-fulfillment passed without disappointment. As Mormons lost their sense of eschatological urgency, the impulse to prepare for Christ's millennial reign through revolution lost its force.

As aggression abroad intensified and nations continued to turn to extremist leaders, Mormon observer opinion about the utility of revolution was further tempered. The Spanish Civil War was a particularly pivotal event. In 1931 a soft revolution deposed Alfonso XIII and es-

---

44. Hugh J. Cannon, "A Stable Mormonism," *Improvement Era* 34 (June 1931): 443.

45. Alexander, *Mormonism in Transition*, 180.

46. Keith E. Norman, "How Long O Lord? The Delay of the Parousia in Mormonism," 55. See also Klaus J. Hansen, "The Metamorphosis of the Kingdom of God: Toward a Reinterpretation of Mormon History," 230.

47. Anthony W. Ivins, October 3, 1926, *Conference Report*, 19.

tablished the Spanish Republic. In 1936 Spain's Popular Front coalition of republicans, democrats, anarchists, and communists won elections against the old regime's monarchist, military, and clerical stalwarts. In July, however, General Francisco Franco, a fascist, led a Nationalist uprising. From his base in Spanish Morocco, Franco invaded Spain. The ensuing war took six hundred thousand lives. Joseph Stalin aided the Republican defenders. The Republic might have survived if England and France had been willing to supply it with arms, but France wanted to contain the fighting and England declined due to its anti-Bolshevik foreign policy. Nazi Germany and Italy were not so shy. Italy sent fifty thousand troops in support of Franco, and the German Air Force (*Luftwaffe*) deployed its Condor Legion to transport Nationalist army divisions and bomb cities. The merciless bombing of Guernica, the subject of Pablo Picasso's cubical art, showed a new, horrific dimension of total war. General Franco's strategic accomplishments were impressive; he was able to obtain help from Germany and Italy without entangling Spain with fascist ambitions leading to World War II. The Republicans, by contrast, fought courageously but never completely unified their efforts. Plagued by poor coordination, insufficient training, and ideological disunity, Republican offensives failed. By March 1938, fascist superiority in supply and firepower turned the tide. A combination of "blitzkrieg" tactics and sieges enabled Franco to capture one leftist stronghold after another until the Republic collapsed in March 1939.[48]

The Spanish Civil War divided the world into fascist and anti-fascist camps. Protestant ministers in the United States overwhelmingly supported the Spanish Republicans and used the conflict as a pretext for reminding the public of Catholic complicity in reactionary anti-republican movements and of Spain's rather sordid history of state-sponsored violence.[49] The Vatican supported the Nationalists, as did the Spanish Catholic Church. But in the United States, the fascist bombing of cities "destroyed Franco's claim to moral superiority" even among

---

48. For overviews of the Spanish Civil War, see Hugh Thomas, *The Spanish Civil War*; and Helen Graham, *The Spanish Republic at War, 1936–1939*. For the impact of aerial bombardment on world opinion, see Ian Patterson, *Guernica and Total War*.

49. Allen Guttman, *The Wound in the Heart: American and the Spanish Civil War*, 67–76.

the Catholic clergy.[50] In the Spanish Civil War, Americans saw a microcosm of a global struggle. On the one side were those who believed that Stalin's involvement was another move in the communization of the world, something many supporters of the Republican side understated. The other side rightly believed that fascism was a repudiation of democracy and liberal thought. Actually, the patchwork of regional and ideological loyalties in Spain that determined on whose side a person stood were more complex than outsiders understood, but that did not stop idealists from taking up arms to support the Republican cause. Twenty-eight hundred American leftists and liberals recruited through communist networks served in the Abraham Lincoln Brigade, one of several international brigades sent to fight the fascists in Spain. Newspaper reporter Ernest Hemingway cataloged his experiences in Spain to write *For Whom the Bell Tolls*, a novel about an American in an international brigade.[51]

J. Reuben Clark took a strong interest in the Spanish Civil War. Before 1936, Clark's understanding of revolution was based on a Russian-style revolution of the Left to advance a putative worker's democracy from below. This view allowed Clark to be a mild proponent of revolution, a perspective that matured during his service as ambassador to Mexico. Confronted with fascism, a model described by Barrington Moore as conservative revolution from the top, Clark reasoned that it, too, satisfied his right-to-revolution principles.[52] This view enabled Clark to accept fascist takeovers in Germany and Italy. But the brutality of Franco's armies shook him. The large collection of books and pamphlets he owned about the Spanish Civil War, now among the Clarkana Papers at Brigham Young University, reveal his concern about the European crisis. Concluding that the Spanish Civil War was just another example of violence caused by empires and would-be empires, Clark said that "what is happening in Spain is but a forecasting shadow of what may be looked for in the next great war."[53] Right-wing revolt in

---

50. Ibid., 49.

51. Peter N. Carroll, *The Odyssey of the Abraham Lincoln Brigade: Americans in the Spanish Civil War*.

52. Barrington Moore Jr., *Social Origins of Dictatorship and Democracy: Lord and Peasant in the Making of the Modern World*, 440, 447–49.

53. "Pres. Clark Joins Attack on Spanish Rebels' Cruelty," *Deseret News*, May 29, 1937, quoted in Quinn, *Elder Statesman*, 287.

Spain challenged Clark's former acceptance of revolution. But instead of questioning revolution in general, Clark used the Spanish Civil War to reinforce his argument for American isolationism.

As challenging as the Spanish Civil War was to his views, the conflict did not end Clark's support for revolution as a means for other nations to effect change. Clark accommodated National Socialism in Germany. Neither did the cruelty of civil war prevent his acceptance of left-wing revolutions following the rise of Soviet power after World War II. In 1947 Clark opposed the Truman Doctrine that committed the United States to contain international communism.[54] Moreover, Clark refused to discount the possibility of peaceful co-existence with the Soviet Union.[55] Up to his death in 1961, Clark supported the right of the people of Vietnam to engage in revolution to establish communism in Indochina.[56] But Clark was unique in his obstinacy. Ever enigmatic, he became the unlikely holdover from Mormonism's first revolutionary imprint. For other Mormon observers revolution had died. Whether the violence sprouted from oppressed peoples or middle-class intelligentsia, efforts to overthrow governments had become associated with new, insidious, repressive forms of state power, and revolution lost its appeal.

Melvin J. Ballard saluted the fading dream in 1939 at a conference of the Eastern States Mission. The Spanish Civil War horrified Ballard. Unlike most contemporary Protestant leaders, Ballard neither ignored Republican atrocities nor blamed everything on the Catholics. He cited how defenders of the Republic had crucified priests, raped nuns, and robbed the treasury; on the other side, he cited how the Nationalists had refused pleas from the Pope to stop the war. Ballard feared that the Luftwaffe, having practiced terror bombing over Spain, could repeat its performance over London.[57] In both fascism and communism, Ballard saw darkness. Fearing the approach of another general war, Ballard struck his own distinctively Mormon tone. Juxtaposing the futility of war with the promise of socialist redistribution, he declared, "If all that science has brought to war were confiscated and secured for the allevia-

---

54. Ibid., 310.

55. Ibid., 314.

56. Ibid., 315–16.

57. Ballard, June 1939, in Ballard, *Crusader for Righteousness*, 262–63, 266. For a similar warning from a non-Mormon source, see L. E. O. Charlton's 1937 book *The Menace of the Clouds*.

tion of poverty and the promotion of brotherhood, what speed we could make toward the golden age!"[58] Ballard stood with university presidents, churchmen, and civic leaders who supported the Spanish Republic not because they were Marxists, but because they believed in democracy, separation of church and state, individual liberty, and Enlightenment rationalism. The war threatened those values. It suggested that perhaps progress is not inevitable; perhaps the Dark Ages could return.[59]

Ballard had lived long enough to know that his hopes—and those of his fellow Mormon observers—had been confounded. In looking back at the First World War, he rendered the peroration:

> Kings and monarchs disappeared, and in their places came republics and democracies. . . . Many of us thought we were on the road to the golden age, an age which prophets and poets have sung and prophesied about, only to see the night of darkness come in disappointment and the old struggle go on.[60]

A month later, on July 30, 1939, cancer killed Melvin J. Ballard.

Conclusion

During the Cold War that followed World War II, American power served as the antidote to Mormon anxiety about the future. Global aspirations remained in terms of missionary work, but the right to revolution as a constructive part of a millennial dream was repealed. Still, pre-World War II Mormon observers' view of progress as a series of revolutions breaking down the old order to make way for the new should inform our understanding of the Church. Indeed, it would have been strange if a church that believed itself established by divine mandate had not expressed itself in revolutionary terms. After all, the proponents of secular revolution relied on religious terminology to broadcast their epiphanies. In a similar vein Mormon observers believed that the restored gospel fulfilled all human aspirations and knowledge. To explain its implications they borrowed from the lexica of secular dreamers.

---

58. Ballard, June 1939, in *Crusader for Righteousness*, 265.
59. Guttman, *Wound in the Heart*, 81–83, 165.
60. Ballard, June 1939, in Ballard, *Crusader for Righteousness*, 261–62.

For a century the discourse of Mormon observers converged on a vision of universal progress and social justice. Utopia was meant for earth, not for a heavenly state of deferred happiness. The quest for utopia, expressed in Mormonism as the millennium, would be accomplished in ways that paralleled Hegel's dialectic: a series of conflicts would create conditions that made theo-democracy inevitable. Time was the medium. For a hundred years Mormon observers exchanged an all-powerful, all-present God for one that was all-knowing. He had mastered the laws of historical development. God's lieutenants—human beings—supplied the muscle. Mormon observers presumed, as did social revolutionaries all over the world, that historical time would produce the final victory.

During the period under study, Mormonism was hardly a world religion; it was limited primarily to North America, a few Pacific islands, and Great Britain. Anxious to break out of their limited purview, Mormon observers expanded these borders through intellectual forays into the larger world. Siding with the aspirations of rising peoples gave them a sense that they were participants in a global utopian transformation. Mormons, of course, had their own script of what would happen to capitalists and empires, republics and monarchs, when historical revolution from below met the millennial revolution from above: the wicked would be crushed as between a hammer and an anvil.

Support for revolution often requires spatial distance between the observer and the doer. In *The End of History and the Last Man*, Francis Fukuyama suggests that by the 1980s American and Western European intellectuals no longer viewed Marxism-Leninism as a role model for their own societies, but continued to legitimate it for other people "in proportion to the geographical and cultural distance" from their own nation.[61] Revolutions elsewhere in the world let Mormon observers assert the Church's pre-1890 political radicalism even in the post-1890 period, when the project of an independent Mormon kingdom had been abandoned in favor of Utah statehood. Confidence in a theocratic empire imploded during the 1890s, marking the end of the revolutionary kingdom of God in the American West, but the utopian dream persisted in the Mormon mind for other nations and peoples.

---

61. Francis Fukuyama, *The End of History and the Last Man*, 9–10.

Even this vestige of the utopian dream, however, eventually faded. Mormonism, born in the Jacksonian age of individualism, democracy, and capitalism, resisted those values until the Church's final merger with mainstream America during the 1930s.[62] One hundred years had passed before the molten core material of Mormonism's original teleology cooled. Only then could Latter-day Saints suppose that the Church's founders had pursued public acceptance and prophetic conservatism all along.

---

62. For the characteristics of the Jacksonian era, see Gordon S. Wood, "The Significance of the Early Republic."

CODA

In 1976 the Church's *Ensign* magazine celebrated the American Bicentennial with a special edition. One section addressed whether revolution remained a people's right. Mormon scholars and officials wrote that revolution remained a theoretical possibility, but it should never be invoked. They counseled members to uphold the "laws of the land." An act of revolution required such preponderant justification that no matter how repressive or corrupt a government had become, prudence required a wait-and-see attitude. The position makes sense. The Church today is not a revolutionary organization. It also needs the permission of foreign governments in order to do missionary work. It is not the calling of our nineteen-year-olds to foment revolution by inciting the poor to revolt.

But the style of the Mormon Church during the first century of its existence offered something that is missing today. The completion of the new Tabernacle without symbolic adornments in Salt Lake City symbolizes the void. The building's designers abandoned esoteric sculpture, but curiosity about the Pythagorean formulations that influenced the architecture of its nineteenth-century counterpart continues in other forms. A book of contemporary Mormon art sold in Church-affiliated Deseret bookstores depicts an abstract rendition of pyramidal and triangular forms. "Egypt is our schoolmaster," the caption suggests.[1] Joseph Smith was familiar with archaic knowledge that enabled him to join Mormon temple symbolism with "eternal life and its connected cosmology"; symbols that remain on older Church architecture remind Mormons that they were once different, but today's members do not fully understand why or how.[2]

---

1. The painting in question is Erich Barsch Wulf's "Toward the Holy Mountain," in *All Things Testify of Him: Inspirational Paintings by Latter-day Saint Artists*, 10.
2. Allen D. Roberts, "Where Are the All-Seeing Eyes? The Origin, Use,

The Latter-day Saint Church was not really designed to exist in normal "calendar time." Joseph Smith did not even plan for a successor. He and most of his followers seem to have expected that during his lifetime Christ would return. Smith's death temporarily defeated Mormon expectations. The divine plan was not supposed to produce martyred prophets and migration to the Rockies; the Saints were supposed to triumph and rule the world with Christ from the New Jerusalem.

After Smith's death, Mormons transplanted their radical vision to the Rockies. Mormon observers railed against the inequalities of capitalism. They sympathized with colonial revolts. They interpreted the revolutions of 1848, 1871, 1905, and 1917 as possible harbingers of utopia's arrival before Christ returned to finish the process. Even after 1890, Mormon observers clung to hope by focusing their attention on revolutions in Mexico and South America. But assimilation finally caught up with the Church in Utah. Mormons became normal Americans concerned with public image and growth statistics. Mormon leaders looked less and less for the transformation of Church into kingdom. They began to assume, more realistically, that tomorrow would be a lot like today. Formulaic Sunday school lessons written by centralized committees no longer know what to do with a Church history vibrant with thoughtful political radicalism and faithful apocalyptic expectation. So they leave it out. The Church now flourishes in calendar time— if not on the strength of its original radicalism, then on a different kind of strength: its ability to adapt.

Today the Church forms a political "popular front" with Southern Baptists and other Evangelical Protestant denominations. As non-Mormon literary critic Harold Bloom has noted, Mormons and Evangelical Protestants tend to vote for the same candidates and champion similar social values despite the fact that most Protestant churches view the Latter-day Saints as cult members. Bloom also highlights the similar grammar of worship: the members of both churches seek God's love on an individual level. Yet despite this Americanized relationship with God, Bloom surmises that Mormons' political and social closeness with Evangelicals may be quite transitory. Mormonism is too different to hold its place in this compound. Bloom goes so far to suggest that Mormons will obtain enough power in the West to revive polygamy in the future

---

and Decline of Early Mormon Symbolism," 40.

should they choose.[3] D. Michael Quinn adds that "Mormonism can never be less than a dormant socioreligious radicalism. Only time will tell whether the continued permeation of middle-class values within Mormonism will turn that dormancy into atrophy."[4] True, the comforts of the status quo make a reversal of assimilation remote. But if the concept of revelation through history is adaptable to modern Church institutions, or if the corporate style of the institutional Church is modified, then it may be possible for Mormonism to contemplate the radical roots of its formation.

In 1998 I climbed Ensign Peak overlooking Salt Lake City. Near the trailhead at the base of the peak stands a Mormon chapel. I walked past two flagpoles. One flew the United States flag; from the other, to my surprise, flapped a "kingdom" flag—blue and white horizontal stripes with three stars in a blue upper-left canton. I felt like William Manchester when he found a well-oiled three-inch Japanese gun atop a hill on the island of Peleliu, mysteriously kept ready for action. I do not know who put the flag there, and I saw no explanation to suggest anyone knew its significance. It stood as a vestige of a forgotten past. Nevertheless, I was thrilled to see it, as I am with all old things reminding me of past inheritances. Maybe one day wards will again sing "High on the mountain top, a banner is unfurled" with a conviction that recalls the day the kingdom flag flew on the summit of the peak, from which it was removed long ago.

---

3. Harold Bloom, *The American Religion: The Emergence of the Post-Christian Nation*, 123.

4. D. Michael Quinn, "Socioreligious Radicalism of the Mormon Church: A Parallel to the Anabaptists," 380.

BIOGRAPHICAL REGISTER
OF MORMON OBSERVERS

Adams, George J. (1811–80)

Founding member of the Council of Fifty in 1844. Appointed as Mormonism's "ambassador to Russia." Freemason. Excommunicated in 1845 for practicing polygamy. Supported the prophetic succession claim of Joseph Smith's twelve-year-old son, Joseph III, then joined the Strangites. Aired revolutionary views as editor of *The Star in the East* in Boston in 1846. Led 156 colonists to Jaffa in 1866 to prepare for the return of the Jews. Failed and returned to the United States. Died in Philadelphia.

Sources: D. Michael Quinn, *Mormon Hierarchy: Origins of Power*, 526, 534; D. Michael Quinn, "Joseph Smith III's 1844 Blessing and the Mormons of Utah," 82; Dean C. Jessee, ed., *The Papers of Joseph Smith: Journal, 1832–1842*, 521.

Anderson, Edward H. (1858–1928)

Born in Sweden and migrated to Utah. Edited the *Contributor* from 1888–90 before being called as president of the Scandinavian Mission. Returned to Utah in October 1892 and held various political and civic offices, including surveyor general in 1901. Additional Church callings included assistant Church historian and assistant editor of the *Improvement Era* starting in 1899, a post held for thirty years. From 1896–1907 served on the General Board of the Young Men's Mutual Improvement Association. A poet by inclination and a self-taught man of letters. Church Historian Andrew Jenson called him "one of the brightest men in the Church." President Heber J. Grant considered him "the ideal type of genuine Latter-day Saint."

Sources: Andrew Jenson, *Latter-day Saint Biographical Encyclopedia: A Compilation of Biographical Sketches of Prominent Men and Women in* the Church of Jesus Christ of Latter-day Saints, 1:715, 4:231; Junius F. Wells and George H. Brimhall, "Edward H. Anderson," *Improvement Era* 31 (March 1928): 363–64.

Appleby, William I. (1811–70)

Heard Mormonism preached around 1837 and was baptized in Recklesstown, New Jersey in 1840. Appointed president of the Eastern States Mission in February 1847. Recorded the revolutions of 1848, believing that there "never was a period in the history of human affairs in which the movements of the Great Powers of the earth were invested with so much grandeur and solemnity as at the present moment." Hoped the Church would accept his chronicle as its official record of European events. Moved to Utah in 1849. On February 21, 1851, Wilford Woodruff recorded that Appleby was "Admitted into our Council today," possibly referring to the Council of Fifty. Held territorial government posts in the 1850s. Between 1856 and 1858 assisted in editing *The Mormon* and served again as president of the Eastern States Mission. Recalled to Utah when US President James Buchanan ordered the Army to occupy the territory. Became chancellor of the University of Deseret (later University of Utah). Also served in the territorial government as a probate judge and treasurer.

Sources: Davis Bitton, *Guide to Mormon Diaries and Autobiographies*, 12; B. H. Roberts, *The Life of John Taylor: Third President of the Church of Jesus Christ of Latter-day Saints*, 270; William I. Appleby, Autobiography and Journal; Jenson, *Latter-day Saint Biographical Encyclopedia*, 4:330–31; Scott G. Kenney, ed., *Wilford Woodruff's Journal, 1833–1889*, February 21, 1851, 4:14.

Ballard, Melvin J. (1873–1939)

Presided over the Northwestern States Mission. Called to the Quorum of the Twelve in 1919 by Church President Heber J. Grant, who overrode his inclination to appoint a close friend, Richard W. Young, and instead selected Ballard, a man he hardly knew. Opened the South American Mission in 1926. Supervised the Church welfare system during the 1930s.

Sources: Francis M. Gibbons, *Heber J. Grant: Man of Steel, Prophet of God*, 175; Bryant S. Hinckley, "Melvin J. Ballard," *Improvement Era* 35

(October 1932): 712–15, 735; Richard R. Lyman, "Melvin J. Ballard: A Beloved Apostle Departs," *Improvement Era* 42 (September 1939): 522–23, 570–72; Melvin J. Ballard, "Our Indian Cousins: Fort Peck Indian Reservation," *Relief Society Magazine* 6 (March 1919): 143–47; Garth L. Mangum and Bruce D. Blumell, *The Mormons War on Poverty: A History of LDS Welfare, 1830–1990*, 130–56.

Bennion, Heber (1858–1932)

Prominent LDS figure and brother-in-law of President Heber J. Grant. Bishop of the Taylorsville (Salt Lake Valley) Ward for several years. Practiced post-Manifesto polygamy with the permission of the First Presidency. Engaged in doctrinal disputes with general authorities. Harbored socialist ideas and vehemently opposed US involvement in World War I.

Sources: Boyd Kirkland, "Jehovah as Father: The Development of the Mormon Jehovah Doctrine," *Sunstone* 9, no. 2 (August 1984): 44 note 71; Blaine Carmon Hardy, *Solemn Covenant: The Mormon Polygamous Passage*, 169, 215, Appendix 2; Heber Bennion, Letter to George Albert Smith, March 14, 1918, George A. Smith Family Papers, box 43, fd. 14; Ronald W. Walker, "Sheaves, Bucklers, and the State: Mormon Leaders Respond to the Dilemmas of War," 298 note 84.

Bertrand, Louis A., born Jean François Élie Flandin (1808–75)

Before conversion to Mormonism in 1850, he was a sailor and would-be photographer until a mugging in the Philippines induced him to return to France. In Paris was the political editor of Étienne Cabet's communist paper *Le Populaire* and participated in the philosophical circles of Christian socialist Philippe Buchez. A member of Paris's Revolutionary Committee in 1848; received a three-month prison sentence for his role. Helped Curtis Bolton translate the first French edition of the Book of Mormon in 1851 (published 1852). His connection to the Red Republicans was viewed with favor by Church officials, leading to his presentation of the Mormon message to Victor Hugo. Preached Mormonism and utopianism at Masonic meetings. Sailed to Utah in 1855. Appointed by Brigham Young to head the French Mission between 1859 and 1863. While in France, published an account of his conversion experience and Mormon Utah in *Memoirs d'un Mormon* (1862), which received favorable reviews. Rebuffed by Napoleon III and unable to preach publicly, returned to Utah. The French Mission closed the next year. Started a silk industry in Utah. Suffered dementia, possibly worsened by death of his wife in 1875. Died in a Salt Lake City public sanatorium.

Sources: Richard D. McClellan, "Not Your Average French Communist Mormon: A Short History of Louis A. Bertrand."

Bolton, Curtis Edwin (1812–90)

Born in Philadelphia. Lived in France several months during the 1830s due to the fact his father was a New York businessman engaged in European trade. Baptized in 1842. Lived with Joseph Smith for five weeks. Claimed he "worked many a day in the [Nauvoo] temple with my rifle and sword hid in the shavings." Fought in the 1846 Battle of Nauvoo. Assisted John Taylor in opening French Mission in 1850–53 and presided over the mission most of that time. Witnessed violent suppression of protest against Napoleon III. Translated Book of Mormon into French and edited *Etoile du Déséret* [*Star of Deseret*], the Church's French periodical. Died in Marysvale, Utah.

Sources: Bitton, *Guide to Mormon Diaries*, 253; S. M. Smith, "Curtis Edwin Bolton"; Cleo H. Evans, comp., *Curtis Edwin Bolton, Pioneer, Missionary: History, Descendants, and Ancestors.*

Brown, Thomas Dunlop (1807–74)

British convert who labored to civilize the Indians of southern Utah during the 1850s with the same devotion he showed as a traveling elder in England in 1848.

Sources: Juanita Brooks, ed., *Journal of the Southern Indian Mission: Diary of Thomas D. Brown.*

Callis, Charles A. (1865–1947)

Born in Dublin, Ireland. Came to Utah in 1875. Called on mission to England in 1893; presided over the Ireland Conference. Elected to the Utah State Legislature in 1908. Admitted to state bar associations in South Carolina and Florida while serving as president of the Southern States Mission. Remained mission president until called to the Quorum of the Twelve in 1933. Died in Florida while organizing the first stake of the Church in the southern United States.

Sources: Lawrence R. Flake, *Prophets and Apostles of the Last Dispensation*, 461–63.

Cannon, George Q. (1827–1901)

Ordained as an apostle in 1860. Polygamist. Member of the Council of Fifty in 1867. Adjutant general of the Utah Nauvoo Legion from 1858 to 1870. At the time of the Paris Commune, edited both the *Deseret News* and the *Juvenile Instructor*. Counselor to four Church presidents from 1874 to 1901. Imprisoned twice for polygamy. Assumed de facto leadership of the Church when presidents were forced underground or weakened by advanced age. Engaged extensively in business and civil service in addition to his ecclesiastical responsibilities. From 1872 to 1882 was the delegate in Washington DC representing Utah Territory.

Sources: Davis Bitton, *George Q. Cannon: A Biography*; D. Michael Quinn, *The Mormon Hierarchy: Extensions of Power*, 645–47.

Cannon, Hugh J. (1870–1931)

Son of George Q. Cannon. Polygamist. Jailed in 1886 for assaulting US attorney for "indecent" questioning of polygamous mother. President of the German-Swiss Mission, 1901–5. President of Salt Lake City's Liberty Stake, 1905–28. Accompanied David O. McKay on world tour in 1920–21. Presided over German Mission, 1925–28. Editor of *Improvement Era*, 1928–31.

Sources: B. H. Roberts, *Comprehensive History of the Church of Jesus Christ of Latter-day Saints, 1830–1930*, 5:91; Hardy, *Solemn Covenant*, 399; Andrew Jenson, comp., *Church Chronology: A Record of Important Events Pertaining to the History of the Church of Jesus Christ of Latter-day Saints*, September 1, 1901; David O. McKay, Diary, 1921–22.

Cannon, John Q. (1857–1931)

Son of George Q. Cannon. Counselor in Presiding Bishopric, 1884–86. Excommunicated in 1886 after first wife charged him with adultery. Rebaptized in 1888 and remarried first wife. Founding president of the Democratic Businessman's Club in Salt Lake City in 1895. Editor-in-chief of *Deseret News* when Spanish-American War began. Captain in "Torrey's Rough Riders" (2nd US Volunteer Cavalry), but a train accident en route to Tampa prevented the regiment's deployment to Cuba.

Held several state and party offices, including delegate at Democratic territorial convention and general in the Utah National Guard. Fled to Canada in 1905 to escape accusations of embezzlement from the Utah Louisiana Purchase Fair Commission; Utah's governor did not seek extradition. Editor of the *Deseret News* again from 1918 to 1922 and 1928 to 1931.

Sources: Jenson, *Church Chronology*, April 1886, October 7, 1886, and May 17, 1898; Quinn, *Mormon Hierarchy: Extensions of Power*, 648–49; "Utah Fugitive Is Caught," *New York Times*, July 20, 1905; Phil Roberts, "The Other Roughriders: Col. Torrey and Wyoming's Volunteer Cavalry"; Wendell J. Ashton, *Voice in the West: Biography of Pioneer Newspaper*, 225.

Clark, J. Reuben (1871–1961)

Lawyer. US undersecretary of state, 1928–29. Ambassador to Mexico, 1930–33. LDS First Presidency, 1933–61. Authored the Clark Memorandum advising non-intervention in Latin America except under a strict interpretation of the Monroe Doctrine. Opposed the League of Nations and US entry into World War II, attracting the suspicion of J. Edgar Hoover and US Army Military Intelligence. A staunch isolationist with conservative proclivities, he nevertheless endorsed the right of all peoples to revolution.

Sources: Frank W. Fox, *J. Rueben Clark: The Public Years*; D. Michael Quinn, *J. Reuben Clark: The Church Years*; Gene A. Sessions, "The Clark Memorandum Myth."

Cordon, Alfred (1817–71)

A potter at the time of his baptism. Probably initiated into Freemasonry at Nauvoo in 1842. As a "political missionary" in 1844, proposed a "Jeffersonian Democracy" convention. Served three more missions and helped settle Utah. Listed with two others as "Presiding and Travelling Bishops among the people" from 1852 to 1853. Polygamist. Ward bishop, 1857–71. Member of Wilford Woodruff prayer circle in 1858.

Source: Quinn, *Mormon Hierarchy: Extensions of Power*, 133, 652.

Darter, Francis M. (1881–1968)

Excommunicated in 1918 for advocating a return to polygamy and the United Order, but still considered himself Mormon. Wrote numerous speculative works on eschatology, housed in the Harold B. Lee Library at BYU. Mentioned by Apostle Anthony W. Ivins in 1931 as "Francis M. Darter of Los Angeles, a member of the Church, in good standing, an experienced engineer and a mathematician of ability."

Sources: Francis M. Darter, *Minutes of Excommunication*; Anthony W. Ivins, October 4, 1931, *Report of the Semi-annual Conference of the Church of Jesus Christ of Latter-day Saints*, 87 (hereafter cited as *Conference Report*).

Eldredge, Horace Sunderlin (1816–87)

Member of the Council of Fifty in 1848. Polygamist. In 1857 was probably one of the fifty men indicted for treason as a result of the Utah War (1857–58). Held numerous civil posts in Utah Territory and served as president of the European Mission from 1870 to 1871.

Sources: Horace Sunderlin Eldredge, Letter to Brigham Young, April 26, 1871; Quinn, *The Mormon Hierarchy: Extensions of Power*, 654–55.

Flanigan, James Henry (1822–52)

Missionary in Kentucky and Tennessee, 1843–45. Died of smallpox in Birmingham in 1852. Eulogized as "an exemplary young man; in fact, an exception among men. His zeal for the cause of truth was unexcelled."

Sources: Bitton, *Guide to Mormon Diaries*, 109; Lyman O. Littlefield, *Reminiscences of Latter-day Saints, Giving an Account of Much Individual Suffering Endured for Religious Conscience*, 40–41.

Fox, Ruth May (1853–1958)

First counselor of the Young Women's Mutual Improvement Association from 1905 to 1929; president from 1929 to 1937. Husband took a second wife without her permission, forcing her to live largely on her own. Committed to women's suffrage and a member of the Utah Woman Suffrage Association. Held several other civil service positions until death at age 104.

Sources: Linda Thatcher, "Fox, Ruth May."

Harris, Franklin S. (1884–1960)

President of BYU, 1921–45. Led a team of agricultural experts to western Siberia to consult with Jewish settlers in 1929. Pushed for higher academic standards at BYU, hiring several faculty members with doctoral degrees. Irritated by J. Reuben Clark's targeting of "heretical" faculty. Resigned from BYU to become president of Utah State Agricultural College. Headed Church branch in Tehran in 1951 while serving as an advisor to the Iranian government. Eulogized as "a kindly man—approachable, tolerant, charitable, and understanding."

Sources: Gary James Bergera and Ronald Priddis, *Brigham Young University: A House of Faith*, 15–19; *Memorial Services for President Franklin Stewart Harris: George Albert Smith Fieldhouse, Monday, May 23, 1960, 10:00 A.M.*, 4.

Hyde, Orson (1805–78)

Selected by the Three Witnesses of the Book of Mormon as one of the original Twelve Apostles. Signed affidavit against Mormonism during the 1838 Missouri War, but was reinstated by Smith as an apostle in 1839. Traveled to Jerusalem and dedicated Palestine for the return of the Jews in 1842. Polygamist, Freemason, Whig. President of the British Mission, 1846–47. Editor of the *Frontier Guardian* at Kanesville, Iowa, 1849–52. Led wagon trains down the Mormon Trail in 1850 and 1852. Helped colonize Utah. Indicted but pardoned by the federal government for role in the 1857–58 Utah War. Advocated range management and introduced irrigation techniques learned from his trip to Palestine. Demoted during the reshuffling of the Quorum of the Twelve in 1875, ensuring that John Taylor would succeed Brigham Young.

Sources: Howard H. Barron, "Hyde, Orson"; Quinn, *Mormon Hierarchy: Origins of Power*, 552–53; Lynn M. Hilton and Hope A. Hilton, "Orson Hyde."

Hyde, William A. (1863–1934)

Born in Kaysville, Utah. Attended Deseret University in Salt Lake City for six months. Called by the Church in 1894 to relocate from Utah to Downey, Idaho, where he became a prosperous general store owner. Appointed bishop the same year. Served in state legislature in 1898–99. Appointed stake president over Pocatello, Idaho Stake in 1901. Formed William A. Hyde Realty Company in 1911. Also became probate judge. Historian Thomas G. Alexander describes him as having strong right-wing tendencies. Contemporary Hiram Taylor French recorded, "Mr.

Hyde maintains an independent attitude, and he is essentially progressive and public spirited. . . . He has great confidence in the future of Idaho, and has pleasure in prophesying political purity." On foreign relations Hyde believed in the cultural and political superiority of the United States and Britain.

Sources: "National Register Properties in Pocatello, Idaho"; Thomas G. Alexander, *Mormonism in Transition: A History of the Latter-day Saints, 1890–1930*, 184; William A. Hyde, "Hands Across the Sea," *Latter-day Saints' Millennial Star* 83 (September 15, 1921): 577–81 (hereafter cited as *Millennial Star*); Hiram T. French, *History of Idaho: A Narrative Account of Its Historical Progress, Its People and Its Principal Interests*, 3:1071.

Ivins, Anthony W. (1852–1934)

In 1877 witnessed the execution of John D. Lee for his role in the infamous Mountain Meadows Massacre of an emigrant wagon train. Called to preside over the Mormon colonies in Chihuahua and Sonora in 1895. Spoke Spanish well. Moved to Salt Lake City in 1907 when called to the Quorum of the Twelve Apostles. Called as counselor to the First Presidency in 1925. Was the figure around whom the Utah Democratic Party rallied in a state generally dominated by Republican Senator Reed Smoot's "Federal Bunch." Rancher by profession, though his interests intersected with college trusteeship, mining, banking, and other enterprises. Representative of the New West type: tough, intellectual, and practical. Noble Warrum, a member of the Mexican Claims Commission during the 1920s, described him this way: "There is no man more dedicated to justice—he is [the] triple combination of the Spartan, the Stoic, and the Christian."

Sources: "Anthony W. Ivins," Anthony W. Ivins Papers, box 1, fd. 2; Quinn, *Mormon Hierarchy: Extensions of Power*, 662–63; Richard S. Van Wagoner and Steven C. Walker, *A Book of Mormons*, 131–34; Thomas Cottam Romney, *The Mormon Colonies in Mexico*; Nelle Spilsbury Hatch and B. Carmon Hardy, *Stalwarts South of the Border*; Bryant S. Hinckley, "President Anthony W. Ivins," *Improvement Era* 35 (November 1931): 5–8, 39; Herman Hoffman Birney, *Zealots in Zion*, 215–18, 293–310; Kristen Smart Rogers, "'Another Good Man': Anthony W. Ivins and the Defeat of Reed Smoot."

Jaques, John, alias Harvey Locksley Birch (1827–1900)

Born in Leicestershire, England. Cabinetmaker before conversion to Mormonism in 1845. Served in the British Mission office during 1848 revolutions and frequently contributed to the *Millennial Star*. May have chosen the pen name Harvey Locksley Birch to hide the fact that he was only twenty years old. Migrated to America and walked in the Martin Handcart Company in 1856, losing his daughter along the way. Called by Brigham Young to serve in the Historian's Office in 1859–63. Employed by the *Daily Telegraph* in Salt Lake City in 1863–69. Called on another mission to Britain in 1869 and served as assistant editor to the *Millennial Star* until 1871. After mission worked for the *Deseret News* until about 1879. Polygamously married a second wife in 1872. Served again in the Church Historian's Office from 1889 until death. Other Church service included a position as private secretary to President Wilford Woodruff. In his civic and professional life, worked as a topographical engineer and served in the Utah Nauvoo Legion, the 12th Ward School Board, and the Utah Territorial Legislative Assembly. Also wrote three songs currently in the LDS hymnal: "Millennial Morning," "The Mountain Standard," and "The Rising Glory of Zion." Was eulogized as a straight talker, strong and steady, a man of many talents, and a believer in "the cause of human redemption." Concerning his literary contributions, the *Deseret News* said, "His first literary efforts were known through the *Millennial Star*. The brightness of that luminary received much of its luster for a considerable period from his facile pen. In poetry and in prose he reflected the light of truth for the benefit of his fellows, and his logical and spiritual sentiments were a comfort and a strength to many honest souls."

Sources: Andrew Jenson, *Latter-day Saint Biographical Encyclopedia*, 1:254–56; Stella Jaques Bell, *Life History and Writings of John Jaques*, 25–26.

King, William H. (1863–1949)

Missionary in England, 1880–82. Utah Congressman, 1896–1900. Elected in 1919 to the US Senate, where he advocated self-determination for Latin America. Styled himself a Constitutional Democrat and opposed several aspects of Roosevelt's New Deal. Lost his seat in 1940 and returned to Salt Lake City to practice law.

Sources: John R. Sillito, "William H. King."

Martin, Thomas L. (1885–1958)

Born into poverty and bad health in England; did not walk until he was five years old. Migrated to Utah at age sixteen. Graduated from BYU in 1912 as valedictorian. Received a PhD from Cornell University in soil technology. Professor at BYU, 1921–55. Toured Soviet communes in 1930. In 1950 was honored by the American Society of Agronomy for "having inspired more young men to go on to advanced degrees in soils than any other teacher in the nation."

Sources: Jeff McClellan, "A Lingering Influence: Top 10 BYU Professors"; Bergera and Priddis, *Brigham Young University*, 191.

Mason, Jane (b. 1809)

Born in Louth, England. Published a poem titled "Truth" in the *Millennial Star* in 1849. The same year migrated with her seven-year-old son to America on the ship *Zetland*. Listed on the ship's manifest as a single, female "Mormon laborer." Republished her poem in the *Frontier Guardian* in 1850. Started overland to Utah in 1852. Told wagon train leaders, "I have not got much to boast of and what I have is in your hands, I am willing to do and to take what you say."

Sources: "Liverpool to New Orleans on the *Zetland* (29 Jan 1849–2 Apr 1849)"; "Council Point Emigrating Company, Journal, 1851 Nov.–1852 Sept."

McClellan, Charles E. (1875–1967)

Lived in Mexico in his early teens. Served as counselor to Bishop Joseph C. Bentley and as a faculty member at the Juárez Stake Academy. Second counselor to Juárez Stake President Junius Romney at the time the Mormons fled the country. Settled in Utah. Served two years as professor of English at BYU; edited BYU's 1914 yearbook. Later appointed superintendent of schools in Rigby, Idaho.

Sources: Thomas C. Romney, *The Mormon Colonies in Mexico*, chapter 13; "Charles McClellan, 'United States Social Security Death Index'"; *The Banyan: A Book of the Year 1914*.

McGhie, William (1811–66)

Born in Galloway, Scotland. Served as minister and schoolmaster. Married Elizabeth Collins in 1830 or 1831. Had eight children, but only three lived to maturity. Converted to Mormonism with his family in

1843. In 1849 published a play titled "Priestcraft in Danger," which was performed throughout Utah. Was active in the Glasgow Conference and presided over the conferences of Newcastle and Devonshire beginning in 1852. Migrated to America with his family aboard the *Windemere*. Arrived in Utah in October 1854 and settled along Big Cottonwood Creek. At some point, abandoned his family and returned to Scotland. Unable to gain back his ministerial teaching job and shunned by old friends because of his Mormon faith, returned to his family in 1865. Died in Mill Creek and was buried in the Salt Lake Cemetery.

Sources: Obituary for Elizabeth Collins McGhie, *Deseret News*, May 8, 1897; Velma B. Casto, "History of Elizabeth Collins McGhie"; Mary McGhie Butler, "History of Elizabeth Collins McGhie"; Joseph Clements and Walter Thomson, *Report of the Glasgow Quarterly Conference, Held in the Mechanics' Institution Hall, Canning St., Calton, Glasgow, June 15th and 16th, 1850.*

McKay, David O. (1873–1970)

School teacher and principal. Graduated from the University of Utah in 1897. Returned from a mission to Scotland in 1899. Ordained as an apostle in 1906. Widening business interests placed him in numerous directorships and on corporate boards. Became Church president in 1951. Considered one of the most congenial and best-loved Church leaders. Known for internationalizing the Church. McKay's Anglophilia contrasted with the Anglophobia of J. Reuben Clark, indicative of a split by which subsequent Church leaders were known as either "Clark men" or "McKay men."

Sources: Quinn, *Mormon Hierarchy: Extensions of Power*, 35, 670–721; James B. Allen, "McKay, David O."; Francis M. Gibbons, *David O. McKay: Apostle to the World, Prophet of God*; Lavina Fielding Anderson, "David O. McKay's Worldwide Travels."

Morgan, John (1842–94)

Born in Indiana. Joined Union Army at age eighteen and fought in several battles. Came to Utah at close of the Civil War and established the Morgan Commercial College in Salt Lake City. Baptized in 1867. Mission to southern states, 1875–77. During a second mission gained a reputation for effective missionary work at a time when the LDS image suffered in the South. Ordained to the Presidency of the Seventy in 1884. Traveled extensively among Mormon settlements. Died in Idaho, and was buried in Salt Lake City.

Source: "John Morgan."

Moyle, James H. (1858–1946)

Father of Henry D. Moyle (1889–1963, counselor to David O. McKay, 1959–63). In 1885 interviewed David Whitmer, last surviving witness to the gold plates of the Book of Mormon. US assistant secretary of the treasury, 1917–21. Eastern States Mission president, 1928–33. Chairman of the Church Welfare Committee during the 1940s.

Sources: James H. Moyle, April 8, 1930, *Conference Report*, 121–22; Ronald W. Walker and Richard W. Sadler, "History of the Church: C. 1898–1945, Transitions: Early Twentieth-Century Period," 634.

Nibley, Charles W. (1849–1931)

Presiding Bishop from 1907 to 1925. Second counselor to President Heber J. Grant from 1925 to 1931. Polygamist. In his younger years was a follower of Henry George. Recommended to President Joseph F. Smith that Republican Apostle Reed Smoot leave the Senate and return to Utah in order to avoid negative press coverage of the Church, counsel Smith rejected. By 1914 was a leading Utah businessman and national investor in the sugar beet industry.

Sources: Milton R. Merrill, *Reed Smoot: Apostle in Politics*, 25, 99 note 28; Bryant S. Hinckley, "President Charles W. Nibley," *Improvement Era* 35 (December 1931): 69–71, 92–93; Quinn, *Mormon Hierarchy: Extensions of Power*, 676–78; Matthew C. Godfrey, *Religion, Politics, and Sugar: The Mormon Church, the Federal Government, and the Utah-Idaho Sugar Company, 1907–1921*, 94.

Paxman, James Walter (1861–1943)

Missionary in England from 1884 to 1886. Later a businessman in Nephi, Utah.

Source: James Walter Paxman, Diaries.

Pratt, Orson (1811–81)

Ordained as one of the original Twelve Apostles in 1835. Freemason. In 1842 became estranged from Joseph Smith upon discovering that Smith had proposed polygamous marriage to Pratt's legal wife. Excommunicated, but rebaptized by Smith in 1843. Polygamist. In 1844 became a member of the Council of Fifty. Served ten missions to the Eastern States, plus seven missions to Britain between 1830 and 1869. From 1848 to 1851 was British Mission president, during which time he wrote some of his most important doctrinal works. A self-styled scientist, tried to unite scientific knowledge with his perception of revealed truth.

Sources: Quinn, *Mormon Hierarchy: Origins of Power*, 526; Breck England, *The Life and Thought of Orson Pratt*; David J. Whittaker, "Orson Pratt: Prolific Pamphleteer"; David J. Whittaker, comp., *The Essential Orson Pratt*, xv–xxv; Richard S. Van Wagoner and Steven C. Walker, *A Book of Mormons*, 211–16; Erich Robert Paul, *Science, Religion, and Mormon Cosmology*, 128–41.

Pratt, Parley P. (1807–57)

Brother of Orson Pratt. Evicted from his New York farm in 1826. Baptized Mormon in 1830 in Ohio. Ordained one of the original Twelve Apostles in 1835. Served several missions, including to Britain, Chile, and Indian Territory (Oklahoma). Authored *Voice of Warning* (1837); *Key to the Science of Theology* (1855), and several other missionary and doctrinal works. Imprisoned with Smith in Missouri in 1839. Founding editor of the *Millennial Star* in 1840. Freemason. Embroiled in polygamy in Nauvoo and accused of unauthorized cohabitations. Crossed plains in Brigham Young's vanguard company in 1846–47. Utah colonizer and territorial official. Murdered in Arkansas in 1857 by the legal husband of his last plural wife.

Sources: Quinn, *Mormon Hierarchy: Origins of Power*, 571–73; Parley P. Pratt, *Autobiography of Parley Parker Pratt*.

Pratt, Rey L. (1878–1931)

The grandson of murdered Apostle Parley P. Pratt. Appointed Mexican Mission president in 1907. Ordained one of seven presidents of the First Council of the Seventy in 1925. Served in both positions until his death. Listed himself as a Republican and was often consulted on Mexican affairs by the party's organ in Salt Lake City, the *Salt Lake Herald-*

Republican. Appointed to head the Zion's Printing and Publishing Company, a Church press in Independence, Missouri, because Church leaders recognized his talents as editor, commentator, and Spanish language translator. Rhetorical skill and concern for the welfare of others magnified the influence he exerted in Church and public circles.

Sources: Quinn, *Mormon Hierarchy: Extensions of Power,* 679; Dale F. Beecher, "Rey L. Pratt and the Mexican Mission," 294–95; Mary Pratt Parrish, "Look to the Rock from Which Ye Are Hewn," 54–112; Elizabeth Hernandez, *Mormonism Comes of Age in Mexico,* 17–18; "A New Member of the Council of Seventy," *Improvement Era* 28 (June 1925): 762–63; Melvin J. Ballard, "President Rey L. Pratt," *Improvement Era* 34 (June 1931): 451.

Reynolds, Alice Louise (1873-1938)

Daughter of George Reynolds, secretary to Brigham Young whose 1875 case in the Supreme Court served notice that the federal government would prosecute polygamy. Educated at University of Michigan, University of Chicago, Columbia University, the University of California at Berkeley, and Queens College in London. Taught English at Brigham Young University from 1894 until death. Instrumental in building the BYU library, and the first woman at BYU to be advanced to professor rank. Edited the Church's monthly periodical for women, the *Young Woman's Journal,* from 1923 to 1930. Lectured and organized women's groups throughout the United States. Praised George Eliot's "heroic" attack on "ignorant clergy" who condemned loving unmarried relationships. Member of the General Board of the Relief Society, the women's organization in the Church. Eulogized by Apostle George Albert Smith for her selfless attitude.

Sources: Van Wagoner and Walker, *A Book of Mormons,* 225–26; Maxine Hanks, *Women and Authority: Re-emerging Mormon Feminism,* 60; Leonard J. Arrington and Davis Bitton, *The Mormon Experience: A History of the Latter-day Saints,* 230–31; Charlene Renberg Winters, "A Lighter of Lamps."

Richards, Franklin D. (1821-99)

Born to a Congregationalist family in Massachusetts. After conversion, served a mission in England in 1846 and edited the *Millennial Star* from 1846 to 1850. Ordained as an apostle during a brief return to the United States in 1849. Returned to England in 1850 as the British Mission president, a post he held until his return to Utah in the summer of 1852. Served as British Mission president again from 1854 to 1856. Blamed by Brigham Young for Willie-Martin handcart disaster of 1856. Polygamist. Served in various elected and appointed offices in Utah Territory. Like other LDS general authorities, served in the Mormon "shadow government" of the territory.

Sources: Andrew Jenson, comp., *Encyclopedic History of the Church of Jesus Christ of Latter-day Saints*, 507; Quinn, *Mormon Hierarchy: Extensions of Power*, 682–84, 729; Edward W. Tullidge, *History of Salt Lake City and Its Founders*, 90–101.

Richards, Phineas (1788–1874)

Converted to Mormonism in 1837. Served on the Kirtland High Council, on the Nauvoo City Council, and as an officer in the Nauvoo Legion. Admitted to the Council of Fifty in 1848. Later elected to the Utah Territorial Legislative Assembly.

Sources: Dean C. Jessee, ed., *The Papers of Joseph Smith: Journal, 1832–1842*, 584; Quinn, *Mormon Hierarchy: Extensions of Power*, 728.

Roberts, B. H. (1857–1933)

Ranks as the preeminent Mormon historian and theologian between the death of Orson Pratt and World War II. When fifty prominent Mormon scholars were asked to name the five most influential intellectuals in Church history, thirty-eight put Roberts at the top of the list. Missionary, polygamist, and newspaper editor. In 1888 became a member of the First Council of Seventy. Used his powerful oratorical skill and writing ability to advance a progressive theology. Polygamist. Embraced the concept of an "unfinished universe" and sought to reconcile Mormon thought with science, especially paleontology. Influenced by William James, whose works provided the intellectual underpinning for the American Left. Authored numerous important works, including *New Witnesses for God* (1909); *The Truth, the Way, the Life* (written in 1928 but not published until 1994); and *Comprehensive History of the Church* (1930).

Sources: Sterling M. McMurrin, "Brigham H. Roberts: A Biographical Essay"; Brigham D. Madsen, introduction to *Studies of the Book of Mormon*, by B. H. Roberts; Davis Bitton, "A Masterwork of Mormon

Theology?"; John Patrick Diggins, *The Rise and Fall of the American Left*, 56.

Sjödahl, Janne M. (1853–1939)

A Baptist minister in Sweden before coming to Utah, where he converted to Mormonism. General director for the *Deseret News* from 1906 to 1914 and editor of the Scandinavian newspapers in Salt Lake City. Editor of the *Millennial Star* from 1916 to 1919. Produced some doctrinal works.

Sources: Jenson, *Encyclopedic History of the Church*, 508; Richard L. Jensen, "Swedish Immigrants and Life in Utah," 538.

Smith, George A. (1817–75)

Ordained as an apostle in 1839. Brigham Young's counselor from 1868 until death. Polygamist. Utah colonizer. Business interests included mining, railroads, and mercantile operations. His inflammatory speeches against non-Mormons were a factor in the 1857 Mountain Meadows Massacre.

Sources: Juanita Brooks, *The Mountain Meadows Massacre*, 36–40, 219; Quinn, *Mormon Hierarchy: Origins of Power*, 581–82.

Smith, George Albert (1870–1951)

Grandson of George A. Smith. Ordained apostle in 1903. Appointed to the Utah Land Office by US Presidents William McKinley and Theodore Roosevelt. Traveled widely. Absent from Church responsibilities from 1909 to 1913 due to frail emotional and physical health. A Republican, but nevertheless supported Wilson's League of Nations as a member of the League to Enforce Peace. Became the eighth president of the LDS Church in 1945. Remembered for moral teachings and support for the Boy Scouts.

Sources: S. George Ellsworth, "Smith, George Albert"; Quinn, *Mormon Hierarchy: Extensions of Power*, 689–90.

Smith, Joseph F. (1838–1918)

Nephew of the founding president of the LDS Church, Joseph Smith Jr. Served missions in Hawaii from 1854 to 1858 and Britain from 1860 to 1863. Polygamist. Ordained as an apostle in 1866. Appointed counselor to the First Presidency in 1880. Went underground to escape federal marshals seeking his arrest on polygamy charges. Became the sixth president of the Church in 1901. Risked prosecution for perjury by testifying in the US Senate that he had not authorized post-1890 polygamous marriages. A conservative Republican, Smith wished that only "sound" doctrine be taught in the Church. His October 1916 General Conference address is considered a landmark, as it acknowledged the deferral of theocracy but legitimized Church history by making the survival of priesthood authority the cardinal point of the Restoration.

Sources: Bruce A. Van Orden, "Smith, Joseph F."; Jan Shipps, *Mormonism: The Story of a New Religious Tradition*, 138–48; Quinn, *Mormon Hierarchy: Extensions of Power*, 694–97.

Smith, Joseph, Jr. (1805–44)

Founder of the Mormon movement and first president of the LDS Church. Claimed a theophany in 1820 in which he saw God and Jesus Christ, who commanded him to reject all established religions and await the restoration of the kingdom of God through his ministry. Published the Book of Mormon and organized the Church in 1830. Established communitarianism in Ohio and Missouri. Imprisoned in the aftermath of the 1838 Mormon War in Missouri, but allowed to escape. Took a more esoteric turn in Nauvoo, Illinois during the 1840s. Established Freemasonry and polygamy, organized the secret Council of Fifty to govern the earthly kingdom of God, and announced his candidacy for president of the United States. Assassinated June 27, 1844. While historian Fawn Brodie portrays Smith as a charlatan, Marvin S. Hill credits him with sincere if overblown intentions. Non-Mormon religious critic Harold Bloom labels Smith an authentic religious genius.

Sources: Fawn McKay Brodie, *No Man Knows My History: The Life of Joseph Smith*; Donna Hill, *Joseph Smith: The First Mormon*, 371; Harold Bloom, *The American Religion: The Emergence of the Post-Christian Nation*, 82–84, 99, 113, 126.

Snow, Eliza R. (1804–87)

Sister of the fifth president of the LDS Church, Lorenzo Snow. Known as a "priestess" and "prophetess" of Zion. Plural wife of Joseph Smith Jr., then Brigham Young. Well-known in Utah for her musical and poetic works. In 1867 became president of the women's Relief Society. In 1872 founded *Woman's Exponent*, which continued circulation until 1970. Supported women's right to vote, but did not play an active role in the suffrage movement. Believed God's order required "submission on the part of women."

Source: Van Wagoner and Walker, *A Book of Mormons*, 321–25.

Snow, Lorenzo (1814–1901)

Descended from New England stock. One historian has described the Snow family as "loyal Americans, socially conscious, . . . religious, educated, and intellectually liberal." School teacher prior to his conversion to Mormonism in 1836. Freemason. Polygamist. Ordained as an apostle in 1848. With Joseph Toronto and T. B. H. Stenhouse, opened the Italian Mission in June 1850. Also served a mission in Hawaii. In Utah filled various posts in the territorial government. Became fifth president of the LDS Church in 1898. Best remembered for revamping Church finances, calling for the issuance of bonds, and making passionate appeals for members to pay tithing.

Sources: James B. Allen and Glen M. Leonard, *Story of the Latter-day Saints*, 448–49; Maureen Ursenbach Beecher, "The Eliza Enigma," 32; Quinn, *Mormon Hierarchy: Extensions of Power*, 701–2; Tullidge, *History of Salt Lake City*, 102–7.

Spence, Robert S. (1844–1916)

Born in Bedford, England. Officer in the British Army before joining the LDS Church in 1876. Served a mission to Tennessee during a time of severe persecution in the South, 1880–82. His missionary experiences were printed in the *Deseret News*. As a school teacher and lawyer, lived in Paris, Idaho; Evanston, Wyoming; and Salt Lake City, Utah. His obituary states that "Spence was a man one could not help liking. His genial disposition, his high type of mind, and his courageous character. . . won him the respect of all classes." B. H. Roberts spoke at his funeral.

Sources: Journal History of the Church, February 21, 1881, 5; ibid., November 22, 1882, 3–4; ibid., December 21, 1916, 3; "Robert S. Spence Succumbs to Peritonitis Attack After Long Illness," *Salt Lake Tribune*, December 28, 1916; "Tribute Is Paid to Robert S. Spence," *Salt Lake Tribune*, January 1, 1917; Missionary Record Index.

Spencer, Orson (1802–55)

Graduated from Union College and Baptist Theological Seminary before converting to Mormonism in 1841. On January 23, 1847, assumed leadership of the British Mission and editorship of the *Millennial Star*. Polygamist. "Professor of languages" for the University of the City of Nauvoo and first chancellor of the University of Deseret founded in 1850 in Salt Lake City. Called on another mission to Europe in 1852. After a failed attempt to establish a mission in Prussia, returned to St. Louis. From there went on a mission to the Cherokee Indians. Became sick and died in St. Louis. Orson Pratt wrote in his obituary that Spencer had forsaken "an enviable position in society, and an extensive circle of influential acquaintances" to cleave to "down-trodden people."

Sources: Jenson, *Latter-Day Saint Biographical Encyclopedia*, 1:337–39; Steven Epperson, *Mormons and Jews: Early Mormon Theologies of Israel*, 182 note 29.

Talmage, James E. (1862–1933)

Professor at the University of Utah, 1893–1907. Fellow of the Royal Society of Edinburgh and the Geological Society of London. Served on several mining and philanthropic boards. Ordained as an apostle in 1911. Did not serve a mission, but was British Mission president from 1924 to 1927. Authored doctrinal works such as *Jesus the Christ* and *Articles of Faith*, which received considerable official endorsement.

Source: Quinn, *Mormon Hierarchy: Extensions of Power*, 704–5.

Tanner, Joseph M. (1859–1927)

One of the most prolific writers the LDS Church has produced. A protégé of Karl G. Maeser, the first president of Brigham Young Academy. Graduated with the first class of that institution in 1877. Between 1879 and 1883 was a railroad surveyor for the Denver & Rio Grande and the city of Provo, Utah. Spent much of his life traveling in Europe and the Middle East. In 1884 began a three-and-a-half-year mission to Germany; in 1885 opened a mission among German colonists living in Palestine. Became president of Brigham Young College in Logan, Utah in 1888, but resigned three years later to attend Harvard University. Forced to return to Utah due to health problems. Among the first three men awarded a doctoral degree by the Utah school system. In 1895 opened a law office in Salt Lake City. Reporter on the Utah Supreme Court after statehood was achieved in 1896. Elected the same year as president of the Utah Agricultural College (later renamed Utah State University), where he was also a professor of constitutional and commercial law. Resigned in 1901 because federal law prevented a polygamist from holding a position in a federally-funded institution. Appointed superintendent of Church schools. Also superintendent of the Deseret Sunday School Union. Church authorities released him from his calling when he refused to abandon polygamy. Moved to Canada to farm and died in Lethbridge largely abandoned by his family, who preferred life in Utah.

Sources: Orson F. Whitney, *History of Utah*, 4:354–55; Jenson, *Biographical Encyclopedia*, 1:709–11; George S. Tanner, *John Tanner and His Family*, 224–25; "Joseph M. Tanner Dies in Canada," *Deseret News*, August 20, 1927; Alan K. Parrish, e-mail message to author, August 18, 1999.

Taylor, John (1808–87)

Born in England. Migrated to Canada, where he witnessed the disruptions caused by Canadian separatists. Converted from Methodism to Mormonism by Parley P. Pratt in 1836. Ordained as an apostle in 1838. Co-designed the arcane seal of the Twelve Apostles. Polygamist. In 1844 survived being struck by four musket balls during the militia attack that resulted in the deaths of Joseph and Hyrum Smith. Visited France in 1849–50 to proselytize and to purchase sugar beet plants. Hauled machinery to Utah in forty-four wagons, but the experiment failed; successful Church-sponsored sugar beet planting would not occur until the establishment of the Utah Sugar Company in 1890. Served on the Utah Territorial Legislative Assembly, 1853–54 and 1857–79. Favored property rights and was unswervingly dedicated to the concept of theocracy. Took over Church leadership after Brigham Young's death in 1877 and was officially sustained as the Church's third president in 1880. In 1885 was anointed as "King, Priest, and Ruler Over Israel on Earth." Forced underground shortly thereafter to elude federal marshals making arrests under the anti-polygamy Edmunds-Tucker Act. Believed polygamy would survive. Died in hiding in 1888.

Sources: Curtis Edwin Bolton, Journal, July 20, 1851; B. H. Roberts, *The Life of John Taylor: Third President of the Church of Jesus Christ of Latter-*

day Saints, 45, 61–63; Van Wagoner and Walker, *A Book of Mormons*, 354–60; Godfrey, *Religion, Politics, and Sugar*, 1–2.

Thatcher, Moses (1842–1909)

Baptized in 1856. Ordained as an apostle in 1879. Polygamist. Regent of the University of Deseret, 1878–79. Trustee of Brigham Young University at Salt Lake City from 1891 to 1895 and of Brigham Young College in Logan, Utah from 1877 to 1897. Served as school superintendent, Utah legislator, and Nauvoo Legion captain. Initiated into the Council of Fifty in 1880. In 1900 spoke in favor of socialism at Logan's Brigham Young College and said there always "had always been a conflict between labor and capital." His socialist ideology and Democratic Party activism offended several fellow general authorities. Was dropped from the Quorum of the Twelve Apostles in 1893 and said he regretted being a Mormon. Avoided excommunication by confessing the error of his ways. Abandoned his socialist beliefs by the time of his death in Logan.

Sources: Quinn, *Mormon Hierarchy: Extensions of Power*, 708–9; John S. McCormick and John R. Sillito, *A History of Utah Radicalism: Startling, Socialistic, and Decidedly Revolutionary*, 61–62.

Vance, Joseph A. (1861–1912)

Prominent Church worker and teacher. Served in the Western States Mission in 1886. Embarked on a mission to England in 1908. Served in Young Men's Mutual Improvement Association about 1910. Appointed by renowned Mormon educator Karl Maeser to superintend Church schools in Brigham City, Utah.

Sources: "Joseph A. Vance Dies Suddenly," *Box Elder News*, October 10, 1912; Jenson, *Church Chronology*, 1912, 56; Missionary Record Index; Early Church Information File, cards 309, 312–14, and 316.

Warrum, Noble (1864–1951)

Member of the Utah Constitutional Convention in 1895. Prolific author of historical works, including *Utah since Statehood* (1919) and *Utah in the World War* (1924). Staff writer for the *Salt Lake Tribune*. Practiced law and served as a probate judge. Appointed Salt Lake City postmaster during the Wilson administration. Member of the Church and intimate friend of several general authorities. His political views leaned toward liberal-capitalist. One historian calls him a "nationalistic chauvinist."

Sources: "Utah Journalist Dies in Hollywood," *Deseret News*, November 2, 1951; "Noble Warrum, Writer, Statesman, Friend," *Salt Lake Tribune*, November 4, 1951; "Noble Warrum, Sr.," *Deseret News*, November 5, 1951; Fox, *J. Reuben Clark*, 483. For Warrum's economic and political views, see "Mexico Needs Stability, Says Claims Man," *Deseret News*, May 10, 1926; and "Mr. Warrum's Address," *Deseret News*, May 20, 1926.

Wells, John (1864–1941)

Businessman. Delegate to the territorial People's Party Convention in 1890. Democratic election judge in the 1890s, Republican during the 1900s. Second counselor in the Presiding Bishopric under Bishop Charles W. Nibley from 1918 to 1938.

Source: Quinn, *Mormon Hierarchy: Extensions of Power*, 712.

Wells, Junius F. (1854–1930)

Served missions in Britain and the United States. One of the founders of the Young Men's Mutual Improvement Association in 1875. Founding editor of the *Contributor* in 1879. In 1919 became assistant editor of the *Millennial Star*, a post held until 1921.

Sources: Jenson, *Latter-day Saint Biographical Encyclopedia*, 1:714; obituary in *Deseret News*, April 15, 1930; obituary in *Salt Lake Tribune*, April 16, 1930.

Whitney, Orson F. (1855–1931)

Ordained to the Quorum of the Twelve in 1906. Polygamist. Edited the *Millennial Star* from 1880 to 1882 and remained intermittently involved until 1885. Led séances and claimed to have seen Christ. Said in 1889 that he would one day lead the Church. Served as Church historian from 1902 to 1906 and wrote a number of works on Utah history. Did not stop seeking additional plural wives until 1911, several years after the Second Manifesto.

Source: Quinn, *Mormon Hierarchy: Extensions of Power*, 713–14.

Woodruff, Wilford W. (1807–98)

Ordained as an apostle in 1839. Member of Zion's Camp in 1834. Enjoyed tremendous proselytizing success during the Twelve's mission to Britain in 1840–41. Polygamist. Held the rank of captain in the Nauvoo Legion. Major leader in the western migration and settlement of Utah. Became the fourth president of the LDS Church in 1887. Issued the Manifesto ending polygamy in 1890. His journal provides important insights into the thinking of the Church's nineteenth-century leadership. A biographer concludes that he had a "firm commitment to building the Kingdom of God" but combined it with a "deep respect and desire for material progress." His holistic view admitted no "discontinuity between heaven and earth."

Sources: Dean C. Jessee, "Woodruff, Wilford"; Thomas G. Alexander, *Things in Heaven and Earth: The Life and Times of Wilford Woodruff, a Mormon Prophet*, 152.

Young, Brigham (1801–77)

Ordained in 1835 as one of the original members of the Quorum of the Twelve. Admitted to the Council of Fifty in 1844. Polygamist. Freemason. After Joseph Smith's death in 1844, headed an apostolic interregnum until his confirmation as second president of the LDS Church in 1849. Led his followers to Utah, where he became territorial governor in 1850. Ranks in American history as a great colonizer and organizer, responsible for a chain of settlements stretching from northern Mexico to Calgary, Canada. Funneled thousands of European immigrants into the Intermountain West. Was deposed as governor after the Utah War in 1857, but remained head of a Mormon "shadow government"; his influence in the territory never diminished. Pragmatic sermons focused on the building of the Mormon kingdom. Attempted to revive the early Mormon communist ideal, but failed as Utah absorbed capitalistic values and Mormon sociopolitical control was slowly diluted. His last words were "Joseph, Joseph, Joseph," referring to Joseph Smith Jr.

Sources: Newell K. Bringhurst, "Brigham Young," 649–50; Leonard J. Arrington, *Brigham Young: American Moses*.

Young, Levi Edgar (1874–1963)

Attended Harvard but did not graduate. Earned an MA from Columbia University in 1910. History professor at the University of Utah, 1899–1939. Missionary in Germany, 1901–4. Blamed Germany for World War I and loathed war on principle. Served as an advisor to the *Salt Lake Tribune* concerning Latter-day Saint viewpoints. Appointed to the First Council of the Seventy in 1910. In 1920 described Mormonism as a "utilitarian-idealistic religion" that that was based on "a mind of the critically-intellectual type." Served as president of the New England Mission from 1939 to 1942. Was threatened with dismissal from the Seventy in 1942 for delivering secular sermons. Participated in numerous civic organizations, including the Utah Sons of the American Revolution (1914), the League to Enforce Peace (1918), the National Conference of Christians and Jews (1936), the Utah Centennial Exposition Committee (1938–1947), and the religion committee of the Utah Association for the United Nations (1946).

Sources: Quinn, *Mormon Hierarchy: Extensions of Power*, 723–24; Levi Edgar Young, Notes on War; Levi Edgar Young, "Sociological Aspect of 'Mormonism,'" *Improvement Era* 23 (July 1920): 822, 824; G. Homer Durham, "Levi Edgar Young—Senior President, First Council of the Seventy," *Improvement Era* 55 (August 1952): 570–73, 612–15.

BIBLIOGRAPHY

Abbreviations

LDS Church History Library. Church History Library of the Church of Jesus Christ of Latter-day Saints, Salt Lake City.

Lee Library. L. Tom Perry Special Collections, Harold B. Lee Library, Brigham Young University, Provo, Utah.

Marriott Library. Special Collections and Archives, J. Willard Marriott Library, University of Utah, Salt Lake City.

Historical Newspapers and Periodicals

American Mercury (New York, 1924–81)
Box Elder News (Brigham City, Utah, 1900–1930)
Children's Friend (Salt Lake City, 1929–70)
Commonweal (New York, 1924–present)
Contributor (Salt Lake City, 1879–96)
Current History (New York, 1914–43; Philadelphia, 1943–present)
Deseret Evening News (Salt Lake City, 1867–1920)
Deseret News (Great Salt Lake City [Salt Lake City], 1850–67, 1920–present)
Deseret Weekly (Salt Lake City, 1888–98)
Ethics: An International Journal of Social, Political, and Legal Philosophy (Chicago, 1938–present)
Evening and Morning Star (Independence, Mo., 1830–33)
Evening Sun (New York, 1887–1920)
Foreign Affairs (New York, 1921–present)
Fortnightly Review (London, 1865–1954)
Forum (New York and Philadelphia, 1886–1930)
Frontier Guardian (Kanesville [Council Bluffs], Iowa, 1849–53)
Harper's Monthly Magazine (New York, 1900–1913)
Improvement Era (Salt Lake City, 1897–1970)
Juvenile Instructor (Great Salt Lake City [Salt Lake City], 1866–1929)
Latter-day Saints' Millennial Star (Manchester and Liverpool, 1840–1940)
Latter-day Saints' Messenger and Advocate (Kirtland, Ohio, 1834–37)
Liahona: The Elder's Journal (Independence, Mo., 1907–45)

Literary Digest (New York, 1890–1938)
Living Age (Boston, 1896–1941)
Mormon (New York, 1855–57)
Nation (New York, 1865–present)
New Republic (New York and Washington, DC, 1914–present)
New York Times (New York, 1851–present)
Outlook (New York, 1870–1928)
Outlook and Independent (New York, 1928–32)
Relief Society Magazine (Salt Lake City, 1915–40)
Rocky Mountain Review (Salt Lake City, 1938–46)
Salt Lake Herald-Republican (Salt Lake City, 1909–18)
Salt Lake Telegram (Salt Lake City, 1915–52)
Salt Lake Tribune (Salt Lake City, 1890–present)
Saturday Evening Post (Philadelphia, 1821–1969)
Scribner's Magazine (New York, 1887–1939)
Seer (Washington, DC, 1853–54)
Times and Seasons (Nauvoo, 1839–46)
Utah Democrat (Salt Lake City, 1921–27)
Weekly Salt Lake Tribune and Utah Mining Gazette (Salt Lake City, 1871–72)
World Affairs Interpreter (Los Angeles, 1932–55)
World Tomorrow (New York, 1918–34)
Young Woman's Journal (Salt Lake City, 1889–1929)

Published and Unpublished Sources

Adams, George J. *A Few Plain Facts, Shewing the Folly, Wickedness, and Imposition of the Rev. Timothy R. Matthews; Also a Short Sketch of the Rise, Faith and Doctrine of the Church of Jesus Christ of Latter-day Saints.* Bedford, England: C. B. Merry, 1841. LDS Church History Library.

_____. *A Letter to His Excellency John Tyler, President of the United States, Touching the Signs of the Times, and the Political Destiny of the World.* New York: C. A. Calhoun, 1844. LDS Church History Library.

Aird, Polly. "Why Did the Scots Convert?" *Journal of Mormon History* 26, no. 1 (Spring 2000): 91–122.

Akgün, Seçil Karal. "Mormon Missionaries in the Ottoman Empire." *Turcica: Revue d'Etudes Turques* 28 (1996): 347–57.

Alexander, Robert J. "Bolivia: Organizations." In Tenenbaum, *Encyclopedia of Latin American History and Culture,* 1:376–77.

_____. *Prophets of the Revolution: Profiles of Latin American Leaders.* New York: Macmillan, 1962.

Alexander, Thomas G. "'To Maintain Harmony': Adjusting to External and Internal Stress, 1890–1930." *Dialogue: A Journal of Mormon Thought* 15, no. 4 (Winter 1982): 44–58.

_____. *Mormonism in Transition: A History of the Latter-day Saints, 1890–1930.* Illini Books ed. Urbana: University of Illinois Press, 1996.

_____. "Between Revivalism and the Social Gospel: The Latter-day Saint Social Advisory Committee, 1916–1922." *BYU Studies* 23 (Winter 1983): 19–39.

_____. *Things in Heaven and Earth: The Life and Times of Wilford Woodruff, a Mormon Prophet.* Salt Lake City: Signature Books, 1991.

_____. *Utah, the Right Place: The Official Centennial History.* Salt Lake City: Gibbs Smith, 1995.

Allen, James B. "Since 1950: Creators and Creations of Mormon History." In Bitton and Beecher, *New Views of Mormon History*, 407–38.

_____. "But Dick Tracy Landed on the Moon." *Sunstone* 7, no. 5 (September–October 1982): 18–19.

_____. "McKay, David O." In Ludlow, *Encyclopedia of Mormonism*, 2:870–75. New York: Macmillan, 1992.

_____. "Personal Faith and Public Policy: Some Timely Observations on the League of Nations Controversy in Utah." *BYU Studies* 14 (Autumn 1973): 77–98.

_____. *Trials of Discipleship: The Story of William Clayton, a Mormon.* Urbana: University of Illinois Press, 1987.

Allen, James B., Ronald K. Esplin, and David J. Whittaker. *Men with a Mission: The Quorum of the Twelve Apostles in the British Isles, 1837–1841.* Salt Lake City: Deseret Book, 1992.

Allen, James B., and Glen M. Leonard. *Story of the Latter-day Saints.* Salt Lake City: Deseret Book, 1976.

Allen, James B., and Malcolm R. Thorp. "The Mission of the Twelve to England, 1840–41: Mormon Apostles and the Working Classes." *BYU Studies* 15, no. 4 (Summer 1975): 499–526.

Allen, James B., Ronald W. Walker, and David J. Whittaker. *Studies in Mormon History, 1830–1997: An Indexed Bibliography.* Urbana: University of Illinois Press, 2000.

All Things Testify of Him: Inspirational Paintings by Latter-day Saint Artists. Salt Lake City: Bookcraft, 1999.

Anderson, C. LeRoy. *For Christ Will Come Tomorrow: The Saga of the Morrisites.* Logan: Utah State University Press, 1981.

Anderson, James. *The Constitution of Free-Masons.* 1st American ed. Philadelphia: Benjamin Franklin, 1723.

Anderson, Lavina Fielding. "David O. McKay's Worldwide Travels." In Brown, Cannon, and Jackson, *Historical Atlas of Mormonism*, 126–27.

Andrew, Laurel B. *The Early Temples of the Mormons: The Architecture of the Millennial Kingdom in the American West.* Albany: State University of New York Press, 1978.

Andrus, Hyrum L. "The Second American Revolution: Era of Preparation." Double issue. *BYU Studies* 1, no. 2 and 2, no. 1 (Autumn 1959 and Winter 1960): 71–99.

Angress, Werner T. *Stillborn Revolution: The Communist Bid for Power in Germany, 1921–1923.* Princeton, N.J.: Princeton University Press, 1963.

Anthony W. Ivins Papers. 1875–1934. Mss B-2, Research Center, Utah State Historical Society, Salt Lake City.

Appleby, William I. Autobiography and Journal. 1848–56. Holograph. MS 1401, fd. 1, LDS Church History Library.

_____. "History of the Signs of the Times for the Benefit of the Church of the Latter-day Saints." 1848. Holograph. MS 1401, fd. 2, LDS Church History Library.

_____. *Lines Suggested and Composed on the Present State of the World.* Philadelphia: Bicking and Guilbert, May 1, 1848. Broadside. LDS Church History Library.

Arrington, Leonard J. *Brigham Young: American Moses.* 1985. Reprint, Urbana: University of Illinois Press, 1986.

_____. *Great Basin Kingdom: An Economic History of the Latter-day Saints, 1830–1900.* Lincoln: University of Nebraska, 1958.

_____. "In Honorable Remembrance: Thomas L. Kane's Services to the Mormons." *BYU Studies* 21 (Fall 1981): 389–402.

Arrington, Leonard J., and Davis Bitton. *The Mormon Experience: A History of the Latter-day Saints.* 1979. Reprint, New York: Vintage Books, 1980.

_____. *Saints without Halos: The Human Side of Mormon History.* Salt Lake City: Signature Books, 1981.

Arrington, Leonard J., Feramorz Y. Fox, and Dean L. May. *Building the City of God: Community and Cooperation among the Mormons.* Salt Lake City: Deseret Book, 1976.

Ashton, Wendell J. *Voice in the West: Biography of Pioneer Newspaper.* New York: Duell, Sloan, and Pearce, 1950.

Atkin, Ronald. *Revolution! Mexico, 1910–1920.* New York: John Day, 1970.

Báez-Camargo, G., and Kenneth G. Grubb. *Religion in the Republic of Mexico.* London: World Dominion Press, 1935.

Bagley, Will. *Blood of the Prophets: Brigham Young and the Massacre at Mountain Meadows.* Norman: University of Oklahoma Press, 2002.

_____, ed. *Scoundrel's Tale: The Samuel Brannan Papers.* Kingdom in the West: The Mormons and the American Frontier 3. Spokane, Wash.: Arthur H. Clarke, 1999.

Bailey, David C. *¡Viva Cristo Rey! The Cristero Rebellion and the Church-State Conflict in Mexico.* Austin: University of Texas Press, 1974.

Bailey, Victor. "The Metropolitan Police, the Home Office, and the Threat of Outcast London." In *Policing and Punishment in Nineteenth Century Britain,* edited by Victor Bailey, 95–104. New Brunswick, N. J.: Rutgers University Press, 1981.

Ballard, M. Russell, ed. *Melvin J. Ballard: Crusader for Righteousness.* Salt Lake City: Bookcraft, 1966.

Balmer, Randall. "Religions." In *The Reader's Companion to American History,* edited by Eric Foner and John A. Garraty, 929. Boston: Houghton Mifflin, 1991.

Bancroft, Hubert Howe. *History of Utah, 1540–1886.* 1889. Reprint, Las Vegas: Nevada Publications, 1982.

The Banyan: A Book of the Year 1914. Provo, Utah: student body of the Brigham Young University, 1914. http://www.archive.org/details/banyan1914brig.

Barlow, Brent A. "The Irish Experience." In Bloxham, Moss, and Porter, *Truth Will Prevail*, 299–331.

Barlow, Philip L. "To Mend a Fractured Reality: Joseph Smith's Project." *Journal of Mormon History* 38, no. 3 (Summer 2012): 28–50.

Barr, James. "Revelation through History in Old Testament and in Modern Theology." In *New Theology*. Vol 1. Edited by Martin E. Marty and Dean G. Peerman, 60–74. New York: Macmillan, 1964.

Barrett, Francis. *The Magus, or Celestial Intelligencer; Being a Complete System of Occult Philosophy.* London: Lackington, Alley, 1801. In *New Mormon Studies: A Comprehensive Resource Library.*

Barron, Howard H. "Hyde, Orson." In Ludlow, *Encyclopedia of Mormonism*, 2:665–67.

Bartholomew, Rebecca. *Audacious Women: Early British Mormon Immigrants.* Salt Lake City: Signature Books, 1995.

Barton, Betty L. "Mormon Poor Relief: A Social Welfare Interlude." *BYU Studies* 18, no. 1 (Fall 1977): 66–88.

Bautista, Margarito. *La evolución de México sus verdaderos progenitores y su origen: el destino de América y Europa.* Mexico, D.F.: Talleres Gráficos Laguna, 1935.

Beals, Carleton. *The Coming Struggle for Latin America.* 2nd ed. New York: Halcyon House, 1940. First published 1938.

_____. *The Great Circle: Further Adventures in Free-Lancing.* Philadelphia: J. B. Lippincott, 1940.

_____. *Mexican Maze.* Philadelphia: J. B. Lippincott, 1931.

Beaver, R. Pierce. *Church, State, and the American Indians: Two and a Half Centuries of Partnership in Missions between Protestant Churches and Government.* St. Louis: Concordia Publishing House, 1966.

Beckett, J. C. *The Making of Modern Ireland, 1603–1923.* New York: Alfred A. Knopf, 1966.

Beecher, Dale F. "Rey L. Pratt and the Mexican Mission." *BYU Studies* 15, no. 3 (Spring 1975): 293–307.

Beecher, Maureen Ursenbach. "The Eliza Enigma." *Dialogue: A Journal of Mormon Thought* 11, no. 1 (Spring 1978): 30–43.

Beezley, William H. *Insurgent Governor: Abraham Gonzalez and the Mexican Revolution in Chihuahua.* Lincoln: University of Nebraska Press, 1973.

Beisner, Robert L. *From the Old Diplomacy to the New, 1865–1900.* 2nd ed. Arlington Heights, Ill.: Harlan Davidson, 1986.

_____. *Twelve against Empire: The Anti-Imperialists, 1898–1900.* New York: McGraw-Hill, 1968.

Bell, Stella Jaques. *Life History and Writings of John Jaques.* Rexburg, Idaho: Ricks College Press, 1978.

Bennett, John C. *The History of the Saints; or, an Exposé of Joe Smith and Mormonism.* 3rd ed. Urbana: University of Illinois Press, 2000. First published 1842.

Bennett, Richard E. "James E. Talmage and the League of Nations." Unpublished manuscript, n.d. Copy in author's possession.

_____. *We'll Find the Place: The Mormon Exodus, 1846–1848.* Salt Lake City: Deseret Book, 1997.

Berenson, Edward. *Populist Religion and Left-Wing Politics in France, 1830–1852.* Princeton, N.J.: University of Princeton Press, 1984.

Bergera, Gary James, ed. "'Let Br. Pratt Do as He Will': Orson Pratt's 29 January 1860 Confessional Discourse—Unrevised." *Dialogue: A Journal of Mormon Thought* 13, no. 2 (Summer 1980): 50–58.

Bergera, Gary James, and Ronald Priddis. *Brigham Young University: A House of Faith.* Salt Lake City: Signature Books, Inc., 1985.

Bertrand, Louis A. *Memoirs of a Mormon.* Translated by Gaston Chappuis. Salt Lake City, 1964. Typescript. LDS Church History Library. First published 1862 in French.

Bethell, Leslie, ed. *The Cambridge History of Latin America.* 11 vols. New York: Cambridge University Press, 1984–2008.

Bickmore, Jean White, ed. *Church, State, and Politics: The Diaries of John Henry Smith.* Salt Lake City: Signature Books/Smith Research Associates, 1990.

Biema, David van. "Kingdom Come." *Time Magazine* 150, no. 5 (August 4, 1997): 52.

Bigler, David L. *Forgotten Kingdom: The Mormon Theocracy in the American West, 1847–1896.* Kingdom in the West: The Mormons and the American Frontier 2. Spokane, Wash.: Arthur H. Clark, 1998.

Billington, James. *Fire in the Minds of Men: The Origins of the Revolutionary Faith.* New York: Basic Books, 1980.

"Biography of Eliza Cook." PoemHunter. Accessed February 15, 2013. http://www. poemhunter.com/eliza-cook/biography/.

Birney, Herman Hoffman. *Zealots in Zion.* Philadelphia: Penn Publishing, 1931.

Bitton, Davis. "Anti-Intellectualism in Mormon History." *Dialogue: A Journal of Mormon Thought* 1, no. 3 (Autumn 1966): 111–34.

_____. *George Q. Cannon: A Biography.* Salt Lake City: Deseret Book, 1999.

_____. *Guide to Mormon Diaries and Autobiographies.* Provo, Utah: Brigham Young University Press, 1977.

_____. "A Masterwork of Mormon Theology?" In Roberts, *The Truth, the Way, the Life,* 561–67.

Bitton, Davis, and Leonard J. Arrington. *Mormons and Their Historians.* Salt Lake City: University of Utah Press, 1988.

Bitton, Davis, and Maureen Ursenbach Beecher, eds. *New Views of Mormon History: A Collection of Essays in Honor of Leonard J. Arrington.* Salt Lake City: University of Utah Press, 1987.

Black, Jan Knippers, ed. *Latin America, Its Problems and Its Promise: A Multidisciplinary Introduction.* 3rd rev. ed. Boulder, Colo.: Westview Press, 1998.

Blancarte, Roberto J. "Recent Changes in Church-State Relations in Mexico: An Historical Approach." *Journal of Church and State.* 35, no. 4 (Autumn 1993): 781–806.

Bloom, Harold. *The American Religion: The Emergence of the Post-Christian Nation.* New York: Simon and Schuster, 1992.

Bloxham, V. Ben, James R. Moss, and Larry C. Porter, eds. *Truth Will Prevail: The Rise of the Church of Jesus Christ of Latter-day Saints in the British Isles, 1837–1987*. Cambridge: Cambridge University Press for the Corporation of the President of the Church of Jesus Christ of Latter-day Saints, 1987.

Bobelian, Michael. *Children of Armenia: A Forgotten Genocide and the Century-long Struggle for Justice*. New York: Simon and Schuster, 2009.

Bober, Mandell Morton. *Karl Marx's Interpretation of History*. 2nd ed., rev. Cambridge, Mass.: Harvard University Press, 1948.

Bolton, Curtis Edwin. Reminiscences and Journals. 2 vols. 1846–53. Holograph. MS 1424, LDS Church History Library.

Bonino, José Miguez. "Protestant Churches in Latin America since 1930." In Bethell, *Cambridge History of Latin America*, vol. 6, pt. 2, 583–604.

Booth, Joseph Wilford. Diaries. 13 vols. 1898–1933. Mormon Missionary Diaries Collection.

Boyer, Paul. *When Time Shall Be No More: Prophecy Belief in Modern American Culture*. Cambridge, Mass.: Belknap Press of Harvard University Press, 1992.

Bozeman, Theodore Dwight. "Inductive and Deductive Politics: Science and Society in Antebellum Presbyterian Thought." *Journal of American History* 64, no. 3 (December 1977): 704–22.

Briceland, Alan V. "The Philadelphia Aurora, the New England Illuminati, and the Election of 1800." *Pennsylvania Magazine of History and Biography* 100, no. 1 (January 1976): 3–36.

Bringhurst, Newell G. "Brigham Young." In Powell, *Utah History Encyclopedia*, 649–50.

Bringhurst, Newell G., and Lavina Fielding Anderson, eds. *Excavating Mormon Pasts: The New Historiography of the Last Half Century*. Salt Lake City: Greg Kofford Books, 2004.

Brinton, Crane. *The Anatomy of Revolution*. Rev. and exp. ed. New York: Vintage Books, 1965. First published 1938.

British Mission. Manuscript History and Historical Reports. 1841–1971. Microfilm. LR 1140 2, Reels 8–9, LDS Church History Library.

Britsch, R. Lanier. *From the East: The History of the Latter-day Saints in Asia, 1851–1996*. Salt Lake City: Deseret Book, 1998.

Britton, John A. *Revolution and Ideology: Images of the Mexican Revolution in the United States*. Lexington: University Press of Kentucky, 1995.

Brodie, Fawn McKay. *No Man Knows My History: The Life of Joseph Smith*. New York: Alfred A. Knopf, 1945.

Brooke, John L. *The Refiner's Fire: The Making of Mormon Cosmology, 1644–1844*. New York: Cambridge University Press, 1994.

Brooks, Juanita, ed. *Journal of the Southern Indian Mission: Diary of Thomas D. Brown*. Western Text Society 4. Logan: Utah State University Press, 1972.

———, ed. *On the Mormon Frontier: The Diary of Hosea Stout, 1844–1861*. 2 vols. 1964. Reprint, Salt Lake City: University of Utah Press, 1982.

———. *The Mountain Meadows Massacre*. Norman: University of Oklahoma Press, 1962.

Brown, Kent S., Donald Q. Cannon, and Richard H. Jackson. *Historical Atlas of*

Mormonism. New York: Simon and Schuster, 1994.

Brown, Matthew B., and Paul Thomas Smith. *Symbols in Stone: Symbolism on the Early Temples of the Restoration.* American Fork, Utah: Covenant Communications, 1997.

Brown, Orson P. Autobiography. 1932. Typescript on microfilm. Taylor O. Macdonald Collection. 1857–1980. MS 9548, Reel 1, item 15, LDS Church History Library.

Brown, Victoria. "Advocate for Democracy: Jane Addams and the Pullman Strike." In Schneirov, Stromquist, and Salvatore, *Pullman Strike and the Crisis of the 1890s,* 130–58.

Browning, Gary L. *Russia and the Restored Gospel.* Salt Lake City: Deseret Book, 1997.

Bruce, Robert V. *1877: Year of Violence.* Indianapolis: Bobbs-Merrill, 1959.

Bryant, M. Darrol, and Donald W. Dayton, eds. *The Coming Kingdom: Essays in American Millennialism and Eschatology.* Barrytown, N.Y.: New Era Books, International Religious Foundation, 1983.

Buber, Martin. *Paths in Utopia.* Translated by R.F.C. Hull. 1949. Reprint, Boston: Beacon Press, 1958.

Buel, Richard, Jr. *Securing the Revolution: Ideology in American Politics, 1789–1815.* Ithaca, N.Y.: Cornell University Press, 1972.

Buerger, David John. *The Mysteries of Godliness: A History of Mormon Temple Worship.* San Francisco: Smith Research Associates, 1994.

Buhle, Mari Jo, Paul Buhle, and Dan Georgakas, eds. *Encyclopedia of the American Left.* Urbana: University of Illinois Press, 1992.

Buhle, Paul. "Socialist Labor Party." In Buhle, Buhle, and Georgakas, *Encyclopedia of the American Left,* 711–16.

———. "Socialist Party." In Buhle, Buhle, and Georgakas, *Encyclopedia of the American Left,* 716–23.

Bullock, Steven C. *Revolutionary Brotherhood: Freemasonry and the Transformation of the American Social Order, 1730–1840.* Chapel Hill: University of North Carolina Press, 1996.

Burgess, Ernest Hungate. Diary. 1905–7. Mormon Missionary Diaries Collection.

Burton, Richard Francis. *The City of the Saints and across the Rocky Mountains to California.* Edited by Fawn McKay Brodie. New York: Alfred A. Knopf, 1963. First published 1861.

Bushman, Richard L. "The Book of Mormon and the American Revolution." In *Book of Mormon Authorship: New Light on Ancient Origins,* edited by Noel B. Reynolds, 189–212. Provo, Utah: Religious Studies Center, Brigham Young University, 1982.

———. *Joseph Smith and the Beginnings of Mormonism.* Urbana: University of Illinois Press, 1984.

———. "Virtue and the Constitution." In Hillam, *"By the Hands of Wise Men,"* 29–38.

Butler, Gregory S. "Visions of a Nation Transformed: Modernity and Ideology in Wilson's Political Thought." *Journal of Church and State* 39 (Winter 1997): 37–51.

Butler, Mary McGhie. "History of Elizabeth Collins McGhie." Darrin and Andrea

Lythgoe's Genealogy Pages. Accessed October 22, 2011. http://lythgoes.net/genealogy/history/ElizabethCollinsMcGhie.php.

Campbell, Eugene E. "Pioneers and Patriotism: Conflicting Loyalties." In Bitton and Beecher, *New Views of Mormon History*, 307–22.

Cannon, George Q. *Gospel Truth: Discourses and Writings of President George Q. Cannon.* 2 vols. Compiled by Jerreld L. Newquist. Salt Lake City: Zion's Book Store, 1957.

Carmack, Noel A. "Of Prophets and Pale Horses: Joseph Smith, Benjamin West, and the American Millenarian Tradition." *Dialogue: A Journal of Mormon Thought* 29, no. 3 (Fall 1996): 173–84.

Carroll, Peter N. *The Odyssey of the Abraham Lincoln Brigade: Americans in the Spanish Civil War.* Stanford, Calif.: Stanford University Press, 1994.

Carvalho, Jose Murilo de. "Armed Forces and Politics in Brazil, 1930–1945." *Hispanic American Historical Review* 62, no. 2 (May 1982): 193–223.

Cashman, Sean Dennis. *America in the Gilded Age: From the Death of Lincoln to the Rise of Theodore Roosevelt.* New York: New York University Press, 1984.

Cassara, Ernest. "The Development of America's Sense of Mission." In Zamora, *Apocalyptic Vision in America*, 64–96.

Castelli, Helen. "June Days (22–26 June 1848)." In Chastain, *Encyclopedia of 1848 Revolutions.* http://www.ohio.edu/chastain/ip/junedays.htm.

Casto, Velma B. "History of Elizabeth Collins McGhie." Darrin and Andrea Lythgoe's Genealogy Pages. Accessed October 22, 2011. http://lythgoes.net/genealogy/history/ElizabethCollinsMcGhie.php.

Chard, Gary Ray. "A History of the French Mission of the Church of Jesus Christ of Latter-day Saints, 1850–1960." MS thesis, Utah State University, 1965.

"Charles Mcclellan, 'United States Social Security Death Index.'" Family Search. Accessed June 3, 2011. https://familysearch.org/pal:/MM9.1.1/V9G1-DJM.

Charlton, L. E. O. *The Menace of the Clouds.* London: William Hodge, 1937.

Chase, Stuart. *Mexico: A Study of Two Americas.* New York: Literary Guild, 1931.

Chastain, James G., ed. *Encyclopedia of 1848 Revolutions.* Ohio University, 2005. http://www.ohio.edu/chastain/index.htm.

Cherry, Conrad, ed. *God's New Israel: Religious Interpretations of American Destiny.* Englewood Cliffs, N.J.: Prentice Hall, 1971.

Cherry, George L. "American Metropolitan Press Reaction to the Paris Commune of 1871." *Mid-America* 32, no. 1 (January 1950): 3–12.

Clark, James R. "The Kingdom of God, the Council of Fifty and the State of Deseret." *Utah Historical Quarterly* 26 (April 1958): 130–48.

———, comp. *Messages of the First Presidency of the Church of Jesus Christ of Latter-day Saints, 1833–1964.* 6 vols. Salt Lake City: Bookcraft, 1965–70.

Clarkana Papers of Joshua Reuben Clark Jr. 1873–1962. MSS 303, Lee Library.

Clayton, James L. "The Challenge of Secularism." *Dialogue: A Journal of Mormon Thought* 3, no. 3 (Autumn 1968): 63–76.

Clements, Joseph, and Walter Thomson. *Report of the Glasgow Quarterly Conference, Held in the Mechanics' Institution Hall, Canning St., Calton,*

Glasgow, June 15th and 16th, 1850. [Glasgow, 1850]. http://archive.org/details/reportofglasgowq00glas.

Clendenen, Clarence C. *Blood on the Border: The United States Army and the Mexican Irregulars.* New York: Macmillan, 1969.

Cloud, Barbara Lee. *The Business of Newspapers on the Western Frontier.* Reno: University of Nevada Press, 1992.

Cobb, John, and Truman G. Madsen. "Theodicy." In Ludlow, *Encyclopedia of Mormonism,* 4:1473–74.

Cohen, Warren I. *Empire without Tears: America's Foreign Relations, 1921–1933.* New York: McGraw-Hill, 1987.

Cohn, Norman. *The Pursuit of the Millennium: Revolutionary Millenarians and Mystical Anarchists of the Middle Ages.* Rev. and exp. ed. New York: Oxford University Press, 1970.

Coil, Henry Wilson. *Coil's Masonic Encyclopedia.* New York: Macoy Publishing and Masonic Supply, 1961.

Cole, Wayne S. *Charles A. Lindbergh and the Battle against American Intervention in World War II.* New York: Harcourt Brace Jovanovich, 1974.

Conniff, Michael L. "The Tenentes in Power: A New Perspective on the Brazilian Revolution of 1930." *Journal of Latin American Studies* 10, no. 1 (May 1978): 61–82.

Conquest, Robert. *Religion in the USSR.* Soviet Studies Series. London: Bodley Head, 1968.

Copeland, Lee. "From Calcutta to Kaysville: Is Righteousness Color-Coded?" *Dialogue: A Journal of Mormon Thought* 21, no. 3 (Fall 1988): 89–99.

Corley, T. A. B. *Democratic Despot: A Life of Napoleon III.* London: Barrie and Rockliff, 1961.

"Council Point Emigrating Company, Journal, 1851 Nov.–1852 Sept." Mormon Pioneer Overland Travel database. Accessed November 16, 2012. http://www.lds.org/churchhistory/library/source/%1,18016,4976-4651,00.html.

Craig, Gordon A. *Germany: 1866–1945.* 1978. Reprint, New York: Oxford University Press, 1980.

Crawley, Peter L. *A Descriptive Bibliography of the Mormon Church.* 2 vols. Provo, Utah: Religious Studies Center, Brigham Young University, 1997–2005.

———, ed. and comp. *The Essential Parley P. Pratt.* Classics in Mormon Thought 1. Salt Lake City: Signature Books, 1990.

Crossman, Virginia. "The Army and Law and Order in the Nineteenth Century." In *A Military History of Ireland,* edited by Thomas Bartlett and Keith Jeffery, 358–78. Cambridge: Cambridge University Press, 1996.

Crowther, Duane S. *Prophecy—Key to the Future.* Salt Lake City: Bookcraft, 1962.

Curti, Merle E. "The Impact of the Revolutions of 1848 on American Thought." *Proceedings of the American Philosophical Society* 93, no. 3 (June 1949): 209–15.

Curtis, Eugene N. "American Opinion of the French Nineteenth-Century Revolutions." *American Historical Review* 29, no. 2 (January 1924): 249–70.

Darter, Francis M. *Minutes of Excommunication.* Salt Lake City: Shepard Book, [1918].

———. *Zion's Redemption: The Return of John the Revelator, the Elias, the Restorer, the Gatherer of All Israel and Forerunner of Christ's Second Coming.* Salt Lake City: Deseret News, 1933.

Davidson, D., and H. Aldersmith. *The Great Pyramid, Its Divine Message: An Original Co-ordination of Historical Documents and Archaeological Evidences.* London: Williams and Norgate, 1924.

Davidson, James W. "Eschatology in New England: 1700–1763." PhD diss., Yale University, 1973.

Davis, David Brion, ed. *The Fear of Conspiracy: Images of Un-American Subversion from the Revolution to the Present.* Ithaca, N.Y.: Cornell University Press, 1971.

_____. "The New England Origins of Mormonism." *The New England Quarterly* 26, no. 2 (June 1953): 147–68.

Davis, Michelle Bray, and Rollin W. Quimby. "Senator Proctor's Cuban Speech: Speculations on a Cause of the Spanish-American War." *Quarterly Journal of Speech* 55, no. 2 (May 1969): 131–41.

Davis, Mollie C. "American Religious and Religiose Reaction to Mexico's Church-State Conflict, 1926–1927: Background to the Morrow Mission." *Journal of Church and State* 13, no. 1 (Winter 1971): 79–96.

Davis, Richard. "Young Ireland." In Chastain, *Encyclopedia of 1848 Revolutions.* http://www.ohio.edu/chastain/rz/youngire.htm.

Dealey, James Quayle. *Sociology: Its Simpler Teachings and Applications.* New York: Silver, Burdett, 1909.

Delpar, Helen. *The Enormous Vogue of Things Mexican: Cultural Relations between the United States and Mexico, 1920–1935.* Tuscaloosa: University of Alabama Press, 1992.

Denny, Ludwell. *We Fight for Oil.* New York: Alfred A. Knopf, 1928.

Deseret News 1993–1994 Church Almanac. Salt Lake City: Deseret News, 1993.

Dewey, John. *A Common Faith.* New Haven, Conn.: Yale University Press, 1934.

_____. *Individualism, Old and New.* In *John Dewey: The Later Works, 1925–1952.* Vol. 5, *1929–1930.* Edited by Jo Ann Boydston, 41–144. Carbondale: Southern Illinois University Press, 1985. First published 1931.

_____. *John Dewey's Impressions of Soviet Russia and the Revolutionary World: Mexico—China—Turkey.* 1929. Reprint, New York: Bureau of Publications, Teachers College, Columbia University, 1964.

Dibble, William E. "The Book of Abraham and Pythagorean Astronomy." *Dialogue: A Journal of Mormon Thought* 8, nos. 3–4 (Autumn–Winter 1973): 135–38.

Diggins, John Patrick. *The Rise and Fall of the American Left.* New York: W. W. Norton, 1992.

Dijk, Teun A. van, ed. *Discourse as Structure and Process.* Vol. 2 of *Discourse Studies: A Multidisciplinary Introduction.* London: Sage Publications, 1997.

Doenecke, Justus D. "Non-Intervention of the Left: The Keep America out of the War Congress, 1938–1941." *Journal of Contemporary History* 12, no. 2 (1977): 221–36.

_____. "U.S. Policy and the European War, 1939–1941." *Diplomatic History* 19, no.

4 (Fall 1995): 669–98.

Dostoevsky, Fyodor. *A Raw Youth.* Translated by Constance Garnett. 1916. Reprint, London: William Heinemann, 1964. First published 1875 in Russian.

Doyle, William. *Origins of the French Revolution.* 2nd ed. Oxford: Oxford University Press, 1988.

Dozer, Donald Marquand. *Are We Good Neighbors? Three Decades of Inter-American Relations, 1930–1960.* Gainesville: University of Florida Press, 1959.

Draper, Richard D. "Maturing toward the Millennium." In Millet and Jackson, *Doctrine and Covenants,* 388–94.

Dubnov, Simon. *History of the Jews: From the Congress of Vienna to the Emergence of Hitler.* Vol. 5. Translated by Moshe Spiegel. Rev. ed. South Brunswick, N.J.: Thomas Yoseloff, 1973.

Duke, James T. "Cultural Continuity and Tension: A Test of Stark's Theory of Church Growth." In *Latter-day Saint Social Life: Social Research on the LDS Church and Its Members,* edited by James T. Duke, 71–104. Religious Studies Center Specialized Monograph Series 12. Provo, Utah: Religious Studies Center, Brigham Young University, 1998.

Dulles, John W. F. *Yesterday in Mexico: A Chronicle of the Revolution, 1919–1936.* Austin: University of Texas Press, 1961.

Durham, Reed C. "Is There No Help for the Widow's Son?" Presidential address before the Mormon History Association Conference, Nauvoo, Ill., April 1974. Typescript. Ernest D. Strack Collection, MS 1839, Box 2, fd. 88, Lee Library.

Durrant, Matthew, and Neal E. Lambert. "From Foe to Friend: The Mormon Embrace of Fiction." *Utah Historical Quarterly* 50, no. 4 (Fall 1982): 325–39.

Early Church Information File. Salt Lake City: Genealogical Society of Utah, 1991. Microfilm. LDS Church History Library.

Edgar, John, and Morton Edgar. *The Great Pyramid Passages and Chambers.* 2 vols. Glasgow: Bone and Hulley, 1910–13.

Edwards, Paul M. "Being Mormon: An RLDS Response." *Dialogue* 17, no. 1 (Spring 1984): 106–12.

———. "The Irony of Mormon History." In Smith, *Faithful History,* 19–34.

———. "Time in Mormon History." In Bitton and Beecher, *New Views of Mormon History,* 387–406.

Edwards, Stewart. *The Paris Commune 1871.* London: Eyre and Spottiswoode, 1971.

Ehat, Andrew F. "'It Seems Like Heaven Began on Earth': Joseph Smith and the Constitution of the Kingdom of God." *BYU Studies* 20 (Spring 1980): 253–79.

Eldredge, Horace Sunderlin. Diaries. Horace Sunderlin Eldredge Papers. 1840–81. MS 1210, Box 2, LDS Church History Library.

———. Letter to Brigham Young. April 26, 1871. Brigham Young Office Files. 1832–78. CR 1234 1, LDS Church History Library.

Elkins, James R. "George Lunt." Strangers to Us All: Lawyers and Poetry. Accessed May 18, 2011. http://myweb.wvnet.edu/~jelkins/lp-2001/lunt.html.

Ellis, David Maldwyn. *Landlords and Farmers in the Hudson-Mohawk Region, 1790–1850.* New York: Octagon Books, 1967.

Ellis, L. Ethan. "Dwight Morrow and the Church-State Controversy in Mexico." *Hispanic American Historical Review* 38, no. 4 (November 1958): 482–505.

———. *Frank B. Kellogg and American Foreign Relations, 1925–1929.* New Brunswick, N.J.: Rutgers University Press, 1961.

Ellis, Peter Berresford. *Eyewitness to Irish History.* Hoboken, N.J.: John Wiley and Sons, 2004.

Ellsworth, S. George. "Smith, George Albert." In Ludlow, *Encyclopedia of Mormonism,* 3:1326–29.

Encyclopaedia Britannica. 29 vols. 11th ed. New York: Cambridge University Press, 1911.

Engelstein, Laura. "Revolution and the Theater of Public Life in Imperial Russia." In Woloch, *Revolution and the Meanings of Freedom,* 315–59.

England, Breck. *The Life and Thought of Orson Pratt.* Salt Lake City: University of Utah Press, 1985.

Enslin, Morton Scott. *Christian Beginnings.* New York: Harper and Row, 1956.

Epperson, Steven. *Mormons and Jews: Early Mormon Theologies of Israel.* Salt Lake City: Signature Books, 1992.

Erickson, Dan. *"As a Thief in the Night": The Mormon Quest for Millennial Deliverance.* Salt Lake City: Signature Books, 1998.

Evans, Cleo H., comp. *Curtis Edwin Bolton, Pioneer, Missionary: History, Descendants, and Ancestors.* Fairfax, Va.: Mrs. Cleo H. Evans, 1968.

Evans, Richard L. *A Century of "Mormonism" in Great Britain.* Salt Lake City: Deseret News, 1937.

Evans, R. J. W., and Hartmut Pogge von Strandmann, eds. *The Revolutions in Europe, 1848–1849: From Reform to Reaction.* Oxford: Oxford University Press, 2000.

Fabre d'Olivet, Antoine. *The Golden Verses of Pythagoras: Explained and Translated into French and Preceded by a Discourse upon the Essence and Form of Poetry among the Principal Peoples of the Earth.* Translated by Nayán Louise Redfield. New York: G. P. Putnam's Sons, 1917.

Falcoff, Mark. "Argentina: The Twentieth Century." In Tenenbaum, *Encyclopedia of Latin American History and Culture,* 1:152–60.

Fales, Susan L. "Artisans, Millhands, and Laborers: The Mormons of Leeds and Their Nonconformist Neighbors." In Jensen and Thorp, *Mormons in Early Victorian Britain,* 156–78.

Farrow, Edward S. *Farrow's Military Encyclopedia: A Dictionary of Military Knowledge.* 3 vols. New York: printed by the author, 1885.

Fausto, Boris. "Brazil: The Social and Political Structure of the First Republic, 1889–1930." In Bethell, *Cambridge History of Latin America,* 5:779–829.

Fäy, Bernard. *Revolution and Freemasonry, 1680–1800.* Boston: Little, Brown, 1935.

Feller, A. H. *The Mexican Claims Commissions, 1923–1934: A Study in the Law and Procedure of International Tribunals.* New York: Macmillan, 1935.

Fetzer, Leland. "Russian Writers Look at Mormon Manners: 1857–72." *Dialogue: A*

Journal of Mormon Thought 13, no. 1 (Spring 1980): 74–84.

Filene, Peter G. *Americans and the Soviet Experiment, 1917–1933.* Cambridge, Mass.: Harvard University Press, 1967.

Finlayson, J. Finlay. *The Symbols and Legends of Freemasonry.* 1889. Reprint, London: G. Kenning and Son, 1910.

Firmage, Edwin Brown, and Richard Collin Mangrum. *Zion in the Courts: A Legal History of the Church of Jesus Christ of Latter-day Saints, 1830–1900.* Urbana: University of Illinois Press, 1988.

Fischer, David Hackett. *Albion's Seed: Four British Folkways in America.* America: A Cultural History 1. New York: Oxford University Press, 1989.

_____. *Paul Revere's Ride.* New York: Oxford University Press, 1994.

Flanders, Robert Bruce. "Dream and Nightmare: Nauvoo Revisited." In Quinn, *New Mormon History,* 75–100.

_____. "The Kingdom of God in Illinois: Politics in Utopia." In Launius and Hallwas, *Kingdom on the Mississippi Revisited,* 147–59.

_____. *Nauvoo: Kingdom on the Mississippi.* Urbana: University of Illinois Press, 1965.

_____. "Some Reflections on the New Mormon History." *Dialogue: A Journal of Mormon Thought* 9, no. 1 (Spring 1974): 34–41.

_____. "To Transform History: Early Mormon Culture and the Concept of Time and Space." *Church History* 40, no. 1 (March 1971): 108–117.

Flanigan, James Henry. Diaries. 4 vols. 1842–51. Holograph. MS 1390, LDS Church History Library.

Flake, Lawrence R. *Prophets and Apostles of the Last Dispensation.* Provo, Utah: Religious Studies Center, Brigham Young University, 2001.

Flynn, Peter. "The Revolutionary Legion and the Brazilian Revolution of 1930." In *Latin American Affairs,* edited by Raymond Carr, 63–105. St. Antony's Papers 22. Oxford: Oxford University Press, 1970.

Foglesong, David S. *America's Secret War against Bolshevism: U.S. Intervention in the Russian Civil War, 1917–1920.* Chapel Hill: University of North Carolina Press, 1995.

Forsberg, Clyde R., Jr. "Retelling the Greatest Story Ever Told: Popular Literature as Scripture in Antebellum America." *Dialogue: A Journal of Mormon Thought* 29, no. 4 (Winter 1996): 69–86.

Foster, Lawrence. *Religion and Sexuality: The Shakers, the Mormons, and the Oneida Community.* Illini Books ed. Urbana: University of Illinois Press, 1984.

Foster, R. F. "Ascendancy and Union." In *Oxford History of Ireland,* edited by R. F. Foster, 134–73. Oxford: Oxford University Press, 1989.

Fox, Frank W. *J. Reuben Clark: The Public Years.* Provo, Utah: Brigham Young University Press, 1980.

Franklin, John Hope, and Alfred A. Moss Jr. *From Slavery to Freedom: A History of African Americans.* 7th ed. New York: McGraw-Hill, 1994.

French, Hiram T. *History of Idaho: A Narrative Account of Its Historical Progress, Its People and Its Principal Interests.* 3 vols. Chicago: Lewis, 1914.

Frierdich, Matt. "Oaxaca and Its Political Culture of Conflict." Paper presented at the Illinois State University Conference for Students of Political Science, Normal, Ill., April 2008. http://pol.illinoisstate.edu/current/conferences/2008.shtml.

Fromkin, David. *A Peace to End All Peace: The Fall of the Ottoman Empire and the Creation of the Modern Middle East.* New York: Avon Books, 1989.

Froom, LeRoy Edwin. *The Prophetic Faith of Our Fathers: The Historical Development of Prophetic Interpretation.* 4 vols. Washington, DC: Review and Herald, 1946–54.

Fukuyama, Francis. *The End of History and the Last Man.* New York: Avon Books, 1992.

Gamble, Richard M. *The War for Righteousness: Progressive Christianity, the Great War, and the Rise of the Messianic Nation.* Wilmington, Del.: ISI Books, 2003.

Gardner, Lloyd C. *Safe for Democracy: The Anglo-American Response to Revolution, 1913–1923.* New York: Oxford University Press, 1984.

_____. "Woodrow Wilson and the Mexican Revolution." In Link, *Woodrow Wilson and a Revolutionary World*, 3–48.

Gaustad, Edwin S. "History and Theology: The Mormon Connection." In Smith, *Faithful History*, 55–66.

Gazley, John Gerow. *American Opinion of German Unification, 1848–1871.* Studies in History, Economics, and Public Law 121. New York: Columbia University, 1926.

George, Henry. *The Irish Land Question: What It Involves, and How Alone It Can Be Settled. An Appeal to the Land Leagues.* New York: D. Appleton, 1881. http://books.google.com/books?id=8ioDAAAAYAAJ.

George A. Smith Family Papers. 1731–1969. Ms0036, Marriott Library.

Gibbons, Francis M. *Heber J. Grant: Man of Steel, Prophet of God.* Salt Lake City: Deseret Book, 1979.

_____. *David O. McKay: Apostle to the World, Prophet of God.* Salt Lake City: Deseret Book, 1986.

Gilbert, Martin. *The First World War: A Complete History.* New York: Henry Holt, 1994.

Gill, Ann M., and Karen Whedbee. "Rhetoric." In Dijk, *Discourse as Structure and Process*, 157–84.

Godfrey, Matthew C. *Religion, Politics, and Sugar: The Mormon Church, the Federal Government, and the Utah-Idaho Sugar Company, 1907–1921.* Lehi: Utah State University, 2007.

Goethe, Johann Wolfgang von. *Goethe's Color Theory.* Arranged and edited by Rupprecht Matthei, translated by Herb Aach. American ed. New York: Van Nostrand Reinhold, 1971.

Golant, William. *The Long Afternoon: British India, 1601–1947.* London: Hamish Hamilton, 1975.

Goldschmidt, Arthur, Jr. *A Concise History of the Middle East.* 7th ed. Boulder, Colo.: Westview Press, 2002.

Goldwert, Marvin. *Democracy, Militarism, and Nationalism in Argentina, 1930–*

1966: An Interpretation. Austin: University of Texas Press, 1972.

Gordon, Sarah Barringer. *The Mormon Question: Polygamy and Constitutional Conflict in Nineteenth-Century America.* Chapel Hill: University of North Carolina Press, 2002.

Gorrell, Donald K. *The Age of Social Responsibility: The Social Gospel in the Progressive Era, 1900–1920.* Macon, Ga.: Mercer University Press, 1988.

Gottlieb, Robert, and Peter Wiley. *America's Saints: The Rise of Mormon Power.* New York: G. P. Putnam's Sons, 1984.

Graham, Helen. *The Spanish Republic at War, 1936–1939.* Cambridge: Cambridge University Press, 2002.

Grant, Heber J. *Diary Excerpts of Heber J. Grant, 1887–1899.* Typescript. In *New Mormon Studies: A Comprehensive Resource Library.*

Green, Arnold H. "Gathering and Election: Israelite Descent and Universalism in Mormon Discourse." *Journal of Mormon History* 25, no. 1 (Spring 1999): 195–228.

———. "A Survey of LDS Proselyting Efforts to the Jewish People." *BYU Studies* 8, no. 4 (Summer 1968): 427–43.

Green, Arnold H., and Lawrence P. Goldrup. "Joseph Smith, an American Muhammad? An Essay on the Perils of Historical Analogy." *Dialogue: A Journal of Mormon Thought* 6, no. 1 (Spring 1971): 46–58.

Green, Paul R., comp. *Science and Your Faith in God: A Selected Compilation of Writings and Talks by Prominent Latter-day Saints Scientists on the Subjects of Science and Religion.* Salt Lake City: Bookcraft, 1958.

Green, Philip Leonard. *Our Latin American Neighbors.* New York: Hastings House, 1941.

Green, Thomas Hill. "Lecture on Liberal Legislation and Freedom of Contract." In *Works of Thomas Hill Green.* Vol. 3, *Miscellanies and Memoir.* Edited by R. L. Nettleship, 365–86. London: Longmans, Green, 1911. http://archive.org/details/worksofthomashil033510mbp.

Griffiths, David B. "Far Western Populism: The Case of Utah, 1893–1900." *Utah Historical Quarterly* 37, no. 4 (Fall 1969): 396–407.

Grover, Mark L. "Execution in Mexico: The Deaths of Rafael Monroy and Vicente Morales." *BYU Studies* 35, no. 3 (1995–96): 6–28.

———. "Maturing of the Oak: The Dynamics of LDS Growth in Latin America." *Dialogue: A Journal of Mormon Thought* 38, no. 2 (Summer 2005): 79–104.

Gruening, Ernest. *Mexico and Its Heritage.* New York: Appleton-Century-Crofts, 1928.

"Guide to the George D. Herron Papers." Elmer Holmes Bobst Library. Last modified March 29, 2012. http://dlib.nyu.edu/findingaids/html/tamwag/tam_008/tam_008.html.

Guttmann, Allen. *The Wound in the Heart: America and the Spanish Civil War.* New York: Free Press of Glencoe, 1962.

Haas, Ernst B. *Nationalism, Liberalism, and Progress: The Rise and Decline of Nationalism.* Ithaca, N.Y.: Cornell University Press, 1997.

Haggard, Robert F. *The Persistence of Victorian Liberalism: The Politics of Social Reform in Britain, 1870–1900.* Westport, Conn.: Greenwood, 2000.

Haggerty, Richard. "Historical Setting." In *Mexico: A Country Study,* edited by

Tim L. Merrill and Ramón Miró, 1–75. 4th ed. Washington, DC: Federal Research Division, Library of Congress, 1997.

Haley, P. Edward. *Revolution and Intervention: The Diplomacy of Taft and Wilson with Mexico, 1910–1917*. Cambridge: Massachusetts Institute of Technology Press, 1970.

Hall, David. "Anxiously Engaged: Amy Brown Lyman and Relief Society Charity Work, 1917–45." *Dialogue: A Journal of Mormon Thought* 27, no. 2 (Summer 1994): 73–91.

"Hall of Great Westerners." National Cowboy and Western Heritage Museum. Accessed June 4, 2011. http://www.nationalcowboymuseum.org/info/awards-hof/Great-Westerners.aspx.

Hallwas, John E. "Mormon Nauvoo from a Non-Mormon Perspective." In Launius and Hallwas, *Kingdom on the Mississippi Revisited*, 160–80.

Hancock, Levi Ward. *Autobiography of Levi Ward Hancock, 1803–36*. Typescript. In *New Mormon Studies: A Comprehensive Resource Library*.

Hancock, Mosiah Lyman. *Autobiography of Mosiah Lyman Hancock*. N.d. Typescript. In *New Mormon Studies: A Comprehensive Resource Library*.

Hanks, Maxine. *Women and Authority: Re-emerging Mormon Feminism*. Salt Lake City: Signature Books, 1992.

Hansen, Klaus J. "The Metamorphosis of the Kingdom of God: Toward a Reinterpretation of Mormon History." In Quinn, *New Mormon History*, 221–46.

_____. *Quest for Empire: The Political Kingdom of God and the Council of Fifty in Mormon History*. East Lansing: Michigan State University Press, 1967.

Hansen, Lorin K. "Some Concepts of Divine Revelation." *Sunstone* 10, no. 5 (May 1985): 51–58.

Hardy, Blaine Carmon. "The Mormon Colonies in Northern Mexico: A History, 1885–1912." PhD diss., Wayne State University, 1963.

_____. "Self-Blame and the Manifesto." *Dialogue: A Journal of Mormon Thought* 24, no. 3 (Fall 1991): 43–57.

_____. *Solemn Covenant: The Mormon Polygamous Passage*. Urbana: University of Illinois Press, 1992.

Hardy, Blaine Carmon, and Melody Seymour. "The Importation of Arms and the 1912 Mormon 'Exodus' from Mexico." *New Mexico Historical Review* 72, no. 4 (October 1997): 297–318.

Harries, Richard. "The Criterion of Success for a Just Revolution." *Theology* 78, no. 658 (April 1975): 190–95.

Harris, Charles H., III, and Louis R. Sadler. *The Secret War in El Paso: Mexican Revolutionary Intrigue, 1906–1920*. Albuquerque: University of New Mexico Press, 2009.

Harrison, John F. C. "The Popular History of Early Victorian Britain: A Mormon Contribution." *Journal of Mormon History* 14 (1988): 3–15.

_____. *The Second Coming: Popular Millenarianism, 1780–1850*. New Brunswick, N.J.: Rutgers University Press, 1979.

Harrison, Royden, ed. *The English Defence of the Commune, 1871*. London: Merlin

Press, 1971.

Hart, John Mason. *Revolutionary Mexico: The Coming and Process of the Mexican Revolution*. Berkeley: University of California Press, 1988.

Harvie, Christopher. "The Rule of Law, 1789–1851." In *The Oxford Illustrated History of Britain*, edited by Kenneth O. Morgan, 419–62. Oxford: Oxford University Press, 1984.

Hastings, James, ed. *Encyclopaedia of Religion and Ethics*. 12 vols. New York: Charles Scribner's Sons, 1908–22.

Hatch, Nelle Spilsbury, and B. Carmon Hardy. *Stalwarts South of the Border*. [Anaheim, Calif.]: privately printed, 1985.

Hawkes, Earl E. "Newspapers, Stern Mormon View." *Time Magazine* (August 4, 1967): 72.

Hayden, Dolores. *Seven American Utopias: The Architecture of Communitarian Socialism, 1790–1975*. Cambridge, Mass.: MIT Press, 1976.

Hayward, Max, and William C. Fletcher, eds. *Religion and the Soviet State: A Dilemma of Power*. New York: Frederick A. Praeger, 1969.

Hazen, Charles Downer. *Contemporary American Opinion of the French Revolution*. Johns Hopkins University Studies in Historical and Political Science 16. 1897. Reprint, Glouscester, Mass.: P. Smith, 1964.

Heale, M. J. *American Anticommunism: Combating the Enemy Within, 1830–1970*. Baltimore: Johns Hopkins University Press, 1990.

Herman, Donald L. *The Comintern in Mexico*. Washington, DC: Public Affairs Press, 1974.

Hernandez, Elizabeth. *Mormonism Comes of Age in Mexico*. Provo, Utah: Brigham Young University Scholar Project, 1975.

Herrera, Agrícol Lozano. *Historia del Mormonismo en México*. Mexico, D.F.: Zarahemla, 1983.

Herron, George D. *The Christian Society*. New York: Fleming H. Revell, 1894.

_____. *The Message of Jesus to Men of Wealth*. New York: Fleming H. Revell, 1891.

Hickman, Martin B. "The Ambassadorial Years: Some Insights." *BYU Studies* 13, no. 3 (Spring 1973): 405–14.

Hill, Donna. *Joseph Smith: The First Mormon*. Salt Lake City: Signature Books, 1999.

Hill, Marvin S. "Counter-Revolution: The Mormon Reaction to the Coming of American Democracy." *Sunstone* 13, no. 3 (June 1989): 24–33.

_____. *Quest for Refuge: The Mormon Flight from American Pluralism*. Salt Lake City: Signature Books, 1989.

_____. "The Shaping of the Mormon Mind in New England and New York." *BYU Studies* 9, no. 3 (Spring 1969): 351–72.

Hillam, Ray C. *"By the Hands of Wise Men": Essays on the U.S. Constitution*. Provo, Utah: Brigham Young University, 1979.

Hilton, Lynn M., and Hope A. Hilton. "Orson Hyde." In Powell, *Utah History Encyclopedia*, 268–69.

Hingley, Ronald. *Joseph Stalin: Man and Legend*. New York: Konecky and Konecky, 1974.

Hinton, Wayne K. "Some Historical Perspective on Mormon Responses to the Great Depression." *Journal of the West* 24, no. 2 (October 1985): 19–26.

Hobsbawm, Eric J. *The Age of Capital, 1848–1875.* New York: Charles Scribners' Sons, 1975.

_____. *The Age of Empire, 1875–1914.* New York: Pantheon Books, 1987.

_____. *Echoes of the Marseillaise: Two Centuries Look Back on the French Revolution.* New Brunswick, N. J.: Rutgers University Press, 1990.

Hodges, Donald, and Ross Gandy. *Mexico 1910–1982: Reform or Revolution?* London: Zed, 1979.

Hoffenberg, Peter H. *Empire on Display: English, Indian, and Australian Exhibitions from the Crystal Palace to the Great War.* Berkeley: University of California Press, 2001.

Hogan, Mervin B. *Mormonism and Freemasonry: The Illinois Episode.* 1977. Reprint, Salt Lake City: Campus Graphics, 1980.

Holdsworth, Mary. "Lenin's *Imperialism* in Retrospect." In *Essays in Honor of E. H. Carr,* edited by C. Abramsky, 341–51. Hamden, Conn.: Archon Books, 1974.

Hollander, Paul. *Political Pilgrims: Travels of Western Intellectuals to the Soviet Union, China, and Cuba, 1928–1978.* New York: Oxford University Press, 1981.

Holyoake, George Jacob. *Bygones Worth Remembering.* 2 vols. London: T. Fisher Unwin; New York: E. P. Dutton, 1905.

Homer, Michael W. "'Similarity of Priesthood in Masonry': The Relationship between Freemasonry and Mormonism." *Dialogue: A Journal of Mormon Thought* 27, no. 3 (Fall 1994): 2–113.

Horn, James J. "U.S. Diplomacy and the 'Specter of Bolshevism' in Mexico (1924–1927)." *The Americas* 32, no. 1 (July 1975): 31–45.

Horne, Alistair. *The Fall of Paris: The Siege and the Commune, 1870–71.* New York: St. Martin's Press, 1965.

Howard, Michael Eliot. *The Franco-Prussian War: The German Invasion of France, 1870–1871.* New York: Macmillan, 1961.

Hrebenar, Ronald J., Melanee Cherry, and Kathanne Greene. "Utah: Church and Corporate Power in the Nation's Most Conservative State." In *Interest Group Politics in the American West,* edited by Ronald J. Hrebenar and Clive S. Thomas, 113–22. Salt Lake City: University of Utah Press, 1987.

Hudson, Rex A., ed. *Peru: A Country Study.* Washington, DC: Federal Research Division, Library of Congress, 1993.

Huff, Kent W. "The United Order of Joseph Smith's Times." *Dialogue: A Journal of Mormon Thought* 19, no. 2 (Summer 1986): 146–49.

Hugo, Victor. *Les Misérables.* Translated by Charles E. Wilbour. New York: Modern Library, 1931. First published 1862 in French.

Hullinger, Robert N. *Joseph Smith's Response to Skepticism.* Salt Lake City: Signature Books, 1992.

Hunt, Lynn. *Politics, Culture, and Class in the French Revolution.* Berkeley: University of California Press, 1984.

Hunt, Michael H. *Ideology and U.S. Foreign Policy.* New Haven, Conn.: Yale

University Press, 1987.

_____. *The Making of a Special Relationship: The United States and China to 1914.* New York: Columbia University Press, 1983.

Hunter, Milton R. *Utah in Her Western Setting.* Salt Lake City: Deseret News Press, 1943.

Huston, Reeve. "Land and Freedom: The New York Anti-Rent Wars and the Construction of Free Labor in the Antebellum North." In *Labor Histories: Class, Politics, and the Working Class Experience,* edited by Eric Arnesen, Julie Greene, and Bruce Laurie, 19–44. Urbana: University of Illinois Press, 1998.

Hyde, Myrtle Stevens. "Orson Hyde and the *Frontier Guardian.*" *Nauvoo Journal* 8, no. 2 (Fall 1996): 62–70.

Hyde, Orson. *A Voice from Jerusalem, or a Sketch of the Travels and Ministry of Elder Orson Hyde, Missionary of the Church of Jesus Christ of Latter Day Saints, to Germany, Constantinople, and Jerusalem.* Liverpool: P. P. Pratt, 1842.

Hymns of the Church of Jesus Christ of Latter-day Saints. Salt Lake City: Church of Jesus Christ of Latter-day Saints, 1985.

Inman, Samuel Guy. *Latin America: Its Place in World Life.* Rev. ed. New York: Harcourt, Brace, 1942.

"International Genealogical Index." Family Search. Accessed December 12, 2012. https://www.familysearch.org/search/collection/igi.

Introvigne, Massimo. "Latter Day Revisited: Contemporary Mormon Millenarianism." In Robbins and Palmer, *Millennium, Messiahs, and Mayhem,* 229–44.

"An Inventory of the William and Mary Howitt Papers, 1827–1886." Friends Historical Library of Swarthmore College. Accessed April 29, 2011. http://www.swarthmore.edu/library/friends/ead/5181howi.xml.

Investigation of Mexican Affairs: Preliminary Report and Hearings of the Committee on Foreign Relations, United States Senate, Pursuant to S. Res. 106, Directing the Committee on Foreign Relations to Investigate the Matter of Outrages on Citizens of the United States in Mexico. 66th Cong., 2nd sess., Document 285. 2 vols. Washington, DC: Government Publication Office, 1920.

Iriye, Akira. *The Globalizing of America, 1913–1945.* Vol. 3 of *The Cambridge History of American Foreign Relations.* New York: Cambridge University Press, 1994.

_____. "Japan as Competitor, 1895–1917." In *Mutual Images: Essays in American-Japanese Relations,* edited by Priscilla Clapp and Akira Iriye, 73–99. Cambridge, Mass.: Harvard University Press, 1975.

Irving, Gordon. "Chile." Latin American Country Histories and Vignettes. 1975–79. CR 100 344, fd. 2, LDS Church History Library.

Israelsen, L. Dwight. "An Economic Analysis of the United Order." *BYU Studies* 18, no. 4 (Summer 1978): 536–62.

_____. "Mormons, the Constitution, and the Host Economy." In Hillam, *"By the Hands of Wise Men,"* 59–81.

Ivins, Anthony W. *Autobiography and Diary Excerpts of Anthony W. Ivins.* N.d. Typescript. In *New Mormon Studies: A Comprehensive Resource Library.*

_____. Diaries. LDS Church History Library.

_____. *The Right Relation of Church and State*. Independence, Mo.: Zion's Printing and Publishing Company, 1926. Lee Library.

Ivins, Stanley S., ed. "Letter from Mexico: Impressions of a Mormon." *Utah Historical Quarterly* 26 (April 1958): 177–82.

Jackson, Kent P. "The Signs of the Times: 'Be Not Troubled.'" In Millet and Jackson, *Doctrine and Covenants*, 186–200.

Jaksíc, Iván. "Masonic Orders." In Tenenbaum, *Encyclopedia of Latin American History and Culture*, 3:542–43.

Jensen, Richard L. "The British Gathering to Zion." In Bloxham, Moss, and Porter, *Truth Will Prevail*, 165–98.

_____. "Swedish Immigrants and Life in Utah." In Powell, *Utah History Encyclopedia*, 537–38.

Jensen, Richard L., and Malcolm R. Thorp, eds. *Mormons in Early Victorian Britain*. Publications in Mormon Studies 4. Salt Lake City: University of Utah Press, 1989.

Jensen, Therald N. "Mormon Theory of Church and State." PhD diss., University of Chicago, 1938.

Jenson, Andrew, comp. *Church Chronology: A Record of Important Events Pertaining to the History of the Church of Jesus Christ of Latter-day Saints*. 2nd ed., rev. and enl. Salt Lake City: Deseret News, 1914.

_____. *Encyclopedic History of the Church of Jesus Christ of Latter-day Saints*. Salt Lake City: Deseret News, 1941.

_____, ed. *Latter-day Saint Biographical Encyclopedia: A Compilation of Biographical Sketches of Prominent Men and Women in the Church of Jesus Christ of Latter-day Saints*. 4 vols. Salt Lake City: Andrew Jenson History Co. and Andrew Jenson Memorial Foundation, 1901–36. Reprint, Salt Lake City: Western Epics, 1971.

Jessee, Dean C., ed. "The John Taylor Nauvoo Journal, January 1845–September 1845," *BYU Studies* 23, no. 3 (Summer 1983): 1–105.

_____, ed. *The Papers of Joseph Smith: Journal, 1832–1842*. Vol. 2 of *The Papers of Joseph Smith*. Salt Lake City: Deseret Book, 1992.

_____. "Woodruff, Wilford." In Ludlow, *Encyclopedia of Mormonism*, 4:1580–84.

"John Morgan." Grandpa Bill's General Authority Pages. Accessed June 3, 2011. http://www.gapages.com/morgaj1.htm.

Johnson, Christopher H. *Utopian Communism in France: Cabet and the Icarians, 1839–1851*. Ithaca, N.Y.: Cornell University Press, 1974.

Jones, Samuel Stephen. Diaries. 3 vols. 1855–73. Mormon Missionary Diaries Collection.

Jones, Zachary R. "'War and Confusion in Babylon': Mormon Reaction to German Unification, 1864–1880." Unpublished manuscript, March 6, 2011. Copy in author's possession.

Journal of Discourses. 26 vols. London: Latter-day Saints' Book Depot, 1854–86.

Journal History of the Church. 263 reels. 1830–1983. Microfilm. CR 100 137, LDS Church History Library.

"Judaic Treasures of the Library of Congress: Mordecai Manuel Noah." *Jewish*

Virtual Library. Accessed May 19, 2011. http://www.jewishvirtuallibrary. org/jsource/loc/noah.html.

Judd, Richard W. *Socialist Cities: Municipal Politics and the Grass Roots of American Socialism*. Albany: State University of New York Press, 1989.

Juhnke, William E. "Anabaptism and Mormonism: A Study in Comparative History." *John Whitmer Historical Association Journal* 2 (1982): 38–46.

Katz, Friedrich. *The Life and Times of Pancho Villa*. Stanford, Calif.: Stanford University Press, 1998.

Katz, Philip M. "'Lessons from Paris': The American Clergy Responds to the Paris Commune." *Church History* 63, no. 3 (September 1994): 393–406.

Kennedy, David M. *Freedom from Fear: The American People in Depression and War, 1929–1945*. New York: Oxford University Press, 1999.

Kenney, Scott G. "E. E. Ericksen: Loyal Heretic." *Sunstone* 3, no. 5 (July/August 1978): 16–27.

———. "Personal and Social Morality in a Religious Context: Reinhold Niebuhr and the Mormon Experience." *Sunstone* 5, no. 2 (March–April 1980): 19–23.

———, ed. *Wilford Woodruff's Journal, 1833–1889, Typescript*. 9 vols. Salt Lake City: Signature Books, 1983–1985.

Kimball, Edward L., ed. *The Teachings of Spencer W. Kimball*. Salt Lake City: Bookcraft, 1982.

King, G. Wayne. "Conservative Attitudes in the United States toward Cuba." *Proceedings of the South Carolina Historical Association* (1973): 94–104.

Kirkland, Boyd. "Jehovah as Father: The Development of the Mormon Jehovah Doctrine." *Sunstone* 9, no. 2 (August 1984): 36–44.

Klaiber, Jeffrey L. "Anticlericalism." In Tenenbaum, *Encyclopedia of Latin American History and Culture*, 1:104–6.

———. "Religion and Revolution in Peru: 1920–1945." *The Americas* 31, no. 3 (January 1975): 289–312.

Klehr, Harvey. *The Heyday of American Communism: The Depression Decade*. New York: Basic Books, 1984.

Klein, Herbert S. *Parties and Political Change in Bolivia, 1880–1952*. Cambridge: Cambridge University Press, 1969.

Knight, Alan. *The Mexican Revolution*. 2 vols. Lincoln: University of Nebraska Press, 1990.

———. "Mexico, c. 1930–1946." In Bethell, *Cambridge History of Latin America*, 7:3–82.

———. "Racism, Revolution, and *Indigenismo*: Mexico, 1910–1940." In *The Idea of Race in Latin America, 1870–1940*, edited by Richard Graham, 71–113. Austin: University of Texas Press, 1990.

———. "Revolutionary Project, Recalcitrant People: Mexico, 1910–1940." In Rodríguez O., *The Revolutionary Process in Mexico*, 227–64.

Knock, Thomas J. *To End All Wars: Woodrow Wilson and the Quest for New World Order*. New York: Oxford University Press, 1992.

Knowlton, David Clark. "Mormonism in Latin America: Toward the Twenty-first Century." *Dialogue: A Journal of Mormon Thought* 29, no. 1 (Spring 1996): 159–176.

_____. "Parley Pratt and the Problem of Separating Latin and Anglo America." *Journal of Mormon History* 37, no. 1 (Winter 2011): 194–200.

Knox, John. *The History of the Reformation of Religion in Scotland.* Edited and revised by Cuthbert Lennox. Twentieth-century ed. London: Andrew Melrose, 1905. First published 1790.

Kolko, Gabriel. "The Decline of American Radicalism in the Twentieth Century." In *For a New America: Essays in History and Politics from Studies on the Left, 1959–1967,* edited by James Weinstein and David W. Eakins, 197–220. New York: Vintage Books, 1970.

Krauze, Enrique. *Mexico: Biography of Power. A History of Modern Mexico, 1810–1996.* New York: Harper Perennial, 1997.

LaFeber, Walter. *The American Search for Opportunity, 1865–1913.* Vol. 2 of *The Cambridge History of American Foreign Relations.* New York: Cambridge University Press, 1993.

Landes, Joan B. *Visualizing the Nation: Gender, Representation, and Revolution in Eighteenth-Century France.* Ithaca, N.Y.: Cornell University Press, 2001.

Lang, Diana. "Chinese Reds." In *Symbols, Myths, and Images of the French Revolution: Essays in Honor of James A. Leith,* edited by Ian Germani and Robin Swales, 307–19. Regina, Saskatchewan: CPRC, 1998.

Langer, Erick D. "Bolivia: Since 1825." In Tenenbaum, *Encyclopedia of Latin American History and Culture,* 1:367–74.

Langer, William L. *Political and Social Upheaval, 1832–1852.* New York: Harper and Row, 1969.

Launius, Roger D., and John E. Hallwas, eds. *Kingdom on the Mississippi Revisited: Nauvoo in Mormon History.* Urbana: University of Illinois Press, 1996.

Lawson, Douglas E., and Arthur E. Lean, eds. *John Dewey and the World View.* Carbondale: Southern Illinois University Press, 1964.

Leach, Eugene E. "Chaining the Tiger: The Mob Stigma and the Working Class, 1863–1894." *Labor History* 35, no. 2 (Spring 1994): 187–215.

Leavitt, Samuel. "Township Coöperation: The Legitimate Fruit of the Protectionist Theory; also, The History of American Socialism: Two Lectures before the New York Liberal Club." New York: S. R. Wells, [1873].

Leech, Geoffrey N. *A Linguistic Guide to English Poetry.* London: Longman, 1969.

Lefebvre, Georges. *The Coming of the French Revolution.* Translated by Robert R. Palmer. Princeton, N.J.: Princeton University Press, 1947. First published 1839 in French.

Lehmann, Paul L. "The Transfiguration of Jesus and Revolutionary Politics." *Christianity and Crisis* 35, no. 3 (March 3, 1975): 44–47.

Lenin, Vladmir I. *Imperialism, the Highest Stage of Capitalism: A Popular Outline.* Peking: Foreign Languages Press, 1975. First published 1917 in Russian.

Lens, Sidney. *Radicalism in America.* New York: Thomas Y. Crowell, 1966.

Leone, Mark P. *Roots of Modern Mormonism.* Cambridge, Mass.: Harvard University Press, 1979.

Lerner, Warren. *A History of Socialism and Communism in Modern Times:*

Theorists, Activists, and Humanists. 2nd ed. Englewood Cliffs, N.J.: Prentice Hall, 1993.

LeSueur, Stephen C. *The 1838 Mormon War in Missouri.* Columbia: University of Missouri Press, 1987.

Levin, N. Gordon, Jr. *Woodrow Wilson and World Politics: America's Response to War and Revolution.* Oxford: Oxford University Press, 1968.

Levine, Lawrence W., and Cornelia R. Levine, eds. *The People and the President: America's Conversation with FDR.* Boston: Beacon Press, 2002.

Lima, Alceu Amoroso. "Voice of Liberty and Reform, in Brazil." In *Freedom and Reform in Latin America,* edited by Frederick B. Pike, 281–302. Notre Dame, Ind.: University of Notre Dame Press, 1959.

Lindemann, Albert S. *A History of European Socialism.* New Haven, Conn.: Yale University Press, 1983.

Link, Arthur S., ed. *Woodrow Wilson and a Revolutionary World, 1913–1921.* Chapel Hill: University of North Carolina Press, 1982.

Lippy, Charles H. "'Waiting for the End': The Social Context of American Apocalyptic Religion." In Zamora, *Apocalyptic Vision in America,* 37–63.

Liss, Sheldon B. *Marxist Thought in Latin America.* Berkeley: University of California Press, 1984.

Littlefield, Lyman O. *Reminiscences of Latter-day Saints, Giving an Account of Much Individual Suffering Endured for Religious Conscience.* Logan: Utah Journal Co., 1888. In *New Mormon Studies: A Comprehensive Resource Library.*

"Liverpool to New Orleans on the *Zetland* (29 Jan 1849 – 2 Apr 1849)." Mormon Migration. Accessed November 15, 2012. http://mormonmigration.lib.byu.edu/.

Livesey, Anthony. *Great Commanders and Their Battles.* New York: Macmillan, 1987.

Livingston, Craig. "From Above and Below: The Mormon Embrace of Revolution, 1840–1940." PhD diss., Temple University, 2002.

Lloyd, Jane-Dale. *El proceso de modernización capitalista en el noroeste de Chihuahua, 1880–1910.* Mexico, D.F.: Universidad Iberoamericana, Departamento de Historia, 1987.

Lobo, Eulália Maria Lahmeyer. "Brazil: Since 1889." In Tenenbaum, *Encyclopedia of Latin American History and Culture,* 1:424–32.

Lovenstein, Meno. *American Opinion of Soviet Russia.* Washington, DC: American Council on Public Affairs, 1941.

Löwith, Karl. *Meaning in History: The Theological Implications of the Philosophy of History.* Chicago: University of Chicago Press, 1949.

Ludlow, Daniel H. "Appendix 3: Church Periodicals." In Ludlow, *Encyclopedia of Mormonism,* 4:1659–64.

———, ed. *Encyclopedia of Mormonism: The History, Scripture, Doctrine, and Procedure of the Church of Jesus Christ of Latter-day Saints.* 5 vols. New York: Macmillan, 1992.

Lund, Anthon Hendrik. Diaries. 1860–1921. Typescript on microfilm. MS 2737, Boxes 60–64, LDS Church History Library.

Lyman, Francis M. Scrapbook. 1878–94. Microfilm. MS 582, LDS Church History Library.

Lyon, John. *Harp of Zion*. Liverpool: S. W. Richards, 1853.

_____. *Songs of a Pioneer*. Edited by David R. Lyon. Salt Lake City: Magazine Printing Co., 1923.

Lyon, T. Edgar, Jr. *John Lyon: The Life of a Pioneer Poet*. Provo, Utah: Religious Studies Center, Brigham Young University, 1989.

_____. "In Praise of Babylon: Church Leadership at the 1851 Great Exhibition in London." *Journal of Mormon History* 14 (1988): 49–61.

Lyons, Eugene. *The Red Decade: The Stalinist Penetration of America*. Indianapolis: Bobbs-Merrill, 1941.

Mabry, Donald J. "Mexican Anticlerics, Bishops, Cristeros, and the Devout during the 1920s: A Scholarly Debate." *Journal of Church and State* 20, no. 1 (1978): 81–92.

Mace, Wandle. *Autobiography of Wandle Mace*. N.d. Typescript. In *New Mormon Studies: A Comprehensive Resource Library*.

MacLachlan, Colin M., and Jaime E. Rodríguez O. *The Forging of the Cosmic Race: A Reinterpretation of Colonial Mexico*. Berkeley: University of California Press, 1980.

Madsen, Brigham D. Introduction to Roberts, *Studies of the Book of Mormon*, 1–33.

Manchester, William. *The Last Lion, Winston Spencer Churchill: Visions of Glory, 1874–1932*. Boston: Little, Brown, 1983.

Mangum, Garth L., and Bruce D. Blumell. *The Mormons' War on Poverty: A History of LDS Welfare, 1830–1990*. Salt Lake City: University of Utah Press, 1993.

Manuel, Frank E. *The Prophets of Paris*. Cambridge, Mass.: Harvard University Press, 1962.

Manuel, Frank E., and Fritzie P. Manuel. *Utopian Thought in the Western World*. Cambridge, Mass.: Belknap Press of Harvard University Press, 1979.

Marsden, George M. *Religion and American Culture*. San Diego: Harcourt, Brace, Jovanovich, 1990.

Marshall, Richard H., Jr., ed. *Aspects of Religion in the Soviet Union, 1917–1967*. Chicago: University of Chicago Press, 1971.

Martin, David. *Tongues of Fire: The Explosion of Protestantism in Latin America*. Cambridge, Mass.: Basil Blackwell, 1990.

Marty, Martin E. *Modern American Religion*. 3 vols. Chicago: University of Chicago, 1986.

_____. "Two Kinds of Two Kinds of Civil Religion." In Richey and Jones, *American Civil Religion*, 139–57.

Masterson, Daniel M. *Militarism and Politics in Latin America: Peru from Sánchez Cerro to Sendero Luminoso*. Westport, Conn.: Greenwood, 1991.

Mauss, Armand L. *All Abraham's Children: Changing Mormon Conceptions of Race and Lineage*. Urbana: University of Illinois Press, 2003.

_____. *The Angel and the Beehive: The Mormon Struggle with Assimilation*. Urbana: University of Illinois Press, 1994.

_____. "Assimilation and Ambivalence: The Mormon Reaction to Americanization."

Dialogue: A Journal of Mormon Thought 22, no. 1 (Spring 1989): 30–67.

———. "In Search of Ephraim: Traditional Mormon Conceptions of Lineage and Race." *Journal of Mormon History* 25, no. 1 (Spring 1999): 131–73.

May, Dean L. "Brigham Young and the Bishops: The United Order in the City." In Bitton and Beecher, *New Views of Mormon History*, 115–37.

May, Ernest R. *The World War and American Isolation, 1914–1917.* 1959. Reprint, Chicago: Quadrangle Books, 1966.

McBrien, Dean D. "The Influence of the Frontier on Joseph Smith." PhD diss., George Washington University, 1929.

McClellan, Jeff. "A Lingering Influence: Top 10 BYU Professors." *Brigham Young Magazine*, Winter 1999. http://magazine.byu.edu/?act=viewanda=172.

McClellan, Richard D. "Not Your Average French Communist Mormon: A Short History of Louis A. Bertrand." *Mormon Historical Studies* 1, no. 2 (Fall 2000): 3–24.

McConkie, Bruce R. *Mormon Doctrine.* 2nd ed. Salt Lake City: Bookcraft, 1966.

McCormick, John S. "Hornets in the Hive: Socialists in Early Twentieth-Century Utah." *Utah Historical Quarterly* 50 (Summer 1982): 225–40.

McCormick, John S., and John R. Sillito. "Henry W. Lawrence: A Life in Dissent." In *Differing Visions: Dissenters in Mormon History*, edited by Roger D. Launius and Linda Thatcher, 220–38. Urbana: University of Illinois Press, 1994.

———. *A History of Utah Radicalism: Startling, Socialistic, and Decidedly Revolutionary.* Logan: Utah State University Press, 2011.

McCue, Robert J. "Similarities and Differences in the Anabaptist Restitution and the Mormon Restoration." MA thesis, Brigham Young University, 1959.

McCurdy, Charles W. *The Anti-Rent Era in New York Law and Politics, 1839–1865.* Chapel Hill: University of North Carolina Press, 2001.

McDougall, Walter A. *Promised Land, Crusader State: The American Encounter with the World since 1776.* Boston, Mass.: Houghton Mifflin, 1997.

McGowan, Thomas. "Mormon Millennialism." In Bryant and Dayton, *Coming Kingdom*, 149–68.

McIntosh, Christopher. *The Rose Cross and the Age of Reason: Eighteenth-Century Rosicrucianism in Central Europe and Its Relationship to the Enlightenment.* New York: E. J. Brill, 1992.

McKay, David O. Diaries. 1897–1961. Photocopies and typescripts. David Oman McKay Papers. Ms0668, Boxes 3–10, Marriott Library.

McLaws, Monty Burr. *Spokesman for the Kingdom: Early Mormon Journalism and the Deseret News, 1830–1898.* Studies in Mormon History 2. Provo, Utah: Brigham Young University Press, 1977.

McLean, Adam. *The Rosicrucian Emblems of Daniel Cramer: The True Society of Jesus and the Rosy Cross.* Magnum Opus Hermetic Sourceworks 4. Grand Rapids, Mich.: Phanes Press, 1991.

McLellan, David, ed. *Karl Marx: Selected Writings.* New York: Oxford University Press, 1977.

McMurrin, Sterling M. "Brigham H. Roberts: A Biographical Essay." In Roberts,

Studies of the Book of Mormon, xiii–xxxi.

_____. *The Theological Foundations of the Mormon Religion.* Salt Lake City: University of Utah Press, 1965.

Mecham, John Lloyd. *Church and State in Latin America: A History of Politico-Ecclesiastical Relations.* Rev. ed. Chapel Hill: University of North Carolina Press, 1966.

Mehew, Ernest, ed. *Selected Letters of Robert Louis Stevenson.* New Haven, Conn.: Yale University Press, 1997.

Meintjes, Johannes. *The Commandant-General: The Life and Times of Petrus Jacobus Joubert of the South African Republic, 1831–1900.* Cape Town: Tafelberg-Uitgewers, 1971.

Melville, Keith J. "Brigham Young's Ideal Society: The Kingdom of God." *BYU Studies* 5, no. 1 (Autumn 1962): 3–18.

_____. "The Reflections of Brigham Young on the Nature of Man and the State." *BYU Studies* 4, no. 3 (1962): 255–67.

Memoir of John C. Lord, D.D.: Pastor of the Central Presbyterian Church for Thirty-Eight Years. Compiled by order of the church session. Buffalo, N.Y.: Courier, 1878.

Memorial Services for President Franklin Stewart Harris: George Albert Smith Fieldhouse, Monday, May 23, 1960, 10:00 A.M. Provo, Utah: Brigham Young University, 1960.

Merrill, Milton R. *Reed Smoot: Apostle in Politics.* Western Experience Series. Logan: Utah State University Press, 1990.

Merriman, John M. "Contested Freedoms in the French Revolutions, 1830–1871." In Woloch, *Revolution and the Meanings of Freedom*, 173–211.

Meyer, Jean A. *The Cristero Rebellion: The Mexican People between Church and State, 1926–1929.* Cambridge: Cambridge University Press, 1976.

Meyer, Michael C. *Mexican Rebel: Pascual Orozco and the Mexican Revolution, 1910–1915.* Lincoln: University of Nebraska Press, 1967.

Michaels, Albert L. "The Modification of the Anti-clerical Nationalism of the Mexican Revolution by General Lázaro Cárdenas and Its Relationship to the Church-State Détente in Mexico." *Americas* 26, no. 1 (July 1969): 35–53.

Mikkelsen, D. Craig. "The Politics of B. H. Roberts." *Dialogue: A Journal of Mormon Thought* 9, no. 2 (Summer 1974): 25–43.

Mill, John Stuart. *Principles of Political Economy with Some of Their Applications to Social Philosophy.* Vols. 2–3 of the *Collected Works of John Stuart Mill.* Edited by J. M. Robson. Toronto: University of Toronto Press, 1965. First published 1848.

Millet, Robert L., and Kent P. Jackson, eds. *The Doctrine and Covenants.* Vol. 1 of *Studies in Scripture.* Salt Lake City: Randall Book, 1984.

Mills, Elizabeth H. "The Mormon Colonies in Chihuahua after the 1912 Exodus." MA thesis, University of Arizona, 1950.

Milner, Clyde A., II, Carol A. O'Connor, and Martha A. Sandweiss, eds. *The Oxford History of the American West.* New York: Oxford University Press, 1994.

Missionary Record Index. 1830–1971. CR 301 43, Reel 19, LDS Church History

Library.

Mitchel, John. *Jail Journal; or, Five Years in British Prisons*. New York, 1854.

Mitchell, Leslie. "Britain's Reaction to the Revolutions." In Evans and Strandmann, *Revolutions in Europe*, 83–98.

Montgomery, David. "Epilogue: The Pullman Boycott and the Making of Modern America." In Schneirov, Stromquist, and Salvatore, *Pullman Strike and the Crisis of the 1890s*, 233–50.

Mooney, Bernice M. "The Catholic Church in Utah." In Powell, *Utah History Encyclopedia*, 78–79.

_____. "Duane Garrison Hunt." In Powell, *Utah History Encyclopedia*, 264.

Moore, Barrington, Jr. *Social Origins of Dictatorship and Democracy: Lord and Peasant in the Making of the Modern World*. Boston: Beacon Press, 1966.

Moore, Laurence R. *Religious Outsiders and the Making of Americans*. New York: Oxford University Press, 1986.

Moore, Matthew S. "'Joseph's Measures': The Continuation of Esoterica by Schismatic Members of the Council of Fifty." *Journal of Mormon History* 25, no. 2 (Fall 1999): 70–100.

Moorhead, James H. *American Apocalypse: Yankee Protestants and the Civil War, 1860–1869*. New Haven, Conn.: Yale University Press, 1978.

_____. "The Erosion of Postmillennialism in American Religious Thought, 1865–1925." *Church History* 53, no. 1 (March 1984): 61–77.

_____. "Between Progress and Apocalypse: A Reassessment of Millennialism in American Religious Thought, 1800–1880." *Journal of American History* 71 (December 1984): 524–42.

Morales, Waltraud Q. *Bolivia: Land of Struggle*. Boulder, Colo.: Westview Press, 1992.

_____. "Daniel Salamanca." In Tenenbaum, *Encyclopedia of Latin American History and Culture*, 5:14–15.

Morgan, William. *Illustrations of Masonry, by One of the Fraternity Who Has Devoted Thirty Years to the Subject*. 3rd ed. Rochester: printed by the author, 1827. In *New Mormon Studies: A Comprehensive Resource Library*.

Mormon Missionary Diaries Collection. Harold B. Lee Library Digital Collections, Brigham Young University. http://lib.byu.edu/digital/mmd/.

Morozov, N. A. *The Revelation in Thunder and Storm: History of the Apocalypse*. Translated by Michael Sergius Kisséll. Northfield, Minn., 1941. First published 1907 in Russian.

Moss, James R., R. Lanier Britsch, James R. Christianson, and Richard O. Cowan. *The International Church*. Provo, Utah: Brigham Young University Publications, 1982.

Mulanax, Richard B. *The Boer War in American Politics and Diplomacy*. Lanham, Md.: University Press of America, 1994.

Mullins, Willard A. "On the Concept of Ideology in Political Science." *American Political Science Review* 66, no. 2 (June 1972): 498–510.

Munslow, Alun. *Discourse and Culture: The Creation of America, 1870–1920*.

London: Routledge, 1992.

Murphy, Thomas W. "Other Mormon Histories: Lamanite Subjectivity in Mexico." *Journal of Mormon History* 26, no. 2 (Fall 2000): 179–214.

_____. "From Racist Stereotype to Ethnic Identity: Instrumental Uses of Mormon Racial Doctrine." *Ethnohistory* 46, no. 3 (Summer 1999): 451–80.

Murray, Robert K. *Red Scare: A Study in National Hysteria, 1919–1920*. New York: McGraw-Hill, 1955.

Myers, Charles Nash. *Education and National Development in Mexico*. Princeton, N.J.: Industrial Relations Section, Department of Economics, Princeton University, 1965.

Nash, Gary B. "The American Clergy and the French Revolution." *William and Mary Quarterly*, 3rd series, 22, no. 3 (July 1965): 392–412.

"National Register Properties in Pocatello, Idaho." National Register of Historic Places. Accessed June 2, 2011. http://esar.imnh.isu.edu/NR/Home.html.

Naylor, Thomas H. "Colonia Morelos and the Mexican Revolution: Consul Dye Inspects an Evacuated Mormon Colony, 1912." *Journal of Arizona History* 20, no. 1 (Spring 1979): 101–20.

Naylor, Thomas H., and Barney T. Burns. "Colonia Morelos: A Short History of a Mormon Colony in Sonora, Mexico." *Smoke Signal* 27 (Spring 1973): 142–80.

Nederhood, Joel H. "Christians and Revolution." *Christianity Today* 15, no. 7 (January 1, 1971): 7–9.

Neu, Charles E. *Troubled Encounter: United States and Japan*. 1975. Reprint, Malabar, Fl.: Robert E. Krieger, 1975.

New Mormon Studies: A Comprehensive Resource Library. CD-ROM. Salt Lake City: Smith Research Associates, 1998.

Nibley, Hugh. *Approaching Zion*. Collected Works of Hugh Nibley 9. Edited by Don E. Norman. Salt Lake City: Deseret Book, 1989.

_____. "How Firm a Foundation! What Makes It So." *Dialogue: A Journal of Mormon Thought* 12, no. 4 (Winter 1979): 29–45.

_____. "The Meaning of the Kirtland Egyptian Papers." *BYU Studies* 11, no. 4 (1971): 350–99.

Noether, Emiliana P. "The American Response to the 1848 Revolutions in Rome and Budapest." *Consortium on Revolutionary Europe, 1750–1850: Proceedings* 15 (1985): 379–97.

_____. "Mazzini and the Nineteenth Century Revolutionary Movement." *Consortium on Revolutionary Europe, 1750–1850: Proceedings* 14 (1984): 277–85.

Nolan, Max. "Materialism and the Mormon Faith." *Dialogue: A Journal of Mormon Thought* 22, no. 4 (Winter 1989): 62–75.

Norgate, Gerald Le Grys. "Cook, Eliza." In *Dictionary of National Biography, 1901 Supplement*, edited by Leslie Stephen and Sidney Lee, 2:53–54. London: Smith, Elder, 1901. http://en.wikisource.org/wiki/Cook,_Eliza_%28DNB01%29.

Norman, Keith E. "How Long O Lord? The Delay of the Parousia in Mormonism." *Sunstone* 8, no. 1–2 (January–April 1983): 48–58.

Northend, Charles, ed. *Elihu Burritt: A Memorial Volume Containing a Sketch of His Life and Labors, with Selections from His Writings and Lectures, and Extracts from His Private Journals in Europe and America*. New York: D. Appleton and Company, 1879.

O'Brien, Thomas F. *The Revolutionary Mission: American Enterprise in Latin America, 1900–1945*. New York: Cambridge University Press, 1996.

O'Connor, John J., and Edmund F. Robertson. "Josef-Maria Hoëné de Wronski." MacTutor History of Mathematics Archive. Accessed November 14, 2012. http://www-groups.dcs.st-and.ac.uk/history/Biographies/Wronski.html.

Oliver, W. H. *Prophets and Millennialists: The Uses of Biblical Prophecy in England from the 1790's to the 1840's*. Auckland: Auckland University Press, 1978.

Oser, Jacob. *Henry George*. The Great Thinkers Series. New York: Twayne, 1974.

Owens, Lance S. "Joseph Smith and Kabbalah: The Occult Connection." *Dialogue: A Journal of Mormon Thought* 27, no. 3 (Fall 1994): 117–94.

Ozinga, James R. *Communism: The Story of the Idea and Its Implementation*. 2nd ed. Englewood Cliffs, N.J.: Prentice Hall, 1991.

Ozouf, Mona. *Festivals and the French Revolution*. Translated by Alan Sheridan. Cambridge, Mass.: Harvard University Press, 1988.

Pace, Gene D. "Brazil's 'Long March': Opposition to the Economic Elite of the Old Regime." *Essays in Economic and Business History* 14 (1996): 133–41.

Palmer, Robert R., and Joel Colton. *A History of the Modern World*. 7th ed. New York: Alfred A Knopf, 1991.

Palmer, Spencer J. *The Church Encounters Asia*. Salt Lake City: Deseret Book, 1970.

Papers Relating to the Foreign Relations of the United States, 1930. 3 vols. Washington, DC: Government Printing Office, 1945.

Papers Relating to the Foreign Relations of the United States, with the Annual Message of the President Transmitted to Congress December 3, 1912. Washington, DC: Government Printing Office, 1919.

Paris Branch, France Mission. Manuscript History and Historical Reports. 1850–1983. Microfilm. LR 6742, LDS Church History Library.

Park, James William. *Latin American Underdevelopment: A History of Perspectives in the United States, 1870–1965*. Baton Rouge: Louisiana State University Press, 1995.

Parrish, Mary Pratt. "Look to the Rock from Which Ye Are Hewn." Unpublished manuscript, n.d. Copy in author's possession.

Patterson, Ian. *Guernica and Total War*. Cambridge, Mass.: Harvard University Press, 2007.

Paul, Erich Robert. *Science, Religion, and Mormon Cosmology*. Urbana, Ill.: University of Illinois Press, 1992.

Pawlikowski, John T. "Jesus and the Revolutionaries: A Jewish-Christian Approach to the Current Debate." *Christian Century* 89, no. 44 (December 6, 1972): 1237–41.

Paxman, James Walter. Diaries. 3 vols. 1884–1927. Mormon Missionary Diaries Collection.

Paxton, John. *Companion to the French Revolution*. New York: Facts on File, 1988.

Peloso, Vincent. "Peru: Since Independence." In Tenenbaum, *Encyclopedia of Latin*

American History and Culture, 4:364–74.

Perez, Louis A. "Cuba, c. 1930–59." In Bethell, *Cambridge History of Latin America*, 7:723–28.

Peterson, Stanley A. "Millennial Star." In Ludlow, *Encyclopedia of Mormonism*, 2:906.

Phillips, Kevin. *The Cousins' Wars: Religion, Politics, Civil Warfare, and the Triumph of Anglo-America*. New York: Basic Books, 1999.

Pike, Albert. *Morals and Dogma of the Ancient and Accepted Scottish Rite of Freemasonry*. Charleston: Supreme Council of the Thirty-Third Degree for the Southern Jurisdiction of the United States, 1871.

Pike, Fredrick B. *FDR's Good Neighbor Policy: Sixty Years of Generally Gentle Chaos*. Austin: University of Texas Press, 1995.

_____. *The United States and Latin America: Myths and Stereotypes of Civilization and Nature*. Austin: University of Texas Press, 1992.

Pinkerton, Allan. *Strikers, Communists, Tramps and Detectives*. New York: G. W. Carleton, 1878.

Pitzer, Donald E., ed. *America's Communal Utopias*. Chapel Hill: University of North Carolina Press, 1997.

Poll, Richard D. "Americanization of Utah." *Utah Historical Quarterly* 44, no. 1 (Winter 1976): 76–93.

Popkin, Jeremy D. *A Short History of the French Revolution*. Englewood Cliffs, N.J.: Prentice Hall, 1995.

Poppino, Rollie E. *International Communism in Latin America: A History of the Movement, 1917–1963*. New York: Free Press of Glencoe, 1964.

_____. "Vargas, Getúlio Dornelles." In Tenenbaum, *Encyclopedia of Latin American History and Culture*, 5:362–65.

Postgate, Raymond. *Story of a Year: 1848*. New York: Oxford University Press, 1956.

Powell, Alan Kent. "Elections in the State of Utah." In Powell, *Utah History Encyclopedia*, 157–67.

_____. "Our Cradles Were in Germany: Utah's German American Community and World War I." *Utah Historical Quarterly* 58 (Fall 1990): 371–87.

_____, ed. *Utah History Encyclopedia*. Salt Lake City: University of Utah Press, 1994.

Pratt, Lucile. "A Keyhole View of Mexican Agrarian Policy as Shown by Mormon Land Problems." MA thesis, Columbia University, 1957.

Pratt, Orson. *Latter-day Kingdom; or, the Preparation for the Second Advent*. Liverpool: L.D.S. Book and Star Depot, March 15, 1857. LDS Church History Library.

_____. *New Jerusalem, and Equality and Oneness of the Saints; a Forecast of Events to Be Established by a Chosen and Dedicated People*. 1849 and 1854. Reprint, Salt Lake City: Parker P. Robison, n.d. Lee Library.

_____. *New Jerusalem; or, the Fulfilment of Modern Prophecy*. Liverpool: R. James, October 1, 1849. LDS Church History Library.

Pratt, Parley P. *Angel of the Prairies; a Dream of the Future*. Salt Lake City: Deseret News, 1880. Written 1843–44. LDS Church History Library.

_____. *The Autobiography of Parley Parker Pratt*. Edited by Parley P. Pratt Jr. Salt

Lake City: Deseret Book, 1961.

_____. *A Proclamation of the Twelve Apostles of the Church of Jesus Christ of Latter-day Saints. To All the Kings of the World; to the President of the United States of America; to the Governors of the Several States; and to the Rulers and Peoples of All Nations.* New York, April 6, 1845. Reprint, Liverpool: Wilford Woodruff, 1845. LDS Church History Library.

_____. *A Voice of Warning and Instruction to All People, or, an Introduction to the Faith and Doctrine of the Church of the Latter-day Saints.* 10th ed. Liverpool: H. S. Eldridge, 1871. First published 1837.

Pratt, Rey L. Diaries. 9 vols. 1906–30. Holograph. Rey L. Pratt Papers, Box 1, fds. 1–5.

_____. *Just Thinking.* [Independence, Mo.: Press of Zion's Printing and Publishing Company], 1928. LDS Church History Library.

Preston, Diana. *The Boxer Rebellion: The Dramatic Story of China's War on Foreigners That Shook the World in the Summer of 1900.* New York: Berkley Books, 2000.

Price, Robert M. "Numbered among the Transgressors, the 'Zealot Hypothesis' Reconsidered." *Drew Gateway* 51, no. 1 (Fall 1981): 28–43.

"Prince L. S. Golitsyn: The Founder of Russian Industrial Winemaking." *Rest in the Pike Perch.* Accessed November 26, 2011. http://i-sudak.com/en/page14.html.

Pringle, Henry F. *The Life and Times of William Howard Taft: A Biography.* 2 vols. New York: Farrar and Rinehart, 1939.

Quinn, D. Michael. "The Council of Fifty and Its Members, 1844–1945." *BYU Studies* 20, no. 2 (Winter 1980): 163–97.

_____. "The Flag of the Kingdom of God." *BYU Studies* 14, no. 1 (Autumn 1973): 105–14.

_____. *Early Mormonism and the Magic World View.* Rev. and enl. ed. Salt Lake City, Signature Books, 1998.

_____. *Elder Statesman: A Biography of J. Reuben Clark.* Salt Lake City: Signature Books, 2002.

_____. *J. Reuben Clark: The Church Years.* Provo, Utah: Brigham Young University Press, 1983.

_____. "Joseph Smith III's 1844 Blessing and the Mormons of Utah." *Dialogue* 15, no. 2 (Summer 1982): 69–90.

_____. "The Mormon Church and the Spanish-American War: An End to Selective Pacifism." *Pacific Historical Review* 43, no. 3 (August 1974): 342–66.

_____. *The Mormon Hierarchy: Extensions of Power.* Salt Lake City: Signature Books/Smith Research Associates, 1997.

_____. *The Mormon Hierarchy: Origins of Power.* Salt Lake City: Signature Books, 1994.

_____, ed. *The New Mormon History: Revisionist Essays on the Past.* Salt Lake City: Signature Books, 1992.

_____. "Socioreligious Radicalism of the Mormon Church: A Parallel to the Anabaptists." In Bitton and Beecher, *New Views of Mormon History,* 363–86.

Quint, Howard H. "American Socialists and the Spanish-American War." *American Quarterly* 10, no. 2 (Summer 1958): 132–54.

Quirk, Robert E. *The Mexican Revolution and the Catholic Church, 1910–1929*. Bloomington: Indiana University Press, 1973.

_____. "Religion and the Mexican Revolution." In *Religion, Revolution, and Reform: New Forces for Change in Latin America*, edited by William V. D'Antonio and Frederick B. Pike, 59–71. New York: Frederick A. Praeger, 1964.

Rachum, Ilan. "The Brazilian Revolution of 1930: A Revision," *Inter-American Economic Affairs* 29, no. 3 (Winter 1975): 59–84.

_____. "Nationalism and Revolution in Brazil, 1922–1930: A Study of Intellectual, Military, and Political Protesters and of the Assault on the Old Republic." PhD diss., Columbia University, 1970.

Racine, Luc. "Paradise, the Golden Age, the Millennium and Utopia: A Note on the Differentiation of Forms of the Ideal Society." *Diogenes* 122 (Summer 1983): 119–36.

Ramírez, Susan E. "Haciendas." In Tenenbaum, *Encyclopedia of Latin American History and Culture*, 3:161–63.

Ramón, Jrade. "Inquiries into the Cristero Insurrection against the Mexican Revolution." *Latin American Research Review* 20, no. 2 (1985): 53–69.

Rapport, Mike. *1848: Year of Revolution*. New York: Basic Books, 2008.

Reed, David. *Ireland: The Key to British Revolution*. London: Larkin, 1984.

Reed, Raymond J. "The Mormons in Chihuahua: Their Relations with Villa and the Pershing Punitive Expedition, 1910–1917." MA thesis, University of New Mexico, 1938.

Reinwand, Louis G. "An Interpretive Study of Mormon Millennialism during the Nineteenth Century with Emphasis on Millennial Developments in Utah." MA thesis, Brigham Young University, 1971.

Renwick, John. "Fabre d'Olivet, Antoine." In *The New Oxford Companion to Literature in French*, edited by Peter France, 296. New York: Oxford University Press, 1995.

Report of the Semi-annual Conference of the Church of Jesus Christ of Latter-day Saints. Salt Lake City: Church of Jesus Christ of Latter-day Saints, 1880–present. Semi-annual series. http://archive.org/details/conferencereport.

Reyes, Antonio Lara. "Mormonism, Americanism, and Mexico." *The American Behavioral Scientist* 40, no. 7 (June–July 1997): 902–13.

Rey L. Pratt Papers. 1901–59. MS 2730, LDS Church History Library.

Reynolds, George F. *The Story of the Book of Mormon*. Salt Lake City: Jos. Hyrum Parry, 1888.

Riasanovsky, Nicholas V. *A History of Russia*. 4th ed. New York: Oxford University Press, 1984.

Richardson, Edward W. *Standards and Colors of the American Revolution*. Philadelphia: University of Pennsylvania Press and the Pennsylvania Society of Sons of the Revolution and its color guard, 1982.

Richey, Russell E., and Donald G. Jones, eds. *American Civil Religion*. New York: Harper and Row, 1974.

_____. "The Civil Religion Debate." In Richey and Jones, *American Civil Religion*, 3–18.

Rickover, Hyman G. *How the Battleship Maine Was Destroyed.* Washington, DC: Department of the Navy, Naval History Division, 1976.

Ridley, Jasper. *The Freemasons: A History of the World's Most Powerful Secret Society.* New York: Arcade Publishing, 2001.

Robbins, Thomas, and Susan J. Palmer, eds. *Millennium, Messiahs, and Mayhem: Contemporary Apocalyptic Movements.* New York: Routledge, 1997.

Roberts, Allen D. "Where Are the All-Seeing Eyes? The Origin, Use, and Decline of Early Mormon Symbolism." *Sunstone* 10, no. 5 (May 1985): 36–48.

Roberts, Allen E. *Freemasonry in American History.* Richmond, Va.: Macoy Publishing and Masonic Supply, 1985.

Roberts, B. H. *Comprehensive History of the Church of Jesus Christ of Latter-day Saints, 1830–1930.* 6 vols. Salt Lake City: Church of Jesus Christ of Latter-day Saints, 1930.

_____. *The Life of John Taylor: Third President of the Church of Jesus Christ of Latter-day Saints.* Salt Lake City, George Q. Cannon and Sons, 1892.

_____. *New Witnesses for God.* 3 vols. Salt Lake City: Deseret News, 1909–11.

_____. *Studies of the Book of Mormon.* Edited by Brigham D. Madsen. Salt Lake City: Signature Books, 1992.

_____. *The Truth, the Way, the Life: An Elementary Treatise on Theology.* Edited by John W. Welch. 2nd ed. Provo, Utah: Brigham Young University Studies, 1996. Written 1927–29.

Roberts, Dale Allen. "Academic Freedom at Brigham Young University: Free Inquiry in Religious Context." In *Religion, Feminism, and Freedom of Conscience: A Mormon/Humanist Dialogue,* edited by George D. Smith, 43–62. Salt Lake City: Signature Books, 1994.

Roberts, Phil. "The Other Roughriders: Col. Torrey and Wyoming's Volunteer Cavalry." Buffalo Bones: Stories of Wyoming's Past. Accessed February 15, 2013. http://uwacadweb.uwyo.edu/robertshistory/Torreys_roughriders.htm.

Roberts, Timothy M., and Daniel W. Howe. "The United States and the Revolutions of 1848." In Evans and Strandmann, *Revolutions in Europe,* 157–79.

Robson, Kent E. "Time and Omniscience in Mormon Theology." *Sunstone* 5, no. 3 (May–June 1980): 17–24.

Rock, David. *Argentina, 1516–1982: From Spanish Colonization to the Falklands War.* Berkeley: University of California Press, 1985.

Rodríguez O., Jaime E., ed. *The Revolutionary Process in Mexico: Essays on Political and Social Change, 1880–1940.* Los Angeles: UCLA Latin American Center, 1990.

Rogers, Kristen Smart. "'Another Good Man': Anthony W. Ivins and the Defeat of Reed Smoot." *Utah Historical Quarterly* 68, no. 1 (Winter 2000): 55–75.

Rogers, Thomas Franklin. "Images and Imaginings: An American in Moscow, 1958." Microfilm of typescript. MS 8229, LDS Church History Library.

Rohrs, Richard C. "American Critics of the French Revolution of 1848." *Journal of the Early Republic* 14, no. 3 (Fall 1994): 359–77.

Romney, Thomas Cottam. *The Mormon Colonies in Mexico.* Salt Lake City: Deseret Book, 1938.

Rosenberg, Emily S. *Spreading the American Dream: American Economic and Cultural Expansion, 1890–1945.* New York: Hill and Wang, 1982.

Rosenberg, John D., ed. *The Genius of John Ruskin: Selections from His Writings.* 2nd ed. Charlottesville: University of Virginia Press, 2000.

Ross, Stanley R. *Francisco I. Madero: Apostle of Mexican Democracy.* New York: Columbia University Press, 1955.

Rubenstein, Richard L. "Religious Modernization and the Millennium." In Bryant and Dayton, *Coming Kingdom,* 223–46.

Ruiz, Eduardo Ramón. *Triumphs and Tragedy: A History of the Mexican People.* New York: W. W. Norton, 1992.

Rutherford, James. *Sir George Grey, K.C.B., 1812–1898: A Study in Colonial Government.* London: Cassell, 1961.

Ryan, Alan. *John Dewey and the High Tide of American Liberalism.* New York: W. W. Norton, 1995.

———. "Liberalism." In *A Companion to Contemporary Political Philosophy,* edited by Robert E. Goodin, Phillip Pettit, and Thomas Pogge, 360–82. Blackwell Companions to Philosophy Series. 2nd ed. Malden, Mass.: Blackwell, 2007.

Sachs, Viola. "The Holy Scriptures and the Scripture of the New Cosmogony." *Amerikastudien/American Studies* 31, no.1 (1986): 51–59.

Sacred Hymns and Spiritual Songs for the Church of Jesus Christ of Latter-day Saints. 15th ed. Liverpool: Latter-day Saints' Book Depot, 1871.

Sandeen, Ernest Robert. *The Roots of Fundamentalism: British and American Millenarianism, 1800–1930.* Chicago, Ill.: University of Chicago Press, 1970.

Schama, Simon. *Citizens: A Chronicle of the French Revolution.* New York: Alfred A. Knopf, 1989.

Schlesinger, Arthur M., Jr. *The Coming of the New Deal, 1933–1935.* Vol. 2 of *The Age of Roosevelt.* Boston: Houghton Mifflin, 1958.

Schlup, Leonard. "William H. King and the Question of League Membership." *Weber: The Contemporary West* 14, no. 3 (Fall 1997). http://weberstudies. weber.edu/archives.htm.

Schmitt, Karl M. *Communism in Mexico: A Study in Political Frustration.* Austin: University of Texas Press, 1965.

Schneider, Ronald M. *"Order and Progress": A Political History of Brazil.* Boulder, Colo.: Westview Press, 1991.

Schneirov, Richard, Shelton Stromquist, and Nick Salvatore, eds. *The Pullman Strike and the Crisis of the 1890s: Essays on Labor and Politics.* Urbana: University of Illinois Press, 1999.

Schopenhauer, Arthur. *The World as Will and Representation.* 2 vols. Translated by E. F. J. Payne. Indian Hills, Colo.: Falcon's Wing, 1958.

Schwartz, Hillel. "Millenarianism: An Overview." In *The Encyclopedia of Religion.* Vol. 9. Edited by Mircea Eliade, 521–32. New York: Macmillan Publishing Company, 1986.

Schwerin, Karl H. "The Indian Populations of Latin America." In Black, *Latin America, Its Problems and Its Promise,* 40–56.

Sessions, Gene A. "The Clark Memorandum Myth." *Academy of American Franciscan History* 34, no. 1 (July 1977): 40–58.

Shalhope, Robert E. "Republicanism in Early American Historiography." *William and Mary Quarterly* 39, no. 3 (1982): 334–56.

Shanks, Andrew. *Civil Society, Civil Religion.* Cambridge, Mass.: Blackwell, 1995.

Sharfman, Glenn R. "Jewish Emancipation, 1848." In Chastain, *Encyclopedia of 1848 Revolutions.* http://www.ohio.edu/chastain/ip/jewemanc.htm.

Shavit, David. *The United States in Latin America: A Historical Dictionary.* New York: Greenwood Press, 1992.

Shepard, Gary, and Gordon Shepard. *A Kingdom Transformed: Themes in the Development of Mormonism.* Salt Lake City: University of Utah Press, 1984.

Shipps, Jan. *Mormonism: The Story of a New Religious Tradition.* Urbana: University of Illinois Press, 1985.

———. *Sojourner in a Promised Land.* Urbana: University of Illinois Press, 2000.

Shoemaker, T. Eugene. "The Office of Prophet: An Intellectual Look." *Sunstone* 5, no. 4 (July/August 1980): 34–35.

Shor, Francis Robert. *Utopianism and Radicalism in a Reforming America, 1888–1918.* Westport, Conn.: Greenwood Press, 1997.

"A Short History of the Department of State: Rise to World Power, 1867–1913." United States Department of State. Accessed December 11, 2012. http://history.state.gov/departmenthistory/short-history/worldpower.

Sillito, John R. "William H. King." In Powell, *Utah History Encyclopedia*, 303–4.

Simkin, John. "George Julian Harney." Spartacus Educational. Accessed November 26, 2011. http://www.spartacus.schoolnet.co.uk/CHharney.htm.

———. "The Northern Star." Spartacus Educational. Accessed November 26, 2011. http://www.spartacus.schoolnet.co.uk/CHnorthern.htm.

Simms, W. Gilmore. *Sabbath Lyrics; or, Songs from Scripture: A Christmas Gift of Love.* Charleston: Walker and James, 1849. http://simms.library.sc.edu/view_item.php?item=100556&tab=overview.

Sjödahl, Janne M. *An Introduction to the Study of the Book of Mormon.* Salt Lake City: Deseret News, 1927.

Smiley, Winn Whiting. "Ammon M. Tenney: Mormon Missionary to the Indians." *Journal of Arizona History* 13, no. 2 (Summer 1972): 82–108.

Smith, Cornelius C., Jr. *Emilio Kosterlitzky: Eagle of Sonora and the Southwest Border.* Frontier Military Series 7. Glendale, Calif.: Arthur H. Clark, 1970.

Smith, David E. "Millenarian Scholarship in America." *American Quarterly* 17 (Fall 1965): 535–49.

Smith, George D., ed. *Faithful History: Essays on Writing Mormon History.* Salt Lake City: Signature Books, 1992.

Smith, Joseph, Jr., et al. *History of the Church of Jesus Christ of Latter-day Saints.* 7 vols. Edited by B. H. Roberts. 2nd ed. rev. Salt Lake City: Deseret Book, 1978.

Smith, Joseph Fielding, Jr. *The Restoration of All Things.* 1945. Reprint, Salt Lake City: Deseret Book, 1973.

———, comp. *Teachings of the Prophet Joseph Smith.* Salt Lake City: Deseret Book,

1938.

_____. *The Way to Perfection: Short Discourses on Gospel Themes.* 9th ed. Salt Lake City: Genealogical Society of the Church of Jesus Christ of Latter-day Saints, 1951.

Smith, Marilyn S. *Living Issues in Philosophy: An Introductory Textbook.* New York: D. Van Nostrand, 1946.

Smith, Robert Freeman. *The United States and Revolutionary Nationalism in Mexico, 1916–1932.* Chicago: University of Chicago Press, 1972.

Smith, Robert W., and Elizabeth A. *Scriptural and Secular Prophecies Pertaining to the Last Days.* Salt Lake City: Pyramid Press, 1931.

Smith, S. M. "Curtis Edwin Bolton." Find a Grave. Last modified January 4, 2011. http://www.findagrave.com/cgi-bin/fg.cgi?page=gr&GRid=63706554.

Smith, W. H. B. *Small Arms of the World: A Basic Manual of Small Arms.* Revised and updated by Joseph E. Smith. 9th ed. Harrisburg, Pa.: Stackpole Books, 1969.

Smith, Wayne S. "The United States and Latin America: Into a New Era." In Black, *Latin America, Its Problems and Its Promise,* 273–95.

Snow, Eliza R., comp. *Biography and Family Record of Lorenzo Snow: One of the Twelve Apostles of the Church of Jesus Christ of Latter-day Saints.* Salt Lake City: Deseret News, 1884.

Snow, Lorenzo. *The Italian Mission.* London: W. Aubrey, 1851. In *New Mormon Studies: A Comprehensive Resource Library.*

Sonne, Conway B. *Saints on the Seas: A Maritime History of Mormon Migration, 1830–1890.* Salt Lake City: University of Utah Press, 1983.

South American Mission. Manuscript History and Historical Reports. 2 vols. 1925–35. Holograph. LR 8458 2, LDS Church History Library.

Spencer, Donald S. *Louis Kossuth and the Young America: A Study of Sectionalism and Foreign Policy, 1848–1852.* Columbus, Mo.: University of Missouri Press, 1977.

Spencer, Herbert. *The Principles of Ethics.* 2 vols. 1892–1893. Reprint, New York: Appleton, 1914.

Spencer, Orson. *The Prussian Mission of the Church of Jesus Christ of Latter-day Saints: Report of Elder Orson Spencer, A.B. to President Brigham Young.* Liverpool: S. W. Richards, 1853. LDS Church History Library.

Sperber, Jonathan. *The European Revolutions, 1848–1851.* New York: Cambridge University Press, 1994.

Stauffer, Vernon. *New England and the Bavarian Illuminati.* New York: Columbia University Press, 1918. Reprint, New York: Russell and Russell, 1967.

Steefel, Lawrence Dinkelspiel. *Bismarck, the Hohenzollern Candidacy, and the Origins of the Franco-German War of 1870.* Cambridge, Mass.: Harvard University Press, 1962.

Steigerwald, David. "The Reclamation of Woodrow Wilson?" *Diplomatic History* 23, no. 1 (Winter 1999): 79–99.

Stein, Leonard. *The Balfour Declaration.* New York: Simon and Schuster, 1961.

Stephanson, Anders. *Manifest Destiny: American Expansion and the Empire of*

Right. New York: Hill and Wang, 1995.

Stewart, George, Dilworth Walker, and E. Cecil McGavin. *Priesthood and Church Welfare: A Study Course for the Quorums of the Melchizedek Priesthood for the Year 1939*. 2nd ed. Salt Lake City: Deseret Book, 1938.

Stocks, Hugh G. "Book of Mormon Translations." In Ludlow, *Encyclopedia of Mormonism*, 1:213–14.

Stokes, Melvyn, and Stephen Conway, eds. *The Market Revolution in America: Social, Political, and Religious Expressions, 1800–1880*. Charlottesville: University Press of Virginia, 1996.

Strakhovsky, Leonid I. *American Opinion about Russia, 1917–1920*. Toronto: University of Toronto Press, 1961.

Stuy, Brian H., ed. and comp. *Collected Discourses Delivered by President Wilford Woodruff, His Two Counselors, the Twelve Apostles, and Others*. 5 vols. Burbank, Calif.: B. H. S. Publishing, 1987–92.

Sundberg, Kenneth M. "The Morning Star, A Study of the Symbolism and Design Inherent in the Holy Priesthood as Administered in the Church of Jesus Christ of Latter-day Saints." Unpublished manuscript, 1972. LDS Church History Library.

Surh, Gerald D. *1905 in St. Petersburg: Labor, Society, and Revolution*. Stanford, Calif.: Stanford University Press, 1989.

Talmage, James E. *The Articles of Faith: A Series of Lectures on the Principal Doctrines of the Church of Jesus Christ of Latter-day Saints*. Salt Lake City: Deseret News, 1899. Page references in the notes are to the 1899 edition unless otherwise specified.

_____. *The Articles of Faith: A Series of Lectures on the Principal Doctrines of the Church of Jesus Christ of Latter-day Saints*. 12th ed. Salt Lake City: Church of Jesus Christ of Latter-day Saints, 1924.

_____. Diaries. 5 vols. 1924–28. Mormon Missionary Diaries Collection.

_____. *Jesus the Christ: A Study of the Messiah and His Mission According to the Holy Scriptures both Ancient and Modern*. Salt Lake City: Deseret News, 1915.

Talmon, Jacob L. *The Origins of Totalitarian Democracy*. New York: Frederick A. Praeger, 1960.

_____. *Political Messianism: The Romantic Phase*. New York: Frederick A. Praeger, 1960.

Tanner, George S. *John Tanner and His Family*. Salt Lake City: John Tanner Family Association, 1974.

Tanner, Obert C., Lewis M. Rogers, and Sterling M. McMurrin, *Toward Understanding the New Testament*. Salt Lake City: Signature Books, 1990.

Tannenbaum, Frank. *Peace by Revolution: Mexico after 1910*. New York: Columbia University Press, 1933.

Taylor, Harold W., comp. *Memories of Militants and Mormon Colonists in Mexico*. Yorba Linda, Calif.: Shumway Family History Services, 1992.

Taylor, John. *The Gospel Kingdom: Selections from the Writings and Discourses of John Taylor*. Compiled by G. Homer Durham. 1st collector's ed. Salt Lake

City: Bookcraft, 1987.

———. *The Government of God.* Liverpool: S. W. Richards, 1852.

———. "John Taylor Letter, Hamburg, Germany, to W. Phillips, Wales, 1851 November 24." Translated by Ronald D. Dennis. MS 6747, LDS Church History Library.

Taylor, Phillip A. M. *Expectations Westward: The Mormons and the Emigration of Their British Converts.* Edinburgh: Oliver and Boyd, 1965.

Taylor, Samuel W. "The Golden Dream and the Nightmare: The Closet Crusade of A. C. Lambert." *Dialogue: A Journal of Mormon Thought* 28, no. 3 (Fall 1995): 51–57.

Tenenbaum, Barbara A., ed. *Encyclopedia of Latin American History and Culture.* 5 vols. New York: Charles Scribner's Sons, 1996.

Thatcher, Linda. "Fox, Ruth May." In Ludlow, *Encyclopedia of Mormonism,* 2:524–25.

Thomas, Hugh. *The Spanish Civil War.* New York: Harper and Brothers, 1961.

Thomas, M. M. "Social Justice and Just Rebellion." *Ecumenical Review* 30, no. 4 (October 1978): 333–38.

Thomas, Mark D. *Digging in Cumorah: Reclaiming Book of Mormon Narratives.* Salt Lake City: Signature Books, 1999.

Thompson, Arthur W., and Robert A. Hart. *The Uncertain Crusade: America and the Russian Revolution of 1905.* [Amherst]: University of Massachusetts Press, 1970.

Thomson, Sandra Caruthers. "Meiji Japan through Missionary Eyes: The American Protestant Experience." *Journal of Religious History* 7, no. 3 (June 1973): 248–59.

Thorp, Malcolm R. "Popular Mormon Millennialism in Nineteenth-Century Britain," *Journal of Mormon History* 32, no. 2 (Summer 2005): 89–111.

———. "The Setting for the Restoration in Britain: Political, Social, and Economic Conditions." In Bloxham, Moss, and Porter, *Truth Will Prevail,* 44–70.

Thrupp, Sylvia L., ed. *Millennial Dreams in Action: Studies in Revolutionary Religious Movements.* New York: Schocken Books, 1970.

Tiller, Ann Quiggins. "The Igniting Spark—Brazil, 1930." *Hispanic American Historical Review* 45, no. 3 (August 1965): 384–92.

Tobler, Douglas F. "Mormonism and the Secular Philosophies: Competing Creeds in the Twentieth Century." In *Mormonism: A Faith for All Cultures,* edited by F. LaMond Tullis, 328–46. Provo, Utah: Brigham Young University Press, 1978.

Tombs, Robert. *The War against Paris, 1871.* Cambridge: Cambridge University Press, 1981.

Toscano, Margaret, and Paul Toscano. *Strangers in Paradox: Explorations in Mormon Theology.* Salt Lake City: Signature Books, 1990.

Trachtenberg, Alexander. "The Lessons of the Paris Commune." Anarchy Archives. Accessed November 26, 2011. http://dwardmac.pitzer.edu/Anarchist_Archives/coldoffthepresses.html.

Trani, Eugene P. *The Treaty of Portsmouth: An Adventure in American Diplomacy.* Lexington: University of Kentucky Press, 1969.

Trask, David F. *The War with Spain in 1898.* New York: Macmillan, 1981.

Trotnow, Helmut. *Karl Liebknecht (1871–1919): A Political Biography*. New York: Archon Books, 1984.

Trumbo, Jean. "Orson Hyde's *Frontier Guardian*: A Mormon Editor Chronicles the Westward Movement through Kanesville, Iowa." *Iowa Heritage Illustrated* 77 (Summer 1996): 74–85.

Tuck, Jim. *Pancho Villa and John Reed: Two Faces of Romantic Revolution*. Tucson: University of Arizona Press, 1984.

Tullidge, Edward W. *History of Salt Lake City and Its Founders*. Salt Lake City: Edward Tullidge, 1886.

_____. *Tullidge's Histories, Containing the History of All the Northern, Eastern, and Western Counties of Utah: Also the Counties of Southern Idaho*. Vol. 2. Salt Lake City: Juvenile Instructor, 1889.

Tullis, F. LaMond. *Mormons in Mexico: The Dynamics of Faith and Culture*. Logan: Utah State University Press, 1987.

_____. "A Shepherd to Mexico's Saints: Arwell L. Pierce and the Third Convention." *BYU Studies* 37, no. 1 (1997–98): 127–57.

Tullis, F. LaMond, and Elizabeth Hernández. *Mormonism Comes of Age: The Third Convention in Mexico*. Provo, Utah: Brigham Young University, 1975.

Turley, Clarence F., and Anna Tenney Turley, comps. *History of the Mormon Colonies in Mexico: The Juarez Stake, 1885–1980*. 2nd ed. Salt Lake City: Publisher's Press, 1996.

Tuveson, Ernest Lee. *Millennium and Utopia: A Study in the Background of the Idea of Progress*. Berkeley: University of California Press, 1949.

_____. *Redeemer Nation: The Idea of America's Millennial Role*. Chicago: University of Chicago Press, 1968.

Underwood, Grant. "Book of Mormon Usage in Early LDS Theology." *Dialogue: A Journal of Mormon Thought* 17, no. 3 (Autumn 1984): 35–74.

_____. *The Millenarian World of Early Mormonism*. Urbana: University of Illinois Press, 1993.

_____. "The Religious Milieu of English Mormonism." In Jensen and Thorp, *Mormons in Early Victorian Britain*, 21–48.

Unterberger, Betty Miller. "Woodrow Wilson and the Russian Revolution." In Link, *Woodrow Wilson and a Revolutionary World*, 40–104.

US Consulate. Letter to US State Department. March 10, 1920. Collected Letters Concerning the Church in the Mexican Colonies. 1912–20. MS 12212, LDS Church History Library.

Vanden, Harry E. *National Marxism in Latin America: José Carlos Mariátegui's Thought and Politics*. Boulder, Colo.: Lynne Rienner, 1986.

Vanderwood, Paul J. "Explaining the Mexican Revolution." In Rodríguez O., *The Revolutionary Process in Mexico*, 97–114.

_____. *The Power of God against the Guns of Government: Religious Upheaval in Mexico at the Turn of the Nineteenth Century*. Stanford, Calif.: Stanford University Press, 1998.

Van Kley, Dale K. *The Religious Origins of the French Revolution: From Calvin to the*

Civil Consitution, 1560–1791. New Haven, Conn.: Yale University Press, 1996.

Van Orden, Bruce A. "Smith, Joseph F." In Ludlow, *Encyclopedia of Mormonism,* 3:1349–52.

Van Wagoner, Richard S., and Steven C. Walker. *A Book of Mormons.* Salt Lake City: Signature Books, 1982.

Varg, Paul A. "William Woodville Rockhill's Influence on the Boxer Negotiations." *Pacific Historical Review* 18, no. 3 (August 1949): 369–80.

Vasconcelos, José. *The Cosmic Race/La raza cósmica: A Bilingual Edition.* Translated and annotated by Didier T. Jaén. Johns Hopkins Paperbacks ed. Baltimore, Md.: Johns Hopkins University Press, 1997.

Vaughan, Mary Kay. "Cultural Approaches to Peasant Politics in the Mexican Revolution." *Hispanic American Historical Review* 79, no. 2 (May 1999): 269–305.

Ventura, Betty G., ed. *The History of the Salt Lake Mexican Branch, 1920–1960.* Salt Lake City, 1998.

Vogel, Dan, ed. and comp. *Early Mormon Documents.* Vol. 1. Salt Lake City: Signature Books, 1996. In *New Mormon Studies: A Comprehensive Resource Library.*

Voss, Stuart F. "Nationalizing the Revolution: Culmination and Circumstance." In *Provinces of the Revolution: Essays on Regional Mexican History, 1910–1929,* edited by Thomas Benjamin and Mark Wasserman, 273–317. Albuquerque: University of New Mexico Press, 1990.

Waite, Arthur Edward. *A New Encyclopaedia of Freemasonry and of Cognate Instituted Mysteries: Their Rites, Literature, and History.* 2 vols. 1921. Reprint, New York: Weathervane, 1970.

Walker, Ronald W. "'A Banner is Unfurled': Mormonism's Ensign Peak." *Dialogue: A Journal of Mormon Thought* 26, no. 4 (Winter 1993): 71–91.

———. "Sheaves, Bucklers, and the State: Mormon Leaders Respond to the Dilemmas of War." In Quinn, *New Mormon History,* 267–301.

———. "When Spirits Did Abound: Nineteenth-Century Utah's Encounter with Free-Thought Radicalism." *Utah Historical Quarterly* 50 (Fall 1982): 304–24.

Walker, Ronald W., and Richard W. Sadler. "History of the Church: C. 1898–1945, Transitions: Early Twentieth-Century Period." In Ludlow, *Encyclopedia of Mormonism,* 2:630–38.

Walker, Ronald W., Richard E. Turley, and Glen M. Leonard. *Massacre at Mountain Meadows: An American Tragedy.* New York: Oxford University Press, 2008.

Walzer, Michael. *The Revolution of the Saints: A Study in the Origins of Radical Politics.* Cambridge, Mass.: Harvard University Press, 1965.

Warman, Arturo. "The Political Project of Zapatismo." In *Riot, Rebellion, and Revolution: Rural Social Conflict in Mexico,* edited by Friedrich Katz, 321–37. Princeton, N.J.: Princeton University Press, 1988.

Warrum, Noble. *Utah in the World War: The Men behind the Guns and the Men and Women behind the Men behind the Guns.* Salt Lake City: Arrow Press, 1924.

Wasserman, Mark. *Capitalists, Caciques, and Revolution: The Native Elite and Foreign Enterprise in Chihuahua, Mexico, 1854–1911.* Chapel Hill: University of North Carolina Press, 1984.

Weber, Alfred. *History of Philosophy.* Translated by Frank Thilly. 1896. Reprint, New York: Charles Scribner's Sons, 1925.

Weber, Timothy P. *Living in the Shadow of the Second Coming: American Premillennialism, 1875–1925.* New York: Oxford University Press, 1979.

Weinberg, Robert. *Stalin's Forgotten Zion. Birobidzhan and the Making of a Soviet Jewish Homeland: An Illustrated History, 1928–1996.* Berkeley: University of California Press, 1998.

Weinstein, James. *Ambiguous Legacy: The Left in American Politics.* New York: New Viewpoints, 1975.

Welch, Richard E., Jr. "Organized Religion and the Philippine-American War, 1899–1902." *Mid-America* 55, no. 3 (July 1973): 184–206.

Weldon, Thomas. "The Turner Thesis and the Mormon Frontier." MA thesis, Stetson University, 1964.

Wells, H. G. *The Outline of History: The Whole Story of Man.* 2 vols. 1919. Reprint, Garden City, N.Y.: Doubleday, 1971.

Wells, John. "Thoughts on the United Order." MS 5531, LDS Church History Library.

Wessinger, Catherine. "Millennialism with and without the Mayhem." In Robbins and Palmer, *Millennium, Messiahs, and Mayhem,* 47–58.

West, Ray B., Jr. *Kingdom of the Saints: The Story of Brigham Young and the Mormons.* New York: Viking Press, 1957.

Westbrook, Robert B. *John Dewey and American Democracy.* Ithaca, N.Y.: Cornell University Press, 1991.

Weyl, Nathaniel and Sylvia. *The Reconquest of Mexico: The Years of Lázaro Cárdenas.* London: Oxford University Press, 1939.

Wheen, Francis. *Karl Marx: A Life.* New York: W. W. Norton, 2000.

Whetten, LaVon Brown. *Colonia Juarez: Commemorating 125 Years of the Mormon Colonies in Mexico.* Bloomington, Ind.: AuthorHouse, 2010.

White, Jean Bickmore, ed. *Church, State, and Politics: The Diaries of John Henry Smith.* Salt Lake City: Signature Books/Smith Research Associates, 1990.

_____. "Utah Voting Patterns in the 20th Century." In Brown, Cannon, and Jackson, *Historical Atlas of Mormonism,* 126–27.

White, O. Kendall, Jr. "The Transformation of Mormon Theology." *Dialogue: A Journal of Mormon Thought* 5, no. 2 (Summer 1970): 9–24.

Whitehead, Laurence. "State Organization in Latin America since 1930." In Bethell, *Cambridge History of Latin America,* vol. 6, pt. 2, 3–95. New York: Cambridge University Press, 1994.

Whitney, Orson F. *History of Utah.* 4 vols. Salt Lake City: George Q. Cannon and Sons, 1892–1904.

_____. *Life of Heber C. Kimball, an Apostle; The Father and Founder of the British Mission.* Salt Lake City, Utah: Kimball Family, 1888.

Whittaker, David J., comp. *The Essential Orson Pratt.* Salt Lake City: Signature Books, 1991.

_____. "Mormons and Native Americans: A Historical and Bibliographical Interpretation." *Dialogue: A Journal of Mormon Thought* 18, no. 4 (Winter

1985): 31–64.

_____. "Orson Pratt: Prolific Pamphleteer." *Dialogue: A Journal of Mormon Thought* 15 (Autumn 1982): 27–41.

_____. "Substituted Names in the Published Revelations of Joseph Smith." *BYU Studies* 23, no. 1 (Winter 1983): 103–12.

Widtsoe, John A. *Evidences and Reconciliations: Aids to Faith in a Modern Day.* Arranged by G. Homer Durham. Reprint, Salt Lake City: Bookcraft, 1960. First published 1943–51 in three volumes.

_____. *Joseph Smith as Scientist: A Contribution to Mormon Philosophy.* Salt Lake City: General Board, Young Men's Mutual Improvement Associations, 1908.

Wilcox, Michael. *Who Shall Be Able to Stand? Finding Personal Meaning in the Book of Revelation.* Salt Lake City: Deseret Book, 2003.

Williams, Frederick S., and Frederick G. Williams. *From Acorn to Oak Tree: A Personal History of the Establishment and First Quarter Century Development of the South American Missions.* Fullerton, Calif.: Et Cetera, Et Cetera Graphics, 1988.

Wilson, Bryan R. *Magic and the Millennium: A Sociological Study of Religious Movements of Protest among Tribal and Third-World Peoples.* London: Heinemann, 1973.

Wilson, Joan Hoff. *Herbert Hoover: Forgotten Progressive.* Library of American Biography Series. Boston: Little, Brown, 1975.

Wimsatt, Mary Ann. "William Gilmore Simms." In *Encyclopedia of Southern Culture*, edited by Charles Reagan Wilson and William Ferris. Chapel Hill: University of North Carolina Press, 1989. http://docsouth.unc.edu/south-lit/simms1/bio.html.

Winn, Kenneth H. *Exiles in a Land of Liberty: Mormons in America, 1830–1846.* Chapel Hill: University of North Carolina Press, 1989.

Winters, Charlene Renberg. "A Lighter of Lamps." *Brigham Young Magazine* (Summer 2006): 49. http://magazine.byu.edu/g/?act=viewanda=1855.

Woloch, Isser, ed. *Revolution and the Meanings of Freedom in the Nineteenth Century.* Stanford, Calif.: Stanford University Press, 1996.

Womack, John, Jr., comp. and ed. *Rebellion in Chiapas: An Historical Reader.* New York: New Press, 1999.

_____. *Zapata and the Mexican Revolution.* New York: Alfred A. Knopf, 1968.

Wood, Gordon S. "The Significance of the Early Republic." *Journal of the Early Republic* 8, no. 1 (Spring 1988): 1–20.

Yates, Frances A. *The Rosicrucian Enlightenment.* London: Routledge and Kegan Paul, 1972.

Young, Brigham. *Discourses of Brigham Young.* Compiled by John A. Widtsoe. 2nd ed. Salt Lake City: Deseret Book, 1926.

Young, Jordan M. *The Brazilian Revolution of 1930 and the Aftermath.* New Brunswick, N.J.: Rutgers University Press, 1967.

_____. "Military Aspects of the 1930 Brazilian Revolution." *Hispanic American Historical Review* 44, no. 2 (May 1964): 180–96.

Young, Levi Edgar. *The Founding of Utah*. New York: C. Scribner's Sons, 1923.
_____. Notes on War. Levi Edgar Young Papers. 1898–1959. Mss B 12, Box 18, fd. 5, Research Center, Utah State Historical Society, Salt Lake City.
Young, Sue. "William Howitt 1792–1879." *Sue Young Histories* (blog). February 18, 2009. http://sueyounghistories.com/archives/2009/02/18/.
Zamora, Lois Parkinson, ed. *The Apocalyptic Vision in America: Interdisciplinary Essays on Myth and Culture*. Bowling Green, Ohio: Bowling Green University Popular Press, 1982.
Zinn, Howard. *The Twentieth Century: A People's History*. Rev. and updated ed. New York: Harper Perennial, 2003.
Zobell, Albert L., Jr. "Thomas L. Kane, Ambassador to the Mormons." MA thesis, University of Utah, 1944.

Index

A

Abyssinia, 330
Adams, George J., 115, 347
Adams, John, 6, 270
Addams, Jane, 129
Aguascalientes Convention, 209–10
Aguinaldo, Emilio, 172
Alexander I of Russia, 73
Alexander II of Russia, 150
Alfonso XIII of Spain, 335
Allenby, Edmund, 181–82
Amaya, Simon, 196
American Civil War, 19, 52, 109, 139, 171, 327, 358
American exceptionalism, 13, 188
American Indians, xxii–xxiii, 45–46, 65, 67, 190, 194–98, 200, 204–8, 214, 218, 222–30, 238–40, 243, 246–47, 249, 252–54, 256–59, 293–305, 309–10, 312–17, 319–21, 323, 350, 360, 366
American Revolution, 6, 10, 12–13, 73, 78–79, 88, 115, 185, 199, 207, 238, 246, 282
Anabaptism, 7, 94
anarchism, 10, 12, 119–20, 131, 142, 148, 189, 192, 202, 336
Anaya, Celso, 196
Anderson, Edward H., 118, 153, 155, 284, 347
anti-colonial revolt, xxi–xxii, 9, 140, 159–90, 285, 300, 344
Antoinette, Marie, 3
Appleby, William I., 43, 48–49, 53, 59, 61, 64, 69, 103, 115, 348
Arámbula, José Doroteo Arango. *See* Villa, Pancho.
Argentina, 251, 295, 298–301, 304–5, 307, 309–16, 318, 321
Argentine War of Independence, 301
Arielism, 207–8

Armenians, 178–80
Articles of Faith, 5
Ataturk, Kemal, 180
Austria, 33, 39–40, 49–50, 52, 58, 180–81, 212, 280–81

B

Babeuf, Francois, 1, 7, 80, 95, 275
Bakunin, Michael, 12, 192
Ballard, Melvin J., xxiii, 182, 251, 267–68, 288–89, 296–97, 300–304, 311–20, 328, 338–39, 348
Balzac, Honoré de, 85
Bamberger, Simon, 277–78
Barmby, Thomas Goodwin, 14, 111
barricade, 5, 40, 59, 61, 63, 68, 70, 121, 286, 315
Batista, Fulgencio, 311
Bautista, Juan, 314
Bautista, Margarito, 205
Bavaria, 50
Beals, Carleton, 225, 245, 252–53, 259, 313
Belgian Congo, 163
Belgium, 265
Bellamy, Edward, 110, 130
Bennett, John C., 32–33, 42, 77
Bennion, Heber, 325–26, 349
Bentley, Joseph C., 212, 334, 357
Benton, William S., 203
Berkman, Alexander, 274
Bernardes, Artur, 305–6
Bertrand, Louis A., xiv, 25–26, 83–84, 103, 121–22, 124, 139, 349–50
Birch, Harvey Locksley. *See* John Jacques.
Bismarck, Otto von, 138, 142, 149
Black Monday, 162
Blanc, Louis, xiv, 39, 125, 132
Blanqui, Augusti, 12, 111, 142
Blok, Alexander, 15

Bloody Sunday massacre, 152, 154
Blum, Robert, 40
Boehme, Jacob, 88
Boer War, 159, 166–70
Bolivar, Simon, 300
Bolivia, 301, 304–5, 307, 309, 312, 314, 316, 320–21
Bolshevik Revolution, 12, 20, 84, 262, 264–65, 267, 269–76, 281–82, 285, 287
Bolton, Curtis Edwin, 46, 67, 349–50
Bonaparte, Louis-Napoléon. *See* Napoleon III of France.
Bonaparte, Napoleon. *See* Napoleon I of France.
Bonneville, Nicholas, 75–76, 80
Book of Mormon, 5, 47, 67, 94, 104, 139, 207–8, 227, 229, 241, 247, 259, 297–98, 300–301, 310, 314, 320, 349–50, 359, 364
Booth, Joseph, 180
Boxer Rebellion, 173–76
Brannan, Samuel, xiv, 105
Brazil, 304–6, 308–9, 311–12
Brazilian Revolution of 1930, 306
Brenner, Anita, 315
Brigham Young University, xiii, xxii, 5
Brinton, Crane, 315
British Mission, xix, 45–46, 55–57, 59, 64, 67, 112, 146, 161, 282, 356
brotherhood. *See* fraternity.
Brown, Thomas Dunlop, 46–47, 59, 350
Brown, William Thurston, 131
Buchanan, James, 348
Buchez, Philippe, 349
Bulgaria, 280
Buonarroti, Filippo, 73, 80, 105
Burgess, Ernest Hungate, 3
Burritt, Elihu, 116–17
Burton, Richard, 79
Bustamante, Daniel Sánchez, 305

C

Cabet, Etienne, 10, 132
Calles, Plutarco, 210, 221–23, 231, 233, 235–36, 239, 242, 247–51, 255, 293
Callis, Charles A., 262, 350
Calvinism, 14–15, 114, 192, 294
Cannon, George Q., xix–xx, 29, 79, 123–25, 137, 141, 144, 146, 148, 351
Cannon, Hugh J., 185, 335, 351

Cannon, John Q., 277, 351–52
capitalism, xi, xiii, xvi–xvii, xxi, 6, 10, 12–13, 39, 59, 64, 70, 86, 109–35, 139, 145, 149, 151, 160, 162–63, 165–66, 174–75, 183, 188, 194–97, 200, 202, 204, 219, 221, 231, 239, 244, 246, 252, 257–58, 262, 277, 280, 282, 285, 291, 293, 308–9, 326–27, 330, 335, 341, 344, 368–70
Carbonari, 72, 77, 86, 89
Cárdenas, Lázaro, 223, 249–50, 254–55, 257
Carlos I of Portugal, 120
Carranza, Victoriano, 204, 206, 209, 213–14, 216–17, 223, 231
Carthage, Illinois, 1, 97
Castro, Fidel, 311
Catholic Church. *See* Roman Catholic Church.
Cavaignac, Eugene, 61
Celman, Miguel Ángel Juárez, 315
Cerro, Luis Miguel Sánchez, 307
Charles II of England, 9
Charles X of France, 10
Chartism, 38–39, 55, 60, 63, 67, 69–70, 91, 104, 113, 150, 161
Chase, Stuart, 253–54
Chile, 295, 312, 318
China, 159, 173–78, 280, 330
church and state, 46, 48, 58, 114, 144, 164, 211, 221, 231–54, 256, 258–59, 273, 290–91, 293, 299, 301–2, 312, 315–16, 318–20, 339
Church of Jesus Christ of Latter-day Saints
   assimilation, xi, xiii –xv, 5, 70, 109–10, 170–71, 219, 229, 291, 193, 323, 329, 335, 339–41, 343–45, 364, 370
   correlation, xiv
   in Missouri, xvi, 17, 30, 33, 74, 82, 87, 97, 120, 137, 215–16, 354, 360, 364
   in Nauvoo, Illinois, 1, 7, 30, 32–33, 38, 47, 66, 71, 74, 77–79, 87–88, 97–98, 107, 215, 350, 352, 360, 366
   in Ohio, xvi, 82, 120, 364
   organizational structure, xvii–xviii, 84–85, 110, 124, 227–28
   periodicals, xix–xx
   priesthood, xvi, 31, 38, 300, 364
   welfare program, 296, 324, 328, 335, 348, 359
Circle of Philadelphians. See Philadelphians.

civil religion, 231–35, 239, 243, 245, 258
Civil War. See American Civil War.
Clark, J. Reuben, 254–57, 278–79, 288, 323–24,
  329, 331–32, 337–38, 352, 354, 358
class struggle, xii–xiii, 7, 10, 11, 14, 31,
  36–37, 55–58, 60–61, 63, 101, 110–13,
  115–20, 124–30, 132, 140–41, 145–46,
  149, 152, 154–56, 161, 164–66, 175, 185,
  188, 192, 198, 203–5, 207–9, 214, 216,
  224–25, 239, 243, 248, 250, 252, 255–56,
  258, 262, 264, 271, 281–82, 285, 287,
  301, 304–7, 309, 312, 316, 320, 324, 327
Clemenceau, Georges, 6
clergy, 146–47, 164, 181, 231, 236, 239, 246,
  248–49, 251, 269
  opposition to revolution, 40–41, 48, 77,
    100, 232, 244, 262, 289, 337, 339
  support for revolution, 40–41, 57, 100,
    232–33, 250, 262, 273, 289, 324, 336
Cold War, 319, 339
Collins, Elizabeth, 357
Colombia, 307
Colonia Díaz, 218
Colonia Dublán, 210, 226
Colonia García, 226
Colonia Juárez, 193, 207, 210, 212, 226–27,
  296, 299, 334, 357
colonialism. See imperialism and anti-
  colonial revolt.
communalism, xi, xv, xxii, 65, 120–24,
  133–34, 194, 200, 219, 224–25, 230, 250,
  253, 281, 325–26, 364
Communards. See Paris Commune.
communism. See socialism and
  communalism.
Communist International, 147, 233, 274,
  332–33
  popular front policy, 332–33, 336, 344
Communist League, 10, 12, 14, 125
Communist Party (Russia), 272–73
Communist Party USA, 332
Comte, Auguste, 197
constitutionalism, xvi, 9, 38, 40, 73–73,
  128, 152, 157, 163, 178, 185, 199, 204,
  209, 211, 216–17, 221, 223, 229, 231,
  236–37, 242, 249, 254–55, 267, 275, 287,
  305–6, 308, 310, 305–6, 308, 310, 367
Cook, Eliza, 67–68
Coolidge, Calvin, 233

Cordon, Alfred, 113, 352
Council of Fifty, xvi–xvii, 77–79, 84, 91, 100,
  347–48, 351, 353, 360, 362, 364, 368, 370
counter-revolution, 17, 19, 28, 33, 38,
  40–41, 49–52, 61, 63, 65–69, 89, 95, 101,
  119–20, 142–47, 151, 166, 173, 196, 198,
  204, 217–18, 250, 279, 307, 336
covenant, 15, 18, 32
Cracow Uprising, 33
Cramer, Daniel, 93
Creighton, Frank W., 243
Cristero Rebellion, 232, 248–52
Croly, Herbert, 243–44
Cromwell, Oliver, 9, 114
Cronje, Pierter A., 169
Crowther, Duane S., 263
Cuba, 159, 172–73
Cutler, John C., 278
Czechoslavakia, 331

D

d'Olivet, Antoine Fabre, 81
Danites, 74, 91, 100
Darter, Francis, 325–26, 352–53
Debs, Eugene, xi, 116
Decembrists, 73–74, 91
deification, 80, 90
Dembowski, Edward, 33
democracy, 3, 15, 18, 22, 25, 39, 47, 49, 55,
  59, 61, 68, 80, 95, 99, 114, 121, 128
  totalitarian democracy, 28–31
Derry, Charles
DeVoto, Bernard, 329
Dewey, George, 173
Dewey, John, 234, 243–45, 303
Díaz, Porfirio, 195–96, 198–99, 204, 208,
  230, 222–23, 235, 240, 250, 257, 293, 333
Díaz y Barreto, Pascual, 251
dispensations, 22–23, 25, 27, 85, 88, 248,
  269, 273, 285, 287, 294, 303, 325
Disraeli, Benjamin, 140, 160
Domenech, Abbé Emmanuel, 237, 239
Dorr Rebellion, 18
Dostoevsky, Fyodor, 144, 303
Durham, G. Homer, 23, 30, 185

E

Ebert, Friedrich, 273–74

economic depression, 98, 116–18, 125, 129, 162–63, 239, 253, 257, 284, 291, 296, 304–10, 320, 323–28, 330, 332
Edgeworth, Vera, 167, 169
Égalité, Philippe, 73
ejidos, 200, 203, 224–25, 230, 240, 250, 252–54
Eldredge, Horace Sunderlin, 146, 353
Eliot, George, 361
Ellsworth, German E., 268
Emerson, William, 15–16
Engels, Friedrich, 39, 73, 92, 113, 132
England. See United Kingdom.
English Civil War, 9
Ensign Peak, 35, 105, 345
Ensign, Horace S., 177–78
equality, 1, 4, 10, 14, 46, 52, 57, 59, 69, 72, 80–82, 85, 94–95, 121, 130, 143, 149, 165, 199, 211, 241, 259, 275, 282, 290, 344
European revolutions of 1848, xii, xvi, xxi, 11, 19, 33, 35–70, 100, 104, 110–11, 125, 149, 154, 192, 317, 348–49, 356

F

fascism, 6, 11, 18, 307–8, 313, 318, 320, 327, 330–33, 336–38
February Revolution. See March revolution.
feminism, 129, 143–44, 353, 364–65
Ferdinand I of the Two Sicilies, 40–41, 50
Ferguson, George C., 208
fiction, 94–96, 107, 117, 144, 337, 358
Flanigan, James, 57, 61, 353
Flemming, Robert, 101
Ford, Thomas, 1, 77
Fourier, Charles, 7, 10, 23, 30, 110–11, 122–23, 130, 132
Fox, Ruth May, 298, 353
France, xiv, xxii, 1, 3, 12, 14, 18–19, 28, 30, 32, 38–41, 48–49, 52–53, 58–59, 60–62, 66–68, 76, 103, 111, 125, 128, 135, 137–50, 144–45, 149, 199, 201, 261–62, 264, 269, 272, 280, 331, 336, 349–50.
Franco, Francisco, 336–37
Franco-Prussian War, xxii, 138–42, 144–45, 149
Frankfurt Assembly, 40, 49, 53
fraternity, 4, 8, 10, 29, 33, 54, 57, 59, 72, 75, 80–81, 106–7, 130, 143, 187, 189–90,

202, 215, 258–59, 263, 266, 275, 282, 326–27, 339
freedom. See liberty and rights.
Freemasonry, xiv, 14, 32, 71–77, 80–81, 86–89, 95, 103, 106, 347, 352, 354, 360, 364–65, 370
French Mission, 47, 83, 121, 139, 349–50
French Revolution, xxi, 2–4, 6, 9–10, 14, 35, 38, 47, 73, 77–78, 81, 85, 87–88, 89, 93, 100–101, 105, 107, 117, 121–22, 147, 185, 199, 201, 241, 265–66, 275–76, 310
slogan of, 4, 10, 56, 81, 95–96, 143, 154
Friedrich Wilhelm IV, 39–40, 67

G

Gaebelein, Arno, 269
Galindo, Carlos Blanco, 305, 313, 316
Gandhi, Mohandas K., 184–85
Gapon, Georgy, 152
Garcia, Diego, 224
Garibaldi, Giuseppe, 4, 40, 50, 68, 101, 138
Gaxiola, C. M., 242
George, Henry, xxii, 110, 124–25, 126, 130, 165, 359
Germany, 11, 20, 24–25, 39–40, 47–48, 52–53, 68, 77, 119, 138–42, 147, 149, 179, 201, 255, 261, 263–66, 269–70, 272–74, 277, 280, 283, 288, 295, 298–99, 307, 313, 327, 330–31, 336–38, 371
Gil, Portas, 255
Glorious Revolution, 9–10
Godbe, William S., 145
Goldman, Emma, 131, 274
Golitsyn, Lev Sergeevich, 167
Gonzalez, Abraham, 199
Gonzalez, Pablo, 213–14
Good Neighbor Policy, 308
Goodwin, Thomas, 101
Gould, Harry, 16
Grant, Heber J., 8, 145, 277–78, 280, 282–83, 289, 296, 347–49, 359
Grant, Jedediah M., 83
Gray, James, 269
Great Britain. See United Kingdom.
Green, Philip L., 310
Gruening, Ernest, 193, 243–44, 250
Gutiérrez, Eulalio, 209

H

Hamid, Abdul, 180
Hancock, Mosiah, 86
Hanly, Frank, 212
Hapsburg Empire, 38–41, 47, 60, 101, 263
Harding, Warren, 235
Harney, George, 91–92, 96, 113
Harris, Franklin S., 253–54, 290, 353–54
Harrison, E. L. T., 145
Hashiguchi, Jeshei, 178
Hay, John, 174
Haya de la Torre, Victor Raúl, 259–60, 307, 315–16, 319–20
Hearst, William Randolph, 233
Hegel, Georg Wilhelm Friedrich, 23–25, 27, 32, 84, 128, 340
Heine, Heinrich, 60
Hemingway, Ernest, 337
Herrick, John, 272
Herring, Hubert, 232
Herron, George D., 129
history
    as dialectic, xii, 14, 23–27, 128, 187, 191, 205, 207, 246, 271, 276, 289, 292, 340
    as revelation, xii, xiv, 16, 27, 138, 162, 191, 245, 276, 286–87, 311, 318, 323, 329, 345
    New Mormon History, xv, 71
Hitler, Adolph, 330–31
Hobbes, Thomas, 9
Hohenzollern Dynasty, 40, 68
Holyoake, George Jacob, 63
Hoover, Herbert, 175, 256, 308, 310
Hoover, J. Edgar, 352
Houtz, Mary E., 131
Huerta, Victoriano, 73, 203–4, 206, 209, 214, 216, 231
Hughes, Evans, 242
Hugo, Victor, 101, 121, 349
Humboldt, Alexander von, 259
Hungary, 11, 39, 41–42, 49, 51, 151, 280
Hunt, Duane Garrison, 236–37, 241–42, 244
Hupay, Joseph-Alexander-Victor, 86
Hyde, Orson, 44–45, 49, 60, 62, 67–68, 99, 103, 354
Hyde, William A., 275–76, 354–55

I

Illuminism, 76–77, 79–80, 84–87, 89, 92–93, 103
imperialism, xiii, xvii, xxiii, 6, 117, 159–90, 208, 224, 261–63, 268, 270, 277–78, 280, 285, 290–1, 301–2, 313, 315, 319, 330, 337
India, xxi, 140, 159, 173, 178, 183–85, 229, 323
Indians. See American Indians.
industrialization, xiii, xxi–xxii, 11, 36–38, 60, 84, 109–35, 148, 152, 155–56, 160, 162–63, 165, 175–76, 189, 230, 254–56, 259, 267, 277, 289, 294, 302, 304, 327
    conflict over oil resources, 223, 231, 233, 255–56, 313
International Workingmen's Association, 11, 116, 132
Ireland, xxi, 39–40, 56, 64–65, 111–13, 140, 159, 164–66, 266
    potato famine, 39, 99, 112
Italy, 11, 38–41, 47–49, 53, 72–73, 86, 103, 141, 188, 280, 282, 330–31, 336–37
Ivins, Anthony W., xii, xxii, 3, 27, 137, 192–93, 195, 197–98, 200–204, 206, 208, 211, 213, 218–19, 224, 227–28, 230, 234–48, 250–51, 257–59, 272, 277, 280, 285–86, 298, 311, 325, 330–31, 335, 353, 355
Ivins, Antoine R., 230

J

Jacobins, 4, 12, 28, 100, 140, 142, 276
Jabotinsky, Vladimir, 182
James, William, 362
Japan, xviii, xxii, 152, 160, 163, 169, 173–78, 280, 330
Jaques, John, 46, 49, 51, 57–58, 65–66, 356
Jay, Peter Augustus, 299
Jefferson, Thomas, 6, 77
Jelaçic, Josip, 50
Jenson, Andrew, 228–29, 295
Jesus Christ, 8–9, 191, 263, 335
    as revolutionary prophet, 15, 37, 76, 117
    second coming, 19–22, 26, 28, 33, 54, 57, 77, 85, 95, 99, 147, 215–16, 248, 271, 311, 317, 319, 325–28, 330, 335, 344
Jews, 144–45, 151, 271, 353
    return to Palestine, xxi, 21, 36–37, 44, 52–54, 154–55, 179–83, 273, 288, 290, 347, 354
Joachim of Fiore, 23

John of Leyden, 7
Jordan, David Starr, 281
Joubert, Piet, 168
Juárez, Benito, 238
Juárez, Isaías, 205
June Days insurrection, 40–41, 61, 65–66, 101, 121

K

Kabbalah, 71–72
Kane, Thomas L., 123
Kant, Immanuel, 24
Kapp, Wolfgang, 274
Kautsky, Karl, 116
Kerensky, Alexander, 264–65, 270–71
Kimball, Heber C., 97–98, 186
Kimball, Spencer W., 191
King, Arthur Henry, xiii, 171
King, William H., 283, 356
kingdom of God, xiii, xiv, xvi–xviii, 12, 18, 22, 25, 27, 30–31, 33, 35, 56, 70, 76, 78–79, 85, 103, 110, 137, 141, 147, 149, 158, 161, 191–92, 219, 259, 264, 294, 317, 319, 326, 329, 334–35, 340, 344, 364, 367, 370
Kitchner, Horatio, 168
Knox, John, 16
Korea, 177–78
Kossuth, Louis, 41–42, 51
Kosterlitzky, Emilio, 196
Kruger, Paul, 167–70

L

La Reforma, 315–16
labor unions, xi, xxi, 10, 109, 111, 116, 124, 129, 131, 147–48, 155, 183, 205, 209, 223–24, 240, 242, 261, 267, 276, 282–83, 285, 307, 326–27, 329
Lamanites. See American Indians.
Lamarque, Maximilien, 96
land reform, xxii, 22, 64–65, 96, 115, 124, 126, 132, 164–65, 198–200, 203, 206, 210, 214, 223–25, 227, 240, 242, 244, 250, 253, 258, 289, 301, 312, 316, 319
Lasalle, Ferdinand, 116
Lawrence, Henry, 134–35, 145
League of Nations, xxiii, 19, 181, 189, 216, 261–64, 269, 272, 274, 276–80, 282–87, 332, 352, 363

League to Enforce Peace, 276–78, 284, 363, 371
Lee, John D., 244, 355
Leguía, Augusto B., 307, 309
Lenin, Vladimir, xii, xiv, xxii, 6, 12, 13, 91, 144, 160, 269–70, 275–76, 340
Leopold II of Belgium, 163
liberty, 4, 10, 15, 28, 32, 46, 57, 62, 75–76, 81, 86, 93, 95, 100, 124, 133, 141, 143, 155, 167, 172, 173, 176, 179, 183, 185, 190, 197–98, 204, 206, 217–18, 221, 239–40, 246, 262–63, 265, 267–68, 275, 282, 288, 300–302, 306, 339
Liebknecht, Karl, 20, 205, 273
Lippman, Walter, 243–44, 248
literary trope, 5, 112
Livingston, John, 101
Locke, John, 234
Lodge, Henry Cabot, 276
London Workingmen's Association, 161–62
Lord, John C., 44, 61–62
Louis XVI of France, 3, 73
Louis-Phillipe I of France, 38, 61
Lund, Anthon H., 278
Lunt, George, 51
Luxembourg, Rosa, 20, 273
Luxembourg Commission, 39–40, 61
Lyman, Francis M., 150
Lyman, Richard R., 277, 327
Lyon, John, 45–46, 50

M

MacDonald, Hector, 169
Madero, Francisco, 194, 198–201, 203, 205, 207, 210, 214, 223, 235
Maeser, Karl G., 131, 366, 368
Mahan, Alfred Thayer, 188
Manchu Dynasty, 176
March revolution (Russia), 264–67, 269–71
Maréchal, Sylvain, 101
Mariátegui, José Carlos, 307, 309, 316, 319–20
Martin, Gabriel-Constant, 142
Martin, Thomas L., 290, 357
Martineau, Joel H., 159
Marx, Karl, xi, xiii, 4, xiv, 6–7, 9–14, 17–18, 20, 23–24, 29, 31, 47, 60, 73, 80, 92, 96, 101, 110–11, 113, 116–17, 122, 125, 127, 131–32, 142, 148, 150, 152, 161, 192, 253, 259, 273, 304–5, 307, 309, 313, 316, 339–40

Mary I of England, 114
Mason, Jane, 91, 357
Maximilian I of Mexico, 139, 237
Mazzini, Giuseppe, 11, 40, 44, 48, 50, 101,
    187–88, 304
McClellan, Charles, 207, 357
McConkie, Bruce R., 102
McGhie, William, 63, 357–58
McKay, David O., 58, 177, 182–83, 278,
    282, 330, 332, 351, 358–59
McKinley, William, 163, 167, 172, 363
Meiji Dynasty, 176
Mendez, Miguel, 238
Mendieta, Carlos, 311
Mercier, Louis Sebastien, 94
Metternich, Klemens von, 39, 50
Mexican Mission, xxii, 192–93, 227, 229–30,
    232, 251, 328–29, 360
Mexican Revolution, xiii, xxii, 3, 73, 110,
    190–219, 242, 250, 255–57, 316, 328
    consolidation of, 221–60
Mexican War of Independence, 159, 239
Mexican War of the Reform, 238
Mexico, xiv, xxii, 9, 73, 139, 159, 190–260,
    293–94, 298–99, 301, 313, 318, 320, 323,
    328–30, 333–34, 337, 352, 357
    Mormon colonies in, 192–200, 202–4,
        208, 210, 215, 226–27, 231, 251, 291,
        296, 334, 355
Michel, Louise, 149–50
Milan, 40–41
militarism, xiii, 11, 117, 119–20, 204, 262,
    304, 339, 371
millennialism, xii–xiii, xv–xviii, xxi, xxiii,
    2, 8, 12, 14, 17, 19, 22, 25, 33, 36, 43, 54,
    59, 65, 69, 89, 95, 98–99, 101, 106, 110,
    116–17, 120, 127, 147, 154, 157–58, 178,
    187–88, 190, 192, 216, 222, 227, 248,
    263–65, 285, 287, 292, 298, 302–3, 314,
    317, 319, 324, 326, 330, 335, 339, 340, 356
    premillennialism, 20–21, 36, 269, 273,
        284, 317
    postmillennialism, 20–21, 33, 36, 43,
        138, 147, 268, 317
missionary work, xii, xvii–xviii, xix, 8,
    21–22, 46, 52, 55, 57–59, 67, 79, 114–15,
    121, 139, 141, 149–50, 155, 159, 160,
    164, 177, 179, 183, 206, 208, 215, 226,
    229, 230, 232, 247, 251, 254, 263, 273,

289, 292, 293–303, 312–14, 317–19,
    321, 339, 343, 348, 350–52, 356, 358–63,
    365–66, 368–71
monarchy, xii, xvii, 10, 19, 25, 36–38,
    48–49, 55, 59, 61–62, 65, 69, 72, 78,
    99–101, 103, 121, 128, 139, 141–42, 144,
    149, 151, 188, 201, 246, 263, 272, 339
monopolies, xii, xxiii, 37, 54, 125, 129, 132,
    160–61, 183, 201, 291
Monroy, Rafael, 252, 333
Morales, Vincente, 252, 333
More, Thomas, 94, 130
Morgan, John, 118, 359–60
Morgan, William, 81
Mormon Reformation, 29, 335
Morris, Joseph, 30, 85
Morris, Nephi L., 277
Morrow, Dwight, 225, 248, 255, 259
Mountain Meadows Massacre, 30, 244,
    355, 363
Moyle, James H., 327–28, 359
Münster, 7
Müntzer, Thomas, 19
Murguía, Francisco, 210
music, xx, 46, 58, 71, 81, 94, 300, 345, 356, 364
Mussolini, Benito, 6

                    N

Naples, 40–41, 49, 99
Napoleon I of France, 38, 82, 89, 186
Napoleon III of France, 26, 41, 47, 49,
    66–67, 83, 103–4, 138–40, 144, 146–47,
    149, 208, 349
Napoleonic Code, 3, 147
Napoleonic Wars, 38, 49
National Socialism, 18, 307, 330–31, 336–38
nationalism, xv, 6, 10, 11, 24, 38, 40–41, 49,
    55, 64, 69, 110, 113, 140, 159, 175, 182,
    184–86, 209–10, 214, 221, 224, 227, 232,
    255, 258, 266, 304–7, 313, 320, 328, 336,
    338, 369
nation-state, 24–25, 221, 226, 230, 235,
    240, 254, 259
Nazi Party. See National Socialism.
Nebuchadnezzar's dream, 25, 59, 99, 273–74
Nehru, Jawaharlal, 185
Netherlands, 52
New Deal, 15, 258, 296, 323–24, 328, 356

New Imperialism, 11, 159–63, 186
New Jerusalem. See Zion.
new world order, xvii, 8, 30–33, 35, 37, 65, 71, 73, 82, 85, 90, 95, 106, 155, 186–90, 261–64, 269, 278, 285–86, 340
Nibley, Charles W., xxii, 125–27, 132, 134–35, 189, 229, 277, 279, 282–83, 328, 359, 369
Nicholas I of Russia, 67, 151
Nicholas II of Russia, 150, 152, 157, 264, 271
Noah, Mordecai Manuel, 37, 45, 53, 58
Noël, Carlos M., 299
Noyes, John Humphrey, 122–23

O

O'Brien, William Smith, 113
O'Connell, Daniel and John, 113
O'Conner, Feargus, 113
Obregón, Álvaro, 210, 221–23, 228, 230, 250–51
Oglethorpe, James, 130
Open Door Notes, 174–75
Order of the Illuminati. See Illuminism.
organized labor. See labor unions and class struggle.
Orozco, Pascual, 199, 201–2, 203, 214
Ottoman Empire, 160, 178–82, 263, 280, 287
Owen, Robert, 10, 111, 122, 130, 132

P

Paine, Thomas, 18, 296
Palestine. See Jews.
Pangaea, 8, 96, 150
Papal States, 40, 50
Paris Commune, xiv, xxii, 6, 12, 119, 137–50, 157, 351
Parnell, Charles Stewart, 165
Party of Movement, 47, 49, 135
Party of Order, 47, 135, 143
Paxman, Walter James, 161–62, 359
Pershing, John J., 210
Persia, 178, 184, 229
Peru, xiv, 260, 299, 301–2, 304, 307, 309, 311–13, 316
Peter the Great, 82, 186
Petrograd Soviet, 199, 271
Petrovitis, Paul, xiv
Philadelphians, 80, 89
Philipot, John, 101
Philippine Insurrection, 172–73

Philippines, 159, 172–73, 178
Piedmont, 41, 102
Pierce, Arwell, 213, 242, 329
Pius IX, 40, 42, 49–50
Plehve, Vyacheslav von, 152
poetry, xx, 15, 36, 44–45, 51, 58, 60, 62, 91, 94, 116, 144, 189, 217–18, 230, 298, 339, 357, 364
Poland, 33, 38–39, 49, 51, 53, 59, 151, 274, 280, 331
Polk, James K., 41
polygamy, xiii, xv, xviii, 7, 29, 32, 75, 109, 131, 134, 148, 179, 229, 237, 241, 244, 294, 344, 347, 349, 351–54, 356, 359–70
Pratt, Orson, xii, 25, 31, 36–37, 45, 58, 63, 65, 76, 90–92, 103–4, 121, 124, 141–42, 147, 360, 362, 366
Pratt, Parley P., 29, 31, 66, 82, 90, 94, 97, 106, 109, 113–15, 193, 295, 360, 367
Pratt, Rey L., xxii, xxiii, 192–94, 204–8, 211, 214–15, 217–19, 227–28, 230, 232, 251, 253–54, 257–58, 263, 296–99, 301, 314–15, 318, 328, 360–61
Prestes, Luís Carlos, 305–6
Priestley, Joseph, 101
Proctor, Redfield, 170
progress, xii, xviii, xxiii, 19, 21, 22–26, 32, 37, 63, 69–70, 94, 124, 127, 130, 135, 178, 197–98, 205, 208, 221–22, 224, 229, 237, 258–59, 262, 268–69, 271, 273, 287, 292, 309–10, 317–18, 327, 330, 332, 339–40, 370
Progressive Movement, 132
proletarian revolution. See class struggle.
Proudhon, Joseph-Pierre, 10–12, 132, 142
Prussia, 19, 33, 38–40, 45, 60, 68, 138–42, 144
Puritanism, 14–16, 26, 32, 81, 334
pyramidology, 247, 285, 325, 340
Pythagoras, 71, 80–82, 84, 87, 325, 343

R

race, 48, 52, 86, 106, 112, 151–52, 154–55, 170–171, 176–78, 189, 200, 202, 205, 207–8, 215, 223–25, 228–30, 234, 243, 253, 258, 263, 266, 278, 295, 297–98, 314–15, 328–29
reason, xxi, 2, 27, 29, 31, 48, 81, 86–87, 89, 93, 95, 121, 134, 143, 245, 286, 339

Rees, Alfred C., 277, 331
Relief Society, xxii, 4, 129, 144, 361, 364
republicanism, xiv, xvi, 9, 18, 35–37, 39–40,
    49–50, 52–55, 65–67, 69, 86–87, 91,
    95, 100, 105, 140, 142–45, 147–49, 152,
    154, 164–66, 172, 175, 180, 189, 198–99,
    201, 208, 211, 223, 228–29, 234, 240–41,
    259, 262, 264–65, 267, 272, 275–78, 280,
    285, 293, 305–7, 309–10, 312, 316–17,
    319–20, 330–34, 336–38, 341, 352
revolution
    organizational structure, 71–79
    as religious practice, 14–16, 32, 61, 63,
        121, 138, 147, 191, 215, 219, 224, 231,
        232, 255, 275, 318, 320
Revolutionary War. See American Revolution.
revolutions of 1848. See European revolutions
    of 1848.
Reynolds, Alice Louise, xxii, 129–31, 148,
    330, 361
Reynolds, George, 361
Rhodankanaty, Plotino, xiv
Rhodes, Cecil, 167–68
Ribbonists, 84, 140
Rice, Arthur L., 289
Richards, Franklin D., 3, 58, 64, 149, 361–62
Richards, George F., 264
Richards, Phineas, 91, 100, 362
Richards, Willard, 43
Riesser, Gabriel, 53
rights, 16, 31, 45–46, 52, 155, 166, 189–90,
    201, 206–7, 211, 241, 249, 260, 276
    freedom of expression, 1, 199, 236
    freedom of religion, 12, 36, 55, 149–50,
        201, 231–32, 234–36, 241, 248–52,
        263, 272–73, 287–90, 299–300
Rio, Moray del, 231
Roberts, B. H., 16, 18–19, 27–28, 117,
    132–34, 149, 228, 251, 263, 268, 281,
    329, 362, 365
Roberts, Frederick, 168
Robespierre, Maximilien de, 1, 4, 28, 67,
    86, 95, 241
Rockhill, William Woodville, 174
Rogers, Thomas Franklin, xiii
Roman Catholic Church, xxii, 72, 101, 114,
    139–41, 144, 147, 149, 164, 201, 205,
    214, 219, 231, 235–39, 243–45, 248–54,
    258–59, 293, 299–301, 308, 312, 315–16,
    319, 321, 336–38
Roman Republic, 40–41, 47, 49–50, 53
Romanov Dynasty, 50, 151, 153, 266, 270–71
Roosevelt, Franklin D., 257–58, 324, 333
Roosevelt, Theodore, 132, 152, 163, 167,
    188, 213, 363
Root, Elihu, 269
Rosicrucianism, 92–93
Rousseau, Jean Jacques, 2
Rubio, Ortiz, 255
Ruskin, John, xxii, 130
Russell, John, 64
Russia, xiv, xxiii, 12, 15, 33, 49, 51–52,
    73–74, 86, 90, 135, 147, 149–57, 160,
    174–76, 181, 188, 229, 260, 263–67,
    269–74, 276, 280–81, 285–87, 289–91,
    303, 313, 320, 327, 331–32, 337, 347
Russian Revolution of 1905, xxii, 137,
    149–57, 276
Russo-Japanese War, 152–53, 184
Russo-Turkish War, 147, 178, 180

S

Sadharia, Daljit Singh, 184–85
Saint-Just, Louis Antoine Léon de. See St. Just.
Saint-Simon, Henri de. See St. Simon,
    Henri de.
Salamanca, Daniel, 305
Salazar, Inez, 203
Sandino, Rafael, 315
Schapper, Karl, 14
Schopenhauer, Arthur, 130
science, xiv, xviii, 7, 17, 21, 24, 69–70, 72,
    76, 122, 124, 197, 221–22, 245, 259,
    296–97, 317, 329, 331–32, 339, 360, 362
Scotland, 36, 45–46, 56
Scott, Hugh, 213
Second Yaqui War, 197–98, 252
Shafter, William, 171
Sharp, Vernon, 300, 321
Sheffield, James, 233
Shih-kai, Yuan, 176
Sicily, 40–41, 50, 138
Siles, Hernando, 304–5, 313–14, 316
Simms, William Gilmore, 51–52
Sjödahl, Janne M., 263, 267, 274, 279, 363
Slav Congress, 40

slavery, 45, 52, 87, 126, 171, 205, 208, 210, 238–39, 256, 301, 305, 327
Smith, Adam, 126
Smith, Asael, 18
Smith, George A., 146, 363
Smith, George Albert, 216, 274, 277, 282, 284, 361, 363
Smith, Hyrum, 2, 74, 96–97, 100, 367
Smith, John Henry, 125
Smith, Joseph, III, 347
Smith, Joseph F., 137, 149, 282, 359, 363
Smith, Joseph Fielding, 278
Smith, Joseph, Jr., xv–xvi, 5, 7, 12, 29, 32–33, 38, 66, 71, 72, 75, 77–79, 82, 85, 87, 90, 94, 96, 100, 113, 124, 133, 262, 279, 294, 328, 334, 343–44, 350, 354, 360, 363–64
    martyrdom, 1–2, 97, 367, 370
Smith, Joseph, Sr., 18
Smith, Robert and Elizabeth, 325
Smoot, Reed, 134, 192, 216, 277–78, 283–84, 359
Snow, Eliza R., 79, 144, 364–65
Snow, Lorenzo, 90, 102, 131, 146, 188–89, 365
social Darwinism, 131
Social Democrat Federation, 161–62
Social Gospel, 118, 262, 309
socialism, xi, xiii, xiv, xxiii, 1–2, 6, 10, 12–15, 14, 17, 24, 29, 47, 49, 61, 68, 70, 72, 86, 91, 96, 116–27, 129–35, 149–50, 152–57, 166, 184–85, 189, 192, 199, 233, 236–37, 249, 255, 259–62, 264, 268, 270–71, 274–75, 281, 287, 289–91, 307, 313, 316, 319–20, 327–28, 331–33, 336–39, 349, 368, 370
Socialist Labor Party, 116
Socialist Party of America, xi, 109, 116, 170
South Africa, 166–70
South American Mission, xxiii, 251–52, 260, 293–303, 310–11, 321, 348
South American revolutions, xiii, xviii, xxiii, 292, 304–21, 327
Soviet Union, xiii, xxiii, 15, 253, 281, 287–92, 323, 330, 332–33, 338, 357
soviets, 152, 157, 267, 271, 289
Spain, 159, 170–73, 206, 224, 238, 335–39
Spanish Civil War, 91, 335–39
Spanish-American War, 170–73, 351
Spartacist Uprising, 20, 205, 273–74

Spence, Robert S., 165, 365
Spencer, Herbert, 130
Spencer, Orson, 45, 49, 53–54, 56, 60, 63, 68, 112, 366
Spry, William, 278
St. Just, 86, 101, 241
St. Simon, Henri de, 7, 10, 23, 84, 123–24, 130, 132, 259, 309
Stalin, Joseph, 15, 287, 289, 331–32, 336–37
Stanford, Leland, 126
statism, 193, 209, 211, 222–24, 226, 240–41, 244–46, 250, 252–54, 259, 307, 338
Steele, Osman, 115
Stenhouse, T. B. H., 365
Stephen, Virginia Snow, 131
Stetzle, Charles, 234
Steward, Ira, 127
Stolypin, Pëter, 156
Stoof, Reinhold, 310, 313
Strong, Josiah, 188
student activism, xiv, 38, 47, 60, 153, 284, 305, 307, 310–11, 313, 315–17, 319
Sun Yat-sen, 176, 184
Switzerland, 99
symbolism, xii, xiv, xv, 14, 35, 71–107
    all-seeing eye, 71, 88–89, 92–93
    architectural, 72, 76, 84, 343
    astronomical, 35, 80–81, 83–84, 88–89, 91–93, 98–99, 105–7, 187, 247, 256, 298
    beehive, 93
    black, 50, 96, 101
    blue, 105–6
    circle, 80, 82–84, 102, 187, 318
    fire and light, xx, 4, 26, 63, 80, 84, 89–91, 102–4, 114, 187, 190, 192, 256, 286, 294, 298, 318, 326
    flags, xiv, 35, 39, 50, 54, 68, 81, 93, 96–98, 100–101, 105–6, 119, 162, 202, 301, 345
    geometric, xxi, 71, 76, 80–85, 87, 106, 186, 247, 318, 325
    meteorological, 104, 112, 272, 275, 302, 311
    numerological, 71, 80–81, 84–87, 325
    pentagram, 80, 84
    Phrygian cap, 87–88, 93, 107
    red, 39, 54, 68, 96–101, 107, 113, 119, 138, 149, 162, 202, 209, 271, 274–75, 281, 284, 349
    seismic, 81, 100–104, 121, 141, 183, 183, 275

Sparta, 86–87, 97, 193, 355
triangle, 80–81, 83–84, 105, 343

T

Taft, William H., 194, 202, 276–77
Talmage, James E., 72, 85, 110, 191, 280–82, 286–87, 366
Tannenbaum, Frank, 13, 194, 245, 253, 312
Tanner, Joseph M., 120, 127–29, 153, 156–57, 160, 163, 168–69, 173, 175, 179, 183, 271, 274, 281, 366–67
Taylor, John, 26, 43, 67, 93, 97, 101–2, 110–11, 275, 350, 354, 367
temples, 75–76, 84, 88, 97, 126, 208, 343, 350
Tenente Revolt, 305
Tenney, Ammon M., 193, 200
terrorism, 4, 144, 151, 189, 271, 275, 338
Thatcher, Moses, 3, 119, 368
theocracy, xv– xvi, 7, 24–25, 28, 30–32, 35, 79–80, 110, 148, 171, 186, 219, 364, 367
theo-democracy, xxi, 27–30, 54, 275, 319, 326, 340
Thiers, Adolphe, 139, 141–42, 144–46
Third Convention, 205, 328–30
time
    sacred, 17, 27, 104, 155, 215, 285, 294
    profane, 17, 149, 279, 340, 344
Toronto, Joseph, 365
Treaty of Brest-Litovsk, 269–70
Treaty of Versailles, 280, 283–85
Turkey, 178–81, 280
Turner, John Kenneth, 204, 217
Tuscany, 40
Tyler, John, 115

U

United Kingdom, 38–39, 45, 55–58, 62–63, 68–69, 72, 97–98, 100, 111–14, 117, 140, 146, 160, 162, 164, 166–70, 173, 175, 178, 181–85, 188, 201, 264, 266, 269, 276, 279, 331, 336
United Order, 29, 123–24, 130, 148, 189, 326, 328, 332, 326, 328, 332, 352
United States
    Constitution, 12–13, 32, 126, 326
    foreign policy, 160, 162–63, 172–75, 198, 204, 206, 210, 212, 216–18, 223, 231, 248, 255, 261, 269, 276–79, 285–87,
        289, 307–8, 310, 313, 338, 352
    founding, 6, 26, 72, 77, 201, 270
    imminent destruction, 25–26, 27, 31, 32, 77, 95–96, 115, 134, 143, 148, 326
    labor agitation, 111, 116, 122, 166
    persecution of Mormons, 36, 110, 147, 169, 236
    public opinion, 62, 139, 143, 146–47, 153, 170, 177, 181, 193, 225, 230, 232–33, 243, 253, 257, 264–65, 270, 274, 276–77, 291, 308–10, 331, 333, 336–37
    as redeemer nation, 13, 83, 188, 234–35, 263, 268, 277, 280, 282–83
Uriburu, José Félix, 304, 310
Utah, xxii, 29–30, 56, 63, 79, 88, 90, 91, 93, 100, 119, 122–25, 127, 131, 135, 143–44, 169, 171, 173, 179, 189, 192, 219, 241–42, 265, 267, 274, 278, 282, 284, 286–87, 289, 323–24, 326, 329–30, 333, 335, 340, 353, 355, 361, 368
    Mormon migration to, 35–36, 44, 46, 57, 66, 68, 82, 95, 105, 107, 109, 344, 347–49, 357–58, 360–61, 363, 370
    Mormon settlement of, xvi, 167, 317, 352, 354, 357, 360, 363, 367, 370
Utah War, 138, 353–54, 370
utopia, xi, xviii, xxi, xxiii, 2, 6, 11, 28, 30, 59, 72, 74, 83, 94, 96, 99, 107, 110, 116–17, 124, 127, 130, 132, 134–35, 137, 150, 189, 192, 202, 215, 226, 245, 253, 260, 294, 298, 303, 340–41, 344, 349

V

Vance, Joseph A., 131, 156, 368
Vargas, Getúlio Dornelles, 306
Vasconcelos, José, 222, 225
Venice, 40–41
Victor Emmanuel II of Italy, 138, 141
Victoria of England, 113–15, 162, 168
Vienna, 38, 50, 59
Villa, Francisco. See Villa, Pancho.
Villa, Pancho, xii, xxii, 199, 204, 206, 208–13, 217–18, 231
violence
    Mormon acceptance of, xii–xiii, 3, 7, 22, 27, 32, 37, 48, 50, 58, 60, 99, 111, 113–15, 117, 120, 134–35, 137–38, 149, 185–86, 201, 207–8, 212–13, 216,

218–19, 221, 245, 256–57, 271, 302, 304, 320, 324, 327
rejection of, 10, 70, 109–10, 118, 122, 124, 153, 165, 184–85, 188, 191, 202, 281, 343
Voltaire, 18

W

Ward, Harry F., 262
Warrum, Noble, 193, 242–43, 280, 355, 368–69
Weishaupt, Adam
Weitling, Wilhelm, 14, 30, 150
Wells, H. G., 4, 15
Wells, John, 127, 369
Wells, Junius F., 2–3, 278, 284–85, 369
Wells, Rulon S., 296
West, Joseph, 271
Whitmer, David, 359
Whitney, Orson F., 3–4, 263, 268, 282, 287, 328, 369
Widtsoe, John A., 277, 332
Wight, Lyman, 97
Wilhelm I, 141
Wilson, Henry Lane, 204, 299
Wilson, Woodrow, 19, 73, 129, 181, 194, 206, 210–11, 216, 261, 264, 266, 269, 272, 274, 276–77, 279, 281, 283–84, 286, 363, 368
Fourteen Points, 261, 280, 283
Winchester, Benjamin, 82
Windischgrätz, Alfred, 40, 50
Winthrop, John, 2
Witte, Serge, 153, 156
Woodbury, John T., 180
Woodruff, Wilford, 22–23, 26–27, 35–36, 43–44, 48–50, 52–53, 58–59, 64, 81, 85, 104, 111–12, 348, 352, 356, 370
World War I, 6, 13, 21, 138, 180–81, 186, 219, 261–62, 264–69, 272, 274, 278–81, 286–87, 294, 316–17, 339, 349, 371
World War II, xiv, 2, 13, 255, 288, 330–31, 336, 338–39, 352, 362
Wronski, Hoëne, 84

Y

Young America, xxi, 41–42, 52
Young, Brigham, xiv, xvi, 25, 27, 29–30, 66, 68, 76, 79, 81–82, 88, 100, 104–5, 110, 123–24, 134, 349, 354, 356, 360–63, 367, 370

Young Europe, 48, 188
Young Hegelians, 24
Young Ireland, 40, 56, 113
Young, Levi Edgar, 4, 24, 31, 85, 190, 230, 277, 371
Young Men's Mutual Improvement Association, 240, 296, 347, 369
Young, Richard W., 173, 348
Young, Seymour Bicknell, 193
Young Turks, 180, 184
Young Women's Mutual Improvement Association, xx, 353
Yrigoyen, Hipólito, 304, 310, 316

Z

Zapata, Emiliano, xiv, xxii, 204, 206, 208–11, 213–15, 218, 250, 259, 334
Zedong, Mao, 205
Zion, 8, 17, 20–22, 33, 48, 56–57, 65–66, 80, 82–83, 90–91, 97, 107, 137, 148, 187, 201, 216, 229, 276, 302, 314, 317, 320, 344, 356, 364
Zion's Cooperative Mercantile Institution, 179
Zionism. See Jews.

Also available from
GREG KOFFORD BOOKS

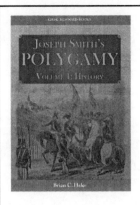

Joseph Smith's Polygamy, 3 Vols.

Brian Hales

Hardcover
Volume 1: History 978-1-58958-189-0
Volume 2: History 978-1-58958-548-5
Volume 3: Theology 978-1-58958-190-6

Perhaps the least understood part of Joseph Smith's life and teachings is his introduction of polygamy to the Saints in Nauvoo. Because of the persecution he knew it would bring, Joseph said little about it publicly and only taught it to his closest and most trusted friends and associates before his martyrdom.

In this three-volume work, Brian C. Hales provides the most comprehensive faithful examination of this much misunderstood period in LDS Church history. Drawing for the first time on every known account, Hales helps us understand the history and teachings surrounding this secretive practice and also addresses and corrects many of the numerous allegations and misrepresentations concerning it. Hales further discusses how polygamy was practiced during this time and why so many of the early Saints were willing to participate in it.

Joseph Smith's Polygamy is an essential resource in understanding this challenging and misunderstood practice of early Mormonism.

Praise for *Joseph Smith's Polygamy*:

"Brian Hales wants to face up to every question, every problem, every fear about plural marriage. His answers may not satisfy everyone, but he gives readers the relevant sources where answers, if they exist, are to be found. There has never been a more thorough examination of the polygamy idea."
—Richard L. Bushman, author of *Joseph Smith: Rough Stone Rolling*

"Hales's massive and well documented three volume examination of the history and theology of Mormon plural marriage, as introduced and practiced during the life of Joseph Smith, will now be the standard against which all other treatments of this important subject will be measured." —Danel W. Bachman, author of "A Study of the Mormon Practice of Plural Marriage before the Death of Joseph Smith"

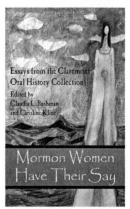

Mormon Women Have Their Say: Essays from the Claremont Oral History Collection

Edited by Claudia L. Bushman and Caroline Kline

Paperback, ISBN: 978-1-58958-494-5

The Claremont Women's Oral History Project has collected hundreds of interviews with Mormon women of various ages, experiences, and levels of activity. These interviews record the experiences of these women in their homes and family life, their church life, and their work life, in their roles as homemakers, students, missionaries, career women, single women, converts, and disaffected members. Their stories feed into and illuminate the broader narrative of LDS history and belief, filling in a large gap in Mormon history that has often neglected the lived experiences of women. This project preserves and perpetuates their voices and memories, allowing them to say share what has too often been left unspoken. The silent majority speaks in these records.

This volume is the first to explore the riches of the collection in print. A group of young scholars and others have used the interviews to better understand what Mormonism means to these women and what women mean for Mormonism. They explore those interviews through the lenses of history, doctrine, mythology, feminist theory, personal experience, and current events to help us understand what these women have to say about their own faith and lives.

Praise for *Mormon Women Have Their Say*:

"Using a variety of analytical techniques and their own savvy, the authors connect ordinary lives with enduring themes in Latter-day Saint faith and history." --Laurel Thatcher Ulrich, author of *Well-Behaved Women Seldom Make History*

"Essential. . . . In these pages, Mormon women will find *ourselves*." --Joanna Brooks, author of *The Book of Mormon Girl: A Memoir of an American Faith*

"The varieties of women's responses to the major issues in their lives will provide many surprises for the reader, who will be struck by how many different ways there are to be a thoughtful and faithful Latter-day Saint woman." --Armand Mauss, author of *All Abraham's Children: Changing Mormon Conceptions of Race and Lineage*

War & Peace in Our Time: Mormon Perspectives

Edited by Patrick Q. Mason, J. David Pulsipher, and Richard L. Bushman

Paperback, ISBN: 978-1-58958-099-2

"This provocative and thoughtful book is sure both to infuriate and to delight. . . . The essays demonstrate that exegesis of distinctly Latter-day Saint scriptures can yield a wealth of disputation, the equal of any rabbinical quarrel or Jesuitical casuistry. This volume provides a fitting springboard for robust and lively debates within the Mormon scholarly and lay community on how to think about the pressing issues of war and peace." - ROBERT S. WOOD, Dean Emeritus, Center for Naval Warfare Studies, Chester W. Nimitz Chair Emeritus, U.S. Naval War College

"This is an extraordinary collection of essays on a topic of extraordinary importance. . . .Whatever your current opinion on the topic, this book will challenge you to reflect more deeply and thoroughly on what it means to be a disciple of Christ, the Prince of Peace, in an era of massive military budgets, lethal technologies, and widespread war." - GRANT HARDY, Professor of History and Religious Studies, University of North Carolina, Asheville, Author, *Understanding the Book of Mormon: A Reader's Guide*

"Mormons take their morality seriously. They are also patriotic. Tragically, the second trait can undermine the first. When calls for war are on the horizon, it is possible for well-intended Saints to be too sure of our selective application of scripture to contemporary matters of life and death, too sure that we can overcome evil by force, that we can control the results of military conflict, that war is the only option for patriots. Yet pacifism has its own critics. This collection of differing views by thoughtful scholars comprises a debate. Reading it may save us in the future from enacting more harm than good in the name of God, country, or presumption." - PHILIP BARLOW, Arrington Chair of Mormon History and Culture, Utah State University, Author, *Mormons and the Bible: The Place of the Latter-day Saints in American Religion*

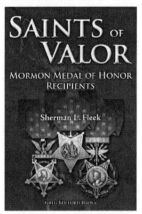

Saints of Valor:
Mormon Medal of Honor Recipients

Sherman L. Fleek

Hardcover, ISBN: 978-1-58958-171-5

Since 1861 when the US Congress approved the concept of a Medal of Honor for combat valor, 3,457 individuals have received this highest military decoration that the nation can bestow. Nine of those have been Latter-day Saints. The military and personal stories of these LDS recipients are compelling, inspiring, and tragic. The men who appear in this book are tied by two common threads: the Medal of Honor and their Mormon heritage.

The purpose of this book is to highlight the valor of a special class of LDS servicemen who served and sacrificed "above and beyond the call of duty." Four of these nine Mormons gave their "last full measure" for their country, never seeing the high award they richly deserved. All four branches of the service are represented: five were Army (one was a pilot with the Army Air Forces during WWII), two Navy, and one each of the Marine Corps and Air Force. Four were military professionals who made the service their careers; five were not career-minded; three died at an early age and never married. This book captures these harrowing historical narratives from personal accounts.

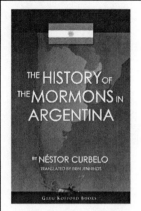

The History of Mormons
in Argentina

Néstor Curbelo

English, ISBN: 978-1-58958-052-7

Originally published in Spanish, Curbelo's The History of the Mormons in Argentina is a groundbreaking book detailing the growth of the Church in this Latin American country.

Through numerous interviews and access to other primary resources, Curbelo has constructed a timeline, and then documents the story of the Church's growth. Starting with a brief discussion of Parley P. Pratt's assignment to preside over the Pacific and South American regions, continuing on with the translation of the scriptures into Spanish, the opening of the first missions in South America, and the building of temples, the book provides a survey history of the Church in Argentina. This book will be of interest not only to history buffs but also to thousands of past, present, and future missionaries.

Translated by Erin Jennings

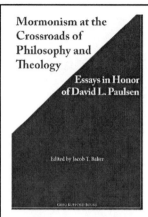

Mormonism at the Crossroads of Philosophy and Theology:
Essays in Honor of David L. Paulsen

Edited by Jacob T. Baker

Paperback, ISBN: 978-1-58958-192-0

"There is no better measure of the growing importance of Mormon thought in contemporary religious debate than this volume of essays for David Paulsen. In a large part thanks to him, scholars from all over the map are discussing the questions Mormonism raises about the nature of God and the purpose of life. These essays let us in on a discussion in progress." —RICHARD LYMAN BUSHMAN, author of *Joseph Smith: Rough Stone Rolling.*

"This book makes it clear that there can be no real ecumenism without the riches of the Mormon mind. Professor Paulsen's impact on LDS thought is well known. . . . These original and insightful essays chart a new course for Christian intellectual life." —PETER A. HUFF, and author of *Vatican II* and *The Voice of Vatican II*

"This volume of smart, incisive essays advances the case for taking Mormonism seriously within the philosophy of religion–an accomplishment that all generations of Mormon thinkers should be proud of." —PATRICK Q. MASON, Howard W. Hunter Chair of Mormon Studies, Claremont Graduate University

"These essays accomplish a rare thing—bringing light rather than heat to an on-going conversation. And the array of substantial contributions from outstanding scholars and theologians within and outside Mormonism is itself a fitting tribute to a figure who has been at the forefront of bringing Mormonism into dialogue with larger traditions." —TERRYL L. GIVENS, author of *People of Paradox: A History of Mormon Culture*

"The emergence of a vibrant Mormon scholarship is nowhere more in evidence than in the excellent philosophical contributions of David Paulsen." —RICHARD J. MOUW, President, Fuller Theological Seminary, author of *Talking with Mormons: An Invitation to Evangelicals*

Excavating Mormon Pasts: The New Historiography of the Last Half Century

Newell G. Bringhurst and Lavina Fielding Anderson

Paperback, ISBN: 978-1-58958-115-9

Special Book Award - John Whitmer Historical Association

Mormonism was born less than 200 years ago, but in that short time it has developed into a dynamic world religious movement. With that growth has come the inevitable restructuring and reevaluation of its history and doctrine. Mormon and non-Mormon scholars alike have viewed Joseph Smith's religion as fertile soil for religious, historical and sociological studies. Many early attempts to either defend or defame the Church were at best sloppy and often dishonest. It has taken decades for Mormon scholarship to mature to its present state. The editors of this book have assembled 16 essays addressing the substantial number of published works in the field of Mormon studies from 1950 to the present. The contributors come from various segments of the Mormon tradition and fairly represent the broad intellectual spectrum of that tradition. Each essay focuses on a particular aspect of Mormonism (history, women's issues, polygamy, etc.), and each is careful to evenhandedly evaluate the strengths and weaknesses of the books under discussion. More importantly, each volume is placed in context with other, related works, giving the reader a panoramic view of contemporary research. Students of Mormonism will find this collection of historiographical essays an invaluable addition to their libraries.

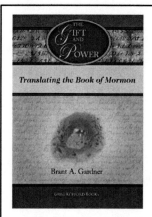

Translating the Book of Mormon

The Gift and Power: Translating the Book of Mormon

Brant A. Gardner

Hardcover, ISBN: 978-1-58958-131-9

From Brant A. Gardner, the author of the highly praised *Second Witness* commentaries on the Book of Mormon, comes *The Gift and Power: Translating the Book of Mormon*. In this first book-length treatment of the translation process, Gardner closely examines the accounts surrounding Joseph Smith's translation of the Book of Mormon to answer a wide spectrum of questions about the process, including: Did the Prophet use seerstones common to folk magicians of his time? How did he use them? And, what is the relationship to the golden plates and the printed text?

Approaching the topic in three sections, part 1 examines the stories told about Joseph, folk magic, and the translation. Part 2 examines the available evidence to determine how closely the English text replicates the original plate text. And part 3 seeks to explain how seer stones worked, why they no longer work, and how Joseph Smith could have produced a translation with them.

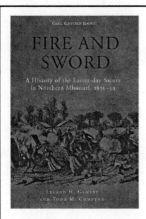

Fire and Sword: A History of the Latter-day Saints in Northern Missouri, 1836-39

Leland Homer Gentry and Todd M. Compton

Hardcover, ISBN: 978-1-58958-103-6

Many Mormon dreams flourished in Missouri. So did many Mormon nightmares.

The Missouri period—especially from the summer of 1838 when Joseph took over vigorous, personal direction of this new Zion until the spring of 1839 when he escaped after five months of imprisonment—represents a moment of intense crisis in Mormon history. Representing the greatest extremes of devotion and violence, commitment and intolerance, physical suffering and terror—mobbings, battles, massacres, and political "knockdowns"—it shadowed the Mormon psyche for a century.

Leland Gentry was the first to step beyond this disturbing period as a one-sided symbol of religious persecution and move toward understanding it with careful documentation and evenhanded analysis. In Fire and Sword, Todd Compton collaborates with Gentry to update this foundational work with four decades of new scholarship, more insightful critical theory, and the wealth of resources that have become electronically available in the last few years.

Compton gives full credit to Leland Gentry's extraordinary achievement, particularly in documenting the existence of Danites and in attempting to tell the Missourians' side of the story; but he also goes far beyond it, gracefully drawing into the dialogue signal interpretations written since Gentry and introducing the raw urgency of personal writings, eyewitness journalists, and bemused politicians seesawing between human compassion and partisan harshness. In the lush Missouri landscape of the Mormon imagination where Adam and Eve had walked out of the garden and where Adam would return to preside over his posterity, the towering religious creativity of Joseph Smith and clash of religious stereotypes created a swift and traumatic frontier drama that changed the Church.

Modern Polygamy and Mormon Fundamentalism:
The Generations after the Manifesto

Brian C. Hales

Paperback, ISBN: 978-1-58958-109-8

**Winner of the John Whitmer Historical Association's
Smith-Pettit Best Book Award**

This fascinating study seeks to trace the historical tapestry that is early Mormon polygamy, details the official discontinuation of the practice by the Church, and, for the first time, describes the many zeal-driven organizations that arose in the wake of that decision. Among the polygamous groups discussed are the LeBaronites, whose "blood atonement" killings sent fear throughout Mormon communities in the late seventies and the eighties; the FLDS Church, which made news recently over its construction of a compound and temple in Texas (Warren Jeffs, the leader of that church, is now standing trial on two felony counts after his being profiled on America's Most Wanted resulted in his capture); and the Allred and Kingston groups, two major factions with substantial membership statistics both in and out of the United States. All these fascinating histories, along with those of the smaller independent groups, are examined and explained in a way that all can appreciate.

Praise for *Modern Polygamy and Mormon Fundamentalism*:

"This book is the most thorough and comprehensive study written on the sugbject to date, providing readers with a clear, candid, and broad sweeping overview of the history, teachings, and practices of modern fundamentalist groups."
—Alexander L. Baugh, Associate Professor of Church History and Doctrine, Brigham Young University

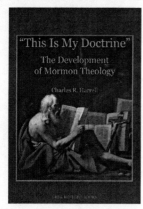

"This is My Doctrine":
The Development of Mormon
Theology

Charles R. Harrell

Hardcover, ISBN: 978-1-58958-103-6

The principal doctrines defining Mormonism today often bear little resemblance to those it started out with in the early 1830s. This book shows that these doctrines did not originate in a vacuum but were rather prompted and informed by the religious culture from which Mormonism arose. Early Mormons, like their early Christian and even earlier Israelite predecessors, brought with them their own varied culturally conditioned theological presuppositions (a process of convergence) and only later acquired a more distinctive theological outlook (a process of differentiation).

In this first-of-its-kind comprehensive treatment of the development of Mormon theology, Charles Harrell traces the history of Latter-day Saint doctrines from the times of the Old Testament to the present. He describes how Mormonism has carried on the tradition of the biblical authors, early Christians, and later Protestants in reinterpreting scripture to accommodate new theological ideas while attempting to uphold the integrity and authority of the scriptures. In the process, he probes three questions: How did Mormon doctrines develop? What are the scriptural underpinnings of these doctrines? And what do critical scholars make of these same scriptures? In this enlightening study, Harrell systematically peels back the doctrinal accretions of time to provide a fresh new look at Mormon theology.

"*This Is My Doctrine*" will provide those already versed in Mormonism's theological tradition with a new and richer perspective of Mormon theology. Those unacquainted with Mormonism will gain an appreciation for how Mormon theology fits into the larger Jewish and Christian theological traditions.

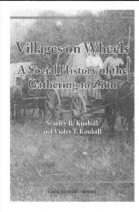

Villages on Wheels: A Social History of the Gathering to Zion

Stanley B. Kimball and Violet T. Kimball

ISBN: 978-1-58958-119-7

The enduring saga of Mormonism is its great trek across the plains, and understanding that trek was the life work of Stanley B. Kimball, master of Mormon trails. This final work, a collaboration he began and which was completed after his death in 2003 by his photographer-writer wife, Violet, explores that movement westward as a social history, with the Mormons moving as "villages on wheels."

Set in the broader context of transcontinental migration to Oregon and California, the Mormon trek spanned twenty-two years, moved approximately 54,700 individuals, many of them in family groups, and left about 7,000 graves at the trailside.

Like a true social history, this fascinating account in fourteen chapters explores both the routines of the trail—cooking, cleaning, laundry, dealing with bodily functions—and the dramatic moments: encountering Indians and stampeding buffalo, giving birth, losing loved ones to death, dealing with rage and injustice, but also offering succor, kindliness, and faith. Religious observances were simultaneously an important part of creating and maintaining group cohesiveness, but working them into the fabric of the grueling day-to-day routine resulted in adaptation, including a "sliding Sabbath." The role played by children and teens receives careful scrutiny; not only did children grow up quickly on the trail, but the gender boundaries guarding their "separate spheres" blurred under the erosion of concentrating on tasks that had to be done regardless of the age or sex of those available to do them. Unexpected attention is given to African Americans who were part of this westering experience, and Violet also gives due credit to the "four-legged heroes" who hauled the wagons westward.

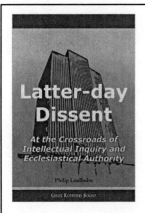

Latter-Day Dissent:
At the Crossroads of Intellectual
Inquiry and Ecclesiastical Authority

Philip Lindholm

Paperback, ISBN: 978-1-58958-128-9

This volume collects, for the first time in book form, stories from the "September Six," a group of intellectuals officially excommunicated or disfellowshipped from the LDS Church in September of 1993 on charges of "apostasy" or "conduct unbecoming" Church members. Their experiences are significant and yet are largely unknown outside of scholarly or more liberal Mormon circles, which is surprising given that their story was immediately propelled onto screens and cover pages across the Western world.

Interviews by Dr. Philip Lindholm (Ph.D. Theology, University of Oxford) include those of the "September Six," Lynne Kanavel Whitesides, Paul James Toscano, Maxine Hanks, Lavina Fielding Anderson, and D. Michael Quinn; as well as Janice Merrill Allred, Margaret Merrill Toscano, Thomas W. Murphy, and former employee of the LDS Church's Public Affairs Department, Donald B. Jessee.

Each interview illustrates the tension that often exists between the Church and its intellectual critics, and highlights the difficulty of accommodating congregational diversity while maintaining doctrinal unity—a difficulty hearkening back to the very heart of ancient Christianity.

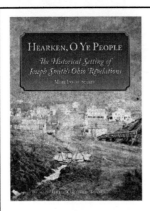

Hearken, O Ye People:
The Historical Setting of Joseph Smith's Ohio Revelations

Mark Lyman Staker

Hardcover, ISBN: 978-1-58958-113-5

2010 Best Book Award - John Whitmer Historical Association

2011 Best Book Award - Mormon History Association

More of Mormonism's canonized revelations originated in or near Kirtland than any other place. Yet many of the events connected with those revelations and their 1830s historical context have faded over time. Mark Staker reconstructs the cultural experiences by which Kirtland's Latter-day Saints made sense of the revelations Joseph Smith pronounced. This volume rebuilds that exciting decade using clues from numerous archives, privately held records, museum collections, and even the soil where early members planted corn and homes. From this vast array of sources he shapes a detailed narrative of weather, religious backgrounds, dialect differences, race relations, theological discussions, food preparation, frontier violence, astronomical phenomena, and myriad daily customs of nineteenth-century life. The result is a "from the ground up" experience that today's Latter-day Saints can all but walk into and touch.

Praise for *Hearken O Ye People*:

"I am not aware of a more deeply researched and richly contextualized study of any period of Mormon church history than Mark Staker's study of Mormons in Ohio. We learn about everything from the details of Alexander Campbell's views on priesthood authority to the road conditions and weather on the four Lamanite missionaries' journey from New York to Ohio. All the Ohio revelations and even the First Vision are made to pulse with new meaning. This book sets a new standard of in-depth research in Latter-day Saint history."
                -Richard Bushman, author of *Joseph Smith: Rough Stone Rolling*

"To be well-informed, any student of Latter-day Saint history and doctrine must now be acquainted with the remarkable research of Mark Staker on the important history of the church in the Kirtland, Ohio, area."
                -Neal A. Maxwell Institute, Brigham Young University

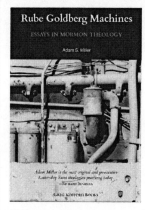

Rube Goldberg Machines: Essays in Mormon Theology

Adam S. Miller

Paperback, ISBN: 978-1-58958-193-7

"Adam Miller is the most original and provocative Latter-day Saint theologian practicing today."

> —Richard Bushman, author of *Joseph Smith: Rough Stone Rolling*

"As a stylist, Miller gives Nietzsche a run for his money. As a believer, Miller is as submissive as Augustine hearing a child's voice in the garden. Miller is a theologian of the ordinary, thinking about our ordinary beliefs in very non-ordinary ways while never insisting that the ordinary become extra-ordinary."

> —James Faulconer, Richard L. Evans Chair of Religious Understanding, Brigham Young University

"Miller's language is both recognizably Mormon and startlingly original. . . . The whole is an essay worthy of the name, inviting the reader to try ideas, following the philosopher pilgrim's intellectual progress through tangled brambles and into broad fields, fruitful orchards, and perhaps a sacred grove or two."

> —Kristine Haglund, editor of *Dialogue: A Journal of Mormon Thought*

"Miller's Rube Goldberg theology is nothing like anything done in the Mormon tradition before."

> —Blake Ostler, author of the EXPLORING MORMON THOUGHT series

"The value of Miller's writings is in the modesty he both exhibits and projects onto the theological enterprise, even while showing its joyfully disruptive potential. Conventional Mormon minds may not resonate with every line of poetry and provocation—but Miller surely afflicts the comfortable, which is the theologian's highest end."

> —Terryl Givens, author of *By the Hand of Mormon: The American Scripture that Launched a New World Religion*

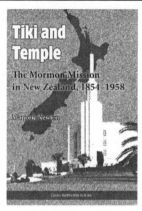

Tiki and Temple:
The Mormon Mission in New Zealand, 1854–1958

Marjorie Newton

Paperback, ISBN: 978-1-58958-121-0

From the arrival of the first Mormon missionaries in New Zealand in 1854 until stakehood and the dedication of the Hamilton New Zealand Temple in 1958, Tiki and Temple tells the enthralling story of Mormonism's encounter with the genuinely different but surprisingly harmonious Maori culture.

Mormon interest in the Maori can be documented to 1832, soon after Joseph Smith organized the Church of Jesus Christ of Latter-day Saints in America. Under his successor Brigham Young, Mormon missionaries arrived in New Zealand in 1854, but another three decades passed before they began sustained proselytising among the Maori people—living in Maori pa, eating eels and potatoes with their fingers from communal dishes, learning to speak the language, and establishing schools. They grew to love—and were loved by—their Maori converts, whose numbers mushroomed until by 1898, when the Australasian Mission was divided, the New Zealand Mission was ten times larger than the parent Australian Mission.

The New Zealand Mission of the Mormon Church was virtually two missions—one to the English-speaking immigrants and their descendants, and one to the tangata whenua—"people of the land." The difficulties this dichotomy caused, as both leaders and converts struggled with cultural differences and their isolation from Church headquarters, make a fascinating story. Drawing on hitherto untapped sources, including missionary journals and letters and government documents, this absorbing book is the fullest narrative available of Mormonism's flourishing in New Zealand.

Although written primarily for a Latter-day Saint audience, this book fills a gap for anyone interested in an accurate and coherent account of the growth of Mormonism in New Zealand.

CPSIA information can be obtained at www.ICGtesting.com
Printed in the USA
BVOW042304040613

322434BV00002B/43/P